Seeking Common Cause

Seeking Common Cause

READING AND WRITING IN ACTION

DIANE BENNETT DURKIN
University of California, Los Angeles

LISA GERRARD
University of California, Los Angeles

Boston   Burr Ridge, IL   Dubuque, IA   Madison, WI   New York
San Francisco   St. Louis   Bangkok   Bogotá   Caracas   Kuala Lumpur
Lisbon   London   Madrid   Mexico City   Milan   Montreal   New Delhi
Santiago   Seoul   Singapore   Sydney   Taipei   Toronto

Higher Education

Published by McGraw-Hill, an imprint of The McGraw-Hill Companies, Inc., 1221 Avenue of the Americas, New York, NY 10020. Copyright © 2008. All rights reserved. No part of this publication may be reproduced or distributed in any form or by any means, or stored in a database or retrieval system, without the prior written consent of The McGraw-Hill Companies, Inc., including, but not limited to, in any network or other electronic storage or transmission, or broadcast for distance learning.

This book is printed on acid-free paper.

2 3 4 5 6 7 8 9 0 DOC/DOC 0 9 8 7

ISBN-13: 978-0-07-244259-5
ISBN-10: 0-07-244259-X

Editor in Chief: *Emily G. Barrosse*
Publisher: *Lisa Moore*
Sponsoring Editor: *Christopher Bennem*
Marketing Manager: *Tamara Wederbrand*
Developmental Editor: *Julie McBurney*
Production Editor: *Brett Coker*
Manuscript Editor: *Joan Pendleton*
Designer: *Gino Cieslik*

Cover Designer: *Laurie Entringer*
Art Editor: *Ayelet Arbel*
Photo Research Coordinator: *Natalia Peschiera*
Photo Researcher: *Robin Sands*
Production Supervisor: *Tandra Jorgensen*
Composition: *Thompson Type*
Printing: *45# New Era Matte by R. R. Donnelley & Sons*

Cover credits: Clockwise, from top left:
Neon sign, Las Vegas (Image Source/Jupiter Images); The Mittens, Monument Valley, Arizona (Robert Glusic/Getty Images); Girls at Coming of Age Party (© Royalty-Free/Corbis)

Credits: The credits section for this book begins on page C-1 and is considered an extension of the copyright page.

Library of Congress Cataloging-in-Publication Data

Durkin, Diane Bennett.
  Seeking common cause: reading and writing in action / Diane Durkin,
Lisa Gerrard.
    p. cm.
  Includes bibliographical references and index.
  ISBN: 978-0-07-244259-5
  MHID: 0-07-244259-X
  1. College readers. 2. English language—Rhetoric—Problems, exercises, etc. 3. Persuasion (Rhetoric)—Problems, exercises, etc. 4. Critical thinking—Problems, exercises, etc. 5. Report writing—Problems, exercises, etc. I. Gerrard, Lisa, 1946- II. Title.

PE1417.D87 2006
808'.0427—dc22

2006046163

The Internet addresses listed in the text were accurate at the time of publication. The inclusion of a Web site does not indicate an endorsement by the authors or McGraw-Hill, and McGraw-Hill does not guarantee the accuracy of the information presented at these sites.

www.mhhe.com

CHAPTER **5**

The Work World 263

ARTWORKS (COLOR PLATES)

Jack Levine, *The Trial* (painting) / Edward Hopper,
New York Office (painting) / Maggi Hambling,
Dorothy Hodgkin (painting) / Florine Stettheimer,
Spring Sale at Bendel's (painting) / John Sloan,
Sun and Wind on the Roof (painting) / Ben Shahn,
Albert Einstein among Other Immigrants (mural) /
Diego Rivera, *Mural, the Great Hall of the Detroit
Institute of Arts* / Daniel DeSiga, *El Campesino*
(painting)

CHAPTER **6**

Connecting to Nature 349

ARTWORKS (COLOR PLATES)

Gutzon Borglum, *Mount Rushmore National
Monument, South Dakota* (photograph) / Korczak
Ziolkowski, *Crazy Horse Memorial* (photograph) /
Dorothea Lange, *Tractored Out, Childress County,
Texas* (photograph) / Alexander Hogue, *Crucified
Land* (painting) / Jasper Francis Cropsey, *Bareford
Mountains, West Milford, New Jersey* / Virginia A.
Stroud, *Doesn't Fall Off His Horse* / Asher B.
Durand, *Kindred Spirits* (painting) / Frederic

Exploring Cyberculture   433

CHAPTER 8

Exploring the Arts 513

TO THE INSTRUCTOR

A New Kind of Reader

We created *Seeking Common Cause* as a new kind of thematic reader, one that tightly interweaves visual and written works. We chose themes that were both intrinsically interesting and thematically visual. And we selected individual pieces that refracted off one another, encouraging students to analyze and synthesize. To support this analysis and synthesis, we knew that we had to provide extensive support—to help students anticipate, understand, connect to, and work with ideas and with images. So we developed four different threads of analysis for each reading and similar threads for the visuals. And we created both short and extended writing projects, with supporting steps and strategies.

In providing this support, we also created a different kind of argument reader. *Seeking Common Cause* emphasizes a form of argument in which writers synthesize points of view rather than polarize them. We wanted to teach critical reading through empathy and belief rather than through disbelief and quick dismissal. So we found ourselves relying less on legal logic—analysis through claim, evidence, and warrant—than on writing strategies for bringing about mutual consent. To help students suspend skepticism or quick judgment of a reading, we ask students to describe what makes each argument credible and to identify underlying commonalities among different points of view. Our introductory chapter explains this approach to argument. It defines argument as credibility, identifies strategies that create mutual consent, takes students through the steps of visual and textual analysis, and provides models of such analysis.

It was important to us to define argument as creating *credibility*. We had seen how argument based on dispute can make readers dismissive. The search for the winning "side" may teach readers to judge before they have identified credible arguments, precluding their finding *common cause* with the author. Rather, we wanted to encourage careful examination of writers' perspectives and their strategies for drawing readers in. Narration, extended example, analogy, telling details, observations, and tone—these are some of the options writers have when they attempt to shape readers' responses. In our first chapter, we discuss each, with a text example. Further, as writers themselves, students can use these strategies to create credible arguments. In our first chapter, we take students through this process, step-by-step. Argument readers that examine warrants and fallacies do not teach such steps and strategies.

Interconnected Readings and Artwork

One way to create credibility is to draw on multiple sources and ideas. We wanted students not only to understand individual readings and artworks but also to have opportunities to weave their understandings into their own arguments. For this reason, *Seeking Common Cause* closely integrates print and visual texts. The works were chosen to connect to one another so that students could synthesize materials. In the extended argument projects at the end of each chapter, we ask students to synthesize selected chapter readings and artwork and bring to bear multiple perspectives on a complex topic. Short writing projects, also at the end of each chapter, prepare students for the extended writing project or can stand on their own. In creating these assignments, and their supporting pedagogy, we kept synthesis as our goal. In one extended argument project, we ask students to analyze an advertisement and to use as support some of the chapter readings on images of gender. In another extended writing project, we ask students to analyze any familiar high school building for what the architecture suggests about how our society educates students; students are asked to draw on multiple readings from the education chapter to analyze the school design. Such assignments help students build knowledge by first analyzing and then synthesizing closely related materials.

Extensive Visual Rhetoric

The visual analysis required for many projects reveals our belief that students need skills in visual rhetoric. We live in an increasingly visual culture: we receive most of our news through visual media; to a great degree, popular culture is shaped by visual images, and many Web sites typically proffer their messages through visual image as much as through text. Further, our lives are shaped by the visual arts—by the architecture we live in, as well as the paintings, photography, film, dance, and sculpture that embody or critique our culture. In response to this need for visual analysis, we created an extensive visual rhetoric, one that we discuss broadly in our first chapter, which we repeat and modify in each subsequent chapter for that chapter's dominant art form, and which we reinforce in the analysis questions for each artwork.

We introduce visual rhetoric in our first chapter. Here we provide students with a step-by-step process for analyzing a visual work. We offer a series of key questions for students' initial response; we provide definitions of key visual elements, including composition, shape and size, line, color, light, and background knowledge, with each element highlighted and explained with reference to a specific work of art; we include a separate section on how to read Web sites; and we present one professional and two student models of analyses of artworks.

Each chapter introduction then modifies this visual rhetoric to fit the featured art form. For the education chapter, which features school architecture, the suggestions help students identify and analyze architectural elements. For the chapter on gender, which features advertisements, the suggestions help students identify and analyze ad features that imply gender behaviors and values. For the chapter on nature, which features American landscape painting, the suggestions help students relate the natural setting to human actions, depicted or implied. Each chapter introduction also offers a sample analysis of one of the visuals in the chapter.

With the presentation of individual works of art in each chapter, we include background information and a prompt to help students connect with the work. Guiding questions then help writers analyze each artwork in detail. Finally, questions at the end of each chapter help students analyze each artwork in light of several readings.

Choice of Themes

We chose our themes because they were intrinsically interesting and thematically visual. We opened with two chapters on identity, Defining Cultural Identity and Constructing

Gender. Images, and in particular self-images, of cultural and gender differences resonate with students. Images of Education and The Work World were chosen because our students are all in college and contemplating the nature of work. Educational values are easily visualized in school architecture. Work, which brings to a head social values and inequities, has long generated social commentary from both writers and artists. Next, Connecting to Nature and Exploring Cyberculture offer two alternative realities—nature and cyberspace. Each spawns very different visualizations, the vast panoramas of American landscape paintings and the technical sophistication of Web pages. We conclude the book with Exploring the Arts, comprising discussions of and images from the various arts.

Four Readers in One

Almost any thematic reader can be used in a variety of ways. Instructors can select themes different from those identified in chapter headings and ask students to read across chapters. In addition, instructors can organize the readings by modes, grouping together readings that illustrate description, narration, definition, argument, analysis, and comparison and contrast. Also, if instructors are using a visual thematic reader, they can select only the visual materials for students to analyze and ignore the print texts, or the reverse.

We created this visual thematic reader with a clear awareness of four additional ways to use this text: as a personal response reader, an argument reader, a source book, and a civic action reader. And we built an extensive pedagogy to support each approach.

First, the book can be used as a personal response reader. For each reading, we have created a series of questions under the heading "Connecting Personally to the Reading." These questions ask students to use personal experience to reflect on each reading, encouraging students to understand through empathy. Students also have the opportunity to respond personally to the visuals, with some of the follow-up questions prompting personal reactions. Furthermore, we have woven personal narrative and reflection into the book as a whole—in the choice of the readings themselves, especially for Chapters 2, 3, and 6; in the introductions to the readings and artwork; in the follow-up questions; and in the short writing projects.

Second, the book can be used as an argument reader. Each reading has follow-up questions under the heading "Focusing on the Argument." These questions prompt students to think about the strategies of argument, identified and illustrated in our first chapter, that each writer uses to create credibility. For instance, students might identify how a writer uses telling examples or analogy or tone to make us believe him or her. Such questions also prepare students for some of the short writing projects that ask them to analyze various arguments. In addition, questions under "Focusing on the Argument" prepare students to analyze arguments in the debate section of each chapter, where writers' arguments support mutually exclusive choices. Finally, instructors can use these strategies of argument to help students create and analyze their own arguments.

Third, the book can be used as a source book, whereby students synthesize multiple readings to draw broad conclusions. For each reading, we have created a series of questions under the heading "Synthesizing Ideas from Multiple Readings." These questions ask students to interpret one writer's ideas in light of other authors' views. Furthermore, at the end of each chapter we have created questions on "Connecting Readings to the Artwork" that ask students to synthesize several readings in order to interpret an artwork. In addition, the debate section for each chapter asks students to synthesize opposing readings, additional information, Web sites, and arguments to help students address mutually exclusive positions. Finally, the short writing projects as well as the extended writing projects typically ask for synthesis.

Fourth, the book can be used as a civic action reader. For each reading we offer a series of questions titled "Writing to Act." These questions encourage specific civic actions, based on the arguments, details, and evidence provided in the readings. Students identify a target audience and write letters, journal articles, editorials, and responses to specific civic events or conditions. This civic action approach is further supported in the short writing projects. And it is carried through the text in that the readings themselves, as well as many of the visuals, imply action. The readings in the debate sections at the end of each chapter specifically call for civic action. Students can choose a wide variety of outlets to write to act.

Acknowledgments

We would first like to acknowledge the help and support we received from so many family members and close friends. Michael Durkin saw this project through from beginning to end, and was lovingly supportive and inspirational at every turn. Celia Durkin was magically complimentary and insightful whenever a college student's view was needed. And to Mike Hobbs, who lived with this project for years, thank you for your patience, love, and encouragement.

Several colleagues helped us in this process. Mike Rose was instrumental in our first meetings with the McGraw-Hill team. Susan Getze gave us good advice on background research. We are also indebted to the Getty Museum, which provided staff and other support for our research. We would especially like to thank the McGraw-Hill team for everything they provided. We are indebted to our acquisitions editor, Lisa Moore, for her faith in us and her open hand in this project. We deeply appreciate the careful help of our editor, Christopher Bennem. Critical to the project's development have been Alexis Walker, Betty Chen, Julie McBurney, Brett Coker, Marty Moga, Natalia Peschiera, Joan Pendleton, and Anne Stameshkin. We would also like to thank the many reviewers of our manuscript, who contributed their thoughtful comments and encouragement.

Alex E. Blazer, University of Louisville
Amy Bolaski, Palomar Community College
Loretta Brister, Tarleton State University
Felicia L. Carr, George Mason University
Nicolette de Csipkay, University at Buffalo, SUNY
David S. Hopcroft, Quinebaug Valley Community College
Dennis G. Jerz, Seton Hill University
Virginia Kuhn, University of Wisconsin, Milwaukee
Steve Luebke, University of Wisconsin, River Falls
Homer Mitchell, State University of New York, Cortland
Patricia A. Moody, Syracuse University
Ted Otteson, University of Missouri, Kansas City
Myra Seaman, College of Charleston
Paula J. Smith, Southeastern Oklahoma State University
Jennifer Widman, South Dakota State University

Seeking Common Cause

Edgar Degas, a French impressionist born in 1834, was fascinated by the actions and positions of his subjects—horses in a race, dancers preparing for the ballet, women bathing, people he knew in telling positions. While best known for his ballet dancers, his portraits are psychologically penetrating.

JOHN SINGER SARGENT Paul Helleu Sketching with His Wife [1889]

John Singer Sargent, an American impressionist born in 1856, painted his friends, Paul Helleu and his wife, each reflectively absorbed in the beauty of the surroundings. Sargent is well known for his landscapes as well as his portraits.

William H. Johnson, an African-American artist born in 1901, is well known for his contributions to the Harlem Renaissance, depicting everyday African-American life. He weaves together his interests in primitive art, modernism, and African-American culture.

GEORGIA O'KEEFE   The Lawrence Tree [1929]

Georgia O'Keefe, an American painter of the Southwest born in 1887, transforms simple images of nature from her beloved Southwest into surprising shapes and sensuous beauty. "I'll paint [the flower] big. . . . I will make even busy New Yorkers take time to see what I see in flowers."

MARY CASSATT   The Child's Bath [1893]

The Art Institute of Chicago.

Mary Cassatt, an American impressionist born in 1844, is drawn to the theme of women caring for children. The intimacy she creates is enhanced by the many ways in which the woman and child are joined as they together peer into their mirrored reflection in the basin.

HENRY OSSAWA TANNER   The Banjo Lesson [1893]

Henry Ossawa Tanner, an African-American artist born in 1859, illustrates the kinship African-Americans feel through music, family, and place. He addresses such stereotypes as the African-American banjo player, and recasts them into subtle images of dignity and human kindness.

PEPÓN OSORIO   El Chandelier [1988]

Smithsonian American Art Museum.

Pepón Osorio, a Puerto-Rican American born in 1955, makes kitsch to comment on social values. This six-foot tall chandelier with its abundance of toys and fake ornaments, humorously chides American excess: "I use kitsch and humor as a way to negotiate with an imposed culture."

LEON GOLUB   Mercenaries II [1979]

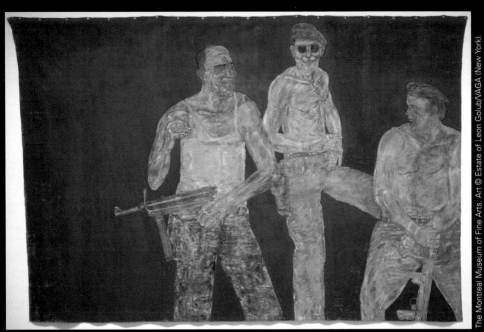

Leon Golub, a post-World War II American painter born in 1922, addresses issues of race, war and human suffering. A political painter, he depicts the violence of the Holocaust and Hiroshima, as well as the brutalities of the 1960s and 1970s. Often, his portraits are of men so callous they kill for money, and enjoy it.

Reading and Writing Arguments

CHAPTER 1

ANALYTICAL READING AS PREPARATION FOR ARGUMENT

Reading Print Texts

Reading thoughtfully involves more than taking in the words and registering the writer's ideas as they unfold—a seemingly passive activity. Rather, reading requires active participation with the text. It entails deciding what the main ideas are, looking for connections, using background knowledge to understand meaning, anticipating arguments, questioning evidence, and focusing on one's purpose for reading. What follows are some suggestions for active reading.

Previewing the Text

Previewing a text helps you quickly identify the overall argument—helps you get the "gist" before looking closely at the individual ideas. Previewing gives you a framework for understanding the details of a text. It also gives you time to recall your previous knowledge about the topic, which will help you anticipate and weigh the ideas you encounter.

- Read the title, subtitles, and any headings within the text.
- Skim the reading to get an overview of its main ideas.
- Read the opening paragraph to anticipate the writer's position on these ideas.
- Look for a summary of the article (often appearing in either the opening paragraph or the conclusion).
- Think about what you already know about this topic.

Bringing your own knowledge to a reading is particularly important. That knowledge provides the context for interaction with a writer's ideas. Also, clarify for yourself your own purpose, preconceptions, and expectations in reading the piece.

Marking Up the Text

To read critically, it helps to have a pen or pencil in hand. Most readers interact with the text by writing out thoughts or questions in the margins or by underlining to identify significant points. These marks help them see the ideas more clearly, as well as guide their reading when they return to the essay a second time.

- Highlight or underline the central ideas.
- Write short summaries of the reading in the margins.
- Write brief comments or questions in the margins.
- Identify sections of the text that you don't understand.
- Look up the meaning of terms you don't know; then write them in the text.

Thinking about the Text

Good readers do much more than decode the words and summarize the ideas. They actively question, wonder, and surmise as they read.

Thinking about the writer's ideas

As you read, ask questions about meaning. Keep the following broad questions in mind and apply them to any reading:

- What is the main point?
- Why does the writer hold that position?
- How are the writer's ideas connected to each other?
- Are you aware of any personal, social, economic, or political conditions that might influence that position?
- Can you think of evidence outside the text that might not fit with the writer's main point? How might the writer have interpreted this evidence?
- Can you think of evidence outside the text that might support the writer's position? How might the writer have interpreted that evidence?
- Are there any beliefs or values that the author seems to take for granted? If so, what are they?
- Does the writer explain the significance of his/her ideas?

You might also note where you find yourself stopping or questioning a connection. If for some reason, you aren't following the logical flow of ideas, ask why. Where, specifically, did you get stuck?

Understanding the writer's methods

As you read, also ask which of these methods the writer uses to convince the reader:

- Offers extensive examples
- Selects telling details
- Describes a person, scene, or object
- Makes an analogy
- Quotes another person
- Summarizes an idea or opinion
- Paraphrases
- Tells a story
- Provides personal testimony

- Reports others' experience
- Defines concepts and terms
- Selects words that express a particular attitude or tone

Ask yourself why the writer chose these methods and what effect they had on you.

Reading Visual Materials

As with reading an essay, reading an ad, photograph, work of architecture, painting, or Web site requires active searching and questioning. Your methods are different, though, for what you take in are immediate images, not words. Here are some general questions to ask yourself as you look at a visual. Some questions apply more readily to one art form than to others.

- What knowledge, if any, do you already have about the artist, the period, or the work's purpose?
- What is your first impression or reaction?
- What subject or form is your eye most drawn to?
- How is the subject or form positioned, and why?
- What is in the foreground, and what is in the background?
- What colors are used for the subjects or central forms, and why?
- What is the overall mood of the work?
- If there are people, where are they looking, and why?
- What did you notice first? What direction did your eye then move in, and why?
- Are there any striking contrasts in color, light, shape, size, or location?
- What is the most subtle feature in the work?

To answer such questions, you may need to use some of the vocabulary of visual art. This vocabulary of key elements is relatively simple, and you may be familiar with it already.

Vocabulary

Composition: the way the work is organized. How do the parts relate? Are they balanced and symmetrical? What elements are in the foreground and what elements in the background? What is in the center or focal point of the work? What is the viewer's line of sight?

Shape and size: the size of the work of art as well as the size and shape of individual elements. Is there a repeated shape? What is the biggest element in the work of art? Are the shapes broken up or whole?

Line: marks that create boundaries between elements. Lines can be sharp or soft, fluid or rigid, heavy or light, angular or flowing. They can also be directional: diagonal (suggesting instability), horizontal (suggesting calm), vertical (suggesting stability), or circular (suggesting movement).

Color: element that creates subjective feelings. What colors dominate? Are the colors complementary (e.g., green and blue) or opposing (e.g., red and blue)? How do the juxtapositions of color affect us? Is the color full (completely saturated) or weak (not fully saturated)?

Light: visual element that determines what we see. Some elements may be lit up and others more shaded. Does the work contrast elements through light and dark? Are some parts illuminated more than others?

As with a print text, you may want to prepare to write by doing some preliminary work.

Getting an Overview of the Artwork

Because images come at us whole, you might begin by summarizing your first impression. How did the work make you feel? It's useful to write a paragraph that distills your initial reactions.

Identifying the Key Elements

Use the questions and the vocabulary provided at the beginning of this section to think about and explain your impression of the visual image you are analyzing. Be as concrete as possible when observing elements in the work. When you write you will need to help the reader see what you see, as this art critic does in analyzing the painting by Degas (insert 1-1) at the beginning of the chapter.

> . . . We know little about Thérèse De Gas beyond what [Degas'] portraits may tell us of her. But these, and, in particular, the double portrait of 1865, tell us a remarkable amount. The position which is assigned to Thérèse in this grouping, seated behind her husband with one hand placed tentatively upon his shoulder, immediately suggests the dependent nature of her relationship to him. At the same time, the startled, almost frightened expression imparted to her face by the staring, widened eyes and the defensive placement of her hand before her slightly parted lips bespeak her timidity in relation to the outside world, a world from which she literally seeks to shield herself by retreating physically behind the imposing and self-assured figure of her protective husband.
> (Norma Broude, "Degas' 'Misogyny'")

Note how Broude helps us see what she sees. First she dismisses the need for background knowledge in interpreting the painting: her first point is that the portrait of husband and wife speaks for itself. She includes her first reaction—that the painting "immediately suggests" that Thérèse depends on her husband. She implies that the eye is initially drawn to the woman's hand placed on her husband's shoulder and to the "startled" expression in her "staring, widened eyes." She also describes the general positions of the subjects, noting that Thérèse is "seated behind her husband." She thus separates foreground from background, the timid Thérèse in the background, the imposing Edmond in the foreground. Note here that Broude's analysis reflects many, though not all, of the questions we suggest you ask of a work of art.

Key elements such as composition, color, line, shape and size, and light and dark can be interwoven into such a discussion. However, you can also focus an entire discussion on a single element, especially when that element strongly affects our response.

Composition

Paul Helleu Sketching with His Wife (1889) by John Singer Sargent (insert 1-2) illustrates how composition, the way a work is organized, shapes our response. To convey feelings of both closeness and separation, as husband and wife take their leisure by water's edge, Sargent makes the figures both intersect and turn away from one another. The wife's reclining figure almost appears to be resting on his shoulder, he leaning toward her—except that his forward-hunched body disconnects the figures. She is actually behind him, not touching. The two near-touching white hats provide the painting's focal point, but they cover faces that are directed away from one another. The man's intense, active gaze is down and left, onto his canvas; the woman's more contemplative gaze is to the right and off the painting.

The intersecting figures form a kind of triangle, with the tip or touching point being the man's hat, and the couple's limbs, stretching away from one another, forming the triangle's sides. Other objects in the painting create triangles, heightening our sense of intersection and division. The red canoe, which the couple must have rowed to this spot, cuts diagonally across the painting, connecting the two figures, but slicing the entire painting into two triangles, one near-empty, with only water and wild grass, the other crowded with the two figures and their various objects of leisure. Forming the bottom of a smaller triangle is the man's canvas, which absorbs our interest as well as his, to the exclusion of the woman and her thoughts. Our gaze then moves from the canvas upward along the canoe to the canoe's tip, which peaks over the couple's heads. Thus Sargent bases his overall composition on a key geometric form to heighten the particular feelings he wishes to convey.

Color

Café by William H. Johnson (insert 1-3) depicts a man and a woman having drinks at a small table in a café. Along with caricature, color is a dominant element in this work, helping us see and be amused by this relationship. The bright primary colors of red, yellow, and blue show us the woman's hold on her man. Red in particular tells us she is in charge of their pleasures. Her red lips, the red bows on her shoes, the partly red wallet, and her red-gloved hands—which grasp both the man and the table—communicate her feminine charm and power. The one gloved hand seems to hold him possessively; the other seems to support the table. She is the couple's support and head. Yellow also contributes to our understanding of the relationship. It suggests the man's more wayward thoughts, coloring not only his suit, in a flamboyant crisscross pattern, but also his jaunty hat. His wandering eyes, which contrast with her direct gaze at him, reinforce this view. Yellow is also the color of the table, which supports their glasses and the bottle, as well as the man's relaxed hand and bent elbow. The yellow of the table shows through the bottle of alcohol to reveal how much has been imbibed. With blue serving as background, these primary reds and yellows, heightened by white, black, and brown, amusingly portray who dictates the "good time" in this café.

Line

The Lawrence Tree, 1929 by Georgia O'Keefe (insert 1-4) demonstrates how line transforms a simple scene. O'Keefe's single tree against a night sky, when viewed diagonally up from the ground, gives us a whole new image, one of dynamic instability. The diagonal itself is unstable, moving our vision from lower right corner to upper left corner and off the canvas. Further, this line puts us on the ground, as if crouching, looking up and sideways. From this angle, the curved lines of the tree trunk and branches make the trunk appear to sprout squidlike tentacles that prod amorphous dark areas—leaves that appear like spreading ink blots above us. These curved lines themselves emphasize movement. In contrast, the night sky, almost blotted out by the curving masses of leaves, appears like flat, motionless blue wallpaper, speckled with white dots that we construe as the stars.

Size and shape

The Child's Bath by Mary Cassatt (insert 1-5) illustrates how size and shape influence our impressions. In this painting of a woman bathing a child, the two subjects take up most of the painting, with both shapes equally prominent. Furthermore, their bodies form parallel shapes that connect and intertwine the two figures. The arms and hands of woman and child are similar to one another. Both subjects' left arms extend down toward the bath, while their left hands similarly hold the child's left leg, between thumb and index finger. Their right hands, parallel to one another, reach around the other person, with fingers equally spread. Both faces, of equal size and on a level plane, look down at the bath water together, and the artist has drawn similar shapes for eyes, hair, eyelids, noses, and mouths.

Light and dark

The Banjo Lesson by Henry Ossawa Tanner (insert 1-6), similar in composition to *The Child's Bath*, illustrates how dark and light can be used to focus attention on the subject. The darkness of the two intertwined and parallel figures is contrasted with the glaring light of the background, which forms a kind of halo of light around the heads of man and boy and outlines the boy's arm as he learns to play the banjo. Softer contrasts of light and dark distinguish the man from the boy, with the boy's young face and the flat face of the banjo lighter than the man's darker face. These gentle variations of darkness against the glaring lightness of the background separate the intimacy of the human connection from the stark coldness of the lit world behind them.

Background knowledge (biographical/cultural)

Background knowledge is not an "element" in a work of art. However, when we know the artist's biography, the time and place of the work, and possibly its purpose, we can better understand the elements and how they contribute to the effect. *El Chandelier* by Pepón Osorio (insert 1-7) illustrates how background knowledge affects our reading of an image. In his book *Arte Latino* (2001), Yorba tells us that Osorio, born in San Juan, Puerto Rico, drew on memories from the island of the extravagant cakes he helped his mother decorate and of his sister's elaborate jewelry. As an adult in Spanish Harlem and the South Bronx, he noticed that in Puerto Rican neighborhoods, every apartment had a chandelier. These "floating crystal islands" (p. 78), as Osorio called them, became emblems of pride in these neighborhoods. Thus, his elaborately constructed and decorated chandelier reflects this cultural past. The decorations themselves—mass-produced toys and fake crystal necklaces, mostly emblems of the popular culture Puerto Rican immigrants experienced in the 1950s and 1960s—indicate pride in one's cultural heritage.

This background knowledge helps us identify and understand the details we see, toys that include "palm trees, soccer balls, Afro-Caribbean saints, cars, dominoes, black and white babies, giraffes and monkeys" (p. 78). Such background information might also include an insightful comment from a Puerto Rican child: "the multifaceted crystals recall the tears of the community" (p. 78).

Background knowledge (historical)

Leon Golub's *Mercenaries II* (1979) (insert 1-8) is part of a series created by the artist to make viewers look at bloodlust among the operants hired—often by "democratic" governments—to carry out subversive operations. These "mercenaries," who kill for a living, are joking, callous, and cruel without thought. Crowded into one side of the canvas, the three figures holding guns look relaxed, unself-conscious, and unashamed, relishing their roles as masters of torture and brutality. Historical background knowledge helps us understand the work. During the 1970s and 1980s foreign agencies, including the CIA, were involved in revolution and counter-revolution in Central and South American countries. Most of the resulting atrocities were not reported in the news. Golub here depicts the human face of savagery—soldiers for hire who epitomize the confluence of money, power, war, and masculinity. These are blunt, brutish shapes, with legs in awkward positions, cut off by the canvas edge, placed against a flat-red background of eroded surfaces. Golub makes the viewer bear witness to this savage human face, a brutal testimony to what happens when one government clandestinely interferes with another.

Reading Web Sites

Web sites almost always combine printed text and visual materials. Unlike most printed texts and pictures, which are static, Web sites change over time: their owners post new information, remove and change text and pictures, add and delete links, and redesign the physical appearance of the site. These changes may occur rarely (once a year or less often) or, as in the case of many Web logs, daily. Furthermore, Web sites may be interactive; that is, unlike print texts and pictures, they can change in response to suggestions from readers. In some cases readers can themselves add materials directly to a Web page, so that the site has multiple, and changing, authors. Thus, when you read a Web site critically, take into consideration how it may change over time and whether it is the work of a single author or many contributors.

Because nearly all Web sites combine printed text and visual elements, all of the strategies you use to analyze readings and pictures apply when you analyze materials on the Web. As you read Web sites critically, then, consider the effect of the language and pictures separately. Then think about the relationship between them: do the graphic elements illustrate the text, do they intensify the effect of the text, do they contrast with or contradict it, or do they offer information that is not in the text? If the visual images dominate the site, you might invert these questions: does the text illustrate the graphic elements, does it intensify the effect of the visual images, does it contrast with or contradict them, or does it offer information that is not in the visual materials? As in any analysis of text or graphics, the more carefully you observe the details of a Web site, the more convincing your writing will be. The passage on page 9 uses specific detail to show how the text and graphics of the Web page b.r.i.l.l.o. reinforce each other:

Click on the box to go...

Archives:

Click on the box to go...
Issue #2: Wetware

Click on the box to go...
Issue #1: Armed and Dangerous

Contact Brillo at brillo@brillomag.net!

Link: http://www.brillomag.net/No3/contents.htm

Web page for *Brillo* magazine, #3—"brillo: the invasion." Reprinted by permission of Virginia Eubanks and Wendy Bryan, *Brillo* magazine.

[The stereotype of] the complaining housewife, shrill and bad-tempered, is the signature image of the zine b.r.i.l.l.o. Located on virago-net, named after a box of wiry pot scrubbers, and subtitled "extra abrasive . . . for today's cranky feminist," b.r.i.l.l.o. glorifies the cantankerous housewife. She stands in classic fishwife posture: her shoulders thrust forward, hands on hips, a scolding face. The rhetoric is aggressive: issue #1 is subtitled "armed and dangerous"; issue #2, "wetware"; and issue #3, "brillo: the invasion," is introduced with candy hearts that say not just "be mine" and "my love," but also "kiss off" and "say no."
(Lisa Gerrard, "Beyond 'Scribbling Women': Women Writing (on) the Web")

Note how this passage describes the interplay between the language of the Web page and its visual images.

Here are some additional questions to guide your analysis of Web sites:

- What is the purpose of the site (e.g., political advocacy, information, self-promotion, public service, humor, marketing)?
- What ideological assumptions underlie the site? If it is affiliated with an organization, is that affiliation apparent in the text or images?
- What adjectives would you use to describe the tone of this site (e.g., playful, serious, urgent, ironic, trendy)? What words and images contribute the most to creating this tone?
- How much text is there relative to visual images, and what is the relationship between them?
- What is the effect of the background elements—e.g., background color, images, or borders?
- What is the effect of the font color, size, and style and of the layout of the text?
- If you see animation or rollovers (text that appears when you move the cursor over a word or picture), how do these contribute to your impression of the site?
- What contrasts do you see, both visually and in the written content?
- What symbols or slogans do you see? What historical or literary references?
- Is there a single authorial voice or several voices? How would you characterize the style(s)?
- How up-to-date is the site, and how does the currency of information affect your experience as a visitor?
- How would you characterize the sites this one links to?
- If you interacted with the site by contributing content to it (e.g., by voting in a poll, writing a letter that got posted on the site), how did this experience affect your impression of the site?

To Sum Up

Through analytical reading, writers are better prepared to write fully and thoughtfully about their subjects. By previewing, marking up a text, and identifying a text's ideas and methods, the writer can generate a variety of ideas and approaches for an essay. Similarly, by reading critically a visual image, including Web sites and architecture, a writer generates a variety of ideas to begin planning an essay. These activities form the groundwork for a paper. While writers still have to sort out their ideas, plan their writing, identify their most convincing evidence, anticipate their readers' responses, and create a first draft, they have ample thoughts to draw from. They are not beginning with a blank page.

ANALYTICAL WRITING AS ARGUMENT

While careful reading and analysis are the beginning points of good writing, they are only the first step in communicating an argument to others. What follows are some of the ways writers convey their ideas to readers.

Credibility

Often people argue to persuade others to take their side: in a court of law, for example, lawyers argue to win jurors to their side of a case; political candidates argue to get voters to choose them over their opponents; students argue to convince the audience in a school debate that their view of an issue is more compelling than that of their competitors. These forms of argument presume two sides: agreement and disagreement, a winner and a loser. Often, the stakes are high.

But arguing is not always a matter of convincing others that your beliefs have more merit than someone else's. Much of the time, arguing is not about persuading someone that you are right, but about being believable. It's about helping others see, by clarifying for yourself and others, one way to interpret a text, picture, or issue. This book is primarily about becoming credible, whether you write to argue a side or to get others to appreciate your point of view.

When you analyze a text or picture, as you will in this book, you look at the work's different elements and you draw conclusions about the significance of what you see. The act of communicating these conclusions to a reader is arguing—that is, you are attempting to convince the reader that your analysis has merit. You may or may not move the reader to agree with you; however, your analysis needs to offer believable evidence, such as research, statistics, details, and examples. And the analysis needs to tie that evidence to your conclusions in reasonable ways, ways others can't dismiss out of hand. Generally, writers who are believable project a strong vision, based on credible ideas; they keep an open mind as they write; they consider and explain multiple points of view when presenting their ideas to a reader; and they draw conclusions that are specific to the evidence, avoiding overgeneralization.

Developing Credible Ideas

One step in being credible is developing your ideas to make sure people see what you see. You can achieve this common vision by using specific writing strategies. Most writers have a repertoire of strategies they use, but may favor some over others—based on subject or personal style. That repertoire might include making an extended analogy, describing an event or picture, telling a story, reporting others' experiences, giving personal testimony, providing the reader firsthand experience with the evidence, quoting, summarizing, defining a central concept, accumulating examples, and choosing a few telling details. If you look at the readings included in this text, you will notice that the writers all employ one or more of these strategies. These writers' primary task is to make the reader see what they see, to give their ideas life and body. At the end of this chapter, we offer paragraphs that exemplify these strategies. In traditional writing terms, the excerpts offer various forms of development.

Getting others to see your subject involves one other strategy, one worth some special attention because it suffuses the writing and often goes unnoticed: the writer's tone. Tone is important because it communicates the persona of the writer. A tone that is appropriate to the subject (e.g., sympathetic, bitter, matter-of-fact, confident, or judicious) presents a trustworthy or believable persona. Imagine the possible disconnects if the writer discussed capital punishment in a cold, distant tone of voice or if the writer spoke about recent medical advances, however new and controversial, in a scolding or sarcastic voice. A good number of readers would not believe the writer.

Notice how the following paragraph uses tone to help readers see the humanity of the people living on death row. The writer, Mumia Abu-Jamal, uses an angry, darkly observant tone to penetrate and counter readers' preconceptions about death-row inmates. Because the tone is appropriate to his subject, we are inclined to believe him.

> Don't tell me about the valley of the shadow of death. I live there. In south-central Pennsylvania's Huntington County, a 100-year-old prison stands, its Gothic towers projecting an air of foreboding, evoking a gloomy mood of the Dark Ages. I and some forty-nine other men spend about twenty-two hours a day in a six-by-ten-foot cell. The additional two hours may be spent outdoors, in a chain-link fenced box, ringed by concertina razor wire, under the gaze of gun turrets. Welcome to Pennsylvania's death row.

In this passage, which argues that prison cells are uncivilized, Abu-Jamal describes his prison surroundings. Suffusing this description is an angry tone that enhances his credibility. We see this anger in his impatient dismissal of commonplace uses of the Bible as a source of comfort ("Don't tell me about the valley of the shadow of death") and in his ironic rendering of the cheery greeting "Welcome to Pennsylvania's death row." Both his dismissal and his ironic cheeriness reveal his bitter reaction to being put in a "six-by-ten-foot cell" for twenty-two hours a day. However, if the passage were merely angry, we might dismiss it as a rant. But he adds to anger a tone of authority. Abu-Jamal establishes his authority on prison architecture with the self-confident "I live there." He then offers us pinpoint details of prison materials and structures that only an insider would know: "chain-link fenced box, ringed by concertina razor wire, under the gaze of gun turrets." These details give him the authority to view his prison as a relic of the Middle Ages ("Gothic towers," "gloomy mood of the Dark Ages"). Here the dual tones, anger and authority, enhance the believability of the description. They help us see what we would not otherwise have seen.

Keeping an Open Mind

A second step in becoming credible is keeping an open mind. As you write, you have opportunities to question your own assumptions and come up with new ideas. For example, when writers begin to report an event, describe a photograph, or exemplify a concept, new thoughts, even contradictory ones, arise. This questioning does not weaken the argument or undermine the writer's resolve. Rather, this review of the words on the page becomes a way to rethink the evidence and conclusion, to shape and strengthen the writer's vision. Ask yourself what you truly "see" in your subject. Do you see the same thing every time? Credible arguments are reinforced by much self-questioning.

Indeed, arguing well is not simply settling on a position and then listing evidence to support it. Experienced writers know that they must remain open to new thoughts every minute, even as they perform a supposedly simple task of, say, describing the elements in a picture that create a certain effect. In describing one element, they might come to "see" a new element and discover a new relationship among the parts of the image. When experienced writers finally stop work on a piece of writing, they often have achieved an unanticipated perspective on their subject. The result may be far more insightful, reasoned, and credible than what they began with.

Presenting Ideas to Others

A third step in becoming credible is to present ideas sympathetically to others, anticipating and giving voice to alternative perspectives. When you create an argument, you need to imagine that others may hold different assumptions, may recall different evidence, and may question your interpretation of the evidence. If throughout the writing process you changed your own mind and considered alternative views, you may already be offering different perspectives in your paper. Giving credence to such views strengthens your own argument. Not only do you engage diverse readers because you understand their points of view, but you are also better able to keep such readers open to your views. Listed below are additional writing strategies that help you anticipate, sympathetically restate, and use alternative views to good purpose.

- Acknowledge and represent accurately other interpretations.
- Grant the validity of certain opposing points, even when they support an unacceptable conclusion.
- Identify shared ground.
- Indicate where you have enlarged your views.
- Use a respectful tone.

You may think that raising and supporting opposing views is not your task and that doing so weakens your argument. However, being able to restate an opposing or alternative view fully and sympathetically is an important skill, not only at times of crisis but also in everyday social relations; we often have more in common with others than we think. If you emphasize that commonality, you put people at ease, making them willing to listen to you. Furthermore, in finding unexpected common ground, you may learn something new. Perhaps the reasons for a seemingly unacceptable view have merit, and in writing about them you come to understand them more fully. As a result, you have deepened your thinking, added significant new insights, and obtained even more credibility.

Tying Your Evidence to Your Ideas

A fourth step in becoming credible involves checking for and enhancing the supporting logic—tying the evidence to the ideas. Novice writers at times leave out the explanations of their evidence, how it supports their ideas. They often make leaps in logic to generalizations that may or may not be justified by the evidence. In fact overgeneralization is the most common logical fallacy plaguing novice writers. The writer intuits the connection between the evidence and the idea it supports, but has not conveyed the relationship to the reader. Or the writer has made too big a claim for the evidence, when a lesser claim is more appropriate. Writers need to lead their readers along, small step by small step, making only those generalizations that are supported by the specific evidence. A sudden leap, a piece of evidence out of the blue, a grandiose generalization, or an unexplained opinion may disrupt that gentle leading. Too many such leaps and disconnects and a sympathetic reader may become a stubborn donkey, feet planted and refusing to go on.

Here is a checklist for creating connections between evidence and idea:

- Provide ample surrounding context for every example or piece of evidence: introduce the example by providing its context or importance; after citing it, discuss how it shows what you say it does.
- Check your generalizations: How global are they? Are you making too big a claim?
- Examine your assumptions. In making the generalization that you do, what are you taking for granted? Will your readers necessarily make the same assumptions? If not, why did you make them?

Here's an example. In our own writing, we, the authors of this book, struggled with just these concerns. In a passage that appears earlier in this chapter (p. 11), for example, we wanted to show how Mumia Abu-Jamal uses two different tones—angry and authoritative—to enhance his credibility. In creating the paragraph, we used examples of both tones. However, we needed to provide important context leading into the quotations. For general context, we decided to indicate Abu-Jamal's subject ("prison cells") and purpose (to show that prison cells are "uncivilized"). Then we sought to provide more specific context, a lead-in to each quote. We had to identify what in particular Abu-Jamal is angry about (for example, "commonplace uses of the Bible as a source of comfort"), and we had to figure out and include what made certain statements reveal an authoritative tone (he offers "pinpoint details" that "only an insider would know"). These lead-ins took us the most time, as we had to choose among various possibilities. (We rejected the possibility that Abu-Jamal was angry at being punished or at religious ideas generally.) We knew that when such context is left out, the reader is not prepared for the quotations or might leap to unexpected conclusions. We also knew that after citing evidence, the writer needs to tie the example to the general point. So we followed each quotation with comments connecting Abu-Jamal's specific words to our claim about his tone. We then tied the various examples to our overriding point, that the dual tone enhances his credibility. These connections were essential to our text because without them, readers might not see what in the examples supported the main point. To repeat our ending:

> Abu-Jamal establishes his authority on prison architecture with the self-confident "I live there." He then offers us pinpoint details of prison materials and structures that only an insider would know: "chain-link fenced box, ringed by concertina razor wire, under the gaze of gun turrets." These details give him the authority to view his prison as a relic of the Middle Ages ("Gothic towers," "gloomy mood of the Dark Ages"). Here the dual tones, anger and authority, enhance the believability of the description.

Creating this tightly connected paragraph proved a further and unexpected challenge: we had to give up certain insights that didn't further our main idea or did so only indirectly. We had to discard ideas about how the passage revealed Abu-Jamal's humanity, his literary and historical knowledge, and his expertise with language. These were some of our favorite ideas, so it was hard to discard them. While in a roundabout way, we might have connected such insights to his authoritative tone, we felt that our strongest evidence lay in his precise knowledge of his prison and cell. So we reluctantly set aside most of these other hard-won insights.

This process of connecting evidence to main ideas through context, lead-ins, and follow-up comments helped us with the other items on the checklist: checking generalizations and examining assumptions. In writing our paragraph, we were trying to avoid overgeneralizing or making problematic assumptions. But we had a hard time with the passage "Don't tell me about the valley of the shadow of death." The passage first suggested Abu-Jamal's rejection of the concept of Hell, then of the Bible, then of religious consolation generally. None of these seemed right. Finally we decided that in the passage, Abu Jamal was only rejecting a facile use of the Bible for easy consolation. We narrowed our generalization and avoided making an assumption that might well have been inaccurate.

The preceding suggestions offer you general guidelines for arguing effectively. What follows are suggestions for specific analyses, analyses of essays and pictures.

www.mhhe.com/durkinl

For more information on writing arguments, go to Writing > Writing Tutors > Arguments

Writing about Texts and Images: The Writing Process

In *Seeking Common Cause,* we suggest that you write about particular essays and visual images we have chosen. It is commonplace that writers see vastly different things in their subjects. In fact, texts and images are valued because they provoke such divergent responses, making them a source of intrigue and speculation. This variation in response might lead you to believe that opinion alone is important, not the attempt to persuade the reader. However, when experienced writers analyze texts or pictures, they do try to change readers' perceptions. They examine closely the elements of the work, they look for unnoticed patterns among the elements, they identify the context of the work, and they include information about the writer or artist if it helps clarify meaning. The writing comes across as detailed, informed, comprehensive, and reasoned. In other words, it is a form of argument and relies on credibility. But how do writers create it?

www.mhhe.com/durkinl

For more information on writing about images, go to Writing > Visual Rhetoric Tutorial

Begin with Concrete Details

When you write about a text or picture, or a group of them, you are forming interpretations about what you see. Some of your first thoughts may not take you very far. They may be too general or opinionated to be credible. Or they may be too specific, a list of observations or descriptions that seem obvious. The first thing you need to do is to generate specifics and then derive ideas closely related to the specifics. Here are some guidelines that may help you:

- Begin by listing all the details that strike you as significant.
- Avoid making quick generalizations. Put observations and details into groups and label them.
- Spend time thinking about what these groups might mean. Think of alternative interpretations. List as many ideas as you can think of.
- Look again at each text or image. Do new details strike you as important? What do they suggest?
- Details of each essay might include its main argument and supporting arguments, tone, different kinds of evidence, assumptions.
- Details of a picture might include a figure (dress, posture, face, gaze), background, actions, objects, colors, shapes. Details of a work of architecture might include site, layout, massing, and style.

Credible arguments reflect careful thought about details. Be sure that you are spending sufficient time looking closely at the reading or visual image, both before you start writing and during the writing process.

Creating a First Draft

Looking closely at your subject, generate a list of key ideas, points that best seem to respond to the question you have chosen. Outlines, clusters of ideas, lists, drawings, visual maps—any overall visualization of key ideas will help you plan and guide the writing process. We suggest that you choose a familiar way to plan your writing, like outlining or clustering, and then use it to keep you writing. Change your plan as you go, but keep a plan in mind. Perhaps put your visualization on your computer or notepad and refer to it as you write. What follows is a visual map for a sample student paper we offer at the end of this chapter.

Ads in *Vanity Fair,* 1985
Ciao! Shoes: conservative picture: white socks and paint = cleanliness and innocence
Benson and Hedges: harmony: elegant dress and smiling faces = agreement, tradition

Ads in *Vanity Fair,* 2003
Prada shoes: edgy: woman on toilet, focus on her legs and stockings = sexually explicit
Camels: glamour: spotlight on woman; shiny background and fancy trays = seduction

Your first draft is just that—a draft, a work in progress. With your outline or visual map in mind, you might try writing sections of the first draft fast, not stopping to correct sentence structure or get down every detail. You can then look back at your map or reread what you have just written to push you forward. Using this strategy, you would not belabor details but would try to capture your main points quickly.

You might also use the first draft process to help you generate and shape ideas. Many writers use the writing process to see what they think. They write more slowly, letting sentences generate other sentences, thinking and rethinking as they go. Their plan or map is a rough list, added to or changed as they go.

You might also try writing first those sections of the paper that seem clearest to you, even though you intend to place them toward the end of the paper. Using this flexible strategy, you might then write other paragraphs as placeholder sections, paragraphs that you sketch in but that will require later attention. With this approach, you might write the introduction last, after you see what you have written. Keep in mind that different writers have different personal preferences for getting words and paragraphs on the page. Use what works for you, but if you get stuck, be open to different approaches.

Development is always a key problem with first drafts. How does a writer expand without merely repeating an idea? The list of writing tools that follows this discussion of the writing process offers a selection of strategies for developing ideas. Credibility depends on the writer's ability to persuade readers through sufficient details, examples, quotations, testimony, or other forms of explanation or evidence. In writing the first draft, you might select from the list those tools you think will best further your argument. For instance, you might decide that vivid details and quotations are the strongest forms of evidence for your thesis. You might then direct your first draft efforts at gathering, introducing, and explaining extensive details and quotations.

Creating a Second Draft

Revising a draft differs significantly from first getting it on paper (or on screen). When you are first drafting or producing ideas, your thinking is often creative and exploratory, the writing often fast-paced and nonlinear; you may elect one strategy and switch to another. As ideas come, you want to get them down. In contrast, revising requires thought that is more focused and deliberate—the writer assesses how the reader might react to what is on the page, rearranges in terms of reader needs, and revises passages with the reader in mind.

When you are satisfied that you have captured the main ideas and evidence from your plan, map, or outline, consider the order of your presentation. Although you may have written your arguments in the order they occurred to you, the final order needs to reflect a logic that the reader can easily identify. Perhaps label the various sections and see whether the labels appear in a logical order. Explain the logic of this sequence to a friend and see whether the order seems logical to him or her. Then reorder your major points to help the reader best take them in.

The persuasiveness of your arguments may vary. Some may seem stronger than others. Ask yourself (and your friends) why the weaker ones seem less persuasive. Are there too few details? Too little reasoning? Questionable assumptions? Overgeneralized, clichéd reasoning? Have you anticipated other points of view? Ask others what they thought about when they read your arguments. What counterexamples, alternative views, or questions occurred to them? Look at some of the checklists offered in this chapter. Use them to help you increase your credibility as a writer.

In revising their writing, most writers are concerned with flow. Connections between ideas may seem natural to the writer, but not to the reader. Reread your paragraphs to see if you notice any leaps in thought. Then use the following steps to help you pinpoint possible disconnections.

- Title each paragraph with a word or phrase. Then ask, Do all the sentences in the paragraph relate to that title? Or do they better fit under a different paragraph title?

- Underline key words in a paragraph. Does the paragraph maintain a focus on these key words? Are those words defined, elaborated, and supported?

- Do the subjects of the sentences remain fairly consistent so that the reader's attention does not jump from one idea to the next?

- Are there too many connectors that set up loose connections as if you were making a list (*also, in addition, furthermore*)? Try to make most connectors indicate logical relations (e.g., causal or sequential) between ideas or concepts.

- Is there a central contrast or opposition in the paragraph? If so, are the two concepts clearly opposing, mutually exclusive concepts, or do they blur, making the reader stumble at an important juncture? Try to emphasize key contrasts through sharply opposing concepts. Use key words that add content to such catchall transition words as *however, in contrast,* and *nevertheless.*

After you have checked for logical order, persuasiveness of arguments, and flow, you are ready for editing. But even as you edit, you may still find yourself discovering new ideas and revising the paper as a whole. Writing is not a linear process but an iterative one. Working on a small editing task may lead you to rethink a major argument.

Creating a Final Draft

With each draft, you are still rereading, rethinking, and rewriting your arguments. However, with the final draft, your task has shifted toward making individual sentences easier for the reader to take in. A number of editing tips can help you with this task.

Reduce wordiness. Read your sentences aloud and see if they are difficult to follow: Do you hear lists of prepositional phrases, two or three verbs that compete for attention, long introductory phrases or clauses, or jargon that could be trimmed or removed? Cut out all inessential words, shorten introductory phrases, keep your subjects and verbs close together, and replace jargon with everyday English. Where possible, choose concrete subjects over abstractions, and select active, informative verbs (e.g., *detected, raved*) over passive, generalized ones (*is, was, has*).

Try to create sentence variety. Too many long sentences dull the reader's mind. Too many short ones jar the reader. When you edit sentences, you try to create smoothness and emphasis. Create short sentences after long ones for the greatest emphasis. Create long sentences out of many short ones by combining sentences, thus increasing smoothness. To combine sentences, reduce the sentence conveying less important information to an introductory clause or phrase; then it becomes a lead-in to the sentence that offers more important information.

Be conscious of word choice. Words are the building blocks of your essay. With every choice, you channel your reader's response. Use special care when you select words for subjects and verbs, for they constitute the foundation of your sentences. Transitions between paragraphs are also key places to focus on word choice. Does the wording of these transitions connect the key concept of the previous paragraph with the key concept of the paragraph to come? Try to make these transition sentences help the reader anticipate the key concepts to come.

When you edit, you also check for mechanics. Typical errors include subject-verb agreement, reference errors, phrasing, word choice, and spelling. It is useful to have a handbook on common errors to help you proofread. Reading aloud, using a computer's spelling checker, and asking friends to proofread are also good approaches to catching errors. However, be wary of computer grammar checkers; these programs often confuse correct and incorrect sentences.

---

www.mhhe.com/durkin1

For more information on the drafting process, go to Writing > Paragraph and Essay Develop. > Drafting and Revising

---

Using the Tools of Your Craft

We suggested a number of approaches to use in creating your initial drafts, including devising a visual map and writing quickly, without thinking about mechanics. But having a map and an approach may not be enough. Writers often wonder how to develop the ideas in their visual map. Following are examples of some of the tools, or strategies, that writers use to develop their ideas convincingly. Typically, writers combine several of these tools, though they may rely especially heavily on one of them.

Accumulating Examples

A series of brief examples, presented one after the other, can make a powerful impact. If individual examples are compelling, an accumulation of them, lined up together, is even more so.

> Since its birth in the United States, the consumer society has moved far beyond American borders, yet its most visible symbols remain American. The Disneyland near Tokyo attracts almost as many visitors each year as Mecca or the Vatican. Coca-Cola products are distributed over 170 countries. Each day, a new McDonald's restaurant opens somewhere in the world. Singaporean youngsters can brush their teeth with the Teenage Mutant Ninja Turtle Talking toothbrush, which says "Hey, Dudes!" in Malay. The techniques of mass marketing first perfected in the United States are now employed on every continent. Teaching former East Germans, for example, to "Taste the West. Marlboro."
> (Alan Durning, *How Much Is Enough? The Consumer Society and the Future of the Earth*)

The power in this passage comes from both the quantity of examples (five) and from their concreteness (we can picture the Teenage Mutant Ninja Turtle Talking toothbrush). Because the author is claiming that consumerism extends "far beyond American borders," it is important that his examples represent both quantity (the "over 170 countries" that sell Coca-Cola; a new McDonald's opening "each day")—and range: countries as diverse as Japan, Singapore, and East Germany. In presenting these examples, the author also draws on telling details: that is, these details   the toothbrush that speaks American slang ("Hey, dudes!") and the Marlboro ad that encourages East Germans to "Taste the West"—show that the United States exports not just products, but a whole culture. Though the passage creates credibility primarily by accumulating these details, a secondary tool it uses is analogy: the popularity of the Tokyo Disneyland is compared with the popularity of two important holy places—Mecca and the Vatican—thus implying that the American icon has almost the status of a world religion.

Choosing Telling Details

Often a specific detail will emerge from a description and evoke the writer's point:

> There is something uneasy in the Los Angeles air this afternoon, some unnatural stillness, some tension. What it means is that tonight a Santa Ana will begin to blow, a hot wind from the northeast whining down through the Cajon and San Gorgonio Passes, blowing up sandstorms out along Route 66, drying the hills and the nerves to the flash point. For a few days now we will see smoke back in the canyons, and hear sirens in the night. I have neither heard nor read that a Santa Ana is due, but I know it, and almost everyone I have seen today knows it too. We know it because we feel it. The baby frets. The maid sulks. I rekindle a waning argument with the telephone company, then cut my losses and lie down, given over to whatever it is in the air. To live with the Santa Ana is to accept, consciously or unconsciously, a deeply mechanistic view of human behavior. (Joan Didion, *Slouching Towards Bethlehem*)

This passage builds on several striking images—the hot, whining wind, the sandstorms, the smoke, the stillness—but two telling details sum up the uneasiness created by these natural phenomena: "The baby frets. The maid sulks." In addition, the tone of the passage reinforces the discomfort Didion describes; through an abrupt, staccato rhythm, Didion creates the tension she is writing about: ". . . I know it, and almost everyone I have seen today knows it too. We know it because we feel it. The baby frets. The maid sulks. I rekindle a waning argument with the telephone company. . . ."

Describing

To describe is to create a visual image or to appeal to other senses—e.g., touch or sound—through words. Description allows the reader to experience your subject as you experience it—to see or feel what you see or feel.

> [The astronauts] were looking at a terrain which lived in a clarity of focus unlike anything they had ever seen on earth. There was no air, of course, and so no wind or clouds, nor dust nor even the finest scattering of light from the smallest dispersal of microscopic particles on a clear day on earth, no, nothing visible or invisible moved in the vacuum before them. All light was pure. No haze was present, not even the invisible haze of the finest day—therefore objects did not go out of focus as they receded into the distance. If one's eyes were good enough,

an object at a hundred yards was as distinct as a rock at a few feet. And their eyes were good enough.
(Norman Mailer, *Of a Fire on the Moon*)

Here Mailer shows us something that scarcely anyone, not even he, has seen: the moon, close up. Since it is difficult to describe the clarity of vision that is unlike anything the reader has experienced, much of his description is indirect; it tells what elements are not there to obscure the astronauts' sight: "no air . . . no wind or clouds, nor dust nor even the finest scattering of light . . . no, nothing visible or invisible moved. . . ." The images are mostly visual, as he brings to mind an absence of clouds, haze, and dust to convey pure light in perfect focus. The admiring tone enhances the sense of awe that he brings to this description. The scene inspires him, and so, as we see in the last sentence, do the astronauts: "And their eyes were good enough."

In another example, the description of the details of two paintings helps us see the paintings as the writer sees them.

In *Ellen Mary Cassatt in a White Coat* and *Girl in the Blue Arm Chair*, the children seem imprisoned and dwarfed by the trappings of respectable life. The lines of Ellen's coat, which create such a powerful framing device, entrap the round armchair and the living child. The sulky little girl in the armchair seems about to be swallowed up by the massive cylinders of drawing room furniture and the strong curves of emptiness that are the floor. In *The Bath*, the little girl has all the unformed charming awkwardness of a young child: the straight limbs, the loose stomach. But these are not the stuff of Gerber babies—or even of the children of Millais. In this picture, the center of interest is not the relationship between the mother and the child, but the strong vertical and diagonal stripes of the mother's dress, whose opposition shapes the picture with an insistence that is almost abstract.
(Mary Gordon, *Good Boys and Dead Girls and Other Essays*)

By carefully describing specific visual details, the writer makes us see relationships and meanings we might not otherwise see. The writer emphasizes the size, location, and power of the entities surrounding the children: the framing "lines of Ellen's coat," the "massive cylinders of drawing room furniture," the "strong curves of emptiness that are the floor," and the "strong vertical and diagonal stripes of the mother's dress." The writer connects these entities to the "respectable life" that forcefully imprisons the children.

In addition to vivid description, the writer uses metaphor and an explicit comparison to develop the writer's view. The writer suggests that the pictures portray middle-class life as a living monster, one that "dwarf[s]," "entrap[s]," and "swallow[s] up" children. In a more extended negative comparison, the writer indicates that these children are not the charming innocents of "Gerber" or "Millais." Rather, they are the victims of powerful abstract forces.

Using Analogies

One way to help readers understand your subject is by comparing it to something they already know. The comparison can thus make the unfamiliar—your subject—familiar.

Conversely, analogies can clarify your point by doing the opposite: they can invite the readers to imagine a familiar subject in a new way, by looking at it against something else.

> Critics of computers say that the computer will alienate people, that people will get so used to transacting business by machine, they'll have little occasion to be with other people. But years ago, critics of the telephone said the same thing: They feared that the telephone would isolate people by making face-to-face contact unnecessary. As it turned out, the phone did not restrict personal contact; it did the opposite, enlarging our world by allowing us to reach people who lived far away. In the same way, computers bring people together. Electronic mail permits instant communication among people all over the world. Some researchers believe computers can even facilitate human relationships; they argue that people are less inhibited when communicating by computer and that email and chat room exchanges often lead to face-to-face meetings.
> (Lisa Gerrard, *The Computer and the Telephone*)

In the passage above, the author draws on a historical analogy to argue that computers bring people together. It compares what critics said about the telephone years ago with what critics say about the computer today: both argued that their respective technologies would drive people apart. By showing us that earlier critics of technology were wrong, it invites us to consider the possibility that today's critics of computers may also be wrong. Another way this comparison works is by making the unfamiliar familiar. It contrasts what we don't know—how computers will affect relationships—with what we know very well—how the telephone brings people together—and thus allows us to imagine the computer enlarging our social worlds as the telephone does. A secondary strategy in this passage is the accumulation of examples: we are told that computer-based communication is "instant," "all over the world," and "less inhibited" than other forms of communication and that it can facilitate "face-to-face meetings."

Using Metaphors

Metaphor helps you see one thing in terms of another. It eliminates explicit comparison words such as *like* or *as* ("He ran as fast as a bird could fly" becomes "he flew") to make the comparison immediate, a joining of two things into one. Writers use metaphor to provide an immediate new vision.

> A friend of mine recently suggested that education is one culture embracing another. It's interesting to think of the very different ways that metaphor plays out. Education can be a desperate, smothering embrace, an embrace that denies the needs of the other. But education can also be an encouraging, communal embrace—at its best an invitation, an opening. Several years ago, I was sitting in on a workshop conducted by the Brazilian educator Paulo Freire. It was the first hour or so and Freire, in his sophisticated, accented English, was establishing the theoretical base of his literacy pedagogy—heady stuff, a blend of Marxism, phenomenology, and European existentialism. I was two seats away from Freire; in front of me and next to him was a younger man, who, puzzled, finally interrupted his speaker to ask a question. Freire acknowledged the question and, as he began

answering, he turned and quickly touched the man's forearm. Not patronizing, not mushy, a look and a tap as if to say: "You and me right now, let's go through this together." Embrace.
(Mike Rose, *Lives on the Boundary*)

In this passage, the writer cites and then examines the metaphor of education as an "embrace" between two cultures. He identifies two abstract kinds of educational embrace—one that smothers and one that encourages. Then he describes education as a real embrace—an actual physical touch. The touch involves two human beings from opposite sides of the teaching-learning spectrum: One a celebrated theoretician, Paulo Freire, ex-postulating on his theories; the other an unknown young man—puzzled, questioning, and hesitant. Freire's physical touching of the student's forearm, helping him along, is the "embrace" of two cultures. The metaphor helps us see education in an entirely new way.

The writer uses other compelling tools, including personal testimony, telling details, and tone. He witnessed Freire's tap on the forearm and testified to its significance ("as if to say: 'You and me right now, let's go through this together.'") We believe him because he was right there—"two seats away." We also believe him because of his telling details—what he thought the tap on the arm was not: "Not patronizing, not mushy." Finally, we believe him because of his tone—observant, modest, and kindly. This writer is happy to examine the simple acts of education and find in them the real meaning of the word *embrace*.

Quoting

Quoting is one of the most powerful ways of establishing a beginning point, supporting a claim, or bringing in a different voice. Quotations also have multiple purposes. They may enrich your ideas by showing that others also have made the same observations, often in particularly apt language. Or you may use them to contrast your views with someone else's. Alternatively, they can function as a point of departure for an idea that you wish to develop, as they do here:

Studying the public perception of [Andy Warhol] in 1966, critic Lucy Lippard noticed that "Warhol's films and his art mean either nothing or a great deal. The choice is the viewer's. . . ." In retrospect, Lippard's early tentative appraisal is revealing. While the images Warhol stumbled across have a deep resonance with the public, the problem of interpreting them is, depending on one's point of view, simple or complex.
(Alan Pratt, "Andy Warhol: The Most Controversial Artist of the 20th Century")

In this passage the quotation is surrounded by helpful information. The opening phrase places it in a context, a study of how the public perceives Andy Warhol's work. Following the quotation is the writer's point, an elaboration on the quoted idea: that Warhol's art elicits both simple and complex interpretations. In this case, the writer uses the quotation as a strategy to advance his own idea about Warhol. Quotations are especially effective when, like this writer, you incorporate them into your text and use them to move your argument forward.

In addition, when you use a quotation to illustrate your point, be sure that the connection between your point and the quotation is obvious. The reader should not have to dig through the quoted text to find the relevant kernel within: quote only the segment that is relevant; then explain the relevance to the reader, as the passage on Warhol does.

Quoting is especially helpful when we want to bring in another's words and then make use of them in our own way.

To understand the immune system, we are to think of it "as a disciplined and effective army that posts soldiers and scouts on permanent duty throughout your body" (Laliberte, 1992:56). These warriors identify a threat, attack and destroy our enemies so quickly that we often do not know that we are threatened: the immune system, "never takes prisoners." The story of the human immune system "reads like a war novel": our lymph nodes are major centers for the breeding "attack dogs," called antibodies (Gates, 1989:16). In sum, the body "has devised a series of defenses so intricate they make war games look like child's play." (National Institute of Allergy and Infectious Diseases 1985:5).
(Emily Martin, *Flexible Bodies: Tracking Immunity in American Culture—from the Days of Polio to the Days of AIDS*)

Here, the writer uses quotations from other researchers, quotations that compare the immune system to a "disciplined and effective army." The writer then makes that analogy into a metaphor and talks directly of "warriors" who "attack and destroy our enemies." For the writer, the immune system "never takes prisoners." The lymph nodes breed "attack dogs." Thus, the writer uses quotations to work together with other tools to extend ideas, detail them more fully, and make them more immediate for the reader. Notice that the writer uses "in-text" quotations—they are part of her sentence, not separate sentences. She thus weaves her own words through these other words, never losing the authority of her own voice.

www.mhhe.com/durkin1

For more information on quoting, go to Research > Avoiding Plagiarism > Using Quotations

Summarizing

Summarizing another writer's ideas or the plot of a story allows you to select the details from an example that are pertinent to your argument.

The entertainment media present working people not only as unlettered and uncouth but also as less desirable . . . than other people, as in *The Three Faces of Eve* (1957), a movie about a woman who suffers from multiple personalities. When we first meet Eve (Joanne Woodward), she is a disturbed, strongly repressed, puritanically religious person, who speaks with a rural, poor-Southern accent. Her second personality is that of a wild, flirtatious woman who also speaks with a rural, poor-Southern accent. After much treatment by her psychiatrist, she is cured of these schizoid personalities and emerges with a healthy third one, the real Eve, a poised, self-possessed, pleasant woman. What is intriguing is that she now speaks with a cultivated, affluent, Smith College accent, free of any

low-income regionalism or ruralism, much like Joanne Woodward herself. This transformation in class style and speech is used to indicate mental health without any awareness of the class bias . . . expressed.
(Michael Parenti, *Make-Believe Media: The Politics of Entertainment*)

Here Parenti uses the plot of a movie to illustrate his assertion that the entertainment industry presents working-class people as less desirable than others. In his summary of *The Three Faces of Eve,* he is careful not to distract us with every event in the story; instead he focuses on his point—he describes how the movie identifies Eve as poor and uneducated when she is mentally ill and as wealthy and cultivated when she is cured.

Giving clout to Parenti's argument is his use of comparison: the sick Eve is alternatively "strongly repressed" or "wild," compared to the healthy Eve, who is "poised, self-possessed, [and] pleasant"; the sick Eve speaks in a rural, poor Southern accent, while the healthy Eve has a cultivated, affluent accent. In addition, by defining the healthy Eve's accent as a "Smith College" accent, the author provides a telling detail that implies a gracious, privileged, sophisticated life.

---

www.mhhe.com/durkinl

For more information on summarizing, go to Research > Avoiding Plagiarism > Summarize/Paraphrase

---

Telling a Story

Everyone loves a good story. If we are drawn in by the characters and the events, the writer has captured our attention and our sympathies.

Today, Baysie works for Reebok as general-merchandise manager—part of the team trying to return Reebok to the position it enjoyed in the mid-nineteen-eighties as the country's hottest sneaker company. . . . The hunt for [what's] cool is an obsession with her. . . . One day last month, Baysie took me on a coolhunt to the Bronx and Harlem, lugging a big black canvas bag with twenty-four different shoes that Reebok is about to bring out, and as we drove down Fordham Road, she had her head out the window like a little kid, checking out what everyone on the street was wearing. We went to Dr. Jay's, which is the cool place to buy sneakers in the Bronx, and Baysie crouched down on the floor and started pulling the shoes out of her bag one by one, soliciting opinions from customers who gathered around and asking one question after another, in rapid sequence. One guy she listened closely to was maybe eighteen or nineteen, with a diamond stud in his ear and a thin beard. He was wearing a Polo baseball cap, a brown leather jacket, and the big, oversized leather boots that are everywhere uptown right now. Baysie would hand him a shoe and he would hold it, look at the top, and move it up and down and flip it over. The first one he didn't like: "Oh-kay." The second one he hated: he made a growling sound in his throat even before Baysie could give it to him, as if to say, "Put it back in the bag—now!" But when she handed him a new DMX RXT—a low-cut run/walk shoe in white and blue and mesh with a translucent "ice" sole, which retails for a hundred and ten dollars—

he looked at it long and hard and shook his head in pure admiration and just said two words, dragging each of them out: "No doubt."
(Malcolm Gladwell, "Annals of Style")

The story about Baysie looking for "cool" does draw us in—the insouciant Reebok manager with her head out the car window in Harlem, and the teenager in Dr. Jay's with the diamond stud in his ear and the cool talk, testing sneakers. Notice that the passage combines several strategies: the story incorporates quotation, telling detail (the "growling sound" the young man makes when he sees a shoe he doesn't like), and description (the man's outfit). The writer has made us see what we could not otherwise have seen.

Providing Personal Testimony

Firsthand experience can advance an argument because the reader is likely to trust what you, the writer, have personally witnessed. It is especially effective if it is detailed and self-revealing.

I have to begin with a few words about androgyny. In grammar school, in the fifth and sixth grades, we were all tyrannized by a rigid set of roles that supposedly determined whether we were boys or girls. The episode in *Huckleberry Finn* where Huck is disguised as a girl and gives himself away by the way he threads a needle and catches a ball—that kind of thing. We learned that the way you sat, crossed your legs, held a cigarette and looked at your nails, your wristwatch, the way you did these things instinctively was absolute proof of your sex. Now obviously most children did not take this literally, but I did. I thought that just one slip, just one incorrect cross of my legs or flick of an imaginary cigarette ash would turn me from whatever I was into the other thing; that would be all it took, really.
(Nora Ephron, "A Few Words about Breasts: Shaping Up Absurd")

What makes this personal testimony especially compelling is its tone, which is both intimate and ironic. The sense of intimacy is created by language that people use in conversation: "I have to begin with a few words . . ."; "that kind of thing"; the use of the second person "you" ("the way you sat, crossed your legs"); "that would be all it took, really." Ephron draws us to her by seeming to confide in us. The ironic tone is created by the disparity between the trivial gestures Ephron describes and the huge importance her childhood self attached to them, an importance reflected in language that suggests extremes: "tyrannized," "absolute proof," and "just one slip."

In addition to personal testimony and tone, the passage gets its power from other tools: a brief summary of an episode in *Huckleberry Finn*, which also serves as a comparison (Huck's gender is defined by ordinary gestures just as Ephron's is), and an accumulation of details ("the way you sat, crossed your legs, held a cigarette, and looked at your nails, your wristwatch . . .").

Reporting Others' Experience

Reporting others' experience, especially through the lens of an intimate relationship, helps build credibility. The relationship itself makes the writer believable; and if the writer is also unusually observant, using telling details, the passage is likely to move us.

Through our bodies, we unconsciously send messages out to the world. Our looks, our gestures say, "Help me, I'm lonely." "Take me, I'm available." "Leave me alone, I'm depressed." Shortly after my grandfather died, I saw how expressive body language could be. My family gathered in the living room to discuss where my grandmother should live. Some felt she'd be better off in a nursing home, while others felt she'd be fine living in her own apartment. Throughout this discussion, my grandmother sat silently on the sofa, fondling her necklace and nodding. All she kept saying was, "Whatever the family decides. I don't want to be a problem to anyone." The family couldn't decide, and after awhile, grandma was fondling objects around her—an ashtray, chess pieces, a teacup. Watching this curious scene, it occurred to me that grandma had become a fondler when she began living alone. Through her fondling, she was saying, "I'm lonely. I'm starved for companionship. Help me!"

By reporting her grandmother's experience and situation, the writer helps us see the meaning of certain small actions in a certain light. The writer combines quotations (real and imagined), descriptions of the family discussion, and telling details about the grandmother's small behaviors—her fondling of various objects—to convince us that her grandmother's body language was saying, "I'm lonely."

Defining a Central Term or Concept

Definitions help us make distinctions. These distinctions then add clarity to our writing, because they separate what something is from what it isn't and require that we give reasons. When we make distinctions, we can expect many readers to question our choice, as it may not be the common choice. Part of defining is anticipating those reactions and giving them credence, as the writer of the following passage does.

I am a cripple. I choose this word to name me. I choose from among several possibilities, the most common of which are "handicapped" and "disabled." . . . People—crippled or not—wince at the word "cripple," as they do not at "handicapped" or "disabled." Perhaps I want them to wince. I want them to see me as a tough customer, one to whom the fates/gods/viruses have not been kind but who can face the brutal truth of her existence squarely. . . .

But to be honest, a certain amount of honesty underlies my choice. "Cripple" seems to me a clean word, straightforward and precise. It has an honorable history, having made its first appearance in the Lindisfarne Gospel in the tenth century. As a lover of words, I like the accuracy with which it describes my condition: I have lost the full use of my limbs. "Disabled," by contrast, suggests any incapacity, physical or mental. And I certainly don't like "handicapped," which implies that I have deliberately been put at a disadvantage . . . in order to equalize chances in the great race of life. These words seem to me to be moving away from my condition, to be widening the gap between word and reality.
(Nancy Mairs, *Plaintext*)

Here, the writer uses definition to tell us who she is. She explains why she chose the word *cripple* over other words such as *handicapped* and *disabled*. She wants to be seen as tough, facing the "brutal truth of her existence," even though she acknowledges that others may not like the word. She does not want to be seen as having a general incapacity or as having been put at a necessary disadvantage—vague impressions that obscure the image of weakened limbs. In defining what she likes about the word *cripple,* she is also defining her own character: honest, straightforward, and precise. Her insistence on a tough definition, and her reasons for it, convince us that she is indeed a "tough customer."

Establishing a Position through Tone

Tone in writing is like tone in speech. The speaker's or writer's voice tells you how to interpret what she says—for instance, whether to take it at face value, whether it's of the utmost importance, whether it's lighthearted and fun, or whether it's ironic (the speaker/writer means the opposite of what he says). And like tone in speech, tone in writing is one of the most powerful ways to control meaning. Tone reveals your attitude toward your subject and is usually described with adjectives—for example, cheerful, serious, formal, wistful, wry, admiring.

> Cooper's gift in the way of invention was not a rich endowment. . . . In his little box of stage-properties he kept six or eight cunning devices, tricks, artifices for his savages and woodsmen to deceive and circumvent each other with, and he was never so happy as when he was working these innocent things and seeing them go. . . . He prized his broken twig above all the rest of his effects, and worked it the hardest. It is a restful chapter in any book of his when somebody doesn't step on a dry twig and alarm all the reds and whites for two hundred yards around. Every time a Cooper person is in peril, and absolute silence is worth four dollars a minute, he is sure to step on a dry twig. There may be a hundred handier things to step on, but that wouldn't satisfy Cooper. Cooper requires him to turn out and find a dry twig; and if he can't do it, go and borrow one. In fact, the Leather Stocking Series ought to have been called the Broken Twig Series.
> (Mark Twain, "Fenimore Cooper's Literary Offenses")

Twain's attitude toward Cooper's novels is belittling, even contemptuous. Rather than tell us in a neutral tone that Cooper had little talent, he begins with ironic understatement: "Cooper's gift . . . was not a rich endowment"—Cooper doesn't merely lack a rich endowment of imagination, but he has no gift at all. The language that follows diminishes Cooper further by describing him as a child playing with his toys—a little boy who is "never so happy" as when he is playing with "his savages and woodsmen," "his little box," and his favorite toy, a broken twig that "he prize[s] . . . and . . . work[s] the hardest." The language also trivializes Cooper's novels by depicting them as contrived—in Cooper's hands the artist's tools are mere "stage-properties," "cunning devices, tricks, artifices," and "effects." Midway through the passage the tone moves from sly contempt to broad ridicule, as Twain, amused that Cooper knows only one way to create suspense, invents an absurd scenario in which a Cooper character in danger has to borrow a broken twig to step on.

The passage also argues through three different metaphors—Cooper is implicitly compared to a child, then to a stage manager (his tools are "stage-properties"), then to a criminal, guilty of "literary offenses." In this latter example, we see that Twain is also laughing at himself for being irritated by Cooper's bad writing. He knows that there are more important "offenses" than an overworked literary device.

As in the Twain passage, the tone of Alice Walker's writing tells us her attitude toward her subject, the stifling of African American women's talent in previous generations.

> What did it mean for a black woman to be an artist in our grandmothers' time? In our great-grandmothers' day? It is a question with an answer cruel enough to stop the blood.
>
> Did you have a genius of a great-great-grandmother who died under some ignorant and depraved white overseer's lash? Or was she required to bake biscuits for a lazy backwater tramp, when she cried out in her soul to paint watercolors of sunsets, or the rain falling on the green and peaceful pasturelands? Or was her body broken and forced to bear children (who were more often than not sold away from her)—eight, ten, fifteen, twenty children—when her one joy was the thought of modeling heroic figures in rebellion, in stone or clay?
> (Alice Walker, *In Search of Our Mothers' Gardens*)

Walker does not merely describe injustice and cruelty, but through her outraged tone, also encourages us to react with equal fervor. The four questions that make up most of the passage force the reader's internal voice to keep rising, the way the pitch of a speaker's voice rises with passion. And the word choices are violent, like the suffering of the women she describes—"cruel enough to stop the blood," "cried out," "broken and forced." The angry tone is also created by the strong contrasts—between the "genius" of a black great-great-grandmother and the "ignorant and depraved" white overseer and "lazy backwater tramp," between the sunsets and "peaceful pasturelands" and the broken body and grief of bearing and losing "eight, ten, fifteen, twenty children"—contrasts that simultaneously emphasize the injustice of an artistic genius controlled and confined by a worthless tramp.

Sample Student Papers

To conclude this chapter, we provide you with two examples of what a student paper might look like after several drafts. In the first example, the writer first analyzed several readings, looked closely at numerous advertisements from different decades, wrote two drafts, and edited for final submission. While the paper is not perfect, it does many things well to create a credible argument.

The assignment was to choose a magazine that has remained in publication over several decades. Students were to examine images of women or men in several ads from the 1980s and compare them with images of women or men from a recent edition of the same magazine. The writer chose to look at ads from *Vanity Fair,* from 1985 and 2003.

YOOSEON ALICE HAM

The Media's Impact on Women's Body Image

Advertisements display captivating images of supermodels who pressure women with standards of impossible perfection. One of the numerous magazines that presents its image of the "flawless" ideal woman is *Vanity Fair*. And while it is now generally acceptable for advertisements to use sex as a marketing tool, the women depicted in an issue of *Vanity Fair* eighteen years ago were presented far more conservatively than they are today. The advertisements geared toward women in the 1985 issue of *Vanity Fair* create tranquil images of innocence and harmony; the same ads today have eschewed these concepts in order to capitalize upon a woman's raw sex appeal.

The advertisers in the 1985 issue of *Vanity Fair* use tranquil environments to market their merchandise. The dominant color of white in the Ciao! ad displaying women's leather shoes sets a peaceful scene for the viewer, bathing the environment in innocence. The demure woman's foot graces a simple leather shoe, covered in a plain white sock. Rather than relying on the scintillating qualities of a naked, pedicured foot, the advertisers opt for a more reserved approach. Also, the wooden paintbrush covered in white paint suits the general cleanliness of the advertisement. The only reference to beauty or excellence is in the fine print that states that Ciao introduces the "hottest" leather shoes only available at "fine" retailers. This advertisement uses pure, natural images to sell Ciao! footwear without exploiting any part of the female body or degrading women.

Similarly, the Benson & Hedges advertisement for cigarettes illustrates a jovial couple relaxing with a cup of tea and coffee. The woman's flower-print suit and yellow hat along with the man's suit all match the bright lighting and bring a sunny tone to the advertisement. The similarity of their dress and attitude creates a comfortable harmony. Though the woman likes English tea while the man prefers Irish coffee, the advertisement explains, "there's one taste they agree on," highlighting their accord. The advertisement presents a desirable peaceful setting.

The advertisement of the Man's Diamond is perhaps the most dramatic example of a harmonious relationship. In this ad from 1985, the central image is of the man and the woman, snuggled together, the man's arm draped around the woman's shoulder. The advertisement promotes togetherness, happiness, and family by showing a happy couple posing for a picture together. The woman, in this case, is not elevated to the status of a sexual demi-goddess the way she is likely to be today; rather, the emphasis is on the family itself.

In contrast, most of the advertisements found in modern women's magazines such as *Vanity Fair* differ drastically from their marketing forebears. The depiction of the woman as a dignified object of affection, perhaps dependent on a good man, has been replaced by a more lascivious, highly sexualized image. In a remarkable instance of art imitating life, the advertisements of the new millennium aim to connect to today's sexually empowered women who do not necessarily need a family or man to succeed.

The Prada shoes ad, run in a 2003 issue of *Vanity Fair,* provides stark contrast to the Ciao! advertisement described before. The page focuses on the woman's long, slender legs dressed seductively in sheer black stockings. Her slim fingers are poised suggestively on the stocking as she draws the thin material closer to her knees. This gesture, while seemingly innocent, is intended to tease and arouse the viewer, as if to say "you can't touch this." Because Prada is a luxurious, expensive brand, many of the facets of the setting show wealth and grandeur, such as the teacup and the fur coat. These details complement her provocative stance. The woman is positioned on the toilet, apparently in a bathroom, a rather curious locale to peddle shoes in. This misplaced focus on the woman's sexuality actually detracts from the ad's intent by making it difficult for the viewer to decipher the product being sold.

Unlike the Benson & Hedges ad, a Camel ad spotlights a beautiful woman, thereby suggesting that smoking a Camel cigarette is sexy. The shiny background and spotlight force the viewer's attention onto the seductive woman enjoying her Camel cigarette. The bright yellow dress matches the Camel sign in the background, as if to show that the cigarette she smokes contributes to her attractiveness. Surprisingly, the men—with their fancy serving trays and smiling faces—are portrayed as submissive to the woman—a marked departure from the practices of the 1985 advertisements and a testament to her seductiveness.

While the 1985 ad for diamonds is directed toward a more family-oriented consumer group, the ad run by Di Modolo in 2003, also promoting diamond jewelry, simply portrays a naked woman. The bright lighting of her exposed body, mixed with the woman's dark hair, illuminates her naked form and averts attention from the diamonds she wears. This blatant nudity, in sharp contrast to the the Man's Diamond ad, focuses solely on the woman as seductress, focusing on her bare skin.

The recent advertisements seem to devalue the product itself and highlight the sexuality of the female models. Often it is hard to distinguish which product the advertisement is trying to sell because of the numerous unrelated, sexualized images that surround and hide it. The six advertisements described show the conspicuous change in methods of advertising—going from a focus on the product's qualities to a focus on the sexual and provocative.

A recurring theme in all three of the ads run in 2003, and in the advertising and modeling industries in general, is the almost exclusive use of thin models. As more women try to mimic their image of sexiness, they are placed upon a precarious perch, often forced to ignore health concerns to maintain a waiflike body. Women live in a world where they are judged by their appearance, a world filled with pressure to meet the expectations of the invisible "public eye." Susan Sontag remarks that being beautiful "is thought to name something essential to women's character and concerns." This sort of self-inflicted pressure sets ridiculous standards for many women, a standard they sadly feel forced to abide by. Unfortunately, to many women across the nation, failing to adhere to the media's definition of sexual attractiveness equates to absolute failure; "nothing less than perfect will do" (Sontag).

Unfortunately, the media is not concerned with social responsibilities, but is rather focused on selling as many products as possible, often by using slim, sexy models. Held up as role models by adoring young girls, these models may seem to preach the value of beauty and thinness over character. In the quest to be sexually attractive, young girls can become not only frail and excessively thin, but also mere objects and images for the pleasure of others.

What most women do not see are the deceptive airbrushing, plastic surgery, makeup, and other tricks of technology that transform a real, imperfect woman into a doll-like, "perfect" figure—an object of sexuality and beauty. In a society where women enhance their breasts despite obvious health risks, where people inject chemicals such as Botox into their faces to obtain youth, clearly something has gone wrong.

Allen Ginsberg, a poet, once said, "whoever controls the image controls the mind." And although people may believe standards of beauty and youth do not affect them, these absurd standards have become so ingrained in our cultural consciousness that it is nigh impossible to be immune to their toxic effects. The struggle to attain a "perfect" image is a struggle that none should undergo; everyone's perfectly unique beauty should be celebrated in its own right. The media's definition of the ideal woman is a trap; thinness does not equal happiness, beauty does not equal power, and sexual attractiveness should never be a measure of success.

A number of features make this essay a credible argument. The author has used various "tools of the trade" effectively—accumulating examples, using telling details, quoting, and establishing her position through tone. The author is especially convincing where she identifies telling details in the ads that might have escaped the reader's attention. These details include one 1985 ad's use of color (white) and simple objects (wooden paintbrush, plain white sock) to connect Ciao! shoes with images of innocence and cleanliness. The details also include one 2003 Prada ad's focus on a woman's legs, over which the woman draws "sheer black stockings" while she sits on a toilet, connecting Prada shoes with provocativeness. The writer also uses quotations effectively, integrating smoothly into the discussion the words of Susan Sontag on the pressures women face to meet high standards of attractiveness. Further, the writer uses an ironic tone to convey her objection to the increasingly sexualized and degrading images of women in advertising (e.g., ". . . as if to say 'you can't touch this' "). The tone is biting, but it reflects a sharp eye for details. Finally, the writer ends the paper with her own views about the media and social responsibility. Such views seem well grounded in the detailed contrasts between *Vanity Fair* ads of 1985 and 2003. The writer speaks with authority because she offers extensive contrasting details tied to reasonable generalizations.

The writer of the second paper also examined a variety of readings, this time on theories related to art and the Surrealist movement, in order to analyze a Surrealist painting by René Magritte. This writer also does many things well: she has a strong organizational plan, uses telling details, weaves in quotations from various sources, and uses an inviting tone.

The assignment was to determine to what extent the painting reflected the historical and conceptual ideas of the Surrealist movement. Students were to examine in close detail this or any other Surrealist painting, using tools of art analysis much like the ones offered in this chapter: subject matter, composition, color, light and dark, line of vision, and focal point.

CELIA DURKIN

Magritte's *Clairvoyance (Self-Portrait)*

René Magritte is considered a Surrealist painter, but what does it mean to be Surrealist? André Breton defines Surrealism in his *Manifesto of Surrealism* as "psychic automatism in its pure state, by which one proposes to express—verbally, by means of the written word, or in any other manner—the actual functioning of thought. Dictated by thought, in the absence of any control exercised by reason, exempt from any aesthetic or moral concern" (Breton 26). According to Breton, Surrealism is the depiction of mental processes. A Surrealist painting is not restricted by the boundaries of reality, only by the boundaries of the human mind. In fact, a key aim of Surrealism is to break the bonds of reality, to allow the artist to use his/her imagination and not be forced to paint what is really there. In his *Manifesto of Surrealism,* André Breton exclaims, "the mere word 'freedom' is the only one that still excites me. I deem it capable of indefinitely sustaining the old human fanaticism. Among all the many misfortunes to which we are heir, it is only fair to admit that we are allowed the greatest degree of freedom of thought" (Breton 5). Breton here presents the Surrealist ideal that expressing freedom of thought, and thus imagination, is essential to our very humanity.

In his painting *Clairvoyance (Self-Portrait),* Magritte depicts the Surrealist ideal of the freedom of the imagination. The painting draws attention to an artist's ability to paint what he/she perceives, not what is necessarily there. However, his painting does not wholeheartedly exclude the boundaries of reality. Although at first glance the painting appears to reflect the Surrealist idea that the artist is free to express mental thought, a deeper look reveals that the painting actually questions how free the artist is to express his/her imagination. Magritte shows that the artist remains partially bound to reality, and the painting ends up exposing a paradox between reality and the artist's imagination. Magritte portrays Surrealism in a new light—not utterly limitless—and presents the Surrealist painter as not utterly free. Thus, Magritte resists being categorized, breaking the bonds not only to reality but also to Surrealist views.

On the surface, Magritte first appears as a Surrealist. Magritte presents freedom as the main theme of his painting *Clairvoyance (Self-Portrait).* The painting portrays an artist sitting in a chair, his gaze fixed on a small, white egg. Although he is painting this egg, what appears on the canvas is a detailed bird, wings outstretched. The subject material seems immediately to correspond with the first part of the painting's title, *Clairvoyance.* The artist is exhibiting clairvoyance, the capacity to see beyond what is really there, in his ability to see an egg and paint a bird. Whether the artist is clairvoyant in the psychic sense and can see into the egg's future, or simply can see beyond the ambiguous shape of the eggshell, is not determined by Magritte. But what is important is that the subject the artist looks at differs from what the artist paints, showing that the artist in the chair has used freedom of thought in his art.

Magritte exhibits the artist's freedom of thought not only through simple subject matter, but also through compositional elements of the painting such as focal point and line of sight. At first glance, Magritte directs the viewer's eye straight to the bird, or more specifically to where the artist's paintbrush touches the canvas. The intersection between paintbrush and canvas serves as the focal point of the painting. This intersection, the center of the painting, is also pointed to by the wings and tail of the bird as well as by the paintbrush stemming from the artist's extended hand. The viewer's eye is first drawn to the focal point, and immediately we are confronted with an animal that is symbolic of freedom, wings outstretched. After we register this animate creature, the paintbrush then directs the viewer's eye to the face of the artist, whose gaze points us in the direction of the small egg, sitting inanimately on the table. The line of sight connects the egg, the artist, and the bird into a triangle, although it prevents the viewer's eye from traveling directly between the egg and the bird. Both the paintbrush and the artist's gaze serve as arrows, forcing the viewer's vision to travel back and forth through the artist, from egg to artist to bird and vice versa, as if the artist were the only connection between reality and the portrayal of reality.

Magritte's line of sight almost serves as a diagram of how artists should use their imaginations to perceive reality freely. The artist's fixed gaze gives the impression that the image of the egg is stable until it reaches the artist's head, where the real egg is transformed by the artist's imagination and the new image is sent through the paintbrush to the painting where it is expressed. Although Magritte's more complex spin on Surrealism will later be revealed, it is important to examine the strong first impression he creates of the freedom of the imagination.

By using another compositional element, balance, Magritte further accentuates the freedom of the imagination by inviting the viewer to use his or her own imagination when looking at the painting. According to Henry Sayre,

> Many works of art utilize an asymmetrical balance in which a perceived center of gravity seems to balance elements around it. It is like balancing a teeter-totter with a very heavy child on one side and a light child on the other: the heavy child moves toward the center of the teeter-totter while the lighter child sits on the very end. Furthermore, relatively darker shapes seem "heavier" to the eye than lighter ones. (Sayre 60)

In Magritte's *Clairvoyance (Self-Portrait)*, the painting is seemingly unbalanced, and heavily weighted to the right side. If the bird defines the central vertical axis of the painting, the artist sitting in his chair occupies much more space than the small egg on the table. Also, the right side of the painting is generally darker than the left side; the dark brown suit of the artist and the shadowing of his back give the right side of the painting a heavier weight. Seemingly, Sayre's teeter-totter would fail in this painting because the right side of the painting would hit the ground with no hope of being pushed back up. However, with the involvement of the viewer's imagination, the teeter-totter becomes functional.

Humans naturally search for balance in a painting, and Magritte relies on that need. By intentionally skewing the balance, Magritte invites the viewer to fix it. On Sayre's teeter-totter, the egg would naturally fly up if balanced against the artist—unless there is something inside the egg that carries weight. By isolating the egg, Magritte emphasizes it, giving it importance. Now it is up to the viewer to imagine what about that egg could be so important for it to be placed opposite a figure many times its size. Furthermore, the egg's ambiguous shape entices the viewer to ponder it, allowing us to try to define the egg for ourselves. But what the viewer comes up with is inconsequential, for the importance lies in Magritte's invitation to the viewer to use his/her own freedom of imagination when looking at the painting. In other words, Magritte evokes the Surrealist idea of active mental processes, not only of the artist, but also of the viewer. The viewer is invited to give the egg an imagined weight in order to balance out the painting. Thus the viewer, along with the artist-subject, expresses his/her own freedom of imagination.

Overall, the egg carries in it potential, and it is this potential that gives the egg its weight. Magritte portrays the artist seeing the potential in the egg and transferring that potential into the form of a bird. The egg by itself in reality is nothing more than a simple white oval, dull and plain. But when the artist uses his imagination, a world of complexities arises. The bird exhibits a complex shape and shading very much in contrast to the simple white oval form of the egg. At first glance, the bird is on a white background, with nothing surrounding it on the canvas. The bird is suspended in nothingness and is free from any boundaries. As the bird is a product of the artist's imagination, the bird's intricate shapes and lines, along with its lack of boundaries, suggest that the artist's imagination is both free and complex.

The complexity of Magritte's imagination extends into the painting as the painting shows itself to be more complex than we first took it to be. Now, we can peel off the outer layer of Magritte's painting that presents the Surrealist ideal of freedom of the imagination and explore how Magritte actually views Surrealism. Although seemingly lacking boundaries, Surrealism in fact consists of rules that the Surrealist artist must adhere to. Although appearing to ignore the restrictions of reality, the Surrealist painter, according to Magritte, actually depends on them. Although the artist may still use his/her imagination, this imagination depends on what is actually seen.

Although Magritte's painting portrays the Surrealist ideal of freedom of imagination, aspects of the painting question just how free the artist actually is. Overall, Magritte's use of line, as well as his positioning of the artist, gives the painting a feeling of rigidity. Many of the lines are straight and produce angles. Interestingly, the artist in the painting himself creates a ninety-degree angle where his arm bends to support his palette. The artist himself is positioned very rigidly, as he is sitting straight up in his chair, his gaze locked on the egg. His set gaze also portrays a lack of freedom. Although the artist uses his imagination to produce the painting, his sight is still locked on reality, suggesting that the imagination depends on what is actually seen. Thus, the imagination is not truly free from the restrictions of reality, as Surrealist ideals suggest.

Furthermore, a key detail that raises questions about how much freedom an artist can truly exercise lies in the painting of the bird, underneath the left corner of the bird's tail. Originating in the tail are two squiggly lines. These two thin lines appear to be fractures in the background of the painting surrounding the bird. Also, the background of the painting is white, the same color as the egg. Together, these details suggest that the bird that the artist is painting is not hovering in space, but in reality is still inside of its egg. The background color coincides with the color of the egg, and the two tiny lines appear to be fractures in the egg's shell. If the artist is indeed painting his imagined bird still inside its shell, the bird, and therefore the artist's imagination, is not completely free, but rather is still confined by the boundaries of reality.

Although Magritte presents the importance of the artist's ability to think freely outside of the boundaries of reality, he ultimately shows that the imagination is dependent on reality. In a few instances, Magritte even turns the relationship between reality and the imagination into a paradox. This paradox can be seen when we contrast the egg and the bird. Although supposedly representing reality, the egg's shape is less defined and more open to interpretation. In contrast, the figure of the imagined bird is detailed and intricate and almost looks more real than the egg does. The paradox is further accentuated by the title of the work. The title has two parts representing opposite methods of painting. The word *clairvoyance* signifies the use of the imagination and mental thought in the creation of a painting. In contrast, *self-portrait* represents a method of painting based on reality, of copying what the artist sees. Again through the title, Magritte analyzes the relationship between the imagination and reality, and the paradox suggests that they are intertwined and that imagination is dependent on reality. As the imagination is not utterly free, Surrealism is not utterly limitless.

Overall, *Clairvoyance (Self-Portrait)* at first suggests that Magritte is presenting the Surrealist ideal of freedom of the imagination. However, if we dig deeper we can uncover Magritte's more complex theory that the imagination is dependent on reality. Just as the imagination is dependent, so is the Surrealist artist. Although Surrealism is mainly viewed as breaking boundaries, Magritte demonstrates that Surrealism actually is restricted by them.

When looking at this painting, we as the viewer must keep in mind that Magritte himself paints the painting with clairvoyance. Interestingly, the background of the entire painting is gray—the same color as the bird. This could signify that the entire painting stems from Magritte's imagination and by looking at this "self-portrait," we are looking through a window into Magritte's mind. According to John Berger, "the painter's way of seeing is reconstituted by the marks he makes on the canvas or paper. Yet, although every image embodies a way of seeing, our perception or appreciation of an image depends also upon our own way of seeing" (Berger 2). The choices that Magritte makes serve to express his desires and inner mental processes. His painting exposes his imagination to whoever chooses to explore. Thus, *Clairvoyance (Self-Portrait)* truly is a self-portrait, for it articulates Magritte's own way of seeing to the viewer—a way of seeing that stems directly from Magritte's imagination, an imagination that still depends on reality.

Various features make this essay a compelling argument. Most compelling is the organization and the way it leads the reader to the writer's conclusions. The author opens with a summary of a key theory that will govern the rest of the essay. This opening orients the reader to the aims and purposes of Surrealist artists who wrote and painted in the 1920s and 1930s. In the second paragraph, the writer applies this theory to Magritte's painting, leading the reader to her stated thesis that Magritte both subscribes to and questions the view that the artist must be freed from bonds to reality.

The next section of the paper addresses the first part of this thesis. The writer uses telling details to support, first, the idea that this artist favors freedom of the imagination and rejects the reality of what he merely sees. She carefully describes the objects in the painting, their size and color, their lack of symmetry, and the viewer's line of sight—using details and analogies. The author next turns to the second part of her thesis, where she complicates the argument. Her point is that the painting also portrays the painter's bonds to reality. Additional telling details—including the subject's rigid body position, the ambiguous "reality" of the imagined bird, and the painting's title—support this more paradoxical relation between imagination and reality. Along the way, the writer uses a highly personable tone, inviting the reader to share with her the exploration of this painting that seems to open up to us as we look at it more closely.

To Sum Up

In summary, this chapter describes a variety of processes and approaches to writing to help you generate credible arguments. It opens with critical reading strategies and takes you through various stages in the writing process. Toward the end we provide an extensive list of writers' "tools of the trade," illustrated through the work of professional writers. The two sample student papers illustrate two possible outcomes of many of these processes. Our hope is that you come to see writing, not as a magical skill or talent, but as something closer to a craft, with specific approaches and processes that can be tried, practiced, and gradually internalized.

STEPHEN SCOTT YOUNG   Flip Flops and Lace

The paintings of Stephen Scott Young often address racial issues, especially through depictions of the individual human figure. In what ways is *Flip Flops and Lace* about race? In what ways is it about childhood?

© Stephen Scott Young. Courtesy of Surovek Gallery, Palm Beach, FL.

1 The little girl appears to be about six years old. Does she seem to be acting her age in the painting? Why or why not?

2 How would you describe the girl's facial expression, posture, and hand and foot position? What do these tell us about her?

3 The painting contains strong contrasts in color, shape, and texture—e.g., the rough texture of the ground and the rock contrasts with the girl's smooth skin and thus suggests the girl's vulnerability in an inhospitable environment. Discuss the significance of two other contrasts in the painting.

4 What is the effect of posing the girl, dressed neatly in a crisp, white dress, in front of a decrepit building? How might you interpret this placement?

JACOB LAWRENCE   The Library [1960]

Lawrence's art takes its themes from African American life and history and it also reflects experiences common to everyone: "This is my genre . . . the happiness, tragedies, and the sorrow of mankind as realized in the teeming black ghetto." How does *The Library* illustrate this idea? How does the painting convey the importance of reading to the people depicted in it?

Smithsonian American Art Museum.

1 Reading is often imagined as a serene activity, yet this painting is full of energy. The vertical and horizontal lines that create the wood furniture seem almost to vibrate with movement. How else does the painting suggest vitality and movement?

2 What do the different positions of the hands and the posture of the people tell us about them?

3 How many people are depicted in this painting? What is the significance of the fact that some of them seem to blend into the walls and furniture?

CARMEN LOMAS GARZA Camas para Sueños (Beds for Dreams) [1985]

Garza's paintings celebrate her childhood in a close-knit Mexican American community in Kingsville, Texas. *Camas para Sueños,* like many of her paintings, tells a story. What is happening in this painting and what do the details—e.g., the objects on the wall, the garden—tell us about this family?

Smithsonian American Art Museum.

1 What is the significance of the childlike quality created by the bright colors, minimal shading, and lack of perspective?

2 What is the relationship between what is going inside and outside the house?

3 The painting contrasts the work of daily living with the imagination, dreams. Which elements in the painting are aligned with dreaming? Which with daily life? How do shape and color support this theme?

HENRY SUGIMOTO   Nisei Babies in Concentration Camp [1943]

Many of Henry Sugimoto's paintings illustrate his experience as a Japanese American interned in a relocation camp during World War II. Although this internment was unconstitutional, it paradoxically reinforced Sugimoto's belief in the ideals of American democracy. What does the flag symbolize in this painting? What do the babies symbolize? What other symbols do you see, and what is their significance?

Japanese American Museum, Los Angeles.

1 What is the significance of the fact that the babies, unlike the guard, have no faces?
2 Find at least four contrasts (e.g., rounded shapes versus linear and jagged ones, innocence versus menace, the gun versus the flag), and explain what they tell us about the concentration camp experience.
3 What do the guard's facial expression and posture tell us about him?
4 Which images in this painting convey a sense of restriction?
5 What is the emotional impact of this painting?

Tomie Arai, whose ancestry is both Chinese and Japanese, often depicts the experiences of Asian Americans in her art. Arai found the photographs depicted in this mixed media work in the archives of the Chinatown History Project in New York City. What is the effect of juxtaposing the three photographs against a painted—and less lifelike—background?

1   What traditional images are there of the Chinese immigrant experience? How does placement and color alter how we see them?

2   Much of the work consists of images that we view through frames—the windows on either side of the women, the photograph held by the seated woman, and the women themselves being framed by red or black. Each of these frames is part of a Chinese immigrant story. What is that story?

PATRICIA RODRIGUEZ, IRENE PEREZ, GRACIELA CARILLO   Fantasy World for Children [mural, 1975]

Rodriguez, Perez, and Carillo are members of the Mujeres muralistas, a collective of Mexican American women artists who together design, build scaffolding for, and paint murals with Latin American themes on public buildings in San Francisco. Painted on a house bordering a playground, this mural evokes an Edenic world where animals, as well as native peoples, play in innocent joy. What images of Latin American culture do you see? Why do you think these images might be important to the Mujeres muralistas?

© Mujeres Muralistas, courtesy of Patricia Rodriguez

1   The mural is on a clapboard house that borders a playground. How might the placement of the mural on wood boards, the siding of a house in a low-income area, next to a playground, fit with an ideal of social harmony?

2   Unlike the Diego Rivera mural on p. 00, this mural does not show struggle and conflict. How do color and composition create feelings of harmony?

FRIDA KAHLO   Self-Portrait on the Borderline between Mexico and the United States [1932]

Frida Kahlo painted this self-portrait while her husband, Mexican muralist Diego Rivera, created the mural at the Detroit Institute of Art (p. 00). Showing herself in traditional Mexican dress, standing on a symbolic border between the United States and Mexico, Kahlo reveals her bicultural roots and conflicts. On the left are emblems of Mexico; on the right, emblems of the United States. What conflicts in cultural identity does the painting suggest?

1   In the foreground, on both left and right sides, different kinds of *roots* go into the ground. Describe these images of roots. What cultural conflicts do they embody?

2   How does Kahlo's portrait of herself suggest a cultural divide?

3   What religious emblems do you see in the painting? What difference between Mexican and U.S. culture do they indicate?

4   Does the image of Frida Kahlo in the middle of the painting embody some common ground between the two cultures? Why or why not?

JUDY CHICAGO   Rainbow Shabbat [1992]

This stained glass window is the final image in Chicago's *The Holocaust Project,* a multimedia series of artworks that depicts the horrors of World War II and culminates here in a vision of multicultural harmony. In Jewish tradition, Shabbat ("Sabbath") is the Friday evening ceremony and meal. Strangers, the poor, or other guests are often invited to share the Shabbat dinner, a long-standing custom meant to unify the community. What images of harmony do you see here?

Courtesy of Through the Flower/Judy Chicago.

1   What is the significance of the rainbow motif?
2   This artwork tells a story. What is that story?
3   What is the significance of the three animals?
4   Although everyone, even the dog, is sitting down, the window has a great deal of energy. What elements of the composition create a sense of movement?

Defining Cultural Identity

The artwork and writings included in this chapter portray people who in some ways live in two cultures, the culture of their family's ethnic ancestry and the larger, multicultural, public culture. The writers and artists represent a spectrum of responses to this duality: some celebrate one or both heritages; some resist the pull of one or the other heritage on them; some reach out from the comfort of one heritage toward another, looking for a fuller integration; and some focus on the discord between them.

CULTURAL IDENTITY IN THE WORKS OF ART

The works of art offer diverse portraits of people living in two cultures. In *Flip Flops and Lace,* Stephen Scott Young depicts an African American girl in rural Florida, whose innocence and purity contrast with her decaying surroundings. In *The Library,* Jacob Lawrence portrays African Americans in a particularly American institution—the public library; at the same time the brilliantly colored shapes and clothing he paints are reminiscent of African textiles. Carmen Lomas Garza, in *Camas para Sueños,* offers an intimate family scene from the Mexican American community of her childhood in Texas. Henry Sugimoto, in *Nisei Babies in Concentration Camp,* depicts the culture clash within World War II concentration camps for Japanese: he pits the innocence of the Japanese babies against the insignia of American power and callousness.

In *The Laundryman's Daughter,* Tomie Arai juxtaposes images from Chinese culture against those of tenements in New York's Chinatown, evoking the immigrant experience of part of her family. *Fantasy World for Children,* a mural painted by Patricia Rodriguez, Irene Perez, and Graciela Carillo (members of a Mexican American women's art collective), depicts icons from Mexican culture on a building in San Francisco, California; while Frida Kahlo, a Mexican artist who lived for a time in the United States, shows the vast differences between the indigenous Mexican culture and the industry-based culture of the United States in her painting *Self-Portrait on the Borderline between Mexico and the United States.* Finally, Judy Chicago, in *Rainbow Shabbat,* offers a utopian view of multicultural harmony, in which people of different backgrounds, their arms around each other, share the Jewish Sabbath. In each of these works, the artist depicts cultures in counterpoint or harmony, straining against each other or blending together.

Analyzing the Paintings

The works of art selected here portray harmony or tension in various ways: through their subjects, the subjects' actions, the background of the painting and the objects it depicts. In the more abstract portrayals, a sense of harmony or tension comes from color and shape. Are the colors vibrant and alive or muted and monochromatic? Are the shapes sharp and jagged or rounded and smooth? When you have identified the individual elements of the painting, you might ask yourself what significance each has.

To unveil this significance, ask how the portrait identifies the figure as part of a subculture and, alternately, whether the painting suggests the larger American culture. Analyze each figure's face, dress, posture, and gaze; or look at the objects and background in the picture. What do such elements suggest about the culture? Furthermore, ask yourself, What are the people doing and what do such actions imply about their culture? In addition, ask how color evokes a particular heritage. Do the colors have symbolic meaning? Overall, what cultural elements does the artist seem to celebrate? What elements are critiqued?

When analyzing a painting, the first step is to identify particular visual elements that have cultural meaning:

- figure(s) (dress, posture, face, expression, hair, placement) How are the people positioned? What do they look like? How are they interacting?
- background (location, detail, relation to figure) What does the background look like? Is the figure comfortable against this background? Is there a conflict?
- objects (what they are; why they are there; what they look like or are made of) How do the objects reflect on the values of the figure? How does the figure use them?
- color (bright, contrasting, monochromatic; associated with certain objects and not others) Do the colors suggest a culture? Are they symbolic? Do they reflect a mood?
- shape (sharp, smooth, large, small, rounded, jagged, symmetrical, or asymmetrical) How do the shapes suggest elements of a specific culture? Are certain shapes related to the figure?

After identifying and characterizing these elements, consider what the elements suggest about the relationship between the people depicted and their cultures:

- What elements are identified with the subculture? In what way?
- What elements are identified with the larger American culture? In what way?
- What is the relationship between those elements and the heritages they represent? (a blending? a tension? a source of inspiration? a conflict?)
- What common ground does the painting suggest? What elements suggest it?

The analysis that follows draws on these questions and is meant to serve as a model for your own analyses of works of art.

Analysis of a Painting

Look at *Flip Flops and Lace* (insert 2-1). Even in the title, you can sense dissonance—the poverty suggested by the flip-flops and the prosperity suggested by the lace. Stephen Scott Young's painting of a young African American girl in a chair offers numerous elements—especially figure (the girl), background (old house), and objects (chair)—that suggest a tension between the girl's poverty and the economic promise of the American dream. The little girl sits demurely in the demeanor of children schooled for proper behavior in an upwardly mobile society: her ankles are crossed neatly, her hands are clasped obediently on her knee, and her head is turned shyly away and down from the viewer, as if she were at a dance. Furthermore, she wears a spotless white dress, with lace trim, and someone has neatly arranged her hair. In contrast, you might notice that her chair, a kitchen chair made of rough metal and cheap plastic, is incongruously placed on empty ground in front of a decrepit white block wall, supported by crumbling white concrete slabs. The girl's youth, tidiness, and innocence are contrasted with the aging, worn-out, hopeless surroundings.

The painting can also be viewed symbolically as if the contrast between the decaying surroundings and the young child reflects the girl's personal situation. One interpretation might be that the painting symbolically depicts a conflict between the limited opportunities available to the girl—because of her poverty and the country's racism—and the American ideal of limitless opportunity. The heritage of deprivation is everywhere in the painting—in the nondescript wall, in the barren ground, even in the faded flip-flops, which the girl holds uncomfortably crossed in order to maintain her demure pose.

In addition to figure, background, and objects, you might note how color and shape emphasize difference. The painting seems composed of sharp white and black contrasts. The white dress, white wall, and white foreground all appear stark against the young girl's dark skin and the dark shadows on the ground. Further, the whiter white of the harsh sunlight on her dress and forehead appear almost glaring—too bright for the girl to look at—heightening the tension. Like color, shape also increases the tension. The girl is depicted in soft curves and gentle shapes; her arms, head, and legs are bent, while her dress curves over her knee. The background, however, is painted in sharp, rough lines. The lines in the broken wall and crumbling concrete are jagged and asymmetrical.

Given such stark contrasts, you might ask where in the painting lies common ground for African Americans and white society in the face of racial and economic tensions? Perhaps the girl's eyes, a focus point, might offer a clue. These eyes gaze past the viewer to someone or something outside of our immediate vision. However, they are neither hopeful nor resistant, but quizzical and sad. Indeed, while the neat appearance of the girl's hair and dress, and the tidy way she sits, might suggest that she can transcend her impoverished background, her posture and expression might suggest the opposite: that the closest she can get to escaping poverty is wearing a clean dress. If this is true, then the common ground may lie only in the viewer's empathy for an innocent girl, well behaved, with little hope of overcoming her circumstances.

▌ CULTURAL IDENTITY IN ESSAYS ▐

The essays in this chapter address the experience of simultaneously living in two cultures, particularly while speaking two languages. Amy Tan, Richard Rodriguez, and Barbara Mellix struggle to establish an identity that either reconciles two heritages or resists the claims of one of them. In each case, the writer experiences the tension between the cultures as a tension between languages or dialects. Tan writes about the indirectness of the Chinese language—which some interpret as discretion—and argues that the subtlety of her family language suggests more than this stereotype would indicate. Rodriguez identifies his Spanish language and Mexican ancestry as belonging to a private culture that conflicts with the "public" culture represented by American English. In a similar way, Barbara Mellix shifts between Standard English and Black English, though she does not favor one over the other; each suits a different context.

Caffilene Allen, Itabari Njeri, Louise Erdrich, and Lydia Minatoya also write about language as a reflection of culture: each shows how personal names reflect cultural identity. Erdrich laments her loss of identity as a Chippewa Native American; much of her culture is lost—what is left are the expressive names, such as Standing Strong or Sky Coming Down. Njeri rejects her American birth name, Jill Lord, and adopts an African name—an action that affirms her African heritage. Lydia Minatoya recounts how her name reflects her Japanese parents' desire for her to fit into American culture and thrive here. Caffilene Allen describes how her teachers changed her East Tennessee "Caffilene" to "Kathleen," disrupting her identity and creating shame in her family. At the same time, leaving behind her Appalachian dialect created opportunities for Allen outside the family, just as learning English did for Rodriguez.

As background for such language tensions, Barbara Wallraff and Haunani-Kay Trask write about the close bond between a language and its culture. Wallraff explores the myth of the world dominance of English. Although she recognizes that English is the principal language of scientific and economic discourse in countries throughout the world, she argues that English has in no way supplanted these countries' native languages. Trask describes how English-speaking historians have devalued Hawaiian culture, an attitude she blames at least partly on their ignorance of the Hawaiian language. Both readings offer an important backdrop to discussions about the significance of specific family languages and heritages within the wider U.S. culture.

Analyzing the Essays

Like the paintings, these readings offer a range of responses to the tension between a private and public culture, from resistance to celebration. When analyzing the essays in this chapter, ask yourself the following questions:

1. What attitudes, values, and concerns does the writer identify as "American"?
2. What are the values, attitudes, and concerns associated with the family heritage or subculture?
3. What are the values, attitudes, and concerns associated with the larger American culture?
4. Does the writer state or imply a common ground? If not, can you posit one?

Analysis of an Essay

Read Itabari Njeri's "What's in a Name?" (p. 71) Then read this example of how you might analyze the essay.

Njeri tries to define the subculture of African Americans and its relation to U.S. culture as a whole through her reflections on her name change. She makes us aware of the ambiguity she feels in identifying her "original name." Although whites and many African Americans consider the "original name" to be Njeri's birth name, Jill Lord, Njeri defines her "original name" as her African ancestral name—unknowable because slavery disrupted family ties. For Njeri, "Jill Lord" is her "slave name," and so she adopts the African name "Itabari Njeri," even against her mother's wishes. While she recognizes that for others, her birth name represents her American rights—for instance, her freedom of speech and right to vote—still she resists being cut off from her African roots. Although she can never know who her specific African ancestors were, she seeks a connection with them through her African name. In so doing, she depicts what may seem an irreconcilable conflict and paradox: she can never know the culture her family lost through slavery, but she wants recognition that it existed.

Taking a step back from this conflict, you might ask yourself, Does Njeri suggest a common ground between her ancestral and American identities? If not, can you posit one? Here are some possibilities: Njeri holds many typically American values, such as material and professional success; she is a well-educated and successful journalist. She also identifies with the American ideal of opportunity and self-transformation. In particular, she sees herself as part of a group of writers and artists who are forging out of cultural conflicts a new African American aesthetic. But while she is thoroughly American in these attitudes, she also takes pride in the connections she makes with some of the Africans she meets, even though these individuals seem also to have been influenced by American culture. Two incidents of personal recognition illustrate this bond. In Tanzania, the hotel operator calls Njeri "sister" and asks her to "Please tell everyone in Harlem hello for us." Later, on the border of Tanzania and Kenya, a woman smiles at her and says, in broken English, "I know you" and "You are from the lost tribe." These two experiences help create the connection to Africa that Njeri seeks.

AMY TAN   Tan, who was born in Oakland, California, confronts a controversial linguistic issue: to what extent does a people's language determine what they can perceive? Comparing her family's native Chinese with her own native English, she speculates that although cultures use language in different ways (e.g., Chinese speakers tend to be less blunt than American English speakers), the languages themselves do not cause them to perceive the world differently. Different language behavior, however, does lead to misunderstandings, as Tan amply illustrates. If you speak more than one language, do you notice that they give rise to different kinds of social behavior? Do you know of language practices that are acceptable, even expected, in one culture, yet considered rude or unusual in another?

TAN is the author of *The Joy Luck Club, The Kitchen God's Wife,* and other novels, memoirs, and essays.

The Language of Discretion (1990) | BY AMY TAN

At a recent family dinner in San Francisco, my mother whispered to me: "Sau-sau [Brother's Wife] pretends too hard to be polite! Why bother? In the end, she always takes everything."

My mother thinks like a *waixiao,* an expatriate, temporarily away from China since 1949, no longer patient with ritual courtesies. As if to prove her point, she reached across the table to offer my elderly aunt from Beijing the last scallop from the Happy Family seafood dish.

Sau-sau scowled. "*B'yao, zhen b'yao!*" (I don't want it, really I don't!) she cried, patting her plump stomach.

"Take it! Take it!" scolded my mother in Chinese.

"Full, I'm already full," Sau-sau protested weakly, eyeing the beloved scallop. 5

"Ai!" exclaimed my mother, completely exasperated. "Nobody else wants it. If you don't take it, it will only rot!"

At this point, Sau-sau sighed, acting as if she were doing my mother a big favor by taking the wretched scrap off her hands.

My mother turned to her brother, a high-ranking communist official who was visiting her in California for the first time: "In American a Chinese person could starve to death. If you say you don't want it, they won't ask you again forever."

My uncle nodded and said he understood fully: Americans take things quickly because they have no time to be polite. I thought about this misunderstanding again—of social contexts failing in translation—when a friend sent me an article from the *New York Times Magazine* (24 April 1988). The article, on changes in New York's Chinatown, made passing reference to the inherent ambivalence of the Chinese language.

Chinese people are so "discreet and modest," the article stated, there aren't even 10 words for "yes" and "no."

That's not true, I thought, although I can see why an outsider might think that. I continued reading.

If one is Chinese, the article went on to say, "One compromises, one doesn't hazard a loss of face by an overemphatic response."

My throat seized. Why do people keep saying these things? As if we truly were those little dolls sold in Chinatown tourist shops, heads bobbing up and down in complacent agreement to anything said!

I worry about the effect of one-dimensional statements on the unwary and guileless. When they read about this so-called vocabulary deficit, do they also conclude that Chinese people evolved into a mild-mannered lot because the language only allowed them to hobble forth with minced words?

Something enormous is always lost in translation. Something insidious seeps 15 into the gaps, especially when amateur linguists continue to compare, one-for-one, language differences and then put forth notions wide open to misinterpretation: that Chinese people have no direct linguistic means to make decisions, assert or deny, affirm or negate, just say no to drug dealers, or behave properly on the witness stand when told, "Please answer yes or no."

Yet one can argue, with the help of renowned linguists, that the Chinese are indeed up a creek without "yes" and "no." Take any number of variations on the old language-and-reality theory stated years ago by Edward Sapir: "Human beings . . . are very much at the mercy of the particular language which has become the medium for their society. . . . The fact of the matter is that the 'real world' is to a large extent built up on the language habits of the group."[1]

This notion was further bolstered by the famous Sapir-Whorf hypothesis, which roughly states that one's perception of the world and how one functions in it depends a great deal on the language used. As Sapir, Whorf, and new carriers of the banner would have us believe, language shapes our thinking, channels us along certain patterns embedded in words, syntactic structures, and intonation patterns. Language has become the peg and the shelf that enables us to sort out and categorize the world. In English, we see "cats" and "dogs"; what if the language had also specified *glatz,* meaning "animals that leave fur on the sofa," and *glotz,* meaning "animals that leave fur and drool on the sofa"? How would language, the enabler, have changed our perceptions with slight vocabulary variations?

And if this were the case—of language being the master of destined thought—think of the opportunities lost from failure to evolve two little words, *yes* and *no,* the simplest of opposites! Ghenghis Khan could have been sent back to Mongolia. Opium wars might have been averted. The Cultural Revolution could have been sidestepped.

There are still many, from serious linguists to pop psychology cultists, who view language and reality as inextricably tied, one being the consequence of the other. We have traversed the range from the Sapir-Whorf hypothesis to est and neurolinguistic programming, which tell us "you are what you say."

I too have been intrigued by the theories. I can summarize, albeit badly, ages-old empirical evidence: of Eskimos and their infinite ways to say "snow," their ability to *see* the differences in snowflake configurations, thanks to the richness of their vocabulary, while non-Eskimo speakers like myself founder in "snow," "more snow," and "lots more where that came from." 20

I too have experienced dramatic cognitive awakenings via the word. Once I added "mauve" to my vocabulary I began to see it everywhere. When I learned how to pronounce *prix fixe,* I ate French food at prices better than the easier-to-say *à la carte* choices.

But just how seriously are we supposed to take this?

Sapir said something else about language and reality. It is the part that often gets left behind in the dot-dot-dots of quotes: ". . . No two languages are ever sufficiently similar to be considered as representing the same social reality. The worlds in which different societies live are distinct worlds, not merely the same world with different labels attached."

When I first read this, I thought, Here at last is validity for the dilemmas I felt growing up in a bicultural, bilingual family! As any child of immigrant parents knows, there's a special kind of double bind attached to knowing two languages. My parents, for example, spoke to me in both Chinese and English; I spoke back to them in English.

"Amy-ah!" they'd call to me. 25

"What?" I'd mumble back.

"Do not question us when we call," they scolded me in Chinese. "It is not respectful."

"What do you mean?"

"Ai! Didn't we just tell you not to question?"

To this day, I wonder which parts of my behavior were shaped by Chinese, which by English. I am tempted to think, for example, that if I am of two minds on some matter it is due to the richness of my linguistic experiences, not to any personal tendencies toward wishy-washiness. But which mind says what? 30

Was it perhaps patience—developed through years of deciphering my mother's fractured English—that had me listening politely while a woman announced over the phone that I had won one of five valuable prizes? Was it respect—pounded in by the Chinese imperative to accept convoluted explanations—that had me agreeing that I might find it worthwhile to drive seventy-five miles to view a time-share resort? Could I have been at a loss for words when asked, "Wouldn't you like to win a Hawaiian cruise or perhaps a fabulous Star of India designed exclusively by Carter and Van Arpels?"

And when this same woman called back a week later, this time complaining that I had missed my appointment, obviously it was my type A language that kicked into gear and interrupted her. Certainly, my blunt denial—"Frankly I'm not interested"—was as American as apple pie. And when she said, "But it's in Morgan Hill," and I shouted, "Read my lips, I don't care if it's Timbuktu," you can be sure I said it with the precise intonation expressing both cynicism and disgust.

It's dangerous business, this sorting out of language and behavior. Which one is English? Which is Chinese? The categories manifest themselves: passive and aggressive, tentative and assertive, indirect and direct. And I realize they are just variations of the same theme: that Chinese people are discreet and modest.

Reject them all!

If my reaction is overly strident, it is because I cannot come across as too emphatic. I grew up listening to the same lines over and over again, like so many rote expressions repeated in an English phrasebook. And I too almost came to believe them. **35**

Yet if I consider my upbringing more carefully, I find there was nothing discreet about the Chinese language I grew up with. My parents made everything abundantly clear. Nothing wishy-washy in their demands, no compromises accepted: "Of course you will become a famous neurosurgeon," they told me. "And yes, a concert pianist on the side."

In fact, now that I remember, it seems that the more emphatic outbursts always spilled over into Chinese: "Not that way! You must wash rice so not a single grain spills out."

I do not believe that my parents—both immigrants from mainland China—are an exception to the modest-and-discreet rule. I have only to look at the number of Chinese engineering students skewing minority ratios at Berkeley, MIT, and Yale. Certainly they were not raised by passive mothers and fathers who said, "It is up to you, my daughter. Writer, welfare recipient, masseuse, or molecular engineer—you decide."

And my American mind says, See, those engineering students weren't able to say no to their parents' demands. But then my Chinese mind remembers: Ah, but those parents all wanted their sons and daughters to be *pre-med*.

Having listened to both Chinese and English, I also tend to be suspicious of any comparisons between the two languages. Typically, one language—that of the person doing the comparing—is often used as the standard, the benchmark for a logical form of expression. And so the language being compared is always in danger of being judged deficient or superfluous, simplistic or unnecessarily complex, melodious or cacophonous. English speakers point out that Chinese is extremely difficult because it relies on variations in tone barely discernible to the human ear. By the same token, Chinese speakers tell me English is extremely difficult because it is inconsistent, a language of too many broken rules, of Mickey Mice and Donald Ducks. **40**

Even more dangerous to my mind is the temptation to compare both language and behavior *in translation*. To listen to my mother speak English, one might think she has no concept of past or future tense, that she doesn't see the difference between singular and plural, that she is gender blind because she calls my husband "she." If one were not careful, one might also generalize that, based on the way my mother talks, all Chinese people take a circumlocutory route to get to the point. It is, in fact, my mother's idiosyncratic behavior to ramble a bit.

Sapir was right about differences between two languages and their realities. I can illustrate why word-for-word translation is not enough to translate meaning and intent. I once received a letter from China which I read to non-Chinese speaking friends. The letter, originally written in Chinese, had been translated by my brother-in law in Beijing. One portion described the time when my uncle at age ten discovered his widowed mother (my grandmother) had remarried—as a number three concubine, the ultimate disgrace for an honorable family. The translated version of my uncle's letter read in part:

> In 1925, I met my mother in Shanghai. When she came to me, I didn't have greeting to her as if seeing nothing. She pull me to a corner secretly and asked me why didn't have greeting to her. I couldn't control myself and cried, "Ma! Why did you leave us? People told me: one day you ate a beancake yourself. Your sister in-law found it and sweared at you, called you names. So . . . is it true?" She clasped my hand and answered immediately. "It's not true, don't say what like this." After this time, there was a few chance to meet her.

"What!" cried my friends. "Was eating a beancake so terrible?"

Of course not. The beancake was simply a euphemism; a ten-year-old boy did not dare question his mother on something as shocking as concubinage. Eating a beancake was his equivalent for committing this selfish act, something inconsiderate of all family members, hence, my grandmother's despairing response to what seemed like a ludicrous charge of gluttony. And sure enough, she was banished from the family, and my uncle saw her only a few times before her death.

While the above may fuel people's argument that Chinese is indeed a language of extreme discretion, it does not mean that Chinese people speak in secrets and riddles. The contexts are fully understood. It is only to those on the *outside* that the language seems cryptic, the behavior inscrutable.

I am, evidently, one of the outsiders. My nephew in Shanghai, who recently started taking English lessons, has been writing me letters in English. I had told him I was a fiction writer, and so in one letter he wrote, "Congratulate to you on your writing. Perhaps one day I should like to read it." I took it in the same vein as "Perhaps one day we can get together for lunch." I sent back a cheery note. A month went by and another letter arrived from Shanghai. "Last one perhaps I hadn't writing distinctly," he said. "In the future, you'll send a copy of your works for me."

I try to explain to my English-speaking friends that Chinese language is more *strategic* in manner, whereas English tends to be more direct; an American business executive may say, "Let's make a deal," and the Chinese manager may reply, "Is your son interested in learning about your widget business?" Each to his or her own purpose, each with his or her own linguistic path. But I hesitate to add more to the pile of generalizations, because no matter how many examples I provide and explain, I fear that it appears defensive and only reinforces the image: that Chinese people are "discreet and modest"—and it takes an American to explain what they really mean.

Why am I complaining? The description seems harmless enough (after all, the *New York Times Magazine* writer did not say "slippery and evasive"). It is precisely the bland, easy acceptability of the phrase that worries me.

I worry that the dominant society may see Chinese people from a limited—and limiting—perspective. I worry that seemingly benign stereotypes may be part of the reason there are few Chinese in top management positions, in mainstream political roles. I worry about the power of language: that if one says anything enough times—in *any* language—it might become true.

Could this be why Chinese friends of my parents' generation are willing to accept the generalization? 50

"Why are you complaining?" one of them said to me. "If people think we are modest and polite, let them think that. Wouldn't Americans be pleased to admit they are thought of as polite?"

And I do believe anyone would take the description as a compliment—at first. But after a while, it annoys, as if the only things that people heard one say were phatic remarks: "I'm so pleased to meet you. I've heard many wonderful things about you. For me? You shouldn't have!"

These remarks are not representative of new ideas, honest emotions, or considered thought. They are what is said from the polite distance of social contexts: of greetings, farewells, wedding thank-you notes, convenient excuses, and the like.

It makes me wonder though. How many anthropologists, how many sociologists, how many travel journalists have documented so-called "natural interactions" in foreign lands, all observed with spiral notebook in hand? How many other cases are there of the long-lost primitive tribe, people who turned out to be sophisticated enough to put on the stone-age show that ethnologists had come to see?

And how many tourists fresh off the bus have wandered into Chinatown expecting the self-effacing shopkeeper to admit under duress that the goods are not worth the price asked? I have witnessed it. 55

"I don't know," the tourist said to the shopkeeper, a Cantonese woman in her fifties. "It doesn't look genuine to me. I'll give you three dollars."

"You don't like my price, go somewhere else," said the shopkeeper.

"You are not a nice person," cried the shocked tourist, "not a nice person at all!"

"Who say I have to be nice," snapped the shopkeeper.

"So how does one say 'yes' and 'no' in Chinese?" ask my friends a bit warily. 60

And here I do agree in part with the *New York Times Magazine* article. There is no one word for "yes" or "no"—but not out of necessity to be discreet. If anything, I would say the Chinese equivalent of answering "yes" or "no" is dis*crete,* that is, specific to what is asked.

Ask a Chinese person if he or she has eaten, and he or she might say *chrle* (eaten already) or perhaps *meiyou* (have not).

Ask, "So you had insurance at the time of the accident?" and the response would be *dwei* (correct) or *meiyou* (did not have).

Ask, "Have you stopped beating your wife?" and the answer refers directly to the proposition being asserted or denied: stopped already, still have not, never beat, have no wife.

What could be clearer? 65

As for those who are still wondering how to translate the language of discretion, I offer this personal example.

My aunt and uncle were about to return to Beijing after a three-month visit to the United States. On their last night I announced I wanted to take them out to dinner.

"Are you hungry?" I asked in Chinese.

"Not hungry," said my uncle promptly, the same response he once gave me ten minutes before he suffered a low-blood-sugar attack.

"Not too hungry," said my aunt. "Perhaps you're hungry?" 70

"A little," I admitted.

"We can eat, we can eat," they both consented.

"What kind of food?" I asked.

"Oh, doesn't matter. Anything will do. Nothing fancy, just some simple food is fine."

"Do you like Japanese food? We haven't had that yet," I suggested. 75

They looked at each other.

"We can eat it," said my uncle bravely, this survivor of the Long March.

"We have eaten it before," added my aunt. "Raw fish."

"Oh, you don't like it?" I said. "Don't be polite. We can go somewhere else."

"We are not being polite. We can eat it," my aunt insisted. 80

So I drove them to Japantown and we walked past several restaurants featuring colorful plastic displays of sushi.

"Not this one, not this either," I continued to say, as if searching for a Japanese restaurant similar to the last. "Here it is," I finally said, turning into a restaurant famous for its Chinese fish dishes from Shandong.

"Oh, Chinese food!" cried my aunt, obviously relieved.

My uncle patted my arm. "You think Chinese."

"It's your last night here in America," I said. "So don't be polite. Act like an 85 American."

And that night we ate a banquet.

Notes

1. Edward Sapir, *Selected Writings*, ed. D. G. Mandelbaum (Berkeley and Los Angeles, 1949).

CONNECTING PERSONALLY TO THE READING

1. Tan is quick to dismiss stereotypes—that Americans have no time to be polite and that the Chinese are "discreet and modest." Think of a stereotype that you used to believe, but no longer do. What changed your mind?

2. If you have visited an area where the culture was different from your own but the language was not, did you ever find it difficult to communicate? Explain your answer.

FOCUSING ON THE ARGUMENT

1. Tan's principal rhetorical device is to move back and forth between a language theory and a first-person experience with language. For example, in her opening paragraph, she narrates a family story and immediately follows that story with a theory, by a writer at the *New York Times,* about the Chinese language and culture. Choose one of the theories Tan discusses

and show how one of the personal experiences reinforces, discredits, or provides a new perspective on this theory.

2. Tan often asks questions that she does not answer or whose answers are implicit in her argument—that is, she answers them indirectly. Choose two of Tan's questions and consider how Tan might answer them directly.

SYNTHESIZING IDEAS FROM MULTIPLE READINGS

1. Richard Rodriguez ("Public and Private Language," p. 51) and Amy Tan both write about their experiences growing up bilingual and bicultural, yet the tone of each article is quite different: Tan is at times humorous, at times outraged, whereas Rodriguez's tone is largely sad, wistful. What accounts for this difference in tone?

2. In "What Global Language?" (p. 93), Barbara Wallraff questions the status of English as a global language. Given Tan's belief that different speakers of different languages have different styles of interacting, do you think any language can truly be global?

WRITING TO ACT

1. According to Tan, "something enormous is always lost in translation." Interview someone you know from another culture, asking them about the behavioral differences they noticed in communicating in their new culture. Pay particularly close attention to a possible "social context that failed in translation." Based on your findings, write a guide for a newcomer to your culture.

2. Survey some of the slang students use on your campus. After you've collected at least ten words, analyze what these terms reveal about your campus's culture. Discuss your analysis and conclusions in an article for your school paper.

READING

RICHARD RODRIGUEZ   The son of Spanish-speaking Mexican Americans, Rodriguez experiences English as a public language that gives him power and confidence to speak in public—and Spanish as a private language that binds his family together. Though he values the public identity English offers him, he regrets the feeling of closeness his family loses as the children, speaking English and Americanized, grow away from their parents, who are tied, in language and custom, to their native country. Do you agree with Rodriguez's assessment of himself as having two distinct identities? What do immigrants lose when they assimilate into U.S. culture?

RODRIGUEZ is the author of numerous essays, and his books include the autobiography *Hunger of Memory* (from which this reading is excerpted), *Days of Obligation: An Argument with My Mexican Father,* and *King's Highway.*

Public and Private Language (1982) | BY RICHARD RODRIGUEZ

Supporters of bilingual education today imply that students like me miss a great deal by not being taught in their family's language. What they seem not to recognize is that, as a socially disadvantaged child, I considered Spanish to be a private language. What I needed to learn in school was that I had the right—and the obligation—to speak the public language of *los gringos*. The odd truth is that my first-grade classmates could have become bilingual, in the conventional sense of that word, more easily than I. Had they been taught (as upper-middle-class children are often taught early) a second language like Spanish or French, they could have regarded it simply as that: another public language. In my case such bilingualism could not have been so quickly achieved. What I did not believe was that I could speak a single public language.

Without question, it would have pleased me to hear my teachers address me in Spanish when I entered the classroom. I would have felt much less afraid. I would have trusted them and responded with ease. But I would have delayed—for how long postponed?—having to learn the language of public society. I would have evaded—and for how long could I have afforded to delay?—learning the great lesson of school, that I had a public identity.

Fortunately, my teachers were unsentimental about their responsibility. What they understood was that I needed to speak a public language. So their voices would search me out, asking me questions. Each time I'd hear them, I'd look up in surprise to see a nun's face frowning at me. I'd mumble, not really meaning to answer. The nun would persist, "Richard, stand up. Don't look at the floor. Speak up. Speak to the entire class, not just to me!" But I couldn't believe that the English language was mine to use. (In part, I did not want to believe it.) I continued to mumble. I resisted the teacher's demands. (Did I somehow suspect that once I learned public language my pleasing family life would be changed?) Silent, waiting for the bell to sound, I remained dazed, diffident, afraid.

Because I wrongly imagined that English was intrinsically a public language and Spanish an intrinsically private one, I easily noted the difference between classroom language and the language of home. At school, words were directed to a general audience of listeners. ("Boys and girls.") Words were meaningfully ordered. And the point was not self-expression alone but to make oneself understood by many others. The teacher quizzed: "Boys and girls, why do we use that word in this sentence? Could we think of a better word to use there? Would the sentence change its meaning if the words were differently arranged? And wasn't there a better way of saying much the same thing?" (I couldn't say. I wouldn't try to say.)

Three months. Five. Half a year passed. Unsmiling, ever watchful, my teachers noted my silence. They began to connect my behavior with the difficult progress my older sister and brother were making. Until one Saturday morning three nuns arrived at the house to talk to our parents. Stiffly, they sat on the blue living room sofa. From the doorway of another room, spying the visitors, I noted the incongruity—the clash of two worlds, the faces and voices of school intruding upon the familiar setting of home. I overheard one voice gently wondering, "Do your children speak only Spanish at home, Mrs. Rodriguez?" While another voice added, "That Richard especially seems so timid and shy."

That Rich-heard!

With great tact the visitors continued, "Is it possible for you and your husband to encourage your children to practice their English when they are home?" Of course, my parents complied. What would they not do for their children's well-being? And how could they have questioned the Church's authority which those women represented? In an instant, they agreed to give up the language (the sounds) that had revealed and accentuated our family's closeness. The moment after the visitors left, the change was observed. "*Ahora,* speak to us *en inglés,*" my father and mother united to tell us.

At first, it seemed a kind of game. After dinner each night, the family gathered to practice "our" English. (It was still then *inglés,* a language foreign to us, so we felt drawn as strangers to it.) Laughing, we would try to define words we could not pronounce. We played with strange English sounds, often over-anglicizing our pronunciations. And we filled the smiling gaps of our sentences with familiar Spanish sounds. But that was cheating, somebody shouted. Everyone laughed. In school, meanwhile, like my brother and sister, I was required to attend a daily tutoring session. I needed a full year of special attention. I also needed my teachers to keep my attention from straying in class by calling out, *Rich-heard*—their English voices slowly prying loose my ties to my other name, its three notes, *Ri-car-do.* Most of all I needed to hear my mother and father speak to me in a moment of seriousness in broken—suddenly heartbreaking—English. The scene was inevitable: One Saturday morning I entered the kitchen where my parents were talking in Spanish. I did not realize that they were talking in Spanish however until, at the moment they saw me, I heard their voices change to speak English. Those *gringo* sounds they uttered startled me. Pushed me away. In that moment of trivial misunderstanding and profound insight, I felt my throat twisted by unsounded grief. I turned quickly and left the room. But I had no place to escape to with Spanish. (The spell was broken.) My brother and sisters were speaking English in another part of the house.

Again and again in the days following, increasingly angry, I was obliged to hear my mother and father: "Speak to us *en inglés.*" (*Speak.*) Only then did I determine to learn classroom English. Weeks after, it happened: One day in school I raised my hand to volunteer an answer. I spoke out in a loud voice. And I did not think it remarkable when the entire class understood. That day, I moved very far from the disadvantaged child I had been only days earlier. The belief, the calming assurance that I belonged in public, had at last taken hold.

Shortly after, I stopped hearing the high and loud sounds of *los gringos.* A more and more confident speaker of English, I didn't trouble to listen to *how* strangers sounded, speaking to me. And there simply were too many English-speaking people in my day for me to hear American accents anymore. Conversations quickened. Listening to persons who sounded eccentrically pitched voices, I usually noted their sounds for an initial few seconds before I concentrated on *what* they were saying. Conversations became content-full. Transparent. Hearing someone's *tone* of voice—angry or questioning or sarcastic or happy or sad—I didn't distinguish it from the words it expressed. Sound and word were thus tightly wedded. At the end of a day, I was often bemused, always relieved, to realize how "silent," though crowded with words, my day in public had been. (This public silence measured and quickened the change in my life.)

10

At last, seven years old, I came to believe what had been technically true since my birth: I was an American citizen.

But the special feeling of closeness at home was diminished by then. Gone was the desperate, urgent, intense feeling of being at home; rare was the experience of feeling myself individualized by family intimates. We remained a loving family, but one greatly changed. No longer so close; no longer bound tight by the pleasing and troubling knowledge of our public separateness. Neither my older brother nor sister rushed home after school anymore. Nor did I. When I arrived home there would often be neighborhood kids in the house. Or the house would be empty of sounds.

Following the dramatic Americanization of their children, even my parents grew more publicly confident. Especially my mother. She learned the names of all the people on our block. And she decided we needed to have a telephone installed in the house. My father continued to use the word *gringo*. But it was no longer charged with the old bitterness or distrust. (Stripped of any emotional content, the word simply became a name for those Americans not of Hispanic descent.) Hearing him, sometimes, I wasn't sure if he was pronouncing the Spanish word *gringo* or saying gringo in English.

Matching the silence I started hearing in public was a new quiet at home. The family's quiet was partly due to the fact that, as we children learned more and more English, we shared fewer and fewer words with our parents. Sentences needed to be spoken slowly when a child addressed his mother or father. (Often the parent wouldn't understand.) The child would need to repeat himself. (Still the parent misunderstood.) The young voice, frustrated, would end up saying, "Never mind"—the subject was closed. Dinners would be noisy with the clinking of knives and forks against dishes. My mother would smile softly between her remarks; my father at the other end of the table would chew and chew at his food, while he stared over the heads of his children.

My *mother!* My *father!* After English became my primary language, I no longer 15 knew what words to use in addressing my parents. The old Spanish words (those tender accents of sound) I had used earlier—*mamá* and *papá*—I couldn't use anymore. They would have been too painful reminders of how much had changed in my life. On the other hand, the words I heard neighborhood kids call *their* parents seemed equally unsatisfactory. *Mother* and *Father; Ma, Papa, Pa, Dad, Pop* (how I hated the all-American sound of that last word especially)—all these terms I felt were unsuitable, not really terms of address for *my* parents. As a result, I never used them at home. Whenever I'd speak to my parents, I would try to get their attention with eye contact alone. In public conversations, I'd refer to "my parents" or "my mother and father."

My mother and father, for their part, responded differently, as their children spoke to them less. She grew restless, seemed troubled and anxious at the scarcity of words exchanged in the house. It was she who would question me about my day when I came home from school. She smiled at small talk. She pried at the edges of my sentences to get me to say something more. (What?) She'd join conversations she overheard, but her intrusions often stopped her children's talking. By contrast, my father seemed reconciled to the new quiet. Though his English improved somewhat, he retired into silence. At dinner he spoke very little. One night his children and even his wife helplessly giggled at his garbled English pronunciation of the Catholic Grace before Meals. Thereafter he made his wife recite the prayer at the start of each meal, even on formal occasions, when there were guests in the house. Hers became the public voice of the family. On official business, it was she, not my father, one would usually hear on the phone or in stores, talking to strangers. His children grew so accustomed to his silence that, years later, they would speak routinely of his shyness. (My mother would often try to explain: Both his parents died when he was eight. He was raised by an uncle who treated him like little more than a menial servant. He was never encouraged to speak. He grew up alone. A man of few words.) But my father was not shy, I realized, when I'd watch him speaking Spanish with relatives. Using Spanish, he was quickly effusive. Especially when talking with other men, his voice would spark, flicker, flare alive with sounds. In Spanish, he expressed ideas and feelings he rarely revealed in English. With firm Spanish sounds, he conveyed confidence and authority English would never allow him.

The silence at home, however, was finally more than a literal silence. Fewer words passed between parent and child, but more profound was the silence that resulted from my inattention to sounds. At about the time I no longer bothered to listen with care to the sounds of English in public, I grew careless about listening to the sounds family members made when they spoke. Most of the time I heard someone speaking at home and didn't distinguish his sounds from the words people uttered in public. I didn't even pay much attention to my parents' accented and ungrammatical speech. At least not at home. Only when I was with them in public would I grow alert to their accents. Though, even then, their sounds caused me less and less concern. For I was increasingly confident of my own public identity.

I would have been happier about my public success had I not sometimes recalled what it had been like earlier, when my family had conveyed its intimacy through a set of conveniently private sounds. Sometimes in public, hearing a stranger, I'd hark back to my past. A Mexican farmworker approached me downtown to ask directions to somewhere. "¿Hijito . . . ?" he said. And his voice summoned deep longing. Another time, standing beside my mother in the visiting room of a Carmelite convent, before the dense screen which rendered the nuns shadowy figures, I heard several Spanish-speaking nuns—their busy, singsong overlapping voices—assure us that yes, yes, we were remembered, all our family was remembered in their prayers. (Their voices echoed faraway family sounds.) Another day, a dark-faced old woman—her hand light on my shoulder—steadied herself against me as she boarded a bus. She murmured something I couldn't quite comprehend. Her Spanish voice came near, like the face of a never-before-seen relative in the instant before I was kissed. Her voice, like so many of the Spanish voices I'd hear in public, recalled the golden age of my youth. Hearing Spanish then, I continued to be a careful, if sad, listener to sounds. Hearing a Spanish-speaking family walking behind me, I turned to look. I smiled for an instant, before my glance found the Hispanic-looking faces of strangers in the crowd going by.

Today I hear bilingual educators say that children lose a degree of "individuality" by becoming assimilated into public society. (Bilingual schooling was popularized in the seventies, that decade when middle-class ethnics began to resist the process of assimilation—the American melting pot.) But the bilingualists simplistically scorn the value and necessity of assimilation. They do not seem to realize that there are *two* ways a person is individualized. So they do not realize that while one suffers a diminished sense of *private* individuality by becoming assimilated into public society, such assimilation makes possible the achievement of *public* individuality.

The bilingualists insist that a student should be reminded of his difference from others in mass society, his heritage. But they equate more separateness with individuality. The fact is that only in private—with intimates—is separateness from the crowd a prerequisite for individuality. (An intimate draws me apart, tells me that I am unique, unlike all others.) In public, by contrast, full individuality is achieved, paradoxically, by those who are able to consider themselves members of the crowd. Thus it happened for me: Only when I was able to think of myself as an American, no longer an alien in *gringo* society, could I seek the rights and opportunities necessary for full public individuality. The social and political advantages I enjoy as a man result from the day that I came to believe that my name, indeed, is *Rich-heard Road-ree-guess*. It is true that my public society today is often impersonal. (My public society is usually mass society.) Yet despite the anonymity of the crowd and despite the fact that the individuality I achieve in public is often tenuous—*because it depends on my being one in a crowd*—I celebrate the day I acquired my new name. Those middle-class ethnics who scorn assimilation seem to me filled with decadent self-pity, obsessed by the burden of public life. Dangerously, they romanticize public separateness and they trivialize the dilemma of the socially disadvantaged. 20

My awkward childhood does not prove the necessity of bilingual education. My story discloses instead an essential myth of childhood—inevitable pain. If I rehearse here the changes in my private life after my Americanization, it is finally to emphasize the public gain. The loss implies the gain: The house I returned to each afternoon was quiet. Intimate sounds no longer rushed to the door to greet me. There were other noises inside. The telephone rang. Neighborhood kids ran past the door of the bedroom where I was reading my schoolbooks—covered with shopping-bag paper. Once I learned public language, it would never again be easy for me to hear intimate family voices. More and more of my day was spent hearing words. But that may only be a way of saying that the day I raised my hand in class and spoke loudly to an entire roomful of faces, my childhood started to end.

CONNECTING PERSONALLY TO THE READINGS

1. If you have spoken a language other than your native one, did you experience a change of identity in the process? If English is the only language you use, how is the way you speak at home different from the way you speak at school or in another public situation?

2. Think of an occasion where you tried hard to fit in—at school, at a social event, at work, or somewhere else. How was your use of language part of this effort?

3. Rodriguez refers often to the power and meaningfulness of silence. Describe a situation in which you experienced silence (your own or that of others) as a form of communication. What was communicated by the silence?

1. The tone of this reading is often nostalgic, suggesting sadness and loss. Where do you feel this tone most strongly, and what individual words contribute to this feeling? How does the tone reinforce Rodriguez's ideas?

2. Rodriguez moves back and forth between narrating his family's story and reflecting on the national controversy over bilingual education. What is his stance on bilingual teaching? Do his personal experiences make his opinions on bilingual teaching more believable? Why or why not?

SYNTHESIZING IDEAS FROM MULTIPLE READINGS

1. Compare Rodriguez's behavior with that of Lydia Minatoya ("Transformation," p. 81) as outsiders at school. How does each child cope with this outsider status?

2. In "The Language of Discretion" (p. 43), Amy Tan objects to an article in the *New York Times Magazine* that polarizes Chinese and U.S. language and behavior. Explain her reasons for questioning this attitude. Then consider the way Rodriguez characterizes English as a public and Spanish as a private language. Do you think Amy Tan would disagree with the way he polarizes English and Spanish? Why or why not?

WRITING TO ACT

1. Research the issue of bilingual education in your state or in a state such as California or Texas. Many of the current programs are controversial. Based upon your findings, write a letter to the state's legislature with recommendations for improvement.

2. Write a glossary in which you define terms that are special to a group you belong to—e.g., the slang that students on your campus use. Be sure to include adequate explanations, assuming that your intended audience does not belong to the group and is not familiar with the slang.

BARBARA MELLIX   Growing up bilingual in Black English and Standard English, Mellix learns how language use is identified with social class and how it can confer insider or outsider status. Mellix's facility with both languages gives her power in several worlds: she can talk comfortably with her family, prove that she is respectable to a white policeman, and share her ideas as a professional writer. What, then, does Mellix mean by this statement: ". . . when we spoke standard English, we acknowledged (to ourselves and to others—but primarily to ourselves) that our customary way of speaking was inferior"? What makes one way of speaking "superior" to another?

MELLIX is a professor at the University of Pittsburgh, where she also serves as assistant dean of the College of Arts and Sciences and the director of the college's Advising Center.

From Outside, In (1987) | BY BARBARA MELLIX

Two years ago, when I started writing this paper, trying to bring order out of chaos, my ten-year-old daughter was suffering from an acute attack of boredom. She drifted in and out of the room complaining that she had nothing to do, no one to "be with" because none of her friends were at home. Patiently I explained that I was working on something special and needed peace and quiet, and I suggested that she paint, read, or work with her computer. None of these interested her. Finally, she pulled up a chair to my desk and watched me, now and then heaving long, loud sighs. After two or three minutes (nine or ten sighs), I lost my patience. "Looka here, Allie," I said, "you too old for this kinda carryin' on. I done told you this is important. You wronger than dirt to be in here haggin' me like this and you know it. Now git on outta here and leave me off before I put my foot all the way down."

I was at home, alone with my family, and my daughter understood that this way of speaking was appropriate in that context. She knew, as a matter of fact, that it was almost inevitable; when I get angry at home, I speak some of my finest, most cherished black English. Had I been speaking to my daughter in this manner in certain other environments, she would have been shocked and probably worried that I had taken leave of my sense of propriety.

Like my children, I grew up speaking what I considered two distinctly different languages—black English and standard English (or as I thought of them then, the ordinary everyday speech of "country" coloreds and "proper" English)—and in the process of acquiring these languages, I developed an understanding of when, where, and how to use them. But unlike my children, I grew up in a world that was primarily black. My friends, neighbors, minister, teachers—almost everybody I associated with every day—were black. And we spoke to one another in our own special language: *That sho is a pretty dress you got on. If she don' soon leave me off I'm gon tell her head a mess. I was so mad I could'a pissed a blue nail. He all the time trying to low-rate somebody. Ain't that just about nastiest thing you ever set ears on?*

Then there were the "others," the "proper" blacks, transplanted relatives and onetime friends who came home from the city for weddings, funerals, and vacations. And the whites. To these we spoke standard English. "Ain't?" my mother would yell at me when I used the term in the presence of "others." "You *know* better than that." And I would hang my head in shame and say the "proper" word.

I remember one summer sitting in my grandmother's house in Greeleyville, South 5 Carolina, when it was full of the chatter of city relatives who were home on vacation. My parents sat quietly, only now and then volunteering a comment or answering a question. My mother's face took on a strained expression when she spoke. I could see that she was being careful to say just the right words in just the right way. Her voice sounded thick, muffled. And when she finished speaking, she would lapse into silence, her proper smile on her face. My father was more articulate, more aggressive. He spoke quickly, his words sharp and clear. But he held his proud head higher, a signal that he, too, was uncomfortable. My sisters and brothers and I stared at our aunts, uncles, and cousins, speaking only when prompted. Even then, we hesitated, formed our sentences in our minds, then spoke softly, shyly.

My parents looked small and anxious during those occasions, and I waited impatiently for our leave-taking when we would mock our relatives the moment we were out of their hearing. "Reeely," we would say to one another, flexing our wrists and rolling our eyes, "how dooo you stan' this heat? Chile, it just too hy*ooo*-mid for words." Our relatives had made us feel "country," and this was our way of regaining pride in ourselves while getting a little revenge in the bargain. The words bubbled in our throats and rolled across our tongues, a balming.

As a child I felt this same doubleness in uptown Greeleyville where the whites lived. "Ain't that a pretty dress you're wearing!" Toby, the town policeman, said to me one day when I was fifteen. "Thank you very much," I replied, my voice barely audible in my own ears. The words felt wrong in my mouth, rigid, foreign. It was not that I had never spoken that phrase before—it was common in black English, too—but I was extremely conscious that this was an occasion for proper English. I had taken out my English and put it on as I did my church clothes, and I felt as if I were wearing my Sunday best in the middle of the week. It did not matter that Toby had not spoken grammatically correct English. He was white and could speak as he wished. I had something to prove. Toby did not.

Speaking standard English to whites was our way of demonstrating that we knew their language and could use it. Speaking it to standard-English-speaking blacks was our way of showing them that we, as well as they, could "put on airs." But when we spoke standard English, we acknowledged (to ourselves and to others—but primarily to ourselves) that our customary way of speaking was inferior. We felt foolish, embarrassed, somehow diminished because we were ashamed to be our real selves. We were reserved, shy in the presence of those who owned and/or spoke *the* language.

My parents never set aside time to drill us in standard English. Their forms of instruction were less formal. When my father was feeling particularly expansive, he would regale us with tales of his exploits in the outside world. In almost flawless English, complete with dialogue and flavored with gestures and embellishment, he told us about his attempt to get a haircut at a white barbershop; his refusal to acknowledge one of the town merchants until the man addressed him as "Mister"; the time he refused to step off the sidewalk uptown to let some whites pass; his airplane trip to New York City (to visit a sick relative) during which the stewardesses and porters—recognizing that he was a "gentleman"—addressed him as "Sir." I did not realize then—nor, I think, did my father—that he was teaching us, among other things, standard English and the relationship between language and power.

My mother's approach was different. Often, when one of us said "I'm gon wash off 10 my feet," she would say, "And what will you walk on if you wash them off?" Everyone would laugh at the victim of my mother's "proper" mood. But it was different when one of us children was in a proper mood. "You think you are so superior," I said to my oldest sister one day when we were arguing and she was winning. "Superior!" my sister mocked. "You mean I'm acting 'biggidy'?" My sisters and brothers sniggered, then joined in teasing me. Finally, my mother said, "Leave your sister alone. There's nothing wrong with using proper English." There was a half-smile on her face. I had gotten "uppity," had "put on airs" for no good reason. I was at home, alone with the family, and I hadn't been prompted by one of my mother's proper moods. But there was also a proud light in my mother's eyes; her children were learning English very well.

Not until years later, as a college student, did I begin to understand our ambivalence toward English, our scorn of it, our need to master it, to own and be owned by it—an ambivalence that extended to the public-school classroom. In our school, where there were no whites, my teachers taught standard English but used black English to do it. When my grammar-school teachers wanted us to write, for example, they usually said something like, "I want y'all to write five sentences that make a statement. Anybody git done before the rest can color." It was probably almost those exact words that led me to write these sentences in 1953 when I was in the second grade:

> The white clouds are pretty.
> There are only 15 people in our room.
> We will go to gym.
> We have a new poster.
> We may go out doors.

Second grade came after "Little First" and "Big First," so by then I knew the implied rules that accompanied all writing assignments. Writing was an occasion for proper English. I was not to write in the way we spoke to one another: The white clouds pretty; There ain't but 15 people in our room; We going to gym; We got a new poster; We can go out in the yard. Rather I was to use the language of "other": clouds *are,* there *are,* we *will,* we *have,* we *may.*

My sentences were short, rigid, perfunctory, like the letters my mother wrote to relatives:

> Dear Papa,
> How are you? How is Mattie? Fine I hope. We are fine. We will come to see you Sunday. Cousin Ned will give us a ride.
>
> Love,
> Daughter

The language was not ours. It was something from outside us, something we used for special occasions.

But my coloring on the other side of that second-grade paper is different. I drew three hearts and a sun. The sun has a smiling face that radiates and envelops everything it touches. And although the sun and its world are enclosed in a circle, the colors I used—red, blue, green, purple, orange, yellow, black—indicate that I was less restricted with drawing and coloring than I was with writing standard English. My valentines were not just red. My sun was not just a yellow ball in the sky.

By the time I reached the twelfth grade, speaking and writing standard English had taken on new importance. Each year, about half of the newly graduated seniors of our school moved to large cities—particularly in the North—to live with relatives and find work. Our English teacher constantly corrected our grammar: "Not 'ain't,' but 'isn't.'" We seldom wrote papers, and even those few were usually plot summaries of short stories. When our teacher returned the papers, she usually lectured on the importance of using standard English: "I *am;* you *are;* he, she, or it *is,*" she would say, writing on the chalkboard as she spoke. "How you gon git a job talking about 'I is,' or 'I isn't' or 'I ain't'?"

In Pittsburgh, where I moved after graduation, I watched my aunt and uncle— 15 who had always spoken standard English when in Greeleyville—switch from black

English to standard English to a mixture of the two, according to where they were or who they were with. At home and with certain close relatives, friends, and neighbors, they spoke black English. With those less close, they spoke a mixture. In public and with strangers, they generally spoke standard English.

In time, I learned to speak standard English with ease and to switch smoothly from black to standard or a mixture, and back again. But no matter where I was, no matter what the situation or occasion, I continued to write as I had in school:

> Dear Mommie,
> How are you? How is everybody else? Fine I hope. I am fine. So are Aunt and Uncle. Tell everyone I said hello. I will write again soon.
>
> Love,
> Barbara

At work, at a health insurance company, I learned to write letters to customers. I studied form letters and letters written by co-workers, memorizing the phrases and the ways in which they were used. I dictated:

> Thank you for your letter of January 5. We have made the changes in your coverage you requested. Your new premium will be $150 every three months. We are pleased to have been of service to you.

In a sense, I was proud of the letters I wrote for the company: they were proof of my ability to survive in the city, the outside world—an indication of my growing mastery of English. But they also indicate that writing was still mechanical for me, something that didn't require much thought.

Reading also became a more significant part of my life during those early years in Pittsburgh. I had always liked reading, but now I devoted more and more of my spare time to it. I read romances, mysteries, popular novels. Looking back, I realize that the books I liked best were simple, unambiguous: good versus bad and right versus wrong with right rewarded and wrong punished, mysteries unraveled and all set right in the end. It was how I remembered life in Greeleyville.

Of course I was romanticizing. Life in Greeleyville had not been so very uncomplicated. Back there I had been—first as a child, then as a young woman with limited experience in the outside world—living in a relatively closed-in society. But there were implicit and explicit principles that guided our way of life and shaped our relationships with one another and the people outside—principles that a newcomer would find elusive and baffling. In Pittsburgh, I had matured, become more experienced: I had worked at three different jobs, associated with a wider range of people, married, had children. This new environment with different prescripts for living required that I speak standard English much of the time, and slowly, imperceptibly, I had ceased seeing a sharp distinction between myself and "others." Reading romances and mysteries, characterized by dichotomy, was a way of shying away from change, from the person I was becoming.

But that other part of me—that part which took great pride in my ability to hold a job writing business letters—was increasingly drawn to the new developments in my life and the attending possibilities, opportunities for even greater change. If I could write letters for a nationally known business, could I not also do something better, more challenging, more important? Could I not, perhaps, go to college and become a school teacher? For years, afraid and a little embarrassed, I did no more than imagine this different me, this possible me. But sixteen years after coming north, when my youngest daughter entered kindergarten, I found myself unable—or unwilling—to resist the lure of possibility. I enrolled in my first college course: Basic Writing, at the University of Pittsburgh.

For the first time in my life, I was required to write extensively about myself. 20 Using the most formal English at my command, I wrote these sentences near the beginning of the term:

> One of my duties as a homemaker is simply picking up after others. A day seldom passes that I don't search for a mislaid toy, book, or gym shoe, etc. I change the Ty-D-Bol, fight "ring around the collar," and keep our laundry smelling "April fresh." Occasionally, I settle arguments between my children and suggest things to do when they're bored. Taking telephone messages for my oldest daughter is my newest (and sometimes most aggravating) chore. Hanging the toilet paper roll is my most insignificant.

My concern was to use "appropriate" language, to sound as if I belonged in a college classroom. But I felt separate from the language—as if it did not and could not belong to me. I couldn't think and feel genuinely in that language, couldn't make it express what I thought and felt about being a housewife. A part of me resented, among other things, being judged by such things as the appearance of my family's laundry and toilet bowl, but in that language I could only imagine and write about a conventional housewife.

For the most part, the remainder of the term was a period of adjustment, a time of trying to find my bearings as a student in a college composition class, to learn to shut out my black English whenever I composed, and to prevent it from creeping into my formulations; a time for trying to grasp the language of the classroom and reproduce it in my prose; for trying to talk about myself in that language, reach others through it. Each experience of writing was like standing naked and revealing my imperfection, my "otherness." And each new assignment was another chance to make myself over in language, reshape myself, make myself "better" in my rapidly changing image of a student in a college composition class.

But writing became increasingly unmanageable as the term progressed, and by the end of the semester, my sentences sounded like this:

> My excitement was soon dampened, however, by what seemed like a small voice in the back of my head saying that I should be careful with my long awaited opportunity. I felt frustrated and this seemed to make it difficult to concentrate.

There is a poverty of language in these sentences. By this point, I knew that the clichéd language of my Housewife essay was unacceptable, and I generally recognized trite expressions. At the same time, I hadn't yet mastered the language of the classroom, hadn't yet come to see it as belonging to me. Most notable is the lifelessness of the prose, the apparent absence of a person behind the words. I wanted those sentences—and the rest of the essay—to convey the anguish of yearning to, at once, become something more and yet remain the same. I had the sensation of being split in two, part of me going into a future the other part didn't believe possible. As that person, the student writer at that moment, I was essentially mute. I could not—in the process of composing—use the language of the old me, yet I couldn't imagine myself in the language of "others."

I found this particularly discouraging because at midsemester I had been writing in a much different way. Note the language of this introduction to an essay I had written then, near the middle of the term:

> Pain is a constant companion to the people in "Footwork." Their jobs are physically damaging. Employers are insensitive to their feelings and in many cases add to their problems. The general public wounds them further by treating them with disgrace because of what they do for a living. Although the workers are as diverse as they are similar, there is a definite link between them. They suffer a great deal of abuse.

The voice here is stronger, more confident, appropriating terms like "physically damaging," "wounds them further," "insensitive," "diverse"—terms I couldn't have imagined using when writing about my own experience—and shaping them into sentences like, "Although the workers are as diverse as they are similar, there is a definite link between them." And there is the sense of a personality behind the prose, someone who sympathizes with the workers: "The general public wounds them further by treating them with disgrace because of what they do for a living."

What caused these differences? I was, I believed, explaining other people's thoughts and feelings, and I was free to move about in the language of "others" so long as I was speaking *of* others. I was unaware that I was transforming into my best classroom language my own thoughts and feelings about people whose experiences and ways of speaking were in many ways similar to mine.

The following year, unable to turn back or to let go of what had become something of an obsession with language (and hoping to catch and hold the sense of control that had eluded me in Basic Writing), I enrolled in a research writing course. I spent most of the term learning how to prepare for and write a research paper. I chose sex education as my subject and spent hours in libraries, searching for information, reading, taking notes. Then (not without messiness and often-demoralizing frustration) I organized my information into categories, wrote a thesis statement, and composed my paper—a series of paraphrases and quotations spaced between carefully constructed transitions. The process and results felt artificial, but as I would later come to realize I was passing through a necessary stage. My sentences sounded like this:

25

> This reserve becomes understandable with examination of who the abusers are. In an overwhelming number of cases, they are people the victims know and trust. Family members, relatives, neighbors and close family friends commit seventy-five percent of all reported sex crimes against children, and parents, parent substitutes and relatives are the offenders in thirty to eighty percent of all reported cases. While assault by strangers does occur, it is less common, and is usually a single episode. But abuse by family members, relatives and acquaintances may continue for an extended period of time. In cases of incest, for example, children are abused repeatedly for an average of eight years. In such cases, "the use of physical force is rarely necessary because of the child's trusting, dependent relationship with the offender. The child's cooperation is often facilitated by the adult's position of dominance, an offer of material goods, a threat of physical violence, or a misrepresentation of moral standards."

The completed paper gave me a sense of profound satisfaction, and I read it often after my professor returned it. I know now that what I was pleased with was the language I used and the professional voice it helped me maintain. "Use better words," my teacher had snapped at me one day after reading the notes I'd begun accumulating from my research, and slowly I began taking on the language of my sources. In my next set of notes, I used the word "vacillating"; my professor applauded. And by the time I composed the final draft, I felt at ease with terms like "overwhelming number of cases," "single episode," and "reserve," and I shaped them into sentences similar to those of my "expert" sources.

If I were writing the paper today, I would of course do some things differently. Rather than open with an anecdote—as my teacher suggested—I would begin simply with a quotation that caught my interest as I was researching my paper (and which I scribbled, without its source, in the margin of my notebook): "Truth does not do so much good in the world as the semblance of truth does evil." The quotation felt right because it captured what was for me the central idea of my essay—an idea that emerged gradually during the making of my paper—and expressed it in a way I would like to have said it. The anecdote, a hypothetical situation I invented to conform to the information in the paper, felt forced and insincere because it represented—to a great degree—my teacher's understanding of the essay, *her* idea of what in it was most significant. Improving upon my previous experiences with writing, I was beginning to think and feel in the language I used, to find my own voices in it, to sense that how one speaks influences how one means. But I was not yet secure enough, comfortable enough with the language to trust my intuition.

Now that I know that to seek knowledge, freedom, and autonomy means always to be in the concentrated process of becoming—always to be venturing into new territory, feeling one's way at first, then getting one's balance, negotiating, accommodating, discovering one's self in ways that previously defined "others"—I sometimes get tired. And I ask myself why I keep on participating in this highbrow form of violence, this slamming against perplexity. But there is no real futility in the question, no hint of that part of the old me who stood outside standard English, hugging to herself a disabling mistrust of a language she thought could not represent a person with her history and experience. Rather, the question represents a person who feels the consequence of her education, the weight of her possibilities as a teacher and writer and human being, a voice in society. And I would not change that person, would not give back the good burden that accompanies my growing expertise, my increasing power to shape myself in language and share that self with "others."

"To speak," says Frantz Fanon, "means to be in a position to use a certain syntax, to grasp the morphology of this or that language, but it means above all to assume a culture, to support the weight of a civilization."[1] To write means to do the same, but in a more profound sense. However, Fanon also says that to achieve mastery means to "get" in a position of power, to "grasp," to "assume." This, I have learned—both as a student and subsequently as a teacher—can involve tremendous emotional and psychological conflict for those attempting to master academic discourse. Although as a beginning student writer I had a fairly good grasp of ordinary spoken English and was proficient at what Labov calls "code-switching" (and what John Baugh in *Black Street Speech* terms "style shifting"), when I came face to face with the demands of academic writing, I grew increasingly self-conscious, constantly aware of my status as a black and a speaker of one of the many black English vernaculars—a traditional outsider. For the first time, I experienced my sense of doubleness as something menacing, a built-in enemy. Whenever I turned inward for salvation, the balm so available during my childhood, I found instead this new fragmentation which spoke to me in many voices. It was the voice of my desire to prosper, but at the same time it spoke of what I had relinquished and could not regain: a safe way of being, a state of powerlessness which exempted me from responsibility for who I was and might be. And it accused me of betrayal, of turning away from blackness. To recover balance, I had to take on the language of the academy, the language of "others." And to do that, I had to learn to imagine myself a part of the culture of that language, and therefore someone free to manage that language, to take liberties with it. Writing and rewriting, practicing, experimenting, I came to comprehend more fully the generative power of language. I discovered—with the help of some especially sensitive teachers—that through writing one can continually bring new selves into being, each with new responsibilities and difficulties, but also with new possibilities. Remarkable power, indeed. I write and continually give birth to myself.

Notes

1. *Black Skin, White Masks* (1952: rpt. New York: Grove Press, 1967). pp. 17–18.

CONNECTING PERSONALLY TO THE READING

1. Think about times when you found it a strain to speak or write. What caused this difficulty? When do you feel most comfortable speaking or writing, and why?

2. What does it mean to "own" a language? What form of English or another language—a form of slang, for example—do you feel you own?

3. Think of prose you have read that you would call "lifeless." What made this writing lifeless?

FOCUSING ON THE ARGUMENT

1. Much of Mellix's argument depends on definition: as the essay unfolds, she defines the differences between Black English and Standard English, indicating not only how their vocabulary and sentence structure differ, but also how the speakers and the occasions for each language differ. Given what Mellix tells us, how would you define these two languages?

2. Mellix uses direct quotation to illustrate the different uses of language she describes. Select three quotations and explain how each one illustrates the point Mellix is making. Pay attention to specific word choices. What adjectives would you use to describe these words?

3. The account of Mellix's growth as a writer, from her basic composition course to her discovery that she had the "power to shape [herself] in language and share that self with 'others,'" is a rhetorical technique called personal testimony. Trace the development of Mellix's ability to write well. Does the personal testimony give her essay credibility? Why or why not?

1. Caffilene Allen ("First They Changed My Name . . . ," below), Richard Rodriguez ("Public and Private Language," p. 51), and Mellix all find that leaving their childhood language is an essential step to gaining personal power and developing a public self. What kind of self does each writer develop, and what role does language play in this development?

2. Barbara Wallraff ("What Global Language?" p. 93) and Mellix both indicate that bilingualism requires more than "a very basic ability to communicate" (Wallraff). How is Mellix bilingual; that is, how does her use of two languages go beyond this basic ability? Why does Wallraff consider such an ability important to a global exchange of ideas?

3. Caffilene Allen ("First They Changed My Name . . . ," p. 65), Amy Tan ("The Language of Discretion," p. 43), and Mellix are all concerned with how the use of language characterizes people from their communities. Compare the reasons for and the nature of this concern. Why does it matter what others think of their communities?

WRITING TO ACT

1. Research the controversy over Ebonics; then consider how Mellix might respond to this issue. Write a report, analyzing the different positions on this issue.

2. Write a brief autobiography of your development as a writer, focusing on two or three significant events in your growth. What obstacles did you encounter? What, if anything, helped you through them? When did you most like your writing, and when did you like it the least?

READING

CAFFILENE ALLEN   For Caffilene Allen, the change, first of her name, later of her speech, marked her entrance into a world outside the Appalachia where she grew up. What is lost when a person leaves her familiar world and enters another culture? What is gained? How does Allen's attitude toward her mother change as the narration progresses?

ALLEN teaches at the University of Maryland in the Professional Writing Program; she has worked as a speechwriter, environmental activist, newspaper reporter, and editor.

First They Changed My Name . . . (1994)

BY CAFFILENE ALLEN

Although I was born in 1951, I grew up speaking the English of an earlier century—a fact I was reminded of one Sunday afternoon at my mother's rest home. A nurse drew me aside and, blushing a little, said uncertainly, "Your mother says Esther has been 'progging' again."

Quickly, I put her mind at ease. How well I knew what progging meant. It had

READING

been the cause of all my spankings as a young child. Progging was the act of going through belongings that were not yours, digging into clothes drawers, purses, anything that contained intriguing items in its mysterious depths.

Though words like "progging" seemed strange to the nurse, the rest home was not more than 12 miles from Tumbling Creek, Tennessee, the town where I grew up. What we called "old" English was the only language that I knew until I was six years old, when I was dragged, wailing and sobbing, onto the school bus. In school, I soon discovered that the lack of communication links from Tumbling Creek to the outside world, as well as the clannish nature of the people who lived there, had allowed two separate cultures, divided by centuries, to exist within miles of each other. At the school, I heard such unfamiliar words as "church," "couch," "living room," "Christ," and "isn't." At home, we used "meetinghouse," "divanette," "front room," "the Good Man," and "ain't." I had vague memories of some of those strange words being spoken occasionally, but whoever had used them had been immediately accused of trying to be like the "town-doogers" (town dwellers). That these were the terms my teachers wanted me to use was incomprehensible.

Perhaps my confusion helps to explain why I was surprisingly meek when my teachers took it upon themselves to change my name, thinking that I had misspelled it. They were probably not too far from the truth. Coming from English, Scottish, Irish, and German stock that never left the Tennessee hill area, I inherited a linguistic pattern that was mostly oral and did not include the "th" sound. My mother was most likely trying to give me the good Irish name of Kathleen, but pronounced the "th" with an "f" sound

and then spelled it phonetically for the nurse. All went well until I got to the first grade, where my teacher first decided that my name must be Caffie Lene but then settled on Kathleen. She told me I had to start writing it that way. My mother had no objection: whatever the God-Teacher said must be done—even if it meant changing my name.

In the second grade, my teacher told 5 me that it was a law that everyone had to have a middle name, and that I should choose one for myself, so she could put it on my permanent record. I was delighted. Here was my chance to be Barbara Allen, the focus of an English ballad in which the heroine rejects "sweet William," supposedly causing his death. When they both eventually die of broken hearts, a rose grows from William's grave and a briar from Barbara Allen's. Why I wished to become the namesake of such a person is something that I have never wanted to examine too closely, but I was absolutely thrilled when my teacher wrote Kathleen Barbara Allen on my permanent record.

If I had known how much frustration would result from these changes, I would have been less thrilled. I soon discovered that Kathleen was one of the most common names in school, and that I was doomed to almost always have a number added after my name to distinguish me from the others with the same name. By the sixth grade I had developed a somewhat oversensitive approach to life, and began to notice that I was never Kathy #1 but always Kathy #2 or #3. I still had enough of my mother's awe for teachers that I was never able to express my displeasure to them.

I was given the chance to reclaim my name when, as a senior in high school, I was required to produce a birth certificate in order to graduate. By that time,

I had almost forgotten about Caffilene, so I was very surprised to see the name on my birth certificate. My teachers were even more surprised, since the ones who had changed my name were long gone. A new problem loomed: I was one name on the school records and another on my birth certificate—therefore, I couldn't graduate. It took several teachers and a great deal of trouble to convince the bureaucracy I should be allowed to graduate.

Changing my name had a profound effect on my sense of identity, but my teachers had an equally long-lasting impact on my relationship with my mother, who believed that if the teacher said it was right, it was so. Having only a third-grade education obtained in a one-room country schoolhouse, she had the same reverence for schoolteachers as she had for the mysterious government, which kept her and her five children alive by sending a monthly Social Security check after my father was killed in the copper mines when I was 16 months old. To her, the government and the teachers were the keepers of some noble and powerful system upon which our survival and well-being depended, and we would be nothing less than ungrateful fools if we questioned their sterling wisdom. My four older brothers and sisters seemed to catch on sooner than I did: if my mother ever found out that the teachers she revered had a low opinion of her way of speech and life, she would be deeply hurt. For her peace of mind, my siblings learned to behave and speak one way at school and another way at home, whereas I would bound home, armed with linguistic rules that created a lifelong conflict between my mother and me. My first demand was that she allow me to call her Mommy rather than Miney (actually, her name was de Sara de Mina de Magdalene Pless Allen, but we couldn't get all of that out).

"What for?" was her reply. None of her ancestors had ever done such a thing.

"Because the teacher said I wasn't 10 showing proper respect."

She became even more puzzled. "What does that mean?"

I had to admit that I didn't know. "But she said I was supposed to call you Mommy, and so I'm going to."

Well, the God-Teacher had said it, so it had to be.

She had an easier time with my second question. After I learned to read about Dick and Jane, I soon realized that everyone—even Jane—was sometimes referred to as "he." Having a strictly literal approach to life, I couldn't understand. When I asked my teachers why only the male pronoun was used, they laughed at me, so I took my question home to my mother. Readily, she replied with the only answer that a good Baptist could give, and one which she sincerely believed: "Because men are better than women." I soon learned to stop asking my mother questions.

By the fourth grade I had become in- 15 creasingly ashamed of my mother and almost came to despise her for her manner and speech. One evening at the supper table when she was speaking improper English, chewing with her mouth open, and propping her elbows on the table, I found myself staring in open disgust. Suddenly, she stopped speaking in mid-sentence and glared at me, her face turning purple. By now, I was familiar enough with this scene to know what was going to happen next. Sure enough, I escaped from my seat just in time to miss being hit by the fork that she threw at my eyes. "Stop looking at me like I was a freak!" she screamed. Later, after the dishes were washed and put away, I went into the kitchen to get a glass of water. Through the screen door, I saw my mother sitting on the back steps, watching the sun go down behind the Blue Ridge Mountains. Her shoulders were shaking with silent sobs. For the first time, I sensed the depth of her isolation and despair; I also got my first inkling that she was not the one who was in the wrong. An intelligent, beautiful woman raised in a fundamentalist culture that assured her that she was nothing simply because she was a woman, she now was confronted with the scorn, brought home to her by her daughter, of those whom she had once revered as her benevolent protectors. Now she was sure that she was truly worthless.

Even though that moment gave me some understanding of my mother, it did not give me enough to change my ways totally. I continued to try to convince her that she needed to speak and act more like the people in town. I didn't have much success by myself, but I eventually got help from a rather surprising source. My mother had adamantly refused to get a telephone or a car, which were becoming more and more common in Tumbling Creek by the mid-1960s, so it was an incredible surprise to me when, one day when I was in the seventh grade, she brought home a television. Never in my life, not before or since, have I felt such a sense of wonder as when the television was first turned on in our house and people showed up on the screen in my living room who were fun to watch and listen to. Suddenly, the mountains seemed a little less lonely and my mother a little less mean.

By this time, I was pretty much considered an oddity by everyone who knew me. Since I always ate first, with the men rather than with the women, who had to wait until the men were fin-

ished before they could even sit down at the table, I became a third sex; people would say, "the men, the women, and Kathy." My love for books and writing seemed especially odd and somewhat slothlike to those working in the fields and the house morning, noon, and night in order to survive (which seemed to include everyone except me). And more than once, students in my class had been sent to the principal's office for calling me a nigger-lover. (No one in Tumbling Creek or Copperhill had ever met a person of color, but racism existed there, and my support of the civil rights movement increased my isolation.) But there, on the television, were people who gave me some inkling of another world out there where I might find others with ideas like mine. Peter, Paul, and Mary showed up singing "Blowing in the Wind" at a civil rights march. One afternoon, while my mother and I were watching *Who Do You Trust?*, newscasters interrupted to report a confrontation between Governor George Wallace and a black student trying to enter the University of Alabama. My spirits rose. Although at first they all seemed to be losing, at least there were people out there fighting for the same things that I thought were right.

I picked up "correct" pronunciation and grammar from TV, as well as an accent that gradually replaced my east Tennessee twang. My mother, on the other hand, changed the words to suit her own style of speech. Once, she told me that her favorite TV show was "Feenanzie." When I told her there was no such show, she retorted that there certainly was: "It's the one that has Hoss Cartwright and Little Joe and advertises Chevrolets."

Nevertheless, my mother did let television temper her cultural approach to life. She stopped trying to compliment my friends by telling them they were "just as fat as a little pig." She learned to stop asking the kids I brought home if they wanted a "dope," which meant a soft drink in Tumbling Creek. Most important, through TV, she learned to understand me and the ways that I had already adopted, and so television made life a little easier for both of us.

Many years have gone by. I grew up 20 and left Tumbling Creek, as my teachers and my mother always knew I would. But even now, thinking back on those times and conflicts, I find my emotions toward my mother and my teachers still bound up in the same love-hate web most of us reserve for our families only. In a way, my teachers were my family.

They were the first to encourage my love for learning, to find scholarships for me, to bring me books to read during the long, lonely summer months, to encourage my writing, to express their belief that I could even make a living as a writer. But at the same time, they taught me to hate my culture, to despise people who had a different linguistic approach to life, even if one of those people was my mother. After many long years, I have managed finally to reconcile to some extent my world with my mother's. Regaining a sense of pride in my Appalachian heritage and an appreciation for who my mother was as a person was one of the hardest and most valuable tasks of my adult life.

CONNECTING PERSONALLY TO THE READING

1. If you have a nickname or have experienced a name or nickname change in your life, what parts of your life do the different names/nicknames represent? Do they reflect different aspects of your personality or of your culture?

2. Think of someone whom you regard or once regarded as a powerful, even intimidating, force in your life, as Allen's teachers are to her and to her mother. How do these people affect your behavior and ideas? What was it about this person that made you trust his/her authority?

3. Allen finds herself "an oddity" both at home and at school. Think of a time when you felt like an oddity. What caused this feeling, and how did you deal with it?

FOCUSING ON THE ARGUMENT

1. Allen's article is built on contrasts—e.g., between the languages she spoke at home and at school and between her behavior at home and that of her brothers and sisters. What other contrasts do you see? How do they help clarify the point of the article?

2. The article is full of telling details, bits of information that Allen doesn't comment on, but that reveal a great deal about the lives and attitudes of the people in her narration. Why, for example, does she tell us that her mother's nurse blushed when reporting her mother's comment about "progging"? How does the fact that Allen's father died when she was

sixteen months old affect your understanding of her mother? What does her sympathy with the civil rights movement tell us about how she has changed? Find three other details and explain what they add to your understanding of the people in this reading.

SYNTHESIZING IDEAS FROM MULTIPLE READINGS

1. Itabari Njeri ("What's in a Name?" p. 71), Richard Rodriguez ("Public and Private Language," p. 51), and Allen each experience name changes. What is the reason for the change of name in each case, and what is its significance for each writer?

2. Teachers are powerful people in Richard Rodriguez's ("Public and Private Language," p. 51), Lydia Minatoya's ("Transformation," p. 81), and Allen's worlds. Compare the way teachers influence each of these three writers as children.

3. Compare Louise Erdrich's ("The Names of Women," p. 76) attitude toward the women in her culture to Allen's attitude toward her mother. What do the women's lives have in common? What do Erdrich and Allen most respect about these women?

WRITING TO ACT

1. Technologies such as television, movies, and computers are sometimes praised and sometimes reviled for homogenizing cultures. Television brought the outside world into Allen's mother's life and made it easier for her to understand her daughter's thinking. Think of a technology that has the potential to allow people from different cultures to understand one another better. Then write an editorial for your campus newspaper in which you explain how this understanding might come about.

2. Itabari Njeri ("What's in a Name?" p. 71), Amy Tan ("The Language of Discretion," p. 43), and Allen imply that it is important for people to try to understand and sympathize with others rather than judge them prematurely. Consider a person or a group of people in your community whom you think are judged unfairly. Write a letter to this group and explain how others can better understand their differences.

READING

ITABARI NJERI   When she changed her name from Jill Lord to Itabari Njeri, the writer of this article sought to "reclaim [her African] culture and synthesize it with [her] present reality." This act is both personal—an effort to clarify her identity as both African and American—and political—a desire to reconnect with the African culture her ancestors lost in slavery: "When I changed my name," she says, "I changed my life." Think about how closely your name is tied to your identity, both as an individual and as a member of an ethnic group. See if you can imagine a name change for yourself that would change your identity. As you read, also consider what objections people make to Njeri's African name and how she counters this criticism.

NJERI is a journalist, critic, and essayist; she is the author of *The Last Plantation* and *Every Goodbye Ain't Gone,* which won the American Book Award in 1990. This essay first appeared in the *Los Angeles Times Magazine,* where Njeri worked as a staff writer.

What's in a Name? (1989) | BY ITABARI NJERI

The decade was about to end when I started my first newspaper job. The seventies might have been the disco generation for some, but it was a continuation of the Black Power, post–civil rights era for me. Of course in some parts of America it was still the pre–civil rights era. And that was the part of America I wanted to explore. As a good reporter I needed a sense of the whole country, not just the provincial Northeast Corridor in which I was raised.

I head for Greenville ("Pearl of the Piedmont"), South Carolina.

"*Wheeere,*" some people snarled, their nostrils twitching, their mouths twisted so their top lips went slightly to the right, the bottom ones way down and to the left, "did you get *that* name from?"

Itabiddy, Etabeedy. Etabeeree. Eat a berry. Mata Hari. Theda Bara. And one secretary in the office of the Greenville Urban League told her employer: "It's Ms. Idi Amin."

Then, and now, there are a whole bunch of people who greet me with: "Hi, Ita." They think "Bari" is my last name. Even when they don't, they still want to call me "Ita." When I tell them my first name is Itabari, they say, "Well, what do people call you for short?"

"They don't call me anything for short," I say. "The name is Itabari."

Sophisticated white people, upon hearing my name, approach me as would a cultural anthropologist finding a piece of exotica right in his own living room. This happens a lot, still, at cocktail parties.

"Oh, what an unusual and beautiful name. Where are you from?"

"Brooklyn," I say. I can see the disappointment in their eyes. Just another homegrown Negro.

Then there are other white people who, having heard my decidedly northeastern accent, will simply say, "What a lovely name," and smile knowingly, indicating that they saw *Roots* and understand.

Then there are others, black and white, who for different reasons take me through this number:

"What's your *real* name?"

"Itabari Njeri is my real, legal name," I explain.

"Okay, what's your original name?" they ask, often with eyes rolling, exasperation in their voices.

After Malcolm X, Muhammad Ali, Kareem Abdul-Jabbar, Ntozake Shange, and Kunta Kinte, who, I ask, should be exasperated by this question-and-answer game?

Nevertheless, I explain, "Because of slavery, black people in the Western world don't usually know their original names. What you really want to know is what my slave name was."

Now this is where things get tense. Four hundred years of bitter history, culture, and politics between blacks and whites in America is evoked by this one term, "slave name."

Some white people wince when they hear the phrase, pained and embarrassed by this reminder of their ancestors' inhumanity. Further, they quickly scrutinize me and conclude that mine was a post–Emancipation Proclamation birth. "You were never a slave."

I used to be reluctant to tell people my slave name unless I surmised that they wouldn't impose their cultural values on me and refuse to use my African name. I

5

10

15

don't care anymore. When I changed my name, I changed my life, and I've been Itabari for more years now than I was Jill. Nonetheless, people will say: "Well, that's your *real* name, you were born in America and that's what I am going to call you." My mother tried a variation of this on me when I legalized my traditional African name. I respectfully made it clear to her that I would not tolerate it. Her behavior, and subsequently her attitude, changed.

But many black folks remain just as skeptical of my name as my mother was.   20

"You're one of those black people who changed their name, huh," they are likely to begin. "Well, I still got the old slave master's Irish name," said one man named O'Hare at a party. This man's defensive tone was a reaction to what I call the "blacker than thou" syndrome perpetrated by many black nationalists in the sixties and seventies. Those who reclaimed their African names made blacks who didn't do the same thing feel like Uncle Toms.

These so-called Uncle Toms couldn't figure out why they should use an African name when they didn't know a thing about Africa. Besides, many of them were proud of their names, no matter how they had come by them. And it should be noted that after the Emancipation Proclamation in 1863, four million black people changed their names, adopting surnames such as Freeman, Freedman, and Liberty. They eagerly gave up names that slave masters had imposed upon them as a way of identifying their human chattel.

Besides names that indicated their newly won freedom, blacks chose common English names such as Jones, Scott, and Johnson. English was their language. America was their home, and they wanted names that would allow them to assimilate as easily as possible.

Of course, many of our European surnames belong to us by birthright. We are the legal as well as "illegitimate" heirs to the names Jefferson, Franklin, Washington, et al., and in my own family, Lord.

Still, I consider most of these names to be by-products of slavery, if not actual slave   25
names. Had we not been enslaved, we would not have been cut off from our culture, lost our indigenous languages, and been compelled to use European names.

The loss of our African culture is a tragic fact of history, and the conflict it poses is a profound one that has divided blacks many times since Emancipation: do we accept the loss and assimilate totally or do we try to reclaim our culture and synthesize it with our present reality?

A new generation of black people in America is reexamining the issues raised by the cultural nationalists and Pan-Africanists of the sixties and seventies: what are the cultural images that appropriately convey the "new" black aesthetic in literature and art?

The young Afro-American novelist Trey Ellis has asserted that the "New Black Aesthetic shamelessly borrows and reassembles across both race and class lines." It is not afraid to embrace the full implications of our hundreds of years in the New World. We are a new people who need not be tied to externally imposed or self-inflicted cultural parochialism. Had I understood that as a teenager, I might still be singing today.

Even the fundamental issue of identity and nomenclature, raised by Baraka and others twenty years ago, is back on the agenda: are we to call ourselves blacks or African-Americans?

In reality, it's an old debate. "Only with the founding of the American Colonization 30
Society in 1816 did blacks recoil from using the term African in referring to themselves and their institutions," the noted historian and author Sterling Stuckey pointed out in an interview with me. They feared that using the term "African" would fuel white efforts to send them back to Africa. But they felt no white person had the right to send them back when they had slaved to build America.

Many black institutions retained their African identification, most notably the African Methodist Episcopal Church. Changes in black self-identification in America have come in cycles, usually reflecting the larger dynamics of domestic and international politics.

The period after World War II, said Stuckey, "culminating in the Cold War years of Roy Wilkins's leadership of the NAACP," was a time of "frenzied integrationism." And there was "no respectable black leader on the scene evincing any sort of interest in Africa—neither the NAACP or the Urban League."

This, he said, "was an example of historical discontinuity, the likes of which we, as a people, had not seen before." Prior to that, for more than a century and a half, black leaders were Pan-Africanists, including Frederick Douglass. "He recognized," said Stuckey, "that Africa was important and that somehow one had to redeem the motherland in order to be genuinely respected in the New World."

The Reverend Jesse Jackson has, of course, placed on the national agenda the importance of blacks in America restoring their cultural, historical, and political links with Africa.

But what does it really mean to be called an African-American? 35

"Black" can be viewed as a more encompassing term, referring to all people of African descent. "Afro-American" and "African-American" refer to a specific ethnic group. I use the terms interchangeably, depending on the context and the point I want to emphasize.

But I wonder: as the twenty-first century breathes down our necks—prodding us to wake up to the expanding mélange of ethnic groups immigrating in record numbers to the United States, inevitably intermarrying, and to realize the eventual reshaping of the nation's political imperatives in a newly multicultural society—will the term "African-American" be as much of a racial and cultural obfuscation as the term "black"? In other words, will we be the only people, in a society moving toward cultural pluralism, viewed to have no history and no culture? Will we just be a color with a new name: African-American?

Or will the term be—as I think it should—an ethnic label describing people with a shared culture who descended from Africans, were transformed in (as well as transformed) America, and are genetically intertwined with myriad other groups in the United States?

Such a definition reflects the historical reality and distances us from the fallacious, unscientific concept of separate races when there is only one: *Homo sapiens*.

But to comprehend what should be an obvious definition requires knowledge and 40
a willingness to accept history.

When James Baldwin wrote *Nobody Knows My Name*, the title was a metaphor—at the deepest level of the collective African-American psyche—for the blighting of black history and culture before the nadir of slavery and since.

The eradication or distortion of our place in world history and culture is most obvious in the popular media. Liz Taylor—and, for an earlier generation, Claudette Colbert—still represent what Cleopatra—a woman of color in a multiethnic society, dominated at various times by blacks—looks like.

And in American homes, thanks to reruns and cable, a new generation of black kids grow up believing that a simpleton shouting "Dy-no-mite!" is a genuine reflection of Afro-American culture, rather than a white Hollywood writer's stereotype.

More recently, *Coming to America,* starring Eddie Murphy as an African prince seeking a bride in the United States, depicted traditional African dancers in what amounted to a Las Vegas stage show, totally distorting the nature and beauty of real African dance. But with every burlesque-style pelvic thrust on the screen, I saw blacks in the audience burst into applause. They think that's African culture, too.

And what do Africans know of us, since blacks don't control the organs of communication that disseminate information about us? 45

"No!" screamed the mother of a Kenyan man when he announced his engagement to an African-American woman who was a friend of mine. The mother said marry a European, marry a white American. But please, not one of those low-down, ignorant, drug-dealing, murderous black people she had seen in American movies. Ultimately, the mother prevailed.

In Tanzania, the travel agent looked at me indignantly. "Njeri, that's Kikuyu. What are you doing with an African name?" he demanded.

I'd been in Dar es Salaam about a month and had learned that Africans assess in a glance the ethnic origins of the people they meet.

Without a greeting, strangers on the street in Tanzania's capital would comment, "Oh, you're an Afro-American or West Indian."

"Both." 50

"I knew it," they'd respond, sometimes politely, sometimes not.

Or, people I got to know while in Africa would mention, "I know another half-caste like you." Then they would call in the "mixed-race" person and say, "Please meet Itabari Njeri." The darker-complected African, presumably of unmixed ancestry, would then smile and stare at us like we were animals in the zoo.

Of course, this "half-caste" (which I suppose is a term preferable to "mulatto," which I hate, and which every person who understands its derogatory meaning—"mule"—should never use) was usually the product of a mixed marriage, not generations of ethnic intermingling. And it was clear from most "half-castes" I met that they did not like being compared to so mongrelized and stigmatized a group as Afro-Americans.

I had minored in African studies in college, worked for years with Africans in the United States, and had no romantic illusions as to how I would be received in the motherland. I wasn't going back to find my roots. The only thing that shocked me in Tanzania was being called, with great disdain, a "white woman" by an African waiter. Even if the rest of the world didn't follow the practice, I then assumed everyone understood that any known or perceptible degree of African ancestry made one "black" in America by law and social custom.

But I was pleasantly surprised by the telephone call I received two minutes after I walked into my Dar es Salaam hotel room. It was the hotel operator. "Sister, welcome to Tanzania. . . . Please tell everyone in Harlem hello for us." The year was 1978, and 55 people in Tanzania were wearing half-foot-high platform shoes and dancing to James Brown wherever I went.

Shortly before I left, I stood on a hill surrounded by a field of endless flowers in Arusha, near the border of Tanzania and Kenya. A toothless woman with a wide smile, a staff in her hand, and two young girls at her side, came toward me on a winding path. I spoke to her in fractured Swahili and she to me in broken English.

"I know you," she said smiling. "Wa-Negro." "Wa" is a prefix in Bantu languages meaning people. "You are from the lost tribe," she told me. "Welcome," she said, touching me, then walked down a hill that lay in the shadow of Mount Kilimanjaro.

I never told her my name, but when I told other Africans, they'd say: "*Emmmm, Itabari.* Too long. How about I just call you Ita."

CONNECTING PERSONALLY TO THE READING

1. To what extent do you see your name as connected to your ancestry? What assumptions do you think people make about you when they first hear your name? Think about the first time you heard a name that was unusual—what impression of the person did that name give you?

2. Why is Njeri pleased when the hotel operator in Dar es Salaam says, "Sister, welcome to Tanzania. . . . Please tell everyone in Harlem hello for us"?

3. What do Africans perceive Njeri's cultural identity to be? What do Americans consider it to be? How does Njeri define her cultural identity?

FOCUSING ON THE ARGUMENT

1. One of Njeri's rhetorical strategies is to quote or paraphrase respected authorities on African American culture: Trey Ellis, Sterling Stuckey, and James Baldwin. What do these sections of her article contribute to her argument? Do you find that they make her writing more convincing?

2. Much of Njeri's writing depends on the reader's recognition of allusions to a wide range of figures from popular culture, literature, and politics: Mata Hari, Theda Bara, Idi Amin, Uncle Tom, Malcolm X, Muhammad Ali, Kareem Abdul-Jabbar, Ntozake Shange, Kunta Kinte, Eddie Murphy, and James Brown, among others. How does recognizing the allusion enrich your understanding of Njeri's argument? What is the effect of mentioning these figures, as Njeri does, without providing a lot of information about them?

3. Before telling us why she changed her name, Njeri gives multiple illustrations of people reacting unsympathetically to her new name. What is the effect of her beginning the essay with several opposing viewpoints?

SYNTHESIZING IDEAS FROM MULTIPLE READINGS

1. Lydia Minatoya's ("Transformation," p. 81) parents are as concerned with choosing the right name for their children as Njeri is in choosing one for herself. In what ways are their motivations alike or different? How do their different historical circumstances explain the similarities or differences you see?

2. Both Louise Erdrich ("The Names of Women," p. 76) and Njeri believe that a person's name and identity are the same thing. Do you agree? What was lost when Njeri's slave ancestors were stripped of their African names? What was lost when Erdrich's ancestors were re-named after Catholic saints?

WRITING TO ACT

1. Njeri argues that the term "African-American" more accurately describes people of African descent who share a common culture than does the word "black." Consider a racial, ethnic, cultural, or other label for a group you belong to. Write a letter to others in the group, and explain why the label does or does not accurately describe the group and, if not, include suggestions for a better label.

2. Njeri believes that popular media such as movies offer distorted images of African Americans. View a movie or TV show or listen to music that presents an image of a group you know well. Then write a review, assessing the accuracy of this portrayal.

READING

LOUISE ERDRICH   Louise Erdrich argues that the names of the Anishinabe, a Native American culture that is largely gone today, "tell stories" about the people whose names these were. What are some of these stories, and what do they tell us about the Anishinabe women? How do these stories represent the Anishinabe people as a whole? Why is it important for Erdrich to tell us these stories?

ERDRICH belongs to the Turtle Mountain band of Chippewa Native Americans. A poet, a short story writer, and a novelist, she is best known for her novel *Love Medicine,* which won the National Book Critics Circle Award in 1984.

The Names of Women (1995) | BY LOUISE ERDRICH

I kwe is the word for woman in the language of the Anishinabe, my mother's people, whose descendants, mixed with and married to French trappers and farmers, are the Michifs of the Turtle Mountain reservation in North Dakota. Every Anishinabe *Ikwe,* every mixed-blood descendant like me, who can trace her way back a generation or two, is the daughter of a mystery. The history of the woodland Anishinabe—decimated by disease, fighting Plains Indian tribes to the west and squeezed by European settlers to the east—is much like most other Native American stories, a confusion of loss, a tale of absences, of a culture that was blown apart and changed so radically in such a short time that only the names survive.

And yet, those names.

The names of the first women whose existence is recorded on the rolls of the Turtle Mountain Reservation, in 1892, reveal as much as we can ever recapture of their personalities, complex natures, and relationships. These names tell stories, or half stories, if only we listen closely.

There once were women named *Standing Strong, Fish Bones, Different Thunder.* There once was a girl called *Yellow Straps.* Imagine what it was like to pick berries with *Sky Coming Down,* to walk through a storm with *Lightning Proof.* Surely, she was struck and lived, but what about the person next to her? People always avoided *Steps Over Truth,* when they wanted a straight answer, and *I Hear,* when they wanted to keep a secret. *Glittering* put coal on her face and watched for enemies at night. The woman named *Standing Across* could see things moving far across the lake. The old ladies gossiped about *Playing Around,* but no one dared say anything to her face. *Ice* was good at gambling. *Shining One Side* loved to sit and talk to *Opposite the Sky.* They both knew *Sounding Feather, Exhausted Wind,* and *Green Cloud,* daughter of *Seeing Iron. Center of the Sky* was a widow. *Rabbit, Prairie Chicken,* and *Daylight* were all little girls. *She Tramp* could make great distance in a day of walking. *Cross Lightning* had a powerful smile. When *Setting Wind* and *Gentle Woman Standing* sang together the whole tribe listened. *Stop the Day* got her name when at her shout the afternoon went still. *Log* was strong, *Cloud Touching Bottom* weak and consumptive. *Mirage* married *Wind.* Everyone loved *Musical Cloud,* but children hid from *Dressed in Stone. Lying Down Grass* had such a gentle voice and touch, but no one dared to cross *She Black of Heart.*

We can imagine something of these women from their names. Anishinabe historian Basil Johnson notes that "such was the mystique and force of a name that it was considered presumptuous and unbecoming, even vain, for a person to utter his own name. It was the custom for a third person, if present, to utter the name of the person to be identified. Seldom, if ever, did either husband or wife speak the name of the other in public." 5

Shortly after the first tribal roll, the practice of renaming became an ecclesiastical exercise, and, as a result, most women in the next two generations bear the names of saints particularly beloved by the French. *She Knows the Bear* became Marie. *Sloping Cloud* was christened Jeanne. *Taking Care of the Day* and *Yellow Day Woman* turned into Catherines. Identities are altogether lost. The daughters of my own ancestors, *Kwayzancheewin—Acts Like a Boy* and *Striped Earth Woman*—go unrecorded, and no hint or reflection of their individual natures comes to light through the scattershot records of those times, although they must have been genetically tough in order to survive: there were epidemics of typhoid, flu, measles, and other diseases that winnowed the tribe each winter. They had to have grown up sensible, hard-working, undeviating in their attention to their tasks. They had to have been lucky. And if very lucky, they acquired carts.

It is no small thing that both of my great-grandmothers were known as women with carts.

The first was Elise Eliza McCloud, the great-granddaughter of *Striped Earth Woman.* The buggy she owned was somewhat grander than a cart. In her photograph, Elise Eliza gazes straight ahead, intent, elevated in her pride. Perhaps she and her daughter Justine, both wearing reshaped felt fedoras, were on their way to the train that would take them from Rugby, North Dakota, to Grand Forks, and back again. Back and forth across the upper tier of the plains, they peddled their hand-worked tourist items—dangling moccasin brooches and little beaded hats, or, in the summer, the wild berries, plums, and nuts that they had gathered from the wooded hills. Of Elise Eliza's industry there remains in the family only an intricately beaded pair of buffalo horns and a piece of real furniture, a "highboy," an object once regarded with some awe, a prize she won for selling the most merchandise from a manufacturer's catalogue.

The owner of the other cart, Virginia Grandbois, died when I was nine years old: she was a fearsome and fascinating presence, an old woman seated like an icon behind the door of my grandparents' house. Forty years before I was born, she was photographed on her way to fetch drinking water at the reservation well. In the picture she is seated high, the reins in her fingers connected to a couple of shaggy fetlocked draft ponies. The barrel she will fill stands behind her. She wears a man's sweater and an expression of vast self-pleasure. She might have been saying *Kaygoh*, a warning, to calm the horses. She might have been speaking to whomever it was who held the camera, still a novel luxury.

Virginia Grandbois was known to smell of flowers. In spite of the potato picking, water hauling, field and housework, she found the time and will to dust her face with pale powder, in order to look more French. She was the great-great-granddaughter of the daughter of the principal leader of the *A-waus-e*, the Bullhead clan, a woman whose real name was never recorded but who, on marrying a Frenchman, was "recreated" as Madame Cadotte. It was Madame Cadotte who acted as a liaison between her Ojibway relatives and her husband so that, even when French influence waned in the region, Jean-Baptiste Cadotte stayed on as the only trader of importance, the last governor of the fort at Sault St. Marie.

By the time I knew Virginia Grandbois, however, her mind had darkened, and her body deepened, shrunk, turned to bones and leather. She did not live in the present or in any known time at all. Periodically, she would awaken from dim and unknown dreams to find herself seated behind the door in her daughter's house. She then cried out for her cart and her horses. When they did not materialize, Virginia Grandbois rose with great energy and purpose. Then she walked towards her house, taking the straightest line.

That house, long sold and gone, lay over one hundred miles due east and still Virginia Grandbois charged ahead, no matter what lay in her path—fences, sloughs, woods, the yards of other families. She wanted home, to get home, to be home. She wanted her own place back, the place she had made, not her daughter's, not anyone else's. Hers. There was no substitute, no kindness, no reality that would change her mind. She had to be tied to the chair, and the chair to the wall, and still there was no reasoning with Virginia Grandbois. Her entire life, her hard-won personality, boiled down in the end to one stubborn, fixed, desperate idea.

I started with the same idea—this urge to get home, even if I must walk straight across the world. Only, for me, the urge to walk is the urge to write. Like my great-grandmother's house, there is no home for me to get to. A mixed-blood, raised in the Sugarbeet Capital, educated on the Eastern seaboard, married in a tiny New England village, living now on a ridge directly across from the Swan Range in the Rocky Mountains, my home is a collection of homes, of wells in which the quiet of experience shales away into sweet bedrock.

Elise Eliza pieced the quilt my mother slept under, a patchwork of shirts, pants, other worn-out scraps, bordered with small rinsed and pressed Bull Durham sacks. As

10

if in another time and place, although it is only the dim barrel of a four-year-old's memory, I see myself lying wrapped under smoky quilts and dank green army blankets in the house in which my mother was born. In the fragrance of tobacco, some smoked in home-rolled cigarettes, some offered to the Manitous whose presence still was honored, I dream myself home. Beneath the rafters, shadowed with bunches of plants and torn calendars, in the nest of a sagging bed, I listen to mice rustle and the scratch of an owl's claws as it paces the shingles.

Elise Eliza's daughter-in-law, my grandmother Mary LeFavor, kept that house of 15 hand-hewed and stacked beams, mudded between. She managed to shore it up and keep it standing by stuffing every new crack with disposable diapers. Having used and reused cloth to diaper her own children, my grandmother washed and hung to dry the paper and plastic diapers that her granddaughters bought for her great-grandchildren. When their plastic-paper shredded, she gathered them carefully together and one day, on a summer visit, I woke early to find her tamping the rolled stuff carefully into the cracked walls of that old house.

It is autumn in the Plains, and in the little sloughs ducks land, and mudhens, whose flesh always tastes greasy and charred. Snow is coming soon, and after its first fall there will be a short, false warmth that brings out the sweet-sour odor of highbush cranberries. As a descendant of the women who skinned buffalo and tanned and smoked the hides, of women who pounded berries with the dried meat to make winter food, who made tea from willow bark and rosehips, who gathered snakeroot, I am affected by the change of seasons. Here is a time when plants consolidate their tonic and drop seed, when animals store energy and grow thick fur. As for me, I start keeping longer hours, writing more, working harder, though I am obviously not a creature of a traditional Anishinabe culture. I was not raised speaking the old language, or adhering to the cycle of religious ceremonies that govern the Anishinabe spiritual relationship to the land and the moral order within human configurations. As the wedding of many backgrounds I am free to do what simply feels right.

My mother knits, sews, cans, dries food and preserves it. She knows how to gather tea, berries, snare rabbits, milk cows, and churn butter. She can grow squash and melons from seeds she gathered the fall before. She is, as were the women who came before me, a repository of all of the homey virtues, and I am the first in a long line who has not saved the autumn's harvest in birch bark *makuks* and skin bags and in a cellar dry and cold with dust. I am the first who scratches the ground for pleasure, not survival, and grows flowers instead of potatoes. I record rather than practice the arts that filled the hands and days of my mother and her mother, and all the mothers going back into the shadows, when women wore names that told us who they were.

CONNECTING PERSONALLY TO THE READING

1. What does Erdrich mean when she states that every descendant of an Anishinabe is "the daughter of a mystery"? Do you have ancestors whom you regard as a "mystery"?

2. What is the significance of being a woman with a cart? What possession or attribute has similar significance for you?

1. Erdrich's article is full of descriptions of women: her great-grandmothers, Elise Eliza McCloud and Virginia Grandbois, and—more briefly—the women named in the fourth paragraph. What personality characteristics do these descriptions reveal? How does Erdrich's characterization of these women support her contention that the Anishinabe had a rich, powerful culture?

2. Although Erdrich quotes an Anishinabe historian, most of her article gives the impression of recollection, as if she were repeating stories handed down through the memories of generations of family members. Explain why you do or do not find this strategy convincing.

SYNTHESIZING IDEAS FROM MULTIPLE READINGS

1. Like Itabari Njeri ("What's in a Name?" p. 71), Erdrich has "an urge to get home," to learn about her ancestral culture. How does Njeri satisfy this need? How does Erdrich? How do words and writing figure into this quest?

2. Both Haunani-Kay Trask ("From a Native Daughter," p. 85) and Erdrich view themselves as native daughters in a land colonized by Europeans. What does each writer see as the consequence for her people of this colonization? In what ways does each writer assert the value of her native culture?

WRITING TO ACT

1. Erdrich describes how she differs from her ancestors:

   I am the first in a long line who has not saved the autumn's harvest in birch bark *makuks*. . . . I am the first who scratches the ground for pleasure, not survival, and grows flowers instead of potatoes. I record rather than practice the arts that filled the hands and days of my mother . . . and all the mothers going back into the shadows.

   Research a specific element of the lives of your ancestors and their contemporaries, such as how they prepared food, their means of transportation, or how they communicated with others. Your research could draw on history books, the Internet, and conversations with family members. Write a magazine article defining how this element of your life and identity differ from those of your grandparents or earlier generations of your family.

2. Research the names of a member of a Native American culture, possibly one that lived or lives in your area. How do the names characterize the people who hold (or held) them? Write a news article reporting on your findings.

READING

LYDIA MINATOYA   In narrating events from her childhood and family history, Japanese American Lydia Minatoya shows the struggle and the price of trying to assimilate into a white, race-conscious culture. Infusing this experience is a historical event: the forced relocation of 120,000 Japanese Americans, including Minatoya's parents, into internment camps during World War II. Responding to racial panic after the bombing of Pearl Harbor, the U.S. government required Japanese Americans to move to detention centers, where they lived in barracks behind barbed wire, guarded by armed troops. Most of those interned lost their homes, farms, businesses, and jobs. As you read, think about how this event, which occurred before Lydia's birth in 1950 in Albany, New York, influences her behavior and that of her family and teachers. Why is it important for the Minatoyas to fit in? What is the American Dream, and what lessons does Lydia draw from her efforts to fulfill it?

MINATOYA's essay first appeared in *Talking to High Monks in the Snow,* a memoir. She is also the author of the novel *The Strangeness of Beauty.*

Transformation (1992) | BY LYDIA MINATOYA

Perhaps it begins with my naming. During her pregnancy, my mother was reading Dr. Spock. "Children need to belong," he cautioned. "An unusual name can make them the subject of ridicule." My father frowned when he heard this. He stole a worried glance at my sister. Burdened by her Japanese name, Misa played unsuspectingly on the kitchen floor.

The Japanese know full well the dangers of conspicuousness. "The nail that sticks out gets pounded down," cautions an old maxim. In America, Relocation was all the proof they needed.

And so it was, with great earnestness, my parents searched for a conventional name. They wanted me to have the full true promise of America.

"I will ask my colleague Froilan," said my father. "He is the smartest man I know."

"And he has poetic soul," said my mother, who cared about such things.   5

In due course, Father consulted Froilan. He gave Froilan his conditions for suitability.

"First, if possible, the full name should be alliterative," said my father. "Like Misa Minatoya." He closed his eyes and sang my sister's name. "Second, if not an alliteration, at least the name should have assonantal rhyme."

"Like Misa Minatoya?" said Froilan with a teasing grin.

"Exactly," my father intoned. He gave an emphatic nod. "Finally, most importantly, the name must be readily recognizable as conventional." He peered at Froilan with hope. "Do you have any suggestions or ideas?"

Froilan, whose own American child was named Ricardito, thought a while.   10

"We already have selected the name for a boy," offered my father. "Eugene."

"Eugene?" wondered Froilan. "But it meets none of your conditions!"

"Eugene is a special case," said my father, "after Eugene, Oregon, and Eugene O'Neill. The beauty of the Pacific Northwest, the power of a great writer."

"I see," said Froilan, who did not but who realized that this naming business would be more complex than he had anticipated. "How about Maria?"

"Too common," said my father. "We want a *conventional* name, not a common one."   15

"Hmmm," said Froilan, wondering what the distinction was. He thought some more and then brightened. "Lydia!" he declared. He rhymed the name with media. "Lydia for *la bonita infanta!*"

And so I received my uncommon conventional name. It really did not provide the camouflage my parents had anticipated. I remained unalterably alien. For Dr. Spock had been addressing *American* families, and in those days, everyone knew all real American families were white.

Call it denial, but many Japanese Americans never quite understood that the promise of America was not truly meant for them. They lived in horse stalls at the Santa Anita racetrack and said the Pledge of Allegiance daily. They rode to Relocation Camps under armed guard, labeled with numbered tags, and sang "The Star-Spangled Banner." They lived in deserts or swamps, ludicrously imprisoned—where would they run if they ever escaped—and formed garden clubs, and yearbook staffs, and citizen town meetings. They even elected beauty queens.

My mother practiced her okoto and was featured in a recital. She taught classes in fashion design and her students mounted a show. Into exile she had carried an okoto and a sewing machine. They were her past and her future. She believed in Art and Technology.

My mother's camp was the third most populous city in the entire state of Wyoming. Across the barren lands, behind barbed wire, bloomed these little oases of democracy. The older generation bore the humiliation with pride. "*Kodomo no tame ni,*" they said. For the sake of the children. They thought that if their dignity was great, then their children would be spared. Call it valor. Call it bathos. Perhaps it was closer to slapstick: a sweet and bitter lunacy. 20

Call it adaptive behavior. Coming from a land swept by savage typhoons, ravaged by earthquakes and volcanoes, the Japanese have evolved a view of the world: a cooperative, stoic, almost magical way of thinking. Get along, work hard, and never quite see the things that can bring you pain. Against the tyranny of nature, of feudal lords, of wartime hysteria, the charm works equally well.

And so my parents gave me an American name and hoped that I could pass. They nourished me with the American dream: Opportunity, Will, Transformation.

When I was four and my sister was eight, Misa regularly used me as a comic foil. She would bring her playmates home from school and query me as I sat amidst the milk bottles on the front steps.

"What do you want to be when you grow up?" she would say. She would nudge her audience into attentiveness.

"A mother kitty cat!" I would enthuse. Our cat had just delivered her first litter of kittens and I was enchanted by the rasping tongue and soft mewings of motherhood. 25

"And what makes you think you can become a cat?" Misa would prompt, gesturing to her howling friends—wait for this; it gets better yet.

"This is America," I stoutly would declare. "I can grow up to be anything I want!" My faith was unshakable. I believed. Opportunity. Will. Transformation.

When we lived in Albany, I always was the teachers' pet. "So tiny, so precocious, so prettily dressed!" They thought I was a living doll and this was fine with me.

My father knew that the effusive praise would die. He had been through this with my sister. After five years of being a perfect darling, Misa had reached the age where students were tracked by ability. Then, the anger started. Misa had tested into the advanced track. It was impossible, the community declared. Misa was forbidden entry into advanced classes as long as there were white children being placed below her. In her defense, before an angry rabble, my father made a presentation to the Board of Education. 30

But I was too young to know of this. I knew only that my teachers praised and petted me. They took me to other classes as an example. "Watch now, as Lydia demonstrates attentive behavior," they would croon as I was led to an empty desk at the head of the class. I had a routine. I would sit carefully, spreading my petticoated skirt neatly beneath me. I would pull my chair close to the desk, crossing my swinging legs at my snowy white anklets. I would fold my hands carefully on the desk before me and stare pensively at the blackboard.

This routine won me few friends. The sixth-grade boys threw rocks at me. They danced around me in a tight circle, pulling at the corners of their eyes. "Ching Chong Chinaman," they chanted. But teachers loved me. When I was in first grade, a third-grade teacher went weeping to the principal. She begged to have me skipped. She was leaving to get married and wanted her turn with the dolly.

When we moved, the greatest shock was the knowledge that I had lost my charm. From the first, my teacher failed to notice me. But to me, it did not matter. I was in love. I watched her moods, her needs, her small vanities. I was determined to ingratiate.

Miss Hempstead was a shimmering vision with a small upturned nose and eyes that were kewpie doll blue. Slender as a sylph, she tripped around the classroom, all saucy in her high-heeled shoes. Whenever I looked at Miss Hempstead, I pitied the Albany teachers whom, formerly, I had adored. Poor old Miss Rosenberg. With a shiver of distaste, I recalled her loose fleshy arms, her mottled hands, the scent of lavender as she crushed me to her heavy breasts.

Miss Hempstead had a pet of her own. Her name was Linda Sherlock. I watched Linda closely and plotted Miss Hempstead's courtship. The key was the piano. Miss Hempstead played the piano. She fancied herself a musical star. She sang songs from Broadway revues and shaped her students' reactions. "Getting to know you," she would sing. We would smile at her in a staged manner and position ourselves obediently at her feet.

Miss Hempstead was famous for her ability to soothe. Each day at rest time, she played the piano and sang soporific songs. Linda Sherlock was the only child who succumbed. Routinely, Linda's head would bend and nod until she crumpled gracefully onto her folded arms. A tousled strand of blond hair would fall across her forehead. Miss Hempstead would end her song, would gently lower the keyboard cover. She would turn toward the restive eyes of the class. "Isn't she sweetness itself!" Miss Hempstead would declare. It made me want to vomit.

I was growing weary. My studiousness, my attentiveness, my fastidious grooming and pert poise: all were failing me. I changed my tactics. I became a problem. Miss Hempstead sent me home with nasty notes in sealed envelopes: Lydia is a slow child, a noisy child, her presence is disruptive. My mother looked at me with surprise, "*Nani desu ka?* Are you having problems with your teacher?" But I was tenacious. I pushed harder and harder, firmly caught in the obsessive need of the scorned.

One day I snapped. As Miss Hempstead began to sing her wretched lullabies, my head dropped to the desk with a powerful CRACK! It lolled there, briefly, then rolled toward the edge with a momentum that sent my entire body catapulting to the floor. Miss Hempstead's spine stretched slightly, like a cat that senses danger. Otherwise, she paid no heed. The linoleum floor was smooth and cool. It emitted a faint pleasant odor: a mixture of chalk dust and wax.

I began to snore heavily. The class sat electrified, There would be no drowsing today. The music went on and on. Finally, one boy could not stand it. "Miss Hempstead," he probed plaintively, "Lydia has fallen asleep on the floor!" Miss Hempstead did not turn. Her playing grew slightly strident but she did not falter.

I lay on the floor through rest time. I lay on the floor through math drill. I lay on the floor while my classmates scraped around me, pushing their sturdy little wooden desks into the configuration for reading circle. It was not until penmanship practice that I finally stretched and stirred. I rose like Sleeping Beauty and slipped back to my seat. I smiled enigmatically. A spell had been broken. I never again had a crush on a teacher. 40

CONNECTING PERSONALLY TO THE READING

1. Think about a situation in which you worried about not fitting in. What were the consequences of being an outsider? What, if anything, did you do to feel part of the group?

2. Naming is an important part of identity. Consider the implications of your name—why your parents chose it and what it implies about you.

3. In what ways are your values and attitudes like or different from your parents'? If you have undergone a transformation like Lydia's, what caused it, and how did it change your thinking?

4. What is the "Japanese way of thinking" that Minatoya refers to? Identify a way of thinking that is common to people of your family's ancestry, and explain, if you can, how it came about. How does this way of thinking affect you?

FOCUSING ON THE ARGUMENT

1. Minatoya's argument relies heavily on situational irony. That is, it reports on actions that the reader and writer know will not work out as the person performing them intends. For example, Minatoya describes her father's hope that his daughter's English first name will ensure that she fit in—while at the same time making clear (in her references to Japanese internment camps) that a change of name will neither disguise Lydia's Japanese heritage nor protect her from racism. What other instances of irony do you see in this reading? How, for example, might Minatoya's description of the Japanese response to internment, her father's reliance on Froilan, her mother's faith in "Art and Technology," and her own eagerness to be a teacher's "dolly" be considered ironic?

2. The reading works by recounting several brief stories—among them, how Lydia got her name, how Japanese Americans adapted to internment, and how four-year-old Lydia entertained her sister's friends. What other stories does the reading tell, what ideas tie them together, and what is the effect of the accumulation of these independent tales?

3. Much of the power of this story comes from the author's use of telling detail—the "snowy white anklets" that seem to encapsulate Lydia as a goody-goody; Lydia's father's presentation "before an angry rabble," a courageous act that defines his own transformation. Find a passage that is especially concrete, and explain how the individual details enhance the point of that passage.

1. Lydia's parents had culturally based ideas about naming children. How would Amy Tan ("The Language of Discretion," p. 43) explain their criteria for choosing the perfect name?

2. Compare Lydia's father's reasons for choosing his daughter's name with the reasons Itabari Njeri ("What's in a Name?", p. 71) gives for changing her name, and the reasons Caffilene Allen's ("First They Changed My Name . . .," p. 65) teacher gives for changing Allen's name. What values motivate each of these decisions?

WRITING TO ACT

1. Find a news article about someone who has suffered from "the dangers of conspicuousness"—someone who was victimized because, for whatever reason, he or she stuck out as an outsider. Write an editorial in response to this story.

2. Research the history of the Japanese American internment. Then create a poster or Web page that uses both language and graphics to describe a part of this experience.

READING

HAUNANI-KAY TRASK   Trask argues that European and American historians have failed to understand Hawaiian culture because they did not know the Hawaiian language. She particularly critiques their misrepresentation of ancient Hawai'i as a feudal system. A feudal system, a hierarchical social structure in which a king owned the land and his serfs worked it for him, was not possible in Hawai'i, which had a tradition of shared land use. Had the historians understood how the Hawaiian language denotes possession, and paid attention to the stories native Hawaiians told about the land, they would have understood that the land did not belong to one person, but to everyone. Why do you think Trask considers the historians' misrepresentation of the Hawaiians' relationship to the land to be deliberate?

TRASK, a Professor of Hawaiian Studies at the University of Hawaii, is also a poet and political activist. She is the author of *The American Indian and the Problem of History,* which includes the essay printed below, and *From a Native Daughter: Colonialism and Sovereignty in Hawaii*; she coproduced the documentary film *Act of War: The Overthrow of the Hawaiian Nation.*

From a Native Daughter (1987) | BY HAUNANI-KAY TRASK

> *E noi'i wale mai no ka haole, a,*
> *'a'ole e pau no hana a Hawai'i 'imi loa*
> Let the *haole* freely research us in detail
> But the doings of deep delving *Hawai'i*
> will not be exhausted.
>
> KEPELINO
> 19th-century Hawaiian historian

Aloha kākou. Let us greet each other in friendship and love. My given name is Haunaniokawēkiu o Haleakalā, native of *Hawai'i Nei.* My father's family is from the *'āina* (land) of Kaua'i, my mother's family from the *'āina* of Maui. I reside today among my native people in the community of *Waimānalo.*

I have lived all my life under the power of America. My native country, Hawai'i, is owned by the United States. I attended missionary schools, both Catholic and Protestant, in my youth, and I was sent away to the American mainland to receive a "higher" education at the University of Wisconsin. Now I teach the history and culture of my people at the University of Hawai'i.

When I was young the story of my people was told twice: once by my parents, then again by my school teachers. From my *'ohana* (family), I learned about the life of the old ones: how they fished and planted by the moon; shared all the fruits of their labors, especially their children; danced in great numbers for long hours; and honored the unity of their world in intricate genealogical chants. My mother said Hawaiians had sailed over thousands of miles to make their home in these sacred islands. And they had flourished, until the coming of the *haole* (whites).

At school, I learned that the "pagan Hawaiians" did not read or write, were lustful cannibals, traded in slaves, and could not sing. Captain Cook had "discovered" Hawai'i and the ungrateful Hawaiians had killed him. In revenge, the Christian god had cursed the Hawaiians with disease and death.

I learned the first of these stories from speaking with my mother and father. I learned the second from books. By the time I left for college, the books had won out over my parents, especially since I spent four long years in a missionary boarding school for Hawaiian children. 5

When I went away I understood the world as a place and a feeling divided in two: one *haole* (white), and the other *kānaka* (native). When I returned ten years later with a Ph.D., the division was sharper, the lack of connection more painful. There was the world that we lived in—my ancestors, my family, and my people—and then there was the world historians described. This world, they had written, was the truth. A primitive group, Hawaiians had been ruled by bloodthirsty priests and despotic kings who owned all the land and kept our people in feudal subjugation. The chiefs were cruel, the people poor.

But this was not the story my mother told me. No one had owned the land before the *haole* came; everyone could fish and plant, except during sacred periods. And the chiefs were good and loved their people.

Was my mother confused? What did our *kūpuna* (elders) say? They replied: Did these historians (all *haole*) know the language? Did they understand the chants? How long had they lived among our people? Whose stories had they heard?

None of the historians had ever learned our mother tongue. They had all been content to read what Europeans and Americans had written. But why did scholars, presumably well-trained and thoughtful, neglect our language? Not merely a passageway to knowledge, language is a form of knowing by itself; a people's way of thinking and feeling is revealed through its music.

I sensed the answer without needing to answer. From years of living in a divided world, I knew the historian's judgment: *There is no value in things Hawaiian; all value comes from things haole.* 10

Historians, I realized, were very like missionaries. They were a part of the colonizing horde. One group colonized the spirit; the other, the mind. Frantz Fanon had been right, but not just about Africans. He had been right about the bondage of my own people: "By a kind of perverted logic, [colonialism] turns to the past of the oppressed people, and distorts, disfigures, and destroys it" (1968:210). The first step in the colonizing process, Fanon had written, was the deculturation of a people. What better way to take our culture than to remake our image? A rich historical past became small and ignorant in the hands of Westerners. And we suffered a damaged sense of people and culture because of this distortion.

Burdened by a linear, progressive conception of history and by an assumption that Euro-American culture flourishes at the upper end of that progression, Westerners have told the history of Hawai'i as an inevitable if occasionally bitter-sweet triumph of Western ways over "primitive" Hawaiian ways. A few authors—the most sympathetic—have recorded with deep-felt sorrow the passing of our people. But in the end, we are repeatedly told, such an eclipse was for the best.

Obviously it was best for Westerners, not for our dying multitudes. This is why the historian's mission has been to justify our passing by celebrating Western dominance. Fanon would have called this missionizing, intellectual colonization. And it is clearest in the historian's insistence that pre-*haole* Hawaiian land tenure was "feudal"—a term that is now applied, without question, in every monograph, in every schoolbook, and in every tour guide description of my people's history.

From the earliest days of Western contact my people told their guests that *no one* owned the land. The land—like the air and the sea—was for all to use and share as their birthright. Our chiefs were *stewards* of the land; they could not own or privately possess the land any more than they could sell it.

But the *haole* insisted on characterizing our chiefs as feudal landlords and our people as serfs. Thus, a European term which described a European practice founded on the European concept of private property—feudalism—was imposed upon a people halfway around the world from Europe and vastly different from her in every conceivable way. More than betraying an ignorance of Hawaiian culture and history, however, this misrepresentation was malevolent in design.

By inventing feudalism in ancient Hawai'i, Western scholars quickly transformed a spiritually-based, self-sufficient economic system of land use and occupancy into an oppressive, medieval European practice of divine right ownership, with the common people tied like serfs to the land. By claiming that a Pacific people lived under a European system—that the Hawaiians lived under feudalism—Westerners could then degrade a successful system of shared land use with a pejorative and inaccurate Western term. Land tenure changes instituted by Americans and in line with current Western notions of private property were then made to appear beneficial to the Hawaiians. But in practice, such changes benefited the *haole,* who alienated the people from the land, taking it for themselves.

The prelude to this land alienation was the great dying of the people. Barely half a century after contact with the West our people had declined in number by eighty percent. Disease and death were rampant. The sandalwood forests had been stripped bare for international commerce between England and China. The missionaries had insinuated themselves everywhere. And a debt-ridden Hawaiian king (there had been

15

no king before Western contact) succumbed to enormous pressure from the Americans and followed their schemes for dividing up the land.

This is how private property land tenure entered Hawai'i. The common people, driven from their birthright, received less than one percent of the land. They starved while huge *haole*-owned sugar plantations thrived.

And what had the historians said? They had said that the Americans "liberated" the Hawaiians from an oppressive "feudal" system. By inventing a false feudal past, the historians justify—and become complicitous in—massive American theft.

Is there "evidence"—as historians call it—for traditional Hawaiian concepts of land use? The evidence is in the sayings of my people and in the words they wrote more than a century ago, much of which has been translated. However, historians have chosen to ignore any references here to shared land use. But there *is* incontrovertible evidence in the very structure of the Hawaiian language. If the historians had bothered to learn our language (as any American historian of France would learn French) they would have discovered that we show possession in two ways: through the use of an "a" possessive, which reveals acquired status, and through the use of an "o" possessive, which denotes inherent status. My body (*ko 'u kino*) and my parents (*ko 'u mākua*), for example, take the "o" form; most material objects, such as food (*ka 'u mea 'ai*) take the "a" form. But land, like one's body and one's parents, takes the "o" possessive (*ko'u 'āina*). Thus, in our way of speaking, land is inherent to the people; it is like our bodies and our parents. The people cannot exist without the land, and the land cannot exist without the people.

Every major historian of Hawai'i has been mistaken about Hawaiian land tenure. The chiefs did not own the land: they *could not* own the land. My mother was right and the *haole* historians were wrong. If they had studied our language they would have known that no one owned the land. But was their failing merely ignorance, or simple ethnocentric bias?

No, I did not believe them to be so benign. As I read on, a pattern emerged in their writing. Our ways were inferior to those of the West, to those of the historians' own culture. We were "less developed," or "immature," or "authoritarian." In some tellings we were much worse. Thus, Gavan Daws (1968), the most famed modern historian of Hawai'i, had continued a tradition established earlier by missionaries Hiram Bingham (1848) and Sheldon Dibble (1909), by referring to the old ones as "thieves" and "savages" who regularly practiced infanticide and who, in contrast to "civilized" whites, preferred "lewd dancing" to work. Ralph Kuykendall (1938), long considered the most thorough if also the most boring of historians of Hawai'i, sustained another fiction—that my ancestors owned slaves, the outcast *Kauwā*. This opinion, as well as the description of Hawaiian land tenure as feudal, had been supported by respected sociologist Andrew Lind (1938).[1] Finally, nearly all historians had refused to accept our genealogical dating of A.D. 400 or earlier for our arrival from the South Pacific. They had, instead, claimed that our earliest appearance in Hawai'i could only be traced to A.D. 1100. Thus at least seven hundred years of our history were repudiated by "superior" Western scholarship. Only recently have archeological data confirmed what Hawaiians had said these many centuries (Tuggle 1979).

Suddenly the entire sweep of our written history was clear to me. I was reading the West's view of itself through the degradation of my own past. When historians wrote that the king owned the land and the common people were bound to it, they were saying that ownership was the only way human beings in their world could relate to the land, and in that relationship, some one person had to control both the land and the interaction between humans.

And when they said that our chiefs were despotic, they were telling of their own society, where hierarchy always results in domination. Thus any authority or elder is automatically suspected of tyranny.

And when they wrote that Hawaiians were lazy, they meant that work must be continuous and ever a burden.   25

And when they wrote that we were promiscuous, they meant that love-making in the Christian West is a sin.

And when they wrote that we were racist because we preferred our own ways to theirs, they meant that their culture needed to dominate other cultures.

And when they wrote that we were superstitious, believing in the *mana* of nature and people, they meant that the West has long since lost a deep spiritual and cultural relationship to the earth.

And when they wrote that Hawaiians were "primitive" in their grief over the passing of loved ones, they meant that the West grieves for the living who do not walk among their ancestors.

For so long, more than half my life, I had misunderstood this written record, thinking it described my own people. But my history was nowhere present. For we had not written. We had chanted and sailed and fished and built and prayed. And we had told stories through the great blood lines of memory: genealogy.   30

To know my history, I had to put away my books and return to the land. I had to plant taro in the earth before I could understand the inseparable bond between people and *'āina*. I had to feel again the spirits of nature and take gifts of plants and fish to the ancient altars. I had to begin to speak my language with our elders and leave long silences for wisdom to grow. But before anything else, I had to learn the language like a lover so that I could rock within her and lay at night in her dreaming arms.

There was nothing in my schooling that had told me of this, or hinted that somewhere there was a longer, older story of origins, of the flowing of songs out to a great but distant sea. Only my parents' voices, over and over, spoke to me of a Hawaiian world. While the books spoke from a different world, a Western world.

And yet, Hawaiians are not of the West. We are of *Hawai'i Nei*, this world where I live, this place, this culture, this *'āina*.

What can I say, then, to Western historians of my place and people? Let me answer with a story.

A while ago I was asked to share a panel on the American overthrow of our government in 1893. The other panelists were all *haole*. But one was a *haole* historian from the mainland who had just published a book on what he called the American anti-imperialists. He and I met briefly in preparation for the panel. I asked him if he knew the language. He said no. I asked him if he knew the record of opposition to our annexation to America. He said there was no real evidence for it, just comments here and there. I told him that he didn't understand and that at the panel I would share the evidence. When we met in public and spoke, I said this: 35

There is a song much loved by our people. It was sung when Hawaiians were forbidden from congregating in groups of more than three. Addressed to our imprisoned Queen, it was written in 1893, and tells of Hawaiian feelings for our land and against annexation. Listen to our lament:

Kaulana na pua a'o Hawai'i	Famous are the children of Hawai'i
Kūpa'a mahope o ka 'āina	Who cling steadfastly to the land
Hiki mai ka 'elele o ka loko 'ino	Comes the evil-hearted with
Palapala 'ānunu me ka pākaha	A document greedy for plunder
Pane mai Hawai'i moku o Keawe	Hawai'i, island of Keawe, answers
Kokua na hono a'o Pi'ilani	The bays of Pi'ilani [of Maui, Moloka'i, and Lana'i] help
Kāko'o mai Kaua'i o Mano	Kaua'i of Mano assists
Pau pu me ke one o Kakuhihewa	Firmly together with the sands of Kakuhihewa
'A'ole a'e kau i ka pūlima	Do not put the signature
Maluna o ka pepa o ka 'enemi	On the paper of the enemy
Ho'ohui 'āina kū'ai hewa	Annexation is wicked sale
I ka pono sīvila a'o ke kānaka	Of the civil rights of the Hawaiian people
Mahope mākou o Lili'ulani	We support Lili'uokalani
A loa'a 'e ka pono o ka 'āina	Who has earned the right to the land
Ha'ina 'ia mai ana ka puana	The story is told
'O ka po'e i aloha i ka 'āina	Of the people who love the land

This song, I said, continues to be sung with great dignity at Hawaiian political gatherings. For our people still share the feelings of anger and protest that it conveys.

But our guest, the *haole* historian, answered that this song, although beautiful, was not evidence of either opposition or of imperialism from the Hawaiian perspective.

Many Hawaiians in the audience were shocked at his remarks, but, in hindsight, I think they were predictable. They are the standard response of the historian who does not know the language and has no respect for its memory.

Finally, I proceeded to relate a personal story, thinking that surely such a tale could not want for authenticity since I myself was relating it. My *tūtū* (grandmother) had told my mother who had told me that at the time of the overthrow a great wailing went up throughout the islands, a wailing of weeks, a wailing of impenetrable grief, a wailing of death. But he remarked again, this too is not evidence.

And so, history goes on, written in long volumes by foreign people. Whole libraries begin to form, book upon book, shelf upon shelf. 40

At the same time, the stories go on, generation to generation, family to family.

Which history do Western historians desire to know? Is it to be a tale of writings by their own countrymen, individuals convinced of their "unique" capacity for analysis, looking at us with Western eyes, thinking about us within Western philosophical contexts, categorizing us by Western indices, judging us by Judeo-Christian morals, exhorting us to capitalist achievements, and finally, leaving us an authoritative-because-Western record of their complete misunderstanding?

All this has been done already. Not merely a few times, but many times. And still, every year, there appear new and eager faces to take up the same telling, as if the West must continue, implacably, with the din of its own disbelief.

But there is, as there has been always, another possibility. If it is truly our history Western historians desire to know, they must put down their books, and take up our practices. First, of course, the language. But later, the people, the *'āina,* the stories. Above all, in the end, the stories. Historians must listen, they must hear the generational connections, the reservoir of sounds and meanings.

They must come, as American Indians suggested long ago, to understand the land. Not in the Western way, but in the indigenous way, the way of living within and protecting the bond between people and *'āina.*

This bond is cultural, and it can be understood only culturally. But because the West has lost any cultural understanding of the bond between people and land, it is not possible to know this connection through Western culture. This means that the history of indigenous people cannot be written from within Western culture. Such a story is merely the West's story of itself.

Our story remains unwritten. It rests within the culture, which is inseparable from the land. To know this is to know our history. To write this is to write of the land and the people who are born from her.

Notes

1. See also Fornander (1878–85). Lest one think these sources antiquated, it should be noted that there exist only a handful of modern scholarly works on the history of Hawai'i. The most respected are those by Kuykendall (1938) and Daws (1968), and a social history of the twentieth century by Lawrence Fuchs (1961). Of these, only Kuykendall and Daws claim any knowledge of pre-*haole* history, while concentrating on the nineteenth century. However, countless popular works have relied on these two studies which, in turn, are themselves based on primary sources written in English by extremely biased, anti-Hawaiian Westerners such as explorers, traders, missionaries (e.g., Bingham [1848] and Dibble [1909]), and sugar planters. Indeed, a favorite technique of Daws's—whose *Shoal of Time* is the most acclaimed and recent general history—is the lengthy quotation without comment of the most racist remarks by missionaries and planters. Thus, at one point, half a page is consumed with a "white man's burden" quotation from an 1886 *Planter's Monthly* article ("It is better for the colored man of India and Australia that the white man rules, and it is better here that the white man should rule . . . ," etc., p. 213). Daws's only comment is, "The conclusion was inescapable." To get a sense of such characteristic contempt for Hawaiians, one has but to read the first few pages, where Daws refers several times to the Hawaiians as "savages" and "thieves" and where he approvingly has Captain Cook thinking, "It was a sensible primitive who bowed before a superior civilization" (p. 2). See also—among examples too numerous to cite—his glib description of sacred *hula* as a "frivolous diversion," which, instead of work, the Hawaiians "would practice energetically in the hot sun for days on end . . . their bare brown flesh glistening with sweat" (pp. 65–66). Daws, who repeatedly displays an affection for descriptions of Hawaiian skin color, taught Hawaiian history for some years at the University of Hawai'i; he now holds the Chair of Pacific History at the Australian National University's Institute of Advanced Studies.

CONNECTING PERSONALLY TO THE READING

1. Think of how people from your own ethnic heritage have been characterized in historical accounts. Which elements of this characterization do you consider accurate and which not?

2. Trask points out that for more than half her life, she believed the account of her people as described by Western historians. Think of a time when you learned something new about

your family or your ethnic group. Did it change your understanding of your heritage? Why or why not?

FOCUSING ON THE ARGUMENT

1. Much of Trask's article is infused with a fervent, angry tone, using language that condemns the Western historians: they are guilty of "colonization," they "insisted on" characterizing Hawai'i as a feudal system, they "imposed" their views on her people, they were "complicitous" in stealing Hawai'i from its people. What other language can you find that conveys Trask's anger? How does the tone of the article affect your reaction to her ideas?

2. Trask contrasts the linear argument typical of Western academic writing, in which the writer advances a thesis and provides facts to illustrate it, with the rhetorical method of her native people, who convey ideas through storytelling. Her own essay combines these two strategies. Where in her essay does she use one strategy, and where does she use the other? What is the effect of juxtaposing the two?

3. What is the effect of the use of the Hawaiian language throughout this article? How does it enhance Trask's argument, even though most of her readers are unlikely to know Hawaiian?

SYNTHESIZING IDEAS FROM MULTIPLE READINGS

1. Like Louise Erdrich ("The Names of Women," p. 76) Trask argues that language and culture are inextricable. How does the language tie people to the culture in each case—or how does it help define the culture?

2. Like Caffilene Allen in "First They Changed My Name . . . ," p. 65), Trask comes to see her culture differently as an adult than she did as a child. What is it about each culture that these writers see in a new way?

3. Both Barbara Wallraff ("What Global Language?" p. 93) and Trask believe that it is important for people to learn other languages. What advantages do they believe multilingualism offers for communication?

WRITING TO ACT

1. Think of a group that you believe is misunderstood, whether it is an entire national culture or a local group, perhaps one on campus. Write an editorial in which you explain why you think popular conceptions of this group are inaccurate.

2. Tell a story that illustrates a value or belief held by your family. Collect your story with those of other students in your class, and produce a Web page or portfolio of your combined work.

READING

BARBARA WALLRAFF   Wallraff argues that though English is spoken throughout the world, it is less pervasive globally than it may seem, and she marshals considerable evidence to support her view: for example, in the United States, a great many people speak a language other than English at home; in a few years, English will no longer be the principal language of the Internet; science and technology courses outside English-speaking countries are taught in the native language; worldwide, far more people speak Chinese than English. Do you agree with Wallraff's conclusion that "we may be well advised to do as people elsewhere are doing: become bilingual"?

WALLRAFF is a senior editor and a columnist at the *Atlantic Monthly* and the author of *Word Court* and *Your Own Words,* books that explore what it means to use language correctly.

What Global Language? (2000)

BY BARBARA WALLRAFF

Because I am interested in what happens to the English language, over the past year or so I've been asking people, at dinner parties and professional gatherings and so on, whether they think that English is well on its way to being the global language. Typically, they look puzzled about why I would even bother to ask such an obvious question. They say firmly, Of course. Then they start talking about the Internet. We're just having a conversation, so I refrain from launching into everything I'm about to tell you. It's not that I believe they're actually wrong. But the idea of English as a global language doesn't mean what they think it does—at least, not according to people I've interviewed whose professions are bound up especially closely in what happens to the English language.

English has inarguably achieved some sort of global status. Whenever we turn on the news to find out what's happening in East Asia, or the Balkans, or Africa, or South America, or practically anyplace, local people are being interviewed and telling us about it in English. This past April [2000] the journalist Ted Anthony, in one of two articles about global English that he wrote for the Associated Press, observed, "When Pope John Paul II arrived in the Middle East last month to retrace Christ's footsteps and addressed Christians, Muslims and Jews, the pontiff spoke not Latin, not Arabic, not Hebrew, not his native Polish. He spoke in English."

Indeed, by now lists of facts about the amazing reach of our language may have begun to sound awfully familiar.

Have we heard these particular facts before, or only others like them? English is the working language of the Asian trade group ASEAN. It is the de facto working language of 98 percent of German research physicists and 83 percent of German research chemists. It is the official language of the European Central Bank, even though the bank is in Frankfurt and neither Britain nor any other predominantly English-speaking country is a member of the European Monetary Union. It is the language in which black parents in South Africa overwhelmingly wish their children to be educated. This little list of facts comes from British sources: a report, *The Future of English?*, and a follow-up newsletter that David Graddol, a language researcher at The Open University, and his consulting firm, The English Company U.K., wrote in 1997 and 1998 for the British Council, whose mission is to promote British culture worldwide; and *English as a Global Language* (1997), a book by David Crystal, who is a professor at the University of Wales.

And yet, of course, English is not sweeping all before it, not even in the United States. According to the U.S. Bureau of the Census, ten years ago about one in seven people in this country spoke a language other than English at home—and since then the proportion of immigrants in the population has grown and grown. Ever-wider swaths of Florida, California, and the Southwest are heavily Spanish-speaking. Hispanic people make up 30 percent of the population of New York City, and a television station there that is affiliated with a Spanish-language network has been known to draw a larger daily audience than at least one of the city's English-language network affiliates. Even Sioux City, Iowa, now has a Spanish-language newspaper. According to the census, from 1980 to 1990 the number of Spanish-speakers in the United States grew by 50 percent.

Over the same decade the number of 5 speakers of Chinese in the United States grew by 98 percent. Today approximately 2.4 million Chinese-speakers live in America, and more than four out of five of them prefer to speak Chinese at home. The rate of growth of certain other languages in the United States has been higher still. From 1980 to 1990 the number of speakers of Korean increased by 127 percent and of speakers of Vietnamese by 150 percent. Small American towns from Huntsville, Alabama, to Meriden, Connecticut, to Wausau, Wisconsin, to El Cenizo, Texas—all sites of linguistic controversy in recent years—have been alarmed to find that many new arrivals do not speak English well and some may not even see the point of going to the trouble of learning it.

How can all of this, simultaneously, be true? How can it be that English is conquering the globe if it can't even hold its own in parts of our traditionally English-speaking country? . . .

A few more definitions will be helpful here. "Second-language" speakers live in places where English has some sort of official or special status. In India, for instance, the national government sanctions the use of English for its business, along with fifteen indigenous languages. . . .

"Foreign-language" speakers of English live in places where English is not singled out in any formal way, and tend to learn it to communicate with people from elsewhere. Examples might be Japanese who travel abroad on business and Italians who work in tourism in their own country. . . .

David Crystal, in his *Cambridge Encyclopedia of the English Language* (1995), observed that only 98 million second-language speakers of English in the world could be totted up with certainty. In *English as a Global Language,* though, he argued that the true number was more nearly 350 million. . . .

Estimates of the number of foreign- 10 language speakers of English range more widely still. Crystal reports that these "have been as low as 100 million and as high as 1,000 million." The estimates *would* vary, because by definition foreign-language speakers live in places where English has no official or special status. They may or may not have been asked in a national census or other poll about their competence in English or other languages; they may or may not have had any formal schooling in English; their assessment of their ability to speak English may or may not be accurate.

This last point is particularly worth bearing in mind. According to recent "Eurobarometer" surveys described by Graddol, "77% of Danish adults and 75% of Swedish adults for example, say they can take part in a conversation in English." And "nearly one third of the citizens of the 13 'non English-speaking' countries in the EU 'can speak English well enough to take part in a conversation.'" However, Richard Parker, in his book *Mixed Signals: The Prospects for Global Television News* (1995), reported this about a study commissioned by Lintas, a major media buyer, in the early 1990s:

> When ad researchers recently tested 4,500 Europeans for "perceived" versus "actual"

English-language skills, the results were discouraging. First, the interviewees were asked to evaluate their English-language abilities, and then to translate a series of sample English phrases or sentences. The study produced, in its own words, "sobering" results: "the number of people really fit for English-language television turned out to be less than half the expected audience." In countries such as France, Spain, and Italy, the study found, fewer than 3 percent had excellent command of English; only in small markets, such as Scandinavia and the Low Countries did the numbers even exceed 10 percent.

So the number of people in the world who speak English is unknown, and how well many of them speak and understand it is questionable. No one is arguing that English is not widely spoken and taught. But the vast numbers that are often repeated—a billion English-speakers, a billion and a half—have only tenuous grounding in reality....

FIRST, SECOND, OR FOREIGN LANGUAGE

People who expect English to triumph over all the other languages are sometimes surprised to learn that the world today holds three times as many native speakers of Chinese as native speakers of English. "Chinese," as language scholars use the word, refers to a family of languages and dialects the most widely spoken of which is Mandarin, and which share a written language although they are not all mutually intelligible when spoken. "English" refers to a family of languages and dialects the most widely spoken of which is standard American English, and which have a common origin in England—though not all varieties of English, either, are mutually intelligible. The versions of English used by educated speakers practically anywhere can be understood by most Americans, but pidgins, creoles, and diverse dialects belong to the same family, and these are not always so generally intelligible. To hear for yourself how far English now ranges from what we Americans are used to, you need only rent a video of the 1998 Scottish film *My Name Is Joe*, which, though in English, comes fully subtitled....

In any case, the numerical gap is impressive: about 1,113 million people speak Chinese as their mother tongue, whereas about 372 million people speak English. And yet English is still the world's second most common native language, though it is likely to cede second place within fifty years to the South Asian linguistic group whose leading members are Hindi and Urdu. In 2050, according to a model of language use that The English Company developed and named "engco" after itself, the world will hold 1,384 million native speakers of Chinese, 556 million of Hindi and Urdu, and 508 million of English. As native languages, Spanish and Arabic will be almost as common as English, with 486 million and 482 million speakers respectively. And among young people aged fifteen to twenty-four English is expected to be in fourth place, behind not only Chinese and the Hindi-Urdu languages but also Arabic, and just ahead of Spanish....

Nonetheless, the gains that everyone 15 expects English to make must come because it is adopted as a second language or a foreign language by most of the people who speak it....

Something else obviously implied by the ascendance of English as a second and a foreign language is that more and more people who speak English speak another language at least as well, and probably better. India may have the third or fourth largest number of English-speakers in the world, but English is thought to be the mother tongue of much less than one percent of the population. This is bound to affect the way the language is used locally. Browsing some English-language Web sites from India recently, I seldom had trouble understanding what was meant. I did, however, time and again come across unfamiliar words borrowed from Hindi or another indigenous Indian language. On the site called India World the buttons that a user could click on to call up various types of information were labeled "*samachar:* Personalised News," "*dhan:* Investing in India," "*khoj:* Search India," "*khel:* Indian Cricket," and so forth. . . .

. . . Much has been made of the Internet as an instrument for circulating English around the globe. According to one estimate that has been widely repeated over the past few years, 80 percent of what's available on the Internet is in English. Some observers, however, have recently been warning that this may have been the high-water mark. It's not that English-speakers are logging off—*au contraire*—but that other people are increasingly logging on, to search out or create content in their own languages. As the newsletter that The English Company prepared for the British Council asserted in September of 1998, "Non English speakers are the fastest growing group of new Internet users." The consensus among those who study these things is that Internet traffic in languages other than English will outstrip English-language traffic within the next few years.

There's no reason this should surprise us—particularly if we recall that there are about 372 million people in the world whose native language is English and about 5,700 million people whose native language is something else. According to the same newsletter, a recent study by Euro Marketing Associates estimated that

> nearly 44% of the world's online population now speak a language other than English at home. Although many of these Internet users are bilingual and speak English in the workplace, Euro Marketing suggest that advertisers of nonbusiness products will more easily reach this group by using their home language. Of the 56 million people who speak languages on the Internet other than English, Spanish speakers represent nearly a quarter.

The study also estimated that 13.1 percent of all Internet users speak an Asian language at home—Japanese, for the most part. A surge in Internet use like the one that began in the United States half a dozen or so years ago is now under way in a number of other populous and relatively well-off places. . . .

No matter how much English-language material there is on the Web, then, or even how much more English material there is than material in other languages, it is naive to assume that home computers around the world will, in effect, become the work stations of a vast English language lab. People *could* use their computers that way—just as we English-speaking Americans could enlist our computers to help us learn Italian, Korean, or Yoruba. But, the glories of learning for its own sake aside, why would we want to do that? Aren't we delighted to be able to gather information, shop, do business, and be entertained in our own language? Why wouldn't others feel the same way? Consider, too, that many people regard high technology as something very much like a new language. Surely it's enough for a person to try to keep his or her hardware and software more or less up-to-date and running smoothly without simultaneously having to grapple with instructions or content in an actual foreign language. . . .

One more fact worth keeping in mind is that the relationship between science or technology and English is, essentially, accidental. It is chiefly because the United States has long been in the vanguard of much scientific and technological research, of course, that English is so widely used in these fields. If the United States were for the most part French-speaking, surely French would be the language of science and technology; there is nothing inherent in English to tie it to these fields. . . .

Here an argument is sometimes advanced that American culture furthers innovation, openness to new ideas, and so forth, and that our culture, whether by accident or not, is inseparable from the English language. But this takes us only so far. Even if the vanguards in all scientific and technological fields, everywhere in the world, used English in their work, once the fruits of their labor became known to ordinary people and began to matter to them, people would coin words in their local languages to describe these things. Theoretical physicists at international conferences may speak English among themselves, but most high school and college physics teachers use their native languages in class with their students. The Microsoft engineers who designed the Windows computer-operating system spoke English, and used English in what they created, but in the latest version, Windows Millennium, the words that users see on the screen are available in twenty-eight languages—and the spell-checker offers a choice of four varieties of English.

In sum, the globalization of English does not mean that if we who speak only English just sit back and wait, we'll soon be able to exchange ideas with anyone who has anything to say. We can't count on having much more around the world than a very basic ability to communicate. Outside certain professional fields, if English-speaking Americans hope to exchange ideas with people in a nuanced way, we may be well advised to do as people elsewhere are doing: become bilingual. . . .

CONNECTING PERSONALLY TO THE READING

1. If you have studied a foreign language, do the conclusions of the Lintas study seem credible to you: is there likely to be a gap between a person's perception of ability to speak a foreign language and the actual ability to converse? If you are comfortable conversing in a foreign language, how long did it take you to develop this proficiency? If not, why not?

2. Visit a Web site written in a language you are studying. How much of the site do you understand?

3. Do you think it is important for people around the world to speak a common language? Why or why not?

1. Wallraff's argument relies heavily on statistics. How persuasive would her argument be without these numbers? Which statistics made you most inclined to accept her argument, and why?

2. In paragraphs 2 and 3, Wallraff presents evidence that might seem to undermine her view that English is not a global language. What is the effect of this evidence on her argument?

3. This reading often works through contrasts—e.g., between what people commonly think the expression "global language" means and what Wallraff means by it. For example, Wallraff compares percentages of native Chinese, Korean, and Vietnamese speakers in the United States; contrasts how well nonnative English speakers think they know English with their actual proficiency; and distinguishes between "second language" and "foreign language" English speakers. Find one contrast in this article, and show how it illuminates Wallraff's argument. What would be lost if only one of the items being compared were described?

1. In "Public and Private Language" (p. 51), Richard Rodriguez distinguishes between a public and private language. What is his definition of a public language, and how might the use of English outside English-speaking countries be described as a public act?

2. Richard Rodriguez ("Public and Private Language"), Itabari Njeri ("What's in a Name?" p. 71), Caffilene Allen ("First They Changed My Name . . . ," p. 65), and Louise Erdrich ("The Names of Women," p. 76) all suggest that there is a close relationship between one's native language and one's identification with the larger culture. Where do you see evidence of this idea in the Wallraff article?

1. Find a Web site written in a language you have studied, but in which you are not entirely fluent. Write an article on the experience of navigating and retrieving information from this Web site.

2. Do a survey in which you ask students on your campus how well they read, write, and speak in another language and how often, outside of a foreign language class, they are called upon to use this language. Then write an article for your campus newspaper, reporting on your results.

Connecting the Readings with the Artworks

Stephen Scott Young, *Flip Flops and Lace*

1. In what ways are Richard Rodriguez in "Public and Private Language" (p. 51) and Lydia Minatoya in "Transformation" (p. 81) at odds with the culture they find themselves in as children? Do you think the girl in *Flip Flops and Lace* (insert 2-1) is at odds with her culture? Why or why not? In what ways can all three children be said to be isolated?

2. How does the painting reflect the cultural division Barbara Mellix describes in "From Outside, In" (p. 57)? What resolution does Mellix find for this problem? What resolution, if any, do you suppose is possible for the girl in the painting?

3. Haunani-Kay Trask's article, "From a Native Daughter" (p. 85), is a protest against white cultural dominance of her people. In what ways does she present this protest, and how might Young's painting be seen as a similar kind of protest?

Jacob Lawrence, *The Library*

1. None of the library patrons are paying attention to each other. Would Lawrence agree with Barbara Mellix ("From Outside, In," p. 57) and Richard Rodriguez ("Public and Private Language," p. 51) that a shared language helps create community? Why or why not?
2. When Caffilene Allen tells us, in "First They Changed My Name . . ." (p. 65), that her teachers have a "low opinion of [her mother's] way of speech," she suggests that they regard her mother as illiterate. How is literacy defined in Allen's essay? How is it defined in Lawrence's painting? What is the value of literacy in each world?

Carmen Lomas Garza, *Camas para Sueños*

1. Caffilene Allen ("First They Changed My Name . . . ," p. 65) and Louise Erdrich ("The Names of Women," p. 76) write about their relationships with their mothers. Compare those mother-child relationships with that between the mother and children in Garza's painting.
2. What was Richard Rodriguez's ("Public and Private Language," p. 51) childhood like? How does it compare with the childhood depicted here?

Henry Sugimoto, *Nisei Babies in Concentration Camp*

1. In arguing that Western historians have deliberately misrepresented Hawaiian history, depicting it in ways that would justify the U.S. takeover of Hawai'i, Haunani-Kay Trask's essay, "From a Native Daughter" (p. 85), advances a political thesis. How does Sugimoto's painting also advance a political viewpoint?
2. Many of the readings, including those by Caffilene Allen ("First They Changed My Name . . . ," p. 65), Richard Rodriguez ("Public and Private Language," p. 51), Lydia Minatoya ("Transformation," p. 81), and Amy Tan ("The Language of Discretion," p. 43), recount what it is like to be treated as an outsider, a common experience for immigrants and their children. In what ways does Sugimoto's painting depict this experience? How does the composition of the painting reinforce this idea?
3. How does the experience represented in the painting parallel or contrast with the experiences Lydia Minatoya's family ("From a Native Daughter," p. 85) had in a Japanese relocation camp? As a child, Minatoya tries hard to fit in, as does her father. Do you think the babies in the painting reflect this same impulse? Why or why not?

Tomie Arai, *The Laundryman's Daughter*

1. In "The Language of Discretion" (p. 43), Amy Tan worries that stereotypes of Chinese Americans limit the ways others perceive them. How would you describe the Chinese Americans in Arai's artwork? How are they like or unlike the people Tan describes? In what ways do they represent or depart from the stereotypes Tan mentions?

2. Both Itabari Njeri ("What's in a Name?" p. 71) and Louise Erdrich ("The Names of Women," p. 76) write about the importance of a name in establishing personal identity, yet Arai does not tell us the names of the people she depicts. What is the effect of this choice?

Patricia Rodriguez, Irene Perez, Graciela Carillo, *Fantasy World for Children*

1. Like Frida Kahlo (*Self-Portrait on the Borderline between Mexico and the United States*), the Mujeres Muralistas celebrate Latino/a cultural values using ancient and modern Mexican images. In what ways are the works of art alike and different in how they depict the differences between two cultures? Does either suggest a possible integration such as Itabari Njeri ("What's in a Name?" p. 71) hopes to achieve? Explain.

2. In "Public and Private Language" (p. 51), Richard Rodriguez sees the division between two cultures as the division between two languages: English is the "public" language of education and work, and Spanish is the "private" language of the family. Do you think that the Mujeres Muralistas would see this division as accurate? Explain, using details from their mural.

3. In "The Names of Women" (p. 76), Louise Erdrich sees herself as the "first in a long line" of Anishinabe women, who "scratches . . . the ground for pleasure, not survival, and grows . . . flowers instead of potatoes." She writes about rather than practices the knitting, sewing, and canning of her forebears. How is Erdrich's integration of two cultures like that of the Mujeres Muralistas? Explain.

Frida Kahlo, *Self-Portrait on the Borderline between Mexico and the United States*

1. In "From a Native Daughter" (p. 85), Haunani-Kay Trask recounts that as a child and later as a new Ph.D, she saw the world divided into two: *haole* (white) and *kānaka* (native). She learned that European and American historians misinterpreted Hawaiian stories about "possession," which was communal, and labeled Hawai'i "feudalistic" and "despotic." How are Trask and Kahlo alike in how they depict American values and culture?

2. In "What Global Language?" (p. 93), Barbara Wallraff argues that English only appears to be a global language—that other languages continually see their numbers rise, even in the United States. Why, according to Wallraff and Kahlo, might language, as well as other cultural values (e.g., religion, work, dress), be particularly valued at the intersection of two cultures?

3. When Itabari Njeri ("What's in a Name?" p. 71) changes her name from Jill Lord, she seeks to "reclaim [her African] culture and synthesize it with [her] present reality." In the face of the loss of African culture—but as part of a new generation of black people—she tries to create a new identity borrowing from both cultures. Do you think that Kahlo's painting also forges a new identity, one that synthesizes two cultures? Explain.

Judy Chicago, *Rainbow Shabbat*

1. Underlying Judy Chicago's stained glass window and Lydia Minatoya's essay "Transformation" (p. 81) are experiences of oppression that took place during World War II: for Chicago, the annihilation of Jews, gypsies, and other groups in the Nazi Holocaust, and, for Minatoya, the forced relocation and internment of Japanese Americans. Using background information you have (or can research) on these two events, what values is Chicago portraying in her artwork, and why?

2. In discussing the use of the English language throughout the world, Barbara Wallraff suggests in "What Global Language?" (p. 93) that the reputed "globalization" of English—and with it, U.S. culture—is not complete. What does Wallraff mean by "globalization"? According to this definition, is Chicago's work of art an image of "globalization"? Why or why not?

3. Chicago's stained glass window offers an image of cross-cultural harmony. How might Haunani-Kay Trask ("From a Native Daughter," p. 85) respond to this image?

FINDING COMMON CAUSE IN CONTROVERSY

When African Americans attempt to eradicate elements of Black English vernacular from their speech, are they "practicing a form of self-hatred"? Or are they exercising their right to "social mobility"?

We typically think of debates as either/or, right/wrong thinking. However, this need not be the case. We view debate as critical thinking about a question of some import. Debate underlies all decision making. In the debate that follows, the decision seems a trivial one—whether or not Earvin "Magic" Johnson should take elocution lessons to eradicate features of his dialect. Underneath the decision, however, lie values and beliefs that are very important to different groups of people. One way to find common ground between the opposing viewpoints is by understanding the values and beliefs behind them.

One's mother tongue—one's language or dialect—is closely tied to one's culture and upbringing. It cannot easily be abandoned for a more prestigious dialect or language at whim. Nor should one's dialect be abandoned, according to many, for it reflects one's heritage. Yet some African Americans, who have learned the prestige dialect, see mastering Standard English as the route to success and respect. Are these blacks "sellouts"? Are they embracing a "slave mentality"? Are they laughable when they make this effort?

READING

KEN PARISH PERKINS   Ken Parish Perkins writes about Black English and the question of assimilation versus cultural identity. His tone is at times amused and at times wistful, even sorrowful—suggesting that he feels empathy for both positions. He writes about dialect differences that split not only blacks and whites, but also blacks and other blacks. In particular, he describes varying reactions among African Americans to Earvin "Magic" Johnson's lessons in Standard English pronunciation. He thinks that holding on to "broken English" for the sake of one's culture is "complete nonsense." Yet he takes great pleasure in the dialect he speaks and the sense of exclusivity and empowerment it gives him, and he speaks of its constructions and rhythm with great pride.

PERKINS is a television critic and columnist for the *Fort Worth Star-Telegram*; he is the recipient of two Griot Awards for his news coverage of African Americans.

The Dilemma of Black English (1998) | BY KEN PARISH PERKINS

A lifelong friend of mine called the other day to shoot the breeze and we began, as we often do, to delve into, dissect, and dispose of subjects large and small with speedy efficiency.

Before long we'd been transported back to our Chicago enclave, and it wasn't until my live-in looked on in perplexed horror that I was aware of our slippage into the netherworld of diction and cultural expression.

He: "What it be like, brah?"

Me: "Just kickin', ma man. Wassup in A-Town?"

He: "Same-o sam-o, knowwhatI'msayin'? I gotta wait for some mo' months before   5
they come through on that promotion."

Me: "So, wassup wit that? Thought dat was promised."

He: "Just another means in keepin' a brother down, youknowwhatI'msayin'?"

My friend Daryl is college-educated with a weighty resume of fine work in banking, and, sure, I know exactly what he's saying. Many may not, my loved one included. She often uses my bilingual services as interpreter when Daryl and I are on one of our verbal rolls, which is almost any time we're within each other's space.

Ours is, to be precise, a black vernacular from the urban section of the Midwest region, a kind of pacing of melodic rhythms weaving speech and expression, where metaphors, similes, and nouns are literally turned into verbs, and the rest is merely tossed in for primitive simplicity.

I explain this in part to be serious and amusing because the whole issue of "Ebonics,"   10
or "black English," took center stage a couple of years back when an Oakland, Calif. school board pushed for permission to teach black English not as a cultural dialect but as a genetically based second language equal in stature to ordinary English. The board figured it was the only way students could academically progress.

But many African-Americans were insulted. Criticism mounted, and the resolution crashed and burned.

Buried under the rubble was a muffled debate about whether critics of "black English" are merely wannabe-white black folk seeking assimilation into the dominant culture.

Well, such a debate has resurfaced, albeit in the underground railroad of black thought (Internet, radio, black barbershops), conjured by a former basketball player who never would have thought he'd be part of a philosophical discussion on cultural linguistics.

Surely you know the dude. Earvin "Magic" Johnson. A former college b-baller who bolted out of Michigan State University early for NBA riches.

A businessman and millionaire many times over, Johnson is also a brother from   15
around the way and speaks that language accordingly. After harsh, though relatively

quiet, criticism of his language skills during a brief stint as a sports commentator, Johnson knew he had to be better prepared for his latest battle.

He has been dutifully taking speech and diction lessons to better communicate with his interviewees, his live audience, and the viewers his show desperately needs to survive in the competitive late-night arena.

Of course, he slips. Johnson's way of saying "dis" for the word "this," "dat" for "that," "I shoulda," and "all's I want to do" has a good number of African-Americans rolling on the floor while others cringe in the embarrassment of a black man butchering the English language.

And that's where the debate begins. Some believe that black critics of black dialect are practicing a form of self-hatred, choosing a white culture over their own, and embracing what they call a slave mentality. Johnson is perfectly fine, since he's just talkin' like a brotha, ya know?

Besides, there's a reason for this. Johnson's dialect, as is mine, is a mixture of accent and sentence construction handed down from enslaved Africans who didn't speak English and weren't taught it. Before you dismiss this as nonsense, consider that slaves picked up words from masters intent on condemning them to a devastating cycle among the lower rungs of society. Some have made it out over the years, while many have not.

Daryl and I grew up in a poor, all-black neighborhood and were educated in cash-strapped all-black schools—my first "educated" peer was a white college roommate from a wealthy suburb whose word usage was jarring to me but considered standard English by my professors. He could barely understand a word I said, and I had to adjust if my plans were to make it through journalism school.   20

For phone conversations with Daryl, black English is our adopted mode of speech, a vernacular chosen with the knowledge that we're both able to employ a more standardized language at will. Call us sellouts if you so please, but our social mobility and respect (from blacks as well as others) hinges on it, even though I have yet to master "ask" without saying "ax," and my editor often appears confused when I'm excited and speaking quickly.

In some ways it's like we're doomed. Past experience keeps black Americans gravely suspicious of anyone wanting to change anything about a way of life that's exclusive and therefore empowering. Our radars will remain keen as long as we witness, for instance, the dilution of the Spanish language in California (bilingual classes will be no more) and other ills.

Still, to adhere to such broken English for the sake of holding on to cultural heritage is false hope and complete nonsense. It's unfortunate that we continue to engage in "who's blacker than whom" contests, attaching the preservation of one's cultural history and identity to, of all things, poor grammar.

Johnson's talk show will go down in flames not because of dis and dat but because he is charming but not entertaining, and late-night television simply isn't his thing. While I've never talked with Johnson, I could see our private conversations dipping into the black vernacular, both of us feeling quite comfortable with the proceedings.

There is, in some ways, a sadness to this truth. But I'll settle for the beauty of this ex-   25
clusivity when it comes, particularly from strangers. Like the other day. Upon leaving the office, a black male city worker emptying the meters noticed me and said quickly, "Wassup, brah?"

"Nothin' much, ma man," I told him. "Nothin' much."

To take a position on this debate, first identify the point of view of African Americans who might resent the idea that their dialect is not good enough. These individuals might feel that replacing features of dialect with Standard English in order to become a host on late-night television was practicing a form of self-hatred.

- Put yourself in the place of Earvin "Magic" Johnson. You are a role model and hero to millions. What do you think it was like to have to worry about saying "dis" instead of "this" and "dat" instead of "that"? Is Johnson really "butchering" English when he says "I shoulda"?

- Perkins offers telling examples of how much his urban Midwest dialect means to him. What do you take from these examples? How would it make you feel to be asked to give up that common dialect?

- Why is there good cause for African Americans to be suspicious of "anyone wanting to change anything about a way of life that's exclusive and therefore empowering"?

- What part of your cultural identity is tied up with the way that you speak? How easy would it be to give up the way you speak and adopt a different way? What would you lose?

- Do you think that Perkins's argument for social mobility and respect is really a justification for his "selling out"? He does seem to disdain Black English by saying that it is "broken," "ungrammatical," and "primitive." Do you think he looks down on the millions of African Americans who haven't been able to learn Standard English?

- What do you think is wrong with asking millions of African Americans to change their speech in order to have higher-paying jobs? Does he mean that many will be condemned to low-paying jobs because they can only speak "broken English"?

Next, put yourself in the place of African Americans who want increased social mobility and respect and don't see themselves as selling out because they learn Standard English.

- If you did not know how to speak Standard English, what kinds of jobs do you think you would have difficulty obtaining? This job stratification may be wrong, but is it a social reality?

- Why might contests of "who's blacker than whom" be pointless? What harmful consequences might they have?

- Perkins and his friend Daryl both speak Standard English as well as their urban Midwest variety of Black English. Do you think that the solution to this debate is to encourage African Americans to speak both? Is this a viable solution?

- Would it be naïve or foolish to assume that African Americans should continue fighting for the prestige of Black English? In what ways does the fight over Ebonics in Oakland suggest that a language's prestige has very little to do with the linguistic stature of the language itself and more to do with social values?

- Perkins's experience learning Standard English suggests that he adapted when he had to. There does not seem to be much self-hatred in his description. Do you agree that success and respect need to be the prime motivations for change?

Once you have thought about these two positions, and decided which side you think is stronger, seek out additional information and arguments that would strengthen or weaken your position.

- We often look to the schools to address questions of language. Investigate the Oakland, California, school board's decision to teach Ebonics. What were the arguments for and against? See these Web sites:

  www.americanstudies.wayne.edu/xchange/3.1/gupta.html

www.rethinkingschools.org/archive/12_01/ebsecret.shtml
www.aawe.com/ebonicsarticle.html

- Investigate what linguists say about Black English vernacular. Is it really "broken" English? Does it reflect "poor grammar"? What is the history of Black English?
- Many of those African Americans who do not speak Black English are unsympathetic to the argument that Black English needs respect. Many would like to move on to larger issues affecting blacks such as jobs and education. Why is it not so easy to dismiss language when one addresses issues of jobs and education?

SEEKING COMMON CAUSE

Before you take a side, identify the points on which the two sides agree so that you can narrow the focus of the debate.

1. Most people agree that Standard English offers greater opportunities for upward mobility and respect on the job.

2. Linguists confirm that Black English offers unique constructions, rhythms, and pronunciation that distinguish it from Standard English, but make it a viable dialect.

3. Speaking one's dialect provides one with a sense of special identity.

4. Language is not the only way by which we establish and maintain our identities.

5. Language can be particularly divisive, perhaps unnecessarily so. We all have personal and public identities that may be in conflict.

6. Speakers of Standard English and of Black English deserve the same access to jobs and education.

DEBATE ESSAY

When an African American like Earvin "Magic" Johnson tries to change the way he speaks to obtain increased "social mobility," is he exercising a form of self-hatred?

In your essay, use ideas from both sides of this issue. Reveal what values both sides share, show why one side offers a stronger argument, and describe the opposing side accurately. You might also draw on your own experience learning a foreign language or different dialect to show how it might feel to be asked to change the way you speak.

WRITING PROJECTS

Writing a Short Essay

1. Write a literacy autobiography in which you trace your efforts to become proficient in a language. You might write about your acquisition of a foreign language or of the kind of academic language you are expected to use in school or of a language special to a group you have joined, possibly a social group on campus. What incentive did you have to learn this language? What was difficult in this effort? What came easily to you? What rewards were there, if any?

2. Write a short essay in which you consider how you switch between languages. These could be two distinct languages, like Spanish and English, or two dialects or language styles that you use with different people—for instance, you may use different syntax and vocabulary

when talking to a professor than when talking to your roommate. Or you might write in a different style when you send e-mail to friends than when you compose a research paper for your history class.

Here are some questions you might address: Do you feel that different aspects of your personality emerge as you write or speak in the two languages or language styles? What is required of you in each situation? Which language or language style is more comfortable for you, and why? How would you define the differences or similarities in these languages? When you switch from one language to the other, what is lost?

3. Meet in groups of three students and take turns interviewing one another about two different language communities that each of you belongs to. Ask such questions as who is part of the language community, what distinguishes the group as such a community, and what is the nature of the language and conversation/writing produced in this language? Each member of the group will take a turn as the person interviewed, the interviewer, and the person who takes notes on what is being said. Then write a report, as a group, on your collective findings.

4. Interview someone you know who speaks more than one language. These could be two different dialects, professional (e.g., legal, finance, computer) languages, or national languages (e.g., Korean, French). Ask whether they ever experience a conflict between the two or whether they move easily from one to the other. Do they find it easy to say what they mean in both languages? Do they favor one over the other? Write an essay based on this interview.

5. Interview someone you know whose native language is not English or who speaks a dialect of English. Ask this person to describe his/her earliest experiences learning English (or Standard American English). Did learning to function in a new language change this person's identity? Were stereotypes attached to the native or new language? You might ask your subject to give you examples of expressions or ways of speaking that don't translate easily into English and to explain them to you. Write up your findings.

6. If you have traveled abroad, consider how much your cultural identity is tied to your native language. What tensions did you feel between your familiar way of behaving and what you felt was expected of you in the foreign country? How did language enter into this experience?

Writing an Extended Argument

Choose two of the paintings for this chapter and consider whether the person or people depicted seem to be in harmony with their culture or in conflict with it. How do the elements of the painting (color, line, composition, etc.) create this impression of harmony or conflict?

Then choose two of the readings, and analyze how the people discussed there fit in or conflict with their ancestral or the larger American culture. Using both the paintings and readings you just analyzed—and drawing upon additional paintings and readings for further evidence—answer *one* of these questions:

1. What is necessary for someone to feel at home in a culture?

   Or

2. What experiences or conditions make a person feel conflicted—caught between two incompatible cultures?

As you think about how the readings and paintings suggest answers to these questions, you might consider these related issues: Where do you see common ground between conflicting experiences? Where do you see tension, and what resolution, if any, do the paintings and readings offer?

Be sure to use ample concrete detail from the readings and paintings to illustrate your essay.

Designing the Extended Writing Project

The following suggestions for constructing a thesis, organizing, adding details, and integrating the thesis and the readings can be generalized to any other writing project you do.

To make your points clearly, we recommend that you include these elements.

A Thesis

The essay prompt under "Writing an Extended Argument" includes several subquestions, which are designed to help you think of ideas for the essay. When you write the essay, you do not necessarily have to answer every one of these questions. In fact, be sure that you have a single thesis that you elaborate on; avoid simply answering each question in turn as if you were writing an exam.

The thesis is the point of your essay; it is a complete sentence (sometimes two sentences) that makes a statement about what it takes to feel at home—or not at home—in a culture.

EXAMPLES | Richard Rodriguez and Caffilene Allen show that not knowing the language of a culture makes them outsiders, whereas in the paintings by Stephen Scott Young (*Flip-Flops and Lace*) and Henry Sugimoto (*Nisei Babies*) the divisive force is racism.

Louise Erdrich and Haunami-Kay Trask suggest that knowing and appreciating one's ancestral history connects them to their culture; this idea is reflected in Frida Kahlo's *Self-Portrait on the Borderline between Mexico and the United States* and Tomie Arai's *The Laundryman's Daughter.*

A Structure Based on the Thesis

One of the most effective ways to organize an essay is to follow the order of ideas set forth in your thesis. There is almost always more than one way to do this. The sample below shows one possibility; the paper based on this outline will have several paragraphs for each section:

Thesis: Richard Rodriguez and Caffilene Allen show that not knowing the language of a culture makes them outsiders, whereas in the paintings by Stephen Scott Young (*Flip Flops and Lace*) and Henry Sugimoto (*Nisei Babies*) the divisive force is racism.

Section one: Describe Rodriguez's and Allen's experiences as children who could not speak the language used at school. Show how this language problem made them feel like outsiders.

Section two: Describe how Rodriguez's and Allen's lives changed—how they began to fit in—once they became fluent in English (Rodriguez) or in the form of English used in school and the workplace (Allen).

Section three: Show how the paintings by Young and Sugimoto illustrate racism.

Section four: Show how the paintings by Young and Sugimoto illustrate one consequence of racism, treating African Americans and Japanese Americans as outsiders.

Detailed Descriptions of the Readings and Visuals

Your description of the *relevant* portions of the readings and visuals is your evidence and will make up the bulk of the essay. Details draw the readers into your writing and persuade them of your interpretation. Be sure to describe the readings and works of art so specifically that a reader who is not familiar with them can picture the visuals and understand your assertions about the readings.

In other words, don't stop with a generalization; add concrete information to illustrate it:

Not

The girl in *Flip Flops and Lace* looks sad.

But

The girl in *Flip Flops and Lace* looks sad. Her shoulders sink forward, her lips are pursed and unsmiling, and she stares into space, looking at nothing in particular.

Not

Barbara Wallraff argues that non-English-speakers routinely integrate words from their native languages into English.

But

Barbara Wallraff argues that people using English in a non-English-speaking country routinely integrate words from their native languages into English. The India World Web site, for example, is mostly in English, but has buttons labeled " '*samachar:* Personalised News,' '*dhan:* Investing in India,' [and] '*khoj:* Search India.'"

Using WEB Resources

Extend the Scope of Your Essay

The Web sites listed below offer information about, and additional works of art by, some of the artists represented in this chapter:

Carmen Lomas Garza
http://www.carmenlomasgarza.com/

The Jacob Lawrence Virtual Archive and Information Center
http://www.jacoblawrence.org/art00.html

Japanese-American National Museum, Henry Sugimoto exhibit
japanese-american-national-museum.visit-los-angeles.com/

Analyze a painting that you find on one of these Web sites and incorporate the analysis into your essay.

Study the Debate over Bilingual Education

Explore some of the Web sites listed below, and familiarize yourself with the arguments for and against bilingual education. Then expand your debate essay by including more information on the benefits and drawbacks of bilingual education. How does the information you find here complicate your understanding of the issues?

Key Legal Cases in Bilingual Education
www.iteachilearn.com/uh/guadarrama/sociopsycho/legal.htm

The Bilingual Families Web Page
http://www.nethelp.no/cindy/biling-fam.html

ACLU Briefing Paper: English Only
http://archive.aclu.org/library/pbp6.html

Comparison of Philosophical Assumptions of English-only L2 Instruction versus Bilingual Education
http://coe.sdsu.edu/people/jmora/Prop227/AssumptionsEOvBE.htm

English First—Bilingual Education Resources
http://www.englishfirst.org/be/begeneral.htm

America's Dairy Farmers and Milk Processors. "Want strong bones? . . ." [2004]

By featuring martial artist, action hero, and stuntman Jackie Chan, this ad draws on stereotypes about professional athletes. Why is the ad using an athlete to sell milk? What associations do people usually have with this product? What type of reader is this ad trying to reach?

1 Chan's hair is disheveled, and he has scratches on his left arm. How do these details contribute to your impression of Chan? What other details add to this impression?

2 Consider the large milk bottle over the ad's text. How might the placement and depiction of this image suggest male sexual prowess?

3 Like the Diet Coke ad, this milk ad uses fantasy as a persuasive technique. What fantasy does each ad invoke?

Like the Jackie Chan ad, this milk ad, featuring actress Hilary Duff, sells milk as a nutritious product necessary for active people. How is this idea approached differently in the two ads?

1. The colors in the ad are bright and playful, like the colors used in children's toys. What else about the ad gives the feeling of playfulness and youth?

2. The ad plays on the words "9 essential nutrients": milk has nine nutrients and Duff has nine shopping bags. What, according to the ad, is essential to Hilary's life? Considering the colors and other elements of the ad, what is your impression of Hilary's values?

3. Compare the facial expressions, clothing, and stance of the celebrities in both milk ads. Discuss whether the ads engage in gender stereotyping.

Givenchy. "Beyond Infinity" [2004]

This is an ad for men's cologne. How much of the ad is used to showcase the product? What does the ad emphasize?

1 How would you characterize the man depicted here? How do the lighting and camera angle create this image?

2 While perfume ads often focus on sexuality, this cologne ad uses images from physics, math, and engineering. Find at least three of these images and explain what they tell us about the man shown (and, by inference, the man who uses Givenchy cologne).

3 How do the shape of the cologne bottle and the colors of this ad reinforce the idea of masculinity depicted here?

Stetson [2004]

While the model in the Givenchy cologne ad wears an astronaut suit, actor Matthew McConaughey, depicted in this Stetson cologne ad, is dressed as a cowboy. What similarities or differences (or both) do you see in the stereotypes associated with these two jobs, astronaut and cowboy?

1 The picture of the cowboy on the cologne bottle, presented in a square frame, looks like a movie still or book illustration. Similarly, McConaughey, with the open shirt, jewelry, and skin-tight jeans looks more like a fantasy cowboy than a real working one. How would you characterize this fantasy man?

2 How else does the ad suggest a movie still rather than a photo of a cowboy on his ranch?

3 The top of the cologne bottle has a phallic shape. How else does the ad highlight McConaughey's sexuality?

Chanel Chance [2003]

Symbolically, women's sexuality is often associated with images that have a round shape and men's sexuality with oblong images. In what other way does this ad emphasize the model's sexuality? How is the shape of a bottle of Chance fragrance different from those of Stetson or Givenchy?

1. What different meanings might you attribute to the slogan "Take It!"?
2. Does the model seem powerful to you? Why or why not?
3. The woman's eyes are closed. How does this compare with the gaze of the men in the Givenchy and Stetson ads?
4. Consider the colors and textures of the different surfaces in this ad—from the woman's hair to the bottle's cap. How do they contribute to the characterization of the woman?

Dior [2003]

This ad persuades by appealing to our senses. Although it shows less of the models' bodies than many other fashion ads do, it highlights the women's sexuality. It also tells a story: what are the women doing, and how would you characterize their relationship?

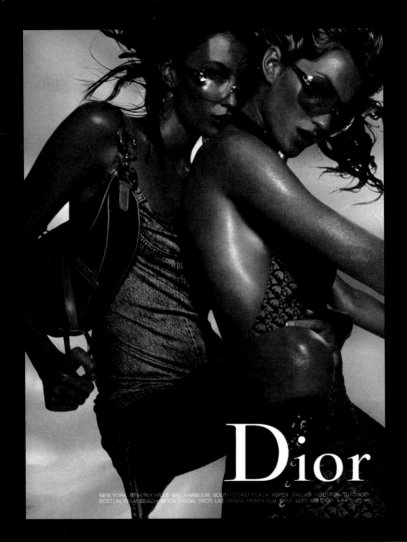

1 Describe the facial expressions and direction of the gaze of the models. How would you define their attitude?

2 The ad's lighting emphasizes the women's skin, which, like their hair, is wet. What other sensual images do you see in the ad?

3 The women's arms create a kind of cage that encircles and contains them. How does that image help define their relationship? What other circular shapes do you see?

4 Compare the clothing and hairstyles of these models to those of the women in the Chanel and Hilary Duff milk ads. How do these styles characterize the appeal of each ad?

Coca-Cola, "Diving into a Diet Coke" [2002]

Both this ad and the Jackie Chan milk ad sell beverages by showing a man flying through the air. But the men's attitudes and the background images are entirely different. How are the depictions of masculinity in the two ads alike or different?

1   Which words in the text suggest action? Looking at the other ads in this chapter, do the ads collectively suggest that being active is more a male than a female attribute? Why or why not?

2   Men rarely smile in ads, and often they look elsewhere than at the viewer. Does this man appear as tough as the men in the Jackie Chan and Stetson ads? Why or why not?

3   What elements of the ad make the man seem approachable and open? How appealing do you find this image?

Pepsi [2001]

Both the Coca-Cola ad and this ad for Pepsi associate "joy" with their product—the Coca-Cola ad by showing a man ecstatically diving through the sky, and the Pepsi ad, with its slogan, "the Joy of Pepsi." Does the woman in this Pepsi ad seem joyful? What is the dominant appeal here, and how does the ad create it?

1   Consider the placement of the text in this ad. How does it draw attention to the woman's sexuality?

2   What different meanings might the expression "workin' it" have in this ad?

3   The plain background of this ad focuses our attention on the woman's body. Compare the function of background colors and images in this ad with that in two other ads in this chapter.

4   Of the four beverage ads, this is the only one that shows the model drinking the product. Given the woman's stance and facial expression, how do you think the Pepsi is affecting her?

Constructing Gender

Researchers are divided over whether the personality characteristics we consider male or female are determined by biology or by culture. Most scholars believe that male and female characteristics reflect both, though these researchers differ in the degree to which they ascribe male and female behavior to genes or social training. Whatever the source of gendered behavior, we know that not all societies define men and women in the same ways and that social forces shape—and often rigidify—conceptions of what the ideal man or woman should be and look like. The readings in this chapter explore how masculinity and femininity are defined in the United States and how advertising influences these definitions.

GENDER IN ADVERTISEMENTS

Advertising is everywhere and affects all of us, whether we think we pay attention to it or not. Advertisers know that readers of magazines and viewers of billboards spend only a second or two looking at their work, so they meticulously design every detail to capture our attention. Most advertisements contain implicit messages about gender: that is, the way they depict the male and female models—their posture, the setting, their clothing, the activity they're shown doing, and even the language the ad uses to describe the product—tell the viewer what a man or woman should be like.

Ads are thus powerful agents for defining masculinity and femininity. Although no one ad is likely to change our notions of gender identity, the cumulative effect of the hundreds of ads we are exposed to each year—combined with the images of men and women we get elsewhere in our lives—help form our notions of men and women, notions that affect what we expect of ourselves and others.

For example, despite its fantasy element, the Jackie Chan ad for America's Dairy Farmers and Milk Processors depicts a conventional view of masculinity: Chan, the central figure in the ad, is muscular, active, and violent—an image of maleness we are accustomed to seeing on TV and in the movies. The preponderance of tough, athletic models standing aggressively in advertisements reinforces the notion that these characteristics are central to masculinity. Rarely do we see a slender, gentle, passive man in advertising. That the model in this milk ad is not just anyone, but a celebrity—actor, martial artist, and action hero Jackie Chan—only makes this notion of masculinity more desirable; here is a man who has used his strength, fierceness, and athletic prowess to forge a successful career. Of course, the advertiser's intent is not to promote a particular view of gender: the ad exists merely to sell a product. But by routinely showing the same images of masculinity and femininity, the ads encourage us not just to buy their goods, but also—whether intentionally or not—to accept a specific view of gender.

Analyzing the Advertisements

Advertisements persuade us by using many of the same rhetorical techniques as print texts; even if an ad contains no words, its picture can tell a story, create a metaphor, advance an idea, or stir the senses or emotions. As you look at the advertisements in this section, think about which argumentative strategies are at play and how *all* the elements of the composition, even the most subtle ones, work together to evoke a particular view of gender.

The questions that follow will help you to identify details in the ads, including those that may not seem significant at first glance, and to consider what each detail contributes to the overall effect:

1. What is the first thing you notice in the ad?
2. What image is depicted in the ad?
3. Which elements of the ad contribute to this image? Be sure to look at every component of the ad, not just the most obvious ones.
4. What is the size of the objects in the ad, relative to one another?
5. What is the relationship between the words and the visual image?
6. How do the small background details contribute to or conflict with the dominant images?
7. Where is the text of the ad located?
8. What do the men and women in the ads seem to be doing or seeking?
9. What is the effect of the use of light, color, and shading?
10. What does the language (if there is any) imply about gender? Consider especially the likelihood that language used to describe the product may contain subtle gender typing.

The following analysis of an advertisement for America's Dairy Farmers and Milk Processors illustrates how you might use these questions to explore the depiction of gender in an ad. It is meant as a model for the kind of analysis you might do with the other ads in this chapter.

Analysis of an Advertisement

The ad for America's Dairy Farmers and Milk Processors provides a visual narrative of male toughness and violence. Though in his movies, Jackie Chan usually plays the action hero who saves others from evil, we cannot tell from this picture whether he is the hero or villain. He is the picture of violence, his body looming at us through the sky, his foot about to kick us in the face, his face grimacing and threatening. In the background, a car is in flames, and even the buildings are off-kilter, intensifying the sense of violent disorder. The milk mustache, which often provides a humorous detail in other ads for this industry, does not detract from Chan's fierceness; if anything, it draws attention to his teeth, which look ready to bite someone. Chan offers a picture of male aggression, and he is presented as a role model for boys and young men: "Want strong bones? Your bones grow until about age 35 and the calcium in milk helps." Presumably the teenage boy who drinks milk can aspire not just to be strong, but to be a fighter as well.

The composition of the ad underlines this point: Chan is placed in the center of the ad and takes up most of its space. Everything else in the ad—the buildings, helicopters, car—recedes behind Chan, making him seem larger and more powerful than his surroundings. The light shines on his face and arms, drawing attention to his muscles and grimace, thus emphasizing the view of man as an athlete, a hero, and a destroyer.

GENDER IN ESSAYS

Each of the essays in this chapter grapples with prevailing ideas about masculinity or femininity in different ways. Most of them critique rigid definitions of gender identity, especially when they are confining or foster dangerous behavior; others explore these definitions and seek ways of building on them. In "The Myth of the Sexual Athlete," Don Sabo argues that the emphasis on male dominance, particularly the treatment of sex as sport, hampers men's friendships with both men and women. In "Just Walk On By," Brent Staples describes how the identification of maleness with dominance is particularly hurtful for an African American man. Staples is subject to both gender and racial stereotyping: he finds himself a threat to strangers, especially women, who not only fear male aggression, but also see black men as potentially violent criminals. In contrast, Lance Strate, in "Beer Commercials: A Manual on Masculinity," shows how many values associated with masculinity, such as seeking challenges and working as a team, are personally fulfilling and productive. At the same time, he believes that other values, such as emotional indifference, are harmful. Such emotional insensitivity is the subject of David Brooks's essay, "The Return of the Pig," which describes a return to "retro-sexism" in which men are encouraged to belittle women and behave boorishly.

While these writers analyze traditional attributes of masculinity, Cindy Jackson, Susan Bordo, Jean Kilbourne, and Mira Jacob believe that women are measured primarily by a narrow standard of physical beauty whose goal is to attract men. In her interview with Danny Danziger, "My Cosmetic Surgery," Cindy Jackson discusses her efforts to achieve this standard of beauty through cosmetic surgery and argues that her new appearance has enriched her life—given her power, a career, the kinds of relationships with men she values, and self-confidence.

In contrast to Jackson, Susan Bordo, in "The Empire of Images in Our World of Bodies," criticizes the media for promoting this obsession with physical perfection; she is especially concerned with the effect of media images on girls. Taken together, Jackson's and Bordo's articles raise questions about where a woman's value as a person lies and whether a devotion to physical appearance is dangerous and shallow or part of a more complex set of values. Like Susan Bordo, Jean Kilbourne, in "'The More You Subtract, the More You Add': Cutting Girls Down to Size," believes conventional ideas about femininity, specifically as conveyed in advertisements, can be "toxic for girls' self-esteem." In addition to seeking physical perfection, girls are taught to be self-effacing, silent, passive, and childlike, while at the same time, seductive. As a woman of color, Mira Jacob finds many of these expectations to be intensified: in "My Brown Face," she describes how strangers find her looks exotic and assume both that she wants to be ogled and that she silently appreciates this attention. Like Jackson, Bordo, and Kilbourne, Jacob finds the cultural obsession with female physical appearance to be a challenge and finds her own way to assert her complexity and individuality. In "Dividing the Consumer Pie," Danae Clark complicates some of these traditional notions of masculinity and femininity as they apply to gay and lesbian communities. Clark argues that a variety of masculine or feminine styles can be found within these communities. Advertisers, by depicting sexually ambiguous men and women, try to appeal to a gay and lesbian market without excluding straight customers.

Analyzing the Essays

As you read these selections, consider what beliefs and values the writers share, where they might disagree, and how you might reconcile apparent contradictions among them. Jackson and Bordo, for example, take opposing positions on cosmetic surgery—Bordo finds it degrading to women, while Jackson believes it made her "childhood dreams come true." Yet both writers seek to give women the power of self-definition: Bordo, by liberating women from the dictates of advertisers, who profit by making women feel unattractive, and Jackson by helping women to look any way they choose, even if they choose to look like her.

In interpreting the readings, you might consider these questions:

1. What image of maleness or femaleness does the writer think makes men or women happy? Unhappy?

2. How are the writer's values similar to or different from the ones he or she ascribes to U.S. culture?

3. How might one define masculinity or femininity in a way that accommodates both the conventional definition that many of the articles critique and an image of men or women that they would support?

The following sample analysis of Susan Bordo's "The Empire of Images in Our World of Bodies" builds on these questions.

Analysis of an Essay

In analyzing Susan Bordo's "The Empire of Images in Our World of Bodies," you might first ask yourself what image of women Susan Bordo objects to and why she thinks it is harmful. Bordo challenges several images promoted by the media: (1) in adult women, a false appearance of eternal youth, (2) in young women, an unhealthy emphasis on extreme thinness, and (3) in girls, a seductiveness, "exuding a sexual knowledge and experience that preteens don't really have." She objects to all these images not only because they are unnatural, but also because they are unhealthy, physically, psychologically, and socially. Older women come to hate the signs of aging on their bodies and to feel inadequate and devalued for looking their age. Some resort to liposuction and Botox injections, procedures that take their toll on the body and that only reinforce the idea that facial lines and body fat are signs of failure. Like older women, young women learn to hate their bodies if they don't resemble those of the models and celebrities they see in magazines. Like the celebrity images of older women, many of the photographs of women in their twenties are digitally altered, yet young women and girls as young as eight go to great lengths to achieve the emaciated look they see everywhere. Many of them diet themselves to starvation and still worry about being fat. Equally insidious is the sexual exploitation of preteens; on television and in advertising, we routinely see girls "in full vixen attire,

with professionally undulating bodies and professionally made-up come-hither eyes."
Bordo argues that this sexualizing of girls contributes to a culture where rape, especially
rape committed by friends and family members, is prevalent.

Bordo's values are clearly at odds with those represented by these images. She wants
her daughter to cultivate her gifts as an athlete, doing what she loves rather than struggling to resemble an unnatural media image; she wants her to be accomplished, proud
of the way she looks, and safe from sexual predators. And while Bordo considers media
representations of the female body to be at odds with the way most women and girls actually look, she also notes trends that are more inclusive, that reflect her values of self-
love, health, and cultural diversity. Bordo cannot reconcile her values with media images
of plastically enhanced, anorexic bodies, but she finds hope in people who resist these
images—such as a young woman who dances without trying to hide her round belly
and athlete Marion Jones, whose shoulders provide a counter-image of self-confidence
and power.

READING

DON SABO   According to Sabo, gender images and behavior derive not only from ads, movies,
and other media, but also from clubs and social groups deeply entrenched in our culture, such
as team sports. He bases his argument on a comparison of sex to "sport," an analogy that underscores the disjunction between men's and women's attitudes toward sex. Is it a loving act, between committed partners, or is it a casual pleasure? Do both sexes share equally and gain
intimacy, or are there winners and losers, the exploiters and the exploited, the debasers and the
debased? Don Sabo shares his own confused early experiences learning about sex in a locker
room culture of boys and later men: "making points," "scoring," and dominating "the game."
Sabo claims that organized sports create "a social setting in which gender learning melds with
sexual learning."

SABO is a sociology professor at D'Youville College in New York. He is the author of *Jock: Sports and Male Identity,*
the coauthor (with Michael Messner) of *Sport, Men, and the Gender Order: Critical Feminist Perspectives,* and the
coeditor of *Prison Masculinities,* as well as a contributor to numerous journals and magazines.

The Myth of the Sexual Athlete (1989) | BY DON SABO

The phrase "sexual athlete" commonly refers to male heterosexual virtuosity in
the bedroom. Images of potency, agility, technical expertise and an ability to attract and satisfy women come to mind. In contrast, the few former athletes like
Dave Meggyesy and Jim Bouton who have seriously written on the subject, and films
such as *Raging Bull* and *North Dallas Forty,* depict the male athlete as sexually uptight,
fixated on early adolescent sexual antics and exploitative of women. The former image
of athletic virility, however, remains fixed within the popular imagination and, partly
for this reason, there has been very little said about the *real* connections between sport
and male sexuality.

LOCKER ROOM SEX TALK

I played organized sports for 15 years and they were as much a part of my "growing up" as Cheerios, television, and homework. My sexuality unfolded within this all-male social world of sport where sex was always a major focus. I remember, for example, when we as prepubertal boys used the old "buying baseball cards" routine as a cover to sneak peeks at *Playboy* and *Swank* magazines at the newsstand. We would talk endlessly after practices about "boobs" and what it must feel like to kiss and neck. Later, in junior high, we teased one another in the locker room about "jerking off" or being virgins, and there were endless interrogations about "how far" everybody was getting with their girlfriends.

Eventually, boyish anticipation spilled into *real* sexual relationships with girls which, to my delight and confusion, turned out to be a lot more complex than I ever imagined. While sex (kissing, necking, and petting) got more exciting, it also got more difficult to figure out and talk about. Inside, most of the boys, like myself, needed to love and be loved. We were awkwardly reaching out for intimacy. Yet publicly, the message that got imparted was to "catch feels," be cool, connect with girls but don't allow yourself to depend on them. Once when I was a high school junior, the gang in the weight room accused me of being wrapped around my girlfriend's finger. Nothing could be further from the truth, I assured them, and in order to prove it, I broke up with her. I felt miserable about this at the time and I still feel bad about it.

Within the college jock subculture, men's public protests against intimacy sometimes became exaggerated and ugly. I remember two teammates, drunk and rowdy, ripping girls' blouses off at a mixer and crawling on their bellies across the dance floor to look up skirts. Then there were the Sunday morning late breakfasts in the dorm. We jocks would usually all sit at one table and be forced to listen to one braggart or another describe his sexual exploits of the night before. Though a lot of us were turned off by such kiss-and-tell, ego-boosting tactics, we never openly criticized them. Real or fabricated, displays of raunchy sex were also assumed to "win points." A junior fullback claimed to have defecated on a girl's chest after she passed out during intercourse. There were also some laughing reports of "gang-bangs."

When sexual relationships *were* "serious," that is, tempered by love and commitment, the unspoken rule was silence. It was rare when we young men shared our feelings about women, misgivings about sexual performance or disdain for the crudeness and insensitivity of some of our teammates. I now see the tragic irony in this: we could talk about superficial sex and anything that used, trivialized or debased women, but frank discussions about sexuality that unfolded within a loving relationship were taboo. Within the locker room subculture, sex and love were seldom allowed to mix. There was a terrible split between inner needs and outer appearances, between our desire for the love of women and our feigned indifference toward them.

SEX AS SPORT

Sport is a social setting in which gender learning melds with sexual learning. Our sense of "femaleness" or "maleness" influences the ways we see ourselves as sexual beings. Indeed, as we develop, *sexual* identity emerges as an extension of an already-formed *gender* identity, and sexual behavior becomes "scripted" by cultural meanings. The prevailing script for manhood in sport is basically traditional; it emphasizes competition, success (winning), domination, aggression, emotional stoicism, goal-directedness and physical strength. Many athletes buy into this hypermasculine image and it affects their relationships with women. Dating becomes a "sport" in itself and "scoring," or seeking sex with little or no regard for emotions, is regarded as a mark of masculine achievement. Sexual relationships get defined as "games" in which women are seen as "opponents," and "winners" and "losers" vie for dominance. Too often, women get used as pawns in men's quests for acceptance among peers and status within the male pecking order. I believe that for many of us jocks, these lessons somehow got translated into a "man-as-hunter/woman-as-prey" approach to sexual relationships.

How did this happen? What transformed us from boys who needed and depended on women to men who misunderstood, felt separated from, and sometimes mistreated women? One part of the problem is the expectation that we are supposed to act as though we want to be alone, like the cowboy who always rides off into the sunset alone. In sport, there is only one "most valuable player" on the team.

Too often this prevents male athletes from understanding women and their life experiences. Though women's voices may reach men's ears from the sidelines and grandstands, they remain distant and garbled by the clamor of male competition. In sport, communication gaps between the sexes are due in part to women's historical exclusion from sport, the failure to create coed athletic programs, and coaching practices which quarantine boys from the "feminizing" taint of female influence. One result of this isolation is that sexual myths flourish. Boys end up learning about girls and female sexuality *from other males,* and the information that gets transmitted within the male network is often inaccurate and downright sexist. I can see in retrospect that as boys we lacked a vocabulary of intimacy which would have enabled us to better share sexual experiences with others. The locker room language that filled our adolescent heads did not exactly foster insights into the true nature of women's sexuality—or our own, for that matter.

PERFORMANCE AND PATRIARCHY

Traditional gender learning and locker room sexual myths can also shape men's lovemaking behavior. Taught to be "achievement machines," many athletes organize their energies and perceptions around a performance ethic which influences sexual relations. The goal-directedness and preoccupation with performance and technique enters into male scripts of lovemaking. In the movie *Joe,* a sexually liberated woman tells her hardhat lover that "making love isn't like running a 50 yard dash."

When intercourse becomes the chief goal of sex, it bolsters men's performance inclinations and limits their ability to enjoy other aspects of sexual experiences. It can also create problems for both men and their partners. Since coitus requires an erection, men are under pressure to get and maintain erections. If erections do not occur, or men ejaculate "too quickly," their self-esteem as lovers and men can be impaired. In fact, sex therapists tell us that men's preoccupation and anxieties about erectile potency and performance can cause the very sexual dysfunctions they fear.

It is important to emphasize that it is not only jocks who swallow this limiting model of male sexuality. Sport is not the only social setting which promotes an androcentric, eroticism-without-intimacy value system. Consider how male sexuality gets socially constructed in fraternities, motorcycle gangs, the armed forces, urban gangs, pornography, corporate advertising, MTV, magazines like *Playboy* or *Penthouse,* and the movies—to name but a few examples. These are not random and unrelated sources of traditional masculine values. They all originate in patriarchy.

10

Sexual relations between men and women in western societies have been conducted under the panoply of patriarchal power. The sexual values which derive from patriarchy emphasize male dominance and the purely erotic dimensions of the sex act while reducing women to delectable but expendable objects. An alternative conception of human sexuality, however, is also gaining ascendancy within the culture. Flowing out of women's experiences and based on egalitarian values, it seeks to integrate eroticism with love and commitment. It is deeply critical of the social forces which reduce women (and men) to sex objects, depersonalize relationships and turn human sexuality into an advertising gimmick or commodity to be purchased. This is the sexual ethos proffered by the women's movement.

Today's young athletes don't seem as hooked on the hypermasculine image that traditional sport has proffered. Perhaps it is because alternative forms of masculinity and sexuality have begun to enter the locker room subculture. Sex segregation in sport is not as pronounced as it was when I was a young man in the mid-sixties. More girls are playing sports than ever before, and coed athletic experiences are more common. As more women enter the traditionally male environments of sport, business, factories or government, men are finding it more difficult to perceive women in one-dimensional terms. Perhaps we are becoming better able to see them for what they really are and, in the process, we are beginning to search for alternative modes of being men.

WHAT DO MEN REALLY WANT ... NEED?

Most of us do not really know what it is we want from our sexual lives. Men seem torn between yearning for excitement and longing for love and intimacy. On one side, we feel titillated by the glitter of contemporary cosmetics and corporate advertising. Eroticism jolts our minds and bodies. We're sporadically turned on by the simple hedonism of the so-called sexual revolution and the sometimes-sleek-sometimes-sleazy veil of soft- and hard-pornography. Many of us fantasize about pursuing eroticism without commitment; some actually live the fantasy. On the other side, more men are recently becoming aware of genuine needs for intimate relationships. We are beginning to recognize that being independent, always on the make and emotionally controlled, are not meeting our needs. Furthermore, the traditional masculine script is certainly not meeting women's expectations or satisfying their emotional needs. More and more men are starting to wonder if sexuality can be a vehicle for expressing and experiencing love.

In our culture many men are suffering from "sexual schizophrenia." Their minds [15] lead them toward eroticism while their heads pull them toward emotional intimacy. What they want rarely coincides with what they need. Perhaps the uneasiness and the ambivalence which permeates male sexuality is due to this root fact: the traditional certainties which men used to define their manhood and sexuality no longer fit the realities of their lives, and until equality between the sexes becomes more of a social reality, no new model of a more humane sexuality will take hold.

As for me, I am still exploring and redefining my sexuality. While I don't have all the answers yet, I do have direction. I am listening more closely to women's voices, turning my head away from the sexist legacy of the locker room and pursuing a pro-feminist vision of sexuality. It feels good to stop pretending that I enjoy being alone. I never did like feeling alone.

1. Reflect on times when single-sex groups get together. Considering your past or recent personal experiences, ask yourself what language they use to talk about members of the opposite sex. Do stereotypes underlie these conversations?

2. How has your experience with a sport—as a player or spectator—contributed to the image you share of men or women?

FOCUSING ON THE ARGUMENT

1. One of Sabo's persuasive techniques is personal testimony, first showing how he and his friends behaved in the "all-male social world of sport," then analyzing this behavior, and finally applying his personal experience to men in general. How persuasive do you find this strategy? Where did you feel most convinced by Sabo's argument? Where did you feel least convinced? Explain your reactions.

2. As you read this article, ask yourself how Sabo's extended analogy works for you. Does it help you better understand his point? How far do you think Sabo's analogy can be taken? Is there a point at which such an analogy might break down? Ask yourself, also, if the analogy helps you think about girls' gender training. Do sports create a similar culture for girls for learning about sex? If so, how?

SYNTHESIZING IDEAS FROM MULTIPLE READINGS

1. What, if anything, does the ideal man in Sabo's world of sports have in common with the image of masculinity that David Brooks decries in "The Return of the Pig" (p. 122)?

2. Jean Kilbourne ("The More You Subtract, the More You Add," p. 149) and Sabo argue that stereotyped images of masculinity have hurt men: in trying to live up to these images, men have been discouraged from having intimate relationships. Furthermore, these authors sometimes suggest that such images undermine men's self-confidence and freedom of choice. What do these authors see as the consequences of this lack of intimacy?

WRITING TO ACT

1. Perhaps collaborating with several classmates, identify a sports association or group that governs the practices of a sport in this country (e.g., United States Tennis Association). Using personal experiences, observations, accounts by others, readings, or other sources, write to this organization at the national level about what values you think their program teaches. Does the organization teach hard work and team effort? Does it downplay courtesy and fair play and reward only winning? What other values does the organization support? Research a similar organization in another country. You might offer suggestions for improved practices to consider.

2. Sabo believes that the analogy between sports and male views of sex—man as jock, woman as opponent, dating as a game, and sex as scoring—reveals a value system shared by institutions besides sports, such as corporate advertising, fraternities, magazines like *Playboy* and *Penthouse,* and motorcycle gangs. First clarify what this value system is. Then test Sabo's claim with your own research. Survey and observe a fraternity, men's residence hall, or other group; study the performance of a rock band; analyze a men's magazine, such as *Playboy* or *Maxim;* or analyze the advertising in a business magazine, such as *Forbes.* Write a report to the institution you studied, outlining your findings and including suggestions for change.

BRENT STAPLES According to Brent Staples, white men and women fear African American men, whom they perceive as potentially violent criminals. How do you think such fears might constrict or otherwise affect the behavior of African American men? Fear of members of a particular group has consequences for both the individual and society. What do you think these consequences are?

STAPLES, an editorial writer at the *New York Times,* won the Anisfield Wolff Book Award for *Parallel Time: Growing Up in Black and White* in 1995.

Just Walk On By (1986) | BY BRENT STAPLES

My first victim was a woman—white, well-dressed, probably in her early twenties. I came upon her late one evening on a deserted street in Hyde Park, a relatively affluent neighborhood in an otherwise mean, impoverished section of Chicago. As I swung onto the avenue behind her, there seemed to be a discreet, uninflammatory distance between us. Not so. She cast back a worried glance. To her, the youngish black man—a broad six feet two inches with a beard and billowing hair, both hands shoved into the pockets of a bulky military jacket—seemed menacingly close. After a few more quick glimpses, she picked up her pace and was soon running in earnest. Within seconds, she disappeared into a cross street.

That was more than a decade ago. I was 22 years old, a graduate student newly arrived at the University of Chicago. It was in the echo of that terrified woman's footfalls that I first began to know the unwieldy inheritance I'd come into—the ability to alter public space in ugly ways. It was clear that she thought herself the quarry of a mugger, a rapist, or worse. Suffering a bout of insomnia, however, I was stalking sleep, not defenseless wayfarers. As a softy who is scarcely able to take a knife to a raw chicken—let alone hold it to a person's throat—I was surprised, embarrassed, and dismayed all at once. Her flight made me feel like an accomplice in tyranny. It also made it clear that I was indistinguishable from the muggers who occasionally seeped into the area from the surrounding ghetto. That first encounter, and those that followed, signified that a vast, unnerving gulf lay between nighttime pedestrians—particularly women—and me. And I soon gathered that being perceived as dangerous is a hazard in itself. I only needed to turn a corner into a dicey situation, or crowd some frightened, armed person in a foyer somewhere, or make an errant move after being pulled over by a policeman. Where fear and weapons meet—and they often do in urban America—there is always the possibility of death.

In that first year, my first away from my hometown, I was to become thoroughly familiar with the language of fear. At dark, shadowy intersections in Chicago, I could cross in front of a car stopped at a traffic light and elicit the *thunk, thunk, thunk, thunk* of the driver—black, white, male, or female—hammering down the door locks. On less traveled streets after dark, I grew accustomed to but never comfortable with people who crossed to the other side of the street rather than pass me. Then there were the standard unpleasantries with police, doormen, bouncers, cab drivers, and others whose business it is to screen out troublesome individuals *before* there is any nastiness.

I moved to New York nearly two years ago and I have remained an avid night walker. In central Manhattan, the near-constant crowd cover minimizes tense one-on-one street encounters. Elsewhere—visiting friends in SoHo, where sidewalks are narrow and tightly spaced buildings shut out the sky—things can get very taut indeed.

Black men have a firm place in New York mugging literature. Norman Podhoretz 5 in his famed (or infamous) 1963 essay, "My Negro Problem—And Ours," recalls growing up in terror of black males; they "were tougher than we were, more ruthless," he writes—and as an adult on the Upper West Side of Manhattan, he continues, he cannot constrain his nervousness when he meets black men on certain streets. Similarly, a decade later, the essayist and novelist Edward Hoagland extols a New York where once "Negro bitterness bore down mainly on other Negroes." Where some see mere panhandlers, Hoagland sees "a mugger who is clearly screwing up his nerve to do more than just *ask* for money." But Hoagland has "the New Yorker's quick-hunch posture for broken-field maneuvering," and the bad guy swerves away.

I often witness that "hunch posture," from women after dark on the warrenlike streets of Brooklyn where I live. They seem to set their faces on neutral and, with their purse straps strung across their chests bandolier style, they forge ahead as though bracing themselves against being tackled. I understand, of course, that the danger they perceive is not a hallucination. Women are particularly vulnerable to street violence, and young black males are drastically overrepresented among the perpetrators of that violence. Yet these truths are no solace against the kind of alienation that comes of being ever the suspect, against being set apart, a fearsome entity with whom pedestrians avoid making eye contact.

It is not altogether clear to me how I reached the ripe old age of 22 without being conscious of the lethality nighttime pedestrians attributed to me. Perhaps it was because in Chester, Pennsylvania, the small, angry industrial town where I came of age in the 1960s, I was scarcely noticeable against a backdrop of gang warfare, street knifings, and murders. I grew up one of the good boys, had perhaps a half-dozen fist-fights. In retrospect, my shyness of combat has clear sources.

Many things go into the making of a young thug. One of those things is the consummation of the male romance with the power to intimidate. An infant discovers that random flailings send the baby bottle flying out of the crib and crashing to the floor. Delighted, the joyful babe repeats those motions again and again, seeking to duplicate the feat. Just so, I recall the points at which some of my boyhood friends were finally seduced by the perception of themselves as tough guys. When a mark cowered and surrendered his money without resistance, myth and reality merged—and paid off. It is, after all, only manly to embrace the power to frighten and intimidate. We, as men, are not supposed to give an inch of our lane on the highway; we are to seize the fighter's edge in work and in play and even in love; we are to be valiant in the face of hostile forces.

Unfortunately, poor and powerless young men seem to take all this nonsense literally. As a boy, I saw countless tough guys locked away; I have since buried several, too. They were babies, really—a teenage cousin, a brother of 22, a childhood friend in his mid-twenties—all gone down in episodes of bravado played out in the streets. I came to doubt the virtues of intimidation early on. I chose, perhaps even unconsciously, to remain a shadow—timid, but a survivor.

The fearsomeness mistakenly attributed to me in public places often has a perilous flavor. The most frightening of these confusions occurred in the late 1970s and early 1980s when I worked as a journalist in Chicago. One day, rushing into the office of a magazine I was writing for with a deadline story in hand, I was mistaken for a burglar. The office manager called security and, with an ad hoc posse, pursued me through the labyrinthine halls, nearly to my editor's door. I had no way of proving who I was. I could only move briskly toward the company of someone who knew me.
10

Another time I was on assignment for a local newspaper and killing time before an interview. I entered a jewelry store on the city's affluent Near North Side. The proprietor excused herself and returned with an enormous red Doberman pinscher straining at the end of a leash. She stood, the dog extended toward me, silent to my questions, her eyes bulging nearly out of her head. I took a cursory look around, nodded, and bade her good night. Relatively speaking, however, I never fared as badly as another black male journalist. He went to nearby Waukegan, Illinois, a couple of summers ago to work on a story about a murderer who was born there. Mistaking the reporter for the killer, police hauled him from his car at gunpoint and but for his press credentials would probably have tried to book him. Such episodes are not uncommon. Black men trade tales like this all the time.

In "My Negro Problem—And Ours," Podhoretz writes that the hatred he feels for blacks makes itself known to him through a variety of avenues—one being his discomfort with that "special brand of paranoid touchiness" to which he says blacks are prone. No doubt he is speaking here of black men. In time, I learned to smother the rage I felt at so often being taken for a criminal. Not to do so would surely have led to madness—via that special "paranoid touchiness" that so annoyed Podhoretz at the time he wrote the essay.

I began to take precautions to make myself less threatening. I move about with care, particularly late in the evening. I give a wide berth to nervous people on subway platforms during the wee hours, particularly when I have exchanged business clothes for jeans. If I happen to be entering a building behind some people who appear skittish, I may walk by, letting them clear the lobby before I return, so as not to seem to be following them. I have been calm and extremely congenial on those rare occasions when I've been pulled over by the police.

And on late-evening constitutionals along streets less traveled by, I employ what has proved to be an excellent tension-reducing measure: I whistle melodies from Beethoven and Vivaldi and the more popular classical composers. Even steely New Yorkers hunching toward nighttime destinations seem to relax, and occasionally they even join in the tune. Virtually everybody seems to sense that a mugger wouldn't be warbling bright, sunny selections from Vivaldi's *Four Seasons*. It is my equivalent of the cowbell that hikers wear when they know they are in bear country.

1. Do you believe that this racist image of black men is reinforced and glamorized by action movies and other popular media? Why or why not?

2. Observe how you react when encountering a stranger whose race is different from yours. Compare your reaction with how you feel and act when you meet a stranger from the same race.

FOCUSING ON THE ARGUMENT

1. Staples uses subtle shifts in point of view and tone to persuade his readers that his blackness alone evokes defensive behavior from others. For instance, he opens humorously with the perspective of a potential female "victim," then quickly adds other views: himself at age twenty-two, young black males who bought into and died for the "tough guy" image, and even the author of a racist tirade. What is the effect of the multiple shifts in perspective?

2. Staples presents himself as a "shadow," someone who is "timid, but a survivor." In addition to this self-effacing persona, he comes across as reasonable, considerate, and sensitive— the opposite of what his "victims" expect him to be. How does his presentation of himself strengthen his argument?

SYNTHESIZING IDEAS FROM MULTIPLE READINGS

1. Both men and women alter their behavior to defend themselves from others' misperceptions of them. What misperceptions do Mira Jacob ("My Brown Face," p. 143) and Brent Staples have to contend with? Why do they choose to change their behavior? When should people whose appearance evokes stereotypes make an effort to accommodate others' prejudices, and when should they simply be themselves?

2. Mira Jacob ("My Brown Face," p. 143) and Brent Staples both become aware of their effect on the opposite sex while they are walking. Walking is an act that has both private and public dimensions: we have private reasons for going somewhere, but we move through public space. How is this balance upset for both Jacob and Staples when they go walking?

3. Staples argues that women react fearfully to him because of his race. At the same time, Jean Kilbourne ("'The More You Subtract, the More You Add,'" p. 149) describes a "climate" of "widespread and increasing violence" against women that might also explain women's fears. What common ground can you find in these two views?

4. Describing the relationship between athletes and women as that of a predator and his prey, in "The Myth of the Sexual Athlete" (p. 113), Don Sabo suggests that we accept violence as a natural part of masculinity. Brent Staples argues that black men are also stereotyped as potentially violent, but in this case, the possibility of aggression is conceived of as frightening and suspect. Think of images of black and white male aggression on campus, in athletics, in the movies, and in the news. Do you think that we expect white men's violence to be heroic—or at least, justified—whereas we expect the same potential in black men to be criminal? Give examples to clarify your response.

WRITING TO ACT

1. Do a study in which you observe women responding to male strangers of a race different from theirs. Do they make eye contact with the stranger? How would you describe the women's behavior? Alternatively, observe men responding to women of a different race.

What do your observations suggest? Write up your findings in an article for your school newspaper.

2. Think of a situation at your former high school in which there were "in groups" and "out groups." Write a letter to your old high school counselor describing these groups and the effects of treating a group of people as outsiders. In what ways did separating these students into insiders and outsiders ignore what they had in common?

3. Think of a movie or a TV show that portrays African American men as predators. Write a letter to the director, asking why s/he depicted the characters in such a way, and include suggestions for a more balanced and fair presentation.

DAVID BROOKS In this article, David Brooks struggles to define a problem that doesn't fall neatly into a category: antifemale images and attitudes that seem simultaneously hostile and satirical. The opportunities to leer at women's bodies offered by such popular phenomena as Hooters restaurants, *The Man Show,* and Lara Croft reduce women's value to that of a sex object and suggest that men, who are presumed to enjoy ogling these women, are crude and lacking empathy. Even worse, women are now encouraged to develop the same attitude toward men's bodies. Is this trend evidence of increased insensitivity to and lack of respect for others, especially for women—or is it a joke? Or is it hostility pretending to be a joke? Or is it all three? While you read, see if Brooks's observations resonate with your own experiences: how widespread is this portrayal of women and men? Do you find it offensive, amusing, harmless, or something else?

BROOKS has been a columnist for the *New York Times* since 2003 and appears on the PBS *Newshour.* He has been a writer or editor at the *Weekly Standard,* the *Atlantic Monthly, Newsweek,* and the *Wall Street Journal.* He is the author of *Bobos in Paradise* and *On Paradise Drive.*

The Return of the Pig (2003)

BY DAVID BROOKS

Have you noticed that male chauvinism is making a comeback? Thirty years after the feminist revolution, if you look at the rap videos on MTV or BET, you'll find that "ho" and "bitch" are just about the nicest words used to describe young women. Hooters is now so mainstream as to be just another link in the chain of familiar eateries. If you turn on *The Man Show,* on Comedy Central, you can watch women in teddies jumping on trampolines and men getting spanked by bikini-clad "juggies"—the show's term for its female cast members.

Elsewhere on the cultural landscape can be found the Wonderbra, Howard Stern, *Joe Millionaire,* Victoria's Secret specials on network TV, Anna Nicole Smith, and Lara Croft. The leading laddie magazine, *Maxim,* has 2.5 million subscribers; its chief competitor, *FHM* ("For Him Magazine"), has more than a million. And then there are *Gear* and *Stuff,* and the various swimsuit monthlies, which among them must have topless, carefully angled models posing on beaches by the hundreds.

To enter the world of *Maxim* is to enter a world entirely free from the taint of polite opinion. Even the editors of *Playboy* and *Penthouse* maintain intellectual pretensions, but the single-minded pursuit of horniness is the *Maxim* editors' most striking trait. Women in the magazine's pages are reduced almost exclusively to cleavage. Men exist solely at the crossroads where babes in lingerie meet power tools and serial-killer computer games. The articles—which tend to fall into the "How to Score at Funerals" genre—are short lessons in ways to become even more shallow than you already are. (To the *Maxim* Man, size matters in every aspect of existence except attention span.)

The men depicted by *Maxim* are not without cultural interests—for instance, they are likely to have participated in prestigious chugging contests. They are capable of emotional bonding—mostly with their remote controls, and with their voyeur buddies at wet-T-shirt contests. And they are not incurious about the world: their wanderlust can be aroused by the mere mention of the word "Tijuana."

But these men have not a hint of any 5 quality that might make them attractive to progressive and mature women. Their world has been vacuumed free of empathy, sensitivity, and sophistication. It is as if millions of American men—many of them well educated—took a look at the lifestyle prescribed by modern feminism and decided, No thanks, we'd rather be pigs.

Considering that for at least a generation polite opinion has been unanimous in the view that women should not be objectified, this chauvinist revival is astonishing. What caused it?

Some believe that it is a product of masculinity in crisis. Insecure men, sensing that their position in the world is threatened by a generation of strong women, have reverted to the most offensive and primal versions of manhood. There's clearly something to this theory. But the lack of any sense of crisis in retro-sexist culture is striking. In the 1970s and 1980s men's magazines were notably defensive in the face of the feminist critique. In the newest men's magazines feminism simply doesn't exist. The women's movement is something that happened in Mom and Dad's time. Now the attitude is, Gather up the boys and girls, and let's all be sexist pigs together. Women are allowed to be as open about their sexuality as men: "hooking up" is common; and we're all free to treat one another as sex objects. We men can leer at your breasts, and you women can leer at our buns. We can all be Bob Gueciones, and we'll call it gender equity.

Another theory is that *Maxim*-style retro-sexism is just a self-conscious, deliberately ironic joke. The men are making fun of themselves as much as they are degrading women. Besides, it's not reality. It's just a normal urge to flout convention, to have some bawdy fun. It doesn't mean anything.

There's some truth to this theory, too. Scanning an excerpt from the theme song for *The Man Show* reveals an obviously playful element.

> Grab a beer and drop your pants,
> Send the wife and kid to France,
> It's *The Man Show*!!!
> Quit your job and light a fart,
> Yank your favorite private part,
> It's *The Man Show*!!!

But there is more than irony at work 10 here. Participants in these bits of public theater are somehow simultaneously engaged in both play and not-play. Readers of *Maxim* may put invisible quotation marks around their leering at women, but they are still leering at women. In fact, the quotation marks constitute an easy escape hatch in the event that anyone ever challenges these men. They can say, not least to themselves, "I'm not a crude ogler or a loser porn addict. I'm a hip ironist. I'm playing a media-savvy game, and therefore I have permission to spend hours looking at women in their underwear."

The most interesting thing about the surge of retro-sexism is how unprepared feminists and other enlightened thinkers are to deal with it. The ironic tone of the material defeats them. Feminists seem to know they are being toyed with. They don't want to appear to be earnest plodders in the face of hip, playful gestures, and they don't want to grant that anyone is more postmodern than they are. The British feminist Imelda Whelehan wrote a book on laddie culture called *Overloaded: Popular Culture and the Future of Feminism,* in which she seemed to be completely flummoxed by the phenomenon. "Classic notions of distinctions between the sexes appear to be reinforced, but it is never easy to determine to what extent parody and irony support or undermine those distinctions," she wrote.

I can't entirely blame the feminists for being flummoxed. It *is* hard to figure out how seriously to take this stuff. On the one hand, if your kid spent a lot of time reading *Maxim* and watching rap videos, you'd know in your gut that it was damaging to his soul. On the other hand, human beings, even at young ages, are pretty good at distinguishing fantasy from reality. A young man can listen to Eminem while driving his Camaro, imagine himself as an angry young badass, and then have dinner with his girlfriend and her mom and be perfectly polite and civilized. Eminem himself is regarded by his neighbors as a pillar of the upscale gated community in which he lives.

Another unnerving feature of retro-sexism is that much of it comes from an unexpected direction. Many progressive thinkers, having inherited a century of radical European thought, assume that the most oppressive and reactionary parts of society are the rich, the powerful, and the wellborn. Partly for that reason they have tended to direct their protests against elites. They know how to handle discrimination when it is found among the corporate muckamucks at the country club.

The rise of misogynistic rap culture dramatizes the inadequacy of that approach. The notion that a self-confident elite exercises cultural hegemony over the masses and that big media corporations and advertising geniuses create ideas and products and then manipulate society into accepting them was always badly oversimplified and often completely misleading. Outsiders, from James Dean to Allen Iverson, have an innate appeal. The cultural elites may have money and position, but the definition of cool, and therefore the influence over what will enter the culture, generally comes from the fringes. Rap and hip-hop came from the urban lower class. N.W.A., 2 Live Crew, Tupac Shakur, and Eminem may have been co-opted by record companies, but they emerged authentically from the streets. As it happens, the parts of society that, according to the class-conflict model, should have been the most reactionary—the affluent classes—have been the quickest to adopt progressive mores. It is the least privileged parts of society that are often the most sexist, reactionary, and even materialistic. We have a dynamic urban culture that treats women like whores and that regards owning a Mercedes as the highest possible human aspiration, and the leading articulators of progressive opinion have almost nothing to say about it. They can't seem to bring themselves to admit out loud that their most effective ideological enemies have turned out to be the same underprivileged people they wanted to rescue from exploitation.

To take just one example: Robin Chandler is a member of the Department of African-American Studies at Northeastern University and teaches a course that includes discussion of hip-hop and rap. A 2001 interview with her in *The Boston Globe* included this exchange:

> Q: How about the misogyny, violence, and profanity in much rap?
> A: As professors with an enormous concern for intellectual freedom, we have to be careful not to indoctrinate or moralize while at the same time providing opportunities for people to explore and clarify their values . . .
> Q: You're a peace activist, and some rap glorifies murder.
> A: I object to it in heavy metal, in Hollywood films, and in rap. I've told students that, but

what's important is the construction of classroom debate and allowing students to have an intellectual space where they can argue and understand the other person's position, increase their tolerance for diversity, and defend their preferences with rational explanations.

Society is not run from the top, or from any one place. Instead it involves a complex dance of different groups rebelling and innovating, co-opting and exploiting. Feminists or progressives or conservatives who blame the cultural elites for most of society's ills are attacking a monster that can't control its own movements. The elites are often a step behind, trying to catch up to the real innovators. All of this raises a set of hard-to-answer questions. How do you react when people further down the social pecking order—whether they are disenfranchised whites or underclass urban minorities—are creating a culture you find degrading? How do you criticize that culture without seeming square, elitist, or even racist? No one has figured out the answers.

CONNECTING PERSONALLY TO THE READING

1. Brooks finds it difficult to determine whether images in media such as rap music are meant to be satirical. How can you tell when an image is meant to be satirical? Think of an image of men or women offered by a particular song, and explain why you think it is or is not satirical.

2. Brooks is concerned about what seem to be regressive and disrespectful images of men and women. Can you think of other images or other trends in our culture that counteract this portrayal of men and women? How effective are they?

3. Brooks argues that it is "the least privileged parts of society that are often the most sexist, reactionary, and even materialistic." What does he mean by this statement? In what ways do your own observations confirm or contradict this idea?

4. What trends define "cool" where you live? Does this version of "cool" originate "from the fringes" of society, as Brooks believes is generally the case?

FOCUSING ON THE ARGUMENT

1. Brooks uses a conversational tone, especially at the opening, where he addresses the reader as "you" and opens with a chatty question, as if he were talking directly to us: "Have you noticed that male chauvinism is making a comeback?" What other techniques does he use to achieve this sense of intimacy? Do you find this style appealing? Why or why not?

2. Brooks's argument assumes the reader is familiar with at least some of his references to popular U.S. culture—among them, MTV, Hooters, the Wonderbra, and Howard Stern—and when Brooks mentions them, he expects to evoke a host of associations in the reader's mind. Which of these references are familiar to you, and what associations do you have with them? How do these associations support or invalidate Brooks's argument? Were any of the references unfamiliar to you? What do you think is lost to the reader who does not recognize these references?

3. What is the purpose of the quotation from the *Boston Globe* interview? How do Professor Chandler's remarks reinforce Brooks's thesis?

4. In what ways is Brooks's article an effort to find common cause in competing interpretations? What techniques does he use to give credence to opposing viewpoints and to reconcile them? Are you disappointed that his article ends with questions rather than answers? Why or why not?

SYNTHESIZING IDEAS FROM MULTIPLE READINGS

1. Both Don Sabo ("The Myth of the Sexual Athlete," p. 113) and David Brooks believe that the masculine ideal separates men from women and makes it hard for men to empathize with, let alone understand, women. According to both writers, what in men's experience causes this problem?

2. How might Brooks explain the male behavior Mira Jacob describes in "My Brown Face" (p. 143)?

3. In what ways do the advertisements you've viewed in this book or elsewhere support the contradictions that Brooks describes in his article?

WRITING TO ACT

1. Write a letter to a television network that produces a show whose images of men or women you find encouraging or offensive. Explain why you object to or support these images. Be sure to name the show(s) and to describe the specific images you're referring to.

2. If there is a Hooters or similar restaurant in your area where the employees are required to wear revealing clothing, write a letter to the management, explaining what you believe to be the effect of its clothing policy. Consider interviewing workers to cite firsthand accounts of the policy's effects.

3. Find a trend in your campus or community whose intent is ambiguous—that could be construed as either offensive or satirical. Then write a short editorial for your campus or local newspaper in which you define the problem and explain why it is ambiguous, using the Brooks essay as a model.

LANCE STRATE   Strate argues that beer commercials provide a traditional image of masculinity: they define men as hardworking, physically active—especially in the outdoors, quick to take risks and overcome challenges, and eager to dominate their environment. Beer drinking is shown as a rite of passage for young men, and drinking beer in groups illustrates the value of teamwork as a marker of masculinity. Women are usually outsiders in these commercials, if they appear at all, and the men tend to be unemotional and cool around them. Do you see these images of men in advertising for other products? Do you agree with Strate that this is a limiting definition of masculinity? How do advertisers incorporate messages of male violence into ads for products that are sold to both sexes? Are advertisers beginning to incorporate other versions of ideal masculinity?

STRATE is the Chair of the Communication and Media Studies Department at Fordham University, where he is also a professor. This essay first appeared in the anthology *Men, Masculinity, and the Media* (edited by Steve Craig). Strate has served as editor on a number of books, including *Communication and Cyberspace: Social Interaction in an Electronic Environment* and *Critical Studies in Media Commercialism.*

Beer Commercials:
A Manual on Masculinity (1992) | BY LANCE STRATE

Jocks, rock stars, and pick-up artists; cowboys, construction workers, and comedians; these are some of the major "social types" (Klapp 1962) found in contemporary American beer commercials. The characters may vary in occupation, race, and age, but they all exemplify traditional conceptions of the masculine role. Clearly, the beer industry relies on stereotypes of the man's man to appeal to a mainstream, predominantly male target audience. That is why alternate social types, such as sensitive men, gay men, and househusbands, scholars, poets, and political activists, are noticeably absent from beer advertising. The manifest function of beer advertising is to promote a particular brand, but collectively the commercials provide a clear and consistent image of the masculine role; in a sense, they constitute a guide for becoming a man, a rulebook for appropriate male behavior, in short, a manual on masculinity. Of course, they are not the only source of knowledge on this subject, but nowhere is so much information presented in so concentrated a form as in television's 30-second spots, and no other industry's commercials focus so exclusively and so exhaustively on images of the man's man. . . .

Myths, according to semioticians such as Roland Barthes (1972), are not falsehoods or fairy tales, but uncontested and generally unconscious assumptions that are so widely shared within a culture that they are considered natural, instead of recognized as products of unique historical circumstances. Biology determines whether we are male or female; culture determines what it *means* to be male or female, and what sorts of behavior and personality attributes are appropriate for each gender role. In other words, masculinity is a social construction (Fejes 1989; Kimmel 1987a). The foundation may be biological, but the structure is manmade; it is also flexible, subject to change over time and differing significantly from culture to culture. Myth, as a form of cultural communication is the material out of which such structures are built, and through myth, the role of human beings in inventing and reinventing masculinity is disguised and therefore naturalized (and "biologicized"). The myth of masculinity is manifested in myriad forms of mediated and nonmediated communication; beer commercials are only one such form, and to a large extent, the ads merely reflect pre-existing cultural conceptions of the man's man. But in reflecting the myth, the commercials also reinforce it. Moreover, since each individual expression of a myth varies, beer ads also reshape the myth of masculinity, and in this sense, take part in its continuing construction.

Myths provide ready-made answers to universal human questions about ourselves, our relationships with others and with our environment. Thus, the myth of masculinity answers the question: What does it mean to be a man? This can be broken down into five separate questions: What kinds of things do men do? What kinds of settings do men prefer? How do boys become men? How do men relate to each other? How do men relate to women? Let us now consider the ways in which beer commercials answer these questions.

What kinds of things do men do? Although advertisers are prevented from actually showing an individual drinking beer in a television commercial, there is no question that drinking is presented as a central masculine activity, and beer as the beverage of choice. Drinking, however, is rarely presented as an isolated activity, but rather is associated with a variety of occupational and leisure pursuits, all of which, in one way or another, involve overcoming challenges. In the world of beer commercials, men work hard and they play hard.

Physical labor is often emphasized in these ads, both on and off the job. Busch beer features cowboys riding horses, driving cattle, and performing in rodeos. Budweiser presents a variety of blue-collar types, including construction workers, lumberjacks, and soldiers (as well as skilled laborers and a few white-collar workers). Miller Genuine Draft shows men working as farm hands and piano movers. But the key to work is the challenge it poses, whether to physical strength and endurance, to skill, patience, and craftsmanship, or to wit and competitive drive in the business world. The ads do associate hard work with the American dream of economic success (this theme is particularly strong in Budweiser's campaign), but it is also presented as its own end, reflecting the Puritan work ethic. Men do not labor primarily out of economic necessity nor for financial gain, but rather for the pride of accomplishment provided by a difficult job well done; for the respect and camaraderie of other men (few women are visible in the beer commercial workplace); for the benefit of family, community, and nation; and for the opportunity to demonstrate masculinity by triumphing over the challenges work provides. In short, work is an integral part of a man's identity.

Beer is integrated with the work world in three ways. *First,* it is represented in some commercials as the product of patient, skillful craftsmanship, thus partaking of the virtues associated with the labor that produced it; this is particularly apparent in the Miller beer commercials in which former football player Ed Marinaro takes us on a tour of the Miller brewery. In effect, an identity relationship between beer and labor is established, although this is overshadowed by the identification between beer and nature discussed below. *Second,* beer serves as a reward for a job well done, and receiving a beer from one's peers acts as a symbol of other men's respect for the worker's ac-

5

complishment—"For all you do, this Bud's for you." Beer is seen as an appropriate reward not just because drinking is pleasurable, but because it is identified with labor, and therefore can act as a substitute for labor. Thus, drinking beer at the end of the day is a symbolic reenactment of the successful completion of a day's work. And *third*, beer acts as a marker of the end of the work day, the signal of quitting time ("Miller time"), the means for making the transition from work to leisure ("If you've got the time, we've got the beer"). In the commercials, the celebration of work completed takes on a ritualistic quality, much like saying grace and breaking bread signal the beginning of meal time; opening the can represents the opening of leisure time.

The men of beer commercials fill their leisure time in two ways: in active pursuits usually conducted in outdoor settings (e.g., car and boat racing, fishing, camping, and sports; often symbolized by the presence of sports stars, especially in Miller Lite ads) and in "hanging out," usually in bars. As it is in work, the key to men's active play is the challenge it provides to physical and emotional strength, endurance, and daring. Some element of danger is usually present in the challenge, for danger magnifies the risks of failure and the significance of success. Movement and speed are often a part of the challenge, not only for the increased risk they pose, but also because they require immediate and decisive action and fine control over one's own responses. Thus, Budweiser spots feature automobile racing; Michelob's music video-like ads show cars moving in fast-motion and include lyrics like "I'm overheating, I'm ready to burn, got dirt on my wheels, they're ready to turn"; Old Milwaukee and Budweiser commercials include images of powerboat, sailboat, and canoe racing; Busch beer features cowboys on galloping horses; and Coors uses the slogan, "The Silver Bullet won't slow you down." Activities that include movement and speed, along with displays of coordination, are particularly troubling when associated with beer, in light of social problems such as drinking and driving. Moreover, beer commercials portray men as unmindful of risks, laughing off danger. For example, in two Miller Genuine Draft commercials, a group of young men are drinking and reminiscing; in one they recall the time when they worked as farm hands, loading bales of hay onto a truck, and the large stack fell over. In the other, the memory is of moving a piano, raising it up by rope on the outside of a building to get it into a third-story apartment; the rope breaks and the piano crashes to the ground. The falling bales and falling piano both appear dangerous, but in the ads the men merely joke about the incidents; this attitude is reinforced visually as, in both cases, there is a cut from the past scene to the present one just before the crash actually occurs.

When they are not engaged in physical activity, the men of beer commercials frequently seek out symbolic challenges and dangers by playing games such as poker and pool, and by watching professional sports. The games pose particular challenges to self-control, while spectator sports allow for vicarious participation in the drama of challenge, risk, and triumph. Even when they are merely hanging out together, men engage in verbal jousts that contain a strong element of challenge, either in the form of good-natured arguments (such as Miller Lite's ongoing "tastes great—less filling" conflict) or in ribbing one another, which tests self-control and the ability to "take it." A sense of proportion and humor is required to overcome such challenges, which is why jokers and comedians are a valued social type in the myth of masculinity. Women may also pose a challenge to the man's ability to attract the opposite sex and, more important, to his self-control.

The central theme of masculine leisure activity in beer commercials, then, is challenge, risk, and mastery—mastery over nature, over technology, over others in good-natured "combat," and over oneself. And beer is integrated into this theme in two ways: one obvious, the other far more subtle. At the overt level, beer functions in leisure activities as it does in work: as a reward for challenges successfully overcome (the race completed, the big fish landed, the ribbing returned). But it also serves another function, never explicitly alluded to in commercials. In several ways drinking, in itself, is a test of mastery. Because alcohol affects judgment and slows reaction time, it intensifies the risks inherent in movement and speed, and thereby increases the challenge they represent. And because it threatens self-control, drinking poses heightened opportunities for demonstrating self-mastery. Thus beer is not merely a reward for the successful meeting of a challenge in masculine work and leisure, but is itself an occasion for demonstrating mastery, and thus, masculinity. Beer is an appropriate award for overcoming challenge because it is a challenge itself, and thereby allows a man to symbolically reenact his feat. It would be all but suicidal for advertisers to present drinking as a challenge by which the masculine role can be acted out; instead, they associate beer with other forms of challenge related to the myth of masculinity.

What kinds of settings do men prefer? In beer commercials, the settings most closely associated with masculinity are the outdoors, generally the natural environment, and the self-contained world of the bar. The outdoors is featured prominently as both a workplace and a setting for leisure activity in ads for Busch beer, Old Milwaukee, Miller Genuine Draft, and Budweiser. As a workplace, the natural environment provides suitable challenge and danger for demonstrating masculinity, and the separation from civilization forces men to rely only on themselves. The height of masculinity can be attained when the natural environment and the work environment coincide, that is, when men have to overcome nature in order to survive. That is why the cowboy or frontiersman is the archetypical man's man in our culture. Other work environments, such as the farm, factory, and office, offer their own form of challenge, but physical danger is usually downplayed and the major risk is economic. Challenge and danger are also reduced, but still present, when nature is presented as a leisure environment; male bonding receives greater emphasis, and freedom from civilization becomes freedom for men to behave in a boyish manner.

In the ads, nature is closely associated with both masculinity and beer, as beer is presented as equivalent to nature. Often, beer is shown to be a product that is natural and pure, implying that its consumption is not harmful, and perhaps even healthy. Moreover, a number of beers, including Rolling Rock, [Heineken's] Old Style, and Molson's Golden, are identified with natural sources of water. This identification is taken even further in one Busch beer commercial: We see a cowboy on horseback, herding cattle across a river. A small calf is overcome by the current, but the cowboy is able to withstand the force of the river and come to the rescue. The voice-over says, "Sometimes a simple river crossing isn't so simple. And when you've got him back, it's your turn. Head for the beer brewed natural as a mountain stream." We then see a six-pack pulled out of clear running water, as if by magic. The raging water represents the power and danger of nature, while the mountain stream stands for nature's gentler aspect. Through the voice-over and the image of the hand pulling the six-pack from the water, beer is presented as identical with the stream, as bottled nature. Drinking beer, then, is a relatively safe way of facing the challenge of raging rivers, of symbolically reenacting the taming of the frontier.

Beer is identified with nature in a more general way in the ads for Old Milwaukee, which are usually set in wilderness environments that feature water, such as the Florida Everglades, and Snake River, Wyoming. In each ad, a group of men is engaged in recreational activities such as high-speed air-boating, flat-bottom boat racing, or fishing. Each commercial begins with a voice-over saying something like, "The Florida Everglades and Old Milwaukee both mean something great to these guys." Each ad includes a jingle, which says, "There's nothing like the flavor of a special place and Old Milwaukee beer." In other words, Old Milwaukee is equivalent to the special place. The place is special because it is untouched by civilization, allowing men to engage in forms of recreation not available elsewhere. It therefore must be fairly inaccessible, but since beer is presented as identical to the place, drinking may act as a substitute for actually going there.

Beer is also identified with nature through animals. For example, the symbol of Busch beer, found on its label and in its commercials, is a horse rearing on its hind legs, a phallic symbol that also evokes the idea of the untamed. And in another Busch ad, a young rodeo rider is quickly thrown from his mount; trying to cheer him up, an older cowboy hands him a beer and says, "Here. This one don't buck so hard." Thus, the identification of beer and nature is made via the horse. Drinking beer is like rodeo-riding, only less strenuous. It is a challenge that the rider can easily overcome, allowing him to save face and reaffirm masculinity. Budweiser beer also uses horses as a symbol: The Budweiser Clydesdales, a breed of "draft" horse. Whereas the Busch Stallion represents the frontier wilderness, the Clydesdales stand for the pastoral. Also, Colt 45 malt liquor, by its very name, invokes images of the Old West, horses, and of course guns, another phallic symbol. Another way in which beer is identified with nature and animals is through Budweiser's "Spuds McKenzie" and Stroh's "Alex," both dogs that behave like humans; both are in turn identified with masculinity as they are male characters, and canines are the animals most closely associated with masculinity.

As a setting for masculine activity, the bar runs a close second to nature, and many commercials seem to advertise bar patronage as much as they do a particular brand of beer. Of course, the drinking hall has a venerable history in Western culture as a center for male socializing and tests of skill, strength, and drinking ability. It is a setting featured prominently in the myths and legends of ancient Greece, and in Norse and Old English sagas. The pub is a popular setting in British literature, as is the saloon in the American Western genre. Like its predecessors, the bar of the beer commercial is presented as a male-dominated environment, although it sometimes serves as a setting for male-female interaction. And it is generally portrayed as a relaxed and comfortable context for male socializing, as well as a place where a man can find entertainment and excitement. The bars are immaculate and smokeless, and the waitresses and bartenders are always friendly; thus, along with nature, bars are the ideal male leisure environment. The only exception is the Bud Light bar, where men who are so uninformed as to ask for "a light" rather than a specific brand are subjected to pranks by the bartenders; still, even in this case the practical jokes are taken in stride, reaffirming the customer's masculinity.

It is worth noting that in the romanticized barroom of beer commercials, no one   15
ever pays for his drinks, either literally or in terms of alcohol's effects. In other words,
there are no consequences to the men's actions, which is consistent with the myth of
masculinity's tendency to ignore or downplay risk and danger. The bar is shown as a
self-contained environment, one that, like the outdoors, frees men from the constraints of civilization, allowing them to behave irresponsibly. Moreover, most settings
featured as drinking-places in beer commercials are probably places that people would
drive to—and drive home from. Because the action is confined to these settings, however, the question of how people arrived and how they will get home never comes up.

How do boys become men? In the world of beer commercials, boys become men
by earning acceptance from those who are already full-fledged members of the community of men. Adult men are identified by their age, their size, their celebrity, and
their positions of authority in the work world and/or status in a bar. To earn acceptance, the younger man must demonstrate that he can do the things that men do: take
risks, meet challenges, face danger courageously, and dominate his environment. In
the workplace, he demonstrates this by seizing opportunities to work, taking pride in
his labor, proving his ability, persisting in the face of uncertainty, and learning to accept failure with equanimity. Having proven that he can act out the masculine role, the
initiate is rewarded with beer. As a reward, beer symbolizes the overcoming of a challenge, the fulfilling of the requirements for group membership. The gift of beer also
allows the adult male to show his acceptance of the initiate without becoming emotional. Beer then functions as a symbol of initiation and group membership.

For example, one of Budweiser's most frequently aired commercials during the
1980s features a young Polish immigrant and an older foreman and dispatcher. In the
first scene, the dispatcher is reading names from a clipboard, giving workers their assignments. Arriving late, which earns him a look of displeasure from the foreman, the
nervous young man takes a seat in the back. When he is finally called, the dispatcher
stumbles over the immigrant's foreign name. The young man walks up to the front of
the room, corrects the dispatcher's mispronunciation—a risky move, given his neophyte status, but one that demonstrates his pride and self-confidence. He receives his
assignment, and the scene then shifts to a montage of the day's work. At the beginning, he drops a toolbox, spilling its contents, a mishap noted by the foreman; by the
end of the day, however, he has demonstrated his ability and has earned the respect of
his co-workers. The final scene is in a crowded tavern; the young man walks through
the door, making his way to the bar, looking around nervously. He hears his name
called, turns around, and the foreman, sitting at the bar, hands him a beer. In both the
first and final scene, the immigrant begins at the back of the room, highlighting his
outsider status, and moves to the front as he is given a chance to prove himself. The
commercial's parallelism is not just an aesthetic device, but a mythic one as well. Having mastered the challenge of work, the neophyte receives the reward of a beer, which
is both a symbol of that mastery and an invitation to symbolically reenact his feat. By
working hard and well, he gains acceptance in the work world; by drinking the beer, he
can also gain acceptance into the social world of the bar. The foreman, by virtue of his
age, his position of authority, and his position sitting at the bar in the center of the
tavern, holds the power of confirmation in both worlds.

The theme of initiation is also present in a subtle way in the Bud Light ads in
which someone orders "a light," is given a substitute such as lamp or torch, and then

corrects himself, asking for a "Bud Light." As one of the commercials revealed, the bartenders play these pranks because they are fed up with uninformed customers. The bizarre substitutions are a form of hazing, an initiation into proper barroom etiquette. The mature male is familiar with brands of beer, knows what he wants, and shows decisiveness in ordering it. Clearly, the individuals who ask for "a light" are inexperienced drinkers, and it is important to keep in mind that, to the barroom novice (and especially to the underage drinker), bars and bartenders can seem very threatening. While the substitute "lights" come as a surprise to the patrons, and thus threaten their composure, they are a relatively mild threat. The customers are able to overcome this challenge to their self-control, correct their order, and thereby gain entry into barroom society.

The biological transition from childhood to adulthood is a gradual one, but in traditional cultures, it is symbolized by formal rituals of initiation, rites of passage which mark the boundary between childhood and adulthood, clearly separating these two social positions. In our own culture, there are no initiation rites, and therefore the adolescent's social position is an ambiguous one. A number of events and activities do serve as symbols of adulthood, however. The commercials emphasize entry into the work world as one such step; financial independence brings the freedom of adulthood, while work is an integral part of the adult male's identity. As a symbol of initiation into the work world, beer also functions as a symbol of adulthood. And although this is never dealt with in the commercials, drinking in and of itself is a symbol of adulthood in our culture, as is driving, particularly in the eyes of underage males. Bars are seen as exclusively adult environments, and so acceptance in bars is a further sign of manhood. In the commercials, bars and workplaces complement each other as environments in which initiation into adulthood can be consummated.

How do men relate to each other? In beer commercials, men are rarely found in 　20 solitary pursuits (and never drink alone), and only occasionally in one-to-one relationships, usually involving father-son or mentor-protégé transactions. The dominant social context for male interaction is the group, and teamwork and group loyalty rank high in the list of masculine values. Individualism and competition, by contrast, are downplayed, and are acceptable only as long as they foster the cohesiveness of the group as a whole. Although differences in status may exist between members of the group and outsiders, within the group equality is the rule, and elitism and intellectualism are disdained. This reflects the American value of egalitarianism and solidifies the importance of the group over individual members. The concept of group loyalty is extended to community and to country, so that patriotism is also presented as an important value for men.

The emotional tenor of relationships among men in beer commercials is characterized by self-restraint. Generally, strong emotions are eschewed, especially overt displays of affection. In the workplace, mutual respect is exhibited, but respect must be earned through ability and attitude. In leisure situations, humor is a major element in male interactions. Conversations among men emphasize joking, bragging, storytelling, and good-natured insults. The insults are a form of symbolic challenge; taking a ribbing in good spirit is a demonstration of emotional strength and self-mastery. By providing a controlled social context for the exchange of challenges and demonstrations of ego strength and self-control, the group provides continuous reinforcement of the members' masculinity. Moreover, gathering in groups provides men with the freedom to act irresponsibly; that is, it allows men to act like boys. This is particularly the case in the Miller Lite ads that feature retired sports stars, comedians, and other celebrities.

In beer commercials, drinking serves several important functions in promoting group solidarity. Beer is frequently the shared activity that brings the group together, and in the ads for Miller Genuine Draft, sharing beer acts as a reminder of the group's identity and history. Thus, beer becomes a symbol of group membership. It also serves as a means for demonstrating the group's egalitarian values. When one man gives a beer to another, it is a sign of acceptance, friendship, or gratitude. In this role, beer is also a substitute for overt display of affection. Although the commercials never deal with why beer takes on this role, the answer lies in the effects of alcohol. Certainly, its function as mood enhancer can have a positive influence on group interaction. And, as previously discussed, alcohol itself constitutes a challenge, so that drinking allows each member of the group to publicly demonstrate his masculinity. Alcohol also lowers inhibitions, making it easier for men to show their affection for one another. The well-known saying that you cannot trust a man who does not drink reflects the popular conception that under the influence of alcohol, men become more open and honest. Moreover, the effects of drinking on physical coordination make a man less of an immediate threat. All these properties contribute to beer's role as a medium of male bonding and a facilitator of group solidarity.

In general, men are not portrayed as loners in beer commercials, and in this respect the ads differ markedly from other expressions of the myth of masculinity. There are no isolated Marlboro men in the Busch frontier, for example, When he saves the calf from being swept away by the river, the Busch cowboy appears to be on his own, but by the time he is ready for his reward, another cowboy has appeared out of nowhere to share his beer. In another Busch ad, a jingle with the following lyrics is heard: "There's no place on earth that I'd rather be, than out in the open where it's all plain to see, if it's going to get done it's up to you and me." In this way, the ideal of individual self-reliance that is so central to the American myth of the frontier is transformed into group self-reliance. In the world of beer commercials, demonstrating one's masculinity requires an audience to judge one's performance and confirm one's status. Moreover, the emphasis the ads place on beer drinking as a group activity undermines the idea that it is in any way problematic. One of the most widespread stereotypes of problem drinkers is that they are solitary and secretive loners. The emphasis on the group in beer commercials plays on the common misconception that drinking, when it is done socially and publicly, cannot be harmful.

How do men relate to women? Although the world of beer commercials is often monopolized by men, some of the ads do feature male-female interaction in the form of courtship, as well as in more established relationships. When courtship is the focus, the image of the man's man gives way to that of the ladies' man, for whom seduction is the highest form of challenge. And while the obvious risk in courtship is rejection by the opposite sex, the more significant danger in beer ads is loss of emotional self-control. The ladies' man must remain cool, confident, and detached when faced with the object of his desires. This social type is exemplified by Billy Dee Williams, who plays on his romantic image in Colt 45 commercials. Strangely enough, Spuds McKenzie, Budweiser's "party animal," also fits into this category, insofar as he, like Alex, is treated like a human being. In his ads, Spuds is surrounded by the Spudettes, three beautiful young women who dance with him, serve him, even bathe him. The women are attractive enough to make most males salivate like Pavlov's dogs, but Spuds receives their attentions with casual indifference (and never betrays the insecurities that haunt his cousin Snoopy when the *Peanuts* dog assumes his "Joe Cool" persona). While the commercials do not go so far as to suggest bestiality, there is no question that Spuds is a stud.

Emotional control is also demonstrated by the male's ability to divide his atten- 25 tion. For example, in one Michelob commercial, a young woman is shown leaning over a jukebox and selecting a song; her expression is one of pure pleasure, and she seems lost in thought. Other scenes, presumably her memories, show her dancing in the arms of a handsome young man. His arms are around her neck, and he is holding in one hand, behind her back, a bottle of beer. This image emphasizes the difference between the myths of masculinity and femininity; her attention is focused entirely on him, while his interests extend to the beer as well as the woman. According to the myth of masculinity, the man who loses control of his emotions in a relationship is a man who loses his independence, and ultimately, his masculinity; dividing attention is one way to demonstrate self-control. Michelob also presents images of ladies' men in the form of popular musicians, such as the rock group Genesis, rock star Eric Clapton, and popular vocalist Frank Sinatra. Many male pop stars have reputations as sexual athletes surrounded by groupies; in the ads, however, they function as modern troubadours, providing a romantic backdrop for lovers and facilitating social interaction. Acting, like Spuds McKenzie, as mascots for the beer companies, they imply that the beer they are identified with serves the same functions.

By far the most sexist of beer commercials, almost to the point of farce, are the Colt 45 ads featuring Billy Dee Williams. One of these, which is divided into three segments, begins with Williams saying: "There are two rules to remember if you want to have a good time: Rule number one, never run out of Colt 45. Rule number two, never forget rule number one." In the next segment, Williams continues: "You want to know why you should keep plenty of Colt 45 on hand? You never know when friends might show up." As he says this, he opens a can and a woman's hand reaches out and takes it. In the third segment, he concludes, "I don't claim you can have a better time with Colt 45 than without it, but why take chances?" As he says this, the camera pulls back to reveal Williams standing, and an attractive woman sitting next to him. The ad ends with a picture of a Colt 45 can and the slogan, "The power of Colt 45: It works every time." There are a number of ways to interpret this pitch. First, malt liquor has a higher alcohol content than beer or ale, and therefore is a more *powerful* beverage. Second, the ad alludes to alcohol's image as an aphrodisiac, despite the fact that it actually reduces male potency. As noted, the Colt 45 pistol is a phallic symbol, while the slogan can be read as a guarantee against impotency—"it works every time." Third, it can be seen as referring to alcohol's ability to make men feel more confident about themselves and more interested in the opposite sex. And fourth, it plays on the popular notion that getting a woman drunk increases her desire for and willingness to engage in sex. Williams keeps Colt 45 on hand not just for himself, but for "friends," meaning "women." His secret of seduction is getting women to drink. In the ad, the woman is eager to drink Colt 45, implying that she will be just as eager to make love. The idea that a woman who drinks is "looking for it" is even clearer in a second ad.

This commercial begins with the title "Billy Dee Williams on Body Language." Moving through an outdoor party, Williams says, "You know, body language tells you a lot about what a person is thinking. For instance, that means she has an interest in the finer things in life." As he says this, the camera pans to show an attractive woman sitting at a bar alone, holding her necklace. She shifts her position and strokes her hair, and Williams says, "That means she also wants a little fun in her life, but only with the right man." At this point, the woman fills her glass with Colt 45, as Williams says, "And now she's pouring Colt 45 and we all know what that means." He then goes over to her and asks if she would mind if he joined her, and she replies, "You must have read my mind." Williams responds, "Something like that," and the ad ends with the same slogan as the first. What is implied in this commercial is that any woman who would sit by herself and drink must be looking to get picked up; she is sending out signals and preparing herself to be seduced. And although she is making herself approachable, she must wait for Williams to make the first move. At the same time, the woman appears to be vain, fondling her jewelry and hair. And in both ads, the women are seated while Williams stands. This portrayal of the woman's woman, based on the myth of femininity, is the perfect counterpart to Williams' image as a ladies' man.

When the commercials depict more established relationships, the emphasis shifts from romance and seduction to male activities in which women are reduced largely to the role of admiring onlookers. Men appear to value their group of friends over their female partners, and the women accept this. Women tend to be passive, not participating but merely watching as men perform physical tasks. In other words, they become the audience for whom men perform. For the most part, women know their place and do not interfere with male bonding. They may, however, act as emotional catalysts for male interaction, bringing men together. Occasionally, a woman may be found together with a group of men, presumably as the girlfriend or wife of one of the group members. Here, the presence of women, and their noninterference, indicates their approval of masculine activity and male bonding, and their approval of the role of beer in these situations. Even when a group of men acts irresponsibly and/or boyishly, the presence of a woman shows that this behavior is socially sanctioned.

Alternate images of femininity can be found in beer commercials, but they are generally relegated to the background; for the most part, the traditional roles of masculinity and femininity are upheld. One exception is a Michelob Light ad that features Madeline Kahn. Introduced by a male voice-over, "Madeline Kahn on having it all," she is lying on her side on a couch, wearing an expensive-looking gown and necklace, and holding a bottle of beer. Kahn does a short humorous monologue in which she acknowledges her wealth and glamour, and the scene shifts to a shot of the beer, as the male voice-over says, "Michelob Light. You *can* have it all." While this represents something of a concession to changing conceptions of femininity, the advertisers hedge their bets. The male voice-over frames, and in a sense controls, Kahn's monologue, while Kahn's position, lying on her side, is a passive and seductive one. To male viewers, the commercial can easily imply that "having it all" includes having a woman like her.

CONCLUSION

In the world of beer commercials, masculinity revolves around the theme of challenge, an association that is particularly alarming, given the social problems stemming from

30

alcohol abuse. For the most part beer commercials present traditional, stereotypical images of men, and uphold the myths of masculinity and femininity. Thus, in promoting beer, advertisers also promote and perpetuate these images and myths. Although targeted at an adult audience, beer commercials are highly accessible to children; between the ages of 2 and 18, American children may see as many as 100,000 of these ads (Postman et al. 1987). They are also extremely attractive to children: humorous, exciting, and offering answers to questions about gender and adulthood. And they do have an impact, playing a role in social learning and attitude formation (Wallack, Cassady, & Grube 1990). As Postman (1979) argues, television constitutes a curriculum, one that children spend more time with than in schoolrooms. Beer commercials are a prominent subject in television's curriculum, a subject that is ultimately hazardous to the intellectual as well as the physical health of the young. The myth of masculinity *does* have a number of redeeming features (facing challenges and taking risks are valuable activities in many contexts), but the unrelenting one-dimensionality of masculinity as presented by beer commercials is clearly anachronistic, possibly laughable, but without a doubt sobering.

References

Atkin, C. K. (1987). Alcoholic-beverage advertising: Its content and impact. *Advances in Substances Abuse (Suppl.) 1*, 267–287.

Barthes, R. (1972). *Mythologies* (A. Lavers, Ed. and Trans.). New York: Hill & Wang. (Original work published 1957).

Craig, S. (1987, March). *Marketing American masculinity; Mythology and flow in the Super Bowl telecasts.* Paper presented at the annual meeting of the Popular Culture Association, Montreal.

Fejes, F. (1989). Images of men in media research. *Critical Studies in Mass Communication, 6*(2), 215–221.

Finn, T. A., & Strickland, D. (1983). The advertising and alcohol abuse issue: A cross media comparison of alcohol beverage advertising content. M. Burgeon (Ed.), *Communication yearbook* (850–872). Beverly Hills, CA: Sage.

Hacker, G. A., Collins, R., & Jacobson, M. (1987). Marketing booze to blacks. Washington, DC: Center for Science in the Public Interest.

Jacobsen, M., Atkins, R., Hacker, G. (1983). *The booze merchants: The inebriating of America.* Washington, DC: Center for Science in the Public Interest.

Kimmel, M. (Ed.) (1987). *Changing men: New directions in research on men and masculinity.* Newbury Park, CA: Sage.

Klapp, Orrin E. (1962). Heroes, villains, and fools: The changing American character. Englewood Cliffs, NJ: Prentice-Hall.

Postman, Neil. (1979). Teaching as a conserving activity. New York: Dell.

Postman, Neil, et al. (1987). Myths, men, and beer. Washington, DC: AAA Foundation for Traffic Safety.

Strate, L. (1989). The mediation of nature and culture in beer commercials. *New Dimensions in Communications, Proceedings of the 47th Annual New York State Speech Communication Association Conference 3,* 92–95.

Strate, L. (1990, October). *The cultural meaning of beer commercials.* Paper presented at the Advances in Consumer Research Conference, New York.

Wallace, L. Cassady, D., & Grube, J. W. (1990). T.V. beer commercials and children: Exposure, attention, beliefs, and expectations about drinking as an adult. Washington, DC: AAA Foundation for Traffic Safety.

Wenner, L. (1991). One part alcohol, one part sport, one part dirt, stir gently: Beer commercials as television sports. In L. R. Vande Berg & L. Wenner (Eds.), *Television criticism: Approaches and applications.* New York: Longman.

1. Watch a beer commercial on TV. Which, if any, of the male attributes described in Strate's essay do you see?

2. Watch a beer commercial. Then imagine changing the gender of the people in the commercial. How does the gender change affect your reaction to the ad?

FOCUSING ON THE ARGUMENT

1. Early in the article, Strate discusses the purpose of myth in our culture. What does this discussion of myth have to do with Strate's analysis of beer commercials?

2. Strate is writing to an audience of academics in the social sciences. What features of the writing style seem especially tailored to this audience?

SYNTHESIZING IDEAS FROM MULTIPLE READINGS

1. Compare the images of femininity offered in the advertisements Jean Kilbourne describes in "'The More You Subtract, The More You Add'" (p. 149) with the images of masculinity presented in beer commercials. Is there any overlap in the male and female images, or are men and women, according to the ads being described, opposites?

2. In "The Return of the Pig" (p. 122), David Brooks argues that the male "chauvinist revival" he observes includes a return to "the most offensive and primal versions of manhood." Do any of the masculine attributes illustrated in the beer commercials fit this description? Why or why not?

WRITING TO ACT

1. Create a poster composed of advertisements showing men acting in nonstereotypical ways—for example, sitting reflectively alone or being overwhelmed by nature. Include text in which you explain the significance of this depiction.

2. What is the role of beer drinking in your campus community? What other rites of masculinity do you see in campus living groups or elsewhere in your community? Do you think these roles and rites should be changed? Why or why not? Write an editorial for your school newspaper in answer to these questions.

READING

CINDY JACKSON   As a child, Cindy Jackson dreamed of being as glamorous as her Barbie doll. After receiving an inheritance at the age of thirty-three, Jackson began what became a series of cosmetic surgeries and procedures: eye lifts, reshaping of the nose and jaw, chin reduction, facelifts, lip enhancement, cheek implants, breast implants, fat transfers, and liposuction, among others. Jackson argues that these cosmetic procedures not only transformed her appearance but, by making her beautiful, also brought her love, respect, career opportunities, and entrance into glamorous society.

In the following interview, Jackson describes her postsurgery self as "the real me" and her previous self as "dead": "I cut her up." Do you agree with Jackson that a major change in physical appearance can transform one's identity? Generally, do you think we can leave old selves behind and fashion new ones? How has a change in appearance, even a small and short-lived one, made you feel different about yourself?

JACKSON grew up in Ohio and moved to England to study. On her Web site www.cindyjackson.com are photographs of her as a child and as an adult and a description of her career as a singer, cosmetic surgery consultant, and celebrity.

My Cosmetic Surgery
(interview with Danny Danziger)

BY CINDY JACKSON

Cindy Jackson was speaking to Danny Danziger.

I have a sister who is three years older than me and very pretty. I always noticed that people talked to her first. I used to think it was because she was the oldest, but it was because she was pretty, and people are attracted to a pretty face. Boys started calling up for her at about 13 or 14, but no one called me. The guys I liked, the football players, the good-looking guys, they were with the cute girls who were cheerleaders, the pretty girls. I couldn't get the attention of the popular boys, because I wasn't pretty. I had a hard, masculine face.

More than anything, I wanted to be one of the in crowd, one of the pretty girls. But they were kind; they let me hang around with them. I remember a girl named Leslie Dye, she had the most perfect turned-up nose. Mine was big, it had no curves to it. I would go home and pull up my nose in front of the mirror and see what I looked like with Leslie's nose. There was a girl with really good lips, Sue Robitski. I would have liked her lips. Mine were very thin.

I would have taken their faces feature by feature, the one girl who had it all was Tina Chevalier. She was perfect. In fact, she looked like Barbie. She had blonde hair that was swept across her forehead, turned-up nose, full lips, and wide clear eyes. I had a problem with my eyes. I used to have tissue around my eyes that retained water, so I had slitty little puffy eyes. I hated those the most.

I never considered cosmetic surgery 5 until my father died in 1988 and left me a small inheritance when I was 33. The first thing I had done was my eyes. Once I saw how my eyes could look, and that I really could change my face, I started planning to have everything done I possibly could. I embarked on a marathon of surgery. With my youth slipping away, I thought: if it all goes horribly wrong, even if I die under the anaesthetic, I've got absolutely nothing to lose.

A man does not have to be good-looking to get a woman, or to get ahead in life. But men value women for their looks. And it's a man's world. I decided to turn myself into something more desirable in this society. If you have a woman who doesn't have looks or money, she's a two-time loser. But if you have a woman who has nothing and you give her looks, for a lot of men, that's enough. They don't even need a brain. That's optional.

As far as choosing which operation to have, I was spoilt for choice. The eyes had bothered me the most. Secondly it was the nose, so I had my nose turned up. I wasn't happy with the first nose job; it

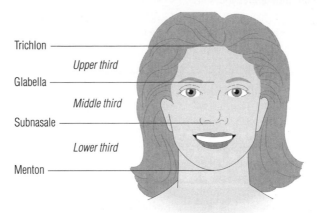

Trichlon
Upper third
Glabella
Middle third
Subnasale
Lower third
Menton

had only made it slightly smaller. So I had it done again and they took more bone out and made my nostrils smaller. My chin bothered me a lot, too. In profile, the chin should be in line from the upper lip, but mine was too far forward; so in this operation, an incision was made along by my lower teeth and the jaw was sawn apart by a circular saw and moved backwards and pinned into place.

I started working on other sections, like my knees: in my 30's I had the usual fat deposits a woman gets. So I had lots and lots of liposuction. The abdominal one hurts quite a bit because it bruises the abdominal muscles, but it got rid of my potbelly, so it was a trade-off—no pain, no gain. I had a lower face-lift because my jaw was a little slack, then I had my lower eyes redone because they needed tightening up again; I had chemical peels to take off one of the layers of my skin because I had freckles and scarring from chickenpox.

I tried collagen injections in my lips but they weren't long lasting, so I had my lower lip cut open and a Teflon implant put into it. I had my upper lip lifted. Then I had fat taken from my thighs and butt and injected into my upper lip and nose to mouth lines. Then I had cheek implants to give me high cheekbones. I also had breast implants, but I had them removed, because they were hard. I never did like them. Besides, I noticed more men staring at me whenever I had my lips enlarged; it's a sexier operation than breast implants.

I had phases where I looked like cer- 10 tain people as my appearance changed. People would tell me I was beginning to look like Ivana Trump or Barbie. But whoever I looked like, I certainly did not look like me, the old me. I was getting better and better looking.

To my amazement, I started getting successful professional men after me, men with money. Those men would not have seen me before. I can remember so many times I'd be out with a guy, walking down the street, and when a prettier girl walked by they would turn and look them up and down. That really used to hurt. I was the sort of woman men would use. Men were unfaithful to me even though I did everything for them: cooked for them, ironed their clothes, did their laundry, scrubbed their floors. Ugly girls have to try harder.

I don't do any of that now. Pretty girls don't have to. I quit letting men treat me like a doormat. Instead of me always being the one trying to please the guy, now men are trying to please me. They bring me flowers, they take me to nice restaurants, they pay me compliments. It means I have the sort of power that I never had before. If a man's going to be with me now, it's going to be because he's going to enrich my life. And now I find that I'm the one men are looking at, and the guy I am with is much more at-tentive, and he realises that if he doesn't treat me right I'll be off. For me, it's a personal triumph. It's saying: okay now I have my ticket into this world, I've got the door open now. I've made myself into Miss Right and I won't settle for anything less than Mr. Right.

This is the real me. I felt like a misfit in my old face and body; it never felt right. This is the way I want to live, and I couldn't do it with my old face and body.

I don't even associate myself with that person. She's dead. I cut her up.

1. Look at Cindy Jackson's photograph. To what extent do you think she resembles a Barbie doll? How would you define Jackson's ideal of female beauty? In what ways is your image of female beauty like or unlike Jackson's? How has this image affected your life?

2. From what you've experienced, are physically beautiful people more likely than less attrac-tive ones to get what they want?

3. Why do you think Jackson speaks so violently of her former self: "I don't even associate myself with that person. She's dead. I cut her up."?

1. As you read this interview, what reactions do you have to Jackson's reasoning and evi-dence, especially to her matter-of-fact telling about the details of her surgeries? Whether or not you agree with her views, do you find her story compelling? How do you account for your reaction?

2. How does the photograph of Cindy Jackson influence your reaction to her argument?

3. Visit www.cindyjackson.com and read about Jackson's interests and accomplishments beyond her association with the cosmetic surgery industry. How do these details give depth to her character and values? Do they change your reaction to her interview? Why or why not?

SYNTHESIZING IDEAS FROM MULTIPLE READINGS

1. Do you think Jackson is a brilliant, (literally) self-made woman and entrepreneur or a victim of a shallow cultural value system, unhappy childhood, and "images, designed to sell products" (Susan Bordo, "The Empire of Images in Our World of Bodies," p. 169)? Explain.

2. Jackson admires a girl she describes as "perfect . . . she looked like Barbie" and later is pleased when she herself is compared to Barbie. Jean Kilbourne ("'The More You Subtract, the More You Add,'" p. 149) believes that efforts to look perfect are futile and destructive: "many girls spend an enormous amount of time and energy attempting to achieve something that is not only trivial but also completely unattainable." How can you reconcile these two views?

3. In "'The More You Subtract, the More You Add'" (p. 149), Jean Kilbourne criticizes advertising for objectifying women, for encouraging them to believe that they "can and should remake [their] bodies into perfect commodities." Do you think that Jackson is objectifying herself when she speaks of her body as parts to be worked on? What in her interview might suggest a more complex person?

WRITING TO ACT

1. Perhaps as a group project, research a common cosmetic medical procedure (e.g., liposuction, Botox injections). Taking note of the risks and potential benefits, write a letter to potential patients (a specific person, if you know one; if not, an open letter to your community) supporting, attacking, or taking a neutral stance on this procedure.

2. Analyze several magazine advertisements for cosmetic medical procedures. What hopes, fears, and values do the ads appeal to? Who are the ads directed to? How are they effective? Ineffective? Write a revised advertisement for the procedure and submit it to the advertising agency.

READING

MIRA JACOB   Mira Jacob writes of her struggle to assert her personal identity when she is pursued by men who expect her, as an Indian American woman, to be a "mystery, waiting to be unfolded." As you read this piece, consider how assumptions about race or ethnicity can complicate ideas about a person's gender. Why does Jacob find it so hard to "evolve in a world that will never stop assuming" her identity? Why do the strangers who harass Jacob behave as if they have the right to do so? What assumptions do they make about Indian women? Why does Jacob feel like an outsider both in India and in the United States?

JACOB, a former writer for VH1's "Pop-Up Video," has contributed essays to numerous periodicals and books, including *Adios, Barbie: Young Women Write about Body Image and Identity*. She is the coauthor of Kenneth Cole's memoir, *Footnotes: What You Stand for Is More Important Than What You Stand In*.

My Brown Face (1998) | BY MIRA JACOB

Next time, I'm going to walk into that warehouse and snap my tongue like a honeyed whip. I'm going to unfurl with grace and fury. I will stand in the dead center of the room, and I will say:

Obviously, you were raised in a goddamn barn. Haven't any of you boys ever gotten near a woman, or was your leash too short? Well, I know you've never come close to my kind because you would know better than to hiss "Hey, Indi" at my passing shadow, or try that where-you-from-baby line with that don't-I-know-it look in your eye. And the next time you see me . . .

Welcome to my morning fantasy. It starts about forty feet from my door and continues between Brooklyn and Sixth Avenue, occasionally bubbling to the surface in waves of "goddamn." It keeps me occupied on the subway and preoccupied at my desk, my mind shuffling out the endless possibilities of what I'll do next time. By mid-afternoon I've usually pep-rallied myself into a proud-to-be Indian state of mind, and by nightfall, in an act of denial or resilience, I've let the whole ritual slip away. Survival of the forgetful.

Worse things have happened in this world, to be sure. A steady tap on my remote control informs me of the multitudes of hell that have yet to befall me. My family hasn't been torn apart by war and disease. I'm not under persecution for my political beliefs, and next to "Mama, Stop Screwing my Boyfriend," even my Ricki Lake potential seems small.

"Mira, you say you feel betrayed by your face?" Ricki asks.   5

"Yes, I do, Ricki," I reply.

"And can you tell the members of our audience what that means?" she asks, gesturing to the rows of scrutiny, hard gazes and arms folded over chests.

"Well, every morning, the guys on the corner scream, 'Indi' at me and ask me what style we go for down there, and some mornings I just can't take it."

"Can't take it. Now what does that mean, Mira? What's the worst thing you've done as a result of this?" Ricki gives me a concerned look.

"Uh, nothing, really, it's a more internal kind of thing."   10

"Okay," Ricki says, not missing a beat. "Our next guest says she is being poisoned by her six-month-old baby. Give a big welcome to . . ."

No, my problem is straightforward and undramatically simple: I was born with a mysterious face. My deep brown eyes and skin, the thick line of my black eyebrows and the slant of my cheekbones have always been described to me as exotic, haunting, elusive. From the day I hit puberty, my Indian-ness has labeled me a box full of secrets, left me wrapped as a package of woman labeled "the other." Why are Indian women mysterious? To answer that question I would have to be outside of myself, claiming a territory I don't inhabit—American, male, most often white. As all outsiders do, I can only hazard a guess, regurgitating the perceptions fed to me: Indian women are quiet, graceful, serene and tranquilized by a thousand blue-skinned gods. We are bent heads looking slyly downward, almond eyes and lotus lips tender with secret knowledge. We are fabulous cooks cloaked in layers of bright silk, bangles dangling in permanent dance from our lithe arms. We are mystery, waiting to be unfolded.

Seattle, late afternoon. The man on the corner is staring at me. I can feel his eyes traveling up my leg, over my stomach and chest, to my face. A smile spread over his face, and I give all my attention to the red DON'T WALK sign across the street.

"Hey, you're Indian, right?" he asks in greeting, stepping in front of me. I walk around him and wait for the light to turn. "Hey, what's up, you don't speak English? I'm just asking you a question. Where are you from?"

I stare at the stoplight, the row of buildings just beyond it. I stare at the businessmen walking around me and glance down at my watch.

"What time is it? Hey, what time is it, baby?" he asks. A slow pool of people gathers at the corner, and the man talks louder, laughing. "Hey, girl, hey! What time is it where you're from? Nighttime?" 15

A quick heat rises to my face, and I watch the cars pass. Two men in suits turn their heads slightly, their eyes scanning my face.

"What, you can't speak to me?" he asks, pushing his face next to mine. He smells like mint gum, sweat and city.

The next time I'm going to look right at you. I'm going to stare into your eyes and wait through twenty lights, and when you are finally mute and embarrassed, I'll walk on.

I wait for the light to turn, my stomach churning, the pulse in my ears growing louder.

"You too good to speak to me? That it?" 20

The WALK sign lights up, and I spring forward, hoping he'll stay behind. He does. "Hey!" he yells after me. "You don't look that good, bitch."

I've been unfolded to the point of splitting. I've had my lid thrust open, my contents investigated by prying eyes, hands, lips. Concealed in compliments, come-ons, gifts, I've been asked to explain the wave of enigma my country of origin arouses in the minds of others.

Indophiles, my Indian friends call the more persistent among them. "Tell me about you," these men ask, the sophisticated version of "Where are you from?" Half listening as I rattle off about anything but my ethnicity, they nod knowingly, more interested in my looks than anything I say. I can see it in them, the hunger for a quiet woman, an erotic encounter, a spicy dish. Some men don't even bother with the formalities, cutting to the chase. "Indian," a man in a bar once said, nodding to me. Then, by way of invitation, his mouth pressed hot against my ear, "*Kamasutra?*"

My mother laughs a tired laugh when I tell her this, her voice weary through the crackling phone line. "Oh, men will do that. You're exciting to them because you're something they do not know, an Indian woman."

An Indian woman. I have been to India several times, and I have watched my aunts and cousins with a mixture of curiosity and awe. I've heard their sing-song chatter and loud-mouthed gossip, watched their deft fingers plucking endless batches of coriander leaves. And while they've never consciously excluded me, my ear cannot follow the lilting mother-tongue conversations, my laugh among them is much too loud. They teasingly call me a tomboy and warn that I may end up marrying my truck, a possibility that repulses them as much as it excites me. Simply put, our graces are instinctually different. My bones and flesh hold the precious truth of a history I can claim more in blood than in experience. 25

Funny that some men can latch on to a part of me I'm still trying to locate. My brown face has made me the recipient of numerous gifts and cryptic cards, mostly from guys I've met in passing. Broken bird wings, wire necklaces and wine bottles filled with rose petals have all found their way to my doorstep, fervid notes tucked under the windshield of my truck. I once opened up a cardboard box to find shattered mirror pieces glued in careful mosaic inside, my own shocked face staring back at me.

Oh, but those gifts were fun when I was younger, in my teens. Just the thought of some stranger thinking enough of me to plot a course of action had me strutting around like a movie star. I rode the drama bull like a rodeo queen, fancied myself a connoisseur of the slightly deranged and obsessed. Heady stuff—all that desire and frisson, electric connection given in doses. I floated outside my body in a state of awe, imagining something in my very soul conducted the energy around me, leading guys to do things they had "never done before" or "felt before" or "dared to think."

The shift from arousal to fear is as hard to pinpoint as it is unmistakable. As I grew older, these gifts were less appreciated, received on days when I needed to stay in my body and be unaware of it. I couldn't understand the loaded intent behind the presents, and instead I began to realize what was being taken away. That old junkie craving for unseen passion left suddenly, replaced by the certain knowledge that these men were not reacting to me, to my mind or words or wit, but to my face, my brown face.

In Denny's, crying to my best friend Laura over coffee, I struggle to keep my eyes averted from the man in the corner, to answer her questions.

"Did you just hear me?" she asks.   30

"No. Yes. I can't concentrate, that man is watching me. Don't turn around and look." The man stares straight at me with such a force I wonder if I don't know him. I feel his eyes hotter on my face with every word I say, my voice fading as I realize he isn't going to look away. I'm embarrassed that he can see me crying, embarrassed that I can't concentrate. Relieved when I see him get up to pay his bill and walk out, the pinch in my throat loosens, and Laura and I can finally talk.

Our conversation comes to an abrupt halt when the man returns half an hour later with earrings in hand. Two silver Egyptian pharaohs dangle in my blurred line of vision as he announces, "I've been watching you all night. I don't know much about India, but I thought these would look nice on you. I *had* to get them for you." He searches my eyes with brooding intensity, as though we've just established spiritual connection over my Grand Slam breakfast combo. "If I give you my number, will you call?"

If I give you a black eye, will you take it and leave?

"She's upset," Laura says, her head shaking, eyes wide. "She crying." The man ignores her, pressing a piece of paper into my palm. "My name is Gil. I think you should call me. You know what I mean." He gives me one last penetrating look, spins on his heel and walks out the door.

God bless my heart of darkness, I think I've stumbled upon a Colonizer Syndrome. It   35
takes seemingly normal men and causes them to lose their minds with brash abandon. It's jarring enough to be snapped in and out of one's body, a phenomenon most women grow accustomed to through experience, resilience. Being sexualized has the remarkable effect of erasing even the most introspective of moments, leaving a

woman utterly aware of nothing but her body, while at the same time making her a spectator of herself. But while every woman I know has been cat-called enough to land up on that hot tin roof, or yanked off her train of thought by some whistling dimwit, my brown face pushes me into the region of the unknown. I am left in a place uninhabited by white sisters, mothers, wives, where common courtesy takes a back seat to wild inspiration. I am uncharted territory, ripe for the conquest.

Hearing the word *India* from a stranger leaves me feeling naked and raw, as though something sacred in me has been cheapened through exposure. The word becomes insulting rolling off certain tongues, the poison of intent harder to trace back to "Pssst . . . Indi" than it is to "nice ass." It's harder to yell back at.

But that's what we're known for, we Indian women: bent heads and shut mouths, quiet grace, the Eastern-girl works. I've seen it so many times before, grown up with it hanging over me like a shadow I would eventually step into and unwillingly claim. Men used to follow my mother through the supermarket, mesmerized at the vegetable court, drooling through the detergents. They drew hearts on her palm at the city dump and made her promise not to wash them off before they let her pass through the gates, curiously blind to the rest of her cargo—me and my brother. They chatted with her at our soccer games, small talk leading to a rush of questions. "Where are you from? You're so unusual looking. You're really quite beautiful . . ." this last part said with a furtive glance in her direction. "India," she would mutter, looking away, a cool weight pressing an invisible screen over her eyes. The same heaviness dulled her eyes sometimes while she cooked or, later, in our nighttime bath ritual. It was a look that hung between boredom and frustration, a thin pulse of anger running through it. But my mother never said anything to these men, who would wait for a thank you, a smile, some sort of acknowledgment. "Why don't you ever smile when people tell you you're pretty?" I asked her once, embarrassed by her rudeness. She never answered me either.

Was she weak? Submissive? Clueless? I can't say that about my mother, She of the Wicked Wit and Ever-Dicing Tongue, an Indian version of a pistol-packing mama, sharpshooting and ready for any showdown. In my house, we know my mother is angry when she yells and, worse, disdainfully apathetic when she is silent, leaving us to boil in our own stew. But the intent behind my mother's deadly quiet, a calm I've seen replayed across the features of many of my other female relatives, isn't often recognized by American men. It's our faces, and our supposed mystery, that they tap into.

My late-teens realization about the powers of mystery, or lack thereof, was followed by the keenest silence my lips have ever observed. Just the mention of my "exotic looks" could shut me up for days on end, a phenomenon previously unwitnessed. Yet contrary to my hasty logic (mute girl = bored guy), my silence only perpetuated the enigma, adding the brute element of interpretation. "I think you're avoiding me," I heard at parties, often only hours after being introduced to a guy. "You're scared of our connection, right? I know you can feel it. I felt it the minute I laid eyes on you." And here it was again, the bond, the miracle, the connection associated with my face, the need to be led into whatever temple I had available. I saw desire thrown back to me in fragments of Taj Mahal, *Kamasutra,* womanly wiles. I felt my body turn into a dark country, my silence permission to colonize.

Next time, I will undress in the middle of the room. I will show you the scar of nightmares on my inner thigh and tuck my vision behind your eyelids. This is what 40 you will remember when you wake sweating at night: the sickened Braille of my skin, the emptiness behind my eyes, the blindness of your desire.

Battle tactics—swing hard and low, use the force of motion. My brother taught me that around the time he bought me a thread bracelet for "protection against freaks." I have a mediocre right hook and a prize-fighting tongue, and at age twenty I storm the fort, beginning an all-out war against anything mysterious in me. I begin to talk. Really talk. From the moment I encounter a man, my mouth becomes a vicious running motor, spewing forth indelectable information at a rapid pace. Pauses, silences and eversneaky meaningful-eye-contact moments become the perfect stage for an update on my bowel movements and skin abrasions. I curse loudly and often enough to leave me free of a docile stereotype. Too much information becomes my best defense against mystery, rattling off my own lid and investigating my contents in front of anyone who dares to watch. Laden with the ammunition of bodily functions and lewd neuroses, I wreck any sacred shrine I could possibly hold inside me, leaving both me and my audience standing in awkward rubble. With each demolition I am chatterboxing, punching behind my words, swinging fast and hard into conversation with my vicious tongue. With each demolition I am breathless, tired, terrified of being caught off guard.

"I can't stop talking," I confess to Laura over the phone. "I never know where the conversation is going to go." I was exhausted, bone bitten, weary of any man I met, on edge with those I already knew. Every part of my body had been itemized into comedic value, and a mere glance would set me smacking any tender portion into a window display, a caricature.

"I know," Laura said quietly. "I'm worried about you. I don't recognize you sometimes." I was hardening inside, a thick callus growing over my ribs. Any hint that I might soften for a minute, crave something kind, threw me into a panic. I knew she was right. I had become no more than a jumble of body parts, a façade raised in perfect opposition to the white man's Indian woman. "I don't recognize me either," I told her.

And that may be the one sticky truth I have to hold on to: I am not so easy to recognize. I am not so easy to taste, to sample or to know. But this truth, far from being an elusive beckoning to an outsider, or one last boundary for the brave to cross, is a mystery that is only mine. It's the puzzle of how to let myself evolve in a world that will never stop assuming my identity.

In trying to be anything but a brown face, an exotic myth, I almost lost the best part of who I am. I dissected myself into a jumble of Indian and American parts, deeming all things Indian as seductive and weak, and trying to find salvation in being an untouchable "lewd American." And yet, after all of my talking and muting, and general abusing of my body, nothing outside of me had changed. Even if I had opened my mouth and poured every last bit of myself into shifting perceptions and the rest of the cosmos, I was, am and will always be seen as "an Indian woman." So the terror for me is also the one realization that offers me hope: I can't change the reactions that my face triggers. It's not my battle to fight.

I also know that *my* Indian woman isn't the shared secret some men imply, with their hissing "Indis," their darting eyes and spice-hungry lips. She isn't the love of curry or the cool crush of silk beneath greedy palms or "chai tea" served redundantly and by the gallon at Starbucks.

My Indian woman is a work in progress. I find her in the grumbling of my daily subway commute, in the damp green smell of coriander leaves and in late-night drives in my truck. She resides in the thousand small deaths my parents lived through to part from their mother country, in the survival skills they have taught me and in the legendary powers of silence. My Indian woman is not the history of submission, but the history of resilience, of beginning again. It's this woman who is at the center of me, the one the men on the street will never see: this woman who is simultaneously on fire and rising from the ashes.

CONNECTING PERSONALLY TO THE READING

1. In what ways do you think Jacob's experience of being harassed by catcalls and other unwanted sexual attention is common to all women? Do you think being different—whether because of race, nationality, or another personal characteristic—intensifies this experience?

2. Jacob's "truth" is that she is "not so easy to taste, to sample or to know." Think of a time when others have imposed their assumptions on you or when you have done the same to someone else. How do you feel when you make facile assumptions about another person or are the object of someone else's misguided views about you?

FOCUSING ON THE ARGUMENT

1. In telling her story, Jacob shifts back and forth between her imaginary conversations with others and the discussion of her treatment as an Indian American woman. How does this narrative strategy illustrate the difference between Jacob's personality and the one others ascribe to her as a "mysterious" Indian? What is this difference?

2. What do the metaphors in this reading—for example, those of war or colonization—reveal about Jacob's experience as an exoticized sex object? How do these analogies allow her to suggest ideas or feelings beyond those that the text explicitly describes?

SYNTHESIZING IDEAS FROM MULTIPLE READINGS

1. Both Brent Staples ("Just Walk On By," p. 118) and Jacob are regarded as outsiders because of their dark skin, but each is stereotyped differently—Staples as potentially violent and Jacob as sexually available. How do these writers adjust their public behavior to defend themselves against others' expectations?

2. Cindy Jackson ("My Cosmetic Surgery," p. 139) sees the ability to attract men's attention as a source of power, whereas Mira Jacob feels oppressed, "colonized," by the same kind of attention. How do you account for this difference?

WRITING TO ACT

1. Write a code of behavior for the men that Jacob describes. Begin the document with a brief paragraph describing the need for such a code. Then create a list of dos and don'ts, indi-

cating how they should and should not behave when they encounter women they perceive as "exotic."

2. Create an anti-sexual harassment poster that uses both words and images to convey what such harassment is and why it is unacceptable.

JEAN KILBOURNE   Kilbourne argues that advertising undermines girls' self-esteem. Not only do ads equate ideal body image with fitting in, but they also diminish girls in more subtle ways. According to Kilbourne, advertisements encourage girls to be silent, passive, childish, and ashamed. In addition, in their passive need for men's attention, they compete with female friends, fostering tension rather than friendship. Can you think of ads that undermine girls in these ways?

KILBOURNE is the author of the book *Buy My Love: How Advertising Changes the Way We Think and Feel,* as well as three documentaries: *Killing Us Softly, Slim Hopes,* and *Calling the Shots.* The *New York Times Magazine* named Kilbourne one of the most popular speakers on college campuses in 2005.

"The More You Subtract, the More You Add": Cutting Girls Down to Size (2000)

BY JEAN KILBOURNE

[. . .] Advertising is one of the most potent messengers in a culture that can be toxic for girls' self-esteem. Indeed, if we looked only at advertising images, this would be a bleak world for females. Girls are extremely desirable to advertisers because they are new consumers, are beginning to have significant disposable income, and are developing brand loyalty that might last a lifetime. Teenage girls spend over $4 billion annually on cosmetics alone.

Seventeen, a magazine aimed at girls about twelve to fifteen, sells these girls to advertisers in an ad that says, "She's the one you want. She's the one we've got." The copy continues, "She pursues beauty and fashion at every turn" and concludes with, "It's more than a magazine. It's her life." In another similar ad, *Seventeen* refers to itself as a girl's "Bible." Many girls read magazines like this and

take the advice seriously. Regardless of the intent of the advertisers, what are the messages that girls are getting? What are they told?

Primarily girls are told by advertisers that what is most important about them is their perfume, their clothing, their bodies, their beauty. Their "essence" is their underwear. "He says the first thing he noticed about you is your great personality," says an ad featuring a very young woman in tight jeans. The copy continues, "He lies." "If this is your idea of a great catch," says an ad for a cosmetic kit from a teen magazine featuring a cute boy, "this is your tackle box." Even very little girls are offered makeup and toys like Special Night Barbie, which shows them how to dress up for a night out. Girls of all ages get the message that they must be flawlessly beautiful and, above all these days, they must be thin.

SUPER SLIM N°7

Only at *Boots*

ANTI-CELLULITE BALM

Even more destructively, they get the message that this is possible, that, with enough effort and self-sacrifice, they can achieve this ideal. Thus many girls spend enormous amounts of time and energy attempting to achieve something that is not only trivial but also completely un-attainable. The glossy images of flawlessly beautiful and extremely thin women that surround us would not have the impact they do if we did not live in a culture that encourages us to believe we can and should remake our bodies into perfect commodities. These images play into the American belief of transformation and ever-new possibilities, no longer via hard work but via the purchase of the right products. As Anne Becker has pointed out, this belief is by no means universal. People in many other cultures may admire a particular body shape without seeking to emulate it. In the Western world, however, "the anxiety of nonrecognition ('I don't fit in') faced by the majority of spectators is more often translated into identifications ('I want to be like that') and attempts at self-alteration than into rage." [. . .]

You can never be too rich or too thin, 5 girls are told. This mass delusion sells a lot of products. It also causes enormous suffering, involving girls in false quests for power and control, while deflecting attention and energy from that which might really empower them. "A declaration of independence," proclaims an ad for perfume that features an emaciated model, but in fact the quest for a body as

WITH SHADOW DUO
AND DEFINER

17

SHADE AND SUBTLY DEFINE YOUR EYES WITH OUR NEW SHADOW DUO AND DEFINER. £2.45.
DERMATOLOGICALLY TESTED AND FRAGRANCE-FREE. EXCLUSIVE TO BOOTS.
17 PRODUCTS ARE NOT TESTED ON ANIMALS.

thin as the model's becomes a prison for many women and girls.

The quest for independence can be a problem too if it leads girls to deny the importance of and need for interpersonal relationships. Girls and young women today are encouraged by the culture to achieve a very "masculine" kind of autonomy and independence, one that excludes interdependence, mutuality, and connection with others. Catherine Steiner-Adair suggests that perhaps eating disorders emerge at adolescence because it is at this point that "females experience themselves to be at a crossroads in their lives where they must shift from a relational approach to life to an autonomous one, a shift that can represent an intolerable loss when independence is associated with isolation." In this sense, she sees eating disorders as political statements, a kind of hunger strike: "Girls with eating disorders have a heightened, albeit confused, grasp of the dangerous imbalance of the culture's values, which they cannot articulate in the face of the culture's abject denial of their adolescent intuitive truth, so they tell their story with their bodies."

Most of us know by now about the damage done to girls by the tyranny of the ideal image, weightism, and the obsession with thinness. But girls get other messages too that "cut them down to size" more subtly. In ad after ad girls are urged to be "barely there"—beautiful but silent. Of course, girls are not just influenced by images of other girls. They are even more powerfully attuned to images of women, because they learn from these images what is expected of them, what they are to become. And they see these images again and again in the magazines they read, even those magazines designed for teenagers, and in the commercials they watch.

"Make a statement without saying a word," says an ad for perfume. And indeed this is one of the primary messages of the culture to adolescent girls. "The silence of a look can reveal more than words," says another perfume ad, this one featuring a woman lying on her back. "More than words can say," says yet another perfume ad, and a clothing ad says, "Classic is speaking your mind (without saying a word)." An ad for lipstick says, "Watch your mouth, young lady," while one for nail polish says, "Let your fingers do the talking," and one for hairspray promises "hair that speaks volumes." In another ad, a young woman's turtleneck is pulled over her mouth. And an ad for a movie soundtrack features a chilling image of a young woman with her lips sewn together.

CHAPTER 3 Constructing Gender

It is not only the girls themselves who see these images, of course. Their parents and teachers and doctors see them and they influence their sense of how girls should be. A 1999 study done at the University of Michigan found that, beginning in preschool, girls are told to be quiet much more often than boys. Although boys were much noisier than girls, the girls were told to speak softly or to use a "nicer" voice about three times more often. Girls were encouraged to be quiet, small, and physically constrained. The researcher concluded that one of the consequences of this socialization is that girls grow into women afraid to speak up for themselves or to use their voices to protect themselves from a variety of dangers.

A television commercial features a 10 very young woman lying on a bed, giggling, silly. Suddenly a male hand comes forward. His finger touches her lips and she becomes silent, her face blank. Another commercial features a very young woman, shot in black and white but with colored contact lenses. She never speaks but she touches her face and her hair as a female voiceover says, "Your eyes don't just see, they also speak. . . . Your eyes can say a lot, but they don't have to shout. They can speak softly. Let your eyes be heard . . . without making a sound." The commercial ends with the

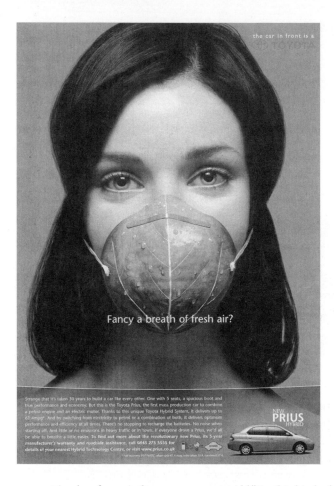

the car in front is a TOYOTA

Fancy a breath of fresh air?

Strange that it's taken 30 years to build a car like every other. One with 5 seats, a spacious boot and true performance and economy. But this is the Toyota Prius, the first mass production car to combine a petrol engine and an electric motor. Thanks to this unique Toyota Hybrid System, it delivers up to 61.4mpg*. And by switching from electricity to petrol or a combination of both, it delivers optimum performance and efficiency at all times. There's no stopping to recharge the batteries. No noise when starting off. And little or no emissions in heavy traffic or in town. If everyone drove a Prius, we'd all be able to breathe a little easier. To find out more about the revolutionary new Prius, its 3-year manufacturer's warranty and roadside assistance, call 0845 275 5555 for details of your nearest Hybrid Technology Centre, or visit www.prius.co.uk

NEW PRIUS HYBRID

young woman putting her finger in her mouth.

"Score high on nonverbal skills," says a clothing ad featuring a young African-American woman, while an ad for mascara tells young women to "make up your own language." And an Italian ad features a very thin young woman in an elegant coat sitting on a window seat. The copy says, "This woman is silent. This coat talks." Girls, seeing these images of women, are encouraged to be silent, mysterious, not to talk too much or too loudly. In many different ways, they are told "the more you subtract, the more you add." In this kind of climate, a Buffalo jeans ad featuring a young woman screaming, "I don't have to scream for attention but I do," can seem like an improvement—until we notice that she's really getting attention by unbuttoning her blouse to her navel. This is typical of the mixed messages so many ads and other forms of the media give girls. The young woman seems fierce and powerful, but she's really exposed, vulnerable.

The January 1998 cover of *Seventeen* highlights an article, "Do you talk too much?" On the back cover is an ad for

Express mascara, which promises "high voltage volume instantly!" As if the way that girls can express themselves and turn up the volume is via their mascara. Is this harmless wordplay, or is it a sophisticated and clever marketing ploy based on research about the silencing of girls, deliberately designed to attract them with the promise of at least some form of self-expression? Advertisers certainly spend a lot of money on psychological research and focus groups. I would expect these groups to reveal, among other things, that teenage girls are angry but reticent. Certainly the cumulative effect of these images and words urging girls to express themselves only through their bodies and through products is serious and harmful.

Many ads feature girls and young women in very passive poses, limp, doll-like, sometimes acting like little girls, playing with dolls and wearing bows in their hair. One ad uses a pacifier to sell lipstick and another the image of a baby to sell BabyDoll Blush Highlight. "Lolita seems to be a comeback kid," says a fashion layout featuring a woman wearing a ridiculous hairstyle and a baby-doll dress, standing with shoulders slumped and feet apart. In women's and teen magazines it is virtually impossible to tell the

fashion layouts from the ads. Indeed, they exist to support each other.

As Erving Goffman pointed out in *Gender Advertisements,* we learn a great deal about the disparate power of males and females simply through the body language and poses of advertising. Women, especially young women, are generally subservient to men in ads, through both size and position. Sometimes it is as blatant as the woman serving as a footrest in the ad for Think Skateboards.

Clarks
For every kid there's a shoe that fits.

The rarest of personal luxuries...

made to order face-powder, evolved from a drift of exquisite
colours to create one special bloom—just for you.
Only Charles of the Ritz can do this. At chosen department stores.

Charles of the Ritz

Other times, it is more subtle but quite 15
striking (once one becomes aware of it).
The double-paged spread for Calvin
Klein's clothing for kids conveys a world
of information about the relative power
of boys and girls. One of the boys seems
to be in the act of speaking, expressing
himself, while the girl has her hand over
her mouth. Boys are generally shown in
ads as active, rambunctious, while girls
are more often passive and focused on
their appearance. The exception to the
rule involves African-American children, male and female, who are often
shown in advertising as passive observers of their white playmates.

That these stereotypes continue, in
spite of all the recent focus on the harm
done to girls by enforced passivity, is evident in the most casual glance at parents' magazines. In the ads in the March
1999 issues of *Child* and *Parents,* all of
the boys are active and all of the girls are
passive. In *Child,* a boy plays on the jungle gym in one ad, while in another, a
girl stands quietly, looking down, holding some flowers. In *Parents,* a boy rides
a bike, full of excitement, while a girl is
happy about having put on lipstick. It's
hard to believe that this is 1999 and not
1959. The more things change, the more
they stay the same.

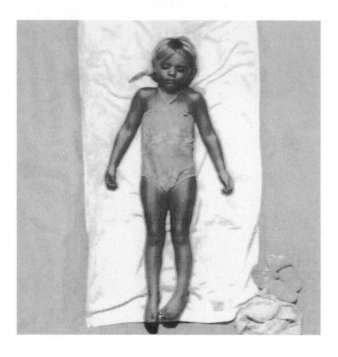

Girls are often shown as playful clowns in ads, perpetuating the attitude that girls and women are childish and cannot be taken seriously, whereas even very young men are generally portrayed as secure, powerful, and serious. People in control of their lives stand upright, alert, and ready to meet the world. In contrast, females often appear off-balance, insecure, and weak. Often our body parts are bent, conveying unpreparedness, submissiveness, and appeasement. We exhibit what Goffman terms "licensed withdrawal"—seeming to be psychologically removed, disoriented, defenseless, spaced out.

Females touch people and things delicately, we caress, whereas males grip, clench, and grasp. We cover our faces with our hair or our hands, conveying shame or embarrassment. And, no matter what happens, we keep on smiling. "Just smiling the bothers away," as one ads says. This ad is particularly disturbing because the model is a young African-American woman, a member of a group

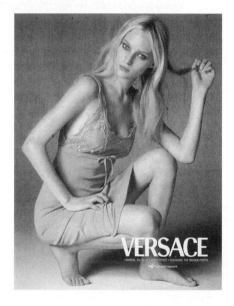

that has long been encouraged to just keep smiling, no matter what. She's even wearing a kerchief, like Aunt Jemima. The cultural fear of angry women is intensified dramatically when the women are African-American.

An extreme example of the shaming and trivialization of girls and women is a recent little trend of ads featuring young women sitting on the toilet, such as the shoe ad with popular MTV star Jenny McCarthy (although the ad offended a lot of people, it also boosted sales of Candies shoes by 19 percent). Unfortunately, this phenomenon is not restricted to the United States. An Italian ad for sneakers and a British one for a magazine use the same image. Such pictures are especially humiliating to self-conscious teenagers.

Girls and young women are often pre- 20 sented as blank and fragile. floating in space, adrift in a snowstorm. A Valentino clothing ad perhaps unwittingly illustrates the tragedy of adolescence for girls. It features a very young woman with her head seemingly enclosed in a glass bubble labeled "Love." Some ads and fashion layouts picture girls as mermaids or underwater as if they were drowning—or lying on the ground as if washed up to shore, such as the Versace makeup ad picturing a young girl caught up in fishing nets, rope, and seashells.

No7
The face of fashion.
AVAILABLE AT LARGER BRANCHES OF BOOTS

An ad for vodka features a woman in the water and the copy, "In a past life I was a mermaid who fell in love with an ancient mariner. I pulled him into the sea to be my husband. I didn't know he couldn't breathe underwater." Of course, she can't breathe underwater either.

Breathe underwater. As girls come of age sexually, the culture gives them impossibly contradictory messages. As the *Seventeen* ad says, "She wants to be outrageous. And accepted." Advertising slogans such as "because innocence is sexier than you think," "Purity, yes. Innocence never," and "nothing so sensual was ever so innocent" place them in a double bind. "Only something so pure

could inspire such unspeakable passion," declares an ad for Jovan musk that features a white flower. Somehow girls are supposed to be both innocent and seductive, virginal and experienced, all at the same time. As they quickly learn, this is tricky. [. . .]

Jane Brown and her colleagues concluded from their years of research that the mass media are important sex educators for American teenagers. Other potential educators, such as parents, schools, and churches, are doing an inadequate job, and even if that were to change dramatically, the media would remain compelling teachers. Brown faults media portrayals for avoiding the "three

CHANEL

BOLD COLOUR COMBINATIONS : HYDRABASE N°98 – LE VERNIS N°28

C's"—commitment, contraceptives, and consequences—and concludes, "It is little wonder that adolescents find the sexual world a difficult and often confusing place and that they engage in early and unprotected sexual intercourse with multiple partners."

The emphasis for girls and women is always on being desirable, not on experiencing desire. Girls who want to be sexually *active* instead of simply being the objects of male desire are given only one model to follow, that of exploitive male sexuality. It seems that advertisers can't conceive of a kind of power that isn't manipulative and exploitive or a way that women can be actively sexual without being like traditional men.

Women who are "powerful" in advertising are uncommitted. They treat men like sex objects: "If I want a man to see my bra, I take him home," says an androgynous young woman. They are elusive and distant: "She is the first woman who refused to take your phone calls," says one ad. As if it were a good thing to be rude and inconsiderate. Why should any of us, male or female, be interested in someone who won't take our phone calls, who either cares so little for us or is so manipulative?

Mostly though, girls are not supposed 25 to have sexual agency. They are supposed to be passive, swept away, overpowered. "See where it takes you," says a perfume ad featuring a couple passionately

American Rag Cie   Candie's 1-888-9CANDIE

embracing. "Unleash your fantasies," says another. "A force of nature." This contributes to the strange and damaging concept of the "good girl" as the one who is swept away, unprepared for sex, versus the "bad girl" as the one who plans for sex, uses contraception, and is generally responsible. A young woman can manage to have sex and yet in some sense maintain her virginity by being "out of control," drunk, or deep in denial about the entire experience.

No wonder most teenage pregnancies occur when one or both parties is drunk. Alcohol and other mind-altering drugs permit sexual activity at the same time that they allow denial. One is al-

most literally not there. The next day one has an excuse. I was drunk, I was swept away. I did not choose this experience.

In adolescence girls are told that they have to give up much of what they *know* about relationships and intimacy if they want to attract men. Most tragically, they are told they have to give up each other. The truth is that one of the most powerful antidotes to destructive cultural messages is close and supportive female friendships. But girls are often encouraged by the culture to sacrifice their relationships with each other and to enter into hostile competition for the attention of boys and men. "What the bitch who's about to steal your man

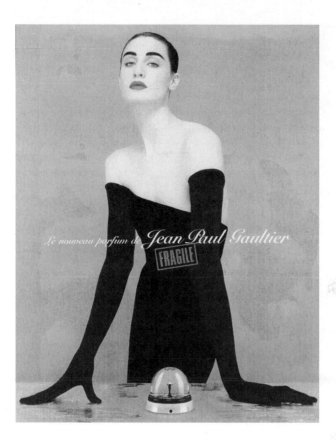

Le nouveau parfum de *Jean Paul Gaultier*
FRAGILE

wears," says one ad. And many ads feature young women fighting or glaring at each other.

Of course, some girls do resist and rebel. Some are encouraged (by someone—a loving parent, a supportive teacher) to see the cultural contradictions clearly and to break free in a healthy and positive way. Others rebel in ways that damage themselves. A young woman seems to have only two choices: She can bury her sexual self, be a "good girl," give in to what Carol Gilligan terms "the tyranny of nice and kind" (and numb the pain by overeating or starving or cutting herself or drinking heavily). Or she can become a rebel— flaunt her sexuality, seduce inappropri-

ate partners, smoke, drink flamboyantly, use other drugs. Both of these responses are self-destructive, but they begin as an attempt to survive, not to self-destruct.

Many girls become women who split themselves in two and do both—have a double life, a secret life—a good girl in public, out of control in private. A feminist in public, involved in an abusive relationship or lost in sadomasochistic fantasies in private. A lawyer by day, a barfly by night. Raiding the refrigerator or drinking themselves into a stupor alone in their kitchens at night, after the children are in bed, the laundry done. Doing well in school, but smoking in order to have a sexier, cooler image. Being sexual only when drunk.

There are few healthy alternatives for girls who want to truly rebel against restrictive gender roles and stereotypes. The recent emphasis on girl power has led to some real advances for girls and young women, especially in the arenas of music and sports. But it is as often co-opted and trivialized. The Indigo Girls are good and true, but it is the Spice Girls who rule. Magazines like *New Moon, Hues,* and *Teen Voices* offer a real alternative to the glitzy, boy-crazy, appearance-obsessed teen magazines on the newsstands, but they have to struggle for funds since they take no advertising. There are some good zines and Websites for girls on the Internet but there are also countless sites that degrade and endanger them. And Barbie

30 continues to rake in two billion dollars a year and will soon have a postal stamp in her honor—while a doll called "Happy to be me," similar to Barbie but much more realistic and down to earth, was available for a couple of years in the mid-1990s (I bought one for my daughter) and then vanished from sight. Of course, Barbie's makers have succumbed to pressure somewhat and have remade her with a thicker waist, smaller breasts, and slimmer hips. As a result, according to Anthony Cortese, she has already lost her waitressing job at Hooter's and her boyfriend Ken has told her that he wants to start seeing other dolls.

Girls who want to escape the stereotypes are viewed with glee by advertisers, who rush to offer them, as always,

fashion v *Style*

french *Connection*

power via products. The emphasis in the ads is always on their sexuality, which is exploited to sell them makeup and clothes and shoes. "Lil' Kim is wearing lunch box in black," says a shoe ad featuring a bikini-clad young woman in a platinum wig stepping over a group of nuns—the ultimate bad girl, I guess, but also the ultimate sex object. A demon woman sells a perfume called Hypnotic Poison. A trio of extremely thin African-American women brandish hair appliances and products as if they were weapons—and the brand is 911. A cosmetics company has a line of products called "Bad Gal." In one ad, eyeliner is shown in cartoon version as a girl, who is holding a dog saying, "grrrr," surely a reference to "grrrrls," a symbol these days of "girl power" (as in cybergrrl.com, the popular Web site for girls and young women). Unfortunately, girl power doesn't mean much if girls don't have the tools to achieve it. Without reproductive freedom and freedom from violence, girl power is nothing but a marketing slogan.

So, for all the attention paid to girls in recent years, what girls are offered mostly by the popular culture is a superficial toughness, an "attitude," exemplified by smoking, drinking, and engaging

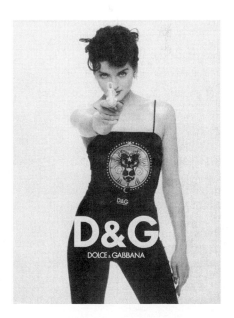

D&G
DOLCE & GABBANA

in casual sex—all behaviors that harm themselves. In 1990 Virginia Slims offered girls a T-shirt that said, "Sugar and spice and everything nice? Get real." In 1997 Winston used the same theme in an ad featuring a tough young woman shooting pool and saying, "I'm not all sugar & spice. And neither are my smokes." As if the alternative to the feminine stereotype was sarcasm and toughness, and as if smoking was somehow an expression of one's authentic self ("get real.")

Of course, the readers and viewers of these ads don't take them literally. But we do take them in—another grain of sand in a slowly accumulating and vast sandpile. If we entirely enter the world of ads, imagine them to be real for a moment, we find that the sandpile has completely closed us in, and there's only one escape route—buy something. "Get the power," says an ad featuring a woman showing off her biceps. "The power to clean anything," the ad continues. "Hey girls, you've got the power of control" says an ad for . . . hairspray. "The possibilities are endless" (clothing). "Never lose control" (hairspray again). "You never had this much control when you were on your own" (hair gel). "Exceptional character" (a watch). "An enlightening experience" (face powder). "Inner strength" (vitamins). "Only Victoria's Secret could make control so sensual" (girdles). "Stronger longer" (shampoo). Of course, the empowerment, the enlightenment, is as impossible to get through products as is anything else— love, security, romance, passion. On one level, we know this. On another, we keep buying and hoping—and buying.

Other ads go further and offer products as a way to rebel, to be a real individual. "Live outside the lines," says a clothing ad featuring a young woman walking out of a men's room. This kind of rebel-

lion isn't going to rock the world. And, no surprise, the young woman is very thin and conventionally pretty. Another pretty young woman sells a brand of jeans called "Revolt." "Don't just change . . . revolt," says the copy, but the young woman is passive, slight, her eyes averted.

"Think for yourself," says yet another 35 hollow-cheeked young woman, demonstrating her individuality via an expensive and fashionable sweater. "Be amazing" (cosmetics). "Inside every woman is a star" (clothing). "If you're going to create electricity, use it" (watches). "If you let your spirit out, where would it go" (perfume). These women are all perfect examples of conventional "femininity," as is the young woman in a Halston perfume ad that says, "And when she was bad she wore Halston." What kind of "bad" is this?

"Nude with attitude" feature[s] an African-American woman in a powerful pose, completely undercut by the brevity of her dress and the focus on her long legs. Her "attitude" is nothing to fear— she's just another sex object. Good thing, given the fear many people have of powerful African-American women.

The British ad "For girls with plenty of balls" is insulting in ways too numerous to count, beginning with the equation of strength and courage and fiery passion with testicles. What this ad offers girls is body lotion.

Some ads do feature women who seem really angry and rebellious, but the final message is always the same. "Today, I indulge my dark side," says an ad featuring a fierce young woman tearing at what seems to be a net. "Got a problem with that?" The slogan is "be extraordinary not ordinary." The product that promises to free this girl from the net that imprisons her? Black nail polish.

Nail polish. Such a trivial solution to such an enormous dilemma. But such triviality and superficiality is common in advertising. How could it be otherwise? The solution to any problem always has to be a product. Change, transformation, is thus inevitably shallow and moronic, rather than meaningful and transcendent. These days, self-improvement seems to have more to do with calories than with character, with abdomens than with absolutes, with nail polish than with ethics.

It has not always been so. Joan Jacobs 40 Brumberg describes this vividly in *The Body Project: An Intimate History of American Girls:*

> When girls in the nineteenth century thought about ways to improve themselves, they almost always focused on their internal character and how it was reflected in outward behavior. In 1892, the personal agenda of an adolescent diarist read: "Resolved, not to talk about myself or feelings. To think before speaking. To work seriously. . . . To be dignified. Interest myself more in others."

A century later, in the 1990s, American girls think very differently. In a New Year's resolution written in 1982, a girl wrote: "I will try to make myself better in every way I possibly can with the help of my budget and baby-sitting money. I will lose weight, get new lenses, already got new haircut, good makeup, new clothes and accessories."

Not that girls didn't have plenty of problems in the nineteenth century. But surely by now we should have come much further. This relentless trivialization of a girl's hopes and dreams, her expectations for herself, cuts to the quick of her soul. Just as she is entering womanhood, eager to spread her wings, to become truly sexually *active*, empowered, independent—the culture moves in to *cut her down to size.*

CONNECTING PERSONALLY TO THE READING

1. Do you agree with Kilbourne that ads tell girls "you can never be too rich or too thin"?

2. In your experience, are girls more likely than boys to be discouraged from being loud or boisterous?

3. To what extent do the girls you know try to emulate the models they see in ads?

FOCUSING ON THE ARGUMENT

1. Kilbourne describes and quotes from dozens of ads. What is the effect on you of the sheer volume of her examples?

2. Most advertisers do not expect readers to analyze ads the way Kilbourne does, but merely to glance at them, taking the images in quickly. Does her analysis make you more critical of ads? Explain.

1. Susan Bordo ("The Empire of Images in Our World of Bodies," p. 169) emphasizes how advertising promotes women's obsession with physical beauty—an obsession that can result in mental and physical health problems. In what ways does Kilbourne build on Bordo's argument and extend it?

2. Cindy Jackson's interview ("My Cosmetic Surgery," p. 139) suggests that she used the physical ideal represented in advertisements as a springboard into a happier life. Do you think that Jackson's actions contradict the cult of silence, passivity, childishness, and shame? Why or why not?

3. In "My Brown Face" (p. 143), Mira Jacob describes how strange men often assume they can address her in public and call attention to her looks. How might their attitude toward her reflect their assumption that women are passive and childish? Does her reaction to this attention contradict or reinforce Kilbourne's belief that women are trained to be passive?

WRITING TO ACT

1. Using evidence from Jean Kilbourne ("'The More You Subtract, the More You Add,'" p. 149) and Susan Bordo ("The Empire of Images in Our World of Bodies," p. 169), write an editorial on the way that advertising creates a climate in which crimes against women become familiar and therefore easier to tolerate.

2. Find an advertisement that you think encourages reciprocal and equal roles for men and women. Then write to the advertiser, describing the features of the ad that you appreciate.

3. Kilbourne refers to "grrrrl" Web sites such as cybergrrl.com, which are meant to promote "girl power." Look at one of these grrl sites (other possibilities are GrrlSpace.com, grrl.org, planetgrrl.com, and riotgrrl.com), and decide whether they in fact promote female power, reinforce the training Kilbourne decries, or do something else entirely. Then do one of the following: (1) e-mail the site owner, expressing your views, or (2) create a Web site that encourages girls to speak out and to be independent, confident, and supportive of their girlfriends.

READING

SUSAN BORDO   Susan Bordo argues that we live in an "empire of images" that have saturated all media with unnatural expectations of female beauty. In the United States and overseas, on television, in magazines, on billboards, in the movies, and just about everywhere we look, we see older women without wrinkles, little girls dolled up as nymphets, and women of all ages and races encouraged to look as thin and white as possible. Though Bordo acknowledges exceptions to this trend—ads that promote female athleticism and a range of body types—she is concerned that the predominance of unhealthy images of women teaches young girls to be dissatisfied with their bodies and contributes to a culture that parades children as objects of sexual desire. Do you believe that people's behavior is affected by these images? Why or why not?

BORDO, a professor of English and Women's Studies at the University of Kentucky, is the author of several books on body studies, including *Unbearable Weight: Feminism, Western Culture, and the Body* and *The Male Body: A New Look at Men in Public and in Private.*

The Empire of Images in Our World of Bodies (2004)

BY SUSAN BORDO

In our Sunday news. With our morning coffee. On the bus, in the airport, at the checkout line.

It may be a 5 a.m. addiction to the glittering promises of the infomercial: the latest in fat-dissolving pills, miracle hair restoration, makeup secrets of the stars. Or a glancing relationship while waiting at the dentist, trying to distract ourselves from the impending root canal. A teen magazine: tips on how to dress, how to wear your hair, how to make him want you. The endless commercials and advertisements that we believe we pay no attention to.

Constant, everywhere, no big deal. Like water in a goldfish bowl, barely noticed by its inhabitants. Or noticed, but dismissed: "eye candy"—a harmless indulgence. They go down so easily, in and out, digested and forgotten.

Just pictures.

Or perhaps, more accurately, perceptual pedagogy: "How To Interpret Your Body 101." It's become a global requirement; eventually, everyone must enroll. Fiji is just one example. Until television was introduced in 1995, the islands had no reported cases of eating disorders. In 1998, three years after programs from the United States and Britain began broadcasting there, 62 percent of the girls surveyed reported dieting. The anthropologist Anne Becker was surprised by the change; she had thought that Fijian aesthetics, which favor voluptuous bodies, would "withstand" the influence of media images. Becker hadn't yet understood that we live in an empire of images and that there are no protective borders.

I am not protected either. I was carded until I was 35. Even when I was 45, people were shocked to learn my age. Young men flirted with me even when I was 50. Having hated my appearance as a child—freckles, Jewish nose, bushy red hair—I was surprised to find myself fairly pleased with it as an adult. Then, suddenly, it all changed. Women at the makeup counter no longer compliment me on my skin. Men don't catch my eye with playful promise in theirs.

I'm 56. The magazines tell me that at this age, a woman can still be beautiful. But they don't mean me. They mean Cher, Goldie, Faye, Candace. Women whose jowls have disappeared as they've aged, whose eyes have become less droopy, lips grown plumper, foreheads smoother with the passing years. They mean Susan Sarandon, who looked older in 1991's *Thelma and Louise* than she does in her movies today. "Aging beautifully" used to mean wearing one's years with style, confidence, and vitality. Today, it means not appearing to age at all. And—like breasts that defy gravity—it's becoming a new bodily norm.

In my 1993 book *Unbearable Weight,* I described the postmodern body, increasingly fed on "fantasies of rearranging, transforming, and correcting, limitless improvement and change, defying the historicity, the mortality, and, indeed, the very materiality of the body. In place of that materiality, we now have cultural plastic."

When I wrote those words, the most recent statistics, from 1989, listed 681,000 surgical procedures performed. In 2001, 8.5 million procedures were performed. They are cheaper than ever, safer than ever, and increasingly used not for correcting major defects but for "contouring" the face and body. Plastic surgeons seem to have no ethical problem with this. "I'm not here to play philosopher king," said Dr. Randal Haworth in a *Vogue* interview. "I don't have a problem with women who already look good who want to look perfect." Perfect. When did "perfection" become applicable to a human body? The word suggests a Platonic form of timeless beauty—appropriate for marble, perhaps, but not for living flesh.

Greta van Susteren: former CNN legal analyst, 47 years old. When she had a face-lift, it was a real escalation in the stakes for ordinary women. She had a signature style: no bullshit, a down-to-earth lack of pretense. (During the O.J. trial, she was the only white reporter many black Americans trusted.) Always stylishly dressed and coiffed, she wasn't really pretty. No one could argue that her career was built on her looks. Perhaps quite the opposite. She sent out a subversive message: Brains and personality still count, even on television.

When Greta had her face lifted, another source of inspiration and hope bit the dust. The story was on the cover of *People,* and folks tuned in to her new show on Fox just to see the change—which was significant. But at least she was open about it. The beauties rarely admit they've had "work." Or if they do, it's

vague, nonspecific, minimizing of the extent. Cher: "If I'd had as much plastic surgery as people say, there'd be another whole person left over!" OK, so how much have you had? The interviewers accept the silences and evasions. They even embellish the lie. How many interviews have you read that began: "She came into the restaurant looking at least 20 years younger than she is, fresh and relaxed, without a speck of makeup."

This collusion, this myth, that Cher or Goldie or Faye Dunaway, unaltered, is what 50-something looks like today has altered my face, however—without benefit of surgery. By comparison with theirs, it has become much older than it is.

My expression now appears more serious, too (just what a feminist needs), thanks to the widespread use of Botox. "It's now rare in certain social circles to see a woman over the age of 35 with the ability to look angry," a *New York Times* reporter observed recently. That has frustrated some film directors, like Baz Luhrmann, who directed *Moulin Rouge.* "Their faces can't really move properly," Luhrmann complained. Last week I saw a sign in the beauty parlor where I get my hair cut. "Botox Party! Sign Up!" So my 56-year-old forehead will now be

judged against my neighbor's, not just Goldie's, Cher's, and Faye's. On television, a commercial describes the product (which really is a toxin, a dilution of botulism) as "Botox cosmetic." No different from mascara and blush, it's just stuck in with a needle, and it makes your forehead numb.

To add insult to injury, the rhetoric of feminism has been adopted to help advance and justify the industries in anti-aging and body-alteration. Face-lifts, implants, and liposuction are advertised as empowerment, "taking charge" of one's life. "I'm doing it for me" goes the mantra of the talk shows. "Defy your age!" says Melanie Griffith, for Revlon. We're making a revolution, girls. Step right up and get your injections.

Am I immune? Of course not. My bathroom shelves are cluttered with the ridiculously expensive age-defying lotions and potions that beckon to me at the Lancôme and Dior counters. I want my lines, bags, and sags to disappear, and so do the women who can only afford to buy their alphahydroxies at Kmart. There's a limit, though, to what fruit acids can do. As surgeons develop ever more extensive and fine-tuned procedures to correct gravity and erase history from the faces of their patients, the difference between the cosmetically altered and the rest of us grows more and more dramatic.

"The rest of us" includes not only those who resist or are afraid of surgery but the many people who cannot afford basic health care, let alone aesthetic tinkering. As celebrity faces become increasingly more surreal in their wide-eyed, ever-bright agelessness, as *Time* and *Newsweek* (and *Discover* and *Psychology Today*) proclaim that we can now all "stay young forever," the poor continue to sag and wrinkle and lose their teeth. But in the empire of images, where even people in the news for stock scandals or producing septuplets are given instant digital dental work for magazine covers, that is a well-guarded secret. The celebrity testimonials, the advertisements, the beauty columns, all participate in the fiction that the required time, money, and technologies are available to all.

I've been lecturing about media images, eating problems, and our culture of body "enhancement" for nearly 20 years now. Undergraduates frequently make up a large share of my audiences, and they are the ones most likely to "get it." My generation (and older) still refers to "air brushing." Many

still believe it is possible to "just turn off the television." They are scornful, disdainful, sure of their own immunity to the world I talk about. No one really believes the ads, do they? Don't we all know those are just images, designed to sell products? Scholars in the audience may trot out theory about cultural resistance and "agency." Men may insist that they love fleshy women.

Fifteen years ago, I felt very alone when my own generation said these things; it seemed that they were living in a different world from the one I was tracking and that there was little hope of bridging the gap. Now, I simply catch the eyes of the 20-year-olds in the audience. They know. They understand that you can be as cynical as you want about the ads—and many of them are—and still feel powerless to resist their messages. They are aware that virtually every advertisement, every magazine cover, has been digitally modified and that very little of what they see is "real." That doesn't stop them from hating their own bodies for failing to live up to computer-generated standards. They know, no matter what their parents, teachers, and clergy are telling them, that "inner beauty" is a big laugh in this culture. If they come from communi-

ties that traditionally have celebrated voluptuous bodies and within which food represents love, safety, and home, they may feel isolation and guilt over the widening gap between the values they've grown up with and those tugging at them now.

In the world in which our children are growing up, there is a size zero, and it's a status symbol. The chronic dieters have been at it since they were 8 and 9 years old. They know all about eating disorders; being preached to about the dangers turns them right off. Their world is one in which anorexics swap starvation-diet tips on the Internet, participate in group fasts, offer advice on how to hide your "ana" from family members, and share inspirational photos of emaciated models. But full-blown anorexia has never been the norm among teenage girls; the real epidemic is among the girls with seemingly healthy eating habits, seemingly healthy bodies, who vomit or work their butts off as a regular form of anti-fat maintenance. These girls not only look "normal" but consider themselves normal. The new criterion circulating among teenage girls: If you get rid of it through exercise rather than purging or laxatives, you don't have a problem.

Theirs is a world in which groups of dorm girls will plow voraciously through pizzas, chewing and then spitting out each mouthful. Do they have a disorder? Of course not—look, they're eating pizza.

Generations raised in the empire of images are both vulnerable and savvy. They snort when magazines periodically proclaim (about once every six months, the same frequency with which they run cover stories about "starving stars") that in the "new" Hollywood one can be "sexy at any size." They are literati, connoisseurs of the images; they pay close attention to the pounds coming and going—on J. Lo, Reese, Thora, Christina Aguilera, Beyoncé. They know that Kate Winslet, whom the director James Cameron called "Kate Weighs-a-lot" on the set of *Titanic*, was described by the tabloids as "packing on," "ballooning to," "swelling to," "shooting up to," "tipping the scales at" a "walloping," "staggering" weight—of 135 pounds. That slender Courtney Thorne-Smith, who played Calista Flockhart's friend and rival on *Ally McBeal*, quit the show because she could no longer keep up with the pressure to remain as thin as the [series'] creator, David E. Kelley, wanted them to be. That Missy Elliot and Queen Latifah are not on diets just for reasons of health.

I track the culture of young girls today with particular concern, because I'm a mother now. My 4-year-old daughter is a superb athlete with supreme confidence in her body, who prides herself on being able to do anything the boys can do—and better. When I see young girls being diminished and harassed by the culture it feels even more personal to me now. I'm grateful that there's a new generation of female athletes to inspire and support girls like my daughter, Cassie. That our icons are no longer just tiny gymnasts, but powerful soccer, softball, and tennis players, broad-shouldered track stars—Mia Hamm, Sarah Walden, Serena Williams, Marion Jones. During a recent visit to a high school, I saw how the eyes of a 14-year-old athlete shone as she talked about what Marion Jones means to her, and that fills me with hope.

But then, I accidentally tune in to the Maury Povich show, and my heart is torn in two. The topic of the day is "back-to-girl" makeovers. One by one, five beautiful 12-, 13-, and 14-year-old "tomboys" (as Maury called them) are "brought back to their feminine side" (Maury again) through a fashion makeover. We first see them in sweatshirts and caps, in-sisting that they are as strong as any boy, that they want to dress for comfort, that they're tired of being badgered to look like girls. Why, then, are they submitting to this one-time, on-air transformation? To please their moms. And indeed, as each one is brought back on stage, in full makeup and glamour outfit, hair swinging (and, in the case of the black girls, straightened), striking vampy supermodel "power" poses, their mothers sob as if they had just learned their daughters' cancers were in remission. The moms are so overwhelmed they don't need more, but Maury is clearly bent on complete conversion: "Do you know how pretty you are?" "Look how gorgeous you look!" "Are you going to dress like this more often?" Most of the girls, unsurprisingly, say yes. It's been a frontal assault, there's no room for escape.

As jaded as I am, this Maury show really got to me. I wanted to fold each girl in my arms and get her out of there. Of course, what I really fear is that I won't be able to protect Cassie from the same assault. It's happening already. I watch public-television kids' shows with her and can rarely find fault with the gender-neutral world they portray. We go to Disney movies and see resourceful, spirited heroines. Some of them, like the Hawaiian girls in *Lilo and Stitch,* even have thick legs and solid bodies. But then, on the way home from the movies, we stop at McDonald's for a Happy Meal, and, despite the fact that Cassie insists she's a boy and wants the boy's toy—a hot-wheels car—she is given a box containing a mini-Barbie. Illustrating the box is Barbie's room, and my daughter is given the challenging task of finding all the matching pairs of shoes on the floor.

Later that day, I open a Pottery Barn catalog, browsing for ideas for Cassie's room. The designated boy's room is in primary colors, the bedspread dotted with balls, bats, catching mitts. The caption reads: "I play so many sports that it's hard to pick my favorites." Sounds like my daughter. On the opposite page, the girls' room is pictured, a pastel planetary design. The caption reads: "I like stars because they are shiny." That, too, sounds like my daughter. But Pottery Barn doesn't think a child can inhabit both worlds. If its catalogs were as segregated and stereotyped racially as they are by gender, people would boycott.

I rent a video—*Jimmy Neutron, Boy Genius*—for Cassie. It's marketed as a kids' movie, and the movie is OK for the most part. But then we get to the music video that follows the movie, unaccompanied by any warnings. A group I've never heard of sings a song called "Kids in America." Two of the girls are 13, two are 15, and one is 16—their ages are emblazoned across the screen as each makes her appearance. They are in full vixen attire, with professionally undulating bodies and professionally made-up, come-hither eyes.

Why are we told their ages, I wonder? Are we supposed to be amazed at the illusion of womanhood created by their performance? Or is their youth supposed to make it all right to show this to little kids, a way of saying, "It's only make-believe, only a dress-up game"? It wasn't so long ago that people were outraged by news clips of JonBenet Ramsey performing in children's beauty pageants. In 2002, toddler versions of Britney Spears were walking the streets on Halloween night. Can it really be that we now think dressing our daughters up like tiny prostitutes is cute? That's what the psychologist Sharon Lamb, author of *The Secret Lives of Girls,* thinks. She advises mothers to chill out if their 9-year-old girls "play lovely little games in high heels, strip teasing, flouncing, and jutting their chests out," to relax if their 11-year-olds go out with "thick blue eye shadow, spaghetti straps and bra straps intertwined, long and leggy with short black dresses." They are "silly and adorable, sexy and marvelous all at once," she tells us, as they "celebrate their objectification," "playing out male fantasies . . . but without risk."

Without risk? I have nothing against girls playing dress-up. But flouncing is one thing; strip teasing is another. Thick blue eye shadow in mommy's bathroom is fine; an 11-year-old's night on the town is not. Reading those words "without risk," I want to remind Sharon Lamb that 22 to 29 percent of all rapes against girls occur when they are 11 and younger. We might like to think that those rapes are the work of deranged madmen, so disconnected from reality as to be oblivious to the culture around them. Or that all we need to do to protect our daughters is simply teach them not to take candy from or go into cars with strangers. The reality, however, is that young girls are much more likely to be raped by friends and family members than by strangers and that very few men, whether strangers or acquaintances, are unaffected by a visual culture of nymphets prancing before their eyes, exuding a sexual knowledge and experience that preteens don't really have. Feminists used to call this "rape culture." We never hear that phrase anymore.

Still, progressive forces are not entirely asleep in the empire of images. I think of *YM* teen magazine, for example. After conducting a survey that revealed that 86 percent of its young readers were dissatisfied with the way their bodies looked, *YM* openly declared war on eating disorders and body-image problems, instituting an editorial policy against the publishing of diet pieces and deliberately seeking out full-size models—without identifying them as such—for all its fashion spreads. A colleague suggested that this resistance to the hegemony of the fat-free body may have something to do with the fact that the editors are young enough to have studied feminism and cultural studies while they got their B.A.'s in English and journalism.

Most progressive developments in the media, of course, are driven by market considerations rather than social conscience. So, for example, the fact that 49 million women are size 12 or more is clearly the motive behind new, flesh-normalizing campaigns created by "Just My Size" and Lane Bryant. Ad campaigns for these lines of clothing proudly show off zaftig bodies in sexy underwear and, unlike older marketing to "plus size" women, refuse to use that term, insisting (accurately) that what has been called plus size is in fact average. It's a great strategy for making profits, but a species of resistance nonetheless. "I won't allow myself to be invisible anymore," these ads proclaim, on our behalf. "But I won't be made visible as a cultural oddity or a joke, either, because I'm not. I'm the norm."

The amorality of consumer capitalism, in its restless search for new markets and new ways to generate and feed desire, has also created a world of racial representations that are far more diverse now than when I wrote *Unbearable Weight*. This is another issue that has acquired special meaning for me, because my daughter is biracial, and I am acutely aware of the world that she sees and what it is telling her about herself. Leafing through current magazines, noting the variety of skin tones, noses, mouths depicted there, I'm glad, for the moment, that Cassie is growing up today rather than in the '70s, when Cheryl Tiegs ruled. It's always possible, of course, to find things that are still "wrong" with these representations; racist codes and aesthetics die hard. The Jezebels and geishas are still with us; and, although black male models and tod- dlers are allowed to have locks and "naturals," straight hair—straighter nowadays than I ever thought it was possible for anyone's hair to be—seems almost mandatory for young black women.

It's easy, too, to be cynical. Today's fashionable diversity is brought to us, after all, by the same people who brought us the hegemony of the blue-eyed blonde and who've made wrinkles and cellulite into diseases. It's easy to dismiss fashion's current love affair with full lips and biracial children as a shameless attempt to exploit ethnic markets while providing ethnic chic for white beauty tourists. Having a child, however, has given me another perspective, as I try to imagine how the models look through her eyes. Cassie knows nothing about the motives of the people who've produced the images. At her age, she can only take them at face value. And at face value, they present a world that includes and celebrates her, as the world that I grew up in did not include and celebrate me. For all my anger, cynicism, and frustration with our empire of images, I cannot help but be grateful for that.

And sometimes, surveying the plastic, digitalized world of bodies that are the norm now, I am convinced that our present state of enchantment is just a moment away from revulsion, or perhaps simply boredom. I see a 20-something woman dancing at a local outdoor swing party, her tummy softly protruding over the thick leather belt of her low-rider jeans. Not taut, not toned, not artfully camouflaged like some unsightly deformity, but proudly, sensuously displayed, reminding me of Madonna in the days before she became the sinewy dominatrix. Is it possible that we are beginning to rebel against the manufactured look of celebrity bodies, beginning to be repelled by their armored perfection?

Such hopeful moments, I have to admit, are fleeting. Usually, I feel horrified. I am sharply aware that expressing my horror openly nowadays invites being thought of as a preachy prude, a relic of an outmoded feminism. At talks to young audiences, I try to lighten my touch, celebrate the positive, make sure that my criticisms of our culture are not confused with being anti-beauty, anti-fitness, or anti-sex. But I also know that when parents and teachers become fully one with the culture, children are abandoned to it. I don't tell them to love their bodies or turn off the television—useless admonitions today, and ones I cannot obey myself—but I do try to disrupt, if only temporarily, their everyday immersion in the culture. For just an hour or so, I won't let it pass itself off simply as "normalcy."

The lights go down, the slides go up. For just a moment, we confront how bizarre, how impossible, how contradictory the images are. We laugh together over Oprah's head digitally grafted to another woman's body, at the ad for breast implants in which the breasts stick straight up in the air. We gasp together as the before and after photos of Jennifer Lopez are placed side by side. We cheer for Marion Jones's shoulders, boo the fact that WNBA Barbie is just the same old Barbie, but with a basketball in her hand. For just a moment, we are in charge of the impact the faked images of "perfect" bodies have on us.

We look at them together and share—just for a moment—outrage.

CONNECTING PERSONALLY TO THE READING

1. Do you agree that "no matter what [your] parents, teachers, and clergy" tell you, "'inner beauty' is a big laugh in this culture"? Why or why not?

2. If you know people, male or female, who are dissatisfied with the way they look, what accounts for this dissatisfaction? What leads us to find some physical attributes—such as the shape of a nose, texture of hair, or body type—to be beautiful, and others not?

FOCUSING ON THE ARGUMENT

1. The first three paragraphs consist almost entirely of sentence fragments that mimic the effect of the bits of visual images that flicker through our lives. What is the point of this opening, and how effective are the fragments in making this point? Read these paragraphs out loud, and notice the rhythm they produce. How would the effect of this opening be different if Bordo had written complete sentences?

2. Bordo introduces personal testimony into her argument. By writing in the first person ("I") and speaking of her feelings about her own body, does Bordo become more or less convincing? Explain your answer.

3. Where in the article does Bordo try to find common ground with those who succumb to media images of women?

SYNTHESIZING IDEAS FROM MULTIPLE READINGS

1. Both Susan Bordo and Mira Jacob ("My Brown Face," p. 143) use metaphors of empire and colonizing to critique the cultural obsession with female beauty. What do these metaphors suggest about the problem each author discusses?

2. Susan Bordo and Jean Kilbourne ("'The More You Subtract, the More You Add,'" p. 149) both fault consumer capitalism for manipulating women's self-image. Using examples from each of their articles, what connections does each writer make between a company's or individual's effort to sell a product—whether it's a movie or a medical procedure—and women's ideas about their beauty?

WRITING TO ACT

1. Do a Web search for Pro-Ana Web sites (you might start with the Pro-Ana links page at http://www.plagueangel.net/grotto/id5.html), which promote eating disorders as a personal choice. Create a Web page that supports, contradicts, or complicates the positions expressed on these sites. Alternatively, send a message to the site owner, expressing your opinion on the ideas advanced on the Web site. For background on the Pro-Ana movement, explore the site Make Up Your Mind (http://ana.makeupyourmind.nu/).

2. Alone or with a group of your classmates, find an advertisement directed toward young girls that promotes the kind of image Bordo critiques. Then create an alternative advertisement for the same product, one that would interest young girls and, at the same time, offer them a healthy self-image. Send your ad to the company that makes the advertised product, along with a letter explaining the rationale for your version.

READING

DANAE CLARK   Clark argues that one way advertisers appeal to gay and lesbian consumers is to create a coded image that gays and lesbians will identify with, but that is subtle enough not to alienate straight men and women. Clark believes that many Calvin Klein menswear ads use this approach, whereas the marketing directors at Calvin Klein deny appealing to a specifically gay market. Find a fashion magazine, and look at the Calvin Klein ads for men's clothing: whose viewpoint do you agree with, and why?

CLARK, a professor of media studies at the University of Pittsburgh, is the author of *Negotiating Hollywood: The Cultural Politics of Actors' Labor.* This is an excerpt from the article "Commodity Lesbianism," which originally appeared in *Camera Obscura,* one of the media-related journals Clark contributes to.

Dividing the Consumer Pie (1991) | BY DANAE CLARK

> *A commodity appears, at first sight, a very*
> *trivial thing, and easily understood. Its analysis*
> *shows that it is, in reality, a very queer thing . . .*
> KARL MARX, *Capital*

. . . Analyses of female consumerism join a substantial body of other feminist work that "assumes, but leaves unwritten, a heterosexual context for the subject" and thus contributes to the continued invisibility of lesbians.

But lesbians too are consumers. Like heterosexual women they are major purchasers of clothing, household goods and media products. Lesbians have not, however, been targeted as a separate consumer group within the dominant configuration of capitalism, either directly through the mechanism of advertising or indirectly through fictional media representations; their relation to consumerism is thus necessarily different. . . .

DIVIDING THE CONSUMER PIE

Lesbians have not been targeted as consumers by the advertising industry for several historical reasons. First, lesbians as a social group have not been economically powerful; thus, like other social groups who lack substantial purchasing power (for example, the elderly), they have not been attractive to advertisers. Second, lesbians have not been easily identifiable as a social group anyway. According to the market strategies commonly used by advertisers to develop target consumer groups, four criteria must be met. A group must be: (1) identifiable, (2) accessible, (3) measurable, and (4) profitable. In other words, a particular group must be "knowable" to advertisers in concrete ways. Lesbians present a problem here because they exist across race, income and age (three determinants used by advertisers to segment and distinguish target groups within the female population). To the extent that lesbians are not identifiable or accessible, they are not measurable and, therefore, not profitable. The fact that many lesbians prefer not to be identified because they fear discrimination poses an additional obstacle to targeting them. Finally, most advertisers have had no desire to identify a viable lesbian consumer group. Advertisers fear that by openly appealing to a homosexual market their products will be negatively associated with homosexuality and will be avoided by heterosexual consumers. Thus, although homosexuals (lesbians and gay men) reputedly comprise 10% of the overall U.S. market population—and up to 20–22% in major urban centers such as New York and San Francisco—advertisers have traditionally stayed in the closet when it comes to peddling their wares.

Recently, however, this trend has undergone a visible shift—especially for gay men. According to a 1982 review in *The New York Times Magazine* called "Tapping the Homosexual Market," several of today's top advertisers are interested in "wooing . . . the white, single, well-educated, well-paid man who happens to be homosexual." This interest, prompted by surveys conducted by *The Advocate* between 1977 and 1980 that indicated that 70% of their readers aged 20–40 earned incomes well above the national median, has led companies such as Paramount, Seagram, Perrier, and Harper & Row to advertise in gay male publications like *Christopher Street* and *The Advocate*.

Their ads are tailored specifically for the gay male audience. Seagram, for example, ran a "famous men of history" campaign for Boodles Gin that pictured men "purported to be gay."

A more common and more discreet means of reaching the gay male consumer, however, is achieved through the mainstream (predominately print) media. As one marketing director has pointed out, advertisers "really want to reach a bigger market than just gays, but [they] don't want to alienate them" either. Thus, advertisers are increasingly striving to create a dual marketing approach that will "speak to the homosexual consumer in a way that the straight consumer will not notice." As one observer explains:

> It used to be that gay people could communicate to one another, in a public place, if they didn't know one another, only by glances and a sort of *code behavior* . . . to indicate to the other person, but not to anybody else, that you, too, were gay. Advertisers, if they're smart, can do that too (emphasis added).

One early example of this approach was the Calvin Klein jeans series that featured "a young, shirtless blond man lying on his stomach" and, in another ad, "a young, shirtless blond man lying on his side, holding a blue-jeans jacket." According to Peter Frisch, a gay marketing consultant, one would "have to be comatose not to realize that it appeals to gay men" (I presume he is referring to the photographs' iconographic resemblance to gay pornography). Calvin Klein marketing directors, however, denied any explicit gay element:

> We did not try *not* to appeal to gays. We try to appeal, period. With healthy, beautiful people. If there's an awareness in that community of health and grooming, they'll respond to the ads.

This dual marketing strategy has been referred to as "gay window advertising." Generally, gay window ads avoid explicit references to heterosexuality by depicting only one individual or same-sexed individuals within the representational frame. In addition, these models bear the signifiers of sexual ambiguity or androgynous style. But "gayness" remains in the eye of the beholder: gays and lesbians can read into an ad certain subtextual elements that correspond to experiences with or representations of gay/lesbian subculture. If heterosexual consumers do not notice these subtexts or subcultural codes, then advertisers are able to reach the homosexual market along with the heterosexual market without ever revealing their aim. . . .

. . . Lesbians have a long tradition of resisting dominant cultural definitions of female beauty and fashion as a way of separating themselves from heterosexual culture politically and as a way of signaling their lesbianism to other women in their subcultural group. This resistance to or reformulation of fashion codes thus distinguished lesbians from straight women at the same time that it challenged patriarchal structures. As Arlene Stein explains in a recent article on style in the lesbian community:

> Lesbian-feminist anti-style was an emblem of refusal, an attempt to strike a blow against the twin evils of capitalism and patriarchy, the fashion industry and the female objectification that fueled it. The flannel-and-denim look was not so much a style as it was anti-style—an attempt to replace the artifice of fashion with a supposed naturalness, free of gender roles and commercialized pretense.

Today, however, many lesbians, particularly younger, urban lesbians, are challenging this look, exposing the constructedness of "natural" fashion, and finding a great deal of pleasure in playing with the possibilities of fashion and beauty. . . .

WHEN DYKES GO SHOPPING . . .

In a recent issue of *Elle* a fashion layout entitled "Male Order" shows us a model who, in the words of the accompanying ad copy, represents "the zenith of masculine allure." In one photograph the handsome, short-haired model leans against the handlebars of a motorcycle, an icon associated with bike dyke culture. Her man-styled jacket, tie, and jewelry suggest a butch lesbian style that offers additional points of purchase for the lesbian spectator. In another photograph from the series, the model is placed in a more neutral setting, a café, that is devoid of lesbian iconography. But because she is still dressed in masculine attire and, more importantly, exhibits the "swaggering" style recommended by the advertisers, the model incorporates aspects of lesbian style. Here, the traditional "come on" look of advertising can be read as the look or pose of a cruising dyke. Thus, part of the pleasure that lesbians find in these ads might be what Elizabeth Ellsworth calls "lesbian verisimilitude," or the representation of body language, facial expression, and general appearance that can be claimed and coded as "lesbian" according to current standards of style within lesbian communities.

Just as early twentieth-century advertisers were more concerned about women's votes in the marketplace than their decisions in the voting booth, contemporary advertisers are more interested in lesbian consumers than lesbian politics. Once stripped of its political underpinnings, lesbianism can be represented as a style of consumption linked to sexual preference. Lesbianism, in other words, is treated as merely a sexual style that can be chosen—or not chosen—just as one chooses a particular mode of fashion for self-expression.

CONNECTING PERSONALLY TO THE READING

1. Do you think images of gays and lesbians in mainstream advertisements make it possible for gays and lesbians to be more openly accepted in society?

2. Find ads that you think might be intended to appeal to both a gay and straight audience. How might you have interpreted the ad before reading Clark's article? Has your impression of the ad changed?

FOCUSING ON THE ARGUMENT

1. One of Clark's persuasive strategies is to quote the opinions of others. Find two examples of these strategies, and explain why you do or do not find them convincing.

2. Clark illustrates her argument by describing specific ads from mainstream magazines that she believes depict gays and lesbians. To what extent does this description strengthen her contention that the sexuality of the models is deliberately ambiguous?

3. Clark sets up her argument by placing it in a historical context, explaining why advertisers have ignored gay and lesbian consumers as a distinct group. Does this context make it

easier for you to accept her thesis: that many ads now try to appeal to both gay and straight consumers?

1. Both Jean Kilbourne ("'The More You Subtract, the More You Add,'", 149) and Clark criticize advertisers, but for different reasons. Kilbourne believes that advertisements trivialize girls; Clark argues that advertisers ignore the real political issues that concern gays and lesbians. Given that advertisers' principal goal is to get consumers to buy products, do you think these are fair criticisms? Or do advertisers have a duty to be socially responsible?

2. Clark believes that advertisers are careful not to make the "gay window dressing" in their ads too noticeable, for fear of losing heterosexual consumers. Yet other consumer groups, such as girls, are targeted directly; no effort is made to disguise the intended audience for the ads that Kilbourne describes in "'The More You Subtract, the More You Add'" (p. 149). What stereotypes do straight people hold about gays and lesbians that make advertisers reluctant to advertise openly to these groups? How are these stereotypes similar to or different from the stereotyping Mira Jacob in "My Brown Face" (p. 143) and Brent Staples in "Just Walk On By" (p. 118) experience?

1. Possibly working with other students, design a poster—using both words and visual images—for a campus event: the poster should be sexually ambiguous, appeal equally to a gay or lesbian or to a straight audience, and offend none of these groups. Display your poster to your classmates, and ask for their responses and suggestions for improvement. Considering your classmates' comments, revise your poster; then get permission from your campus's student event office to display the poster.

2. Choose a public communication medium in which you think gays or lesbians may be largely invisible—such as television news—and analyze the depiction of gender in this medium. Write an editorial describing your findings.

Connecting the Readings with the Advertisements

America's Dairy Farmers and Milk Processors, "Want strong bones? . . ."

1. In "Just Walk On By" (p. 118), Brent Staples describes how he is stereotyped by both gender and race. Do you think the same is true of Jackie Chan in the milk ad? Why or why not?

2. In "Beer Commercials: A Manual on Masculinity" (p. 127), Lance Strate argues that beer ads perpetuate myths about male behavior. Although culturally, we have very different associations with milk than we do with beer, some of the myths described in Strate's essay appear in this milk advertisement. Show which myths are or are not represented in the ad.

America's Dairy Farmers and Milk Processors, "Shop and Not Drop"

1. In "'The More You Subtract the More You Add'" (p. 149), Jean Kilbourne argues that advertising undermines girls' self-confidence by showing them as passive, powerless, and childish. Explain whether the ad supports this criticism.

2. One interpretation of this ad is that Duff is identified with the shopping bags, which hang off her, like extensions of her body; that is, Duff herself has become an object, to be admired and eventually possessed. How might Susan Bordo ("The Empire of Images in Our World of Bodies," p. 169), Cindy Jackson ("My Cosmetic Surgery," p. 139), and Don Sabo ("The Myth of the Sexual Athlete," p. 113) respond to this interpretation?

Givenchy

1. The man in this ad has an expression of awe and inspiration on his face. Given the way Lance Strate (in "Beer Commercials: A Manual on Masculinity," p. 127) characterizes the depiction of men in beer commercials, do you think a beer commercial might show a man the same way? Why or why not?

2. How is this man like or unlike the athletes Don Sabo describes in "The Myth of the Sexual Athlete" (p. 113)?

Stetson

1. In "Dividing the Consumer Pie" (p. 177), Danae Clark argues that advertisers sometimes use "gay coding," images that speak to gay and lesbian readers without alienating straight readers. Do you see "gay coding" in this ad? Why or why not?

2. Lance Strate ("Beer Commercials: A Manual on Masculinity," p. 127) points out that TV commercials often identify masculinity with nature, showing men herding cattle or crossing a raging stream. How would you characterize the natural setting in this ad? Does it enhance or detract from the man's toughness?

Chanel Chance

1. How old do you think the woman in the ad is? Do you think Susan Bordo ("The Empire of Images in Our World of Bodies," p. 169) would approve of this ad? Why or why not?

2. What does Mira Jacob ("My Brown Face," p. 143) mean by this statement—"Being sexualized . . . [leaves] a woman utterly aware of nothing but her body"—and how might this ad contribute to the experience she describes?

Dior

1. How might Danae Clark ("Dividing the Consumer Pie," p. 177) interpret this ad? How would you interpret the relationship being depicted if the models were male?

2. In "The Return of the Pig" (p. 122), David Brooks argues that men's magazines like *Maxim* encourage men to leer at women, to view them as objects. Do you think that this ad and others like it encourage women to view themselves and other women as sex objects? Why or why not?

Coca-Cola

1. Lance Strate ("Beer Commercials: A Manual on Masculinity," p. 127) argues that in commercials, a young man must prove his masculinity by doing the things that mature men do: "take risks, meet challenges, face danger courageously, and

dominate his environment." Compare the ways the young men in the Coca-Cola ad and the milk ad ("Want strong bones? . . .") fulfill these expectations. Does one man seem more successful than the other?

2. Jean Kilbourne ("'The More You Subtract, the More You Add,'" p. 149), Susan Bordo ("The Empire of Images in Our World of Bodies," p. 169), Mira Jacob ("My Brown Face," p. 143), and Cindy Jackson ("My Cosmetic Surgery," p. 139) all argue that a woman's value is identified primarily with her body. The man in this ad is wearing nothing but a bathing suit. What personal characteristics does the ad ascribe to him, and to what extent are they associated with his body?

Pepsi

1. According to Susan Bordo ("The Empire of Images in Our World of Bodies," p. 169), ads often suggest that women must be beautiful to have power. What forms of power does the Pepsi ad offer women?

2. Mira Jacob ("My Brown Face," p. 143) notes that her mother doesn't smile when strange men tell her she's pretty, a way of resisting being objectified. Jacob herself resorts to "battle tactics": "I have a mediocre right hook and a prize-fighting tongue." Like Jacob and her mother, the model in the Pepsi ad is responding to being ogled (by the viewers of the ad). How would you describe her attitude? How is it like or unlike Jacob's reaction to being objectified?

FINDING COMMON CAUSE IN CONTROVERSY
Should Same-Sex Marriage Be Legalized?

In 2004, the city of San Francisco and the state of Massachusetts began to permit marriages between couples of the same sex, thus prompting a debate over the legality and appropriateness of same-sex marriage. An issue that touches people's lives as personally as this one does can evoke so much emotion that it polarizes people, making common cause hard to find. What shared beliefs can you find among the different sides of this debate? What ideas could you propose that might make it easier for each side to listen to the other?

Same-sex marriages have a controversial history. In 1989, Denmark recognized same-sex unions by allowing gay and lesbian couples to register as partners. In 1991, three same-sex couples sued the state of Hawaii for the right to get married. In response, the voters amended the Hawaiian constitution to limit marriage to a man and a woman. Similarly, in 1996, President Clinton signed the Defense of Marriage Act prohibiting federal recognition of same-sex marriage. As of early 2006, the Netherlands, Belgium, Spain, and Canada all allow gays and lesbians to marry, and Denmark, Sweden, Greenland, Iceland, Hungary, France, Finland, Germany, Great Britain, and New Zealand have legalized civil unions between partners of the same sex. In the United States, only Vermont and Connecticut have legalized civil unions between couples of the same sex.

The debate on this issue depends heavily on one's personal values. Those who believe homosexuality to be unnatural do not approve of same-sex unions of any kind, whereas those who accept homosexuality as innate, rather than as a choice, consider any prohibition against same-sex marriages to be discriminatory and unconstitutional. What arguments does Andrew Sullivan make for gay marriage in "Why the *M* Word Matters to Me"? In "Deathblow to Marriage," why does Stanley Kurtz argue against gay marriage? What common cause can you find in their positions?

ANDREW SULLIVAN   Andrew Sullivan, a senior editor at the *New Republic,* contributes frequently to other publications, including *Time* magazine, and he writes a column for the *Sunday Times* of London. Sullivan is one of the first established journalists to keep a blog, www.andrewsullivan.com, where he regularly posts commentary and links to articles about politics and culture. His book *Virtually Normal: An Argument about Homosexuality* makes a case for civil marriage rights for same-sex couples.

Why the *M* Word Matters to Me
Only marriage can bring a gay person home

BY ANDREW SULLIVAN

As a child, I had no idea what homosexuality was. I grew up in a traditional home—Catholic, conservative, middle class. Life was relatively simple: education, work, family. I was raised to aim high in life, even though my parents hadn't gone to college. But one thing was instilled in me. What mattered was not how far you went in life, how much money you earned, how big a name you made for yourself. What really mattered was family and the love you had for one another. The most important day of your life was not graduation from college or your first day at work or a raise or even your first house. The most important day of your life was when you got married. It was on that day that all your friends and all your family got together to celebrate the most important thing in life: your happiness—your ability to make a new home, to form a new but connected family, to find love that put everything else into perspective.

But as I grew older, I found that this was somehow not available to me. I didn't feel the things for girls that my peers did. All the emotions and social rituals and bonding of teenage heterosexual life eluded me. I didn't know why. No one explained it. My emotional bonds to other boys were one-sided; each time I felt myself falling in love, they sensed it, pushed it away. I didn't and couldn't blame them. I got along fine with my buds in a nonemotional context, but something was awry, something not right. I came to know almost instinctively that I would never be a part of my family the way my siblings might one day be. The love I had inside me was unmentionable, anathema. I remember writing in my teenage journal one day, "I'm a professional human being. But what do I do in my private life?"

I never discussed my real life. I couldn't date girls and so immersed myself in schoolwork, the debate team, school plays, anything to give me an excuse not to confront reality. When I looked toward the years ahead, I couldn't see a future. There was just a void. Was I going to be alone my whole life? Would I ever have a most important day in my life? It seemed impossible, a negation, an undoing. To be a full part of my family, I had to somehow not be me. So, like many other gay teens, I withdrew, became neurotic, depressed, at times close to suicidal. I shut myself in my room with my books night after night while my peers developed the skills needed to form real relationships and loves. In wounded pride, I even voiced a rejection of family and marriage. It was the only way I could explain my isolation.

It took years for me to realize that I was gay, years more to tell others and more time yet to form any kind of stable emotional bond with another man. Because my sexuality had emerged in solitude—and without any link to the idea of an actual relationship—it was hard later to reconnect sex to love and self-esteem. It still is. But I persevered, each relationship slowly growing longer than the last, learning in my 20s and 30s what my straight friends had found out in their teens. But even then my parents and friends never asked the question they would have asked automatically if I were straight: So, when are you going to get married? When will we be able to celebrate it and affirm it and support it? In fact, no one—no one—has yet asked me that question.

When people talk about gay marriage, 5 they miss the point. This isn't about gay marriage. It's about marriage. It's about family. It's about love. It isn't about religion. It's about *civil* marriage licenses. Churches can and should have the right to say no to marriage for gays in their congregations, just as Catholics say no to divorce, but divorce is still a civil option. These family values are not options for a happy and stable life. They are necessities. Putting gay relationships in some other category—civil unions, domestic partnerships, whatever—may alleviate real human needs, but by their very euphemism, by their very separateness, they actually build a wall between gay people and their families. They put back the barrier many of us have spent a lifetime trying to erase.

It's too late for me to undo my past. But I want above everything else to remember a young kid out there who may even be reading this now. I want to let him know that he doesn't have to choose between himself and his family anymore. I want him to know that his love has dignity, that he does indeed have a future as a full and equal part of the human race. Only marriage will do that. Only marriage can bring him home.

STANLEY KURTZ   Stanley Kurtz is a contributing editor at the *National Review* and a research fellow at the Hoover Institute. His essays and articles appear in the *Weekly Standard,* the *Wall Street Journal,* and the *Chronicle of Higher Education,* among other periodicals. He is the author of the book *All the Mothers Are One: Hindu India and the Cultural Reshaping of Psychoanalysis.*

Deathblow to Marriage

BY STANLEY KURTZ

On Wednesday, the Massachusetts Supreme Judicial Court unambiguously mandated the granting of marriage licenses to same-sex couples. The decision will take effect in about three and a half months. The time will come to debate the tactics of the gay-marriage battle. Right now is a moment for sober reflection on what is at stake.

At issue in the gay-marriage controversy is nothing less than the existence of marriage itself. This point is vehemently denied by the proponents of gay marriage, who speak endlessly of marriage's adaptability and "resilience." But if there is one thing I think I've established in my recent writing on Scandinavia, it is that marriage can die—and is in fact dying—somewhere in the world. In fact, marriage is dying in the very same place that first recognized gay marriage.

In setting up the institution of marriage, society offers special support and encouragement to the men and women who together make children. Because marriage is deeply implicated in the interests of children, it is a matter of public concern. Children are helpless. They depend upon adults. Over and above their parents, children depend upon society to create institutions that keep them from chaos. Children cannot articulate their needs. Children cannot vote. Yet children are society. They are us, and they are our future. That is why society has the right to give special support and encouragement to an institution that is necessary to the well being of children—even if that means special benefits for some, and not for others. The dependence intrinsic to human childhood is why unadulterated libertarianism can never work.

The "discrimination" inherent in the legal institution of marriage is relatively minor. Single people are "discriminated against" by the benefits granted to married couples. Those who prefer to live with multiple lovers are also "discriminated against" by the institution of marriage. So, too, are same-sex couples "discriminated against" by marriage. Each of these groups is now demanding redress from this "discrimination." Such redress will spell the end of marriage.

The difficulties and challenges of gays 5 are special precisely because they do not derive from the "discrimination" of marriage. The real source of the challenges of gay life is the problem of sexual difference. It is terribly difficult to grow up with a different sort of sexuality than most of the world around you. Marriage does not cause this problem, and it cannot solve it.

Yet, out of understandable compassion for the sorrows and difficulties of gays, many Americans want to offer marriage as a kind of consolation or remedy for the challenges inherent in the gay situation. The increased social tolerance for gays in America is largely a good thing, as far as I'm concerned. But using marriage to accomplish a purpose for which it was not intended—and which it cannot fulfill—will not fundamentally alter the situation of gays. It will, however, spell the end of marriage, and of the protection marriage offers to vulnerable children who cannot vote or articulate their interests. The number of children potentially endangered by the collapse of marriage is far larger than the number of gays or "polyamorists." The number of single people who will never marry is substantial and growing, yet society is right to "discriminate" against these single people in ways that are relatively modest—but which sustain an institution that protects children.

THE ROOT CAUSE

I believe I have established that marriage in Scandinavia is dying. No one has disputed this. Instead it is objected that gay marriage is not a cause of this demise, but only an effect. I would like someone to explain how gay marriage could be only an effect of the decline of marriage, without also being a reinforcing cause. How can a change that becomes imaginable only after marriage has been separated from parenthood fail to lock in and reinforce that very separation?

In Sweden, where marriage was already radically separated from parenthood, and largely equalized with cohabitation in legal-financial terms, gay marriage was more effect than cause. But in Norway, where the decline of marriage was only partial, gay marriage had a greater role as a facilitator of marital decline than it did in Sweden. In the United States, the effect of gay marriage would be massive.

As of now (and in substantial contrast to Scandinavia), the legal distinction between marriage and cohabitation in America is strong. Yet important proposals from the American Law Institute would put us on the Scandinavian path. In America, gay marriage would be the leading edge of the Scandinavian system—not the tail-end, as it was in Sweden. Gay marriage would accustom us to think about marriage in Scandinavian terms—to think of marriage as

substantially unrelated to parenthood. And that would lead us to adopt legal reforms that already loom—reforms that would lock us in to the Scandinavian pattern of marital decline.

Everywhere, gay marriage is both an 10 effect and a cause of marital decline. But in America, gay marriage would have even more causal impact than it did in Norway—and far more than in Sweden. [...]

In addition to some preliminary indications that same-sex registered partnerships may not be as stable as heterosexual marriages, it's of interest that a much higher proportion of same-sex spouses tend to be over 40 years of age. In Sweden, for example, half of all male partnerships are entered into by at least one spouse over 40. In contrast, only 14 percent of opposite-sex marriages involved such senior spouses. This suggests that even when same-sex couples do marry, the effect on sexual behavior is minimal. That's because they wait until their later years to wed. True, some of this age discrepancy may be due to same-sex couples who might have married at younger ages "catching up" after legalization. Even so, the age discrepancy is striking, and may have more general significance.

In short, current data on same-sex registered partnerships in Scandinavia suggest that the effect of marriage on gay monogamy will be minimal. Exceedingly few couples marry. Those few who do marry are significantly older. And in Sweden at least, same-sex couples divorce at a significantly higher rate. But the biggest imponderable here is Sullivan's assumption that marriage does in fact indicate monogamous behavior—or even monogamy as an ideal—among same-sex couples. In my earlier piece, "Beyond Gay Marriage," I showed that this can by no means be assumed. So in

Scandinavia, exceedingly few gays marry at all. And we don't even know if those very few who do marry practice or strive for monogamy. [...]

Most people who get married are planning to have children. The fact that older couples have kids off in college does nothing to change that fact. The striking thing about Americans—and it's evident immediately on comparison with Scandinavia—is just how closely we continue to associate marriage with parenthood. Every time Andrew Sullivan makes his case that marriage and parenthood are not connected, he is harming marriage. I know this is far from Sullivan's intention (and I respect his intentions). But the harm to marriage is real nonetheless.

The debate will go on. I believe the coming weeks and months will show that we are just beginning to learn what is really at stake in the gay-marriage controversy. The Massachusetts Supreme Judicial Court has acted precipitously, and without due regard to the immensity and complexity of the institution they are tampering with. The mere fact that the real situation of marriage in Scandinavia—and Europe as a whole—is almost entirely unknown in the United States should be enough to give us pause. Unfortunately, we are now obliged to do battle against judges who haven't the foggiest notion of the real implications of their actions (much less respect for the democratic process).

EMPATHIZING WITH DIFFERENT POINTS OF VIEW

Before you choose sides in this debate, try to understand why some people feel so strongly in favor of same-sex marriage and why others reject it with equal vehemence. Try to empathize with each side of this issue.

Favoring those who support same-sex marriage:

- Imagine yourself as so much in love with another person that you want to spend your lives together. How would you feel if the law refused to recognize your emotional bond with your partner by denying the two of you the right to marry?
- How would you feel if you and your life partner—after decades together as a same-sex couple—were denied the right to make medical decisions for each other in an emergency, receive tax advantages as a couple, and get health benefits for each other, rights that are automatically granted to heterosexual married couples?
- Same-sex couples frequently adopt children, providing them with a loving and stable home. How would you counter the argument that only married heterosexual couples should have a family?
- Homosexuals have faced discrimination and violence for centuries. How might legalizing same-sex marriage encourage parents, teachers, and others to respect homosexuals?
- You have friends who have been with their life partners for many years. How do you answer opponents who argue that same-sex marriages are less likely to be monogamous than heterosexual marriages? What assumptions about homosexual and heterosexual behavior lie beneath their views? Beneath your views?

Siding with those who oppose same-sex marriage:

- What arguments might one make for the idea that the purpose of marriage is procreation?
- Kurtz argues that the lack of marriage didn't create the problem of "difference" and that marriage won't solve it. What is Sullivan's problem, and why is marriage a poor solution for it?
- Put yourself in the position of someone who believes marriage is a sacrament, a religious institution that unites a man and a woman. In what ways would same-sex marriage offend you?
- How might changing the definition of marriage be a risky social experiment that threatens heterosexual marriage?
- Take the position of someone who believes that the special benefits of marriage should accrue to those men and women who bring up children because of the special duties and responsibilities needed to protect children. Explain how only a heterosexual couple can fulfill these duties.

ADDING MORE INFORMATION

- The online version of Stanley Kurtz's article has links to other articles supporting his points: http://www.nationalreview.com/kurtz/kurtz200402050842.asp. How convincing do you find these arguments?
- Consider the arguments about gay marriage at http://grove.ufl.edu/~ggsa/gaymarriage.html.
- The following article includes many arguments in favor of same-sex marriage and links for additional information: http://www.bidstrup.com/marriage.htm.

SEEKING COMMON CAUSE

- Both Sullivan and Kurtz believe that marriage celebrates a couple's love and commitment to each other.
- Both believe that marriage is not just a personal arrangement, but a powerful institution that stabilizes society.
- Both value tradition and believe that a loving family provides the best place to raise children.
- Both believe in monogamy as the basis for a good relationship.
- Neither supports discrimination against any minority group.

DEBATE ESSAY

Do the arguments that Sullivan presents for gay marriage outweigh the opposing arguments discussed in Kurtz's article? What additional arguments about same-sex marriage make you lean toward one side or another?

WRITING PROJECTS

Writing a Short Essay

The following short writing projects can prepare you for writing the long essay in the Writing an Extended Argument section or can be done independently.

Writing to Understand a Reading

Write a summary of and personal response to any one of the readings in this chapter. The summary should occupy at least one-third of this paper and should do the following:

- Indicate the main point of the article.
- Indicate some of the key subordinate points the article makes.
- Explain some of the evidence the author offers.
- Use your own words, though you can quote the article briefly, if you like.

The response should occupy at least one-third of the paper. The best responses go beyond simple opinion to discuss concrete evidence. These are some possible approaches:

- Agree or disagree with the article's thesis or any of its ideas.
- Evaluate the evidence (e.g., how convincing is it to you? how does it measure up to your experience?).
- Consider the effectiveness of the article's other persuasive strategies.
- Discuss your own experiences.
- Indicate any points the author should have mentioned.
- Explain what you liked or disliked about the article (e.g., its style, ideas, evidence, attitude).

Evaluating the Personal Influence of Advertising

1. Consider the following statement: "Advertisements depict for us not necessarily how we actually behave as men and women but how we *think* men and women behave. This depiction serves the social purpose of convincing us that this is how men and women are, or want to be, or should be." (Vivian Gornick).

2. After you have analyzed the depiction of men or women in an advertisement, compare the image in the ad with your own understanding of how men or women behave. Do you think the ad accurately represents actual men or women you know? Does it idealize men or women? Does it make them unappealing? Do you think you are influenced by these images of men or women?

Comparing Written and Visual Forms of Persuasion

Cindy Jackson's interview ("My Cosmetic Surgery," p. 139) appears on her Web site (http://www .cindyjackson.com), which functions partly to advertise Jackson's services as a consultant on cosmetic surgery. What rhetorical strategies does the article use to persuade the reader that cosmetic surgery can improve his or her life? Compare the persuasive devices used in Jackson's interview in the *Sunday Times* of London, which relies primarily on words, with those used in the Jackie Chan "Got Milk?" ad (insert 3-1), which combines words and images. In what ways are the persuasive strategies of the reading and the ad alike? In what ways are they different?

Writing to Protest Abusive Gender Images

Log on to the Web site for Media Watch (http://www.mediawatch.com), an organization that educates the public about offensive images in the media. If you find an ad you would like to protest, write a letter to the company sponsoring the ad at the address given on the Web site and describe the elements of the ad that strike you as offensive. If you disagree with the Web site's contention that an ad is oppressive, write to the e-mail address given on the site, explaining your position.

Writing a Petition to Protest Offensive Gender Images

Log on to the Archives of the Web site Media Watch (http://www.mediawatch.com/boycott.html), and read the descriptions of offensive media images in the Media Watch Endorsed Boycott List. Or log on to the National Organization for Women's Web site and go to the Love Your Body pages (http:// www.nowfoundation.org/health/lybdkit/index.html). Following these examples, write a petition protesting a particular ad or other media image you find offensive. Get signatures on your petition, and mail it to the studio or manufacturer responsible for the image. You will find a sample petition (that you can also sign and e-mail) at http://www.nowfoundation.org/health/lybdkit/petition.html.

Comparing ads from another era

Go to the library and find a popular magazine from an earlier decade (e.g., *Vanity Fair,* c. 1910; *McCall's,* c. 1920; *Life,* c. 1940; *Esquire,* c. 1950; *Glamour* c. 1960). Compare the image of men or women that you find in the ads in this chapter with what you see in the magazine. What has changed? What hasn't? What cultural changes account for the differences you see?

When you turn in your first draft, include photocopies of several of your ads, so your instructor can help you add descriptive details, if necessary.

Writing An Extended Argument

The following assignment asks you to incorporate numerous sources into a complex argument—that is, to use the readings to interpret your observations about the ads.

Write an essay in which you use ideas from the readings to interpret two different images of men or women (choose one) depicted in the advertisements in this chapter.

Your thesis might be—but doesn't necessarily have to be—an answer to one of these questions:

1. Do the ads support the images of men or women described in the readings? Do they contradict them? Do they complicate them?

2. What happens when real men or women try to live up to the images depicted in the ads?

3. How is the concept of masculinity (or femininity) seen in the ads reinforced or nullified in other areas of life (e.g., sports, movies, the military)?

4. In what ways do the authors of the readings accept, promote, or resist values implied by the ads?

5. In instances where a reading seems to condemn a gender image represented in an ad, how might these conflicting views of masculinity (or femininity) find common ground?

Designing the Extended Writing Project

The following writing suggestions for constructing a thesis, organizing, adding details, and integrating the thesis and the readings can be generalized to any other writing project you do.

To make your points clearly, we recommend that you include these elements:

A Thesis

This is the point of your essay; it is a complete sentence that names the male or female characteristics you see in the ads and the significance of this portrayal.

EXAMPLE | The ads for America's Dairy Farmers and Milk Processors ("Want Strong Bones? . . .") and for Stetson show men looking cold and tough, qualities that Don Sabo ("The Myth of the Sexual Athlete") and David Brooks ("The Return of the Pig") ascribe to traditional concepts of masculinity.

A Structure Based on the Thesis

One of the most effective ways to organize an essay is to follow the order of ideas set forth in your thesis. There is almost always more than one way to do this. The sample below shows one possibility; the paper based on this outline is likely to have several paragraphs for each section:

Thesis   America's Dairy Farmers and Milk Processors and Stetson ads show men who are cold and tough, qualities that Don Sabo and David Brooks ascribe to traditional concepts of masculinity.

Section one   Describe the elements in the America's Dairy Farmers and Milk Processors and Stetson ads that indicate that men are emotionally distant.

Section two   Describe the elements in the America's Dairy Farmers and Milk Processors and Stetson ads that indicate that men are tough.

Section three   Discuss Sabo's and Brooks's critiques of the social values that encourage men to be emotionally distant.

Section four   Discuss Sabo's and Brooks's critiques of the social values that encourage men to be tough.

Detailed Description of the Ads

Your description of the *relevant* portions of the ads is your evidence and will make up the bulk of the essay. Details draw the readers into your writing and persuade them of your interpretation. Be sure to describe the ads specifically enough that a reader who is not looking at the ads can picture them. Also note the following:

- If you make statements such as "the woman is beautiful" or "the man is handsome," be sure to define the specific physical characteristics that constitute male or female beauty. Don't assume that there is a single standard of physical attractiveness.

- Avoid statements such as "the woman is feminine" or "the man is masculine"; these sentences are circular. Instead, describe the visual images and language that create an impression of masculinity or femininity.

Note that in the example below, we don't need to have the ad in front of us to picture it because the writer has provided ample detail.

EXAMPLE | The ads suggest that the ideal man is successful at work. In several business-related advertisements, we see the man climbing the career ladder, becoming the best in his field. In the Parker Duofold pen advertisement, a smiling, well-groomed businessman reaches out his hand cordially to the reader. We know he is successful because he is wearing a dark, neatly pressed suit, crisp white shirt, perfectly placed tie, and confident smile. Next to him is a large, expensive looking pen. The placement of the man and the pen suggests that the two are being compared, and, in fact, the man is just like a Parker: he looks rich ("23K gold plated trim"), he focuses on high performance ("smooth and uninterrupted flow to writing"), and he is precise ("precisely engineered ink flow system"). The message above the man's head says that he "never settles for second best." The text at the bottom praises the pen's superior performance, which is designed to "bring out the best in a man." The word "best" appears four times in this ad, linking the attributes of the pen with those of the successful businessman: a man who is precise, obsessed with performance, ambitious, and a perfectionist.

Detailed Discussion of the Relevant Parts of the Readings

After you have shown how the ads define masculinity or femininity, relate these findings to some of the readings. Use the readings to show the significance of what you've said about the ads: that is, demonstrate how the readings support, explain, or raise questions about the depiction of men or women you observe in the ads. For example, the readings might suggest a consequence of this depiction, explain a reason for it, indicate that this image is promoted in many places in our culture (besides advertising), or show that it coexists with an alternative image.

Using WEB Resources

Extending the Scope of Your Essay

The following Web sites offer information, articles, and graphics concerning depictions of men and women in advertising and other media.

Masculinity and Representation. http://www.newcastle.edu.au/department/so/kibby.htm
About-Face. http://www.about-face.org/index.html
Gender and Advertising Database. http://www.genderads.com
Jean Kilbourne. http://www.jeankilbourne.com

Browse one of these Web sites and consider how some of the sources you find there challenge, confirm, or complicate the ideas raised in the readings or your analysis of the ads. Revise your paper to include this new information.

Incorporating Ads from Another Era

Consult the Web site Ad Access (http://scriptorium.lib.duke.edu/adaccess), which reproduces advertisements from the past. Compare the image of men or women that you found in your paper with what you see in these magazines. What has changed? What hasn't? What cultural changes account for the differences you see?

Analyzing Gender Images on the World Wide Web

Find three or four online zines or other Web sites that address primarily men (or women). Considering the graphics, language style, choice of links, subject matter, and audience, what image of men (or women) do you see here? How does this image compare with the ones in the ads?

---

www.mhhe.com/durkinl

Using the Web for resources on constructing gender. Go to Web Resources

Photograph: University High School, Los Angeles, California [1924]

The school pictured here is a traditional high school. The school site is a typical one—in a dense suburban neighborhood, not far from central thoroughfares. Why would you have liked (or not liked) to attend a high school like this one?

1   Look at the design of the main school building, including the façade, the orientation (vertical? horizontal?), the materials, and style. What image of education do these features suggest? (e.g., personal betterment? community-based learning?)

2   With all classrooms of equal size (suggested by the uniform window design), what does the architecture say about the relationship between different school subjects, class activities, and teacher-student relationships?

3   What role of education is underscored by locating a school in the center of a residential and business district? Explain.

4   Describe an architectural element in these school buildings that appeals to you. Why is it appealing?

Photograph: Diamond Ranch High School, Diamond Bar, California
[Thom Mayne, 2000]

This modern high school is located on an isolated hilltop overlooking a large southern California valley impacted by freeways and businesses. Why would you have liked (or not liked) to attend a high school similar to this one?

1   Looking at the modern qualities of this high school, what image of education do you think this design projects to students? What kind of curriculum does it suggest?

2   How do you think the site itself makes students feel about the purpose of education? Consider the long drive up a winding walled road and the sudden view of the school, with its unexpected shapes, roof lines, and materials. Consider also the isolation, tiered site, and vistas.

3   What message do you think this design communicates to teachers about the kind of education they should provide? Why?

Photograph: Engineering Building, Utah State University [MHTN Architects, 2003]

The photograph shows little of the building's site, layout, shape, or massing, although its shape appears conventionally boxlike. However, we see the striking interior style and materials. What kind of learning do you think engineering students would derive from this building?

1 What do you think that the industrial materials convey to students about what they need to learn?

2 What do you think that the exposed materials, cavities, and structures convey to students about how one learns engineering?

3 The gray and white colors and patterns convey the impression of symmetry and coherence. Why do you think these may be important concepts in engineering?

Photograph: The Brown Center, Maryland Institute College of Art
[Zeigner/Sneed Architects, 2003]

This cutting-edge arts building is on a difficult site—other campus buildings and a high-way hem it in on all sides. Yet it creates an image of artistic creation conquering spatial and environmental constraints. Why might it be important that this building sharply contrasts with its surroundings?

1 The Brown Center houses digital art classes, experimental animation, and interactive media. Do you think that the materials of blue-white glass, letting in light from every angle, suggest to art students something about the nature and purpose of their subject? Explain.

2 What do you think that the building's shape and massing—its angular forms, tilts, and jutting roofline—convey about how digital art fits into the modern world?

3 What does the building's urban site and its relationship to surrounding buildings and structures convey about the nature and products of learning?

Photograph: Dormitory, Illinois Institute of Technology [Helmut Jahn, 2003]

This modern dormitory, with its curved walls and rooflines, redefines dorm life. Rather than resembling a home away from home, the structure looks highly industrial and work-related, with every convenience. Symmetrical cutouts in the roofline reveal large open spaces. The interior consists of apartments, where students each have their own bedroom but share a living room, kitchen, and bath. Does this design appeal to you?

1   How would students (yourself included) relate in a dormitory with symmetrical floors, individual bedrooms, and high-tech features? What impediments to socializing might there be? What encouragements?

2   The layout of the building is a conventional rectangle, on a flat site. The building is lined with symmetrical trees providing shaded walkways, walkways with high-intensity lights for good night visibility. What values do these features suggest?

Photograph: Interior of the Graduate Reading Room at Suzzallo Library, University of Washington [Carl F. Gould, Sr., and Charles H. Bebb, 1923]

The architecture of the reading room featured here epitomizes the lofty goals of seeking truth. The larger library that houses the reading room is flanked by terra-cotta sculptures of great thinkers and artists, including Homer, Plato, Shakespeare, Pasteur, Goethe, Beethoven, and Darwin. Students then climb a designed stairway leading to this reading room. This entry sequence reinforces the idea of being physically elevated yet sequestered, away from distractions. Originally, all the reading tables placed readers at a perpendicular to the west-facing windows, to keep students' focus inward. The stained glass windows, carved bookcases, cathedral ceilings, hanging chandeliers that cast light on the ceiling, and expansive 240-foot length remind readers of why they are there. What might be the reason behind making a reading room feel like a cathedral?

1   What are some of the geometric patterns that you notice in the building's interior architecture? What is the effect of these patterns?

2   What materials do you most notice? What do these materials suggest about the specific values this institution promotes?

3   If you were sitting at one of these tables, along with hundreds of other students, what kind of expectations would you feel that the institution had for you? What do these expectations have to do with the architectural elements? Explain.

Painting: Winslow Homer, *Snap the Whip* [1872]

This painting offers an image of the little red schoolhouse typifying the nineteenth century's view of education. The building, groupings of children of different ages, and the
teacher herself convey an image of education that no longer informs our schools. What
might be the advantages and disadvantages of mixed-grade-level schooling and a single
teacher who knows all the children well?

© Butler Institute of American Art, Youngstown, OH.

1   Describe the architecture of the schoolhouse (size, shape, materials, color, etc.) What does it
     suggest about how education fits with other everyday activities?

2   Describe the relationship between the schoolhouse and the setting. What does this relation-
     ship indicate about how education fits with the environment?

3   Pointing to specific details, describe the game of Snap the Whip in the painting. What rela-
     tionship do you think the game has to education? What kind of human relationships are
     central to this image of education?

tall on a flat horizon, the two- or three-room schoolhouse is now in disrepair. What values may have disappeared with the abandonment of this building?

1 What do the spire and arched window and doorway suggest to you about the value of education, as seen by the community? Do other architectural features such as layout and massing support this view? Explain.

2 The building site is located in the midst of miles of empty, flat prairie land. Given such a remote site, and the difficulty in getting there, what kind of knowledge do you think parents might have wanted teachers to provide? Explain.

3 The photographer shot the schoolhouse from a place on the ground looking up, making the schoolhouse look large against the sky. What contrast does the angle create? Why do you suppose he wanted to create this contrast?

Images of Education

In this chapter, the readings—together with images of architecture in academic settings—present a range of views concerning the content, purposes, and methods of education. One issue is the substance of what is taught: Is education supposed to teach students critical thinking or the skills necessary for work? Further, should educators go beyond traditional subject matter and teach good character, personal skills, and caring? A second issue is whether or not our educational system provides equal opportunity for all students, regardless of race, ethnicity, language background, or socioeconomic status. A third issue concerns teaching methods and measurements. Is there only one kind of intelligence and one kind of measurement? What do other intelligences look like, and how could they be taught?

Such questions about the content, purpose, and methods of education interest not only educators but also architects who design schools. Their designs offer implicit answers to such questions, for schools are environments for learning. The high school and college campus buildings (shown here in photographs), as well as the paintings of schoolhouses, embody different answers. For instance, the architecture of the high school built in 1924 suggests a different purpose and method for public education than is suggested by the architecture of the high school built in 2000. The modern college campus architecture reflects new ideas about what and how students learn. All of these images contrast with paintings of schoolhouses from a different era.

IMAGES OF EDUCATION IN ARCHITECTURE

The architecture pictured here reflects different views of the goals and methods of education. For instance, University High School, in Los Angeles, California, built in the first half of the twentieth century, illustrates the view of education as shared knowledge and values. The entrance of the imposing brick two-story structure, with decorative Italianate detailing and symmetrical windows, opens out into the community, facing the intersection of two apartment-lined streets. Students are drawn up a processional walkway that suggests the importance of their transition from the community into the school. When students pass through the main building to the steps leading down to the school grounds, they face a panorama of the school site, including the fields and peripheral buildings below. If they descend these steps, they flow into the main walkway that links most of the buildings of the school. In choosing a costly traditional style, the architect conveys the idea of common knowledge, pride, and shared beliefs.

However, over the years, as other buildings were added, the style and campus changed. Rectangular utilitarian buildings took over circulation areas. Temporary buildings filled in other spaces, where students had once congregated, and became permanent. Some temporary buildings were added so far from the central core that they cannot be seen from the main building. To get there, students (more each year are from low-income families) must walk around patches of weed-ridden terrain. In addition, fewer windows were built, and existing windows came to have grilles or wire mesh over them. The emphasis shifted from community pride to safety and utility. The campus architecture, however, still reflects the struggle to maintain educational traditions.

In contrast, the avant-garde style of Diamond Ranch High School, in Diamond Bar, California, completed in January 2000, disrupts all impressions of continuity. This is not like any traditional high school. Different school buildings jut out at different angles. Walls are not perpendicular but lean inward along a jagged walkway that forms the spine of the site. Roof lines are not parallel to the ground. Further, the shape of each structure differs from the others. There are no uniform window plans or classroom size. Some parts of buildings cantilever over space, in abrupt, sharp angles. Nor are the materials conventional, but rather feature concrete benches and corrugated steel walls. Furthermore, the school was built on a site once deemed impossible for a school. Two years of grading preceded its construction, and the sports fields are positioned both above and below the main structures. These fields, as well as the school's walkways, open spaces, and windows, overlook miles of valley industries, housing, freeways, and distant mountains. The dramatic hilltop site is removed from any immediate neighborhood and business district. Such architectural elements emphasize modernity, discontinuity, instability and a radically new future that students must prepare for.

The four college campus buildings are equally interesting for what they reflect about education. Two of the buildings, the engineering building at Utah State University and the Brown Center at the Maryland Institute College of Art, reveal college architecture that models the educational enterprise the buildings house. The first calls attention to engineering feats, the second to artistic design. Both use industrialized materials and reveal state-of-the art technology. Both expose such functions as air shafts and radiators to indicate new technologies and materials.

The engineering building exposes part of the concrete foundation, the major braces, and the interiors of cavities, such as ceiling space, that are usually closed off. The building replicates the construction processes and products taught in its classrooms. The Brown Center embodies artistic creation conquering environmental constraints. Its white-blue glass exterior soars above the buildings and highway that hem it in. This arts building, on a difficult site on the campus in downtown Baltimore, leans out over a street, pointing toward the campus's main building. The glass, creating an iridescent look, absorbs and reflects sunlight.

The third building, a new college residence hall at Illinois Institute of Technology, suggests student life in a modern age, with an increasing emphasis on privacy and high-tech services over communal life. Residence halls in general provide an environment for student learning outside the classroom. Some dorms encourage socialization; others emphasize privacy. Before the 1960s, economy drove most choices, and campuses across the country still have a legacy of high-rise boxes featuring double rooms and shared baths. The modern dormitory pictured here reflects a new economy—one of marketing and services.

The fourth college campus building, the interior of the Graduate Reading Room at Suzzallo Library, University of Washington, reflects the educational traditions that the college values. The interior, replicating the size and architectural features of halls at Oxford and Cambridge, in Gothic style, recalls centuries-old traditions of liberal arts education. The 240-foot reading room, on the third floor of the library, includes high cathedral ceilings, stained glass windows, and hanging chandeliers to cast light upwards, to remind students of the lofty goals of higher education.

In contrast to images of school buildings that are currently in use are two images of now obsolete nineteenth-century schoolhouses. These artistic images reveal historical conceptions of education. The buildings' size, materials, color, and design reflect an earlier view of the purpose and methods of education, against which to contrast more modern views. Winslow Homer's "Snap the Whip" depicts a traditional little red schoolhouse in a lush rural setting, with children linked together in play in the foreground. The school building, a one-room "house," reflects the continuity between home and school, buildings and nature, family and school relationships. Alan Bauer's photograph of an abandoned schoolhouse in the prairie, with its steeple revealing its churchlike role, tells the story of a lost struggle to make religion the center of education, especially on the plains.

Analyzing the Architecture

To discuss school and campus architecture as it reflects educational ideals, you need to analyze architectural elements. The elements of the school and college campus buildings presented here embody different views of schooling. These architectural elements include the building's site, or relationship to the surrounding environment; its layout; its overall shape and massing, including roof lines; and its style. For instance, ask yourself, What is the site and layout like at University High School and how does the school relate to the surrounding community? Existing traditional high schools, representing community values, are located in a neighborhood near central transportation arteries. The layout typically includes a main entrance that funnels students from the larger community into the school's administration building. Other school buildings typically relate to the main building by paralleling it or being perpendicular to it.

The following questions can be asked in analyzing architectural elements that may have meaning for education:

1. Identify particular visual elements that have educational meaning:
   - **Site** Is it in a neighborhood? Removed hillside? Business district? (What does the site tell you about how the school is supposed to relate to other city activities, such as business or home life? How does the site relate to the surrounding topography?)
   - **Layout** What buildings are placed where? How do they relate to one another? Is there a main building? If so, how do the other buildings relate to it? How do students get from one building to the next? (What relationship between administration and teaching is suggested by the layout? What connection between subjects is suggested by the layout?)
   - **Massing** What shapes are the buildings? Are the masses symmetrical or asymmetrical? Densely packed together or open and diffused? Do they have a vertical or horizontal orientation, or do they cut across these orientation systems? How would you describe their tops and bottoms, fronts and backs, and left and right sides? (How do the building masses orient students in space—do they put them off balance or reinforce balance? How might this massing affect the way subjects are taught?)

- **Style** What other kinds of buildings does this one remind you of? A Greek temple? An office building? A stone and ivy elite college? A prison? (How does the style suggest a view of the purpose and methods of education?)
- **Materials** What materials predominate? Wood and plaster? Concrete and steel? Brick and other stone? What is the roof made of? (How do the materials convey a message about the purpose and methods of education?)

2. Consider what these elements suggest about education.

- What do particular elements suggest about the way people are educated?
- What kind of social interactions are suggested by these elements?
- What do these elements suggest about how new knowledge is produced and used?

Analysis of an Engineering Building (Photograph)

The new engineering building at Utah State University (insert 4-3) draws attention to the feats of this profession. While the building shape and massing present a conventionally large, spacious entry with smaller spaces for classrooms and computer labs, less conventional are the exposed supports that make the building work. The steel supports of the building—especially those that cross diagonally—draw attention to themselves as engineering solutions. Viewers see what holds the building up. Further, in its materials and unfinished style, the building teaches the observer what it is about. The white and gray marble, steel, and glass surfaces reinforce the sense of technological achievement. What is more, viewers see how hidden elements work together. Openings into the ceilings reveal the innards of the construction. As Scott Carlson states, because the ceiling tiles in the entry are absent, "you see the guts of the structure—blue computer cables, ventilation ducts wrapped in silver insulation, and hot-water pipes coursing through the building" (*Chronicle of Higher Education*, March 26, 2004, B12).

IMAGES OF EDUCATION IN ESSAYS

The essays in this chapter offer multiple perspectives on current education debates. They provide history, theory, and personal experiences that will help you converse about education with well-informed opinions and a judicious tone.

The first three essays look at education in broad social, historical, or humanistic terms. David Tyack, in a historical account of public education ("School: The Story of American Public Education"), thinks that public education's changing purpose reflects a remarkable adaptability to changing social values. In "Learning in the Key of Life," Jon Spayde makes us think philosophically about education: What is it for? How does it help us as human beings? John Dewey ("The School and the Life of the Child") argues for experiential learning by doing as opposed to an artificial learning of discrete chunks of information, fitted to the twelve years of a child's school life.

The next three essays feature personal experiences on issues related to equal opportunity. In "Savage Inequalities," Jonathan Kozol uses observations and interviews, at schools in impoverished and affluent areas, to reveal the "savage inequalities" among public schools. Less concerned with equity and more with individual achievement, David Brooks, from the perspective of a middle-class parent, argues the benefits of a "meritocracy" in "The Merits of Meritocracy." His view presumes that children gain self-fulfillment by striving to do better than others to achieve "merit." While he addresses only after-school activities, the same arguments have been applied to public education. Robert Barr tells the personal story of his preconceptions about a child from an impoverished background in "Who Is This Child?" He sees new hope for this child in a single teacher's ability to care.

The next two essays offer alternative values, definitions, and methods for education. These include teaching and valuing other "intelligences" such as interpersonal, musical, or kinesthetic, and creating a different kind of school culture for students who cross boundaries. Howard Gardner ("Human Intelligence Isn't What We Think It Is") wants schools to recognize and enhance forms of "intelligence" other than those measured by IQ tests. He feels that schools should be responsible for finding "roles in which [children] can use their abilities" and should resist tracking students on the basis of narrow measurements. In "Epilogue: Lilia," Mike Rose describes the ways in which the culture of a school changes how an immigrant student sees herself and how others see her. When the student comes to recognize her own special experience and language, she finds herself better able to succeed and to help others like her succeed.

The last essay, "Forget Classrooms. How Big Is the Atrium in the New Student Center?" by Michael J. Lewis examines how the architecture of college student centers, focal buildings on college campuses, reflects hidden hierarchies of associations and values. He compares the earliest student center in the 1890s to today's student centers to show how we increasingly view education as a commercial product.

Analyzing the Essays

The steps listed here can help you analyze these essays:

- Identify the dominant view of education in each essay. What are the assumptions underlying this view? How are the learner and the teacher depicted? What activities are most important in developing students?
- What contrasting views does the essay present? What do these contrasts consist of?
- Is there possible common ground between the contrasting views? What do both groups want to see happen?

Analysis of an Essay

Consider Robert Barr's "Who Is This Child?" Notice the key contrast on which the essay turns. Barr contrasts his own research-based perspective on education with the hands-on, intuitive knowledge of a teacher working with an individual child. Barr, full of statistics and predictions, holds out little hope for the young child. Yet he sees in the teacher's simple welcoming behaviors, and the child's happy response, a reply to such despairing views. Barr's reversal, his openness to a different view, indicates that he can still learn. The contrasts in the essay clarify for us the message about the importance of a single connection. Barr is old; the teacher and child are young. He is full of educational theories and terminology, statistics and trends; the teacher is full of simple loving words for the child, words and gestures that make all the difference. Barr is an outsider looking in, uncomfortable with the child's hugs, quick to categorize her; the teacher knows the individual child, hugs her easily, and envisions the day with her. Despite these radical differences, Barr learns. He is ready to shed his preconceptions. We, then, experience the new hope generated by the child's unexpected smiles. It is hope that flies in the face of decades of pessimistic educational research.

DAVID TYACK   Why did Americans, in the mid-nineteenth century, institute public schools? The Americans of this time might seem an unlikely group to have desired a universal, government-sponsored, system of education. They were clearly tax aversive, independent, and suspicious of government. As further arguments against public schools, literacy rates in the 1800s were already high, private schools flourished, and affluent parents had ample choice. So what were the motives? And how have Americans' motives and thinking changed since this time? In this introduction to a Public Broadcasting series on schools, David Tyack argues that public schools have always represented a sense of common purpose. To make this point, he provides a short history of public schools in this country. The history touches on the original purpose and common values of public schools, including the overriding desire to teach good character. Tyack then documents the changes in Americans' view of public education; he attributes these changes to Americans' shifting views of democracy. In contrast to so many critics, Tyack depicts public education as remarkably adaptive.

TYACK is a professor of history and education at Stanford University. His books include *The One Best System: A History of American Urban Education* and *Tinkering toward Utopia: A Century of Public School Reform*, with coauthor Larry Cuban.

READING

School: The Story of American Public Education (2002) | BY DAVID TYACK

Schools are the most familiar of all civic institutions. You find them in city slums and leafy suburbs, Appalachian valleys and mining towns high in the Rockies. If you fly over the prairies that stretch endlessly across the middle of the United States, you see below you a patchwork of the farms and municipalities neatly laid out in townships, each composed of thirty-six sections. More than two centuries ago the federal government laid out these civic checkerboards and pledged that the inhabitants of the western territories could use the revenue generated from the sixteenth section of each township to support education. The public ("common") schools supported by these land grants were emblems of a common citizenship across the new nation and even newer western states, but they were also civic centers of their local communities in long-established towns as well as frontier settlements.

One article of faith among the founding fathers was that a republic could survive only if its citizens were educated. School has continued to shape the core of our national identity. "The free common school system," Adlai Stevenson once said, is "the most American thing about America."

Early in the nineteenth century, Thomas Jefferson argued that locally controlled public schools were key democratic institutions in two ways. By teaching correct political principles to the young, they could nurture virtuous citizens. Equally important, local control gave adult citizens a chance to exercise self-rule. In the twentieth century, John Dewey voiced a similar commitment to education in democracy through an emphasis on political socialization and wise collective choices. For these philosophers of democracy, education was a common good, not simply an individual consumer good.

But achieving a sense of common purpose has never been easy. For two centuries, public school districts have been political arenas in which citizens have contended with one another. In a society as socially diverse as the United States, controversies about purposes and practices in public schooling are hardly surprising. Such policy debates express both hopes and fears about the nation. When citizens deliberate about the education of the young, they are also debating the shape of the future for the whole nation.

Talk about schooling has been part of a larger attempt to define what historian 5 Thomas Bender calls "the public culture." He says that the struggle of groups for "legitimacy and justice" has created and recreated this public culture and established "our common life as a people and as a nation." It is essential, he adds, to understand "why some groups and some values have been so much—or so little—represented in public life and in mainstream culture and schooling at any given moment in our history."

To some people, the notion of common values taught in a common school seems outdated or naïve at this time in history. Today, some critics deride "government schools" as inefficient, bureaucratic, and coercive. Some say that Americans are so different that shared civic values are impossible. Ethnic and racial groups attack bias in traditional accounts of American history, and debates over what should be a canon of standard knowledge reverberate in Congress and state capitals as well as the groves of academe.

By many accounts, public schools are in trouble today. Grim stories appear daily in the media about violence, high dropout rates, and low test scores. Beyond such immediate concerns lies an uneasiness about purpose, a sense that we have lost our way. As the larger purposes that once gave resonance to public education have become muted, constituencies that at one time supported public education have become splintered and confused about what to do.

Policy talk about education has always contained plenty of hype and alarm at the hellfire-and-damnation sermon followed by the certain solution. Recent talk may set a record for moving without missing a beat from tales of catastrophe to promises of revolutionary reform.

School does not gloss over the recent crisis of confidence or the array of practical problems in education. But it suggests that the recent maelstrom of criticism and defense of public schooling has left little space for deliberation about what unites as well as divides citizens, what part broad civic goals have played within a pluralistic society, what features of the common school are worth preserving, and how education has (and has not) adapted to the remarkable pluralism of the American population.

Perhaps one reason many Americans feel that we have lost our way in education 10 is that we have forgotten where we have been. Reformers often say that they don't want to look backwards, arguing that amnesia is a virtue when it comes to reinventing education. The problem with that stance is that it is impossible. Everyone uses some sense of the past in everyday life, and leaders cannot escape thinking in time. The real question is whether the histories we all use in decision making enrich and ground our understanding of the choices we face.

History does not proffer simple lessons. If it did, historians would probably not disagree so much with each other. But study of the past can provide context for decisions and images of possibility and constraint.

The story that *School* tells is complex and controversial and open-ended, in keeping with the aspirations, fears, achievements, and failures of citizens and educators, past and present. It explores how Americans have sought to shape their society through public education. It invites readers to step back from today's formulations of problems and solutions, to think about where we have been and where we might go.

Foreign observers of American society during the century following independence often commented on how much U.S. citizens distrusted government at a distance, whether that of King George III or spendthrift state legislatures. Voters wanted to keep legislators on a short leash and kept rewriting their state constitutions to weaken government. Partly because of this deep-rooted distrust of government, Americans have, over the years, been slow to provide social and health services through public agencies (a fact well known to proponents of medical coverage for all citizens today).

Thus in the middle of the nineteenth century, the advocates of public education realized that they had a job to do. They faced rugged competition from a host of private schools of many varieties. Families with resources had many choices in the educational marketplace—some public, some private, some charitable and some for profit, some sectarian and some secular. The results of this miscellaneous schooling were impressive: well before the majority of children attended public schools, both attendance in school and literacy rates were quite high. By 1890, public schools became dominant and enrolled about nine in ten pupils.

Government-distrusting, tax-pinching, independent Americans might well have   15
chosen to continue to rely on this diverse collection of schools to educate their children. They did not. Instead, they chose, collectively and decisively, to establish and sustain the world's most universal and popular system of education.

In doing so, they stayed close to their roots and formed the most decentralized system of school governance in the world. They controlled and financed schools locally. Public education would not have thrived without this self-rule. It enabled citizens to keep a close eye on their schools and to resolve issues by local majority rule. American school board members constituted the largest group of public officials in the world during the late nineteenth century. They outnumbered teachers in a number of rural states.

But considering local self-rule leads to a puzzle: why was this grassroots schooling so similar, at least across the North, when no central ministry of education set standards and enforced regulations? Adam Smith claimed that the "invisible hand" of the market worked more effectively than a directive government. In the United States, it was a common set of political and social values that helped to produce similar common schools scattered across the nation. Shared beliefs encouraged people to build institutions, and over time citizens came to believe that schooling was a public good essential to the health of the nation. Individuals did benefit from schooling, yes, but even more important, civic society depended on instilling common values.

But what were these values to be? An inclination to compete lay deep in the American grain. Throughout the nineteenth century, churches vied with each other for souls and members; how could they agree on common principles? The nineteenth century was also a time of lusty contest between the political parties; they delighted in puncturing the claims and pretenses of the opposition. And raw conflict—red in tooth and claw—marked much of the economic history of the time. So why did Americans hope that they could agree about the moral and civic lessons that schools should teach when they clashed so vigorously in most other arenas?

Horace Mann, the great nineteenth-century school reformer, and thousands of other state and local leaders had a plan. Surely, they said, the warring religious groups could call a truce at the door of the common school for the sake of the children and the nation. They developed an argument that they thought was self-evident: the main purpose of public education is to develop good character; character is based on religion; religion is based on the central teachings of the Bible; therefore, moral education should be based on reading the Bible without sectarian comment. This "nonsectarian" religion of consensus appealed to the Protestant mainstream that supplied most of the leadership of public education. Catholics clearly saw that this set of propositions did not match their doctrine. In response, they decided to challenge the common school by creating their own schools.

Hand in hand with this doctrine of nonsectarian moral teaching was the claim 20 that political education could be nonpartisan. In this theory, the common school should teach only those pure republican principles and practices that united Americans. This pedagogy of patriotism is most obvious in American history textbooks that glorified the founding fathers. The compilers of the famous McGuffey readers promised that they contained no sectarian or partisan accounts and included solely those values that everyone subscribed to (or should subscribe to). There was a huge market for such a political and religious common denominator: the McGuffey readers racked up sales of over 122 million copies.

The creation of the common school, with its grassroots governance and consensual curriculum, was one of the triumphs of nineteenth-century reform. Fueled by a powerful republican ideology and aspiring to create universal education, the common school movement appealed to millennial hope and fear. But by the turn of the twentieth century, reformers grew dissatisfied with local self-rule and a shared curriculum.

Once again, the country came to a turning point in the development of its system of education, as leaders redefined democracy in the new urban and industrial society of the early twentieth century. Their vision of democracy in the twentieth century exalted experts and denigrated widespread lay participation.

Local control by elected school committees had set a democratic stamp on public education, but policy elites at the turn of the twentieth century complained that the efforts of rural school trustees fell short. They gave local citizens just what they wanted: schooling that was cheap, that reflected local notions of useful learning, and that gave employment to local teachers who fit in well with the community. One leader denounced local control by district trustees as "democracy gone to seed." How could penny-pinching and provincial rural trustees prepare youth for the twentieth century?

Elite reformers also believed that the leadership in urban districts was poor. They felt that the central urban school committees were far too large and delegated decisions to subcommittees of trustees rather than to the experts. They felt that too many of the wrong people ran things, and they pointed especially to corrupt machine politicians and to immigrants who wanted the schools to respect their cultures and to hire their daughters. How could urban schools become efficient and professional, how could they "Americanize" immigrants, with all these foxes in the chicken coops? Worse, many cities still retained ward boards that were relics of the old decentralized district system.

"Take the schools out of politics!" In the early twentieth century, that was the call 25 to battle of advocates of a new concept of democracy in public education. These policy elites decided that the older concepts of common school governance and curriculum were antediluvian. Democracy, they insisted, did not mean laypeople running the schools, as trustees did all over the country. Democracy at its best meant administration of public schools by specially trained experts (superintendents and their staffs). A school system resembled a public hospital: a lay board might provide general oversight, but professionals should be in charge.

The reformers wanted to consolidate small rural districts and assert more control of country schools by counties and states. Taking city schools out of politics meant radically reducing the size of city school boards and abolishing ward boards.

As they sought to centralize and standardize education, they rejected the old idea that democracy demanded a common curriculum for all students. The intelligence and future destiny of pupils clearly differed, and thus the curriculum should be differentiated to match their abilities and needs. Democratic schools provided opportunities to all students to find niches suited to their various talents. Equality meant difference, not sameness, of treatment.

The public school, then, became an "instrument of democracy" run by apolitical experts, with authority "in the hands of those who will really represent the interests of the children." Such leaders would be able to educate all children according to their abilities and destiny in life. The people owned the schools, but experts ran them, just as corporate CEOs managed their firms. Such was the new version of democracy in governance: a socially and economically efficient system that adapted schooling to different kinds of students, thereby guaranteeing equality of opportunity.

The redefinition of democracy and reorganization of schools became the conventional wisdom of educators for the following decades. Big districts and big schools, they said, were better than small ones. A centralized, specialized administrative structure was more efficient and accountable than a decentralized, simple one. Differentiation of the curriculum into several tracks and hundreds of electives generated greater equality of opportunity for students of varied ability and for the numerous ethnic and "racial" groups.

Beginning in the 1960s, in another effort to change the course of history, reformers set 30 out once again to redefine democracy and to challenge the organizational changes introduced in the first half of the twentieth century. They argued that small schools are better, that big districts should be decentralized, that all students should be helped to meet the same high academic standards, that academic segregation of students into tracks limits their learning, and that schools can benefit from parents' involvement in educational reform.

Reformers today recognize that no amount of wishful thinking can transform politics of education into neutral administration, for schooling is and always has been intrinsically value-laden. The question is not *whether* politics but *whose* politics. In the last fifty years the history of school governance is in large part the story of efforts to breach the buffers erected around schools during the first half of the twentieth century to protect them from participatory democracy.

Groups that were excluded or unfairly treated—for example, African Americans, Latinos, the handicapped, women—have organized in social movements and have sought access and influence in public education. Besides employing traditional political strategies, these new voices have also expanded notions of democracy; they speak, for example, of *cultural* democracy, of equal respect and equal rights for all cultural groups, and of *economic* democracy to close the gap between rich and poor school districts.

The politics of education has never been more fluid and complicated than today. As in earlier periods of contentiousness, some critics—especially various advocates of vouchers and school choice—have put a new spin on the concept of democracy. The challenge this time is even more fundamental than the earlier attempt to rely on experts. These critics do not seek to replace politics with professional administration. Indeed, they consider public education already too bureaucratic, too constrained by government regulations inflicted by special-interest groups.

The solution, they say, is to replace politics with markets. Treating schooling as a consumer good and giving parents vouchers for the education of their children solves the problem of quality and decision making: parents choose the schools that will best suit their children. The collective choices engendered by democratic institutions produced bureaucracy and gridlock, they say; the invisible hand of the market will lead the individual to the best personal choice. The market in education will satisfy and liberate families through competition.

But wait. Is education primarily a consumer good or a common good? *School*   35 provides a context for answering that question. If Thomas Jefferson, Horace Mann, and John Dewey were now to enter policy discussions on public education, they might well ask if Americans have lost their way. Democracy is about making wise collective choices, not individual consumer choices. Democracy in education and education in democracy are not quaint legacies from a distant and happier time. They have never been more essential to wise self-rule than they are today.

CONNECTING PERSONALLY TO THE READING

1. The beginning of the twentieth century saw the rise of the expert, including the manager. School reformers thought democracy and thus public schools needed experts in management, not laypeople, to run schools. As a result, public schools began to lose their common curriculum in civics, and students became "tracked" so that some students could become

experts. How does understanding this history of tracking help you better assess its value today?

2. What learning experiences (such as religious training or language courses) have you had that did not involve separating learners out according to their abilities or goals? What differences in experience did you notice?

3. Tyack questions the analogy many use today of schooling as a commodity (it produces workers whose skills can be bought and sold). What benefits and/or liabilities do you think this analogy has had for you personally?

4. Tyack stresses that common beliefs still underlie our system of public education. What evidence do you see of such common beliefs? What benefits or dangers do you see in them?

FOCUSING ON THE ARGUMENT

1. Tyack uses broad historical knowledge of the democratic institutions that unite us, and of schools in particular, to create *credibility* for his argument. He argues that public schools have always represented a sense of common purpose. Do you think that Tyack's use of broad historical trends proves more convincing than extensive numerical facts? Explain.

2. What is the effect of Tyack's addressing our skepticism by giving reasons why Americans would *not* want a system of public education? What kind of persona does he convey by addressing these reasons?

3. Current attacks on public education claim that Americans now lack shared civic values. How does it help Tyack's argument that he addresses these attacks? How important is his tone here to his credibility?

SYNTHESIZING IDEAS FROM MULTIPLE READINGS

1. According to Tyack, American public education reflects its citizens' changing views of democracy. What might John Dewey ("The School and the Life of the Child," p. 211) critique in the twentieth-century view of democracy that emphasizes efficiency? What negative effects on public schools would Dewey identify?

2. Tyack mentions more recent expanded notions of democracy—including "cultural democracy," which "respects the equal rights of all cultural groups." How does the UCLA program Lilia attended (in Mike Rose's "Epilogue: Lilia," p. 242) reflect this expanded notion? In "Forget Classrooms" (p. 246), how does Michael J. Lewis's view of the architecture of recent student centers also reflect that idea?

3. In "Savage Inequalities" (p. 214), Jonathan Kozol portrays schools' inequality, reflected in tracking. This view conflicts with the corporate view that tracks create equality of opportunity by offering different schooling to different kinds of students. How do you think Kozol would challenge this view, one that Tyack thinks is based on a model of corporate efficiency?

4. In chapter 5, Malcolm Gladwell ("The Physical Genius," p. 268) and Mike Rose ("The Working Life of a Waitress," p. 278) both praise work that is highly efficient. Interestingly, Tyack criticizes efficiency as a key educational value. Although appearing to differ on the surface, what might these writers share in their views on efficiency?

WRITING TO ACT

1. Tyack seems critical of a recent corporate view of public education, one that claims that markets will shape education. Identify an area in education—for instance, the increase in

timed test taking—where you think that a market view of education as commodity has replaced an older view. Write a letter to a leader in education (for instance, an assistant principal) either supporting this view or not. If not, be sure to include reasons for your position.

2. Write an opinion/editorial for or against the overall idea of education as a commodity. Use some of Tyack's history of public education as support, if applicable.

READING

JON SPAYDE   What kind of learning is best for our entire society? This essay on the meaning of education places us at the feet of Plato and other philosophers who ask the big questions: What sort of society do we want? How do we learn best? What is the Good? Spayde seems skeptical of answers given by those who think they may know—policy experts, multiculturalists, and organized religious groups. He is especially skeptical of the idea of high-tech "training"—which he equates with computer expertise and other short-lived competencies. Instead, he argues for dialogue—thinking and arguing about ideas—for slow learning, and for learning infused with love. Do you think such learning is possible in the schools? Is it only possible for the well-off and leisured?

SPAYDE spent more than a decade studying classical Japanese at Harvard and Stanford, but he decided to become a journalist and, more recently, a fiction writer. Today he is an editor at *Utne* magazine and an MFA candidate at the University of Minnesota. Previously, he worked on the staffs of several magazines, including *Travel and Leisure*.

Learning in the Key of Life (1998) | BY JON SPAYDE

What does it mean—and more important, what *should* it mean—to be educated?

This is a surprisingly tricky and two-sided question. Masquerading as simple problem-solving, it raises a whole laundry list of philosophical conundrums: What sort of society do we want? What is the nature of humankind? How do we learn best? And—most challenging of all—what is the Good? Talking about the meaning of education inevitably leads to the question of what a culture considers most important.

Yikes! No wonder answers don't come easily in 1998, in a multiethnic, corporation-heavy democracy that dominates the globe without having much of a sense of its own soul. For our policyheads, education equals something called "training for competitiveness" (which often boils down to the mantra of "more computers, more computers"). For multiculturalists of various stripes, education has become a battle line where they must duke it out regularly with incensed neo-traditionalists. Organized religion and the various "alternative spiritualities"—from 12-step groups to Buddhism, American style—contribute their own kinds of education.

Given all these pushes and pulls, is it any wonder that many of us are beginning to feel that we didn't get the whole story in school, that our educations didn't prepare us for the world we're living in today?

We didn't; we couldn't have. So what do we do about it?   5

The first thing, I firmly believe, is to take a deep, calm breath. After all, we're not the first American generation to have doubts about these matters. One of the great ages of American intellectual achievement, the period just before the Civil War, was ruled by educational misfits. Henry David Thoreau was fond of saying, "I am self-educated; that is, I attended Harvard College," and indeed Harvard in the early 19th century excelled mainly in the extent and violence of its food fights.

Don't get me wrong: Formal education is serious stuff. There is no divide in American life that hurts more than the one between those we consider well educated and those who are poorly or inadequately schooled. Talking about education is usually the closest we get to talking about class; and no wonder—education, like class, is about power. Not just the power that Harvard- and Stanford-trained elites have to dictate our workweeks, plan our communities, and fiddle with world financial markets, but the extra power that a grad school dropout who, let's say, embraces voluntary simplicity and makes $14,000 a year, has over a high school dropout single mom pulling down $18,000. That kind of power has everything to do with attitude and access: an attitude of empowerment, even entitlement, and access to tools, people, and ideas that make living—at any income level—easier, and its crises easier to bear.

That's something Earl Shorris understands. A novelist and journalist, Shorris started an Ivy League–level adult education course in humanities for low-income New Yorkers at the Roberto Clemente Family Guidance Center on the Lower East Side, which he described in his book *New American Blues* (Norton, 1977). On the first day of class, Shorris said this to the students, who were Asians, whites, blacks, and Hispanics at or near the poverty line: "You've been cheated. Rich people learn the humanities; you didn't. The humanities are a foundation for getting along in the world, for thinking, for learning to reflect on the world instead of just reacting to whatever force is turned against you. . . . Do all rich people, or people who are in the middle, know the humanities? Not a chance. But some do. And it helps. It helps to live better and enjoy life more. Will the humanities make you rich? Absolutely. But not in terms of money. In terms of life." And the Clemente course graduates did get rich in this way. Most of them went on to further higher education, and even the hard-luck Abel Lomas (not his real name), who got mixed up in a drug bust after he graduated, dumbfounded the classics-innocent prosecutor with arguments drawn from Plato and Sophocles.

By deliberately refusing to define poor Americans as nothing more than economic units whose best hope is "training" at fly-by-night computer schools, Shorris reminds us all that genuine education is a discourse—a dialogue—carried on within the context of the society around us, as well as with the mighty dead. School helps, but it's just the beginning of the engagement between ideas and reality—as Abel Lomas can attest.

Shorris' radical idea—more controversial even than expecting working-class stu-   10
dents to tackle a serious college curriculum—was to emphasize the humanities, those subtle subjects that infuse our minds with great, gushing ideas but also equip us to think and to argue. As more and more colleges, goaded by demands for "global competitiveness" from government officials and business leaders, turn themselves into glorified trade schools churning out graduates with highly specialized skills but little intellectual breadth, you might think humanities would go the way of the horse and buggy.

"It's an enormous error to believe that technology can somehow be the content of education," says John Ralston Saul, a Canadian historian and critic with years of experience in the business world. "We insist that everyone has to learn computer technology, but when printing came in with Gutenberg and changed the production and distribution of knowledge profoundly, nobody said that everyone should learn to be a printer. Technical training is training in what is sure to be obsolete soon anyway; it's self-defeating, and it won't get you through the next 60 years of your life." Training, says Saul, is simply "learning to fit in as a passive member of a structure. And that's the worst thing for an uncertain, changing time."

Oberlin College environmental studies professor David Orr poses an even fiercer challenge to the argument that education in the 21st century should focus primarily on high-tech training. In a recent article in the British magazine *Resurgence* (No. 179), he defines something he calls "slow knowledge": It is knowledge "shaped and calibrated to fit a particular ecological and cultural context," he writes, distinguishing it from the "fast knowledge" that zips through the terminals of the information society. "It does not imply lethargy, but rather thoroughness and patience. The aim of slow knowledge is resilience, harmony, and the preservation of long-standing patterns that give our lives aesthetic, spiritual, and social meaning." Orr says that we are focusing far too much of our energy and resources on fast knowledge, ignoring all the richness and meaning slow knowledge adds to our lives. Indeed, slow knowledge is what's needed to save the planet from ecological disaster and other threats posed by technological, millennial society.

"Culturally, we just are slow learners, no matter how fast individuals can process raw data," he says. "There's a long time gap between original insights and the cultural practices that come from them. You can figure out what you *can* do pretty quickly, but the ethical understanding of what you *ought* to do comes very slowly."

Miles Harvey, a Chicago journalist who assembled a list of environmental classics for *Outside* magazine (May 1996), reminds us that much of the divisiveness in contemporary debates on education boils down to a time issue. "The canon makers say you've only got so much time, so you have to choose between, say, Shakespeare and Toni Morrison, on the assumption that you can't get to both," he says. "Well, it is hard. The level of creativity and intellectual activity in this country would jump up if we had a four-day workweek."

But suppose we redefined this issue from the very beginning. Suppose we abandoned the notion that learning is a time-consuming and obligatory filling of our heads, and replaced it with the idea, courtesy of Goethe, that "people cannot learn what they do not love"—the idea of learning as an encounter infused with eros. We always find time for what we truly love, one way or another. Suppose further that love, being an inclusive spirit, refused to choose between Shakespeare and Toni Morrison (or Tony Bennett, for that matter), and we located our bliss in the unstable relationship between the two, rattling from book to book, looking for connections and grandly unconcerned about whether we've read "enough," as long as we read what we read with love.

And we wouldn't just read. We would reflect deeply on the relationship between our everyday lives and big philosophical questions—for, as Nietzsche memorably said,

15

"Metaphysics are in the street." The Argentine novelist Ernesto Sabato glosses him this way: "[By metaphysics Nietzsche means] those final problems of the human condition: death, loneliness, the meaning of existence, the desire for power, hope, and despair." The whole world's a classroom, and to really make it one, the first thing is to believe it is. We need to take seriously the proposition that reflection and knowledge born out of contact with the real world, an education carpentered out of the best combination we can make of school, salon, reading, online exploration, walking the streets, hiking in the woods, museums, poetry, classes at the Y, and friendship, may be the best education of all—not a makeshift substitute that must apologize for itself in the shadow of academe.

One of the things I like about this in-the-streets definition of education is how classical it is. In what's still one of the best concise summaries of classical education, Elizabeth Sutton Lawrence notes in *The Growth of Modern Education* (1971), that ancient Greek education "came largely from firsthand experience, in the marketplace, in the Assembly, in the theater, and in the religious celebration; through what the Greek youth saw and heard." Socrates met and challenged his adult "pupils" in the street, at dinner parties, after festivals, not at some Athenian Princeton.

Educational reactionaries want to convince us that the Western classical tradition is a carefully honed reading list. But as the dynamic classicist and philosopher Martha Nussbaum, who teaches at the University of Chicago Law School, insists, "The very idea that we should have a list of Great Books would have horrified the ancients. If you take to heart what the classical philosophers had to say, you'll never turn them into monuments. Their goal was to enliven the mind, and they knew that to enliven the mind you need to be very alert to what is in the world around you."

To really believe this casts a new light, to say the least, on the question of what the content of our learning ought to be. In her latest book, *Cultivating Humanity: A Classical Defense of Reform in Liberal Education* (Harvard University Press, 1997), Nussbaum argues compellingly that study of the non-Western world, of women's issues, of alternative sexuality, and of minority cultures is completely in line with classical principles, in particular the Stoic ideal of the "world citizen" with a cultivated ability to put her- or himself into the minds and lives of the members of divergent groups and cultures.

And New York jazz and rock writer Gene Santoro—trained in the classics and Dante studies—points out there's nothing frivolous about paying attention to popular culture: "Popular culture, and particularly popular music, is the place where the dominant culture is most heavily affected by marginal cultures. Jazz, for example, became wide enough to take in much of the range of American reality, from the African American experience to the European classical tradition to the Latin and Caribbean spirit. It's the artistic version of the American social experience, and if you care about this culture, you'll look at it." And, he adds in a Socratic vein, "Jazz can help you think. It's both disciplined and unpredictable. It gives you tradition but doesn't let you settle into preconceived notions."

Colin Greer—co-editor of *The Call to Character* and *The Plain Truth of Things*, progressive responses to William Bennett's *Book of Virtues*—suggests further ways to make the most of the relationship between books and what's going on in the streets.

"You could study the moments of major change in the world," he proposes. "The end of slavery. The early struggle against child labor. Woman suffrage. The organization of labor. People have forgotten what it really took to accomplish these things: What pragmatic things were done and how people learned to be generous and decent to their opponents. It's important to know the real story of how change works, and recognize that to fall short of your highest goals is OK as long as you stick to the struggle."

You get the idea. The American tradition, in learning as well as jazz and activism, is improvisatory. There are as many ways to become an educated American as there are Americans. To fall short of your highest goals—mastering that imaginary "complete" reading list, say—is OK as long as you stuck to the struggle. And the joy.

CONNECTING PERSONALLY TO THE READING

1. Spayde argues that low-income students need the humanities just as much as high-income students. Do you agree with Spayde, or do you think that he is being unrealistic in his attack on trade schools and other schools turning out graduates with highly specialized and marketable skills? Explain.

2. Describe a time when you have experienced "slow learning." What does this concept mean to you? Did the experience help you achieve any of the aims Spayde notes of "resilience, harmony, and the preservation of long-standing patterns . . ."? Explain.

3. What do you think are the problems with Spayde's attack on technical knowledge? Do you think that all technical knowledge is quickly obsolete? What about expert knowledge, such as the knowledge of aviation? What category do you think that knowledge falls under?

FOCUSING ON THE ARGUMENT

1. Although Spayde's subject is abstract, he interacts with the reader while he continues his line of thought: "Yikes!"; "The first thing, I firmly believe, is to take a deep, calm breath." How do such pauses, exclamations, and direct addresses help the reader follow his thinking? How do such expressions make the reader feel?

2. How does Spayde's constant questioning and "supposing" reflect his point about how people learn—they learn when they take the time to react to new ideas, discuss them with their classmates, and do the kind of repeated questioning that Spayde does in his article?

SYNTHESIZING IDEAS FROM MULTIPLE READINGS

1. Spayde thinks that the content of education should be humanistic, not technical. This means that the instruction should address large debatable questions, instigate dialogue and critical thinking, and involve personal contact and feeling. How do Rose's and Lilia's stories (in Mike Rose's "Epilogue: Lilia," p. 242), as well as Robert Barr's (in "Who Is This Child?" p. 229), support that view?

2. What do you think would be Spayde's reaction to David Brooks's description in "The Merits of Meritocracy" (p. 224) of the rushed, busy quality of middle-class children's after-school activities? What would he think of the ethic of self-improvement?

3. Spayde thinks Americans need to be seen as something more than "economic units" and that they need to learn how to have a dialogue about ideas. Explain why you think either John Dewey ("The School and the Life of the Child," p. 211) or Michael J. Lewis ("Forget Classrooms," p. 246) would agree or disagree.

4. Both Jonathan Kozol ("Savage Inequalities," p. 214) and Spayde are concerned with the unfair treatment in schools of poor Americans. Compare and contrast their concerns for curricula. Would Kozol think that Spayde's ideas for "slow knowledge" are feasible in a poverty-stricken school? Explain.

WRITING TO ACT

1. Identify a high school with an extensive technical training track, such as auto shop or computer repair. Examine the curriculum for students tracked into these courses. Do you think that the school is teaching these students basic humanistic values and skills, such as reading and thinking critically? If not, write a letter to the principal explaining that these students need courses designed to prepare them as citizens and adults. Include details on the skills taught in such classes.

2. Examine the curriculum of a specialized field such as computer programming at a college or university. If you have access to several instructors in this program, briefly interview them about the changing nature of the field. What do you (and they) think are the dangers in preparing students to earn a living in a field that changes so rapidly? Write a letter to the department chair at this or a similar college voicing your concerns.

READING

JOHN DEWEY   Dewey collapses the separation between schooling and living. He underscores that children need to learn through active experiences, like the ones they have outside of school, rather than through passive memorization of a set body of knowledge. Through these active experiences, each individual child should be encouraged to "construct, create, and actively enquire." In emphasizing active learning and individuality, Dewey questions some of the tacit assumptions we make about schooling and learning. What is the relationship between teacher and student? How might it be like parent and child? How does one "learn" something? What is the effect of an educational system that offers a uniform curriculum and masses students together in schoolrooms with set desks and ready-made accomplishments? In your own questioning of education practices, what are some unexamined assumptions about education that you have been asked to accept?

DEWEY, American philosopher, psychologist, and educator (1859–1952), wrote many influential works including *Democracy and Education, How We Think, Human Nature and Conduct,* and *The Public and Its Problems.*

The School and the Life
of the Child (1915) | BY JOHN DEWEY

There is very little place in the traditional schoolroom for the child to work. The workshop, the laboratory, the materials, the tools with which the child may construct, create, and actively inquire, and even the requisite space, have been for the most part lacking. The things that have to do with these processes have not even a definitely recognized place in education. They are what the educational authorities who write editorials in the daily papers generally term "fads" and "frills." A lady told me yesterday that she had been visiting different schools trying to find one where activity on the part of the children preceded the giving of information on the part of the teacher, or where the children had some motive for demanding the information. She visited, she said, twenty-four different schools before she found her first instance. I may add that that was not in this city.

Another thing that is suggested by these schoolrooms, with their set desks, is that everything is arranged for handling as large numbers of children as possible; for dealing with children *en masse*, as an aggregate of units; involving, again, that they be treated passively. The moment children act they individualize themselves; they cease to be a mass and become the intensely distinctive beings that we are acquainted with out of school, in the home, the family, on the playground, and in the neighborhood.

On the same basis is explicable the uniformity of method and curriculum. If everything is on a "listening" basis, you can have uniformity of material and method. The ear, and the book which reflects the ear, constitute the medium which is alike for all. There is next to no opportunity for adjustment to varying capacities and demands. There is a certain amount—a fixed quantity—of ready-made results and accomplishments to be acquired by all children alike in a given time. It is in response to this demand that the curriculum has been developed from the elementary school up through the college. There is just so much desirable knowledge, and there are just so many needed technical accomplishments in the world. Then comes the mathematical problem of dividing this by the six, twelve, or sixteen years of school life. Now give the children every year just the proportionate fraction of the total, and by the time they have finished they will have mastered the whole. By covering so much ground during this hour or day or week or year, everything comes out with perfect evenness at the end—provided the children have not forgotten what they have previously learned. The outcome of all this is Matthew Arnold's report of the statement, proudly made to him by an educational authority in France, that so many thousands of children were studying at a given hour, say eleven o'clock, just such a lesson in geography; and in one of our own western cities this proud boast used to be repeated to successive visitors by its superintendent.

I may have exaggerated somewhat in order to make plain the typical points of the old education: its passivity of attitude, its mechanical massing of children, its uniformity of curriculum and method. It may be summed up by stating that the center of gravity is outside the child. It is in the teacher, the textbook, anywhere and everywhere you please except in the immediate instincts and activities of the child himself. On that basis there is not much to be said about the *life* of the child. A good deal might be said about the studying of the child, but the school is not the place where the child *lives.* Now the change which is coming into our education is the shifting of the center of gravity. It is a change, a revolution, not unlike that introduced by Copernicus when the astronomical center shifted from the earth to the sun. In this case the child becomes the sun about which the appliances of education revolve; he is the center about which they are organized.

If we take an example from an ideal home, where the parent is intelligent enough 5 to recognize what is best for the child, and is able to supply what is needed, we find the child learning through the social converse and constitution of the family. There are certain points of interest and value to him in the conversation carried on: statements are made, inquiries arise, topics are discussed, and the child continually learns. He states his experiences, his misconceptions are corrected. Again the child participates in the household occupations, and thereby gets habits of industry, order, and regard for the rights and ideas of others, and the fundamental habit of subordinating his activities to the general interest of the household. Participation in these household tasks becomes an opportunity for gaining knowledge. The ideal home would naturally have a workshop where the child could work out his constructive instincts. It would have a miniature laboratory in which his inquiries could be directed. The life of the child would extend out of doors to the garden, surrounding fields, and forests. He would have his excursions, his walks and talks, in which the larger world out of doors would open to him.

Now, if we organize and generalize all of this, we have the ideal school. There is no mystery about it, no wonderful discovery of pedagogy or educational theory. It is simply a question of doing systematically and in a large, intelligent, and competent way what for various reasons can be done in most households only in a comparatively meager and haphazard manner.

CONNECTING PERSONALLY TO THE READING

1. Recount a key personal experience in school of "ready-made results and accomplishments." Did you struggle to individualize yourself? How might the lesson have been transformed into one that addressed your "instincts and activities"?

2. Dewey discusses the passivity that results from the treatment of students as a group, not as individuals. In your experience, how does passivity result from crowded classrooms, with set desks and limited space?

3. In your opinion, how might a school become a place where "a child lives"?

FOCUSING ON THE ARGUMENT

1. Dewey's argument for experiential learning is fairly straightforward. Yet, with an ironic tone, he cites reports, from educational authorities, that support the opposite view. How does Dewey's use of irony further our belief in experiential learning?

2. Dewey says he "may have exaggerated somewhat in order to make plain" his attack on the "old education." How has he exaggerated? Has the exaggeration made plain his point? Explain.

3. Dewey creates an analogy between an ideal education and the social makeup of the family. How does this analogy further his argument? What new values does this analogy attach to education?

SYNTHESIZING IDEAS FROM MULTIPLE READINGS

1. In "The Merits of Meritocracy" (p. 224), David Brooks writes about meritocracy as fundamental to education. One element of meritocracy is that individuals separate themselves from others on the basis of merit—individual achievement. How might Dewey agree with the individualism underlying this view? What would Dewey like about separating oneself from others?

2. Howard Gardner ("Human Intelligence Isn't What We Think It Is," p. 232), Mike Rose ("Epilogue: Lilia," p. 242), and Dewey all explore the knowledge and abilities that students might hold but that traditional schools devalue. What are the similarities and differences in these writers' views of such abilities?

3. How would Dewey's idea of "intensely distinctive beings" help explain Robert Barr's ("Who Is This Child?" p. 229) narrative about the teacher and the little girl? How does Dewey's contrast between "uniformity of method" and addressing "the life of the child" help explain the girl's transformation?

4. In "Learning in the Key of Life" (p. 205), Jon Spayde's idea of education involves questioning the purpose of education. Do you think he is advocating the same kind of questioning as Dewey? Explain.

5. In Chapter 2, various writers—Lydia Minatoya in "Transformation" (p. 81), Richard Rodriguez in "Public and Private Language" (p. 51), Itabari Njeri in "What's in a Name?" (p. 71), among others—who have experienced language and cultural differences, describe a transformative process of creating a new identity. Choose one of these writers and analyze how that person might have suffered in the educational system Dewey attacks. Do you think the writer would have benefited from the one he advocates? Explain.

WRITING TO ACT

1. Write a letter to a former teacher explaining to him or her the unconscious assumptions he or she may hold about how a child learns. Does the teacher assume that knowledge is uniform or individualistic? If the former, offer a different, more experiential way of teaching a lesson or class you had with this teacher.

2. Consider a field that interests you, and research the skills essential for a specific job. Write a letter to a potential employer asking which skills—memorized knowledge about the field or experiences related to the field—would be most essential to the job and why.

3. Conduct research on your local school district and determine whether the district stresses test results at the expense of active inquiry and critical thinking. If so, write an editorial for your local paper outlining why skills of active inquiry are more important than test results.

READING

JONATHAN KOZOL Do we have equality of educational opportunity in this country? Our belief in such opportunity motivates our continuing support of public education. Most Americans believe that, based on merit, the least-advantaged Americans can receive an education that could bring them out of poverty into affluence. David Brooks, in his article "The Merits of Meritocracy," implies that most middle-class parents believe in merit and seek extracurricular activities to further their children's opportunities. But is there equality of educational opportunity for lower- and working-class children? Jonathan Kozol makes a powerful case for the lack of such equality. How, according to Kozol, does public education serve to maintain a class system?

KOZOL, an educator and activist, began his teaching career in 1965 at a public school in Roxbury, Massachusetts, where he was fired for reading Langston Hughes's poetry to students. His book *Death at an Early Age: The Destruction of the Hearts and Minds of Negro Children in the Boston Public Schools,* recounts his experiences at that school and explores many problems faced by minority students in low-income school districts; it received the National Book Award in 1968. Kozol continues to teach in poor, urban neighborhoods (such as the South Bronx) and to write about race, poverty, and education. Recent books by Kozol include *Amazing Grace: The Lives of Children and the Conscience of a Nation* (1995) and *Ordinary Resurrections: Children in the Years of Hope* (2000).

Savage Inequalities (1991) | BY JONATHAN KOZOL

In order to find Public School 261 in District 10, a visitor is told to look for a mortician's office. The funeral home, which faces Jerome Avenue in the North Bronx, is easy to identify by its green awning. The school is next door, in a former roller-skating rink. No sign identifies the building as a school. A metal awning frame without an awning supports a flagpole, but there is no flag.

In the street in front of the school there is an elevated public transit line. Heavy traffic fills the street. The existence of the school is virtually concealed within this crowded city block.

In a vestibule between the outer and inner glass doors of the school there is a sign with these words: "All children are capable of learning."

Beyond the inner doors a guard is seated. The lobby is long and narrow. The ceiling is low. There are no windows. All the teachers that I see at first are middle-aged white women. The principal, who is also a white woman, tells me that the school's "capacity" is 900 but that there are 1,300 children here. The size of classes for fifth and sixth grade children in New York, she says, is "capped" at 32, but she says that class size in the school goes "up to 34." (I later see classes, however, as large as 37.) Classes for younger children, she goes on, are "capped at 25," but a school can go above this limit if it puts an extra adult in the room. Lack of space, she says, prevents the school from operating a pre-kindergarten program.

I ask the principal where her children go to school. They are enrolled in private 5 school, she says.

"Lunchtime is a challenge for us," she explains. "Limited space obliges us to do it in three shifts, 450 children at a time."

Textbooks are scarce and children have to share their social studies books. The principal says there is one full-time pupil counselor and another who is here two days a week: a ratio of 930 children to one counselor. The carpets are patched and sometimes taped together to conceal an open space. "I could use some new rugs," she observes.

To make up for the building's lack of windows and the crowded feeling that results, the staff puts plants and fish tanks in the corridors. Some of the plants are flourishing. Two boys, released from class, are in a corridor beside a tank, their noses pressed against the glass. A school of pinkish fish inside the tank are darting back and forth. Farther down the corridor a small Hispanic girl is watering the plants.

Two first grade classes share a single room without a window, divided only by a blackboard. Four kindergartens and a sixth grade class of Spanish-speaking children have been packed into a single room in which, again, there is no window. A second grade bilingual class of 37 children has its own room but again there is no window.

By eleven o'clock, the lunchroom is already packed with appetite and life. The kids line up to get their meals, then eat them in ten minutes. After that, with no place they can go to play, they sit and wait until it's time to line up and go back to class.

On the second floor I visit four classes taking place within another undivided space. The room has a low ceiling. File cabinets and movable blackboards give a small degree of isolation to each class. Again, there are no windows.

The library is a tiny, windowless and claustrophobic room. I count approximately 700 books. Seeing no reference books, I ask a teacher if encyclopedias and other reference books are kept in classrooms.

"We don't have encyclopedias in classrooms," she replies. "That is for the suburbs."

The school, I am told, has 26 computers for its 1,300 children. There is one small gym and children get one period, and sometimes two, each week. Recess, however, is not possible because there is no playground. "Head Start," the principal says, "scarcely exists in District 10. We have no space."

The school, I am told, is 90 percent black and Hispanic; the other 10 percent are Asian, white or Middle Eastern.

In a sixth grade social studies class the walls are bare of words or decorations. There seems to be no ventilation system, or, if one exists, it isn't working.

The class discusses the Nile River and the Fertile Crescent.

The teacher, in a droning voice: "How is it useful that these civilizations developed close to rivers?"

A child, in a good loud voice: "What kind of question is that?"

In my notes I find these words: "An uncomfortable feeling—being in a building with no windows. There are metal ducts across the room. Do they give air? I feel asphyxiated. . . ."

On the top floor of the school, a sixth grade of 30 children shares a room with 29 bilingual second graders. Because of the high class size there is an assistant with each teacher. This means that 59 children and four grown-ups—63 in all—must share a room that, in a suburban school, would hold no more than 20 children and one teacher. There are, at least, some outside windows in this room—it is the only room with windows in the school—and the room has a high ceiling. It is a relief to see some daylight.

I return to see the kindergarten classes on the ground floor and feel stifled once again by lack of air and the low ceiling. Nearly 120 children and adults are doing what they can to make the best of things: 80 children in four kindergarten classes, 30 children in the sixth grade class, and about eight grown-ups who are aides and teachers. The kindergarten children sitting on the worn rug, which is patched with tape, look up at me and turn their heads to follow me as I walk past them.

As I leave the school, a sixth grade teacher stops to talk. I ask her, "Is there air conditioning in warmer weather?"

Teachers, while inside the building, are reluctant to give answers to this kind of question. Outside, on the sidewalk, she is less constrained: "I had an awful room last year. In the winter it was 56 degrees. In the summer it was up to 90. It was sweltering."

I ask her, "Do the children ever comment on the building?"   25

"They don't say," she answers, "but they know."

I ask her if they see it as a racial message.

"All these children see TV," she says. "They know what suburban schools are like. Then they look around them at their school. This was a roller-rink, you know. . . . They don't comment on it but you see it in their eyes. They understand."

On the following morning I visit P.S. 79, another elementary school in the same district. "We work under difficult circumstances," says the principal, James Carter, who is black. "The school was built to hold one thousand students. We have 1,550. We are badly overcrowded. We need smaller classes but, to do this, we would need more space. I can't add five teachers. I would have no place to put them."

Some experts, I observe, believe that class size isn't a real issue. He dismisses this   30
abruptly. "It doesn't take a genius to discover that you learn more in a smaller class. I have to bus some 60 kindergarten children elsewhere, since I have no space for them. When they return next year, where do I put them?

"I can't set up a computer lab. I have no room. I had to put a class into the library. I have no librarian. There are two gymnasiums upstairs but they cannot be used for sports. We hold more classes there. It's unfair to measure us against the suburbs. They have 17 to 20 children in a class. Average class size in this school is 30.

"The school is 29 percent black, 70 percent Hispanic. Few of these kids get Head Start. There is no space in the district. Of 200 kindergarten children, 50 maybe get some kind of preschool."

I ask him how much difference preschool makes.

"Those who get it do appreciably better. I can't overestimate its impact but, as I have said, we have no space."

The school tracks children by ability, he says. "There are five to seven levels in   35
each grade. The highest level is equivalent to 'gifted' but it's not a full-scale gifted program. We don't have the funds. We have no science room. The science teachers carry their equipment with them."

We sit and talk within the nurse's room. The window is broken. There are two holes in the ceiling. About a quarter of the ceiling has been patched and covered with a plastic garbage bag.

"Ideal class size for these kids would be 15 to 20. Will these children ever get what white kids in the suburbs take for granted? I don't think so. If you ask me why, I'd have to speak of race and social class. I don't think the powers that be in New York City understand, or want to understand, that if they do not give these children a sufficient education to lead healthy and productive lives, we will be their victims later on. We'll pay the price someday—in violence, in economic costs. I despair of making this appeal in any terms but these. You cannot issue an appeal to conscience in New York today. The fair-play argument won't be accepted. So you speak of violence and hope that it will scare the city into action."

While we talk, three children who look six or seven years old come to the door and ask to see the nurse, who isn't in the school today. One of the children, a Puerto Rican girl, looks haggard. "I have a pain in my tooth," she says. The principal says, "The nurse is out. Why don't you call your mother?" The child says, "My mother doesn't have a phone." The principal sighs. "Then go back to your class." When she leaves, the principal is angry. "It's amazing to me that these children ever make it with the obstacles they face. Many *do* care and they *do* try, but there's a feeling of despair. The parents of these children want the same things for their children that the parents in the suburbs want. Drugs are not the cause of this. They are the symptom. Nonetheless, they're used by people in the suburbs and rich people in Manhattan as another reason to keep children of poor people at a distance."

I ask him, "Will white children and black children ever go to school together in New York?"

"I don't see it," he replies. "I just don't think it's going to happen. It's a dream.   40 I simply do not see white folks in Riverdale agreeing to cross-bus with kids like these. A few, maybe. Very few. I don't think I'll live to see it happen."

I ask him whether race is the decisive factor. Many experts, I observe, believe that wealth is more important in determining these inequalities.

"This," he says—and sweeps his hand around him at the room, the garbage bag, the ceiling—"would not happen to white children."

In a kindergarten class the children sit cross-legged on a carpet in a space between two walls of books. Their 26 faces are turned up to watch their teacher, an elderly black woman. A little boy who sits beside me is involved in trying to tie bows in his shoelaces. The children sing a song: "Lift Every Voice." On the walls are these handwritten words: "Beautiful, also, are the souls of my people."

In a very small room on the fourth floor, 52 people in two classes do their best to teach and learn. Both are first grade classes. One, I am informed, is "low ability." The other is bilingual.

"The room is barely large enough for one class," says the principal.   45

The room is 25 by 50 feet. There are 26 first graders and two adults on the left, 22 others and two adults on the right. On the wall there is the picture of a small white child, circled by a Valentine, and a Gainsborough painting of a child in a formal dress.

"We are handicapped by scarcity," one of the teachers says. "One fifth of these children may be at grade level by the year's end."

A boy who may be seven years old climbs on my lap without an invitation and removes my glasses. He studies my face and runs his fingers through my hair. "You have nice hair," he says. I ask him where he lives and he replies, "Times Square Hotel," which is a homeless shelter in Manhattan.

I ask him how he gets here.

"With my father. On the train," he says.   50

"How long does it take?"

"It takes an hour and a half."

I ask him when he leaves his home.

"My mother wakes me up at five o'clock."

"When do you leave?"   55

"Six-thirty."

I ask him how he gets back to Times Square.

"My father comes to get me after school."

From my notes: "He rides the train three hours every day in order to attend this segregated school. It would be a shorter ride to Riverdale. There are rapid shuttle-vans that make that trip in only 20 minutes. Why not let him go to school right in Manhattan, for that matter?"

At three o'clock the nurse arrives to do her recordkeeping. She tells me she is here 60 three days a week. "The public hospital we use for an emergency is called North Central. It's not a hospital that I will use if I am given any choice. Clinics in the private hospitals are far more likely to be staffed by an experienced physician."

She hesitates a bit as I take out my pen, but then goes on: "I'll give you an example. A little girl I saw last week in school was trembling and shaking and could not control the motions of her arms. I was concerned and called her home. Her mother came right up to school and took her to North Central. The intern concluded that the child was upset by 'family matters'—nothing more—that there was nothing wrong with her. The mother was offended by the diagnosis. She did not appreciate his words or his assumptions. The truth is, there was nothing wrong at home. She brought the child back to school. I thought that she was ill. I told her mother, 'Go to Montefiore.' It's a private hospital, and well respected. She took my advice, thank God. It turned out that the child had a neurological disorder. She is now in treatment.

"This is the kind of thing our children face. Am I saying that the city underserves this population? You can draw your own conclusions."

Out on the street, it takes a full half hour to flag down a cab. Taxi drivers in New York are sometimes disconcertingly direct in what they say. When they are contemptuous of poor black people, their contempt is unadorned. When they're sympathetic and compassionate, their observations often go right to the heart of things. "Oh . . . they neglect these children," says the driver. "They leave them in the streets and slums to live and die." We stop at a light. Outside the window of the taxi, aimless men are standing in a semicircle while another man is working on his car. Old four-story buildings with their windows boarded, cracked or missing are on every side.

I ask the driver where he's from. He says Afghanistan. Turning in his seat, he gestures at the street and shrugs. "If you don't, as an American, begin to give these kids the kind of education that you give the kids of Donald Trump, you're asking for disaster."

Two months later, on a day in May, I visit an elementary school in Riverdale. The dog- 65 woods and magnolias on the lawn in front of P.S. 24 are in full blossom on the day I visit. There is a well-tended park across the street, another larger park three blocks away. To the left of the school is a playground for small children, with an innovative jungle gym, a slide and several climbing toys. Behind the school there are two playing fields for older kids. The grass around the school is neatly trimmed.

The neighborhood around the school, by no means the richest part of Riverdale, is nonetheless expensive and quite beautiful. Residences in the area—some of which are large, free-standing houses, others condominiums in solid red-brick buildings—sell for prices in the region of $400,000; but some of the larger Tudor houses on the winding and tree-shaded streets close to the school can cost up to $1 million. The excellence of P.S. 24, according to the principal, adds to the value of these homes. Advertisements in the *New York Times* will frequently inform prospective buyers that a house is "in the neighborhood of P.S. 24."

The school serves 825 children in the kindergarten through sixth grade. This is approximately half the student population crowded into P.S. 79, where 1,550 children fill a space intended for 1,000, and a great deal smaller than the 1,300 children packed into the former skating rink; but the principal of P.S. 24, a capable and energetic man named David Rothstein, still regards it as excessive for an elementary school.

The school is integrated in the strict sense that the middle- and upper-middle-class white children here do occupy a building that contains some Asian and Hispanic and black children; but there is little integration in the classrooms since the vast majority of the Hispanic and black children are assigned to "special" classes on the basis of evaluations that have classified them "EMR"—"educable mentally retarded"—or else, in the worst of cases, "TMR"—"trainable mentally retarded."

I ask the principal if any of his students qualify for free-lunch programs. "About 130 do," he says. "Perhaps another 35 receive their lunches at reduced price. Most of these kids are in the special classes. They do not come from this neighborhood."

The very few nonwhite children that one sees in mainstream classes tend to be Japanese or else of other Asian origins. Riverdale, I learn, has been the residence of choice for many years to members of the diplomatic corps. 70

The school therefore contains effectively two separate schools: one of about 130 children, most of whom are poor, Hispanic, black, assigned to one of the 12 special classes; the other of some 700 mainstream students, almost all of whom are white or Asian.

There is a third track also—this one for the students who are labeled "talented" or "gifted." This is termed a "pull-out" program since the children who are so identified remain in mainstream classrooms but are taken out for certain periods each week to be provided with intensive and, in my opinion, excellent instruction in some areas of reasoning and logic often known as "higher-order skills" in the contemporary jargon of the public schools. Children identified as "gifted" are admitted to this program in first grade and, in most cases, will remain there for six years. Even here, however, there are two tracks of the gifted. The regular gifted classes are provided with only one semester of this specialized instruction yearly. Those very few children, on the other hand, who are identified as showing the most promise are assigned, beginning in the third grade, to a program that receives a full-year regimen.

In one such class, containing ten intensely verbal and impressive fourth grade children, nine are white and one is Asian. The "special" class I enter first, by way of contrast, has twelve children of whom only one is white and none is Asian. These racial breakdowns prove to be predictive of the schoolwide pattern.

In a classroom for the gifted on the first floor of the school, I ask a child what the class is doing. "Logic and syllogisms," she replies. The room is fitted with a planetarium. The principal says that all the elementary schools in District 10 were given the same planetariums ten years ago but that certain schools, because of overcrowding, have been forced to give them up. At P.S. 261, according to my notes, there was a domelike space that had been built to hold a planetarium, but the planetarium had been removed to free up space for the small library collection. P.S. 24, in contrast, has a spacious library that holds almost 8,000 books. The windows are decorated with attractive, brightly colored curtains and look out on flowering trees. The principal says that it's inadequate, but it appears spectacular to me after the cubicle that holds a meager 700 books within the former skating rink.

The district can't afford librarians, the principal says, but P.S. 24, unlike the poorer schools of District 10, can draw on educated parent volunteers who staff the room in shifts three days a week. A parent organization also raises independent funds 75 to buy materials, including books, and will soon be running a fund-raiser to enhance the library's collection.

In a large and sunny first grade classroom that I enter next, I see 23 children, all of whom are white or Asian. In another first grade, there are 22 white children and two others who are Japanese. There is a computer in each class. Every classroom also has a modern fitted sink.

In a second grade class of 22 children, there are two black children and three Asian children. Again, there is a sink and a computer. A sixth grade social studies class has only one black child. The children have an in-class research area that holds some up-to-date resources. A set of encyclopedias (World Book, 1985) is in a rack beside a window. The children are doing a Spanish language lesson when I enter. Foreign languages begin in sixth grade at the school, but Spanish is offered also to the kindergarten children. As in every room at P.S. 24, the window shades are clean and new, the floor is neatly tiled in gray and green, and there is not a single light bulb missing.

Walking next into a special class, I see twelve children. One is white. Eleven are black. There are no Asian children. The room is half the size of mainstream classrooms. "Because of overcrowding," says the principal, "we have had to split these rooms in half." There is no computer and no sink.

I enter another special class. Of seven children, five are black, one is Hispanic, one is white. A little black boy with a large head sits in the far corner and is gazing at the ceiling.

"Placement of these kids," the principal explains, "can usually be traced to neurological damage." 80

In my notes: "How could so many of these children be brain-damaged?"

Next door to the special class is a woodworking shop. "This shop is only for the special classes," says the principal. The children learn to punch in time cards at the door, he says, in order to prepare them for employment.

The fourth grade gifted class, in which I spend the last part of the day, is humming with excitement. "I start with these children in the first grade," says the teacher. "We pull them out of mainstream classes on the basis of their test results and other factors such as the opinion of their teachers. Out of this group, beginning in third grade, I pull out the ones who show the most potential, and they enter classes such as this one."

The curriculum they follow, she explains, "emphasizes critical thinking, reasoning and logic." The planetarium, for instance, is employed not simply for the study of the universe as it exists. "Children also are designing their own galaxies," the teacher says.

A little girl sitting around a table with her classmates speaks with perfect poise: 85 "My name is Susan. We are in the fourth grade gifted program."

I ask them what they're doing and a child says, "My name is Laurie and we're doing problem-solving."

A rather tall, good-natured boy who is half-standing at the table tells me that his name is David. "One thing that we do," he says, "is logical thinking. Some problems, we find, have more than one good answer. We need to learn not simply to be logical in our own thinking but to show respect for someone else's logic even when an answer may be technically incorrect."

When I ask him to explain this, he goes on, "A person who gives an answer that is not 'correct' may nonetheless have done some interesting thinking that we should examine. 'Wrong' answers may be more useful to examine than correct ones."

I ask the children if reasoning and logic are innate or if they're things that you can learn.

"You know some things to start with when you enter school," Susan says. "But we also learn some things that other children don't."

I ask her to explain this.

"We know certain things that other kids don't know because we're *taught* them."

She has braces on her teeth. Her long brown hair falls almost to her waist. Her loose white T-shirt has the word TRI-LOGIC on the front. She tells me that Tri-Logic is her father's firm.

Laurie elaborates on the same point: "Some things you know. Some kinds of logic are inside of you to start with. There are other things that someone needs to teach you."

David expands on what the other two have said: "Everyone can think and speak in logical ways unless they have a mental problem. What this program does is bring us to a higher form of logic."

The class is writing a new "Bill of Rights." The children already know the U.S. Bill of Rights and they explain its first four items to me with precision. What they are examining today, they tell me, is the very *concept* of a "right." Then they will create their own compendium of rights according to their own analysis and definition. Along one wall of the classroom, opposite the planetarium, are seven Apple II computers on which children have developed rather subtle color animations that express the themes—of greed and domination, for example—that they also have described in writing.

"This is an upwardly mobile group," the teacher later says. "They have exposure to whatever New York City has available. Their parents may take them to the theater, to museums. . . ."

In my notes: "Six girls, four boys. Nine white, one Chinese. I am glad they have this class. But what about the others? Aren't there ten black children in the school who could enjoy this also?"

The teacher gives me a newspaper written, edited and computer-printed by her sixth grade gifted class. The children, she tells me, are provided with a link to kids in Europe for transmission of news stories.

A science story by one student asks if scientists have ever falsified their research. "Gregor Mendel," the sixth grader writes, "the Austrian monk who founded the science of genetics, published papers on his work with peas that some experts say were statistically too good to be true. Isaac Newton, who formulated the law of gravitation, relied on unseemly mathematical sleight of hand in his calculations. . . . Galileo Galilei, founder of modern scientific method, wrote about experiments that were so difficult to duplicate that colleagues doubted he had done them."

Another item in the paper, also by a sixth grade student, is less esoteric: "The Don Cossacks dance company, from Russia, is visiting the United States. The last time it toured America was 1976. . . . The Don Cossacks will be in New York City for two weeks at the Neil Simon Theater. Don't miss it!"

The tone is breezy—and so confident! That phrase—"Don't miss it!"—speaks a volume about life in Riverdale.

"What makes a good school?" asks the principal when we are talking later on. "The building and teachers are part of it, of course. But it isn't just the building and the teachers. Our kids come from good families and the neighborhood is good. In a three-block area we have a public library, a park, a junior high. . . . Our typical sixth grader reads at eighth grade level." In a quieter voice he says, "I see how hard my colleagues work in schools like P.S. 79. You have children in those neighborhoods who live in virtual hell. They enter school five years behind. What do they get?" Then, as he spreads his hands out on his desk, he says: "I have to ask myself why there should be an elementary school in District 10 with fifteen hundred children. Why should there be an elementary school within a skating rink? Why should the Board of Ed allow this? This is not the way that things should be."

Stark as the inequities in District 10 appear, educators say that they are "mild" in comparison to other situations in the city. Some of the most stunning inequality, according to a report by the Community Service Society, derives from allocations granted by state legislators to school districts where they have political allies. The poorest districts in the city get approximately 90 cents per pupil from these legislative grants, while the richest districts have been given $14 for each pupil.

Newspapers in New York City have reported other instances of the misallocation 105 of resources. "The Board of Education," wrote the *New York Post* during July of 1987, "was hit with bombshell charges yesterday that money earmarked for fighting drug abuse and illiteracy in ghetto schools was funneled instead to schools in wealthy areas."

In receipt of extra legislative funds, according to the *Post,* affluent districts were funded "at a rate 14 times greater than low-income districts." The paper said the city's poorest areas were underfunded "with stunning consistency."

The report by the Community Service Society cites an official of the New York City Board of Education who remarks that there is "no point" in putting further money "into some poor districts" because, in his belief, "new teachers would not stay there." But the report observes that, in an instance where beginning teacher salaries were raised by nearly half, "that problem largely disappeared"—another interesting reminder of the difference money makes when we are willing to invest it. Nonetheless, says the report, "the perception that the poorest districts are beyond help still remains. . . ." Perhaps the worst result of such beliefs, says the report, is the message that resources would be "wasted on poor children." This message "trickles down to districts, schools, and classrooms." Children hear and understand this theme—they are poor investments—and behave accordingly. If society's resources would be wasted on their destinies, perhaps their own determination would be wasted too. "Expectations are a powerful force . . . ," the CSS observes.

Despite the evidence, the CSS report leans over backwards not to fuel the flames of racial indignation. "In the present climate," the report says, "suggestions of racism must be made with caution. However, it is inescapable that these inequities are being perpetrated on [school] districts which are virtually all black and Hispanic. . . ." While the report says, very carefully, that there is no "evidence" of "deliberate individual discrimination," it nonetheless concludes that "those who allocate resources make decisions over and over again which penalize the poorest districts." Analysis of city policy, the study says, "speaks to systemic bias which constitutes a conspiracy of effect. . . . Whether consciously or not, the system writes off its poorest students."

1. Kozol describes what others see and confide in him. Do you have any telling personal experiences, stories, or observations that support his view of "savage inequalities" in education? If so, choose one and imagine that you are responding to a question he has asked you. Tell your story.

2. According to Kozol, the architecture of the schools imparts a strong message to children about what they are worth and what they are capable of. What details strike you as conveying the most significant messages to children? Why?

3. If you were to change the conditions of a poor school, and you had a $200,000 grant, what would be the first thing you would do? Why?

1. Kozol's argument is especially credible because of his use of concrete details. How do his specific observations and interviews, quotations from various sources such as school principals, teachers, and students, as well as telling statistics, help persuade you?

2. What voice does Kozol use? (personal? emotional? strident? objective?) What is the effect of this voice?

3. What is the effect of letting the reader draw his or her own conclusions from what others say as well as from what Kozol has recorded in his notes? Do you find this strategy particularly persuasive? Explain.

1. In "The Merits of Meritocracy" (p. 224), David Brooks describes the busy activities of children from obviously affluent homes. He sees this activity as representative of an American "meritocracy." How might Kozol respond to such a view?

2. John Dewey argues in "The School and the Life of the Child" (p. 211) against the traditional schoolroom with its set desks, where information is memorized by essentially passive minds. How would Dewey analyze the education of the children Kozol describes? Do you think that questions such as "How is it useful that these civilizations [along the Nile and Fertile Crescent] developed close to rivers?" indicate a set curriculum? Explain.

3. In "School: The Story of American Public Education" (p. 198), David Tyack emphasizes that public education has always reflected common ideals, yet the schools Kozol describes do not seem to embody any such common values. What would Tyack think went wrong?

4. The children in the impoverished schools Kozol describes likely grow up to take jobs such as those described by Barbara Ehrenreich ("Nickel and Dimed," p. 322) and Gary Soto ("Black Hair," p. 296) in Chapter 5. What in these children's education prepares them to work in such jobs? What might be the educational reason they cannot move out of such jobs?

1. From personal experience, write to a school administrator or teacher about some evidence of "savage inequalities" you have seen: You can describe in detail a school building or

classroom, an exchange between a teacher and student, or a watered-down curriculum that you think contributes to such inequalities. Pinpoint what you think this person could do.

2. Investigate the curriculum of a typical teacher training program at a local college or university. What changes should be made? Revise the curriculum to include those changes, and describe the skills and qualities to be developed.

READING

DAVID BROOKS Beginning with the assumption that "we live amid plenty," David Brooks writes about how children's extensive after-school activities contribute to children's moral education. Brooks contrasts the busy life of today's young children—whose frenetic activities adults supervise and support—with the life of previous generations of children who were working and independent of adults. In defense of children's busy life, Brooks says the activities create a "meritocracy"—an emphasis on individual achievement that helps children realize their potential. Do you agree with this? What positive values do you think are taught by such after-school activities as soccer, dance, art, skateboarding, Little League baseball, and horseback riding, especially when they involve coaching, competition, and parental support?

BROOKS has been a columnist for the *New York Times* since 2003 and appears on the PBS *Newshour.* He has been a writer or editor at the *Weekly Standard,* the *Atlantic, Newsweek,* and the *Wall Street Journal.* He is the author of the books *Bobo in Paradise* and *On Paradise Drive.*

The Merits of Meritocracy (2002)

BY DAVID BROOKS

My daughter is a four-helmet kid. She has a regular helmet she wears bike riding, pogo sticking, and when she borrows her older brother's skateboard. She has a pink batting helmet, which she wears during her Little League baseball games. She has a helmet for horseback-riding lessons, on Sundays. And she has a helmet for ice hockey, which she plays on Friday afternoons. (For hockey she also has an equipment bag large enough to hold several corpses.) My daughter's not even a jock (although she is something of a live wire). Her main interest is art, which she does in an after-school program on Tuesdays and at home on her own.

But it's her helmets that really got me thinking. They're generally scattered around the equipment racks in our garage, along with her brothers' helmet collections and all manner of sleds, mitts, scooters, bicycles, and balls, and they represent a certain sort of childhood—a childhood that has now become typical in middle-class America.

It's a busy childhood, filled with opportunities, activities, teams, coaches, and, inevitably, gear. It's a safety-conscious childhood, with ample adult supervision. And it is, I believe (at least I want to believe), a happy and fulfilling childhood that will prepare my daughter for a happy adult life.

This sort of childhood is different from the childhoods Americans have traditionally had. It's not an independent childhood, like Huck Finn's or the Bowery Boys'. Today's middle-class kids, by and large, don't live apart from adult society, free to explore and experiment and, through adventure and misadventure, teach themselves the important lessons of life. Nor is it a Horatio Alger childhood. Middle-class kids by definition haven't come from poverty and deprivation. Nor do they build self-discipline from having to work on a farm. If they hunger for success, it's not because they started at the bottom.

Today's mode of raising kids generates [5] a lot of hand-wringing and anxiety, some of it on my part. We fear that kids are spoiled by the abundance and frenetic activity all around them. We fear that the world of suburban sprawl, Game Boys, Britney Spears CDs, and shopping malls will dull their moral senses. We fear that they are too deferential to authority, or that they are confronted with so many choices that they never have to make real commitments. Or we fear that they are skipping over childhood itself. The toy companies call this phenomenon "age compression": Kids who are ten no longer want toys that used to appeal to ten-year-olds. Now it is three-to-five-year-olds who go for Barbie dolls. By the time a girl is seven she wants to be a mini-adult.

But I've come to believe that our fears are overblown. The problem is that the way kids (and, for that matter, the rest of us) live is estranged from the formulaic ideas we have about building character. We assume that character is forged through hardship—economic deprivation, war, and so on—and that we who have had it easy, who have grown up in this past half century of peace and pros-

perity, must necessarily have weak or suspect souls.

It's true that we live amid plenty; even in time of war we are told to keep shopping. But today's kids have a way of life that entails its own character-building process, its own ethical system. They live in a world of almost crystalline meritocracy. Starting at birth, middle-class Americans are called on to master skills, do well in school, practice sports, excel in extracurricular activities, get into college, build their résumés, change careers, be good in bed, set up retirement plans, and so on. This is a way of life that emphasizes individual achievement, self-propulsion, perpetual improvement, and permanent exertion.

The prime ethical imperative for the meritocrat is self-fulfillment. The phrase sounds New Agey; it calls to mind a Zen vegan sitting on the beach at dawn contemplating his narcissism. But over the past several years the philosophers Charles Taylor, of McGill University, and Alan Gewirth, of the University of Chicago, have argued that a serious moral force is contained in the idea of self-fulfillment. Meritocrats may not necessarily be able to articulate this morality, but they live by it nonetheless.

It starts with the notion that we have a lifelong mission to realize our capacities. "It is a bringing of oneself to flourishing completion, an unfolding of what is strongest or best in oneself, so that it represents the successful culmination of one's aspirations or potentialities," Gewirth wrote in *Self-Fulfillment* (1998). The way we realize our potential is through our activities. By ceaselessly striving to improve at the things we enjoy, we come to define, enlarge, and attain our best selves. These activities are the bricks of our identities; if we didn't write or play baseball or cook or litigate (or whatever it is we do well), we would cease to be who we are. This is what Karl Marx was describing when he wrote, "Milton produced *Paradise Lost* as a silkworm produces silk, as the activation of his own nature."

In this mode of living, character isn't 10 something one forges as a youth and then retains thereafter. Morality doesn't come to one in a single revelation or a grand moment of epiphany. Instead, virtue and character are achieved gradually and must be maintained through a relentless struggle for self-improvement. We are in an ongoing dialogue with our inadequacies, and we are happiest when we are most deeply engaged in overcoming them.

This is not a solitary process. Once ensconced in an activity, we find ourselves surrounded by mentors, coaches, teachers, colleagues, teammates, consultants, readers, and audience members. Society helps us in two ways. First, it gives us opportunities to participate in the things that will allow us to realize our capacities: Parents earnestly cast about for activities their children will love, and then spend their weekends driving them from one to another. Good schools have extracurricular offerings. Good companies and organizations allow their employees and members to explore new skills, and great nations have open, fluid societies—so that individuals can find their best avenues and go as far as their merit allows.

Second, society surrounds the individual with a web of instruction, encouragement, and recognition. The hunger for recognition is a great motivator for the meritocrat. People define themselves in part by the extent to which others praise and appreciate them. In traditional societies recognition was determined by birth, breeding, and social station, but in a purified meritocracy

people have to win it through performance. Each person responds to signals from those around him, working hard at activities that win praise and abandoning those that don't. (America no doubt leads the world in trophy production per capita.) An individual's growth, then, is a joint project of the self and society.

In this joint project individuals not only improve their capacities; they also come to realize that they cannot fully succeed unless they make a contribution to the society that helped to shape them. A scientist may be good at science, but she won't feel fulfilled unless she has made important discoveries or innovations that help those around her. Few meritocrats are content to master pointless tasks.

Social contributions—giving back—flow easily and naturally from the meritocrat's life mission. Baseball players enjoy clinics where they share tips with younger players. Parents devote many hours to coaching, or they become teachers, managers, and mentors. In the best relationships what follows is a sort of love affair. Mentor and pupil work hard to help each other and to honor each other's effort. Most find that they glimpse their best selves while working with others on an arduous undertaking, whether it is staging a play, competing for a championship, or arguing a case in court.

The great moral contest for the merit- 15 ocrat is not between good and evil or virtue and vice. Most meritocrats are prudent, so they don't commit terrible crimes or self-destructive follies. The great temptation is triviality. Society recognizes the fulfillment of noble capacities, but it also rewards shallow achievements. A person can be famous simply for being rich or good-looking. Sometimes it's the emptiest but splashiest activities that win the most attention. It can be easy to fall into a comfortable pattern of self-approval. Society seems to be rewarding you for what you are doing. Your salary goes up. You get promoted. You win bonuses. But you haven't tapped your capacities to the fullest.

Meritocrats therefore face a continual struggle to choose worthy opportunities over trivial ones. Charles Taylor argues that each of us has an intuitive ability to make what he calls "strong evaluations" of which aspirations are noblest. We do this, he believes, by tapping into any of a variety of moral frameworks, which have been handed down through time and which have "significance independent of us or our desires." It is necessary, then, to dig deep into what it means to be a Christian or a Jew or an American or a doctor. By this way of thinking, society's rebels had it all wrong when they tried to find self-fulfillment by breaking loose from tradition. Their rebellions created selves without roots or moral reference points. Burrowing down into an inherited tradition allows the meritocrat to strive upward.

For decades social critics have sold Americans short. All those books about the Organization Man, the culture of narcissism, the last man, and the flat, commercial materialism of American life underestimated the struggles and opportunities to build character that are embedded in the meritocratic system. The critics applied bygone codes to today's way of life. Inevitably, they have found kids, and us, wanting, and not in the areas where we truly are wanting (chief among these being that we don't sufficiently educate our children in the substance of the moral traditions they are inheriting—the history of Christianity, the history of Judaism, the history of America).

Today's kids live amid peace and prosperity, true. But theirs is not an easy life. Has there ever been a generation compelled to accomplish so much—to establish an identity, succeed in school, cope with technological change, maneuver through the world of group dating and diverse sexual orientation, and make daily decisions about everything from cell-phone rate plans to brands of sugar substitute? The meritocrat's life is radically open, but its very openness creates a series of choices and challenges that are demanding and subtle because they are never-ending and because they are embedded in the pattern of everyday life—rather than being faced, say, at one crucial, life-determining moment on the battlefield.

There is virtue in trying to articulate the codes we live by, open and diverse and sprawling as those codes may be. Perhaps if we can reach a reasonably accurate understanding of the moral landscape of our lives, we will be better able to achieve our dreams and guide our ethical debates—though we will no doubt still have need of protective headgear.

CONNECTING PERSONALLY TO THE READING

1. What are some of the after-school activities through which you have defined your identity? Write about one in particular and how it helped form your character.

2. Do you think that today's middle-class children are formed by an "almost crystalline meritocracy"? Explain.

3. Brooks writes that according to the ethic of meritocracy, "virtue and character are achieved gradually and must be maintained through a relentless struggle for self-improvement." Do you agree? Explain, using your own experience or personal reflection.

4. What do you think are the strengths and weaknesses of an ethic based on self-fulfillment?

FOCUSING ON THE ARGUMENT

1. Brooks begins his argument with personal experience, his role as the middle-class parent of a busy daughter, a "four-helmet kid." With some consternation, he then reflects on the acute differences between her childhood experiences and those of previous generations. What is the effect on the reader of this contrast in personal experience?

2. Conscious of the "hand-wringing and anxiety" of today's parents concerned about spoiling their children, Brooks comes across as moderate and reasonable, mixing humor, self-parody, telling details, and research. How does this persona help make the reader believe him? What kind of persona does he carefully avoid?

SYNTHESIZING IDEAS FROM MULTIPLE READINGS

1. How would John Dewey ("The School and the Life of the Child," p. 211) view Brooks's idea of an education through activities? Would Dewey think that parents today have seen the failure of public schools and looked to after-school activities as key learning opportunities? Explain.

2. Contrast the opportunities children have in Brooks's view of education with those Jonathan Kozol's children have in "Savage Inequalities" (p. 214). Do you think that the poor children Kozol describes lack the opportunity to forge character?

3. In "Human Intelligence Isn't What We Think It Is" (p. 232), Howard Gardner identifies five kinds of intelligence not typically valued by the schools. Some of these, especially musical and bodily-kinesthetic intelligences, might seem to support Brooks's argument for children's extensive after-school activities. Do you think that Gardner's view does support Brooks? If so, how?

WRITING TO ACT

1. Write a letter to David Brooks from the point of view of someone not in the middle class. What assumptions does Brooks make about character and identity that you would challenge?

2. Using Brooks's theories of moral development, write an article in an education journal in support of after-school programs. Explain the importance of making them available to all children. Detail at least one possible offering and how it might address a child's moral development.

READING

ROBERT BARR   Robert Barr, an experienced education researcher, writes about his own fallible judgment through a story about his interactions with a young child. His interactions with her are kindly, and he is sadly skeptical about her prospects. Circumstances seem against her. Yet Barr's story tells of a quick about-face in his view of the child's future. What are our own preconceptions about children of poverty who come from single-parent families? What kinds of interactions with adults do you think would most make a difference in their lives?

BARR is internationally known for his research on education and at-risk children. A speaker, consultant, and writer, he currently works as senior analyst at the Boise State University Center for School Improvement; previously, he served as dean of the Boise State University College of Education and dean of the Oregon State University College of Education. Barr is widely published in education journals, makes occasional television appearances, and has coauthored eight books, which include *Saving Our Students, Saving Our Schools: 50 Proven Strategies for Revitalizing At-Risk Students and Low-Performing Schools* and *How to Create Alternative, Magnet and Charter Schools That Work* (both written with William H. Parrett).

Who Is This Child? (1996)

BY ROBERT BARR

During my spring vacation, I visited my grandson Sam's first-grade classroom in Eugene, Oregon—home of author Ken Kescy, the University of Oregon's Fighting Ducks, and a T-shirt that proudly proclaims, "Me Tarzan, Eugene." Eager to start the day, Sam and I traded a couple of high-fives and sallied forth. He carried his books and an authentic Mighty Morphin Power Ranger lunch box; I carried a note pad and wore a sappy grin. This was the essence of grandparenting: a bright spring day in Oregon and off to school, hand-in-hand with Sam.

On arrival, Sam threw down his things and yelled over his shoulder, "Watch my stuff," as he ran off to join his friends in a soccer game. Almost immediately, I felt a small arm slide around my waist. Surprised, I looked down into the face of a little girl. "Who is this child?" I wondered. She flashed me a ragged smile that was missing half a dozen teeth. "I am from Chicago," she said and buried her head in my side. Suddenly uneasy, I looked around for some other adult. Having served on teacher licensure boards in two states and having sat through a dozen or so hearings to revoke the certification of child molesters, I was well aware of the taboos governing interactions between old guys like me and this small child.

As I tried to disentangle myself, she looked up at me with huge, longing eyes. "We don't have a father in our family," she said in her small voice. Then, as if repeating from a script, she whispered, "My father is a deadbeat dad. He ran away because he couldn't pay his bills." She blew her bangs up out of her eyes and sighed. "They found him, though. He is somewhere, I forgot . . . maybe in Portland, but I don't know where that is." She stared up at me with moist eyes. "But it's all right. My mom says we don't need him." Once again she burrowed into my side.

The longing and need of this small child caught me off guard. Her yearning for affection was almost palpable. And suddenly I knew this child—not her name or her address, but her identity. In her ragged dress, with her dirty fingernails, she carried the staggering weight of research predictability, of statistical probability. I had pored over the data far too long; I knew where she came from, where she was bound, and where her sad journey would end. I knew that a deep yearning for denied love can soon wither into anger—perhaps even hate—and that one generation will impose its tragic story on the next.

Was there even a chance that this small 5 child would one day graduate from the University of Oregon School of Law and walk crisply into the world, clad in a Brooks Brothers pin-striped jacket and miniskirt, swinging an Armani briefcase? More likely, she was a teenage parent in the making. I could envision a burned-out, unemployed 28-year-old, recovering from a messy second divorce and pregnant with her third child. Yes, I thought, I knew this child.

Just then a bell rang, setting off a wild rush to classes. My little friend gave me a final squeeze, waved goodbye, and skipped away. Sam ran up laughing—and, after he had gathered his things, we walked hand-in-hand into the school.

Still troubled by my encounter with the little girl, I watched her up ahead as she turned into a classroom. When I came abreast of that particular classroom door, I paused and looked in. What I saw was a teacher kneeling to hug the little girl and to say, "Melody, it's so good to see you! I'm so glad you made it to school today!" The teacher held the little girl at arm's length and gave her a thousand-watt smile that lit up the entire classroom. Then she took the little girl's hand and walked her to a desk. "Won't we have a great time today?" the teacher asked. "We'll paint today and sing—and of course we'll read some books." Bathed in the warmth of the teacher's care, the little girl seemed almost to glow.

Watching this touching tableau reminded me that researchers often jump to hasty conclusions, overgeneralizing from far too little data. I knew all the grim predictions that could be derived from the research literature, but I also knew the power of a good school and of caring and demanding teachers. I knew that schools could make a difference, could transform the lives of children, could overcome the deficiencies of the home and the dysfunctions of the family. I knew about resilient children and about the power of education, done well, to transform.

With a sigh of relief, I turned back to Sam, who was impatiently tugging at my hand. "Come on, Bob," he said. "We're gonna be late for class." With a final wave at the little girl, this 55-year-old researcher—now filled with hope—headed once again into a first-grade classroom.

CONNECTING PERSONALLY TO THE READING

1. Recall a teacher who has made a difference in your life. What interactions, comments, and gestures communicated to you how much that teacher cared?

2. The little girl clearly had a need for love and physical contact, and the researcher and teacher reacted differently to this need. Why do you think that each responded so differently? Do you think both reactions were appropriate? Explain.

3. What conceptions about the little girl did you form as you read Barr's description of her? Did they change? What did you learn personally from the reading?

FOCUSING ON THE ARGUMENT

1. How does Barr use personal experience, detailed observations, and a humble tone to draw us into the narrative? Why do we think he is credible when he sees in the young girl a familiar pattern of failure?

2. Little in the story prepares the reader for what happens at the end. Why does Barr want to surprise the reader with the exchange between teacher and child? How does Barr's own surprise, coming from an experienced, grandfatherly man, give credibility to his hopeful-ness about teaching?

SYNTHESIZING IDEAS FROM MULTIPLE READINGS

1. Like Mike Rose ("Epilogue: Lilia," p. 242), Barr sees hope as key to transformation. How is Barr's vision of hope like that of Rose?

2. John Dewey ("The School and the Life of the Child," p. 211) argues against education as a place where "everything is arranged for handling as large numbers of children as possible" in that a child's individuality is lost. In Barr's story, do you think that the teacher's way of interacting with the little girl illustrates this view? Explain.

3. In "Savage Inequalities" (p. 214), Jonathan Kozol's examination of New York schools—especially their lack of facilities, supplies, qualified teachers, and challenging subjects—suggests a pervasive hopelessness contrary to Barr's one example. Do you think Barr is unfair in holding up this one example? Does Kozol's portrayal of so many students without hope appear less convincing in light of this one example? Explain.

4. In Chapter 2, Richard Rodriguez ("Public and Private Language," p. 51) discusses the differ-ence between public and private worlds, as defined for him by language. How is the story of the little girl's hope also a story of separating the public and the private? Do you think that the public world of school will, as for Rodriguez, provide the girl with a chance to be successful?

WRITING TO ACT

1. Recall a teacher who had a significant impact on your life. Write a thank-you letter to the teacher for some important intervention in your life. Detail the words, actions, and guidance this teacher offered you.

2. Write an opinion letter to an education journal such as *Education Weekly* calling for an on-site teacher preparation class focused on unconscious bias. How do you think such a class might be put together? What elements would be crucial?

READING

HOWARD GARDNER   Howard Gardner strikes a chord in most of us who have abilities that public education does not measure. In this article from *U.S. News & World Report,* which we combined with sections from his book *Multiple Intelligences: The Theory in Practice* (1993), Gardner argues that people have multiple intelligences, not one. He also argues that the two forms of intelligence now in favor in the schools—linguistic and mathematical intelligences—have not always been favored. Looking back on your experiences with tests, do you think you have abilities beyond those that have been measured by IQ tests, aptitude tests, and other scholastic measures of intelligence? Have many of your abilities remained invisible? Do you know others who may have such abilities?

GARDNER is the award-winning author of more than twenty books, which include *Intelligence Reframed: Multiple Intelligences for the 21st Century* (2000) and *Changing Minds: The Art and Science of Changing Our Own and Other People's Minds* (2004). A professor of cognition and education at the Harvard Graduate School for Education, he also teaches psychology courses and serves as senior director of Harvard Project Zero, where his theory of multiple intelligences serves as foundation for the group's mission to develop less standardized, more personalized forms of assessment.

Human Intelligence Isn't What We Think It Is (1984)
and excerpt from Multiple Intelligences (1993)

BY HOWARD GARDNER

"PEOPLE HAVE MULTIPLE INTELLIGENCES"

Intelligence is not an absolute such as height that can be measured simply, largely because people have multiple intelligences rather than one single intelligence.

In all, I have identified seven forms of intelligence. The two that are valued most highly in this society are linguistic and logical-mathematical intelligences. When people think of someone as smart, they are usually referring to those two, because individuals who possess linguistic and logical-mathematical abilities do well on tests that supposedly measure intelligence.

But there are five other kinds of intelligence that are every bit as important: Spatial, musical, bodily-kinesthetic and two forms of personal intelligence—interpersonal, knowing how to deal with others, and intrapersonal, knowledge of self. None of these ought to have a priority over others.

"SHIFTING IMPORTANCE" OF THE SEVEN VARIETIES

The relative importance of these seven intelligences has shifted over time and varies from culture to culture. In a hunting society, for example, it is a lot more important to have extremely good control of your body and know your way around than to add or subtract quickly. In Japanese society, interpersonal intelligence—the ability to work well in groups and to arrive at joint decisions—is very important.

Historically, different systems of education have emphasized different blends of 5
intelligence. In the old apprenticeship system, bodily, spatial and interpersonal abilities were valued. In old-fashioned religious schools, the focus was on linguistic and interpersonal abilities. The modern secular school emphasizes the linguistic and logical-mathematical, but in the school of the near future I think that linguistic will become much less crucial. For working with computers, logical-mathematical intelligence will be important for programming, and intrapersonal intelligence will be important for individual planning.

What I'm saying is that while both logical-mathematical and linguistic are important today, it won't always be that way. We need to be sensitive to the fact that blends of intelligences keep shifting so that in the future we don't get locked into a specific blend.

SECRETS UNLOCKED BY BIOLOGICAL RESEARCH

Research in biology has laid the foundation for the theory of multiple intelligences.

Studies show that when someone suffers damage to the nervous system through a stroke or tumor, all abilities do not break down equally. If you have an injury to areas of the left hemisphere of the brain, you will lose your language ability almost entirely, but that will not affect your musical, spatial or interpersonal skills to the same extent.

Conversely, you can have lesions in your right hemisphere that leave language capacity intact but that seriously compromise spatial, musical or interpersonal abilities. So we have a special capacity for language that is unconnected to our capacity for music or interpersonal skills, and vice versa.

I'm not suggesting that this analysis is the last word. I would like to think of it as 10
the first word in a new way of looking at human abilities.

"AMERICA WASTES POTENTIAL!"

In America, we are wasting a lot of human potential by focusing on only linguistic and logical intelligence. If an individual doesn't happen to be good in these, he or she often gets thrown on society's scrap heap.

What happens is that a youngster takes an IQ test and doesn't do very well. He gets labeled as not very smart and the teacher treats him accordingly.

But there are many roles in society in which it is not important that a person have a high intelligence in language and logic so long as he or she can function at a basic level in these domains.

For example, somebody good at working with his hands and figuring out how machines function might find a responsible position in a science lab or working backstage in a theater. If kids with such abilities were encouraged—rather than discouraged because they can't figure out who wrote the *Iliad*—they could be extremely valuable to society.

IQ TESTS "HAVE DESTRUCTIVE SOCIAL EFFECTS"

I would like to get rid of intelligence and aptitude tests; they measure only two forms of intelligence and have destructive social effects. These tests have been successful because they serve as a good predictor of how people will do in school in the short run. But how much does doing well in school predict success outside of school? Very little.

Those of us who take a position against IQ tests have the burden of coming up with ways of assessing abilities that are not completely impractical. My notion is something between a report card and a test score.

I would assess intellectual propensities from an early age. I used the word *propensities* because I don't believe intelligences are fixed for many years. The earlier a strength is discovered, the more flexibility there is to develop it. Similarly, if a child has a low propensity, the earlier intervention begins, the easier it is to shore up the child. So early diagnosis is important.

PRESCHOOLS WHERE "CHILDREN CAN DO EXPLORING"

I would not assess abilities through traditional paper-and-pencil tests. Instead, we need learning environments—preschools—in which children can do a lot of exploring on their own or with help from adults.

All children play with blocks, for example, but what do they do with them? How complex are the structures they make? How well can they remember them? Can they revise them in various ways? All of these questions can be answered by adults observing and playing with the children.

The same environment could be equipped with musical materials, and, again, children could explore on their own and with adults. If we had such environments, with periodic monitoring we could develop very good profiles of a child's propensities. This would give parents and teachers a better way of thinking about children than one or two test scores. Instead of looking at a child and saying, "He's smart" or "He's dumb," people would talk in terms of a child's strengths and weaknesses. It is a much more realistic view.

But no theory is going to tell people what to do once a child's propensities are assessed. That decision would depend on the value of those around the child. Some people would say, "Let's go with the child's strengths for all they are worth." Others would say, "It's very important to be good in language, so even though this kid isn't good in it, we're going to work on it."

"THE CHALLENGE FOR EDUCATION"

As children mature, the assessments would continue in a different vein. By the age of 10 or 11, the monitoring would shift to "domains," where you might come up with analyses such as "this person has the talent to be a doctor."

While having a high intelligence in an area doesn't predict exactly what you are going to do, it predicts the direction you are likely to move in. If somebody has a very highly developed bodily intelligence, he or she could become an athlete, dancer or surgeon. If somebody has a highly developed spatial intelligence, he or she might be at home in architecture, engineering, sculpture or painting.

The challenge for the educational community is to figure out profiles of young people and then to help them find roles in which they can use their abilities in a productive way.

RECOGNIZING THE DIVERSITY OF OUR CAPABILITIES

The Suzuki method of teaching music, developed in Japan, shows what can be done to foster a specific intelligence when the effort is undertaken intensively at an early age and a lot of energy is put into it. This method creates an environment that is rich with music; mothers play with the youngsters for 2 hours a day from the time they reach age 2. Within a few years, all participants become decent musicians. 25

In theory, we could "Suzuki" everything. The more time and energy invested early in life on a particular intelligence, the more you can buoy it up. I am not advocating this approach, merely pointing out the possibilities. But before we can make these kinds of decisions, we have to take a first step—recognizing the diverse intelligences of which human beings are capable.

[The following excerpt from *Multiple Intelligences* (*Basic Books,* 1993) details these diverse intelligences.]

MUSICAL INTELLIGENCE

When he was three years old, Yehudi Menuhin was smuggled into the San Francisco Orchestra concerts by his parents. The sound of Louis Persinger's violin so entranced the youngster that he insisted on a violin for his birthday and Louis Persinger as his teacher. He got both. By the time he was ten years old, Menuhin was an international performer.[1]

Violinist Yehudi Menuhin's musical intelligence manifested itself even before he had touched a violin or received any musical training. His powerful reaction to that particular sound and his rapid progress on the instrument suggest that he was biologically prepared in some way for that endeavor. In this way evidence from child prodigies supports our claim that there is a biological link to a particular intelligence. Other special populations, such as autistic children who can play a musical instrument beautifully but who cannot speak, underscore the independence of musical intelligence.

A brief consideration of the evidence suggests that musical skill passes the other tests for an intelligence. For example, certain parts of the brain play important roles in perception and production of music. These areas are characteristically located in the right hemisphere, although musical skill is not as clearly "localized," or located in a specifiable area, as language. Although the particular susceptibility of musical ability to brain damage depends on the degree of training and other individual differences, there is clear evidence for "amusia" or loss of musical ability.

Music apparently played an important unifying role in Stone Age (Paleolithic) societies. Birdsong provides a link to other species. Evidence from various cultures supports the notion that music is a universal faculty. Studies of infant development suggest that there is a "raw" computational ability in early childhood. Finally, musical notation provides an accessible and lucid symbol system.

In short, evidence to support the interpretation of musical ability as an "intelli- 5 gence" comes from many different sources. Even though musical skill is not typically considered an intellectual skill like mathematics, it qualifies under our criteria. By definition it deserves consideration; and in view of the data, its inclusion is empirically justified.

BODILY-KINESTHETIC INTELLIGENCE

Fifteen-year-old Babe Ruth played third base. During one game his team's pitcher was doing very poorly and Babe loudly criticized him from third base. Brother Mathias, the coach, called out, "Ruth, if you know so much about it, YOU pitch!" Babe was surprised and embarrassed because he had never pitched before, but Brother Mathias insisted. Ruth said later that at the very moment he took the pitcher's mound, he KNEW he was supposed to be a pitcher and that it was "natural" for him to strike people out. Indeed, he went on to become a great major league pitcher (and, of course, attained legendary status as a hitter).[2]

Like Menuhin, Babe Ruth was a child prodigy who recognized his "instrument" immediately upon his first exposure to it. This recognition occurred in advance of formal training.

Control of bodily movement is, of course, localized in the motor cortex, with each hemisphere dominant or controlling bodily movements on the contra-lateral side. In right-handers, the dominance for such movement is ordinarily found in the left hemisphere. The ability to perform movements when directed to do so can be impaired even in individuals who can perform the same movements reflexively or on a nonvoluntary basis. The existence of specific *apraxia* constitutes one line of evidence for a bodily-kinesthetic intelligence.

The evolution of specialized body movements is of obvious advantage to the species, and in humans this adaptation is extended through the use of tools. Body movement undergoes a clearly defined developmental schedule in children. And there is little question of its universality across cultures. Thus it appears that bodily-kinesthetic "knowledge" satisfies many of the criteria for an intelligence.

The consideration of bodily-kinesthetic knowledge as "problem solving" may be less intuitive. Certainly carrying out a mime sequence or hitting a tennis ball is not solving a mathematical equation. And yet, the ability to use one's body to express an emotion (as in a dance), to play a game (as in a sport), or to create a new product (as in devising an invention) is evidence of the cognitive features of body usage. The specific computations required to solve a particular bodily-kinesthetic *problem,* hitting a tennis ball, are summarized by Tim Gallwey:

At the moment the ball leaves the server's racket, the brain calculates approximately where it will land and where the racket will intercept it. This calculation includes the initial velocity of the ball, combined with an input for the progressive decrease in velocity and the effect of wind and after the bounce of the ball. Simultaneously, muscle orders are given: not just once, but constantly with refined and updated information. The muscles must cooperate. A movement of the feet occurs, the racket is taken back, the face of the racket kept at a constant angle. Contact is made at a precise point that depends on whether the order was given to hit down the line or cross-court, an order not given until after a split-second analysis of the movement and balance of the opponent.

To return an average serve, you have about one second to do this. To hit the ball at all is remarkable and yet not uncommon. The truth is that everyone who inhabits a human body possesses a remarkable creation.[3]

LOGICAL-MATHEMATICAL INTELLIGENCE

In 1983 Barbara McClintock won the Nobel Prize in medicine or physiology for her work in microbiology. Her intellectual powers of deduction and observation illustrate one form of logical-mathematical intelligence that is often labeled "scientific thinking." One incident is particularly illuminating. While a researcher at Cornell in the 1920s McClintock was faced one day with a problem; while *theory* predicted 50-percent pollen sterility in corn, her research assistant (in the "field") was finding plants that were only 25- to 30-percent sterile. Disturbed by this discrepancy, McClintock left the cornfield and returned to her office where she sat for half an hour, thinking:

> Suddenly I jumped up and ran back to the (corn) field. At the top of the field (the others were still at the bottom) I shouted "Eureka, I have it! I know what the 30% sterility is!" . . . They asked me to prove it. I sat down with a paper bag and a pencil and I started from scratch, which I had not done at all in my laboratory. It had all been done so fast; the answer came and I ran. Now I worked it out step by step—it was an intricate series of steps—and I came out with [the same result]. [They] looked at the material and it was exactly as I'd said it was; it worked out exactly as I had diagrammed it. Now, why did I know, without having done it on paper? Why was I so sure?[4]

This anecdote illustrates two essential facts of the logical-mathematical intelligence. First, in the gifted individual, the process of problem solving is often remarkably rapid—the successful scientist copes with many variables at once and creates numerous hypotheses that are each evaluated and then accepted or rejected in turn.

The anecdote also underscores the *nonverbal* nature of the intelligence. A solution to a problem can be constructed *before* it is articulated. In fact, the solution process may be totally invisible, even to the problem solver. This need not imply, however, that discoveries of this sort—the familiar "Aha!" phenomenon—are mysterious, intuitive, or unpredictable. The fact that it happens more frequently to some people (perhaps Nobel Prize winners) suggest the opposite. We interpret this as the work of logical-mathematical intelligence.

Along with the companion skill of language, logical-mathematical reasoning provides the principal basis for IQ tests. This form of intelligence has been heavily investigated by traditional psychologists, and it is the archetype of "raw intelligence" or the problem-solving faculty that purportedly cuts across domains. It is perhaps ironic, then, that the actual mechanism by which one arrives at a solution to a logical-mathematical problem is not as yet properly understood.

This intelligence is supported by our empirical criteria as well. Certain areas of the brain are more prominent in mathematical calculation than others. There are idiots savants who perform great feats of calculation even though they remain tragically deficient in most other areas. Child prodigies in mathematics abound. The development of this intelligence in children has been carefully documented by Jean Piaget and other psychologists.

LINGUISTIC INTELLIGENCE

At the age of ten, T. S. Eliot created a magazine called "Fireside" to which he was the sole contributor. In a three-day period during his winter vacation, he created eight complete issues. Each one included poems, adventure stories, a gossip column, and humor. Some of this material survives and it displays the talent of the poet.[5]

As with the logical intelligence, calling linguistic skill an "intelligence" is consis- 15
tent with the stance of traditional psychology. Linguistic intelligence also passes our empirical tests. For instance, a specific area of the brain, called "Broca's Area," is responsible for the production of grammatical sentences. A person with damage to this area can understand words and sentences quite well but has difficulty putting words together in anything other than the simplest of sentences. At the same time, other thought processes may be entirely unaffected.

The gift of language is universal, and its development in children is strikingly constant across cultures. Even in deaf populations where a manual sign language is not explicitly taught, children will often "invent" their own manual language and use it surreptitiously! We thus see how an intelligence may operate independently of a specific input modality or output channel.

SPATIAL INTELLIGENCE

Navigation around the Caroline Islands in the South Seas is accomplished without instruments. The position of the stars, as viewed from various islands, the weather patterns, and water color are the only sign posts. Each journey is broken into a series of segments; and the navigator learns the position of the stars within each of these segments. During the actual trip the navigator must envision mentally a reference island as it passes under a particular star and from that he computes the number of segments completed, the proportion of the trip remaining, and any corrections in heading that are required. The navigator cannot *see* the islands as he sails along; instead he maps their locations in his mental "picture" of the journey.[6]

Spatial problem solving is required for navigation and in the use of the notational system of maps. Other kinds of spatial problem solving are brought to bear in visualizing an object seen from a different angle and in playing chess. The visual arts also employ this intelligence in the use of space.

Evidence from brain research is clear and persuasive. Just as the left hemisphere has, over the course of evolution, been selected as the site of linguistic processing in right-handed persons, the right hemisphere proves to be the site most crucial for spatial processing. Damage to the right posterior regions causes impairment of the ability to find one's way around a site, to recognize faces or scenes, or to notice fine details.

Patients with damage specific to regions of the right hemisphere will attempt to compensate for their spacial deficits with linguistic strategies. They will try to reason aloud, to challenge the task, or even make up answers. But such nonspatial strategies are rarely successful.

Blind populations provide an illustration of the distinction between the spatial intelligence and visual perception. A blind person can recognize shapes by an indirect method: running a hand along the object translates into the length of time of movement, which in turn is translated into the size of the object. For the blind person, the perceptual system of the tactile modality parallels the visual modality in the seeing person. The analogy between the spatial reasoning of the blind and the linguistic reasoning of the deaf is notable.

There are few child prodigies among visual artists, but there are idiots savants such as Nadia.[7] Despite a condition of severe autism, this preschool child made drawings of the most remarkable representational accuracy and finesse.

INTERPERSONAL INTELLIGENCE

With little formal training in special education and nearly blind herself, Anne Sullivan began the intimidating task of instructing a blind and deaf seven-year-old Helen Keller. Sullivan's efforts at communication were complicated by the child's emotional struggle with the world around her. At their first meal together, this scene occurred:

> Annie did not allow Helen to put her hand into Annie's plate and take what she wanted, as she had been accustomed to do with her family. It became a test of wills—hand thrust into plate, hand firmly put aside. The family, much upset, left the dining room. Annie locked the door and proceeded to eat her breakfast while Helen lay on the floor kicking and screaming, pushing and pulling at Annie's chair. [After half an hour] Helen went around the table looking for her family. She discovered no one else was there and that bewildered her. Finally, she sat down and began to eat her breakfast, but with her hands. Annie gave her a spoon. Down on the floor it clattered, and the contest of wills began anew.[8]

Anne Sullivan sensitively responded to the child's behavior. She wrote home: "The greatest problem I shall have to solve is how to discipline and control her without breaking her spirit. I shall go rather slowly at first and try to win her love."

In fact, the first "miracle" occurred two weeks later, well before the famous incident at the pumphouse. Annie had taken Helen to a small cottage near the family's house, where they could live alone. After seven days together, Helen's personality suddenly underwent a profound change—the therapy had worked:

> My heart is singing with joy this morning. A miracle has happened! The wild little creature of two weeks ago has been transformed into a gentle child.[9]

It was just two weeks after this that the first breakthrough in Helen's grasp of language occurred; and from that point on, she progressed with incredible speed. The key to the miracle of language was Anne Sullivan's insight into the *person* of Helen Keller.

Interpersonal intelligence builds on a core capacity to notice distinctions among others; in particular, contrasts in their moods, temperaments, motivations, and intentions. In more advanced forms, this intelligence permits a skilled adult to read the intentions and desires of others, even when these have been hidden. This skill appears in a highly sophisticated form in religious or political leaders, teachers, therapists, and parents. The Helen Keller–Anne Sullivan story suggests that this interpersonal intelligence does not depend on language.

All indices in brain research suggest that the frontal lobes play a prominent role in interpersonal knowledge. Damage in this area can cause profound personality changes while leaving other forms of problem solving unharmed—a person is often "not the same person" after such an injury.

Alzheimer's disease, a form of presenile dementia, appears to attack posterior brain zones with a special ferocity, leaving spatial, logical, and linguistic computations severely impaired. Yet, Alzheimer's patients will often remain well groomed, socially proper, and continually apologetic for their errors. In contrast, Pick's disease, another variety of presenile dementia that is more frontally oriented, entails a rapid loss of social graces.

Biological evidence for interpersonal intelligence encompasses two additional factors often cited as unique to humans. One factor is the prolonged childhood of primates, including the close attachment to the mother. In those cases where the mother is removed from early development, normal interpersonal development is in serious jeopardy. The second factor is the relative importance in humans of social interaction. Skills such as hunting, tracking, and killing in prehistoric societies required participation and cooperation of large numbers of people. The need for group cohesion, leadership, organization, and solidarity follows naturally from this.

INTRAPERSONAL INTELLIGENCE
In an essay called "A Sketch of the Past," written almost as a diary entry, Virginia Woolf discusses the "cotton wool of existence"—the various mundane events of life. She contrasts this "cotton wool" with three specific and poignant memories from her childhood: a fight with her brother, seeing a particular flower in the garden, and hearing of the suicide of a past visitor:

> These are three instances of exceptional moments. I often tell them over, or rather they come to the surface unexpectedly. But now for the first time I have written them down, and I realize something that I have never realized before. Two of these moments ended in a state of despair. The other ended, on the contrary, in a state of satisfaction.
>
> The sense of horror (in hearing of the suicide) held me powerless. But in the case of the flower, I found a reason; and was thus able to deal with the sensation. I was not powerless.
>
> Though I still have the peculiarity that I receive these sudden shocks, they are now always welcome; after the first surprise, I always feel instantly that they are particularly valuable. And so I go on to suppose that the shock-receiving capacity is what makes me a writer. I hazard the explanation that a shock is at once in my case followed by the desire to explain it. I feel that I have had a blow; but it is not, as I thought as a child, simply a blow from an enemy hidden behind the cotton wool of daily life; it is or will become a revelation of some order; it is a token of some real thing behind appearances; and I make it real by putting it into words.[10]

This quotation vividly illustrates the intrapersonal intelligence—knowledge of the internal aspects of a person: access to one's own feeling life, one's range of emotions, the capacity to effect discriminations among these emotions and eventually to label

30

them and to draw upon them as a means of understanding and guiding one's own behavior. A person with good intrapersonal intelligence has a viable and effective model of himself or herself. Since this intelligence is the most private, it requires evidence from language, music, or some other more expressive form of intelligence if the observer is to detect it at work. In the above quotation, for example, linguistic intelligence is drawn upon to convey intrapersonal knowledge; it embodies the interaction of intelligences, a common phenomenon to which we will return later.

We see the familiar criteria at work in the intrapersonal intelligence. As with the interpersonal intelligence, the frontal lobes play a central role in personality change. Injury to the lower area of the frontal lobes is likely to produce irritability or euphoria; while injury to the higher regions is more likely to produce indifference, listlessness, slowness, and apathy—a kind of depressive personality. In such "frontal-lobe" individuals, the other cognitive functions often remain preserved. In contrast, among aphasics who have recovered sufficiently to describe their experiences, we find consistent testimony: while there may have been a diminution of general alertness and considerable depression about the condition, the individual in no way felt himself to be a different person. He recognized his own needs, wants, and desires and tried as best he could to achieve them.

The autistic child is a prototypical example of an individual with impaired intrapersonal intelligence; indeed, the child may not even be able to refer to himself. At the same time, such children often exhibit remarkable abilities in the musical, computational, spatial, or mechanical realms.

Evolutionary evidence for an intrapersonal faculty is more difficult to come by, but we might speculate that the capacity to transcend the satisfaction of instinctual drives is relevant. This becomes increasingly important in a species not perennially involved in the struggle for survival.

In sum, then, both interpersonal and intrapersonal faculties pass the tests of an intelligence. They both feature problem-solving endeavors with significance for the individual and the species. Interpersonal intelligence allows one to understand and work with others; intrapersonal intelligence allows one to understand and work with oneself. In the individual's sense of self, one encounters a melding of inter- and intrapersonal components. Indeed, the sense of self emerges as one of the most marvelous of human inventions—a symbol that represents all kinds of information about a person and that is at the same time an invention that all individuals construct for themselves.

Notes

1. Menuhin, Y. (1977). *Unfinished journey.* New York: Knopf.
2. Connor, A. (1982). *Voices from Cooperstown.* New York: Collier. (Based on a quotation taken from *The Babe Ruth Story,* Babe Ruth & Bob Considine. New York: Dutton, 1948.)
3. Gallwey, T. (1976). *Inner tennis.* New York: Random House.
4. Keller, E. (1983). *A feeling for the organism* (p. 104). Salt Lake City: W. H. Freeman.
5. Soldo, J. (1982). Jovial juvenilia: T. S. Eliot's first magazine. *Biography,* 5, 25–37.
6. Gardner, H. (1983). *Frames of mind: The theory of multiple intelligences.* New York: Basic Books.
7. Selfe, L. (1977). *Nadia: A case of extraordinary drawing in an autistic child.* New York: Academic Press.
8. Lash, J. (1980). *Helen and teacher: The story of Helen Keller and Anne Sullivan Macy* (p. 52). New York: Delacorte.
9. Lash (p. 54).
10. Woolf, V. (1976). *Moments of being* (pp. 69–70). Sussex: The University Press.

1. Gardner taps into readers' personal experience to persuade us. To what extent does your experience confirm his point that there are multiple intelligences?

2. What effect has knowing IQ or aptitude test scores had on you or someone you know?

3. Gardner says he thinks that the education community should be responsible for figuring out profiles for children to "find roles in which [children] can use their abilities in productive ways." What problems can you anticipate if teachers tried to guide children toward specific occupations? What might be the benefits?

1. How does Gardner make his argument more credible by his examples of other cultures and other historical periods that have valued a different intelligence—for instance, interpersonal intelligence?

2. How does Gardner use recent research in biology, as well as recent criticism of IQ tests, to lend credibility to his argument? How persuasive is this evidence? Explain.

1. Gardner hopes to offer students many options for being successful. He wants schools to value intelligences other than the linguistic and mathematical and to encourage career paths that reflect these intelligences. Do you think that John Dewey ("The School and the Life of the Child," p. 211) would agree with Gardner? Explain.

2. In "Savage Inequalities" (p. 214), Jonathan Kozol states his belief that schools offer students unequal facilities, supplies, and opportunities to learn. How do you think he would respond to Gardner's concerns that schools recognize only linguistic and mathematical intelligence? What benefits do you think poor students would derive from teachers encouraging a musical or interpersonal curriculum?

3. In "The Merits of Meritocracy" (p. 224), David Brooks discusses the value of a wide range of children's after-school activities, such as soccer, in which pure merit counts. These activities teach ethical knowledge, not school-based linguistic or mathematical knowledge. How are Brooks and Gardner alike in encouraging different forms of knowledge and ability?

4. In their appreciation of nature, Barry Lopez ("Ice and Light," p. 397), Ian Frazier ("Terminal Ice," p. 408), Wendell Berry ("An Entrance to the Woods," p. 372) and others (Chapter 6) illustrate a different kind of intelligence than the linguistic-mathematical. How do you think Gardner would describe their intelligence?

1. According to Gardner, schools are not set up to recognize children's diverse intelligences. Write a letter to Gardner emphasizing how you think your high school could have done a better job of recognizing different abilities.

2. Researchers in education are increasingly critical of the nature and extent of testing in the schools. Consider the form of assessment used at your high school. Then write a letter to your high school principal either praising the school for using multiple assessments or arguing in favor of such assessments.

MIKE ROSE What does it take to succeed when you come from poverty, attend schools where tracking lands you in the "dumb" classes, and see only models of failure? What special qualities of intelligence characterize those who "cross over" into college preparatory classes? In this epilogue to his book *Lives on the Boundary,* Mike Rose meditates on the meaning of intelligence. His own story, interwoven with that of his student Lilia, tells of the psychological damage young students sustain when they are tracked into remedial courses, as so often happens to immigrants or kids from poor neighborhoods. But rather than rethinking school testing, facilities, and curricula, Rose looks at the cultural elements of intelligence. He claims that intelligence embodies a "feeling" and a "culture." When Lilia leaves one school for another, she goes from "dumb to normal." The different school culture was responsible for this change in view. Later, as a college student tutoring low-achieving children, she discovers her own special language for communicating with students like herself, from immigrant families. Mike Rose's own story, like Lilia's, is about crossing cultural boundaries. Are stories of students "crossing over" familiar to you?

ROSE, a former public school teacher, is currently professor of social research methodology at the UCLA Graduate School of Education and Information Studies. His books include the award-winning *Lives on the Boundary* (1990), *Possible Lives: The Promise of Public Education in America* (1996), and *The Mind at Work* (2004), from which "The Working Life of a Waitress" is reprinted on p. 278 of this book.

Epilogue: Lilia (1990) | BY MIKE ROSE

I sit with Lilia, the tape recorder going. "We came from Mexico when I was four years old. When I went into school, I flunked the first grade. The first grade! I had to repeat it, and they put me in classes for slow learners. I stayed in those classes for five years. I guess there was a pattern where they put me in those really basic classes and then decided I would go through my elementary school years in those classes. I didn't learn to read or write. My parents got my cousins—they came here prior to us, so they knew English really well—and they had me read for them. I couldn't. They told my parents I didn't know anything. That's when my parents decided they would move. They moved to Tulare County. My aunt was there and told them that the schools were good and that there was work in agriculture. I picked grapes and cotton and oranges—everything—for six straight summers. I kinda liked it, out there with all the adults, but I knew it wasn't what I wanted for the future. The schools *were* good. The teachers really liked me, and I did very well. . . . Between the eighth and ninth grades I came to UCLA for six weeks in the summer. It was called the MENTE program— Migrants Engaged in New Themes of Education—I came here and loved the campus. It was like dreamland for me. And I made it my goal to come here."

The school that designated Lilia a slow learner is two miles from my old neighborhood on South Vermont. She arrived as a child about eight years after I left as an adult. The next generation. We make our acquaintance in an office of the University of California at Los Angeles. Lilia is participating in an unusual educational experiment, one developed by some coworkers of mine at UCLA Writing Programs. Lilia and fifteen other freshmen—all of whom started UCLA in remedial writing courses themselves—are tutoring low-achieving students in Los Angeles area schools. The tutoring is connected to a special composition class, and Lilia and her partners write papers on their tutorial work and on issues of schooling. Lilia is writing a paper on the academic, social, and psychological effects of being placed in the remedial track. Her teacher suggested she come to see me. I can't stop asking her questions about growing up in South L.A.

Desire gets confused on South Vermont. There were times when I wanted so much to be other than what I was, to walk through the magical gate of a television cottage. But, strange blessing, we can never really free ourselves from the mood of early neighborhoods, from our first stories, from the original tales of hope and despair. There are basic truths there about the vulnerability and power of coming to know, about the way the world invites and denies language. This is what lies at the base of education—to be tapped or sealed over or distorted, by others, by us. Lilia says the tutoring makes her feel good. "Sometimes I feel that because I know their language, I can communicate. I see these kids and I see myself like I was in elementary school." Lilia stops. She asks me what it was like in South L.A. when *I* was there, when I was going to school. Not much different then, I say. Not as tough probably. She asks me if I've ever gone back. I tell her I did, just recently. . . .

The place was desolate. The power plant was still standing, smaller than I remembered it, surrounded now by barbed wire. All the storefront businesses were covered with iron grating; about half of them, maybe more, were shut down. The ones that were open had the grating pulled back the width of the door, no further. The hair and nails shop was closed. The Stranger's Rest Baptist Church was closed. Teddy's Rough Riders—an American Legion post—was battered and closed. The Huston Mortuary looked closed. My house had been stuccoed over, a dark dirty tan with holes in the walls. 9116 South Vermont. My old neighborhood was a blighted island in the slum. Poverty had gutted it, and sealed the merchants' doors. "It's worse now," I tell Lilia, "much worse. No one comes. No one goes." At Ninety-sixth Street two men were sitting on the curb outside a minimart. East on Ninety-first a girl sat in the shadows of steps tucked back from the pavement. At Eighty-ninth Street, a woman walked diagonally in front of me, moving unsteadily in a tight dress, working the floured paper off an X-L-NT burrito. As I drove back by my house, I saw a little boy playing with two cans in the dirt. Imagination's delivery. Fantasy in cylinders and tin.

Lilia is telling me about one of her fellow classmates who had also been designated a slow learner. "She said it was awful. She had no friends because everyone called her dumb, and no one wanted to be seen with a dumb person. . . . Because they were calling her dumb, she started to believe she was really dumb. And with myself and my brother, it was the same thing. When we were in those courses we thought very low of ourselves. We sort of created a little world of our own where only we existed. We became really shy."

What we define as intelligence, what we set out to measure and identify with a number, is both in us and out of us. We have been socialized to think of intelligence as internal, fixed, genetically coded. There is, of course, a neurophysiology to intelligence, but there's a feeling to it as well, and a culture. In moving from one school to

5

another—another setting, another set of social definitions—Lilia was transformed from dumb to normal. And then, with six powerful weeks as a child on a university campus—"opening new horizons for me, scary, but showing me what was out there"—she began to see herself in a different way, tentatively, cautiously. Lilia began the transition to smart, to high school honors classes, to UCLA. She could go back, then, to the schools, to the place where, as she says, she "knows the language."

The promise of community and equality is at the center of our most prized national document, yet we're shaped by harsh forces to see difference and to base judgment on it. The language Lilia can speak to the students in the schools is the language of intersection, of crossed boundaries. It is a rich language, filled with uncertainty. Having crossed boundaries, you sometimes can't articulate what you know, or what you know seems strange. What is required, then, is for Lilia and her students to lean back against their desks, grip the firm wood, and talk about what they hear and see, looking straight ahead, looking skyward. What are the gaps and discordances in the terrain? What mix of sounds—eerie and compelling—issues from the hillside? Sitting with Lilia, our lives playing off each other, I realize that, finally, this is why the current perception of educational need is so limited: it substitutes terror for awe. But it is not terror that fosters learning, it is hope, everyday heroics, the power of the common play of the human mind.

CONNECTING PERSONALLY TO THE READING

1. How do you think the different cultures of two places can enable someone to go from "dumb" to "normal"? What do you think Rose means when he says that intelligence is also a "feeling" and a "culture"? How is intelligence both "in us" and "out of us"?

2. What do you think it means to speak the "language of intersection"? Have you crossed any boundaries that required you to speak differently? If so, how did your language change? What did you struggle with the most?

3. Do you agree with Rose that we don't need to focus on low-achieving students' "educational need"? Why do you think such a focus leads to "terror" rather than "hope"?

FOCUSING ON THE ARGUMENT

1. To draw the reader in, Rose, like Jonathan Kozol in "Savage Inequalities" (p. 214), uses his presence as a sympathetic but objective recorder and observer of others' lives. How does this role as listener, which features Lilia's and other students' words, give him credibility?

2. Rose uses Lilia's story to help him tell about his own childhood neighborhood and early years. He too has crossed boundaries and acquired a special language that reflects his experience. How do these details of neighborhoods, school experiences, and early feelings give special weight to his words on crossing boundaries?

1. Rose, like Howard Gardner in "Human Intelligence Isn't What We Think It Is" (p. 232), complicates our notions of intelligence. What kind of intelligence does Lilia show, according to Gardner? Do you think her intelligence falls outside the categories Gardner offers? Explain.

2. Rose ties Lilia's boundary crossing to her ability to transform herself, once she spent six weeks on the campus of UCLA. On what points would Jonathan Kozol ("Savage Inequalities," p. 214) and Rose agree concerning the power of a setting to transform a young student's life?

3. John Dewey ("The School and the Life of the Child," p. 211), Robert Barr ("Who Is This Child?" p. 229), and Rose all envision young people being transformed by education. How are their visions of what is essential to this process similar and different?

4. What kinds of skills has Lilia learned that will make it possible for her to move beyond such jobs as those Gary Soto ("Black Hair," p. 296) and Barbara Ehrenreich ("Nickel and Dimed," p. 322) describe in Chapter 5?

1. Design a curriculum in which low-achieving students have a chance to use their special knowledge to help others like them and along the way gain confidence in their own knowledge and language skills. Find an on-campus tutoring site that might be interested in this curriculum.

2. Write an editorial to a local newspaper describing your own border crossing or that of a friend. Discuss the implications for high school educators, especially in the area of language.

3. Write a contribution to an education journal such as *Education Weekly* describing which teaching strategies reduce low-income or minority children's sense of their own intelligence. Offer some strategies on what schools should do to increase all children's views of their own abilities.

MICHAEL J. LEWIS   What does the architecture of a college student center tell us about the culture of the campus? Michael J. Lewis argues that a college campus is more than a collection of facilities, that there is an "invisible campus, a mental hierarchy of associations and sentiments," to which people become emotionally attached. Lewis examines some of the associations embedded in the architecture of the student center, arguing that student centers have increasingly reflected the consumerism of the modern university. Students shop for colleges, comparing them as they would any other expensive product, and colleges offer such commercial services as convenience stores and ATM machines. The student center itself becomes a marketing tool, as colleges seek to attract students. Does your school have a student center? If not, are there other places on campus where students socialize, university products are sold, and where the school markets itself? If so, what does your school's student center suggest about the campus culture?

LEWIS is the chair of the art department at Williams College, where he teaches art and architecture courses. He has contributed numerous essays (including the one that follows) to art journals and other periodicals, and his book *Frank Furness: Architecture and the Violent Mind* was published in 2001.

Forget Classrooms. How Big Is the Atrium in the New Student Center? (2003)

BY MICHAEL J. LEWIS

Has any American college not yet built a new student center? If so, it is probably interviewing architects at this moment. All across the country, from Bowdoin to Pomona, colleges are scrambling to renovate, expand, or replace aging student unions, with their battered billiard tables and subterranean TV lounges. So great is the demand that one Pittsburgh-based firm, WTW Architects, has designed more than 30 in the past few years. The student-center craze is upon us, and not even the stormy economy seems able to slow its eager advance.

The modern student center is a versatile breed. It might be a sprawling creation, like the $75-million, 330,000-square-foot leviathan at the University of Massachusetts at Boston. Or a restrained and subtle affair, like the taut, 50,000-square-foot building at Sweet Briar College, which cost only about $14-million. But large or small, it is certain to contain a multistory atrium, cafe seating, and the obligatory food court. And it boasts an extravagant quantity of glass, so that it can blaze away cheerfully in those nocturnal views that are so often used to depict the buildings. Such is the state-of-the-art student center in 2003.

This is not the first time that a new building type has spread from campus to campus. After the Civil War came a great wave of memorial auditoriums, built to honor fallen classmates. The 1920s clamored for football stadiums. Those earlier booms were prompted by sweeping changes in the nature of student life and alumni identity. Our era—for better or worse—has embraced the student center. It speaks of our time—but what precisely does it say?

As a building type, the student center is barely a century old. It was not part of the traditional university, which preserved the basic building types of its monastic roots: the dormitory, the refectory, and the library. In the late 19th century there came a great explosion of new and specialized building types, including the laboratory and the gymnasium. There also came the first student union, Houston Hall, built in 1894 by the University of Pennsylvania. A robust Jacobean pile, part clubhouse and part country estate, it was an Anglophiliac reverie, every possible surface liberally paneled with oak. Its great achievement was to wed two distinct ideas, domesticity and masculinity, in a single architectural solution of great conviction.

It is no coincidence that student centers were born in the decade of the 1890s. It was just then that the college student body was starting to diversify; students were now both wealthier and poorer than the homogeneous student body of the past. Faculty members and students were also likely to be further apart, both socially and intellectually. The modern professor was typically a product of the Continental system, a scholar devoted to research, while the student was more likely to be in college for purposes of social grooming. As the college population ramified and diversified, its collective identity was no longer a given. The student center offered a new focus of identity, organized around

₅

the activities and social life of the institution rather than around the solidarity of class and religion that had previously bound classmates.

Houston Hall was widely imitated at the turn of the century, with each version adjusted to the character of its college. On campuses with a vigorous fraternity life—like Williams College—or where dormitories provided a great variety of social spaces—like Bryn Mawr College—such student unions were superfluous, and their creation lagged. But at those where that was not the case, like large universities, they flourished in stately profusion. Thus the University of Virginia opened Madison Hall in 1934 as a student union, while Princeton University—with its tradition of eating clubs—did without until the early 1950s.

After the student center's origination, a century passed before a fundamental rethinking of the model occurred—fit-

tingly enough—at Houston Hall. In 1980 the architect Robert Venturi remodeled the building for the first time (he did so again more recently), giving it linoleum floors, eye-popping signage, and a jaunty welter of neon. The coziness of the clubroom gave way to the sensory jumble of the commercial highway strip, which Venturi had praised in *Learning from Las Vegas* (MIT Press, 1972). The choice of model was no mere affectation; it acknowledged that student centers were being opened to outside concessions and franchises, and that their essential character was, increasingly, commercial rather than institutional. . . .

The student center has dispensed with the essentially private character of its predecessors, as epitomized by Penn's Houston Hall. Not only do the modern center's public spaces open onto one another, but they unfold to the world outside as well. The place is extroverted to

Collections of the University of Pennsylvania Archives

the point of exhibitionism. Having lost its sense of being a rather oversized living room, the student center has assumed something of the impersonal quality of a visitors' center at a national park, or a bus terminal—buildings whose task it is to orient strangers. And, in truth, the student center is designed in large measure for strangers. It must serve not only college students but also prospective students. And while it is the former who will use the building regularly, it is the latter who, in the scheme of things—even though many will visit it no more than once—matter most.

The essence of the modern student center is to be a recruiting instrument, a fact that pardons its many infelicities: its self-consciousness, its nervous unctuousness, its relentless transparency. If its character is shaped by the world of commercial architecture, that is because it is itself an advertisement. It is the principal highlight of the standard college tour, along with the fitness center. And it communicates exceptionally well. Directors of admissions note that a quick meal in the student center conveys more information about life at a college, and with more credibility, than the lengthiest formal presentation. There the visitor can observe at a glance how students act and interact, how they dress, their relative stress level, and how they relate to their professors. As one admissions director told me, "It's a veritable vibe fest."

Because the prospective student, parents in tow, will probably visit a battery of campuses in quick succession, it is inevitable that these facilities will be carefully compared. Colleges have not failed to note this. As students increasingly select colleges based on what they can see, colleges will spend more money on that which can be seen. Rigor in the classroom and intellect in the faculty cannot easily be seen—certainly not as easily as

a fitness center or a three-story granite fireplace. . . .

The emergence of a new building type, whether cathedral or skyscraper, always expresses a new impulse in the structure of society, one that could not be expressed within the existing range of buildings. What new forces does the student center express? At a minimum, it suggests that the process by which students select colleges is increasingly made as a consumer decision, through comparison shopping among competing brands. The student center serves as a crucial device of product differentiation, exaggerating the differences among brands that are generally equivalent. Of course, we hardly need the student center to tell us that consumerism has touched the academy.

The modern student union also expresses startling changes in the nature of student life. Since the American campus was wired for computers, a process essentially completed a decade or so ago, studying is no longer a private affair of reading and typing, which involved prolonged and quiet concentration. Studying has become more intermittent, more gregarious, and more mobile. As workstations and terminals have been dispersed across the campus, the clear hierarchy between public and private spaces has dissolved. That, too, is written across the eloquent face of the modern student center—hospitable, industrious, and somewhat prone to insomnia.

10   Smith College's new campus center is a splendid example of the type, a sinuous viaduct with glazed walls and a skylight along its meandering spine. It is not so much a building as a roofed-over street. But that is precisely what its architects, Weiss/Manfredi, intended. "Imagined as an en-route passage through the campus, the building is defined by various interconnecting paths that challenge the boundary between inside and outside,"

© Jeff Goldberg/Esto

says a description on Smith's Web site. In other words, movement rather than repose is its leitmotif. Here the student center is no longer the gentleman's club-room but a kind of medieval market square, under a glass roof rather than a tent.

Besides technological change, demographic change has occurred. The modern dorm room may well be plugged in, but it is liable to be a lonelier place than it used to be. The college roommate is gradually becoming a thing of the past. As more students come from single-child families, fewer and fewer have had to share rooms with siblings, or are willing to share as young adults. Colleges have increasingly been forced to convert dormitories from double rooms and suites to singles—and, in the process, have sacrificed a great many dormitory lounges. As those public spaces have been squeezed out of residences, it becomes all the more necessary to provide them in a student center. This concentration of recreation space has not been resisted by college administrations. On the contrary, as colleges have become increasingly legalistic and paternalistic, the centralization of social activities in a single building has made them easier to monitor.

If the student center increasingly ca- 15 ters to consumers, then consumers have shaped them in turn. No academic building has ever been subjected to as much student involvement. Students have played crucial roles on building committees, as is apparent on the large number of Web sites devoted to student-center projects. Not only are these sites used as clearinghouses during the planning process, but many of them charmingly provide Webcams, which broadcast the subsequent course of construction in real time (surely one of the more esoteric species of Internet entertainment). Some campus centers can even be said to be student-designed, to the extent that their functions were democratically chosen. Smith College, for example, surveyed students about what services the campus center should offer. The highest vote-getter was an ATM machine, far outstripping the bookstore, convenience store, and performance space that were the closest contenders.

It is easy to see how the contemporary college has changed the student center; it is less clear how the new student center will change the college. In the end, every campus is simply a collection of facilities, encased within so many sheds that are arranged in functional proximity to one another. But there is also an invisible campus, a mental hierarchy of associations and sentiments, which in their totality form a living tradition, capable of inspiring great affection and loyalty. It is for that reason that a college has traditionally been known by its administration building, the stately classical box with a weather-beaten white cupola. Whether Founders Hall or Old Main, this was the physical manifestation of the college that projected its image across the campus and across memory, and around which sentimental attachments once congealed.

Such buildings no longer serve the same symbolic role. Many have lost the classrooms that once took up most of their space, dislodged by the administrative staffs that burgeoned everywhere during the course of the 1960s and '70s. Students visit those buildings—once an integral part of academic life—only intermittently and for reasons that are either tedious or unpleasant. As administration buildings become increasingly remote, and as student centers become increasingly commercial in character, it is likely that the sentimental attachment to the physical landmarks of the campus, that great wellspring of alumni loyalty, will be diminished, or transferred in ways yet unforeseeable.

The student-center building boom, at a conservative estimate, has already consumed several billion dollars. More will

be spent in the coming years, recession or no recession, for those brash buildings have become indispensable. They bring to the staid campus all that is vital about commercial architecture: its energy, newness, and wide-awake readiness to face the demands of the present. But they bring, alas, the weaknesses of commercial architecture as well—superficiality, flimsiness, and a very limited shelf life. In their very swagger is a cringing insecurity, which is foreign to the plodding and deliberate way that campuses used to grow.

Fashions in architecture, as in clothing, are ephemeral, and every building eventually takes its place in the great faceless mass of nondescript, somewhat dowdy structures that compose most older institutions. But nothing grows so soon stale as novelty, and commercial architecture is predicated on novelty. The Piranesian ramp at Columbia, the skylighted viaduct at Smith, the countless atriums with their granite fireplaces and cafe seating: It is not at all clear whether they are destined to be the beloved landmarks of the next generation or as outdated as the fern-and-pastel décor of 1980s nightspots.

It was once true that the buildings of 20 each college bore a family resemblance to one another, linked by a common scale or palette of materials and textures, and a shared sensibility. The new student center, with some exceptions, tends to be a stranger. It is more likely to resemble distant student centers at other colleges than its immediate neighbors. Let us give it its due. It is a lovely object, and it speaks with unerring honesty about the college today. But its tragedy is that in seeking so frantically to be state-of-the-art, it very likely will wound that most fragile of artifacts, the state of the place.

1. Lewis believes that education has become a consumer product: students shop for schools, and colleges market themselves to prospective students. Do you agree with this analysis? If not, why not? If so, in what other areas do you see consumerism on your campus? For example, your school might cater to tourists, or it might sell items advertising the football team.

2. Lewis argues that the architecture of the student center reflects the relationships between students and faculty (in the nineteenth century, a distant relationship). How would you define the relationship the school promotes between students and faculty? In what ways does the student center support this relationship?

3. Lewis states that student centers were unnecessary throughout most of the nineteenth century because the student population was homogeneous: students were Protestant; came from the wealthy, leisured social class; and were attending college for the same reason—to acquire social polish. Why does Lewis believe that a homogeneous student body doesn't need a student center, whereas a more diverse group of students does? Do you agree with his view? Explain.

4. If your school has a student center, what do you like best about its design, and why? What associations does the design of the center convey to you?

1. Lewis begins his article with a discussion of the history of the student center, beginning with the first center, the University of Pennsylvania's Houston Hall, built in 1894. How does this history support Lewis's argument about modern student centers?

2. In what ways can the photographs that accompany the article be said to be strategies of persuasion? What do they offer Lewis's argument?

3. Lewis often personifies buildings in his article, describing them as if they were people. Some are made to sound unattractive—one is accused of "nervous unctuousness"—while others are complimented for appearing "hospitable" and "industrious" (if a little "prone to insomnia"). Discuss the trade-off, in trying to be persuasive, between making images vivid and memorable and merely appearing glib to your readers.

1. Both David Tyack ("School: The Story of American Public Education," p. 198) and Lewis use historical analysis to demonstrate that the purpose of education has changed. Tyack says that the purpose used to be to build character; Lewis claims it was to give social polish. In what ways are these ideas different from and similar to one another? Do you think that building character and acquiring social polish are still among the goals of a college education? Explain.

2. Lewis claims that new campus student centers reflect the increasing democratization of students, as well as different relationships between faculty and students. Do you think that such student centers offer special supports to students like Lilia, whom Mike Rose describes in "Epilogue: Lilia" (p. 242)? If so, how?

3. Like Lewis, John Dewey ("The School and the Life of the Child," p. 211) is concerned with how physical space can affect learning. How do you think Dewey would react to all the ways in which Lewis sees physical space as affecting learning? Explain.

4. A commercialized image of feminine beauty has certainly affected people like Cindy Jackson ("My Cosmetic Surgery," p. 139 in Chapter 3), whose multiple surgeries have transformed her image. What dangers might lie ahead in the commercialization of education? How might we become "products" of an educational system—the way Jackson has become a product?

1. Study the architecture of the student center at your own college or at another. What adjectives would you use to describe the style of the building? What features of the building contribute to this style? What message to prospective students does the external appearance and internal floor plan of the building convey? Then write an article for your campus newspaper stating your conclusions.

2. Consider the facilities (e.g., bookstore, study areas, game room) that your student center offers. How do these facilities reflect the center's purpose? Do they serve the students' interests, the university's interests, the faculty's interests, or a combination of these? Write a letter to the administrator of the student center, praising the facilities and/or suggesting ways the center might better serve the campus.

Connecting the Readings to the Architecture

University High School, Los Angeles, California

1. In "Savage Inequalities," Jonathan Kozol describes how a deteriorating physical school building undermines children's sense of self-esteem. The physical environment at University High School may give mixed messages to children. What elements of the site send those mixed messages?

2. Public education was not kind to Mike Rose ("Epilogue: Lilia"), who in other works tells how he was mistakenly tracked into remedial courses. He did, however, succeed. Robert Barr ("Who Is This Child?") is also aware of the dismal record of education in turning the tide for many low-income children who enter public schools. David Tyack ("School: The Story of American Public Education"), however, seems more optimistic about the future of public schooling. Without rebuilding any buildings, how could the physical environment of a school like University High be changed to reflect hope? What would you do first?

Diamond Ranch High School, Diamond Bar, California

1. In "School: The Story of American Public Education," David Tyack states that public schools were instituted to achieve a common purpose. Do you think that the architecture of Diamond Ranch High School illustrates such a purpose? Look carefully at the walkway and the different building shapes that students pass by. What features suggest to you a common purpose for the school and what architectural features do not?

2. In "Epilogue: Lilia," Mike Rose describes the importance to Lilia of her six-week stay at UCLA. What similar transformative powers do you think the architecture of Diamond Ranch High School has? Describe what you think low-income minority

students who have been tracked into remedial classes might gain from an experience in this high school.

3. In "Human Intelligence Isn't What We Think It Is," Howard Gardner discusses the need to recognize multiple intelligences in children. What aptitudes does the architecture of this school seem to suggest are important? Would they fit with Gardner's multiple intelligences? Explain.

4. Michael J. Lewis's photograph (in "Forget Classrooms") of the student center at Smith College reveals a focal building with an asymmetrical design and use of windows to channel students' vision. In what ways are the building shapes and use of windows similar to those of Diamond Ranch High School? What views of education are suggested by these shapes and window designs? Do you think that the design of Diamond Ranch High School also reflects an increasing commercialism in our society? Explain.

Engineering Building, Utah State University

1. A number of writers, including Robert Barr ("Who is This Child?"), Mike Rose ("Epilogue: Lilia"), and John Dewey ("The School and the Life of the Child"), indicate that we learn through exchanges with people. Can we also learn through interactions with the physical environment? What do you think that these writers might say about the interactions encouraged by a building that is meant to teach?

2. Jonathan Kozol ("Savage Inequalities") indicates that a building's interior reflects back to students the image educators have of them. What image of self do you think this interior is creating for engineering students?

3. In "Human Intelligence Isn't What We Think It Is," Howard Gardner emphasizes that we have different kinds of intelligences. What kind of intelligence does this building suggest is needed to build such a building? Explain.

4. John Dewey ("The School and the Life of the Child") critiques the modern emphasis in education on efficiency. Do you think this building emphasizes this value? Explain.

The Brown Center, Maryland Institute College of Art

1. In "Forget Classrooms," Michael J. Lewis discusses the "mental hierarchy of associations and sentiments" attached to campus student centers. What hierarchy of associations and sentiments do you think a building such as the Brown Center creates? Explain.

2. Jon Spayde ("Learning in the Key of Life") asks us to think critically about education, to ask questions about what education is for and how it helps us as human beings. What statement about the purpose of digital art, and its benefit to humanity, does this building imply? Explain.

3. David Tyack argues in "School: The Story of American Education" against the view of education as a commodity to produce workers whose skills become commodities. Do you think that this architecture suggests that education is a commodity? Explain.

Dormitory, Illinois Institute of Technology

1. Michael J. Lewis ("Forget Classrooms") indicates that campus architecture can be driven by consumerism rather than education. Do you think his point holds true for the architectural features of this dormitory? What elements of the building might be designed to appeal to consumerist motives in students and their parents?

2. Dormitories used to offer few amenities to students. Today, campuses compete with one another to offer students more housing features. What educational inequities, described by Jonathan Kozol in "Savage Inequalities," are embedded in this competition? Why might the features of this dormitory reflect such inequities?

3. Students with many different kinds of intelligence come to college campuses and occupy the dormitories. What might students, who display intelligences other than linguistic and mathematical, feel in this environment?

Reading Room, Suzzallo Library, University of Washington

1. Michael J. Lewis ("Forget Classrooms") describes modern student centers as an attempt to market colleges. Suzallo Library, in particular the Reading Room, might also be considered a marketing tool. What might the University of Washington be marketing? Explain.

2. In "Human Intelligence Isn't What We Think It Is," Howard Gardner suggests that there are multiple intelligences undervalued by many educational institutions. Looking at the architecture of Suzzallo Library, what intelligences seem to you most valued here? Which might be undervalued? Explain.

3. John Dewey ("The School and the Life of the Child"), David Brooks ("The Merits of Meritocracy"), and Jonathan Kozol ("Savage Inequalities") might look at the architecture of Suzzallo Library with very different eyes. They might argue about tradition, privilege, or merit. Imagine that you and they are all first-year students at the University of Washington. Write a dialogue where you and they discuss one of these topics.

"Snap the Whip"

1. David Tyack ("School: The Story of American Public Education") validates the traditional values of public education. Do you think that Homer's painting embodies those values? Explain.

2. Robert Barr ("Who Is This Child?") and John Dewey ("The School and the Life of the Child") indicate the importance of the school as a place to live. How might their views be used to explain the education imagined here?

3. Although the schoolhouse in the painting is small and crude, the education portrayed here suggests positive values. Do you think that Jonathan Kozol ("Savage Inequalities") places too much emphasis on the decreptitude of many public school buildings and not enough on what teachers can do to connect to students? Explain.

"Schoolhouse"

1. Bauer's photograph reminds us that the view of education once embodied in this school no longer exists. What is this view? Then, drawing on David Brooks ("The Merits of Meritocracy"), David Tyack ("School: The Story of American Public Education"), and John Dewey ("The School and the Life of the Child"), describe what views you think have replaced it.

2. Students attending this school likely came from families who made a subsistence living from the land. How might those conditions affect the purpose parents saw for educating their children? How do you think that these parents might have responded to Jon Spayde's ideas in "Learning in the Key of Life"? Explain.

FINDING COMMON CAUSE IN CONTROVERSY
Who Becomes Valedictorian? A Question of Merit

This is a book about finding common reasons or cause. And finding commonality is hardest where feelings run strong. While educators and citizens, and especially politicians, uniformly tout education as a panacea to societal ills, controversy still abounds, with issues of merit bumping up against issues of fairness and compassion. At times an issue arises that distills this controversy and requires a debate and a clear answer. While the issue of who is named valedictorian may seem a trivial one in education, it disguises a host of opposing assumptions and beliefs. Only one person can receive the award of being valedictorian. Can the numbers be manipulated? What is fairness when the student has a disability but has received significant extra help?

READING

HANS ALLHOFF   The following news report details a controversy that students and school officials might find extremely interesting. What does it mean and what value do we attach to being first or best? In a meritocracy, don't we all want to be best, especially when the award, being chosen valedictorian, represents being the best after many years of schooling? The student whom the article describes, Blair Hornstine, wants the courts to ensure that she be ruled sole valedictorian because her GPA was just slightly higher than two other students' GPAs. She does not want to share the award, for she thinks that this would undermine its value. However, she had been home-schooled because of chronic fatigue syndrome. Others declare that she may have had an unfair advantage in the home schooling, in the guise of a disadvantage.

ALLHOFF is a law student at Stanford University.

She's Almost Too Good to Be True, and to Prove It She's Going to Sue (2003)

BY HANS ALLHOFF

"Who is Blair Hornstine?" may be a tougher question for most Americans than "Where is Osama bin Laden?"

It shouldn't be. Hornstine is a high school senior and straight-A student from Moorestown, N.J., who thinks she should be the sole valedictorian of her graduating class.

Her school district wants her to share this honor with two other students, whose GPAs are only slightly lower than hers—essentially because they took gym classes, which receive no special weight in a GPA calculation. Hornstine was excused from gym because she suffers from chronic fatigue syndrome.

Now, Hornstine has asked a federal judge to intervene on her behalf. What's more, she has sued her school district for $200,000 in compensatory damages and $2.5 million in punitive damages.

She is being discriminated against and humiliated on account of her disability, she claims. (Her father is a state Superior Court judge and is on her side publicly.)

"Not only does the conferral of co-valedictorian status inaccurately suggest that plaintiff Blair Hornstine was not at the top of her class, but it actually raises a derogatory implication that her performance is not what it seems," said her attorney, Edwin J. Jacobs Jr.

One hopes Hornstine will either drop her case or lose it, and then stand proudly with her two equally accomplished classmates on graduation day, June 19. It is a little too early to tell, however. U.S. District Judge Freda Wolfson has scheduled a hearing for Thursday. The Moorestown Board of Education has planned a May 12 meeting of its own.

Meanwhile, Princeton, Stanford, Harvard, Duke and Cornell all admitted Hornstine to their classes of 2007. And for understandable reasons: Aside from her stellar academic record, she scored a 1570 on her SAT, is an accomplished orator and debater and founded the Tri-County Prom Dress Drive, which collected and distributed more than 400 prom dresses to girls from low-income families.

She also helped raise money for 10 Chinese orphans to have oral surgery, which earned her an invitation to China to address a global conference there.

She was even an Olympic torchbearer.

Yet while her academic and extracurricular accomplishments are not up for discussion, Hornstine's character now is: What kind of student decides that simply doing well is not enough? What kind of person, when asked to share such an honor as valedictorian, claims an exclusive right to it?

Although Princeton—just to pick a school—has a compelling interest in filling its classrooms and dormitories with accomplished young men and women just like Hornstine, it also has an interest in making sure those young men and women have an appropriate attitude toward learning and academic success.

It is unclear whether Hornstine—whose ego and litigious instinct appear to drive her—has such an attitude. Someone who simply loves to learn would not do what she is doing.

It is too late for Princeton to rescind its offer of admission to Hornstine. She has reportedly decided to go to Harvard. This timing is unfortunate. Princeton, and every other school to which she was admitted, could have—and should have—made a powerful statement by saying, "Blair Hornstine, we were wrong about you."

Hornstine may seem to possess something special; but in fact, she's just a member of a hyper-accomplished generation for whom getting good grades and doing good deeds has become a way of life.

It would be better for the nation's elite colleges and universities to offer admission to those candidates with a more sophisticated sense of success and deeper appreciation for academic life.

EMPATHIZING WITH DIFFERENT POINTS OF VIEW

When you encounter such clearly opposing positions, we recommend that you first identify the feelings, values, and perspectives of each side. Try to empathize with each person or group.

Taking the student's (plaintiff's) side:

- Assume that you had worked for four years to achieve A's in every class, had taken all the Advanced Placement classes you could, and worked with the disability of chronic fatigue, in order to be the best in your class. How would you feel if the school asked you to share your award with students whose GPAs were lower than yours?
- How would you feel if your family had spent time and resources securing teachers to teach private AP classes in order for you to compete with your classmates? You knew that only one student would be valedictorian. What would you feel about the school's decision to have you share the award?
- What motives do you think the school had for not naming you valedictorian when your GPA was clearly higher than anyone else's? How would this make you feel?

Taking the school administration's (defendant's) side:

- If you were the superintendent, how would you feel if, according to your review of Blair Hornstine and two other students whose GPAs were very close, Hornstine appears to have had an unfair advantage. She did not have to take the state-mandated physical education classes, which are non-weighted courses (a weighted course is one for which students receive an extra point toward GPA because of its difficulty level). Instead, she took weighted AP courses, from teachers her family selected. This arrangement made possible a higher GPA than other students could possibly obtain. Explain your feelings to the judge.
- Assume that you had made numerous concessions to Hornstine's family, had made available teachers and materials, and helped the family in any way you could to create an equal playing field. Explain how their refusal to "share" the award makes you feel.
- Explain why you think that the school administrators have the right to award valedictorian status in any way they see fit.

ADDING MORE INFORMATION

Perhaps you have made up your mind which side you would take. How would your thinking change (or not) with each additional piece of information?

- Blair Hornstine had already been accepted by Harvard, Stanford, Princeton, Yale, and other schools, as was K.M., one student with whom she was to share the award. Hornstine claimed that sharing the award would affect her career.
- Hornstine's GPA was 4.689 and K.M.'s was 4.634. If subjected to the same scheduling difficulties as K.M., Hornstine's may have been lower than K.M.'s.
- Hornstine's father is a state superior court judge, and he is suing the school for $200,000 in court costs and $2.5 million in punitive damages.
- According to the suit, during Hornstine's high school years, the school superintendent ordered an independent medical review of Hornstine, which recommended that she drop one course in second semester because of her chronic fatigue syndrome. However, the superintendent ruled that she would have to carry a full load, but recommended she drop all AP and honors courses. This would have ensured that she not make valedictorian. She refused.
- Hornstine co-founded a program that raised $30,000 for the needy and raised funds to pay for ten harelip operations for Chinese kids. Not only did she face a disability to complete her schoolwork, but she also faced one in finding the time to do significant community service. Her community service was far more extensive than that of either of the two other candidates.
- Hornstine was reputed to have avoided taking classes from Moorestown High teachers known to have "difficult grading standards" for AP students. She was known to have dropped difficult courses at the high school and finished them through home school, with private tutors whom she selected.

For additional information: A number of editorials were written about this case. Use Blair Hornstine as a keyword to search on the Web for further information and opinions. Also, *Newsweek* ran an article on Blair Hornstine on June 23, 2003.

SEEKING COMMON CAUSE

Before you take a side, first identify where the two people or groups agree. This will narrow the points of disagreement and allow you to focus on the key issues.

- Both sides seek "fairness," but define it differently. Do they share any views of fairness? Can you envision a view of fairness that both parties could accept?
- What views of a meritocracy do both Hornstine and the superintendent share? What alternate views of success should both consider?

DEBATE ESSAY

Take a side on whether or not the courts should force the superintendent to make Hornstine sole valedictorian. What principles are at stake here? Use arguments from both sides to support your determination, revealing what values both sides have in common but also why one side is stronger than the other. Avoid being dismissive or glib, and give both sides their due. Your task is to make your argument reasoned and judicious.

WRITING PROJECTS

Writing a Short Argument

The following short writing projects can prepare you for writing the long essay in the Writing an Extended Argument section or can be done independently.

1. In groups of three students, discuss the features of a local school. Does the architecture seem to support or undermine a sense of community? You might look at the way buildings are clustered, the massing, the pathways students take to go from one building to another, the building materials, and the school's orientation to the outside community and topography. What features of the architecture have helped either to bring students together and encourage community or to silence and isolate students? Explain, using detailed descriptions of the school's architecture.

2. Describe a day of schooling in your old high school. Describe the experience itself, what you typically thought about, what experiences with the courses you had, what feelings were evoked. Be very detailed. Take us on a walk from class to class. At the end of the day what did you feel about your learning experience? Using some of the readings from this chapter, what conclusions can you draw about your educational experience?

3. Describe the most important learning experience of your life. It could be an experience learning a sport, understanding an ethical idea, or comprehending a subject. What made this experience important? (Was it your sense of involvement? Your sense of joy in accomplishment? The subject matter? The teacher? The exchange among many minds? The application?) Recount the experience in detail, as a narrative, even if the learning experience entails more than a single event and takes place over many months. At the end, comment on what elements you think are essential to learning.

4. Interview individually three students whom you have identified as having some extraordinary talent such as the ability to dance, play a sport, empathize with others, or work with animals. Create a list of questions about what abilities they think they have that distinguish them from other people. Also, ask them what they think matters most in developing this talent. Encourage them to give examples. In your paper, first describe your purpose for these interviews and what you intend to ask each of them. Then describe these interviewees, your basis for selecting them, and their responses to your questions. Next, explain how their responses are similar and different. Finally, explain what you learned from their responses (what conclusions you drew about what matters in education in promoting extraordinary talent).

5. Observe two seminars or small classes on different subjects (preferably, not classes you yourself are taking). Take notes on the behavior of the students, the strategies of the teacher, and the interactions you see. Look for details such as students taking notes or not, any signs of the "slow learning" Jon Spayde discusses in "Learning in the Key of Life," any appeal to multiple intelligences, any signs of personal caring, or any attempts to reinforce a meritocracy. In your paper, describe what you saw in detail, and develop an opinion on which experience helped students learn more. Draw on several of the readings to support your viewpoint.

6. Interview three college students who came from large urban public schools, where less than 50 percent of the student body goes on to college. Ask them what obstacles they faced and how they overcame them. What single change, given that budgets are tight everywhere, do these students think would most ensure equal opportunity for all students (e.g., more counseling, more after-school programs, better parent education programs)? Write a paper identifying the dominant themes these students suggest.

Writing an Extended Argument

The following assignment asks you to incorporate numerous sources, and references, as well as photographs of schools, into a complex argument; that is, it asks you to use the readings and visuals to support a position you have arrived at after careful thought and consideration.

Write an essay in which you explain what kind of K–12 education you think all students should have if they are to have equal opportunities for success. What skills must they learn? What classroom experiences best support learning? What subjects should they study? What physical environment should the school provide?

Your thesis might be an answer to one of these questions:

- How might the architecture of a school enhance or undermine the essential competencies, experience, and knowledge students need to succeed?

- What happens to students when they are tracked into specific classes based on standardized tests, grades, and teacher evaluations? Do you think that curriculum, teacher expectations, and required student work in such classes reinforce or undermine equal opportunity?

- Many writings in this chapter emphasize that caring for students and teaching them critical-thinking skills are important to education. How might these two elements be combined to give all students an opportunity to succeed?

- Compare the architecture and physical condition of two different high schools. What messages do you think that the physical environment of the two schools conveys to students about what behaviors the school values? Does it value risk-taking and independent thought? Obedience and orderly procedures?

- Describe how you think schools can encourage both competition and caring to provide equal opportunities for all students.

Designing the Extended Writing Project

As we have indicated before, we suggest that you design your extended writing project to include key elements of a paper. These include your thesis, a structure based on the thesis, detailed descriptions (including quotes and comments on quotes), and discussions of the significance of the thesis. These elements can be addressed in any order. Sometimes, it takes a draft before you realize what your thesis is. Also, you may find that your structure evolves while you write your draft, given that your details and discussions of details may change the direction of your thinking. What follows are reminders about what these elements are and how they might look in schematic form.

A Thesis

A thesis is the point of your essay. It may be a claim, a specific perspective, or a position in a debate.

EXAMPLE OF AN OPENING PARAGRAPH WITH THE THESIS AT THE END | If schools wish to succeed in providing equal opportunity to all students, the foremost thing they need to do is to recognize and reward what Howard Gardner ("Human Intelligence Isn't What We Think It Is") calls "multiple intelligences." This means that they develop each student's unique intelligence, such as musical or kinesthetic ability. While I agree that schools also need to ensure that all students learn to think critically about subject matter, and be taught in caring ways, I think that schools best support equality of opportunity when they recognize and enhance students' differing aptitudes.

A Structure Based on the Thesis.

What follows are three possible ways you might structure your essay:

- Order your ideas of the essay around the order of ideas set forth in the thesis.

- Order the ideas in a problem-solution structure.
- Order your ideas around a pro-con structure.

EXAMPLE OF A PROBLEM-SOLUTION STRUCTURE

Section 1: statement of the "problem"—inequality of opportunity in public schools.
Section 2: possible solution 1—teaching critical thinking; why this is not enough.
Section 3: possible solution 2—caring for students; why this is not enough.
Section 4: solution 3 (favored here)—identify and support each student's aptitude.
Section 5: significance of solution—students have high self-esteem; later in life they become very productive.

Detailed Description (Essays and Photographs of School Architecture)

When you weave quotes, descriptions, paraphrasing, and other forms of evidence into your paper, assume that your reader has not read the selections in this chapter or seen the photographs of the schools. Where needed, introduce each specific detail, to give it context and to indicate your purpose in using it. Following the detail, discuss how it supports your point. If you refer to photographs of schools, describe what you see so that the reader can picture what you have seen. What follows is an example of a paragraph from the paper whose thesis and structure are outlined above. Notice the number of specific details.

EXAMPLE | In "Human Intelligence Isn't What We Think It Is," Howard Gardner encourages educators to support children's different aptitudes. One school, Diamond Ranch High School, uses architectural design and physical environment to encourage students' artistic and technical creativity. It took creativity to imagine a school on this steep, removed hillside site. The playing fields were literally carved out of the hillside. The building shapes, geometric but asymmetrical, are also unique. Some lean inward; others project upward with sharp angles. The classroom sizes and shapes also vary, suggesting the diverse activities that students engage in. Furthermore, the building materials, concrete and corrugated steel, are high tech, their use suggesting innovative design and research. The environment itself encourages technical creativity.

Conclusion or Significance of the Thesis

One of the best ways to conclude an essay is to write about significance. Ask yourself, So what? This is always a difficult question, because we tend to think that significance is self-evident. Keep probing. Ask yourself, Who cares? You can use a number of strategies to convey significance. What follows are three possibilities:

- Imagine consequences for individuals (e.g., We do not need citizens who have learned to memorize facts in books but not to solve problems).
- Create an analogy that vivifies significance (e.g., The building looks like a space station from *Star Wars*).
- Introduce a pertinent quotation and explain what it means (e.g., "You can never learn what you do not love").

What follows is an example of imagining consequences for individuals.

EXAMPLE | Teachers who believe in and support the idea of multiple intelligences help students become more productive later in life. When a teacher praises a student's ability such as empathy with others, the student is motivated to further develop that ability. The teacher may have guided that student toward a career in counseling or therapy. As a result, the student may seek further schooling after high school, even if he or she has not done well in traditional subjects.

Geometry in Architecture: Students Design Schools
http://ali.apple.com/ali_sites/glefli/exhibits/1000048/The_Lesson.html

This page from the George Lucas Educational Foundation Web site describes a project undertaken by a high school geometry class in Seattle, Washington. The class designed a school:
they consulted with architects, researched such architectural features as solar panels, and constructed models of their proposed building. After reading about this project, write a paper showing how the project illustrates one of the theories of learning discussed in this chapter. How do you think the project enhances or limits the students' education? What did the students learn by doing it?

Teacher Heroes
http://myhero.com/hero.asp?hero=jkozol

This site provides information about Jonathan Kozol ("Savage Inequalities") and several other teachers who have had a progressive impact on education. Read what the site has to say about four or five of the teachers it describes. Then write a short essay indicating what these teachers have in common and which of the ideas in the readings these teachers seem to represent.

www.mhhe.com/durkinl

Using the Web for Resources on Images on Education. Go to Web Resources

JACK LEVINE   The Trial [1953–1954]

In trials, final decisions are made to determine right and wrong, guilt and redress. In the background of all parts of the legal profession—contract law, patent law, constitutional law, and family law, for example—is the trial, or threat of trial. Given such an important event, what do you find surprising in this rendition of a trial?

1 What do the expressions on the faces of the subjects and the direction of their gaze suggest about the nature of the legal work depicted here? Explain.

2 The symbol of justice, the balanced weights, is placed in the center of the painting. What does this placement suggest about how the painter wants you to see the legal profession depicted here? Explain.

3 What do the various people in the painting appear to be doing? How do their activities relate? What might the painter be trying to convey by these activities?

4 What objects can you identify in the painting? What expertise, values, experience, and concerns do these objects convey about the people in the room?

EDWARD HOPPER   New York Office [1962]

Office work is one of the most common forms of work today. We think of millions of people rushing around doing office work, keeping the economy alive. How does the impression here contradict some of your stereotypes of office life?

Montgomery Museum of Fine Arts, Montgomery, Alabama.

1 What do qualities of the woman's gaze tell you about what she might be doing or thinking? How does the painting direct our gaze to her gaze?

2 Through the plate glass window, we see into the office life of the central figure. What is that life like? What do the objects and background figures tell you about that life?

3 While the exposing plate glass window is framed in glaring light, we cannot see into the small dark windows of the shadowed adjacent building. What does this stark contrast suggest about office work? What other elements of exposure do you see in the painting?

4 The woman's dress and hair stand out in striking contrast to this office context. Describe the nature of this contrast and explain what the artist might be suggesting about office work.

1 Detail the woman's characteristics (face, body position, clothes, hair, hands, expression) and activities. What do these suggest about the nature of her work?

2 Describe the objects in the chemist's physical surroundings. What do they tell you about her and the nature of her work?

3 The viewer's eye moves from the chemical model (foreground) to the figure, desk, and notes (middle ground) to the window (background). What connection do you make between these three? Explain.

4 Why do you think the woman's glasses are the focal point of the painting? What kinds of "seeing" occur in the painting?

5 How many hands seem to be portrayed? What image do these hands create about the nature of the work Hodgkin does?

1 Detail the various activities you see in this lighthearted painting of a department store sale. How do the actions of the customers differ from those of the salespeople?

2 What in the painting seems circuslike or carnival-like? Why might this atmosphere be important in a "sale"? How might it also affect the work and attitudes of the salespeople? Explain, using details in the painting.

3 Describe the artist's use of color. How does color reinforce the contrast in behavior we see in the painting?

JOHN SLOAN   Sun and Wind on the Roof [1915]

This image of a single woman doing domestic work contrasts sharply with Hopper's image of a single woman in an office. Sloan's figure and surroundings do not have the static quality of Hopper's. Why might motion be so important in Sloan's portrayal of work?

Maier Museum of Art. Fine Arts Fund, 1947.

1 In what ways are the woman's garments shaped and colored like the garments on the clothesline? What does this similarity suggest about the woman's relationship to her work?

2 While the buildings in the background (upper half) are dark and unmoving, the woman and the clothing are bright and active. What contrast might the painter be suggesting between this woman's work and that performed in the dark buildings?

3 The woman's clothes cling to her body and reveal its curves. In what ways might this painting represent a man's view of the nature of this work?

BEN SHAHN *Albert Einstein among Other Immigrants,* Jersey
Homesteads [1937–1938]

Shahn's mural depicts the entry of immigrants, in particular Jewish immigrants, including
Albert Einstein and the artist's mother, into the United States through Ellis Island. At the
upper left we see a Nazi soldier. Below him, two women weep over the coffins of the
unjustly executed Sacco and Vanzetti. At the lower right we see garment workers toiling
over their sewing machines, the kind of work immigrants typically perform. Does the
mural create an overall impression of work or competing impressions?

Community Center, Jersey Homestead
Roosevelt, New Jersey, U.S.A. Art © Estate of Ben Shahn/Licensed by VAGA,
New York, NY.

1 The lower-left section opens onto the halls of the Ellis Island Registry Center. What does this
   image suggest about how immigrants enter the United States?

2 The right side of the mural depicts the work awaiting these immigrants. What is that work
   like? What is Shahn suggesting by placing Einstein at the center of the image?

3 What comment is Shahn making by placing a small American flag in the left background, as
   well as a small window opening up a view to the Statue of Liberty?

DIEGO RIVERA Mural, Great Hall of Detroit Institute of Arts
[1932–1933]

Factory work dominated American life after the Industrial Revolution. Humans worked with machines, often assembling parts. The size and scale of this mural reflects the extent to which this work dominated the nineteenth and early twentieth centuries—and continues to do so today. Why do you think the mural is placed in the Detroit Institute of Arts?

1 Three larger-than-life workers placed at the lower center of the mural draw the viewer's eye. What do their body positions, face, dress, and relationship to each other, as well as other physical features you might notice, suggest about the nature of the work they do? Explain.

2 Describe the most dominant machinery depicted in the mural. What image of work does it portray?

3 Different rectangular sections of the painting allow the viewer to see into the work done in various parts of a factory. Choose two of these sections and describe the work portrayed there. What do your descriptions suggest about the overall nature of factory work?

DANIEL DESIGA   El Campesino [1977]

Field work has been the employment of millions of workers. Typically, this has been low-paying, back-breaking work. What qualities of this painting emphasize not only the labor but also the strength of such work?

Private Collection.

1 The generic figure of a field worker, bent over to hoe the ground, takes up most of the canvas of this painting. Why do you think that the painter chose to make the figure so large, to paint him from the particular angle he does, and to avoid depicting the worker's face?

2 The viewer's eye is drawn to the gold color of the field worker's back. What does the gold, in contrast to other colors in the painting, suggest about the worker and the work he does?

3 How are the land and sky depicted in the scene? What do you think the painter is suggesting about the relationship between the worker and his surroundings? Explain.

The Work World

The writers and artists in this chapter offer views of the experience as well as the value of different kinds of work. What are certain jobs like? Does work have to be professional to be valuable? What gives value to any job? Many of the writers and artists in this chapter emphasize the need to engage in work that brings out our humanity—our ability to engage in and care about what we do and who benefits from it. They vividly portray this human element of work, or they depict how some work deprives men and women of their humanity.

While professions that receive celebrity status in the media—law, medicine, secret intelligence—may look appealing for their high drama, most Americans work in low-paying, routine jobs that serve essential functions. While this chapter discusses a wide range of jobs, professions, and work issues, it delves most deeply into the lives of every-day workers. Our goal is a humanistic one, to help you experience the day-to-day events, inner conflicts, and values of others in their work—their feelings, concerns, and choices.

▌ THE WORK WORLD IN THE ARTWORKS ▌

The artworks in this chapter represent several media—and the artists offer individual portraits or broad images that convey key insights into the nature and value of work.

Jack Levine's *The Trial* depicts the legal profession in action during one of those key moments in a trial when all participants reveal something about the nature of legal work. To convey his vision, Levine has painted the central people—the judge, the attorneys and the witnesses—interacting and doing their work. Edward Hopper's *New York Office* portrays, through a large glass window, a female office worker reading correspondence, standing exposed in pinpoint light. The elegantly dressed worker, framed in the window and motionless as she reads, contrasts sharply with the bleak walls and buildings both inside and outside the office, as well as the cut-off, shadowy figures of busy coworkers in the background. Maggi Hambling's *Dorothy Hodgkin* depicts the 1985 Nobel Prize winner for chemistry. The painting emphasizes the constant intellectual actions of the woman sitting at her desk, hunched over, hair awry. While intellectual activity is difficult to paint, the figure, surrounding objects, and color convey the intensity of her work.

Other artworks focus on workers' physical actions. Florine Stettheimer's *Spring Sale at Bendel's* portrays the work of department store salespeople, especially in the carnival atmosphere of a sale. The energetic playfulness, posturing, people watching, and self-admiration of the customers contrasts with the drab stasis of the employees. John Sloan's *Sun and Wind on the Roof,* which depicts a woman hanging out her wash, offers a luxurious image of ordinary work. As the woman hangs up clothes to dry, these clothes wave sensuously in the wind while the woman's own dress wraps around her body.

Broader social issues of work are seen in two murals and a painting. The panel from Ben Shahn's *Jersey Homesteads Mural* addresses such concerns as immigration, prejudice, and exploitation. This mural panel portrays the entry of immigrants, including Albert Einstein, through Ellis Island, with sections revealing rows of garment workers, the coffins of wrongly executed Italian radicals Sacco and Vanzetti, and a Nazi soldier standing next to anti-Jewish signs. Diego Rivera's large mural depicts the physical labor of factory workers in a complex series of images that intertwine machinery and human forms in a factory work environment. The mural, placed in the Great Hall of the Detroit Institute of Arts, covers a complete building wall, conveying a strong message about the nature of work in the early twentieth century, especially in such industrialized cities as Detroit. Daniel DeSiga's *El Campesino* portrays a bent-over field-worker, whose back and bowed head occupy most of the painting. The pose itself reflects both the grueling nature of the work and the powerful but generic body that is bent to do it.

Each image takes a particular view of the work depicted. The artists communicate that view through their subjects, the subjects' expressions and actions, the background of the picture, and the objects in the scene. Where the portrayal is more abstract, the artist's choice of color, shape, contrasts of light and dark, line, and movement communicate the vision: Are the contrasts sharp or blurred? Are the shapes jagged or smooth? Do the lines complement one another or do they intersect and conflict, creating tension?

Analyzing the Artworks

To analyze the artist's perspective on work, the viewer needs to ask what the artist's chosen subjects communicate about their feelings (conveyed through posture, face, attire, etc). The gaze is especially significant. Where is each subject looking? How does the subject interact with other subjects in the portrayal? The objects surrounding the subjects are also important. Is the background space crowded with objects? If so, what do the objects imply about the nature of the work? Do they reflect the values of the subjects or do they contrast ironically with what the subjects are doing? Overall, what is the artist trying to say about the nature of the work portrayed?

Here is a list of steps that can help you analyze the works of art included in this chapter. These are the same elements we include for other chapters, but we adjust some of the questions for this theme.

1. Identify particular visual elements that tell us something about the work being done:

   - Figures (dress, posture, face, expression, hair, placement). How are the people positioned? What do they look like? How are they interacting?
   - Background (location, detail, relation to figure). What does the background look like? Is the figure comfortable against this background? Is there a conflict?
   - Objects (what they are; why they are there; what they look like or are made of). How do the objects reflect the values of the figure? How does the figure use them? What do the objects suggest about the work being done?

- Color (bright, contrasting, monochromatic; associated with certain objects and not others). Do the colors suggest an attitude toward work? Are they symbolic? Do they reflect a mood?
- Shape (sharp, smooth, large, small, rounded, jagged, symmetrical, or asymmetrical). How are the shapes related to the nature of the work? Are certain shapes related to the central figure?

2. After identifying and characterizing these elements, consider what these elements suggest about the nature of the work being portrayed.

- Is there a central contrast in the painting, say between a subject and the background? Between human postures and machines? Between foreground and background? Between people and objects? Between bright light and dark shadow?
- What contrast or harmony in views, ideas, values, or behaviors is suggested?

Analysis of a Painting

Edward Hopper's *New York Office* presents a deceptive simplicity. A woman standing and reading correspondence is seen through a large plate-glass window. Glaring light from outside, as well as from overhead lighting, illuminates her face and bare shoulders and arms. Two other office workers, turning away and partly cut off, are in the background. The glass window is framed by a spare but glaring building façade and juxtaposed to an empty street corner and a shadowed adjacent building with darkened windows. Except for the three figures in the office, nothing human or active exists in the painting. Yet this starkness seems to indicate something about office work, as Hopper sees it.

Contrasts in light and dark, interior office and exterior street, the drab office workers in the background and the striking woman in the foreground, contribute to our sense of the starkness of work in a big-city office. The woman, whose intimate act of reading is lit up as with a spotlight, appears alone and exposed. The viewer, like anyone on the street, can see through the large window into her life, whose human connections are visualized in the letter and unused telephone. The shadowed coworkers, dressed more modestly in business apparel, are moving out of the picture, in different directions, disconnected, and absorbed in disparate tasks. The darkened anonymous windows of the adjacent building heighten our sense of the woman's exposure and aloneness. Her work, by implication, is lonely, anonymous, and scrutinized.

▌ THE WORK WORLD IN THE ESSAYS ▌

Many of the writers featured in this chapter offer insight into the nature and value of work. Malcolm Gladwell addresses a special kind of work that requires what he calls "physical genius." He analyzes the nature of this "genius," yet the qualities he identifies would help anyone excel in any work—qualities such as vision, anticipation, awareness, practice, and a struggle for perfection. In parallel fashion, Mike Rose ("The Working Life of a Waitress") examines the cognitive aptitudes of everyday work, exploring the high level of physical and mental abilities needed in the work of a waitress. In "Work Makes Life Sweet," bell hooks speculates about what makes one happy in work, noting that African American women are at a particular disadvantage in finding work that reflects their passions and abilities. She questions conventional views of work as onerous and unfulfilling. Similarly anxious to contradict conventional views of work, Daniel Levine ("Take This Job and Love It") rejects the traditional view that low-paying, entry-level jobs are dead-end jobs and that they undermine one's self-confidence. He focuses on the values that such jobs teach us and the need to instill those values in young people.

Other writers portray the texture of daily lives in a variety of low-paying jobs. In contrast to the view that low-paying jobs teach valuable lessons, in "Black Hair," Gary Soto, detailing his work in a tire factory, shows such work to be dehumanizing. In his experience, many of the workers in this factory become lifers, and their personal lives reflect the degradation of their work lives. David Sedaris, also doing low-paying work, describes a holiday job for which his commitment is minimal in "SantaLand Diaries." The job amuses him because it provides insight into the people he meets and because he can look at his own behavior and laugh. Another writer concerned with low-paying work is Barbara Ehrenreich ("Nickel and Dimed"), who takes a job as an employee at Wal-Mart, as well as other low-paying jobs across the country, in order to speak from the inside about such jobs in this country. She indicates that the extensive application process, low salaries, and constant oversight keep employees' expectations low and fears high.

Still other writers describe the texture of work in a variety of businesses and professions. In *Voices from the Workplace*, selected writers describe their specific careers, recounting their activities, roles, and feelings. The voices include those of a muralist, a psychiatrist, and a journalist.

These chapter readings, which address an array of issues, portray on-the-job decisions, reactions, and meanings involved in particular kinds of work. The readings thus provide valuable insight into what people do with their lives and why. The writers' attitudes range from cynical to joyous, with some writers choosing a playful or ironic perspective.

Analyzing the Essays

To help you address these readings, here are some steps to follow in your analysis:

1. What attitudes, values, and concerns does the writer associate with the particular job?
2. What contrasting attitudes, values, and concerns does the writer reject?
3. How do these job attitudes, values, and concerns fit with the larger social values associated with American culture?
4. If there is a disconnection, does the writer state or imply a common ground? If not, can you posit one?

Analysis of an Essay

In "Interview with a Psychiatrist," the narrator talks about the values that make her job interesting and fulfilling. She cites her connections to the families of her patients, her dealings with schools and other agencies affecting her patients' well-being, her sense of connectedness to the community, and the lifelong learning required of her. She aligns these values with her personal values as a woman and mother. She wants time to be both a wife and a mother in addition to being a doctor. Indeed, she brings her imagination and understanding as wife and mother to bear on her work with families.

In promoting these values, the psychiatrist rejects a number of traditional views about her work. For one, she rejects the view that some jobs in the medical profession are ill-suited to women. She insists that her choice of specialization represents personal interest and individual fulfillment, not social acquiescence. For another, she rejects the current emphasis on the "expert." She demonstrates that the job demands, not just professionalism, but also caring and imagination, as well as humility and self-knowledge. The work is not limited to "cases" and professional expertise—indeed, she talks with the whole family and is sensitive to their cultural values in a multicultural environment.

The values she demonstrates in working as a psychiatrist fit with the larger American culture. Just on the surface, they embody the American work ethic (she spent eleven years in medical training); in particular they represent the American dream of being rewarded for hard work, even work one doesn't like. More deeply, the psychiatrist's values fit with the American values of individualism, self-determination, and self-improvement; she continuously increases her knowledge and her impact on the profession. Finally her work values fit the larger ethical values of the community—of honesty and humility—within a larger framework of public service.

READING

People who are very happy in the work they choose seem to do it well. Yet few of us know what enables people to do something with expertise. For instance, what enables a person to perform extraordinary feats of physical skill, such as neurosurgery? Is one simply born with a physical "talent"—a uniform entity combining neurons, muscles, and instincts that help one to perform a physical act extraordinarily well? To what extent is the mind involved, and what role does practice play?

MALCOLM GLADWELL describes professionals who demonstrate a number of exceptional *physical* abilities—from a neurosurgeon to famous athletes to a renowned cellist. In describing physical genius, he rejects the view that such genius involves a "single factor"—one that can be measured in terms of athleticism or technique. He also rejects the idea of physical genius as mostly fine-motor ability. Instead, Gladwell views it as comprising multiple abilities, all tied to a person's vision of what is possible at the moment. These include decision making, anticipation, preparation, and visualization. What emerges in Gladwell's discussion of physical genius is the importance of imagination—for instance, the ability to visualize an entire musical score—and attitude, the willingness to review and practice. Significantly, physical coordination seems least important. What role do you think imagination and attitude play in professions that don't require physical ability?

GLADWELL was born in England, grew up in Canada, and now lives in New York. A former reporter for the *Washington Post,* he has been a staff writer for the *New Yorker* magazine since 1996. Gladwell is the author of two books—*Blink: The Power of Thinking without Thinking* and *The Tipping Point: How Little Things Can Make Big Differences*—both of which draw connections between seemingly disparate ideas or modes of thinking.

The Physical Genius (1999) | BY MALCOLM GLADWELL

Early one recent morning, while the San Francisco fog was lifting from the surrounding hills, Charlie Wilson performed his two thousand nine hundred and eighty-seventh transsphenoidal resection of a pituitary tumor. The patient was a man in his sixties who had complained of impotence and obscured vision. Diagnostic imaging revealed a growth, eighteen millimetres in diameter, that had enveloped his pituitary gland and was compressing his optic nerve. He was anesthetized and covered in blue surgical drapes, and one of Wilson's neurosurgery residents—a tall, slender woman in her final year of training—"opened" the case, making a small incision in his upper gum, directly underneath his nose. She then tunnelled back through his nasal passages until she reached the pituitary, creating a cavity several inches deep and about one and a half centimetres in diameter.

Wilson entered the operating room quickly, walking stiffly, bent slightly at the waist. He is sixty-nine—a small, wiry man with heavily muscled arms. His hair is cut very close to his scalp, so that, as residents over the years have joked, he might better empathize with the shaved heads of his patients. He is part Cherokee Indian and has high, broad cheekbones and large ears, which stick out at almost forty-five-degree angles. He was wearing Nike cross-trainers, and surgical scrubs marked with the logo of the medical center he has dominated for the past thirty years—Moffitt Hospital, at the University of California, San Francisco. When he was busiest, in the nineteen-eighties, he would routinely do seven or eight brain surgeries in a row, starting at dawn and ending at dusk, lining up patients in adjoining operating rooms and striding from one to the other like a conquering general. On this particular day, he would do five, of which the transsphenoidal was the first, but the rituals would be the same. Wilson believes that neurosurgery is best conducted in silence, with a scrub nurse who can anticipate his every step, and a resident who does not have to be told what to do, only shown. There was no music in the O.R. To guard against unanticipated disturbances, the door was locked. Pagers were set to "buzz," not beep. The phone was put on "Do Not Disturb."

Wilson sat by the patient in what looked like a barber's chair, manipulating a surgical microscope with a foot pedal. In his left hand he wielded a tiny suction tube, which removed excess blood. In his right he held a series of instruments in steady alternation: Cloward elevator, Penfield No. 2, Cloward rongeur, Fulton rongeur, conchatome, Hardy dissector, Kurze scissors, and so on. He worked quickly, with no wasted motion. Through the microscope, the tumor looked like a piece of lobster flesh, white and fibrous. He removed the middle of it, exposing the pituitary underneath. Then he took a ring curette—a long instrument with a circular scalpel perpendicular to the handle—and ran it lightly across the surface of the gland, peeling the tumor away as he did so.

It was, he would say later, like running a squeegee across a windshield, except that in this case the windshield was a surgical field one centimetre in diameter, flanked on either side by the carotid arteries, the principal sources of blood to the brain. If Wilson were to wander too far to the right or to the left and nick either artery, the patient might, in the neurosurgical shorthand, "stroke." If he were to push too far to the rear, he might damage any number of critical nerves. If he were not to probe aggressively, though, he might miss a bit of tumor and defeat the purpose of the procedure entirely.

It was a delicate operation, which called for caution and confidence and the ability to distinguish between what was supposed to be there and what wasn't. Wilson never wavered. At one point, there was bleeding from the right side of the pituitary, which signalled to Wilson that a small piece of tumor was still just outside his field of vision, and so he gently slid the ring curette over, feeling with the instrument as if by his fingertips, navigating around the carotid, lifting out the remaining bit of tumor. In the hands of an ordinary neurosurgeon, the operation—down to that last bit of blindfolded acrobatics—might have taken several hours. It took Charlie Wilson twenty-five minutes.

Neurosurgery is generally thought to attract the most gifted and driven of medical-school graduates. Even in that rarefied world, however, there are surgeons who are superstars and surgeons who are merely very good. Charlie Wilson is one of the superstars. Those who have trained with him say that if you showed them a dozen videotapes of different neurosurgeons in action—with the camera focussed just on the hands of the surgeon and the movements of the instruments—they could pick Wilson out in an instant, the same way an old baseball hand could look at a dozen batters in silhouette and tell you which one was Willie Mays. Wilson has a distinctive fluidity and grace.

There are thousands of people who have played in the National Hockey League over the years, but there has been only one Wayne Gretzky. Thousands of cellists play professionally all over the world, but very few will ever earn comparison with Yo-Yo Ma. People like Gretzky or Ma or Charlie Wilson all have an affinity for translating thought into action. They're what we might call physical geniuses. But what makes them so good at what they do?

The temptation is to treat physical genius in the same way that we treat intellectual genius—to think of it as something that can be ascribed to a single factor, a physical version of I.Q. When professional football coaches assess the year's crop of college prospects, they put them through drills designed to measure what they regard as athleticism: How high can you jump? How many pounds can you bench press? How fast can you sprint? The sum of the scores on these tests is considered predictive of athletic performance, and every year some college player's stock shoots up before draft day because it is suddenly discovered that he can run, say, 4.4 seconds in the forty-yard dash as opposed to 4.6 seconds. This much seems like common sense. The puzzling thing about physical genius, however, is that the closer you look at it the less it can be described by such cut-and-dried measures of athleticism.

Consider, for example, Tony Gwynn, who has been one of the best hitters in baseball over the past fifteen years. We would call him extraordinarily coördinated, by which we mean that in the course of several hundred milliseconds he can execute a series of perfectly synchronized muscular actions—the rotation of the shoulder, the movement of the arms, the shift of the hips—and can regulate the outcome of those actions so that his bat hits the ball with exactly the desired degree of force. These are abilities governed by specific neurological mechanisms. Timing, for example, appears to be controlled by the cerebellum. . . .

What sets physical geniuses apart from other people, then, is not merely being able to do something but knowing what to do—their capacity to pick up on subtle patterns that others generally miss. This is what we mean when we say that great athletes have a

5

"feel" for the game, or that they "see" the court or the field or the ice in a special way. Wayne Gretzky, in a 1981 game against the St. Louis Blues, stood behind the St. Louis goal, laid the puck across the blade of his stick, then bounced it off the back of the goalie in front of him and into the net. Gretzky's genius at that moment lay in seeing a scoring possibility where no one had seen one before. "People talk about skating, puck-handling, and shooting," Gretzky told an interviewer some years later, "but the whole sport is angles and caroms, forgetting the straight direction the puck is going, calculating where it will be diverted, factoring in all the interruptions." Neurosurgeons say that when the very best surgeons operate they always know where they are going, and they mean that the Charlie Wilsons of this world possess that same special feel— an ability to calculate the diversions and to factor in the interruptions when faced with a confusing mass of blood and tissue.

When Charlie Wilson came to U.C. San Francisco, in July of 1968, his first case   10
concerned a woman who had just had a pituitary operation. The previous surgeon had done the one thing that surgeons are not supposed to do in pituitary surgery— tear one of the carotid arteries. Wilson was so dismayed by the outcome that he re-solved he would teach himself how to do the transsphenoidal, which was then a relatively uncommon procedure. He carefully read the medical literature. He practiced on a few cadavers. He called a friend in Los Angeles who was an expert at the proce-dure, and had him come to San Francisco and perform two operations while Wilson watched. He flew to Paris to observe Gerard Guiot, who was one of the great transsphenoidal surgeons at the time. Then he flew home. It was the equivalent of someone preparing for a major-league tryout by watching the Yankees on television and hitting balls in an amusement-arcade batting cage. "Charlie went slowly," recalls Ernest Bates, a Bay-area neurosurgeon who scrubbed with Wilson on his first transsphenoidal, "but he knew the anatomy and, boom, he was there. I thought, My God, this was the first? You'd have thought he had done a hundred. Charlie has a skill that the rest of us just don't have."

This is the hard part about understanding physical genius, because the source of that special skill—that "feel"—is still something of a mystery. "Sometimes during the course of an operation, there'll be several possible ways of doing something, and I'll size them up and, without having any conscious reason, I'll just do one of them," Wil-son told me. He speaks with a soft, slow drawl, a remnant of Neosho, Missouri, the lit-tle town where he grew up, and where his father was a pharmacist, who kept his store open from 7 A.M. to 11 P.M., seven days a week. Wilson has a plainspoken, unpreten-tious quality. When he talks about his extraordinary success as a surgeon, he gives the impression that he is talking about some abstract trait that he is neither responsible for nor completely able to understand. "It's sort of an invisible hand," he went on. "It begins almost to seem mystical. Sometimes a resident asks, 'Why did you do that?' and I say"—here Wilson gave a little shrug—"'Well, it just seemed like the right thing.'"

There is a neurosurgeon at Columbia Presbyterian Center, in Manhattan, by the name of Don Quest, who served two tours in Vietnam flying A-1s off the *U.S.S. Kitty Hawk*. Quest sounds like the kind of person who bungee jumps on the weekend and has per-sonalized license plates that read "Ace." In fact, he is a thoughtful, dapper man with a carefully trimmed mustache, who plays the trombone in his spare time and quite cheerfully describes himself as compulsive. "When I read the *New York Times,* I don't speed-read it," Quest told me. "I read it carefully. I read everything. It drives my wife crazy." He was wearing a spotless physician's coat and a bow tie. "When I'm reading a novel—and there are so many novels I want to read—even if it's not very good I can't throw it away. I stick with it. It's quite frustrating, because I don't really have time for garbage." Quest talked about what it was like to repair a particularly tricky aneurysm compared to what it was like to land at night in rough seas and a heavy fog when you are running out of fuel and the lights are off on the carrier's landing strip, because the skies are full of enemy aircraft. "I think they are similar," he said, after some thought, and what he meant was that they were both exercises in a certain kind of exhaustive and meticulous preparation. "There is a checklist, before you take off, and this was drilled into us," Quest said. "It's on the dashboard with all the things you need to do. People forget to put the hook down, and you can't land on an aircraft carrier if the hook isn't down. Or they don't put the wheels down. One of my friends, my roommate, landed at night on the aircraft carrier with the wheels up. Thank God, the hook caught, because his engine stopped. He would have gone in the water." Quest did not seem like the kind of person who would forget to put the wheels down. "Some people are much more compulsive than others, and it shows," he went on to say. "It shows in how well they do their landing on the aircraft carrier, how many times they screw up, or are on the wrong radio frequency, or get lost, or their ordinances aren't accurate in terms of dropping a bomb. The ones who are the best are the ones who are always very careful."

Quest isn't saying that fine motor ability is irrelevant. . . . And, like Tony Gwynn, he's probably an adept and swift decision maker. But these abilities, Quest is saying, are of little use if you don't have the right sort of personality. Charles Bosk, a sociologist at the University of Pennsylvania, once conducted a set of interviews with young doctors who had either resigned or been fired from neurosurgery-training programs, in an effort to figure out what separated the unsuccessful surgeons from their successful counterparts. He concluded that, far more than technical skills or intelligence, what was necessary for success was the sort of attitude that Quest has—a practical-minded obsession with the possibility and the consequences of failure. "When I interviewed the surgeons who were fired, I used to leave the interview shaking," Bosk said. "I would hear these horrible stories about what they did wrong, but the thing was that they didn't *know* that what they did was wrong. In my interviewing, I began to develop what I thought was an indicator of whether someone was going to be a good surgeon or not. It was a couple of simple questions: Have you ever made a mistake? And, if so, what was your worst mistake? The people who said, 'Gee, I haven't really had one,' or, 'I've had a couple of bad outcomes but they were due to things outside my control'—invariably those were the worst candidates. And the residents who said, 'I make mistakes all the time. There was this horrible thing that happened just yesterday and here's what it was.' They were the best. They had the ability to rethink everything that they'd done and imagine how they might have done it differently."

What this attitude drives you to do is practice over and over again, until even the smallest imperfections are ironed out. After doing poorly in a tournament just prior to this year's Wimbledon, Greg Rusedski, who is one of the top tennis players in the world, told reporters that he was going home to hit a thousand practice serves. One of the things that set Rusedski apart from lesser players, in other words, is that he is the kind of person who is willing to stand out in the summer sun, repeating the same physical movement again and again, in single-minded pursuit of some fractional improvement in his performance. Wayne Gretzky was the same way. He would frequently stay behind after practice, long after everyone had left, flipping pucks to a specific spot in the crease, or aiming shot after shot at the crossbar or the goal post.

And Charlie Wilson? In his first few years as a professor at U.G.S.F., he would disappear at the end of the day into a special laboratory to practice his craft on rats: isolating, cutting, and then sewing up their tiny blood vessels, and sometimes operating on a single rat two or three times. He would construct an artificial aneurysm using a vein graft on the side of a rat artery, then manipulate the aneurysm the same way he would in a human being, toughening its base with a gentle coagulating current—and return two or three days later to see how successful his work had been. Wilson sees surgery as akin to a military campaign. Training with him is like boot camp. He goes to bed somewhere around eleven at night and rises at 4:30 A.M. For years, he ran upward of eighty miles a week, competing in marathons and hundred-mile ultramarathons. He quit only after he had a hip replacement and two knee surgeries and found himself operating in a cast. Then he took up rowing. On his days in the operating room, at the height of his career, Wilson would run his morning ten or twelve miles, conduct medical rounds, operate steadily until six or seven in the evening, and, in between, see patients, attend meetings, and work on what now totals six hundred academic articles. . . . [T]o Wilson the perfect operation requires a particular grace and rhythm. "In every way, it is analogous to the routine of a concert pianist," he says. "If you were going to do a concert and you didn't practice for a week, someone would notice that, just as I notice if one of my scrub nurses has been off for a week. There is that fraction-of-a-second difference in the way she reacts."

"Wilson has a certain way of positioning the arm of the retractor blade"—an instrument used to hold brain tissue in place—"so that the back end of the retractor doesn't stick up at all and he won't accidentally bump into it," Michon Morita told me. "Every once in a while, though, I'd see him when he didn't quite put it in the position he wanted to, and bumped it, which caused a little bit of hemorrhage on the brain surface. It wasn't harming the patient, and it was nothing he couldn't handle. But I'd hear 'That was stupid,' and I'd immediately ask myself, What did I do wrong? Then I'd realize he was chastising himself. Most people would say that if there was no harm done to the patient it was no big deal. But he wants to be perfect in everything, and when that perfection is broken he gets frustrated."

This kind of obsessive preparation does two things. It creates consistency. Practice is what enables Greg Rusedski to hit a serve at a hundred and twenty-five miles per hour again and again. It's what enables a pianist to play Chopin's double-thirds Étude at full speed, striking every key with precisely calibrated force. More important, practice changes the *way* a task is perceived. A chess master, for example, can look at a game in progress for a few seconds and then perfectly reconstruct that same position on a blank chessboard. That's not because chess masters have great memories (they don't have the same knack when faced with a random arrangement of pieces) but because hours and hours of chess playing have enabled them to do what psychologists call "chunking." Chunking is based on the fact that we store familiar sequences—like our telephone number or our bank-machine password—in long-term memory as a single unit, or chunk. If I told you a number you'd never heard before, though, you would be able to store it only in short-term memory, one digit at a time, and if I asked you to re-peat it back to me you might be able to remember only a few of those digits—maybe the first two or the last three. By contrast, when the chess masters see the board from a real game, they are able to break the board down into a handful of chunks—two or three clusters of pieces in positions that they have encountered before.

In "The Game of Our Lives," a classic account of the 1980–81 season of the Ed-monton Oilers hockey team, Peter Gzowski argues that one of the principal explana-tions for the particular genius of Wayne Gretzky was that he was hockey's greatest chunker. Gretzky, who holds nearly every scoring record in professional hockey, baffled many observers because he seemed to reverse the normal laws of hockey. Most great of-fensive players prefer to keep the rest of the action on the ice behind them—to try to make the act of scoring be just about themselves and the goalie. Gretzky liked to keep the action in front of him. He would set up by the side of the rink, or behind the oppos-ing team's net, so that the eleven other players on the ice were in full view, and then slide the perfect pass to the perfect spot. He made hockey look easy, even as he was playing in a way that made it more complicated. Gzowski says that Gretzky could do that because, like master chess players, he wasn't seeing all eleven other players individually; he was seeing only chunks. Here is Gzowski's conclusion after talking to Gretzky about a game he once played against the Montreal Canadians. It could as easily serve as an explana-tion for Charlie Wilson's twenty-five-minute transsphenoidal resection:

> What Gretzky perceives on a hockey rink is, in a curious way, more simple
> than what a less accomplished player perceives. He sees not so much a set of
> moving players as a number of situations. . . . Moving in on the Montreal
> blueline, as he was able to recall while he watched a videotape of himself, he
> was aware of the position of all the other players on the ice. The pattern they
> formed was, to him, one fact, and he reacted to that fact. When he sends a pass
> to what to the rest of us appears an empty space on the ice, and when a team-
> mate magically appears in that space to collect the puck, he has in reality
> simply summoned up from his bank account of knowledge the fact that in a
> particular situation, someone is likely to be in a particular spot, and if he is
> not there now he will be there presently.

. . . "A good [tennis] player knows where the ball is going," [Charlie] Wilson says. "He anticipates it. He is there. I just wasn't." What Wilson is describing is a failure not of skill or of resolve but of the least understood element of physical genius—imagina-tion. For some reason, he could not make the game come alive in his mind.

When psychologists study people who are expert at motor tasks, they find that al-most all of them use their imaginations in a very particular and sophisticated way. Jack Nicklaus, for instance, has said that he has never taken a swing that he didn't first mentally rehearse, frame by frame. Yo-Yo Ma told me that he remembers riding on a bus, at the age of seven, and solving a difficult musical problem by visualizing himself playing the piece on the cello. Robert Spetzler, who trained with Wilson and is widely considered to be the heir to Wilson's mantle, says that when he gets into uncharted territory in an operation he feels himself transferring his mental image of what ought to happen onto the surgical field. Charlie Wilson talks about going running in the morning and reviewing each of the day's operations in his head—visualizing the entire procedure and each potential outcome in advance. "It was a virtual rehearsal," he says, "so when I was actually doing the operation, it was as if I were doing it for the second time." Once, he says, he had finished a case and taken off his gloves and was walking down the hall away from the operating room when he suddenly stopped, because he realized that the tape he had been playing in his head didn't match the operation that had unfolded before his eyes. "I was correlating everything—what I saw, what I expected, what the X-rays said. And I just realized that I had not pursued one particular thing. So I turned around, scrubbed, and went back in, and, sure enough, there was a little remnant of tumor that was just around the corner. It would have been a disaster."

The Harvard University psychologist Stephen Kosslyn has shown that this power 20 to visualize consists of at least four separate abilities, working in combination. The first is the ability to generate an image—to take something out of long-term memory and reconstruct it on demand. The second is what he calls "image inspection," which is the ability to take that mental picture and draw inferences from it. The third is "image maintenance," the ability to hold that picture steady. And the fourth is "image transformation," which is the ability to take that image and manipulate it. If I asked you whether a frog had a tail, for example, you would summon up a picture of a frog from your long-term memory (image generation), hold it steady in your mind (image maintenance), rotate the frog around until you see his backside (image transformation), and then look to see if there was a tail there (image inspection). These four abilities are highly variable. Kosslyn once gave a group of people a list of thirteen tasks, each designed to test a different aspect of visualization, and the results were all over the map. You could be very good at generation and maintenance, for example, without being good at transformation, or you could be good at transformation without necessarily being adept at inspection and maintenance. Some of the correlations, in fact, were negative, meaning that sometimes being good at one of those four things meant that you were likely to be bad at another. Bennett Stein, a former chairman of neurosurgery at Columbia Presbyterian Center, says that one of the reasons some neurosurgery residents fail in their training is that they are incapable of making the transition between the way a particular problem is depicted in an X-ray or an M.R.I., and how the problem looks when they encounter it in real life. These are people whose capacities for mental imaging simply do not match what's required for dealing with the complexities of brain surgery. Perhaps these people can generate an image but are unable to transform it in precisely the way that is necessary to be a great surgeon; or perhaps they can transform the image but they cannot maintain it. . . .

"Certain aneurysms at the base of the brain are surrounded by very important blood vessels and nerves, and the typical neurosurgeon will make that dissection with a set of microinstruments that are curved, each with a blunt end," Craig Yorke, who trained with Wilson and now practices neurosurgery in Topeka, recalls. "The neurosurgeon will sneak up on them. Charlie would call for a No. 11 blade, which is a thin, very low-profile scalpel, and would just cut down to where the aneurysm was. He would be there in a quarter of the time." The speed and the audacity of Wilson's maneuvers, Yorke said, would sometimes leave him breathless. "Do you know about Gestalt psychology?" he continued. "If I look at a particular field—tumor or aneurysm— I will see the gestalt after I've worked on it for a little while. He would just glance at it and see it. It's a conceptual, a spatial thing. His use of the No. 11 blade depended on his ability to construct a gestalt of the surgical field first. If just anybody had held up the eleven blade in that way it might have been a catastrophe. He could do it because he had the picture of the whole anatomy in his head when he picked up the instrument."

If you think of physical genius as a pyramid, with, at the bottom, the raw components of coördination, and, above that, the practice that perfects those particular movements, then this faculty of imagination is the top layer. This is what separates the physical genius from those who are merely very good. Michael Jordan and Karl Malone, his longtime rival, did not differ so much in their athletic ability or in how obsessively they practiced. The difference between them is that Jordan could always generate a million different scenarios by which his team could win, some of which were chunks stored in long-term memory, others of which were flights of fancy that came to him, figuratively and literally, in midair. Jordan twice won championships in the face of unexpected adversity: once, a case of the flu, and, the second time, a back injury to his teammate Scottie Pippen, and he seemed to thrive on these obstacles, in a way Karl Malone never could.

Yo-Yo Ma says that only once, early in his career, did he try for a technically perfect performance. "I was seventeen," he told me. "I spent a year working on it. I was playing a Brahms sonata at the 92nd Street Y. I remember working really hard at it, and in the middle of the performance I thought, I'm bored. It would have been nothing for me to get up from the stage and walk away. That's when I decided I would always opt for expression over perfection." It isn't that Ma doesn't achieve perfection; it's that he finds striving for perfection to be banal. He says that he sometimes welcomes it when he breaks a string, because that is precisely the kind of thing (like illness or an injury to a teammate) that you cannot prepare for—that you haven't chunked and, like some robot, stored neatly in long-term memory. The most successful performers improvise. They create, in Ma's words, "something living." Ma says he spends ninety per cent of his time "looking at the score, figuring it out—who's saying this, who wrote this and why," letting his mind wander, and only ten per cent on the instrument itself. Like Jordan, his genius originates principally in his imagination. If he spent less time dreaming and more time playing, he would be Karl Malone.

Here is the source of the physical genius's motivation. After all, what is this sensation—this feeling of having what you do fit perfectly into the dimensions of your imagination—but the purest form of pleasure? Tony Gwynn and Wayne Gretzky and Charlie Wilson and all the other physical geniuses are driven to greatness because they have found something so compelling that they cannot put it aside. Perhaps this explains why a great many top neurosurgeons are also highly musical. . . .Wilson . . . is a cellist and, when he was a student in New Orleans, he would play jazz piano at Pat O'Brien's, in the French Quarter. Music is one of the few vocations that offer a kind of sensory and cognitive immersion similar to surgery: the engagement of hand and eye, the challenge of sustained performance, the combination of mind and motion—all of it animated by the full force of the imagination.

Once, in an E-mail describing his special training sessions on rats, Wilson wrote 25 that he worked on them for two years and "then trailed off when I finally figured that

I was doing it for fun, not for practice." For fun! When someone chooses to end a twelve-hour day alone in a laboratory, inducing aneurysms in the arteries of rats, we might call that behavior obsessive. But that is an uncharitable word. A better explanation is that, for some mysterious and wonderful reason, Wilson finds the act of surgery irresistible, in the way that musicians find pleasure in the sounds they produce on their instruments, or in the way Tony Gwynn gets a thrill every time he strokes a ball cleanly through the infield. Before he was two years old, it is said, Wayne Gretzky watched hockey games on television, enraptured, and slid his stockinged feet on the linoleum in imitation of the players, then cried when the game was over, because he could not understand how something so sublime should have to come to an end. This was long before Gretzky was any good at the game itself, or was skilled in any of its aspects, or could create even the smallest of chunks. But what he had was what the physical genius must have before any of the other layers of expertise fall into place: he had stumbled onto the one thing that, on some profound aesthetic level, made him happy. . . .

CONNECTING PERSONALLY TO THE READING

1. Have you had any unpleasant or neutral jobs that require mostly motor abilities? Did you find that attitude and/or imagination could transform such a job? How might attitude and/or imagination have helped you improve your coordination and perhaps your pleasure in the job?

2. Think of a job that you enjoyed. What did it call from you (preparation? attitude? vision?) that made you feel good about the work?

3. Gladwell recounts sociologist Charles Bosk's work on what makes some neurosurgeons successful whereas others fail: "a practical-minded obsession with the possibility and the consequences of failure." Describe an activity you or someone you know does well because of a similar obsession. What kinds of "possibilities and consequences of failure" are important to keep in mind for this job?

4. Wayne Gretzky, according to Peter Gyowski, could "chunk," or see clusters of hockey moves in one mental image. Have you ever had such an experience? Describe the closest thing to such "chunking" that you have experienced.

FOCUSING ON THE ARGUMENT

1. Where does Gladwell use vivid description to most heighten his credibility? What do you find particularly effective about these descriptions?

2. Gladwell makes an analogy between the fluid movements of a neurosurgeon and the fluid movements of professional sports players. Do you think this analogy furthers Gladwell's argument? Explain.

3. Gladwell discusses not only the physical skill of a neurosurgeon but also that of a musician and great athletes. How does it help his argument to accumulate examples of different kinds of professions?

1. Gladwell emphasizes the importance of visualization. In his Christmas job as a Photo Elf for Santa Claus, in "SantaLand Diaries" (p. 303), David Sedaris visualizes the motives of those coming to visit Santa. How is Sedaris's visualization similar to and different from the visualization that Gladwell discusses?

2. Both bell hooks in "Work Makes Life Sweet" (p. 285) and Gladwell describe what they think makes people like their work. How do their ideas differ? Are there any similarities? Explain.

3. In Chapter 6, Ian Frazier ("Terminal Ice," p. 408) and Jane Goodall (selection from *In the Shadow of Man,* p. 402) demonstrate the expertise needed for their scientific work. Do you think their notions of expertise reflect Gladwell's ideas of decision making, anticipation, preparation, and visualization? Explain.

4. Do you think that Gladwell's ideas of physical genius (especially preparation, attitude, and vision) help explain what makes a great dancer, as described by Martha Graham in "Blood Memory" (Chapter 8, p. 591)? Explain.

1. We all know that teachers, parents, coaches, and employers like to stress practice (doing math problems, writing a memo, passing the ball, etc). Gladwell, citing Bosk, offers a rationale that goes beyond the traditional "practice makes perfect." Bosk notes that skilled practitioners practice because they have "the ability to rethink everything that they'd done and imagine how they might have done it differently." Write a letter to a parent, coach, or teacher explaining how this view of practice could help you or others better perform a job or activity.

2. According to Gladwell, Gretzky "stumbled onto the one thing that, on some profound aesthetic level, made him happy." In an opinion/editorial, write about whether you think that corporate America is helping or hindering young people "stumble onto something" that will make them happy, and explain your views.

MIKE ROSE In the previous reading, "The Physical Genius," Malcolm Gladwell discusses the feeling of "flow" experienced by celebrated physical geniuses. In the reading that follows, Rose depicts "flow" as part of the everyday rush experience of a waitress, juggling multiple tasks and demands, yet occupying what has been called "the least skilled lower class occupations." Rose is impressed with the number and kinds of decisions waitresses make on the fly and with the cognitive, social, and physical skills needed, including balance, economy of motion, memory, vigilance, organization, and social interaction. What do you think are the competing demands a waitress faces with every move? Who besides the customer makes these demands? How might physical, social, and cognitive skills be necessary to keep the work going smoothly, increase revenues for the restaurant, and provoke the highest tips?

ROSE, a former public school teacher, is currently professor of social research methodology at the UCLA Graduate School of Education and Information Studies. He is the author of numerous articles and essays, and his books include *Possible Lives: The Promise of Public Education in America* and the award-winning *Lives on the Boundary* (from which "Epilogue: Lilia," a reading in Chapter 4 of this text, is excerpted.)

The Working Life of a Waitress (2004) | BY MIKE ROSE

Several years ago, I sat down at my mother's kitchen table with a tape recorder and began a series of interviews with her about her work. . . .

I was particularly curious about the thinking involved in doing a waitress's work well. How did she remember all those orders? How did she organize the many tasks that emerged minute by minute? How did she decide what to do first? How, in fact, did she learn how to do these things? As we talked, she would use the kitchen table, cluttered with pill bottles and letters, as an imaginary four-top. She and I would sketch out the floor plan or counter space of Norm's or of Coffee Dan's. She would get up, steadying herself on the back of my chair, and demonstrate how she placed all those plates along her arm. Her memory for the particulars appeared sharp, and her demonstrations were precise. . . .

Consider the restaurant in terms of multiple streams of time and motion. Customers enter with expectations: they will be seated without much delay and, once seated, a series of events will unfold along a familiar time line, from ordering through salad, entrée, dessert, delivery of the check. Their satisfaction—physical and emotional—is affected by the manner in which these expectations are met. But customers are entering the restaurant at different times, each with his or her own schedule, so tables (or places at the counter) proceed through meals at different paces. This staggering of customers facilitates the flow of trade but also increases the cognitive demands on the waitress: what she must attend to, keep in mind, prioritize. This situation intensifies during peak hours, for the number of customers expected can be estimated, but not known—coffee shops and family-style restaurants typically do not take reservations. If the numbers swell beyond capacity or an employee calls in sick or is late or quits, then, as the younger waitresses I interviewed vividly put it, you're "slammed," abruptly pushed to the limits of physical and mental performance.

Another timetable kicks in as soon as an order is placed with the cook. Different items have different prep times, and once the item is prepared, there is a limited amount of time—pretty restricted for hot items—during which it can be served. As well, the serving area needs to be cleared quickly so that the cook can deliver further items. The waitress, therefore, is aware of the kitchen as she moves among her customers.

Both waitress and management work by the clock. Profit is related to time; the quicker the turnover, the more revenue for the owner—and the greater the number of tips. There can be exceptions to this principle for the waitress—but not the management—for example, the regulars who may hold a table or stool longer but tip more. Still, generally, the waitress, like her manager, is ever mindful of clearing a plate, closing out a tab, moving the process along.   5

Imagine these streams of time and motion as co-occurring and related but not synchronous. Any given customer may hem and haw over an order, or want a refill while the waitress is occupied, or send an item back. The cook may deliver a waitress's hot dish while she is in the middle of taking an order and is being summoned by two other customers. Tables may be filled with variously contented customers while the manager feels the press of new customers gathering inside the door.

Once more observation about this environment. No matter how efficiently designed the physical layout of the restaurant—let's say that coffeepots, water, soft drinks, cups, glasses, and ice are all located in the same area—the waitress's motion will be punctuated by the continual but irregular demands made of her. For example, all requests for coffee do not come at the same time or in regular intervals. So one request comes during an order, and another as she's rushing back to get extra mayonnaise, and another as she's clearing a table. The waitress must learn how to move efficiently through a vibrant environment that, for all its structural regularities, is dynamically irregular. A basic goal, then, is to manage irregularity and create an economy of movement. And she does this through effective use of body and mind. The work calls for strength and stamina; for memory capacity and strategy; for heightened attention, both to overall layout and to specific areas and items; for the ability to take stock, prioritize tasks, cluster them, and make decisions on the fly. I'll consider each of these qualities in further detail, beginning with physical prowess.

What bodily skill does a waitress need? She must be able to balance and carry multiple items, using the hand, forearm, and biceps, creating stability by locking arms to torso and positioning the back. Then she moves, fast, in bursts, navigating tables, customers, other help. And since this occurs in a public space, it must be done with a certain poise. As waitress and writer Lin Rolens nicely puts it: "You learn a walk that gets you places quickly without looking like you are running. . . . This requires developing a walk that is all business from the waist down, but looks fairly relaxed from the waist up." With time and practice, all this becomes routine, automatic. But early in a career, the waitress will undoubtedly be conscious of various aspects of this physical performance, have to think about it, monitor herself. . . .

I ask her, then, how she learned to do it. Beginning with her own restaurant, "you watch the other waitresses, what they do." She was "cautious" at first, starting with two plates, being deliberate. Then she began adding plates, responding to the demands of the faster pace of the restaurants in Los Angeles. "Norm's was much busier. So you had to stack as many plates as you possibly could." And, with continued practice in these busy settings, you get to where "you don't even have to think about it." I'm struck by the similarity between my mother's description and the studies I've read on the role of cognition in the development of athletic skill. My mother mixed observation and practice, got some pointers from coworkers, tricks of the trade, monitored her performance, and developed competence. As she achieved mastery, her mind was cleared for other tasks—such as remembering orders.

To be a good waitress, my mother says emphatically, "you have to have one hell of a good memory." Her observation is supported by a small body of psychological research demonstrating that the competent waiter and waitress have techniques that enable them to override the normal limits on human "short-term" or "working" memory. Though there are some differences in the results of the studies, they point to four commonalities: The waiter and waitress know things about food and drink—ingredients, appearance, typical combinations—and this knowledge from "long-term" memory plays continually into their ability to remember orders. Furthermore, they have developed various visual, spatial, and linguistic techniques to aid memory: abbreviating

10

items, grouping them in categories, repeating orders, utilizing customer appearance and location. The routines and physical layout of the restaurant also contribute to remembering orders. And, finally, though not strictly a characteristic of memory—as defined and studied in the psychologist's laboratory—the waiter's and waitress's memory is profoundly goal-directed: to make their work efficient and to enhance their tips. My mother attests to each of these elements.

As she stood before a table, taking orders, sometimes repeating them back while writing them out, sometimes not, making small talk, my mother would "more or less make a picture in my mind" of the person giving her the order, what that person ordered, and where around a table (or at a counter) he or she was located. Though, surely, there was variation in the way my mother did this, her picture could include dress and physical appearance: items of clothing—a red blouse, a splashy tie—and physical features like a birthmark or an unusually shaped nose. Broad social markers such as gender, race, age, body type, and weight also aided in memorization. ("Of course, a child's plate, you can always tell" where that will go, my mother laughingly notes.) My mother's beliefs and biases about these markers could play into the construction of the picture. . . .

Sometimes, it's a social expectation that is salient and an aid to memory. For example, cocktail waitresses make distinctions between the drinks men and women typically order, and other waitresses I interviewed spoke of these gender distinctions as well. My mother describes a couple ordering. The man orders a T-bone steak, and the woman "would order something smaller, so naturally you're gonna remember that." And if an order violates expectation—the woman orders the steak, the man a chef's salad—that will stand out, the memorable deviation. . . .

Finally, a customer's attitude, the way he or she interacts with the waitress, contributes to her recall of the order. My mother comments on "how a customer would say something—you remember this dish is on the second table because so and so acted this way." She especially notes if "somebody is giving me a rough time." Of course, a particularly abrasive customer would stick in one's mind, but this raises an interesting broader issue: the way one's personal history and social position, the *feelings* related to these, play into cognition on the job.

One of the things that strikes me about my mother's report is the number of techniques it contains, the mix of strategies and processes: imagistic, spatial, verbal, and the role of emotion. Such complexity seems necessary when one is hurriedly tending to seven to nine tables, with two to six people at each. As my mother puts it: "Even though you're very busy, you're *extremely* busy . . . you're still, in your mind, you have a picture . . . you use all these [strategies], and one thing triggers something else." The strategies are interactive and complementary, and they enable us to get a sense of how much and what kind of work is going on in the working memory of a waitress during peak hours in a family-style restaurant.

Remembering an array of orders, then, takes place in a rush of activity that demands   15
attention to the environment, organizing and sequencing tasks that emerge in the stream of that activity, and occasional problem solving on the fly. My mother's interviews contain more than ten references to the pace and conflicting demands of waitressing. She describes a setting where an obnoxious regular is tapping the side of his coffee cup with a spoon while she is taking an order. The cook rings her bell indicating

another order is ready, and a few seconds later the manager seats two new parties at two of her tables that have just cleared. And, oh, as she is rushing back to the kitchen, one customer asks to modify an order, another signals for more coffee, and a third requests a new fork to replace one dropped on the floor. "Your mind is going so fast," she says, "thinking what to do first, where to go first . . . which is the best thing to do . . . which is the quickest." She is describing multiple demands on cognition—and the challenge is not a purely cognitive one.

There is a powerful affective component to all this, one with economic consequences. The requests made of the waitress have emotional weight to them. Customers get grumpy, dissatisfied if they have to wait too long or if their request is bungled or forgotten. The relationship with the cook is fraught with tension—orders need to be picked up quickly and returns handled diplomatically—and the manager is continually urging the movement of customers through a waitress's station. As my mother puts it, you attend to your orders or "the cook will yell at you"; you try to get customers their checks quickly, "because you'll get hell from the manager." The waitress's assessment of the emotional—blended with the economic—consequences of her decisions and actions plays back into the way she thinks through the demands of the moment.

One more thing. Depending on the restaurant, the flow of work can be facilitated (or impeded) by the arrangements and negotiations, mostly informal, made among the waitresses themselves and among the waitresses and those who bus the tables. These negotiations involve, at the least, the clearing of plates and glassware, assisting each other at rush hour, compensating for absent staff, and transitioning between shifts.

What do we know about the cognitive processes the waitress uses to bring some control to these multiple and conflicting demands? A good place to begin is with the psychological research on attention.

Attention is described in terms of its selectivity, a focusing on particular aspects of the environment; of the sustaining of that selective focus, a concentration as well as a vigilance for similar anticipated events or objects; and of the ability to control and coordinate the focus. In expert performance, these processes may become more refined and automatic. As one researcher puts it, attention serves "the purpose of allowing for and maintaining goal-directed behavior in the face of multiple, competing distractions."

There are periods in the waitress's day, lulls in activity, when she can stop and 20
survey her station. My mother talks about a pause, standing back where she can "keep an eye on the register and all the way down the counter." But often the waitress is attending to things while on the move. Every waitress I interviewed commented on the necessity of attending in transit to requests, empty cups, plates moved to the edge of the table. As one waitress explained: "As you walk, every time you cross the restaurant, you're never doing just a single task. You're always looking at the big picture and picking up things along the way." . . .

. . . A waitress could attend to all [these demands] and know what it means, and yet not know what to do next. How does she decide what her next move should be? . . .

. . . She organizes tasks by type or location. She combines tasks in ways that greatly economize movement, that make activity, in my mother's words, "smooth." As one waitress puts it, she is always asking "which pieces of what I need to do fit together best." Though some prioritizing of tasks—guided by rules of thumb—does occur, the more common move (noted as a mark of experience by several of the waitresses) is to quickly see what tasks can be grouped and executed with least effort.

. . . [R]estaurant routines aid in this organizing of tasks. My mother and the other waitresses I interviewed all refer in some way to a circuit through one's station that is watchful and that takes advantage of the restaurant's physical layout. As one waitress explains it:

> I always think of it as kind of a circle, because there's the tables, there's the bar, there's the coffee station, and it kind of becomes a flow of organizing what can be in one full circle, how many tasks can be accomplished, as opposed to back and forth, back and forth. I think the waitresses who get going back and forth are the ones who get crazy with four tables.

This description resonates with the earlier discussion of attention—the blend of anticipation, vigilance, and motor skill—but in a way that underscores the dynamic interaction of the waitress's ability and the structure and conventions of the restaurant.

Perhaps the thing that most impressed me in all this—and it emerged in every interview—is the claim the waitresses made that they work best when the restaurant is busy. On the face of it, this doesn't make sense. I would imagine that one could remember three or four orders with more accuracy than six or seven, that one could handle refills easier with a half-full station. These numbers would result in a more relaxed pace but, the waitresses claim, not in more skillful performance. In fact, my mother insists she could never have developed her level of skill in slower restaurants. "You're not as alert . . . not thinking that quick"; you're not anticipating orders; "you're making a couple of trips" rather than a single efficient one. "In a slow place, you think slower." One waitress notes the feeling of working "like a well-oiled machine" during rush hour. Another says that "when it gets the craziest, that's when I turn on. I'm even better than when it's dead."

. . . [I]t is telling how my mother and the other waitresses all comment on the satisfaction that they feel when they perform well under stress. Several use language similar to that of the currently celebrated "flow" experience, felt during those times when a person responds successfully to significant challenges from the environment. "There's a sense of accomplishment in just the mechanics of it," says one waitress, "just knowing that . . . I'm handling it all." 25

Remembering orders, being vigilant, and regulating the flow of work all play out in an emotional field. . . .

The service encounter provides the tips that enable the waitress to make a living, but in concert with the financial need, other needs of hers, depending on the waitress, can be met as well. Some waitresses gain satisfaction from contributing to a customer's enjoyment: "You supply nurturing and sustenance, the things that make life pleasurable." Some respond to the hustle and stimulation of a busy restaurant, the sense of being in the middle of things. (This was a big one for my mother, and its loss has been difficult for her.) Some like the attention ("the spotlight's on you") and the safe flirtation. Some comment on the pleasure of the brief human interaction: "Though we'll never get to know each other, there's a really nice feeling that goes back and forth." Some waitresses comment on the feeling of independence the job affords;

anthropologist Paules characterizes the waitress as a private entrepreneur. And some gain satisfaction from the display of their skill ("I get to show off my memory") and, as we saw, gain a feeling of competence by performing the job well. . . .

Waitressing enabled my mother "to be among the public." This phrase carried a certain pride for her, as it reflected a social facility that the once-shy girl had to develop. The work provided the opportunity for a low-responsibility social exchange— "I like that part. I like to be with people, associated with people"—that must have been pleasant for someone with so many cares at home. (This casual sociability has traditionally been more afforded to male occupational roles.) To be among the public was also a sign of attainment: it was not the kind of solitary labor she had known as a girl, and it brought her into contact with a range of people whose occupations she admired. There's paradox here, but the logic goes like this: yes, you are serving the doctor or the businessman, but it's your ability that makes everything work right; you are instrumental in creating their satisfaction. As she is fond of saying, not everyone can do that. . . .

And the restaurant provided a context for other kinds of learning. Educational researchers are increasingly studying learning in nonschool settings—workplace programs, social and civic clubs—but still very much unexplored is the learning that occurs in everyday, informal social exchange. Given the restrictions of my mother's formal education, her personal predilections (she did not, for example, read for pleasure), and all the demands on her life, she had limited time and means to gain information and learn new things. Yet, to this day, she possesses an alert curiosity. The educational medium available to her was the exchange with her customers, regulars particularly. ("How else can I learn about people?" asks Dolores Dante, the waitress Studs Terkel interviewed for *Working*. "How else does the world come to me?") Through the waitress-customer interaction, she acquired knowledge about a range of everyday activities—gardening, cooking, home remedies—and, as well, fed a curiosity that my mother had for as long as I can remember for topics related to medicine, psychology, and human relations: "There isn't a day that goes by in the restaurant that you don't learn something." Some of what she learned was a fact or a procedure (for example, on planting roses), and some was more experiential and relational. The restaurant became a kind of informal laboratory for her to observe behavior and think through questions of human motivation. This aspect of waitressing engaged her; "you learn a lot, and it interests me." . . .

CONNECTING PERSONALLY TO THE READING

1. Have you or a friend ever held a low-paying job that required extensive mental and physical skill? If so, what skills do you think were involved? Why do you think that they go unrewarded?

2. Describe the daily tasks of a parent or guardian. What is a typical day like? What choices and priorities does that person make in order to advance the flow of work and keep a certain flow going?

3. From your own experience, what satisfactions are gained by being in the world, relating to customers, and making things work right? Why do you think so?

1. Rose interweaves a report of his mother's experience, quotations from interviews, and summaries from the literature on work and waitressing to meld together a story about the cognitive, social, and physical skills that waitresses display. How do such varied strategies increase the credibility of Rose's views?

2. Rose lets the reader know many intimate details about his life. We see the kitchen table where he interviewed his mother, the pills that reflect her ill health, the images of her carrying plates at Coffee Dan's. How does this window into his personal life—the telling details and the personal testimony—create a bond between reader and writer?

3. Rose invites the reader to "consider" or to "imagine" analogous ways of interpreting scenes. ("Imagine these streams of time and motion as co-occurring and related but not synchronous"; "Consider the restaurant in terms of multiple streams of time and motion.") How do such analogies help the reader visualize everyday occurrences in the restaurant as high-level cognitive activities?

4. What kind of tone does Rose use? Do you think it is effective? Why or why not?

1. Gary Soto ("Black Hair," p. 296) and Barbara Ehrenreich ("Nickel and Dimed," p. 322), also describing low-paying jobs, detail the automatic, high-energy movements of their jobs. Based on details in the readings, what kind of cognitive skills do these jobs require? How are these skills similar to and/or different from those required of a waitress?

2. Both Malcolm Gladwell ("The Physical Genius," p. 268) and Rose break down the skills needed to perform a job at an "expert" level. How are their views similar? How are they different?

3. In "Voices from the Workplace" (p. 328), individuals describe what their jobs are like. Choose one job that interests you and describe what you think are the cognitive skills involved. These might include memory, attention, visualization, or any of the other skills Rose mentions.

4. Like Rose, bell hooks ("Work Makes Life Sweet," p. 285) believes in the integrity of low-paying jobs. In what ways is her perspective different from and/or similar to Rose's views?

5. Rose identifies the cognitive skills of waitressing. What cognitive skills do we see in the work of Jane Goodall from *In the Shadow of Man* (Chapter 6, p. 402)—especially memory, vigilance, organization, and social interaction—as she observes and records the behaviors of chimpanzees?

1. Like Rose, interview a parent, grandparent or guardian about the daily events, environment, skills, and job pressures of the work he or she performed. What were the physical skills needed? What cognitive skills? What social skills? Discuss what changes the interviewee would make preparing for his or her career. Write your findings as an article for a journal on working.

2. Using any writer in this chapter for support, write an argument that we need to reexamine what it means to become an "expert." What assumptions do people typically make about this word? How do the readings make us rethink its meaning? What implications would this reexamination have for our labor system? Submit your views to the editorial section of a journal on work.

BELL HOOKS   What is it that makes work sweet? According to bell hooks, most black women in the United States do not like their work, yet they grow up knowing that they will be workers. Black women lack choice, sense they have skills superior to the jobs available, and are denied satisfaction—all of which create job-related stress. In response, hooks advocates the concept of "right livelihood" based on the teachings of Buddha. She espouses "work consciously chosen, done with full awareness and care, and leading to enlightenment." What do these concepts mean to you? Why do you think they are particularly relevant to black women?

HOOKS (Gloria Watkins's pen name) is Distinguished Professor of English at City College in New York. As a critic and author, she has devoted much of her work to feminist and African American studies, but she also writes on topics of class, education, and the media. Her best-known scholarly books include *Ain't I a Woman: Black Women and Feminism* and *Talking Back: Thinking Feminist, Thinking Black*. She is also the author of the children's book *Happy to be Nappy*.

Work Makes Life Sweet (1993) | BY BELL HOOKS

"**W**ork makes life sweet!" I often heard this phrase growing up, mainly from old black folks who did not have jobs in the traditional sense of the word. They were usually self-employed, living off the land, selling fishing worms, picking up an odd job here and there. They were people who had a passion for work. They took pride in a job done well. My Aunt Margaret took in ironing. Folks brought her clothes from miles around because she was such an expert. That was in the days when using starch was common and she knew how to do an excellent job. Watching her iron with skill and grace was like watching a ballerina dance. Like all the other black girls raised in the fifties that I knew, it was clear to me that I would be a working woman. Even though our mother stayed home, raising her seven children, we saw her constantly at work, washing, ironing, cleaning, and cooking (she is an incredible cook). And she never allowed her six girls to imagine we would not be working women. No, she let us know that we would work and be proud to work.

The vast majority of black women in the United States know in girlhood that we will be workers. Despite sexist and racist stereotypes about black women living off welfare, most black women who receive welfare have been in the workforce. In *Hard Times Cotton Mill Girls*, one can read about black women who went to work in the cotton mills, usually leaving farm labor or domestic service. Katie Geneva Cannon remembers: "It was always assumed that we would work. Work was a given in life, almost like breathing and sleeping. I'm always surprised when I hear people talking about somebody taking care of them, because we always knew that we were going to work." Like older generations of southern black women, we were taught not only that we would be workers, but that there was no "shame" in doing any honest job. The black women around us who worked as maids, who stripped tobacco when it was the season, were accorded dignity and respect. We learned in our black churches and in our schools that it "was not what you did, but how you did it" that mattered.

A philosophy of work that emphasizes commitment to any task was useful to black people living in a racist society that for so many years made only certain jobs (usually service work or other labor deemed "undesirable") available to us. Just as many Buddhist traditions teach that any task becomes sacred when we do it mindfully and with care, southern black work traditions taught us the importance of working with integrity irrespective of the task. Yet these attitudes towards work did not blind anyone to the reality that racism made it difficult to work for white people. It took "gumption" to work with integrity in settings where white folks were disrespectful and downright hateful. And it was obvious to me as a child that the black people who were saying "work makes life sweet" were the folks who did not work for whites, who did what they wanted to do. For example, those who sold fishing worms were usually folks who loved to fish. Clearly there was a meaningful connection between positive thinking about work and those who did the work that they had chosen.

Most of us did not enter the workforce thinking of work in terms of finding a "calling" or a vocation. Instead, we thought of work as a way to make money. Many of us started our work lives early and we worked to acquire money to buy necessities. Some of us worked to buy school books or needed or desired clothing. Despite the emphasis on "right livelihood" that was present in our life growing up, my sisters and I were more inclined to think of work in relation to doing what you needed to do to get money to buy what you wanted. In general, we have had unsatisfying work lives. Ironically, Mama entered the paid workforce very late, after we were all raised, working for the school system and at times in domestic service, yet there are ways in which she has found work outside the home more rewarding than any of her children. The black women I talked with about work tended to see jobs primarily as a means to an end, as a way to make money to provide for material needs. Since so many working black women often have dependents, whether children or other relatives, they enter the workforce with the realistic conviction that they need to make money for survival purposes. This attitude coupled with the reality of a job market that remains deeply shaped by racism and sexism means that as black women we often end up working jobs that we do not like. Many of us feel that we do not have a lot of options. Of the women I interviewed, the ones who saw themselves as having options tended to have the highest levels of education. Yet nearly all the black women I spoke with agreed that they would always choose to work, even if they did not need to. It was only a very few young black females, teenagers and folks in their early twenties, who talked with me about fantasy lives where they would be taken care of by someone else.

Speaking with young black women who rely on welfare benefits to survive economically, I found that overall they wanted to work. However, they are acutely aware of the difference between a job and a fulfilling vocation. Most of them felt that it would not be a sign of progress for them to "get off welfare" and work low-paying jobs, in situations that could be stressful or dehumanizing. Individuals receiving welfare who are trying to develop skills, to attend school or college, often find that they are treated with much greater hostility by social-service workers than if they were just sitting at home watching television. One woman seeking assistance was told by an angry white woman worker, "welfare is not going to pay for you to get your B.A." This young woman had been making many personal sacrifices to try and develop skills and educational resources that would enable her to be gainfully employed and she was

5

constantly disappointed by the level of resentment toward her whenever she needed to deal with social services.

Through the years, in my own working life, I have noticed that many black women do not like or enjoy their work. The vast majority of women I talked to . . . agreed that they were not satisfied with their working lives even though they see themselves as performing well on the job. That is why I talk so much about work-related stress in [*Remembered Rapture*]. It is practically impossible to maintain a spirit of emotional well-being if one is daily doing work that is unsatisfying, that causes intense stress, and that gives little satisfaction. Again and again, I found that many black women I interviewed had far superior skills than the jobs they were performing called for but were held back because of their "lack of education," or in some cases, "necessary experience." This routinely prevented them from moving upward. While they performed their jobs well, they felt added tension generated in the work environment by supervisors who often saw them as "too uppity" or by their own struggle to maintain interest in their assigned tasks. One white woman administrator shared that the clearly overly skilled black woman who works as an administrative assistant in her office was resented by white male "bosses" who felt that she did not have the proper attitude of a "subordinate." When I spoke to this woman she acknowledged not liking her job, stating that her lack of education and the urgent need to raise children and send them to college had prevented her from working towards a chosen career. She holds to the dream that she will return to school and someday gain the necessary education that will give her access to the career she desires and deserves. Work is so often a source of pain and frustration.

Learning how to think about work and our job choices from the standpoint of "right livelihood" enhances black female well-being. Our self-recovery is fundamentally linked to experiencing that quality of "work that makes life sweet." In one of my favorite self-help books, Marsha Sinetar's *Do What You Love, the Money Will Follow*, the author defines right livelihood as a concept initially coming from the teachings of Buddha which emphasized "work consciously chosen, done with full awareness and care, and leading to enlightenment." This is an attitude toward work that our society does not promote, and it especially does not encourage black females to think of work in this way. As Sinetar notes:

> Right Livelihood, in both its ancient and its contemporary sense, embodies self-expression, commitment, mindfulness, and conscious choice. Finding and doing work of this sort is predicated upon high self-esteem and self-trust, since only those who like themselves, who subjectively feel they are trustworthy and deserving dare to choose on behalf of what is right and true for them. When the powerful quality of conscious choice is present in our work, we can be enormously productive. When we consciously choose to do work we enjoy, not only can we get things done, we can get them done well and be intrinsically rewarded for our effort.

Black women need to learn about "right livelihood." Even though I had been raised in a world where elderly black people had this wisdom, I was more socialized by the get-ahead generation that felt how much money you were making was more important than what you did to make that money. We have difficult choices ahead.

As black females collectively develop greater self-esteem, a greater sense of entitlement, we will learn from one another's example how to practice right livelihood. Of the black women I interviewed the individuals who enjoyed their work the most felt they were realizing a particular vocation or calling. C.J. (now almost forty) recalls that generations of her family were college-educated. She was taught to choose work that would be linked with the political desire to enhance the overall well-being of black people. C.J. says, "I went to college with a mission and a passion to have my work be about African-Americans. The spirit of mission came to me from my family, who taught us that you don't just work to get money, you work to create meaning for yourself and other people." With this philosophy as a guiding standpoint, she has always had a satisfying work life.

When one of my sisters, a welfare recipient, decided to return to college, I encouraged her to try and recall her childhood vocational dreams and to allow herself adult dreams, so that she would not be pushed into preparing for a job that holds no interest for her. Many of us must work hard to unlearn the socialization that teaches us that we should just be lucky to get any old job. We can begin to think about our work lives in terms of vocation and calling. One black woman I interviewed, who has worked as a housewife for many years, began to experience agoraphobia. Struggling to regain her emotional well-being, she saw a therapist, against the will of her family. In this therapeutic setting, she received affirmation for her desire to finish her undergraduate degree and continue in a graduate program. She found that finishing a master's and becoming a college teacher gave her enormous satisfaction. Yet this achievement was not fully appreciated by her husband. A worker in a factory, whose job is long and tedious, he was jealous of her newfound excitement about work. Since her work brings her in touch with the public, it yields rewards unlike any he can hope to receive from his job. Although she has encouraged him to go back to school (one of his unfulfilled goals), he is reluctant. Despite these relational tensions, she has found that "loving" her work has helped her attend to and transform previous feelings of low self-esteem.

A few of the black women I interviewed claimed to be doing work they liked but complained bitterly about their jobs, particularly where they must make decisions that affect the work lives of other people. One woman had been involved in a decisionmaking process that required her to take a stance that would leave another person jobless. Though many of her peers were proud of the way she handled this difficult decision, her response was to feel "victimized." Indeed, she kept referring to herself as "battered." This response troubled me for it seemed to bespeak a contradiction many women experience in positions of power. Though we may like the status of a power position and wielding power, we may still want to see ourselves as "victims" in the process, especially if we must act in ways that "good girls, dutiful daughters" have been taught are "bad."

I suggested to the women I interviewed that they had chosen particular careers that involved "playing hardball" yet they seemed to be undermining the value of their choices and the excellence of their work by complaining that they had to get their hands dirty and suffer some bruises. I shared with them my sense that if you choose to play hardball then you should be prepared for the bruises and not be devastated when they occur. In some ways it seemed to me these black women wanted to be "equals" in a man's world while they simultaneously wanted to be treated like fragile "ladies." Had

10

they been able to assume full responsibility for their career choices, they would have enjoyed their work more and been able to reward themselves for jobs well done. In some cases it seemed that the individuals were addicted to being martyrs. They wanted to control everything, to be the person "in power" but also resented the position. These individuals, like those I describe in the chapter on stress, seemed not to know when to set boundaries or that work duties could be shared. They frequently over-extended themselves. When we over-extend ourselves in work settings, pushing ourselves to the breaking point, we rarely feel positive about tasks even if we are performing them well.

Since many people rely on powerful black women in jobs (unwittingly turning us into "mammies" who will bear all the burdens—and there are certainly those among us who take pride in this role), we can easily become tragically over-extended. I noticed that a number of us (myself included) talk about starting off in careers that we really "loved" but over-working to the point of "burn-out" so that the pleasure we initially found dissipated. I remember finding a self-help book that listed twelve symptoms of "burn-out," encouraging readers to go down the list and check those that described their experience. At the end, it said, "If you checked three or more of these boxes, chances are you are probably suffering from burn-out." I found I had checked all twelve! That let me know it was time for a change. Yet changing was not easy. When you do something and you do it well, it is hard to take a break, or to confront the reality that I had to face, which was that I really didn't want to be doing the job I was doing even though I did it well. In retrospect it occurred to me that it takes a lot more energy to do a job well when you really do not want to be doing it. This work is often more tiring. And maybe that extra energy would be better spent in the search for one's true vocation or calling.

In my case, I have always wanted to be a writer. And even though I have become just that and I love this work, my obsessive fears about "not being poor" have made it difficult for me to take time away from my other career, teaching and lecturing, to "just write." Susan Jeffers' book, *Feel the Fear and Do It Anyway,* has helped me to finally reach the point in my life where I can take time to "just write." Like many black women who do not come from privileged class backgrounds, who do not have family we can rely on to help if the financial going gets rough (we in fact are usually the people who are relied on), it feels very frightening to think about letting go of financial security, even for a short time, to do work one loves but may not pay the bills. In my case, even though I had worked with a self-created financial program aimed at bringing me to a point in life when I could focus solely on writing, I still found it hard to take time away. It was then that I had to tap into my deep fears of ending up poor and counter them with messages that affirm my ability to take care of myself economically irrespective of the circumstance. These fears are not irrational (though certainly mine were a bit extreme). In the last few years, I have witnessed several family members go from working as professionals to unemployment and various degrees of homelessness. Their experiences highlighted the reality that it is risky to be without secure employment and yet they also indicated that one could survive, even start all over again if need be.

My sister V. quit a job that allowed her to use excellent skills because she had major conflicts with her immediate supervisor. She quit because the level of on-the-job stress had become hazardous to her mental well-being. She quit confident that she would find a job in a few months. When that did not happen, she was stunned. It had not occurred to her that she would find it practically impossible to find work in the area she most wanted to live in. Confronting racism, sexism, and a host of other unclear responses, months passed and she has not found another job. It has changed her whole life. While material survival has been difficult, she is learning more about what really matters to her in life. She is learning about "right livelihood." The grace and skill with which she has confronted her circumstance has been a wonderful example for me. With therapy, with the help of friends and loved ones, she is discovering the work she would really like to do and no longer feels the need to have a high-paying, high-status job. And she has learned more about what it means to take risks.

In *Do What You Love, the Money Will Follow,* Sinetar cautions those of us who have not been risk-takers to go slowly, to practice, to begin by taking small risks, and to plan carefully. Because I have planned carefully, I am able to finally take a year's leave from my teaching job without pay. During this time, I want to see if I enjoy working solely as a writer and if I can support myself. I want to see if (like those old-time black folks I talk about at the start of the essay) doing solely the work I feel most "called" to do will enhance my joy in living. For the past few months, I have been "just writing" and indeed, so far, I feel it is "work that makes life sweet." 15

The historical legacy of black women shows that we have worked hard, long, and well, yet rarely been paid what we deserve. We rarely get the recognition we deserve. However, even in the midst of domination, individual black women have found their calling, and do the work they are best suited for. Onnie Lee Logan, the Alabama midwife who tells her story in *Motherwit,* never went to high school or college, never made a lot of money in her working life, but listened to her inner voice and found her calling. Logan shares:

> I let God work the plan on my life and I am satisfied at what has happened to me in my life. The sun wasn't shinin' every time and moon wasn't either. I was in the snow and the rain at night by my lonely self. . . . There had been many dreary nights but I didn't look at em as dreary nights. I had my mind on where I was going and what I was going for.
>
> Whatever I've done, I've done as well as I could and beyond. . . . I'm satisfied at what has happened in my life. Perfectly satisfied at what my life has done for me. I was a good midwife. One of the best as they say. This book was the last thing I had planned to do until God said well done. I consider myself—in fact if I leave tomorrow—I've lived my life and I've lived it well.

The life stories of black women like Onnie Logan remind us that "right livelihood" can be found irrespective of our class position, or the level of our education.

To know the work we are "called" to do in this world, we must know ourselves. The practice of "right livelihood" invites us to become more fully aware of our reality, of the labor we do and of the way we do it. Now that I have chosen my writing more fully than at any other moment of my life, the work itself feels more joyous. I feel my whole being affirmed in the act of writing. As black women unlearn the conventional thinking about work—which views money and/or status as more important than the work we do or the way we feel about that work—we will find our way back to those moments celebrated by our ancestors, when work was a passion. We will know again that "work makes life sweet."

1. Do you know of anyone who has followed the advice, *Do What You Love, the Money Will Follow*? Did their experience bear out the advice? Explain.

2. What do you think it means to have a "calling"? Have you ever thought that you had one? If so, what is it and how did you recognize it?

3. What difficulties do you anticipate that black women face when they attempt to do what they love, irrespective of class position or level of education? What barriers to finding work that you love have you faced? How might you overcome them?

1. In this essay, bell hooks uses a wide array of evidence. She reports others' experiences (e.g., her Aunt Margaret who took in ironing). She quotes from published accounts of black women's work experiences. She summarizes broad social history, in particular southern black work traditions, to explain black women's traditional views of work. And she quotes from her extensive interviews with black women, as well as white employers, to expose the roots of black women's frustrations with work. Which of these forms of evidence do you find most compelling and why?

2. The writer's tone is not the bland tone of a neutral scientist collecting data but that of a passionate, conflicted black woman struggling to find her own "right livelihood." Do you think bell hooks's tone increases her credibility? Explain why or why not.

1. In "Nickel and Dimed" (p. 322), Barbara Ehrenreich describes work that employees clearly do not love. These employees understand that they are small pieces in a corporate plan whose bottom line is profit. What do you think that hooks would recommend that these employees do?

2. Gary Soto ("Black Hair," p. 296), David Sedaris ("SantaLand Diaries," p. 303), and hooks condemn the boredom of low-paying work. While the work they describe may not "make life sweet," their ability to think and write about such work may. Explain why writing about such work, for Soto, Sedaris, and hooks, may be different from doing the work itself.

3. Do any of the people in "Voices from the Workplace" (p. 328) seem to be doing what they love? Is the work "consciously chosen" and full of "care"? Explain.

4. Doing what you love is advice typically taken to heart by artists. In what ways do Rosanne Cash's and Martha Graham's writings ("The Ties That Bind," p. 586, and "Blood Memory," p. 591, respectively, Chapter 8) show the importance of "doing what you love"?

1. With several friends, create a proposal for your own self-help book on finding meaningful work for teenagers. What key advice would you offer? What do you think most teenagers need to understand about seeking a job?

2. Interview a number of friends who have held unpleasant summer jobs. Why did they choose these jobs? What did they do to make them bearable? Write up your results as a short study on what teenagers should seek and avoid in summer work.

DANIEL LEVINE   According to Levine, low-paying, entry-level jobs teach youth good work habits and self-respect. They do so by providing valuable work experience. While many would argue that such jobs undermine self-respect, Levine sees them as "an introduction to the real world," where one learns the values of punctuality, getting along with others, and presenting oneself well. What is your view of such jobs? Do they build character or degrade it? Are most low-paid jobs exploitative or do they reward effort and skill?

LEVINE is a senior editor in the Washington bureau of *Reader's Digest.* In the 1990s, he collected stories from a variety of people about their first experiences in the work world and published a series of articles called "My First Job." The essay that follows, written for the academic journal *Policy Review,* attempts to synthesize their experiences and, by doing so, dispel what he calls "liberal myths" about entry-level jobs.

Take This Job and Love It (1997) | BY DANIEL LEVINE

For more than 30 years, the federal government has been trying to figure out ways to get people to work. It spends billions of taxpayer dollars each year on job-training and placement programs with questionable results.

For the past six years I have written a series of articles for *Reader's Digest* titled "My First Job," in which successful people discuss the value of their early work experiences. Their jobs were not part of government-sponsored training or placement programs; they were simply low-level jobs earned through diligent effort. And what they learned in these jobs goes a long way toward dispelling several liberal myths about the workplace in general and entry-level jobs in particular.

MYTH #1: LOW-PAYING JOBS ARE A DEAD-END.
Roberto Suarez fled Cuba after Castro came to power and arrived in Miami with just $5 in his pocket and a small duffel bag of clothes. He doggedly pursued every job lead. When he heard about openings at "the Herald," he had no idea what it was, but he went there anyway and stood in line for hours, hoping to be called for temporary work. Eventually he was picked for a 10-hour night shift bundling newspapers. Leaving work at 5 a.m., he was told to come back in five hours if he wanted to work again. He returned every day; after three months he was given a regular five-day shift. Suarez went on to become president of the Miami Herald Publishing Co.

Nothing makes Herman Cain, the CEO of Godfather's Pizza, quite so angry as youngsters who refuse jobs or complain about them because they do not pay enough or because they consider the work beneath them. Cain held a number of early jobs including mowing lawns, washing dishes, and handling a jackhammer on a construction crew. He expresses a view shared by all those interviewed: "In every job I've held, I have learned something that helped me in my next job. If you look hard enough, you can learn from any job you do."

All their jobs were low-paying, but they were also among the most valuable and   5 enriching experiences of their lives. These jobs were their introduction to the real world. They were exposed, often for the first time, to some of the basic requirements necessary to succeed, such as arriving on time, working with others, being polite, and dressing presentably. Their first jobs also helped them develop a strong work ethic and character.

The lessons that New Jersey developer and trucking magnate Arthur E. Imperatore learned while working in a candy store at age 10 made such an impression on him that he can recall them today—more than 60 years later. One day while sweeping the store, he found 15 cents under a table and gave it to the owner. Imperatore was shocked when the owner admitted placing the coins there to see if he could be trusted. Imperatore went on to work for him for several years and learned a lasting lesson: "I've never forgotten that honesty is what kept me in that job."

Oklahoma congressman J. C. Watts was a dishwasher in a diner when he discovered that his hard work and professionalism were not going unnoticed. A local clothing store extended him a line of credit because the owner had heard he was diligent and trustworthy. Watts was just 12.

When Norman Augustine, the CEO of Lockheed-Martin Corp., worked on a roofing crew as a young man, he was responsible for spreading tar out of barrels. He learned to appreciate his work according to his own private standard of value: "Since it took two hours to spread a barrel and I earned $1.69 an hour, that came out to about $3.38 a barrel. A ball game was a half-barrel event, a date was a two-barrel affair, and the prom was a six-barrel night."

MYTH #2: LOW-PAYING JOBS DESTROY CONFIDENCE.

Author and former presidential speechwriter Peggy Noonan said the first time she felt truly self-assured was when she worked as a 14-year-old summer-camp counselor. Says Noonan, "That first job showed me I could be responsible and more than the class clown."

Jeane Kirkpatrick, a former U.S. ambassador to the United Nations, worked as a small-town newspaper reporter in Mount Vernon, Illinois, when she was 15. She says the job taught her "to be on time and meet deadlines. In return, I was treated with respect. It gave me an overwhelming sense of pride and taught me the fundamentals of professionalism."

10

Gordon M. Bethune, the chairman and CEO of Continental Airlines, worked for his father's small crop-dusting business in Mississippi when he was 15. Bethune was responsible for loading chemicals onto planes and helping guide them in for landings. He always knew that without his help, the business would not have been able to function effectively. Bethune and the others interviewed agreed that the confidence gained from these first jobs made it possible for them to master jobs of greater responsibility later on.

Other first jobs were equally unglamorous: Actress Patricia Richardson, star of the ABC sit-com *Home Improvement,* scrubbed bathroom floors and toilets in a hotel. Telecommunications executive John J. Sie worked on the assembly line of a stapler factory. Ivan Seidenberg, the chairman and CEO of NYNEX, was a janitor. Herman Cain expresses a sentiment shared by most of those interviewed: "My job was not glamorous or high-paying, but that didn't matter. It taught me that any job is a good job and that whatever I was paid was more than I had before."

MYTH #3: ENTRY-LEVEL EMPLOYEES NEED THE GUIDANCE ONLY JOB-TRAINING PROGRAMS CAN GIVE.

A parent's advice, encouragement, and love help a child develop the confidence necessary to tackle a first job much more effectively than any government program.

Jack Faris, the president and CEO of the National Federation of Independent Business, recalls his parents teaching him when he was 13 to budget his earnings from his first job as a gas-station attendant. Ten percent of whatever he earned went into a mason jar that he took to church every Sunday. Twenty percent was set aside for room and board (but his parents actually saved it for his college education). Another 20 percent went toward his own savings, and he was free to spend the remaining 50 percent on whatever he pleased.

Elaine L. Chao, a former president of the United Way of America, remembers her   15
father working three jobs and still making time to help her with homework in the evenings. When she took her first job, as a library assistant, she remembered the wise advice that motivated her to succeed. He once told her, "You have a responsibility to develop your God-given talents. America is a wonderful country where if you work hard, anything is possible."

Today show host Katie Couric worked as a counselor at a camp for blind children because her parents wanted her to learn the importance of helping those less fortunate.

Lt. General William G. Pagonis (Ret.), who directed the movement and supply of the allied troops during the Persian Gulf War, was six years old when he started shining shoes in his father's diner. By age 10, he was clearing tables and working as a janitor. One of his proudest moments came when his father told him he was the best "mop guy" he'd ever had. Says Pagonis, who now handles logistics for Sears, Roebuck and Co., "My father made it clear I had to meet certain standards. I had to be punctual, hard-working, and polite to the customers."

J. C. Watts recalls that his father, who worked three jobs, told his son at an early age, "If you understand sacrifice and commitment, there are not many things in life you can't have."

MYTH #4: EMPLOYERS LOOK FOR WAYS TO EXPLOIT THEIR LOW-PAID WORKERS.

Wendy's founder R. David Thomas worked in a diner and says he will never forget the owners, Greek immigrant brothers named Frank and George Regas. Says Thomas, "They taught me the importance of being polite and of praising people for a job well done. From them I learned that if you work hard and apply yourself, you succeed. It's really not that complicated."

Thomas applied many of the lessons from that first job to the successful restau-   20
rant chain he founded years later. After taking a chance on hiring Thomas, who was just a young boy, the owners exposed him to real-world experiences that affected the course of his life. Thomas considered the Regas brothers his role models. They never asked him or any other employee to do a job that they would not do themselves. This made a deep impression on Thomas and motivated him to adopt similar principles.

Those I interviewed said they still use the skills they learned in their first jobs and are forever grateful to the employers who hired them. Their employers made a point of watching and nurturing them while providing advice and personal guidance.

Country music star Shania Twain was 14 when she landed her first job at a McDonald's. The manager assigned her to work the cash register and provided encouragement when he noticed her strong work habits and polite manner. She was soon stationed at the drive-through window. Motivated by her manager's trust and encouragement, Twain strove to take on new responsibilities. She was eventually promoted to training new hires.

One of the best ways for young people to learn effective work habits is by watching employers practice them. This, combined with the practical experience of working, will enhance a young person's self-respect and teach important values. There is no more effective job-training program than experience and no better teacher than an employer who cares enough to help a young person develop a solid work ethic.

CONNECTING PERSONALLY TO THE READING

1. Have you ever had a low-paying job that you felt taught you valuable life lessons? If so, what was the job and how did it teach you these lessons?

2. What jobs have you held that taught you self-respect? Did they necessarily pay well? What were the key ingredients of each job that enabled you to gain self-respect?

3. Do you feel that the arguments against low-paying jobs, arguments that Levine calls "myths," are necessarily all fictions? What truths might they embody?

FOCUSING ON THE ARGUMENT

1. Levine's essay is a policy article that reflects a political slant, and he starts out by summing up the cost to taxpayers of the opposing position. Levine is against expensive, government-sponsored job-training programs and supports low-paying jobs as a way to learn valuable work lessons. How do his opening sentences establish a particular tone? Describe this tone and decide whether it helps or hinders his argument.

2. Levine attacks the "myths" that such low-paying jobs undermine one's self-confidence and fail to provide valuable guidance. How does his accumulation of examples, which includes reporting others' experiences, support or not support his case?

SYNTHESIZING IDEAS FROM MULTIPLE READINGS

1. In "Black Hair" (p. 296), Gary Soto does not indicate that he gained any self-respect from his temporary low-paying job at Valley Tire Factory. Do you think Levine would have thought he learned some valuable life lessons from this summer job? Explain.

2. In "The Working Life of a Waitress" (p. 278), Mike Rose's mother does not hold a temporary, entry-level job, but a life's vocation. How do Levine's attitudes and assumptions about low-paying work differ from those of Mike Rose, even though both discuss the value of such work?

3. In "Work Makes Life Sweet" (p. 285), bell hooks does not see the intrinsic value of work as teaching a person the "basic requirements necessary to succeed." She might think Levine's view is overly utilitarian. In contrast, how might he interpret her view? What differences do you see in their views? Explain.

4. Would Levine have thought that David Sedaris's Christmas job in "SantaLand Diaries" (p. 303) taught him such valuable lessons as "arriving on time, working with others, being polite, and dressing presentably"? Would he have had a similar or different view of the lessons learned by the Wal-Mart employees that Barbara Ehrenreich describes in "Nickel and Dimed" (p. 322)? Explain.

5. Several of the people in the section "Voices from the Workplace" (p. 328) describe some drudgery as part of the work they clearly love. What are some of the lessons from early jobs that might have helped prepare these people for the jobs they now hold?

WRITING TO ACT

1. Write a similar policy article arguing the opposite view, that only through government-sponsored job-training programs can we ensure that young people obtain the training they need to succeed. First, research what some of these job-training programs offer.

2. Interview a number of people you know who have been successful. Ask them about any low-paying entry-level jobs they held. What did they learn from these jobs? Try to come up with common themes and ideas. Using these themes, write a letter of response to Levine either supporting or refuting his views.

READING

GARY SOTO Gary Soto, a Mexican American, describes a summer job he took as a runaway, fixing and replacing used tires in a tire store. This is a job that seems to offer no possibility of advancement, dignity, or self-fulfillment. What qualifies a job as "dead-end"? Most of the coworkers Soto describes seem to hate the work and to be degraded by it. Soto finds it worse than the fieldwork chopping cotton and picking grapes he had done as a boy. Given the low salary, at first he can't get enough money together to rent an apartment, clean himself up, and get a night's rest. The permanent workers themselves seem to live personal lives that reflect the squalor of the job. Yet these men return to this work each day. Why do you think someone would come back to such work?

SOTO, who teaches writing at the University of California, Riverside, has lived in California for most of his life. A prolific essayist, poet, and fiction writer, he writes—largely for children and teens—about Mexican American life in and around Fresno; some of his most widely read books are *Baseball in April and Other Stories, Too Many Tamales,* and *Living Up the Street* (from which the following essay was taken). Soto's poetry is widely anthologized and has appeared in literary journals such as the *Iowa Review* and *Ploughshares.*

READING

Black Hair (1985) | BY GARY SOTO

There are two kinds of work: One uses the mind and the other uses muscle. As a kid I found out about the latter. I'm thinking of the summer of 1969 when I was a seventeen-year-old runaway who ended up in Glendale, California, to work for Valley Tire Factory. To answer an ad in the newspaper I walked miles in the afternoon sun, my stomach slowly knotting on a doughnut that was breakfast, my teeth like bright candles gone yellow.

I walked in the door sweating and feeling ugly because my hair was still stiff from a swim at the Santa Monica beach the day before. Jules, the accountant and part owner, looked droopily through his bifocals at my application and then at me. He tipped his cigar in the ashtray, asked my age as if he didn't believe I was seventeen, but finally after a moment of silence, said, "Come back tomorrow. Eight-thirty."

I thanked him, left the office, and went around to the chain link fence to watch the workers heave tires into a bin; others carted uneven stacks of tires on hand trucks. Their faces were black from tire dust and when they talked—or cussed—their mouths showed a bright pink.

From there I walked up a commercial street, past a cleaners, a motorcycle shop, and a gas station where I washed my face and hands; before leaving I took a bottle that hung on the side of the Coke machine, filled it with water, and stopped it with a scrap of paper and a rubber band.

The next morning I arrived early at work. The assistant foreman, a potbellied 5 Hungarian, showed me a timecard and how to punch in. He showed me the Coke machine, the locker room with its slimy shower, and also pointed out the places where I shouldn't go: The ovens where the tires were recapped and the customer service area, which had a slashed couch, a coffee table with greasy magazines, and an ashtray. He introduced me to Tully, a fat man with one ear, who worked the buffers that resurfaced the white walls. I was handed an apron and a face mask and shown how to use the buffer: Lift the tire and center, inflate it with a footpedal, press the buffer against the white band until cleaned, and then deflate and blow off the tire with an air hose.

With a paint brush he stirred a can of industrial preserver. "Then slap this blue stuff on." While he was talking a co-worker came up quietly from behind him and goosed him with the air hose. Tully jumped as if he had been struck by a bullet and then turned around cussing and cupping his genitals in his hands as the other worker walked away calling out foul names. When Tully turned to me smiling his gray teeth, I lifted my mouth into a smile because I wanted to get along. He has to be on my side, I thought. He's the one who'll tell the foreman how I'm doing.

I worked carefully that day, setting the tires on the machine as if they were babies, since it was easy to catch a finger in the rim that expanded to inflate the tire. At the day's end we swept up the tire dust and emptied the trash into bins.

At five the workers scattered for their cars and motorcycles while I crossed the street to wash at a burger stand. My hair was stiff with dust and my mouth showed pink against the backdrop of my dirty face. I then ordered a hotdog and walked slowly in the direction of the abandoned house where I had stayed the night before. I lay under the trees and within minutes was asleep. When I woke my shoulders were sore and my eyes burned when I squeezed the lids together.

From the backyard I walked dully through a residential street, and as evening came on, the TV glare in the living rooms and the headlights of passing cars showed against the blue drift of dusk. I saw two children coming up the street with snow cones, their tongues darting at the packed ice. I saw a boy with a peach and wanted to stop him, but felt embarrassed by my hunger. I walked for an hour only to return and discover the house lit brightly. Behind the fence I heard voices and saw a flashlight poking at the garage door. A man on the back steps mumbled something about the refrigerator to the one with the flashlight.

I waited for them to leave, but had the feeling they wouldn't because there was 10
the commotion of furniture being moved. Tired, even more desperate, I started walking again with a great urge to kick things and tear the day from my life. I felt weak and
my mind kept drifting because of hunger. I crossed the street to a gas station where I
sipped at the water fountain and searched the Coke machine for change. I started
walking again, first up a commercial street, then into a residential area where I lay
down on someone's lawn and replayed a scene at home—my Mother crying at the
kitchen table, my stepfather yelling with food in his mouth. They're cruel, I thought,
and warned myself that I should never forgive them. How could they do this to me.

When I got up from the lawn it was late. I searched out a place to sleep and found
an unlocked car that seemed safe. In the backseat, with my shoes off, I fell asleep but
woke up startled about four in the morning when the owner, a nurse on her way to
work, opened the door. She got in and was about to start the engine when I raised my
head up from the backseat to explain my presence. She screamed so loudly when I said
"I'm sorry" that I sprinted from the car with my shoes in hand. Her screams faded,
then stopped altogether, as I ran down the block where I hid behind a trash bin and
waited for a police siren to sound. Nothing. I crossed the street to a church where I
slept stiffly on cardboard in the balcony.

I woke up feeling tired and greasy. It was early and a few street lights were still lit,
the east growing pink with dawn. I washed myself from a garden hose and returned to
the church to break into what looked like a kitchen. Paper cups, plastic spoons, a coffee pot littered on a table. I found a box of Nabisco crackers which I ate until I was full.

At work I spent the morning at the buffer, but was then told to help Iggy, an old
Mexican, who was responsible for choosing tires that could be recapped without the
risk of exploding at high speeds. Every morning a truck would deliver used tires, and
after I unloaded them Iggy would step among the tires to inspect them for punctures
and rips on the side walls.

With a yellow chalk he marked circles and Xs to indicate damage and called out
"junk." For those tires that could be recapped, he said "goody" and I placed them on
my hand truck. When I had a stack of eight I kicked the truck at an angle and balanced
them to another work area where Iggy again inspected the tires, scratching Xs and
calling out "junk."

Iggy worked only until three in the afternoon, at which time he went to the locker 15
room to wash and shave and to dress in a two-piece suit. When he came out he glowed
with a bracelet, watch, rings, and a shiny fountain pen in his breast pocket. His shoes
sounded against the asphalt. He was the image of a banker stepping into sunlight with
millions on his mind. He said a few low words to workers with whom he was friendly
and none to people like me.

I was seventeen, stupid because I couldn't figure out the difference between an
F 78 14 and 750 14 at sight. Iggy shook his head when I brought him the wrong tires,
especially since I had expressed interest in being his understudy. "Mexican, how can
you be so stupid?" he would yell at me, slapping a tire from my hands. But within
weeks I learned a lot about tires, from sizes and makes to how they are molded in iron
forms to how Valley stole from other companies. Now and then we received a truck-
load of tires, most of them new or nearly new, and they were taken to our warehouse
in the back where the serial numbers were ground off with a sander. On those days the
foreman handed out Cokes and joked with us as we worked to get the numbers off.

Most of the workers were Mexican or black, though a few redneck whites worked there. The base pay was a dollar sixty-five, but the average was three dollars. Of the black workers, I knew Sugar Daddy the best. His body carried two hundred and fifty pounds, armfuls of scars, and a long knife that made me jump when he brought it out from his boot without warning. At one time he had been a singer, and had cut a record in 1967 called *Love's Chance,* which broke into the R and B charts. But nothing came of it. No big contract, no club dates, no tours. He made very little from the sales, only enough for an operation to pull a steering wheel from his gut when, drunk and mad at a lady friend, he slammed his Mustang into a row of parked cars.

"Touch it," he smiled at me one afternoon as he raised his shirt, his black belly kinked with hair. Scared, I traced the scar that ran from his chest to the left of his belly button, and I was repelled but hid my disgust.

Among the Mexicans I had few friends because I was different, a *pocho* who spoke bad Spanish. At lunch they sat in tires and laughed over burritos, looking up at me to laugh even harder. I also sat in tires while nursing a Coke and felt dirty and sticky because I was still living on the street and had not had a real bath in over a week. Nevertheless, when the border patrol came to round up the nationals, I ran with them as they scrambled for the fence or hid among the tires behind the warehouse. The foreman, who thought I was an undocumented worker, yelled at me to run, to get away. I did just that. At the time it seemed fun because there was no risk, only a good-hearted feeling of hide-and-seek, and besides it meant an hour away from work on company time. When the police left we came back and some of the nationals made up stories of how they were almost caught—how they out-raced the police. Some of the stories were so convoluted and unconvincing that everyone laughed *mentiras,* especially when one described how he overpowered a policeman, took his gun away, and sold the patrol car. We laughed and he laughed, happy to be there to make up a story.

If work was difficult, so were the nights. I still had not gathered enough money to 20 rent a room, so I spent the nights sleeping in parked cars or in the balcony of a church. After a week I found a newspaper ad for room for rent, phoned, and was given directions. Finished with work, I walked the five miles down Mission Road looking back into the traffic with my thumb out. No rides. After eight hours of handling tires I was frightening, I suppose, to drivers since they seldom looked at me; if they did, it was a quick glance. For the next six weeks I would try to hitchhike, but the only person to stop was a Mexican woman who gave me two dollars to take the bus. I told her it was too much and that no bus ran from Mission Road to where I lived, but she insisted that I keep the money and trotted back to her idling car. It must have hurt her to see me day after day walking in the heat and looking very much the dirty Mexican to the many minds that didn't know what it meant to work at hard labor. That woman knew. Her eyes met mine as she opened the car door, and there was a tenderness that was surprisingly true—one for which you wait for years but when it comes it doesn't help. Nothing changes. You continue on in rags, with the sun still above you.

I rented a room from a middle-aged couple whose lives were a mess. She was a school teacher and he was a fireman. A perfect setup, I thought. But during my stay there they would argue with one another for hours in their bedroom.

When I rang at the front door both Mr. and Mrs. Van Deusen answered and didn't bother to disguise their shock at how awful I looked. But they let me in all the same. Mrs. Van Deusen showed me around the house, from the kitchen and bathroom to the living room with its grand piano. On her fingers she counted out the house rules as she walked me to my room. It was a girl's room with lace curtains, scenic wallpaper of a Victorian couple enjoying a stroll, canopied bed, and stuffed animals in a corner. Leaving, she turned and asked if she could do laundry for me and, feeling shy and hurt, I told her no; perhaps the next day. She left and I undressed to take a bath, exhausted as I sat on the edge of the bed probing my aches and my bruised places. With a towel around my waist I hurried down the hallway to the bathroom where Mrs. Van Deusen had set out an additional towel with a tube of shampoo. I ran the water in the tub and sat on the toilet, lid down, watching the steam curl toward the ceiling. When I lowered myself into the tub I felt my body sting. I soaped a wash cloth and scrubbed my arms until they lightened, even glowed pink, but still I looked unwashed around my neck and face no matter how hard I rubbed. Back in the room I sat in bed reading a magazine, happy and thinking of no better luxury than a girl's sheets, especially after nearly two weeks of sleeping on cardboard at the church.

I was too tired to sleep, so I sat at the window watching the neighbors move about in pajamas, and, curious about the room, looked through the bureau drawers to search out personal things—snapshots, a messy diary, and a high school yearbook. I looked up the Van Deusen's daughter, Barbara, and studied her face as if I recognized her from my own school—a face that said "promise," "college," "nice clothes in the closet." She was a skater and a member of the German Club; her greatest ambition was to sing at the Hollywood Bowl.

After awhile I got into bed and as I drifted toward sleep I thought about her. In my mind I played a love scene again and again and altered it slightly each time. She comes home from college and at first is indifferent to my presence in her home, but finally I overwhelm her with deep pity when I come home hurt from work, with blood on my shirt. Then there was another version: Home from college she is immediately taken with me, in spite of my work-darkened face, and invites me into the family car for a milkshake across town. Later, back at the house, we sit in the living room talking about school until we're so close I'm holding her hand. The truth of the matter was that Barbara did come home for a week, but was bitter toward her parents for taking in boarders (two others besides me). During that time she spoke to me only twice: Once, while searching the refrigerator, she asked if we had any mustard; the other time she asked if I had seen her car keys.

But it was a place to stay. Work had become more and more difficult. I not only worked with Iggy, but also with the assistant foreman who was in charge of unloading trucks. After they backed in I hopped on top to pass the tires down by bouncing them on the tailgate to give them an extra spring so they would be less difficult to handle on the other end. Each truck was weighed down with more than two hundred tires, each averaging twenty pounds, so that by the time the truck was emptied and swept clean I glistened with sweat and my T-shirt stuck to my body. I blew snot threaded with tire dust onto the asphalt, indifferent to the customers who watched from the waiting room.

The days were dull. I did what there was to do from morning until the bell sounded at five; I tugged, pulled, and cussed at tires until I was listless and my mind drifted and caught on small things, from cold sodas to shoes to stupid talk about what we would do with a million dollars. I remember unloading a truck with Hamp, a black man.

25

"What's better than a sharp lady?" he asked me as I stood sweaty on a pile of junked tires. "Water. With ice," I said.

He laughed with his mouth open wide. With his fingers he pinched the sweat from his chin and flicked at me. "You be too young, boy. A woman can make you a god."

As a kid I had chopped cotton and picked grapes, so I knew work. I knew the fatigue and the boredom and the feeling that there was a good possibility you might have to do such work for years, if not for a lifetime. In fact, as a kid I imagined a dark fate: To marry Mexican poor, work Mexican hours, and in the end die a Mexican death, broke and in despair.

But this job at Valley Tire Company confirmed that there was something worse than field work, and I was doing it. We were all doing it, from foreman to the newcomers like me, and what I felt heaving tires for eight hours a day was felt by everyone— black, Mexican, redneck. We all despised those hours but didn't know what else to do. The workers were unskilled, some undocumented and fearful of deportation, and all struck with an uncertainty at what to do with their lives. Although everyone bitched about work, no one left. Some had worked there for as long as twelve years; some had sons working there. Few quit; no one was ever fired. It amazed me that no one gave up when the border patrol jumped from their vans, baton in hand, because I couldn't imagine any work that could be worse—or any life. What was out there, in the world, that made men run for the fence in fear?

Iggy was the only worker who seemed sure of himself. After five hours of "junking," he brushed himself off, cleaned up in the washroom, and came out gleaming with an elegance that humbled the rest of us. Few would look him straight in the eye or talk to him in our usual stupid way because he was so much better. He carried himself as a man should—with that old world "dignity"—while the rest of us muffed our jobs and talked dully about dull things as we worked. From where he worked in his open shed he would now and then watch us with his hands on his hips. He would shake his head and click his tongue in disgust.

The rest of us lived dismally. I often wondered what the others' homes were like; I couldn't imagine that they were much better than our work place. No one indicated that his outside life was interesting or intriguing. We all looked defeated and contemptible in our filth at the day's end. I imagined the average welcome at home: Rafael, a Mexican national who had worked at Valley for five years, returned to a beaten house of kids who were dressed in mismatched clothes and playing kick-the-can. As for Sugar Daddy, he returned home to a stuffy room where he would read and reread old magazines. He ate potato chips, drank beer, and watched TV. There was no grace in dipping socks into a wash basin where later he would wash his cup and plate.

There was no grace at work. It was all ridicule. The assistant foreman drank Cokes in front of the newcomers as they laced tires in the afternoon sun. Knowing that I had a long walk home, Rudy, the college student, passed me waving and yelling "Hello," as I started down Mission Road on the way home to eat out of cans. Even our plump secretary got into the act by wearing short skirts and flaunting her milky legs. If there was love, it was ugly. I'm thinking of Tully and an older man whose name I can no longer recall fondling one another in the washroom. I had come in cradling a smashed finger to find them pressed together in the shower, their pants undone and partly pulled down. When they saw me they smiled their pink mouths but didn't bother to push away.

How we arrived at such a place is a mystery to me. Why anyone would stay for years is even a deeper concern. You showed up, but from where? What broken life? What ugly past? The foreman showed you the Coke machine, the washroom, and the yard where you'd work. When you picked up a tire, you were amazed at the black it could give off.

CONNECTING PERSONALLY TO THE READING

1. What is the most dehumanizing job you have ever held? What were the people like, and how did they treat you? What were you expected to do?

2. According to Soto, how did the way the workers were treated on the job and the job conditions affect their behavior when not on the job? Why do you think this is the case? Have you ever held a job so completely without dignity that it affected your behavior at home or with friends? Explain.

FOCUSING ON THE ARGUMENT

1. Soto records the tedious but exhausting events of his days and nights with an eye for telling details. How does his detailed personal testimony persuade readers of the indignity of this job?

2. How would you characterize Soto's tone? Do you think it builds credibility? Explain.

3. Soto offers us quick portraits, to convey a sense of other people's lives: where they go after work, how they love, how they treat others and are treated. Do you find these portraits compelling? Explain why or why not.

SYNTHESIZING IDEAS FROM MULTIPLE READINGS

1. In what ways is the work Soto describes similar to the work that many black women face, according to bell hooks in "Work Makes Life Sweet" (p. 285)? Why would individuals prefer to remain on welfare rather than take such jobs?

2. Like David Sedaris in "SantaLand Diaries" (p. 303), Soto looks back on a job he held for a short time, viewing the job from a distance. Although she writes in the present, in "Nickel and Dimed" (p. 322), Barbara Ehrenreich also reflects on her work at Wal-Mart. How would you describe the different feelings Soto, Sedaris, and Ehrenreich convey about their temporary jobs? What tone of voice do they use and why?

3. Soto suggests that he derived no benefit from his dead-end job. What makes the restaurant work described by Mike Rose in "The Working Life of a Waitress" (p. 278) more gratifying than this tire repair job? Is it the job itself, the way employers treat the employees, the hours, or the money that matters most? Explain your views.

4. The environment that Soto works in, both social and physical, seems to devalue him as a person. What would Jonathan Kozol ("Savage Inequalities," Chapter 4, p. 214) notice in this environment? What would both agree are essential in the physical environment for one to grow as a person?

1. Soto finds the sarcasm and cruelty among low-paid workers at Valley Tire Factory as wearing and difficult as the dirty work itself. With a group of friends, identify a job in which the environment made the work even more terrible than it had to be. Write a letter to the employer explaining how this climate made people feel.

2. Write an op-ed article on the need for a decent minimum wage, one that allows a person enough dignity to perform the work with self-respect and want to do the job with some care.

READING

DAVID SEDARIS   What constitutes a "fun" job? Despite the irritations and abuse from customers, Sedaris seems to enjoy his short stint in Macy's SantaLand during a Christmas break. He comments on the people who bring their children to such places, what they expect of a Santa's elf, the job "requirements," and the kids and adults who take these jobs. What would you imagine would not be fun about playing Santa or a Santa's elf at Macy's? What privileged attitude can someone take who only needs a two-week job?

SEDARIS is a frequent contributor to *This American Life* on National Public Radio; he made his debut by reading the following essay on the air. In addition to being a well-known humorist, social critic, playwright (with his sister, the actress Amy Sedaris), and essayist, he is one of the most sought-after public speakers today. His books include *Barrel Fever, Naked, Me Talk Pretty One Day, Holidays on Ice,* and *Dress Your Family in Corduroy and Denim,* and his essays appear regularly in the *New Yorker* and other magazines. He lives in France.

SantaLand Diaries (1994) | BY DAVID SEDARIS

I was in a coffee shop looking through the want ads when I read, "Macy's Herald Square, the largest store in the world, has big opportunities for outgoing, fun-loving people of all shapes and sizes who want more than just a holiday job! Working as an elf in Macy's SantaLand means being at the center of the excitement. . . ."

I circled the ad and then I laughed out loud at the thought of it. The man seated next to me turned on his stool, checking to see if I was a lunatic. I continued to laugh, quietly. Yesterday I applied for a job at UPS. They are hiring drivers' helpers for the upcoming Christmas season and I went to their headquarters filled with hope. In line with three hundred other men and women my hope diminished. During the brief interview I was asked why I wanted to work for UPS and I answered that I wanted to work for UPS because I like the brown uniforms. What did they expect me to say?

"I'd like to work for UPS because, in my opinion, it's an opportunity to showcase my substantial leadership skills in one of the finest private delivery companies this country has seen since the Pony Express!"

I said I liked the uniforms and the UPS interviewer turned my application face-down on his desk and said, "Give me a break."

I came home this afternoon and checked the machine for a message from UPS but the only message I got was from the company that holds my student loan, Sallie Mae. Sallie Mae sounds like a naive and barefoot hillbilly girl but in fact they are a ruthless and aggressive conglomeration of bullies located in a tall brick building somewhere in Kansas. I picture it to be the tallest building in that state and I have decided they hire their employees straight out of prison. It scares me.

The woman at Macy's asked, "Would you be interested in full-time elf or evening and weekend elf?"

I said, "Full-time elf."

I have an appointment next Wednesday at noon.

I am a thirty-three-year-old man applying for a job as an elf.

I often see people on the streets dressed as objects and handing out leaflets. I tend to avoid leaflets but it breaks my heart to see a grown man dressed as a taco. So, if there is a costume involved, I tend not only to accept the leaflet, but to accept it graciously, saying, "Thank you so much," and thinking, "You poor, pathetic son of a bitch. I don't know what you have but I hope I never catch it." This afternoon on Lexington Avenue I accepted a leaflet from a man dressed as a camcorder. Hot dogs, peanuts, tacos, video cameras, these things make me sad because they don't fit in on the streets. In a parade, maybe, but not on the streets. I figure that at least as an elf I will have a place; I'll be in Santa's Village with all the other elves. We will reside in a fluffy wonderland surrounded by candy canes and gingerbread shacks. It won't be quite as sad as standing on some street corner dressed as a french fry.

I am trying to look on the bright side. I arrived in New York three weeks ago with high hopes, hopes that have been challenged. In my imagination I'd go straight from Penn Station to the offices of "One Life to Live," where I would drop off my bags and spruce up before heading off for drinks with Cord Roberts and Victoria Buchannon, the show's greatest stars. We'd sit in a plush booth at a tony cocktail lounge where my new celebrity friends would lift their frosty glasses in my direction and say, "A toast to David Sedaris, the best writer this show has ever had!!!"

I'd say, "You guys, cut it out." It was my plan to act modest.

People at surrounding tables would stare at us, whispering, "Isn't that . . . ? Isn't that . . . ?"

I might be distracted by their enthusiasm and Victoria Buchannon would lay her hand over mine and tell me that I'd better get used to being the center of attention.

But instead I am applying for a job as an elf. Even worse than applying is the very real possibility that I will not be hired, that I couldn't even find work as an elf. That's when you know you're a failure.

This afternoon I sat in the eighth-floor SantaLand office and was told, "Congratulations, Mr. Sedaris. You are an elf."

In order to become an elf I filled out ten pages' worth of forms, took a multiple choice personality test, underwent two interviews, and submitted urine for a drug test. The first interview was general, designed to eliminate the obvious sociopaths. During the second interview we were asked why we wanted to be elves. This is always a problem question. I listened as the woman ahead of me, a former waitress, answered the question, saying, "I really want to be an elf? Because I think it's about acting? And before this I worked in a restaurant? Which was run by this really wonderful woman who had a dream to open a restaurant? And it made me realize that it's really really . . . important to have a . . . dream?"

Everything this woman said, every phrase and sentence, was punctuated with a question mark and the interviewer never raised an eyebrow.

When it was my turn I explained that I wanted to be an elf because it was one of the most frightening career opportunities I had ever come across. The interviewer raised her face from my application and said, "And . . . ?"

I'm certain that I failed my drug test. My urine had roaches and stems floating in it, but still they hired me because I am short, five feet five inches. Almost everyone they hired is short. One is a dwarf. After the second interview I was brought to the manager's office, where I was shown a floor plan. On a busy day twenty-two thousand people come to visit Santa, and I was told that it is an elf's lot to remain merry in the face of torment and adversity. I promised to keep that in mind.

I spent my eight-hour day with fifty elves and one perky, well-meaning instructor in an enormous Macy's classroom, the walls of which were lined with NCR 2152's. A 2152, I have come to understand, is a cash register. The class was broken up into study groups and given assignments. My group included several returning elves and a few experienced cashiers who tried helping me by saying things like, "Don't you even know your personal ID code? Jesus, I had mine memorized by ten o'clock."

Everything about the cash register intimidates me. Each procedure involves a series of codes: separate numbers for cash, checks, and each type of credit card. The term *Void* has gained prominence as the filthiest four-letter word in my vocabulary. Voids are a nightmare of paperwork and coded numbers, everything produced in triplicate and initialed by the employee and his supervisor.

Leaving the building tonight I could not shake the mental picture of myself being stoned to death by restless, angry customers, their nerves shattered by my complete lack of skill. I tell myself that I will simply pry open my register and accept anything they want to give me — beads, cash, watches, whatever. I'll negotiate and swap. I'll stomp their credit cards through the masher, write "Nice Knowing You!" along the bottom of the slip and leave it at that.

All we sell in SantaLand are photos. People sit upon Santa's lap and pose for a picture. The Photo Elf hands them a slip of paper with a number printed along the top. The form is filled out by another elf and the picture arrives by mail weeks later. So really, all we sell is the idea of a picture. One idea costs nine dollars, three ideas cost eighteen.

My worst nightmare involves twenty-two thousand people a day standing before my register. I won't always be a cashier, just once in a while. The worst part is that after I have accumulated three hundred dollars I have to remove two hundred, fill out half a dozen forms, and run the envelope of cash to the drop in the China Department or to the vault on the balcony above the first floor. I am not allowed to change my clothes beforehand. I have to go dressed as an elf. An elf in SantaLand is one thing, an elf in Sportswear is something else altogether.

This afternoon we were given presentations and speeches in a windowless conference room crowded with desks and plastic chairs. We were told that during the second week of December, SantaLand is host to "Operation Special Children," at which time poor children receive free gifts donated by the store. There is another morning set aside for terribly sick and deformed children. On that day it is an elf's job to greet the child at the Magic Tree and jog back to the house to brace our Santa.

"The next one is missing a nose," or "Crystal has third-degree burns covering 90 percent of her body."

Missing a nose. With these children Santa has to be careful not to ask, "And what would *you* like for Christmas?"

We were given a lecture by the chief of security, who told us that Macy's Herald Square suffers millions of dollars' worth of employee theft per year. As a result the store treats its employees the way one might treat a felon with a long criminal record. Cash rewards are offered for turning people in and our bags are searched every time we leave the store. We were shown videotapes in which supposed former employees hang their heads and rue the day they ever thought to steal that leather jacket. The actors faced the camera to explain how their arrests had ruined their friendships, family life, and, ultimately, their future.

One fellow stared at his hands and sighed, "There's no way I'm going to be admit- 30 ted into law school. Not now. Not after what I've done. Nope, no way." He paused and shook his head of the unpleasant memory. "Oh, man, not after this. No way."

A lonely, reflective girl sat in a coffee shop, considered her empty cup, and moaned, "I remember going out after work with all my Macy's friends. God, those were good times. I loved those people." She stared off into space for a few moments before continuing, "Well, needless to say, those friends aren't calling anymore. This time I've *really* messed up. Why did I do it? Why?"

Macy's has two jail cells on the balcony floor and it apprehends three thousand shoplifters a year. We were told to keep an eye out for pickpockets in SantaLand.

Interpreters for the deaf came and taught us to sign "MERRY CHRISTMAS! I AM SANTA'S HELPER." They told us to speak as we sign and to use bold, clear voices and bright facial expressions. They taught us to say "YOU ARE A VERY PRETTY BOY/GIRL! I LOVE YOU! DO YOU WANT A SURPRISE?"

My sister Amy lives above a deaf girl and has learned quite a bit of sign language. She taught some to me and so now I am able to say, "SANTA HAS A TUMOR IN HIS HEAD THE SIZE OF AN OLIVE. MAYBE IT WILL GO AWAY TOMORROW BUT I DON'T THINK SO."

This morning we were lectured by the SantaLand managers and presented with a 35 Xeroxed booklet of regulations titled "The Elfin Guide." Most of the managers are former elves who have worked their way up the candy-cane ladder but retain vivid memories of their days in uniform. They closed the meeting saying, "I want you to remember that even if you are assigned Photo Elf on a busy weekend, YOU ARE NOT SANTA'S SLAVE."

In the afternoon we were given a tour of SantaLand, which really is something. It's beautiful, a real wonderland, with ten thousand sparkling lights, false snow, train sets, bridges, decorated trees, mechanical penguins and bears, and really tall candy canes. One enters and travels through a maze, a path which takes you from one festive environment to another. The path ends at the Magic Tree. The Tree is supposed to resemble a complex system of roots, but looks instead like a scale model of the human intestinal tract. Once you pass the Magic Tree, the light dims and an elf guides you to Santa's house. The houses are cozy and intimate, laden with toys. You exit Santa's house and are met with a line of cash registers.

We traveled the path a second time and were given the code names for various posts, such as "The Vomit Corner," a mirrored wall near the Magic Tree, where nauseous children tend to surrender the contents of their stomachs. When someone vomits, the nearest elf is supposed to yell "VAMOOSE," which is the name of the janitorial product used by the store. We were taken to the "Oh, My God, Corner," a position near the escalator. People arriving see the long line and say "Oh, my God!" and it is an elf's job to calm them down and explain that it will take no longer than an hour to see Santa.

On any given day you can be an Entrance Elf, a Water Cooler Elf, a Bridge Elf, Train Elf, Maze Elf, Island Elf, Magic Window Elf, Emergency Exit Elf, Counter Elf, Magic Tree Elf, Pointer Elf, Santa Elf, Photo Elf, Usher Elf, Cash Register Elf, Runner Elf, or Exit Elf. We were given a demonstration of the various positions in action, performed by returning elves who were so animated and relentlessly cheerful that it embarrassed me to walk past them. I don't know that I could look someone in the eye and exclaim, "Oh, my goodness, I think I see Santa!" or "Can you close your eyes and make a very special Christmas wish!" Everything these elves said had an exclamation point at the end of it!!! It makes one's mouth hurt to speak with such forced merriment. I feel cornered when someone talks to me this way. Doesn't everyone? I prefer being frank with children. I'm more likely to say, "You must be exhausted," or "I know a lot of people who would kill for that little waistline of yours."

I am afraid I won't be able to provide the grinding enthusiasm Santa is asking for. I think I'll be a low-key sort of an elf.

Today was elf dress rehearsal. The lockers and dressing rooms are located on the 40 eighth floor, directly behind SantaLand. Elves have gotten to know one another over the past four days of training but once we took off our clothes and put on the uniforms everything changed.

The woman in charge of costuming assigned us our outfits and gave us a lecture on keeping things clean. She held up a calendar and said, "Ladies, you know what this is. Use it. I have scraped enough blood out from the crotches of elf knickers to last me the rest of my life. And don't tell me, 'I don't wear underpants, I'm a dancer.' You're not a dancer. If you were a real dancer you wouldn't be here. You're an elf and you're going to wear panties like an elf."

My costume is green. I wear green velvet knickers, a yellow turtleneck, a forest-green velvet smock, and a perky stocking cap decorated with spangles. This is my work uniform.

My elf name is Crumpet. We were allowed to choose our own names and given permission to change them according to our outlook on the snowy world.

Today was the official opening day of SantaLand and I worked as a Magic Window Elf, a Santa Elf, and an Usher Elf. The Magic Window is located in the adult "Quick Peep" line. My job was to say, "Step on the Magic Star and look through the window, and you can see Santa!" I was at the Magic Window for fifteen minutes before a man approached me and said, "You look so fucking stupid."

I have to admit that he had a point. But still, I wanted to say that at least I get paid to look stupid, that he gives it away for free. But I can't say things like that because I'm supposed to be merry.   45

So instead I said, "Thank you!"

"Thank you!" as if I had misunderstood and thought he had said, "You look terrific."

"Thank you!"

He was a brawny wise guy wearing a vinyl jacket and carrying a bag from Radio Shack. I should have said, real loud, "Sorry man, I don't date other guys."

Two New Jersey families came together to see Santa. Two loud, ugly husbands with   50
two wives and four children between them. The children gathered around Santa and had their picture taken. When Santa asked the ten-year-old boy what he wanted for Christmas, his father shouted, "A WOMAN! GET HIM A WOMAN, SANTA!" These men were very loud and irritating, constantly laughing and jostling one another. The two women sat on Santa's lap and had their pictures taken and each asked Santa for a Kitchen-Aide brand dishwasher and a decent winter coat. Then the husbands sat on Santa's lap and, when asked what he wanted for Christmas, one of the men yelled, "I WANT A BROAD WITH BIG TITS." The man's small-breasted wife crossed her arms over her chest, looked at the floor, and gritted her teeth. The man's son tried to laugh.

Again this morning I got stuck at the Magic Window, which is really boring. I'm supposed to stand around and say, "Step on the Magic Star and you can see Santa!" I said that for a while and then I started saying, "Step on the Magic Star and you can see Cher!"

And people got excited. So I said, "Step on the Magic Star and you can see Mike Tyson!"

Some people in the other line, the line to sit on Santa's lap, got excited and cut through the gates so that they could stand on my Magic Star. Then they got angry when they looked through the Magic Window and saw Santa rather than Cher or Mike Tyson. What did they honestly expect? Is Cher so hard up for money that she'd agree to stand behind a two-way mirror at Macy's?

The angry people must have said something to management because I was taken off the Magic Star and sent to Elf Island, which is really boring as all you do is stand around and act merry. At noon a huge group of retarded people came to visit Santa and passed me on my little island. These people were profoundly retarded. They were rolling their eyes and wagging their tongues and staggering toward Santa. It was a large group of retarded people and after watching them for a few minutes I could not begin to guess where the retarded people ended and the regular New Yorkers began.

Everyone looks retarded once you set your mind to it.   55

This evening I was sent to be a Photo Elf, a job I enjoyed the first few times. The camera is hidden in the fireplace and I take the picture by pressing a button at the end of a cord. The pictures arrive by mail weeks later and there is no way an elf can be identified and held accountable but still, you want to make it a good picture.

During our training we were shown photographs that had gone wrong, blurred frenzies of an elf's waving arm, a picture blocked by a stuffed animal, the yawning Santa. After every photograph an elf must remove the numbered form that appears at the bottom of the picture. A lazy or stupid elf could ruin an entire roll of film, causing eager families to pay for and later receive photographs of complete, beaming strangers.

Taking someone's picture tells you an awful lot, *awful* being the operative word. Having the parents in the room tends to make it even worse. It is the SantaLand policy to take a picture of every child, which the parent can either order or refuse. People are allowed to bring their own cameras, video recorders, whatever. It is the multimedia groups that exhaust me. These are parents bent over with equipment, relentless in their quest for documentation.

I see them in the Maze with their video cameras instructing their children to act surprised. "Monica, baby, look at the train set and then look back at me. No, look at *me*. Now wave. That's right, wave hard."

The parents hold up the line and it is a Maze Elf's job to hurry them along. 60

"Excuse me, sir, I'm sorry but we're sort of busy today and I'd appreciate it if you could maybe wrap this up. There are quite a few people behind you."

The parent then asks you to stand beside the child and wave. I do so. I stand beside a child and wave to the video camera, wondering where I will wind up. I picture myself on the television set in a paneled room in Wapahanset or Easternmost Meadows. I picture the family fighting over command of the remote control, hitting the fast-forward button. The child's wave becomes a rapid salute. I enter the picture and everyone in the room entertains the same thought: "What's that asshole doing on our Christmas Memory tape?"

The moment these people are waiting for is the encounter with Santa. As a Photo Elf I watch them enter the room and take control.

"All right, Ellen, I want you and Marcus to stand in front of Santa and when I say, 'now,' I want you to get onto his lap. Look at me. Look at Daddy until I tell you to look at Santa."

He will address his wife who is working the still camera and she will crouch low 65 to the ground with her light meter and a Nikon with many attachments. It is heavy and the veins in her arms stand out.

Then there are the multimedia families in groups, who say, "All right, now let's get a shot of Anthony, Damascus, Theresa, Doug, Amy, Paul, *and* Vanity — can we squeeze them all together? Santa, how about you let Doug sit on your shoulders, can we do that?"

During these visits the children are rarely allowed to discuss their desires with Santa. They are too busy being art-directed by the parents.

"Vanity and Damascus, look over here, no, look *here*."

"Santa, can you put your arm around Amy and shake hands with Paul at the same time?"

"That's good. That's nice." 70

I have seen parents sit their child upon Santa's lap and immediately proceed to groom: combing hair, arranging a hemline, straightening a necktie. I saw a parent spray their child's hair, Santa treated as though he were a false prop made of cement, turning his head and wincing as the hair spray stung his eyes.

Young children, ages two to four, tend to be frightened of Santa. They have no interest in having their pictures taken because they don't know what a picture is. They're not vain, they're babies. They are babies and they act accordingly—they cry. A Photo Elf understands that, once a child starts crying, it's over. They start crying in Santa's house and they don't stop until they are at least ten blocks away.

When the child starts crying, Santa will offer comfort for a moment or two before saying, "Maybe we'll try again next year."

The parents had planned to send the photos to relatives and place them in scrapbooks. They waited in line for over an hour and are not about to give up so easily. Tonight I saw a woman slap and shake her sobbing daughter, yelling, "Goddamn it, Rachel, get on that man's lap and smile or I'll give you something to cry about."

I often take photographs of crying children. Even more grotesque is taking a picture of a crying child with a false grimace. It's not a smile so much as the forced shape of a smile. Oddly, it pleases the parents.   75

"Good girl, Rachel. Now, let's get the hell out of here. Your mother has a headache that won't quit until you're twenty-one."

At least a third of Santa's visitors are adults: couples, and a surprising number of men and women alone. Most of the single people don't want to sit on Santa's lap; they just stop by to shake his hand and wish him luck. Often the single adults are foreigners who just happened to be shopping at Macy's and got bullied into the Maze by the Entrance Elf, whose job it is to hustle people in. One moment the foreigner is looking at china, and the next thing he knows he is standing at the Magic Tree, where an elf holding a palm-sized counter is asking how many in his party are here to see Santa.

"How many in your party?"

The foreigner answers, "Yes."

"How many in your party is not a yes or no question."   80

"Yes."

Then a Santa Elf leads the way to a house where the confused and exhausted visitor addresses a bearded man in a red suit, and says, "Yes, OK. Today I am good." He shakes Santa's hand and runs, shaken, for the back door.

This afternoon a man came to visit Santa, a sloppy, good-looking man in his mid-forties. I thought he was another confused European, so I reassured him that many adults come to visit Santa, everyone is welcome. An hour later, I noticed the same man, back again to fellowship with Santa. I asked what he and Santa talk about, and in a cracked and puny voice he answered, "Toys. All the toys."

I noticed a dent in the left side of his forehead. You could place an acorn in a dent like this. He waited in line and returned to visit a third time. On his final visit he got so excited he peed on Santa's lap.

So far in SantaLand, I have seen Simone from "General Hospital," Shawn from "All My   85
Children," Walter Cronkite, and Phil Collins. Last year one of the elves was suspended after asking Goldie Hawn to autograph her hand. We have been instructed to leave the stars alone.

Walter Cronkite was very tall, and I probably wouldn't have recognized him unless someone had pointed him out to me. Phil Collins was small and well groomed. He arrived with his daughter and an entourage of three. I don't care about Phil Collins one way or the other but I saw some people who might and I felt it was my duty to tap them on the shoulder and say, "Look, there's Phil Collins!"

Many of Santa's visitors are from out of town and welcome the opportunity to view a celebrity, as it rounds out their New York experience. I'd point out Phil Collins and people would literally squeal with delight. Seeing as it is my job to make people happy, I didn't have any problem with it. Phil Collins wandered through the Maze, videotaping everything with his camcorder and enjoying himself. Once he entered the Magic Tree, he was no longer visible to the Maze audience, so I began telling people that if they left immediately and took a right at the end of the hall, they could probably catch up with Phil Collins after his visit with Santa. So they did. People left. When Phil Collins walked out of SantaLand, there was a crowd of twenty people waiting for autographs. When the managers came looking for the big mouth, I said, "Phil Collins, who's he?"

I spent a few hours in the Maze with Puff, a young elf from Brooklyn. We were standing near the Lollipop Forest when we realized that *Santa* is an anagram of *Satan*. Father Christmas or the Devil—so close but yet so far. We imagined a SatanLand where visitors would wade through steaming pools of human blood and feces before arriving at the Gates of Hell, where a hideous imp in a singed velvet costume would take them by the hand and lead them toward Satan. Once we thought of it we couldn't get it out of our minds. Overhearing the customers we would substitute the word *Satan* for the word *Santa*.

"What do you think, Michael? Do you think Macy's has the real Satan?"

"Don't forget to thank Satan for the Baby Alive he gave you last year."   90

"I love Satan."

"Who doesn't? Everyone loves Satan."

I would rather drive upholstery tacks into my gums than work as the Usher Elf. The Usher stands outside Santa's exit door and fills out the photo forms. While I enjoy trying to guess where people are from, I hate listening to couples bicker over how many copies they want.

It was interesting the first time I did it, but not anymore. While the parents make up their minds, the Usher has to prevent the excited children from entering Santa's back door to call out the names of three or four toys they had neglected to request earlier.

When things are slow, an Usher pokes in his head and watches Santa with his vis-   95
itors. This afternoon we were slow and I watched a forty-year-old woman and her ancient mother step in to converse with Santa. The daughter wore a short pink dress, decorated with lace—the type of dress that a child might wear. Her hair was trained into pigtails and she wore ruffled socks and patent leather shoes. This forty-year-old girl ran to Santa and embraced him, driving rouge into his beard. She spoke in a baby voice and then lowered it to a whisper. When they left I asked if they wanted to purchase the photo and the biggest little girl in the world whispered something in her mother's ear and then she skipped away. She skipped. I watched her try and commune with the youngsters standing around the register until her mother pulled her away.

This morning I spent some time at the Magic Window with Sleighbell, an entertainer who is in the process of making a music video with her all-girl singing group. We talked about one thing and another, and she told me that she has appeared on a few television shows, mainly soap operas. I asked if she has ever done "One Life to Live," and she said, yes, she had a bit part as a flamenco dancer a few years ago when Cord and Tina remarried and traveled to Madrid for their honeymoon.

Suddenly I remembered Sleighbell perfectly. On that episode she wore a red lace dress and stomped upon a shiny nightclub floor until Spain's greatest bullfighter entered, challenging Cord to a duel. Sleighbell intervened. She stopped dancing and said to Cord, "Don't do it, Señor. Yoot be a fool to fight weeth Spain's greatest boolfighter!"

Sleighbell told me that the honeymoon was filmed here in the New York studio. That surprised me as I really thought it was shot in Spain. She told me that the dancing scene was shot in the late morning and afterwards there was a break for lunch. She took her lunch in the studio cafeteria and was holding her tray, when Tina waved her over to her table. Sleighbell had lunch with Tina! She said that Tina was very sweet and talked about her love for Smokey Robinson. I had read that Tina had driven a wedge between Smokey and his wife, but it was thrilling to hear it from someone who had the facts.

Later in the day I was put on the cash register where Andrea, one of the managers, told me that her friend Caroline was the person responsible for casting on "One Life to Live." It was Caroline who replaced the old Tina with the new Tina. I loved the old Tina and will accept no substitutes, but I told Andrea that I liked the new Tina a lot, and she said, "I'll pass that along to Caroline. She'll be happy to hear it!" We were talking when Mitchell, another manager, got involved and said that he'd been on "One Life to Live" seven times. He played Clint's lawyer five years ago when the entire Buchannon family was on trial for the murder of Mitch Laurence. Mitchell knows Victoria Buchannon personally and said that she's just as sweet and caring in real life as she is on the show.

"She's basically playing herself, except for the multiple personality disorder," he said, pausing to verify a check on another elf's register. He asked the customer for another form of ID, and while the woman cursed and fished through her purse, Mitchell told me that Clint tends to keep to himself but that Bo and Asa are a lot of fun. 100

I can't believe I'm hearing these things. I know people who have sat around with Tina, Cord, Nicki, Asa, and Clint. I'm getting closer, I can feel it.

This evening I was working as a Counter Elf at the Magic Tree when I saw a woman unzip her son's fly, release his penis, and instruct him to pee into a bank of artificial snow. He was a young child, four or five years old, and he did it, he peed. Urine dripped from the branches of artificial trees and puddled on the floor.

Tonight a man proposed to his girlfriend in one of the Santa houses. When Santa asked the man what he wanted for Christmas, he pulled a ring out of his pocket and said he wanted this woman to be his wife. Santa congratulated them both and the Photo Elf got choked up and started crying.

A spotted child visited Santa, climbed up on his lap, and expressed a wish to recover from chicken pox. Santa leapt up.

I've met elves from all walks of life. Most of them are show business people, actors and   105
dancers, but a surprising number of them held real jobs at advertising agencies and
brokerage firms before the recession hit. Bless their hearts, these people never imagined there was a velvet costume waiting in their future. They're the really bitter elves.
Many of the elves are young, high school and college students. They're young and cute
and one of the job perks is that I get to see them in their underpants. The changing
rooms are located in the employee bathrooms behind SantaLand. The men's bathroom is small and the toilets often flood, so we are forced to stand on an island of
newspapers in order to keep our socks dry. The Santas have a nice dressing room
across the hall, but you don't want to see a Santa undress. Quite a few elves have taken
to changing clothes in the hallway, beside their lockers. These elves tend to wear
bathing suits underneath their costumes—jams, I believe they are called.

The overall cutest elf is a fellow from Queens named Snowball. Snowball tends to
ham it up with the children, sometimes literally tumbling down the path to Santa's
house. I tend to frown on that sort of behavior but Snowball is hands down
adorable—you want to put him in your pocket. Yesterday we worked together as Santa
Elves and I became excited when he started saying things like, "I'd follow *you* to Santa's
house any day, Crumpet."

It made me dizzy, this flirtation.

By mid-afternoon I was running into walls. At the end of our shift we were in the
bathroom, changing clothes, when suddenly we were surrounded by three Santas and
five other elves—all of them were guys that Snowball had been flirting with.

Snowball just leads elves on, elves and Santas. He is playing a dangerous game.

This afternoon I was stuck being Photo Elf with Santa Santa. I don't know his real   110
name; no one does. During most days, there is a slow period when you sit around the
house and talk to your Santa. Most of them are nice guys and we sit around and laugh,
but Santa Santa takes himself a bit too seriously. I asked him where he lives, Brooklyn
or Manhattan, and he said, "Why, I live at the North Pole with Mrs. Claus!" I asked
what he does the rest of the year and he said, "I make toys for all of the children."

I said, "Yes, but what do you do for money?"

"Santa doesn't need money," he said.

Santa Santa sits and waves and jingles his bell sash when no one is there. He actually recited "The Night Before Christmas," and it was just the two of us in the house,
no children. Just us. What do you do with a nut like that?

He says, "Oh, Little Elf, Little Elf, straighten up those mantel toys for Santa." I reminded him that I have a name, Crumpet, and then I straightened up the stuffed animals.

"Oh, Little Elf, Little Elf, bring Santa a throat lozenge." So I brought him a lozenge.   115

Santa Santa has an elaborate little act for the children. He'll talk to them and give
a hearty chuckle and ring his bells and then he asks them to name their favorite
Christmas carol. Most of them say "Rudolph, the Red-Nosed Reindeer." Santa Santa
then asks if they will sing it for him. The children are shy and don't want to sing out
loud, so Santa Santa says, "Oh, Little Elf, Little Elf! Help young Brenda to sing that favorite carol of hers." Then I have to stand there and sing "Rudolph, the Red-Nosed
Reindeer," which I hate. Half the time young Brenda's parents are my age and that certainly doesn't help matters much.

This afternoon I worked as an Exit Elf, telling people in a loud voice, "THIS WAY OUT OF SANTALAND." A woman was standing at one of the cash registers paying for her idea of a picture, while her son lay beneath her kicking and heaving, having a tantrum.

The woman said, "Riley, if you don't start behaving yourself, Santa's not going to bring you *any* of those toys you asked for."

The child said, "He is too going to bring me toys, liar, he already told me."

The woman grabbed my arm and said, "You there, Elf, tell Riley here that if he doesn't start behaving immediately, then Santa's going to change his mind and bring him coal for Christmas."   120

I said that Santa no longer traffics in coal. Instead, if you're bad he comes to your house and steals things. I told Riley that if he didn't behave himself, Santa was going to take away his TV and all his electrical appliances and leave him in the dark. "All your appliances, including the refrigerator. Your food is going to spoil and smell bad. It's going to be so cold and dark where you are. Man, Riley, are you ever going to suffer. You're going to wish you never heard the name Santa."

The woman got a worried look on her face and said, "All right, that's enough."

I said, "He's going to take your car and your furniture and all the towels and blankets and leave you with nothing."

The mother said, "No, that's enough, really."

I spend all day lying to people, saying, "You look so pretty," and, "Santa can't wait to   125
visit with you. You're all he talks about. It's just not Christmas without you. You're Santa's favorite person in the entire tri-state area." Sometimes I lay it on real thick: "Aren't you the Princess of Rongovia? Santa said a beautiful Princess was coming here to visit him. He said she would be wearing a red dress and that she was very pretty, but not stuck up or two-faced. That's you, isn't it?" I lay it on and the parents mouth the words "Thank you" and "Good job."

To one child I said, "You're a model, aren't you?" The girl was maybe six years old and said, "Yes, I model, but I also act. I just got a second call-back for a Fisher Price commercial." The girl's mother said, "You may recognize Katelyn from the 'My First Sony' campaign. She's on the box." I said yes, of course.

All I do is lie, and that has made me immune to compliments.

Lately I am feeling trollish and have changed my elf name from Crumpet to Blisters. Blisters — I think it's cute.

Today a child told Santa Ken that he wanted his dead father back *and* a complete set of Teenage Mutant Ninja Turtles. Everyone wants those Turtles.

Last year a woman decided she wanted a picture of her cat sitting on Santa's lap, so she   130
smuggled it into Macy's in a duffel bag. The cat sat on Santa's lap for five seconds before it shot out the door, and it took six elves forty-five minutes before they found it in the kitchen of the employee cafeteria.

A child came to Santa this morning and his mother said, "All right, Jason. Tell Santa what you want. Tell him what you want."

Jason said, "I . . . want . . . Prokton and . . . Gamble to . . . stop animal testing."

The mother said, "Procter, Jason, that's Procter and Gamble. And what do they do to animals? Do they torture animals, Jason? Is that what they do?"

Jason said, Yes, they torture. He was probably six years old.

This week my least favorite elf is a guy from Florida whom I call "The Walrus." The Walrus has a handlebar mustache, no chin, and a neck the size of my waist. In the dressing room he confesses to being "a bit of a ladies' man." 135

The Walrus acts as though SantaLand were a single's bar. It is embarrassing to work with him. We'll be together at the Magic Window, where he pulls women aside, places his arm around their shoulders, and says, "I know you're not going to ask Santa for good looks. You've already got those, pretty lady. Yes, you've got those in spades."

In his mind the women are charmed, dizzy with his attention.

I pull him aside and say, "That was a *mother* you just did that to, a married woman with three children."

He says, "I didn't see any ring." Then he turns to the next available woman and whistles, "Santa's married but I'm not. Hey, pretty lady, I've got plenty of room on my knee."

I Photo Elfed all day for a variety of Santas and it struck me that many of the parents don't allow their children to speak at all. A child sits upon Santa's lap and the parents say, "All right now, Amber, tell Santa what you want. Tell him you want a Baby Alive and My Pretty Ballerina and that winter coat you saw in the catalog." 140

The parents name the gifts they have already bought. They don't want to hear the word "pony," or "television set," so they talk through the entire visit, placing words in the child's mouth. When the child hops off the lap, the parents address their children, each and every time, with, "What do you say to Santa?"

The child says, "Thank you, Santa."

It is sad because you would like to believe that everyone is unique and then they disappoint you every time by being exactly the same, asking for the same things, reciting the exact same lines as though they have been handed a script.

All of the adults ask for a Gold Card or a BMW and they rock with laughter, thinking they are the first person brazen enough to request such pleasures.

Santa says, "I'll see what I can do." 145

Couples over the age of fifty all say, "I don't want to sit on your lap, Santa, I'm afraid I might break it!"

How do you break a lap? How did so many people get the idea to say the exact same thing?

I went to a store on the Upper West Side. This store is like a Museum of Natural History where everything is for sale: every taxidermic or skeletal animal that roams the earth is represented in this shop and, because of that, it is popular. I went with my brother last weekend. Near the cash register was a bowl of glass eyes and a sign reading "DO NOT HOLD THESE GLASS EYES UP AGAINST YOUR OWN EYES: THE ROUGH STEM CAN CAUSE INJURY."

I talked to the fellow behind the counter and he said, "It's the same thing every time. First they hold up the eyes and then they go for the horns. I'm sick of it."

It frightened me that, until I saw the sign, my first impulse was to hold those eyes up to my own. I thought it might be a laugh riot. 150

All of us take pride and pleasure in the fact that we are unique, but I'm afraid that when all is said and done the police are right: it all comes down to fingerprints.

There was a big "Sesame Street Live" extravaganza over at Madison Square Garden, so thousands of people decided to make a day of it and go straight from Sesame Street to Santa. We were packed today, absolutely packed, and everyone was cranky. Once the line gets long we break it up into four different lines because anyone in their right mind would leave if they knew it would take over two hours to see Santa. Two hours — you could see a movie in two hours. Standing in a two-hour line makes people worry that they're not living in a democratic nation. People stand in line for two hours and they go over the edge. I was sent into the hallway to direct the second phase of the line. The hallway was packed with people, and all of them seemed to stop me with a question: which way to the down escalator, which way to the elevator, the Patio Restaurant, gift wrap, the women's rest room, Trim-A-Tree. There was a line for Santa and a line for the women's bathroom, and one woman, after asking me a dozen questions already, asked, "Which is the line for the women's bathroom?" I shouted that I thought it was the line with all the women in it.

She said, "I'm going to have you fired."

I had two people say that to me today, "I'm going to have you fired." Go ahead, be my guest. I'm wearing a green velvet costume; it doesn't get any worse than this. Who do these people think they are?

"I'm going to have you fired!" and I wanted to lean over and say, "I'm going to have you killed." 155

In the Maze, on the way to Santa's house, you pass spectacles—train sets, dancing bears, the candy-cane forest, and the penguins. The penguins are set in their own icy wonderland. They were built years ago and they frolic mechanically. They stand outside their igloo and sled and skate and fry fish in a pan. For some reason people feel compelled to throw coins into the penguin display. I can't figure it out for the life of me—they don't throw money at the tree of gifts or the mechanical elves, or the mailbox of letters, but they empty their pockets for the penguins. I asked what happens to that money, and a manager told me that it's collected for charity, but I don't think so. Elves take the quarters for the pay phone, housekeeping takes the dimes, and I've seen visitors, those that aren't throwing money, I've seen them scooping it up as fast as they can.

I was working the Exit today. I'm supposed to say, "This way *out* of SantaLand," but I can't bring myself to say it as it seems like I'm rushing people. They wait an hour to see Santa, they're hit up for photo money, and then someone's hustling them out. I say, "This way *out* of SantaLand if you've decided maybe it's time for you to go home."

"You can exit this way if you feel like it."

We're also supposed to encourage people to wait outside while the parent with money is paying for a picture. "If you're waiting for someone to purchase a photo, wait *outside* the double doors."

I say, "If you're waiting for someone to purchase a picture, you might want to 160 wait *outside* the double doors where it is pleasant and the light is more flattering."

I had a group of kids waiting this afternoon, waiting for their mom to pay for pictures, and this kid reached into his pocket and threw a nickel at me. He was maybe twelve years old, jaded in regard to Santa, and he threw his nickel and it hit my chest and fell to the floor. I picked it up, cleared my throat, and handed it back to him. He threw it again. Like I was a penguin. So I handed it back and he threw it higher, hitting me in the neck. I picked up the nickel and turned to another child and said, "Here, you dropped this." He examined the coin, put it in his pocket, and left.

Yesterday was my day off, and the afflicted came to visit Santa. I Photo Elfed for Santa Ira this afternoon, and he told me all about it. These were severely handicapped children who arrived on stretchers and in wheelchairs. Santa couldn't put them on his lap, and often he could not understand them when they voiced their requests. He made it a point to grab each child's hand and ask what they wanted for Christmas. He did this until he came to a child who had no hands. This made him self-conscious, so he started placing a hand on the child's knee until he came to a child with no legs. After that he decided to simply nod his head and chuckle.

I got stuck with Santa Santa again this afternoon and had to sing and fetch for three hours. Late in the afternoon, a child said she didn't know what her favorite Christmas carol was. Santa said, " 'Rudolph'? 'Jingle Bells'? 'White Christmas'? 'Here Comes Santa Claus'? 'Away in the Manger'? 'Silent Night'?"

The girl agreed to "Away in the Manger," but didn't want to sing it because she didn't know the words.

Santa Santa said, "Oh, Little Elf, Little Elf, come sing 'Away in the Manger' for us." 165

It didn't seem fair that I should have to solo, so I told him I didn't know the words.

Santa Santa said, "Of course you know the words. Come now, sing!"

So I sang it the way Billie Holiday might have sung it if she'd put out a Christmas album. "Away in the manger, no crib for a bed, the little Lord, Jesus, lay down his sweet head."

Santa Santa did not allow me to finish.

This afternoon we set a record by scooting fourteen hundred people through Santa- 170 Land in the course of an hour. Most of them were school groups in clots of thirty or more. My Santa would address them, saying, "All right, I'm going to count to three, and on three I want you all to yell what you want and I need you to say it as loud as you can."

Then he would count to three and the noise was magnificent. Santa would cover his ears and say, "All right—one by one I want you to tell me what you're planning to leave Santa on Christmas Eve."

He would go around the room and children would name different sorts of cookies, and he would say, "What about sandwiches? What if Santa should want something more substantial than a cookie?"

Santa's thrust this afternoon was the boredom of his nine-year relationship. He would wave the children good-bye and then turn to me, saying, "I want an affair, Goddamn it—just a little one, just something to get me through the next four or five years."

Some of these children, they get nervous just before going in to visit Santa. They pace and wring their hands and stare at the floor. They act like they're going in for a job interview. I say, "Don't worry, Santa's not going to judge you. He's very relaxed about that sort of thing. He used to be judgmental but people gave him a hard time about it so he stopped. Trust me, you have nothing to worry about."

I was Photo Elf tonight for the oldest Santa. Usually their names are written on the water cups they keep hidden away on the toy shelf. Every now and then a Santa will call out for water and an elf will hold the cup while his master drinks through a straw. I looked on the cup and saw no name. We were busy tonight and I had no time for an introduction. This was an outstanding Santa, wild but warm. The moment a family leaves, this Santa, sensing another group huddled upon his doorstep, will begin to sing. 175

He sings, "A pretty girl . . . is like a melody."

The parents and children enter the room, and if there is a girl in the party, Santa will take a look at her, hold his gloved hands to his chest, and fake a massive heart attack—falling back against the cushion and moaning with a combination of pleasure and pain. Then he slowly comes out of it and says, "Elf, Elf . . . are you there?"

"Yes, Santa, I'm here."

"Elf, I just had a dream that I was standing before the most beautiful girl in the world. She was right here, in my house."

Then I say, "It wasn't a dream, Santa. Open your eyes, my friend. She's standing before you." 180

Santa rubs his eyes and shakes his head as if he were a parish priest, visited by Christ. "Oh, heavenly day," he says, addressing the child. "You are *the* most beautiful girl I have seen in six hundred and seventeen years."

Then he scoops her into his lap and flatters every aspect of her character. The child is delirious. Santa gestures toward the girl's mother, asking, "Is that your sister I see standing there in the corner?"

"No, that's my mother."

Santa calls the woman over close and asks if she has been a good mother. "Do you tell your daughter that you love her? Do you tell her every day?"

The mothers always blush and say, "I try, Santa." 185

Santa asks the child to give her mother a kiss. Then he addresses the father, again requesting that he tell the child how much he loves her.

Santa ends the visit, saying, "Remember that the most important thing is to try and love other people as much as they love you."

The parents choke up and often cry. They grab Santa's hand and, on the way out, my hand. They say it was worth the wait. The most severe cases open their wallets and hand Santa a few bucks. We're not supposed to accept tips, but most Santas take the money and wink, tucking it into their boot. This Santa looked at the money as if it were a filthy Kleenex. He closed his eyes and prepared for the next family.

With boys, this Santa plays on their brains: each one is the smartest boy in the world.

The great thing about this Santa is that he never even asks what the children want. Most times he involves the parents to the point where they surrender their urge for documentation. They lay down their video recorders and gather round for the festival of love. 190

I was the Pointer Elf again this afternoon, one of my favorite jobs. The Pointer stands inside the Magic Tree and appoints available Santa Elves to lead parties of visitors to the houses. First-time visitors are enthusiastic, eager that they are moments away from Santa. Some of the others, having been here before, have decided to leave nothing to chance.

Out of all the Santas, two are black and both are so light-skinned that, with the beard and makeup, you would be hard-pressed to determine their race.

Last week, a black woman became upset when, having requested a "Santa of color," she was sent to Jerome.

After she was led to the house, the woman returned to the Pointer and demanded to speak with a manager.

"He's not black," the woman complained.   195

Bridget assured this woman that Jerome was indeed black.

The woman said, "Well, he isn't black enough."

Jerome is a difficult Santa, moody and unpredictable. He spends a lot of time staring off into space and tallying up his paycheck for the hours he has worked so far. When a manager ducks in encouraging him to speed things up, Jerome says, "Listen up, I'm playing a role here. Do you understand? A dramatic role that takes a great deal of preparation, so don't hassle me about 'Time.'"

Jerome seems to have his own bizarre agenda. When the children arrive, he looks down at his boots and lectures them, suggesting a career in entomology.

"Entomology, do you know what that is?"   200

He tells them that the defensive spray of the stink bug may contain medicinal powers that can one day cure mankind of communicable diseases.

"Do you know about holistic medicine?" he asks.

The Photo Elf takes a picture of yawning children.

The other black Santa works during weeknights and I have never met him but hear he is a real entertainer, popular with Photo Elves and children.

The last time I was the Pointer Elf, a woman approached me and whispered, "We   205
would like a *traditional* Santa. I'm sure you know what I'm talking about."

I sent her to Jerome.

Yesterday Snowball was the Pointer and a woman pulled him aside, saying, "Last year we had a chocolate Santa. Make sure it doesn't happen again."

I saw it all today. I was Pointer Elf for all of five minutes before a man whispered, "Make sure we get a white one this year. Last year we were stuck with a black."

A woman touched my arm and mouthed, "White—white like *us*."

I address a Santa Elf, the first in line, and hand these people over. Who knows   210
where they will wind up? The children are antsy, excited—they want to see Santa. The children are sweet. The parents are manipulative and should be directed toward the A&S Plaza, two blocks away. A&S has only two Santas working at the same time—a white Santa and a black Santa, and it's very clear-cut: whites in one line and blacks in another.

I've had requests from both sides. White Santa, black Santa, a Pointer Elf is instructed to shrug his shoulders and feign ignorance, saying, "There's only one Santa."

Today I experienced my cash register nightmare. The actual financial transactions weren't so bad—I've gotten the hang of that. The trouble are the voids. A customer will offer to pay in cash and then, after I have arranged it, they examine their wallets and say, "You know what, I think I'll put that on my card instead."

This involves voids and signatures from the management.

I take care of the paperwork, accept their photo form and staple it to the receipt. Then it is my job to say, "The pictures taken today will be mailed January twelfth."

The best part of the job is watching their faces fall. These pictures are sent to a lab to be processed; it takes time, all these pictures so late in the season. If they wanted their pictures to arrive before Christmas, they should have come during the first week we were open. Lots of people want their money back after learning the pictures will arrive after Christmas, in January, when Christmas is forgotten. Void. 215

We were very crowded today and I got a kick out of completing the transaction, handing the customer a receipt, and saying, "Your photos will be mailed on August tenth."

August is much funnier than January. I just love to see that look on someone's face, the mouth a perfect O.

This was my last day of work. We had been told that Christmas Eve is a slow day, but this was the day a week of training was meant to prepare us for. It was a day of nonstop action, a day when the managers spent a great deal of time with their walkie-talkies.

I witnessed a fistfight between two mothers and watched while a woman experienced a severe, crowd-related anxiety attack: falling to the floor and groping for breath, her arms moving as though she were fighting off bats. A Long Island father called Santa a faggot because he couldn't take the time to recite "The Night Before Christmas" to his child. Parents in long lines left disposable diapers at the door to Santa's house. It was the rowdiest crowd I have ever seen, and we were short on elves, many of whom simply did not show up or called in sick. As a result we had our lunch hours cut in half and had to go without our afternoon breaks. Many elves complained bitterly, but the rest of us found ourselves in the moment we had all been waiting for. It was us against them. It was time to be a trouper, and I surrendered completely. My Santa and I had them on the lap, off the lap in forty-five seconds flat. We were an efficient machine surrounded by chaos. Quitting time came and went for the both of us and we paid it no mind. My plane was due to leave at eight o'clock, and I stayed until the last moment, figuring the time it would take to get to the airport. It was with reservation that I reported to the manager, telling her I had to leave. She was at a cash register, screaming at a customer. She was, in fact, calling this customer a bitch. I touched her arm and said, "I have to go now." She laid her hand on my shoulder, squeezed it gently, and continued her conversation, saying, "Don't tell the store president I called you a bitch. Tell him I called you a fucking bitch, because that's exactly what you are. Now get out of my sight before I do something we both regret."

CONNECTING PERSONALLY TO THE READING

1. What kind of vacation jobs have you taken? How does the temporary nature of the job change your attitude toward it? What observations did you make that were funny or ironic?

2. Do you think that Sedaris learned anything about work in this job, or do you think he just wanted to mock his employers and those who came to SantaLand? Explain.

3. What might you have done if you held this job? Would you have sabotaged it? Explain.

FOCUSING ON THE ARGUMENT

1. Tone is important in this essay. Because he does not need this job to survive, Sedaris can poke fun at its requirements, job "training," and the people he must please. What does the humorous tone help us see about such work?

2. Sedaris provides explicit descriptions of what people do and say, making fun of them while appearing simply to record what he sees in his "diary." Do you think that this obvious pretense of objectivity makes us believe him more? Explain.

SYNTHESIZING IDEAS FROM MULTIPLE READINGS

1. Malcolm Gladwell ("The Physical Genius," p. 268) sees attitude as essential to good work. Sedaris's attitude toward his job would seem to undermine his ability to be a good elf. Do you think this is true? Explain.

2. Both Gary Soto ("Black Hair," p. 296) and Sedaris are writers who took work they either knew or sensed would not be permanent. Both look back on that work with a certain amount of detachment and irony. What insights do they share about why this work was not meaningful? What made the work dehumanizing? How did this work make bitter or resigned those who needed it for survival?

3. Harvey the mural painter (in "Voices from the Workplace," p. 328) and Sedaris both seem able to sabotage their work in some way without alienating their employers. What element of creativity or self-expression is involved in such acts? Why are they important to gaining fulfillment in a job?

4. In Michael Lewis's "Pyramids and Pancakes" (Chapter 7, p. 438), Marcus Allen, the 15-year-old who gave adults legal advice over the Internet, seems to sabotage the regulations of the legal profession. Do you think that either he or Sedaris did any harm by sabotaging regulations? Explain.

WRITING TO ACT

1. Write a former employer about the ways in which his or her employees played with or sabotaged their jobs. Explain how important this act of creativity was to the job and why the motive was less malicious than expressive.

2. Fabricate a letter to someone who might have the power to offer you a dream job. Humorously describe what you see as the job requirements and how you would meet them in special ways. Describe what you could contribute and how this contribution might be received. Find a journal on humor and submit it.

READING

BARBARA EHRENREICH   In her study of low-paying work, Barbara Ehrenreich takes a job at Wal-Mart, describing not only what she does but also how she does it, the mental pictures and thoughts that flood her mind as she does the work put before her. She witnesses how women shop, why they leave the store in disarray for her to reorder, and her role as "therapist" to frustrated women who in their own homes pick up after others. Further, she describes the other employees' attitudes, their reluctance to try to find work elsewhere, their sense of intimidation facing the application process, and their resignation to ill treatment and low pay. She creates a picture of the lives of millions of employees who work at the Wal-Marts and Targets and other conglomerates. What do you think their lives are like?

EHRENREICH, a journalist and writer, is a columnist for *The Progressive* and contributes to—among many publications—*Mother Jones,* the *New York Times,* the *Atlantic Monthly,* and *Ms.;* from 1991 to 1997, she wrote a regular column for *Time.* She is the author of the bestselling *Nickel and Dimed: On (Not) Getting By in America* (2002), from which this excerpt is taken, as well as eleven other books, most recently *Global Woman: Nannies, Maids, and Sex Workers in the New Economy* (2004).

Selection from *Nickel and Dimed* (2002)

BY BARBARA EHRENREICH

The breakthrough comes on a Saturday, one of your heavier shopping days. There are two carts waiting for me when I arrive at two, and tossed items inches deep on major patches of the floor. The place hasn't been shopped, it's been looted. In this situation, all I can do is everything at once—stoop, reach, bend, lift, run from rack to rack with my cart. And then it happens—a magical flow state in which the clothes start putting *themselves* away. Oh, I play a part in this, but not in any conscious way. Instead of thinking, "White Stag navy twill skort," and doggedly searching out similar skorts, all I have to do is form an image of the item in my mind, transpose this image onto the visual field, and move to wherever the image finds its match in the outer world. I don't know how this works. Maybe my mind just gets so busy processing the incoming visual data that it has to bypass the left brain's verbal centers, with their cumbersome instructions: "Proceed to White Stag area in the northwest corner of ladies', try bottom racks near khaki shorts . . ." Or maybe the trick lies in understanding that each item *wants* to be reunited with its sibs and its clan members and that, within each clan, the item *wants* to occupy its proper place in the color/size hierarchy. Once I let the clothes take charge, once I understand that I am only the means of their reunification, they just fly out of the cart to their natural homes.

On the same day, perhaps because the new speediness frees me to think more clearly, I make my peace with the customers and discover the purpose of life, or at least of my life at Wal-Mart. Management may think that the purpose is to sell things, but this is an overly reductionist, narrowly capitalist view. As a matter of fact, I never see anything sold, since sales take place out of my sight, at the cash registers at the front of the store. All I see is customers unfolding carefully folded T-shirts, taking dresses and pants off their hangers, holding them up for a moment's idle inspection, then dropping them somewhere for us associates to pick up. For me, the way out of resentment begins with a clue provided by a poster near the break room, in the back of the store where only associates go: "Your mother doesn't work here," it says. "Please pick up after yourself." I've passed it many times, thinking, "Ha, that's all I do—pick up after people."

Then it hits me: most of the people I pick up after are mothers themselves, meaning that what I do at work is what *they* do at home—pick up the toys and the clothes and the spills. So the great thing about shopping, for most of these women, is that here *they* get to behave like brats, ignoring the bawling babies in their carts, tossing things around for someone else to pick up. And it wouldn't be any fun—would it?—unless the clothes were all reasonably orderly to begin with, which is where I come in, constantly re-creating orderliness for the customers to maliciously destroy. It's appalling, but it's in their nature: only pristine and virginal displays truly excite them.

I test this theory out on Isabelle: that our job is to constantly re-create the stage setting in which women can act out. That without us, rates of child abuse would suddenly soar. That we function, in a way, as therapists and should probably be paid accordingly, at $50 to $100 an hour. "You just go on thinking that," she says, shaking her head. But she smiles her canny little smile in a way that makes me think it's not a bad notion.

With competence comes a new impatience: *Why does anybody put up with the wages we're paid?* True, most of my fellow workers are better cushioned than I am; they live with spouses or grown children or they have other jobs in addition to this one. I sit with Lynne in the break room one night and find out this is only a part-time job for her—six hours a day—with the other eight hours spent at a factory for $9 an hour. Doesn't she get awfully tired? Nah, it's what she's always done. The cook at the Radio Grill has two other jobs. You might expect a bit of grumbling, some signs here and there of unrest—graffiti on the hortatory posters in the break room, muffled guffaws during our associate meetings—but I can detect none of that. Maybe this is what you get when you weed out all the rebels with drug tests and personality "surveys"—a uniformly servile and denatured workforce, content to dream of the distant day when they'll be vested in the company's profit-sharing plan. They even join in the "Wal-Mart cheer" when required to do so at meetings, I'm told by the evening fitting room lady, though I am fortunate enough never to witness this final abasement.[1]

5

But if it's hard to think "out of the box," it may be almost impossible to think out of the Big Box. Wal-Mart, when you're in it, is total—a closed system, a world unto itself. I get a chill when I'm watching TV in the break room one afternoon and see . . . *a commercial for Wal-Mart.* When a Wal-Mart shows up within a television within a Wal-Mart, you have to question the existence of an outer world. . . .

The only thing to do is ask: Why do you—why do *we*—work here? Why do you stay? So when Isabelle praises my work a second time (!), I take the opportunity to say I really appreciate her encouragement, but I can't afford to live on $7 an hour, and how does she do it? The answer is that she lives with her grown daughter, who also works, plus the fact that she's worked here two years, during which her pay has shot up to $7.75 an hour. She counsels patience: it could happen to me. Melissa, who has the advantage of a working husband, says, "Well, it's a job." Yes, she made twice as much when she was a waitress but that place closed down and at her age she's never going to be hired at a high-tip place. I recognize the inertia, the unwillingness to start up with the apps and the interviews and the drug tests again. She thinks she should give it a year. *A year?* I tell her I'm wondering whether I should give it another week.

A few days later something happens to make kindly, sweet-natured Melissa mad. She gets banished to bras, which is terra incognita for us—huge banks of shelves bearing barely distinguishable bi-coned objects—for a three-hour stretch. I know how she feels, because I was once sent over to work for a couple of hours in men's wear, where I wandered uselessly through the strange thickets of racks, numbed by the sameness of colors and styles.[2] It's the difference between working and pretending to work. You push your cart a few feet, pause significantly with item in hand, frown at the ambient racks, then push on and repeat the process. "I just don't like wasting their money," Melissa says when she's allowed back. "I mean they're *paying* me and I just wasn't accomplishing anything over there." To me, this anger seems badly mis-aimed. What does she think, that the Walton family is living in some hidden room in the back of the store, in the utmost frugality, and likely to be ruined by $21 worth of wasted labor? I'm starting in on that theme when she suddenly dives behind the rack that separates the place where we're standing, in the Jordache/No Boundaries section, from the Faded Glory region. Worried that I may have offended her somehow, I follow right behind. "*Howard*," she whispers. "Didn't you see him come by? We're not allowed to talk to each other, you know."

"The point is our time is so cheap they don't care if we waste it," I continue, aware even as I speak that this isn't true, otherwise why would they be constantly monitoring us for "time theft"? But I sputter on: "That's what's so insulting." Of course, in this outburst of militance I am completely not noticing the context—two women of mature years, two very hard-working women, as it happens, dodging behind a clothing rack to avoid a twenty-six-year-old management twerp. That's not even worth commenting on. . . .

Then I get a little reckless. When an associate meeting is announced over the loudspeaker that afternoon, I decide to go, although most of my coworkers stay put. I don't understand the purpose of these meetings, which occur every three days or so and consist largely of attendance taking, unless it's Howard's way of showing us that there's only one of him compared to so many of us. I'm just happy to have a few minutes to sit down or, in this case, perch on some fertilizer bags since we're meeting in lawn and garden today, and chat with whoever shows up, today a gal from the optical department. She's better coifed and made up than most of us female associates—forced to take the job because of a recent divorce, she tells me, and sorry now that she's found out how crummy the health insurance is. There follows a long story about preexisting conditions and deductibles and her COBRA running out. I listen vacantly because, like most of the other people in my orientation group, I hadn't opted for the health insurance—the employee contribution seemed too high. "You know what we need here?" I finally respond. "We need a union." There it is, the word is out. Maybe if I hadn't been feeling so footsore I wouldn't have said it, and I probably wouldn't have said it either if we were allowed to say "hell" and "damn" now and then or, better yet, "shit." But no one has outright banned the word *union* and right now it's the most potent couple of syllables at hand. "We need *something*," she responds.   10

After that, there's nothing to stop me. I'm on a mission now: *Raise the questions! Plant the seeds!* . . . Almost everyone is eager to talk, and I soon become a walking repository of complaints. No one gets paid overtime at Wal-Mart, I'm told, though there's often pressure to work it.[3] Many feel the health insurance isn't worth paying for. There's a lot of frustration over schedules, especially in the case of the evangelical lady who can never get Sunday morning off, no matter how much she pleads. And always there are the gripes about managers: the one who is known for sending new hires home in tears, the one who takes a ruler and knocks everything off what he regards as a messy shelf, so you have to pick it up off the floor and start over.

Sometimes, I discover, my favorite subject, which is the abysmal rate of pay, seems to be a painful one. . . .

At the other extreme, there are people like Marlene. I am sitting out there talking to a doll-like blonde whom I had taken for a high school student but who, it turns out, has been working full-time since November and is fretting over whether she can afford to buy a car. Marlene comes out for her break, lights a cigarette, and emphatically seconds my opinion of Wal-Mart wages. "They talk about having spirit," she says, referring to management, "but they don't give us any reason to have any spirit." In her view, Wal-Mart would rather just keep hiring new people than treating the ones it has decently. You can see for yourself there's a dozen new people coming in for orientation every day—which is true. Wal-Mart's appetite for human flesh is insatiable; we've even been urged to recruit any Kmart employees we may happen to know. They don't care that they've trained you or anything, Marlene goes on, they can always get someone else if you complain. Emboldened by her vehemence, I risk the red-hot word again. "I know this goes against the whole Wal-Mart philosophy, but we could use a union here." She grins, so I push on: "It's not just about money, it's about dignity." She nods fiercely, lighting a second cigarette from her first. *Put that woman on the organizing committee at once,* I direct my imaginary coconspirators as I leave.

. . . Someone has to puncture the prevailing fiction that we're a "family" here, we "associates" and our "servant leaders," held together solely by our commitment to the "guests." After all, you'd need a lot stronger word than *dysfunctional* to describe a family where a few people get to eat at the table while the rest—the "associates" and all the dark-skinned seamstresses and factory workers worldwide who make the things we sell—lick up the drippings from the floor: *psychotic* would be closer to the mark.[4] And someone has to flush out the mysterious "we" lurking in the "our" in the "Our people make the difference" statement we wear on our backs. It might as well be me because I have nothing to lose. . . .

I could use some amusement. I have been discovering a great truth about low-wage work and probably a lot of medium-wage work, too—that nothing happens, or rather the same thing always happens, which amounts, day after day, to nothing. This law doesn't apply so strictly to the service jobs I've held so far. In waitressing, you always have new customers to study; even housecleaning offers the day's parade of houses to explore. But here—well, you know what I do and how it gets undone and how I just start all over and do it again. How did I think I was going to survive in a factory, where each *minute* is identical to the next one, and not just each day? There will be no crises here, except perhaps in the pre-Christmas rush. There will be no "Code M," meaning "hostage situation," and probably no Code F or T (I'm guessing on these letters, which I didn't write down during my note taking at orientation and which may be a company secret anyway), meaning fire or tornado—no opportunities for courage or extraordinary achievement or sudden evacuations of the store. Those breaking-news moments when a disgruntled former employee shoots up the place or a bunch of people get crushed in an avalanche of piled-up stock are one-in-a-million events. What my life holds is carts—full ones, then empty ones, then full ones again.

You could get old pretty fast here. In fact, time does funny things when there are 15
no little surprises to mark it off into memorable chunks, and I sense that I'm already
several years older than I was when I started. In the one full-length mirror in ladies'
wear, a medium-tall figure is hunched over a cart, her face pinched in absurd concentration—surely not me. How long before I'm as gray as Ellie, as cranky as Rhoda, as
shriveled as Isabelle? When even a high-sodium fast-food diet can't keep me from
needing to pee every hour, and my feet are putting some podiatrist's kid through college? Yes, I know that any day now I'm going to return to the variety and drama of my
real, Barbara Ehrenreich life. But this fact sustains me only in the way that, say, the
prospect of heaven cheers a terminally ill person: it's nice to know, but it isn't much
help from moment to moment. What you don't necessarily realize when you start selling your time by the hour is that what you're actually selling is your *life*. . . .

Notes

1. According to Wal-Mart expert Bob Ortega, Sam Walton got the idea for the cheer on a 1975 trip to Japan,
"where he was deeply impressed by factory workers doing group calisthenics and company cheers." Ortega describes Walton conducting a cheer: " 'Gimme a W!' he'd shout. 'W!' the workers would shout back, and on
through the Wal-Mart name. At the hyphen, Walton would shout 'Gimme a squiggly!' and squat and twist his
hips at the same time; the workers would squiggle right back" (*In Sam We Trust*, p. 91).
2. "During your career with Wal-Mart, you may be cross-trained in other departments in your facility. This will
challenge you in new areas, and help you be a well-rounded Associate" ("Wal-Mart Associate Handbook," p. 18).
3. Wal-Mart employees have sued the retail chain for unpaid overtime in four states—West Virginia, New Mexico, Oregon, and Colorado. The plaintiffs allege that they were pressured to work overtime and that the company then erased the overtime hours from their time records. Two of the West Virginia plaintiffs, who had been
promoted to management positions before leaving Wal-Mart, said they had participated in altering time
records to conceal overtime work. Instead of paying time and a half for overtime work, the company would reward workers with "desired schedule changes, promotions and other benefits," while workers who refused the
unpaid overtime were "threatened with write-ups, demotions, reduced work schedules or docked pay"
(Lawrence Messina, "Former Wal-Mart Workers File Overtime Suit in Harrison County," *Charleston Gazette*,
January 24, 1999). In New Mexico, a suit by 110 Wal-Mart employees was settled in 1998 when the company
agreed to pay for the overtime ("Wal-Mart Agrees to Resolve Pay Dispute," *Albuquerque Journal*, July 16, 1998).
In an e-mail to me, Wal-Mart spokesman William Wertz stated that "it is Wal-Mart's policy to compensate its
employees fairly for their work and to comply fully with all federal and state wage and hour requirements."
4. In 1996, the National Labor Committee Education Fund in Support of Worker and Human Rights in Central America revealed that some Kathie Lee clothes were being sewn by children as young as twelve in a sweat-
shop in Honduras. TV personality Kathie Lee Gifford, the owner of the Kathie Lee line, tearfully denied the
charges on the air but later promised to give up her dependence on sweatshops.

CONNECTING PERSONALLY TO THE READING

1. Have you ever engaged in work so trivial that you begin to do it unconsciously, all the activities at once, in a kind of "magical flow state" that Ehrenreich describes? If so, what was
this state like for you?

2. Have you ever looked past the stated purpose of your work (to sell something or to provide
service, for example) to some other meaning it may have? What was that experience like?
What meaning did you derive from your work?

3. Ehrenreich questions the reasons why people take low-paying, trivial work in which employers debase their employees. Do you think that she answers this question adequately? Explain.

1. Ehrenreich does not use a linear sociological argument to persuade her readers, but rather her own experiences and thought processes. We follow her stream-of-consciousness, from her "flow state" of work to her reflections on the purpose of her life in Wal-Mart to her speculations about other employees' motivations to her "crusades" to change things. Why do you think she chose to use this inner monologue of personal experience?

2. The tone Ehrenreich uses is personable, but it borders on outrage. The colloquial and often metaphoric language (e.g., "The place hasn't been shopped, it's been looted") intensifies the anger. What is the effect of this tone? Does she seem more or less credible because of it?

3. Ehrenreich's idea of the globalization of Wal-Mart–type corporations is depicted in her images of TVs within Wal-Mart showing Wal-Mart stores. How do such images help her convey her point?

4. Ehrenreich develops her ideas by telling her own story as well as reporting others' experiences. Her own story includes an attempt to act on a mission to help workers organize a union. Do you think her own perceptions, anger, and interventions distort the study and thus make her descriptions less credible? Or do you think that they make the study more credible? Explain.

1. In "The Physical Genius" (p. 268), Malcolm Gladwell also describes a "magical flow" that characterizes the physical genius of certain professionals and athletes. How is the magical flow that Ehrenreich describes similar to and different from that which Gladwell describes?

2. Ehrenreich clearly does not love her work at Wal-Mart. Yet, according to bell hooks ("Work Makes Life Sweet," p. 285), one can love work that one does well, no matter how ordinary. What prevents Ehrenreich and other employees from loving their work in the way hooks describes?

3. Both David Sedaris ("SantaLand Diaries," p. 303) and Ehrenreich take on jobs in order to study them. What might this role make them miss about the work they are performing? How do their different purposes shape what they see? Explain.

4. One of the cognitive skills Mike Rose ("The Working Life of a Waitress," p. 278) describes in depth is memory. How does memory play a key role in the Wal-Mart job Ehrenreich describes? How would visualization and economy of motion also be important?

5. Ehrenreich thinks Wal-Mart is like a box within a box—everywhere, one is bombarded with Wal-Mart advertising and Wal-Mart-like stores. Do you think that John Dewey ("The School and the Life of the Child," Chapter 4, p. 211) might see conventional schooling as preparing young minds to accept Wal-Mart ideals? Explain.

1. Imagine that you were going to start a union at Wal-Mart. What would be your first step? How would you organize people? Write out a list of key complaints that you think you could get workers to support.

2. Using details from this study, write a letter to Wal-Mart on their employee practices. Suggest a different treatment of employees, one that includes not only a moderate increase in pay but also different treatment. Explain what you think may be the cost/benefits to Wal-Mart.

Voices from the Workplace What follows are three short pieces that give voice to people engaged in various kinds of work. Together these voices suggest a variety of activities and approaches to work. In each, an individual describes the particulars of a certain kind of work, the value he or she sees in it, and the conflicts that arise. Ask yourself, Do these descriptions reflect any of the theories put forth so far, by Malcolm Gladwell ("The Physical Genius"), Mike Rose ("The Working Life of a Waitress"), bell hooks ("Work Makes Life Sweet"), or Daniel Levine ("Take This Job and Love it")? For instance, does the work require cognitive skills such as memory or anticipation? Does it teach basic requirements of good work habits? Is it "sweet"? Overall, which jobs sound most enticing to you?

Mural Painter: Harvey (from *Sabotage*)

BY MARTIN SPROUSE

I work for a company that produces custom murals and decorative paintings. We do a lot of work for cruise ships, hotels, restaurants and casinos in Vegas and Atlantic City. As far as I know, there aren't many companies that do what we do. Art consultants bring us jobs from all over the world.

We mainly do pictorial murals. We don't do anything abstract. My bosses have a real chip on their shoulders against anything conceptual whatsoever; the more vapid the subject, the more they like it. In fact, they try to keep human figures out of the compositions as much as possible because the human figure can be a very controversial thing. If the painting is in a public space and it contains a group of figures, you're almost guaranteed to offend someone. The piece we're working on right now has absolutely no figures in it at all. It's a big architectural painting of classic Greek columns with a landscape in the background. It has a couple of animals in it. It's impressive to someone who doesn't want to think about an image and just wants to be struck by its surface as they glide past. It's made to sit against the wall as a whisper instead of a shout.

I do my best not to focus on the down side of my job but I'm not a hopeless optimist either. I have to watch it while I'm working there because if I let my cynicism be known I'll just fuck myself out of a job. It's more important that I keep this veneer of calmness and satisfaction.

Since I'm able to do more than just paint, I don't really fall into a monotonous routine. I think the frustration with my job comes more from the fact that what I consider to be worthy and beautiful art is opposed to my bosses' opinions. They put a lot more emphasis on money and let their artistic standards be dictated by it. I'd like to think that mine are associated with something other than cash. True, it's a business, but they love to pose as artists. My bosses' notion of what good painting is really annoys me. It's all fluff. All false. We have to pump up the colors in the paintings to these absurdly tacky proportions. I can have this twisted grin on my face, just wallow in the cheesiness of it and really run with it, and my boss will think that I'm really into it. In reality I'm mocking it. I play the role and ape my boss. Then it ceases to be fun, and it becomes dreary and I have to look for other ways to keep myself amused.

Recently we did a job for the Walt Disney Corporation. They specifically re- 5 quested the Great Gatsby as the theme, which basically is about rich people in the good old days. The idea was to make the people look happy and create the ideal that people off the streets should strive to get a white suit, Panama hat and a croquet mallet. One of my favorite scenes was a hotel scene where people were seated at tables. In the background there was this balcony where I painted this little SS Stormtrooper. It was my little comment on what was happening in the rest of the world while the Great Gatsbys were whittling away their hours with cocktails. My boss noticed it and said that it looked like a soldier, but I convinced him it was a security guard. He dropped it at that. All of the people that I worked with noticed it was a Nazi right away.

I changed some of the pictures as I worked my way down the panel. The scene had framed pictures hanging on the background wall which I changed to paintings by Francis Bacon: weird-shaped monsters with pear-shaped bodies sitting on a wobbly table with claws hanging over their heads. My boss didn't say anything about those either. There were some very large figures of two men and two women in the foreground which I improved by adding a psychological element. I made it look like the two men were ready to fight it out in sort of a territorial mating battle over the women. There were fifteen people painted into the middleground who were all looking very alarmed, shocked and dismayed. The foreground had the two men about to fight, the middleground had these shocked onlookers, and the background had Francis Bacon paintings and a Nazi. My bosses repainted the foreground figures but never fixed anything else. It's now installed in a hotel. That gave me a lot of satisfaction. It's pretty minor but it did make me feel better.

I did a series of reproductions of Pompeii wall frescoes for an Italian restaurant in Vegas. I changed figures in that too. I painted one guy with cloven hooves instead of feet, and put a knife in his hand. I painted a few severed heads in that one, too. When I worked on some paintings of the New Orleans French Quarter, I was appalled that these paintings had to go over slot machines and compete with them for attention. So I put three figures in the balcony scene. One is pointing at the person who would be below at the slot machine; one has a martini and is looking very aristocratic and sneering at the slot-machine player. Then there's this other guy who is more of a caricature: he's got big buck teeth, a monocle, and an iron cross pinned to his lapel and has his head back, also laughing at the person playing the machine.

It's really hard to get away with anything more. I've been told to repaint fruit in still lifes because they were too suggestive. I didn't do it on purpose, but once they called my attention to it, I started to figure out ways that I could do it and get away with it.

Interview with a Psychiatrist (Anna Balas)

BY DIANE BENNETT DURKIN

I am fifty-five and nearly the age of some people about ready to retire. I don't even think about retirement. I feel that I am just reaching the height of my abilities. I always wanted to be a psychiatrist, even in medical school. Some of my friends in medical school said, "That's a good profession for a woman." I took offense at that. I thought, if I had loved surgery, I would have done that. But as it turned out, being a psychiatrist has been good for me as a woman. Not only have I spent eleven years in medical training, first medical school, then a residency in psychiatry, another in childhood psychiatry, then in liason work that applies psychiatry to pediatrics, and finally in psychoanalytic training, but I became a wife and mother. If I had loved surgery, it would have been more difficult. Psychiatry is more flexible than other medical professions. There has been some cost when I cut back my hours, but not much. With my son in college, I have built my practice back up.

I love my work. The day is full of activities. For much of the day, I see patients—some of whom I've been seeing for a long time, some in consultation as possible new patients. I do some phone work with patients, for those in a crisis or needing a prescription. I also spend time at the hospital supervising aspiring psychiatrists. I go over cases. Cases are the pivots of my day. I particularly like my work with children and adolescents.

Working with children involves so much—I have to work with the whole family, finding out what's going on with the kid, giving advice to the family. There is always something unexpected. A patient, say an adolescent, is in crisis, she "worsens," has what used to be called a "nervous breakdown." Then I am involved in a huge amount of additional work, something that may distinguish me from other therapists. I get involved in lengthy phone conferences with the family, perhaps with a college administrator, a head of a department. I go way beyond the immediate problem—arrange for the parents to pick up the student, get permits to allow a parent to "get into" the school, alerting those involved as to what might happen should the crisis worsen. I have to caution parents to lower the pressure on the adolescent. Also, even though I am a psychiatrist and a psychoanalyst, I don't have special expertise in pharmacology. I have to call a specialist.

I have to use all of my skills, skills in collaboration, analytical skills, techniques for working with kids and with parents. On top of this, New York is so multicultural. Practicing psychiatry in a multicultural environment is not like practicing psychiatry in a homogeneous environment. I am like a cultural anthropologist. I need to know a family's social class, education, values, and cultural traditions.

My analytical skills took a long time to develop. I remember watching a senior person comment on one of the "cases" I was studying in my residency. She identified the patient's underlying "complexes," complexes I couldn't see at all. It was like magic. How did she figure out the case? It was like reading Braille. Then I couldn't imagine that analyzing cases would become second nature. Later, I began to see. I could figure things out. So many of the people around me are getting older and worrying about their cholesterol and their bone density. I'm also worried about my cholesterol and my

5

bone density, but professionally I am just hitting my stride. I love to teach, I take great pleasure in sharing what I have learned, I am working with aspiring child psychiatrists, and I am on several foundation boards. I am appreciating what has come with age—a new sense of the quality of my work. This is a major shift.

One of the analytic parts I find most intriguing is the intrapsychic conflicts—the inner world of the person—how a conflict is organized. For instance, a three-year-old child is torn between a desire for independence—say, riding a hobby horse—and dependence—the need for help from an adult. How does the child organize the conflict? Children hide information. I need to act like a detective. Intrapsychic conflict gets more and more complex as the person gets older, and so is more challenging. The dimension of trauma, for instance. Some of the people I see have been touched by traumatic events, and the trauma gets incorporated and digested, gets hidden, but because of some event or news later in life the person becomes retraumatized. For instance, a woman with three children, ten, twelve and fourteen, who as a ten-year-old experienced her mother's sudden death, was retraumatized when she found out she had cancer. She imagined not only her own death but the trauma of her children suddenly left motherless, as she had been. I had to understand her symptoms in terms of early trauma, not just the facts of the case at hand. Trauma takes special expertise, yet I am expected to understand it. It is part of my general knowledge.

As with most jobs, there is a potential for abuse. I work in the privacy of my own place, no one is watching. There is potential for overstepping bounds. One has to have internalized good ethics. The abuse is not always obvious—as with asking for some insider stock tips or seducing a patient. A therapist can be overly friendly, accept presents, enjoy the patient's transference. Nothing obvious. Yet these violations can have profound effects. They can undermine a patient, who is extremely vulnerable. Even the most innocuous questions may have to be resisted. One patient asked me if I wasn't the oldest child, as she was. It would have been easy to answer, yes, and let her just a little into my personal life. It might have seemed like an easy, even a conversational thing to do. But it wouldn't have been good for the patient. Further, a therapist may have his or her own problems with boundaries. A patient who was molested as a child might try to seduce a therapist in a drive to re-create the dramatic situation. The therapist, who may have his or her own problems with early seduction, might have a negative reaction, called "counter transfer," in which the therapist develops negative feelings about the patient. The therapist might diagnose the patient as "borderline," which means a difficult patient, a kind of name calling.

Therapists, of course, are human beings too, with their own complexes. But they need to be alert, to be skilled, to be highly trained. This is why I work as a discussant in so many cases, helping to train other analysts. I remember a training case of abandonment. A patient suddenly decides to leave, to stop treatment. This may trigger an analyst's own abandonment issues: Why is this patient leaving? Why so dismissive of the treatment? The therapist, who is reenacting a childhood event, is "transferring" his or her own anxiety to the patient and becomes extremely agitated at the patient's behavior. What is so clear from the outside is obscure to the untrained analyst. We can all have blind spots, be out of tune, take on grandiose views of ourselves, or just lose perspective. Training helps give one the tools to treat patients fairly, with humility, without doing harm. They also shift one's entire view of oneself and the world.

This is not a job for people who are concrete, who need "the answer." These people won't do well as psychiatrists. I find I have to be creative, multidimensional, complex, and at the same time extremely responsible. As I put it, a psychiatrist needs to have his or her "feet on the ground and head in the sky." Empathy is what is most needed. I try to go back and forth between the practical grounded reality and the imagination. I need both to do my job well. I can connect with patients, yet I am a solid, no-nonsense person. I don't idealize my training or my role. I always wanted to become a doctor, to take on that responsibility, not to skirt it, but I didn't like medical school. Especially not the procedural stuff. But I learned to do things I didn't like. I was happier in my residency, which required a more dynamic understanding. The profession is always changing. My patients as well as the aspiring psychiatrists are increasingly multicultural—East Asian, Mediterranean, Indian—so I am constantly learning.

Interview with a Journalist (Claudia Luther)

BY DIANE BENNETT DURKIN

When I started out as a journalist in the mid-1960s, women still were relegated to food and fashion and the society sections, so let's fast forward a bit to when I covered a lot more—city councils, state commissions, county supervisors—actually all the basic levels of government. For several years, I covered the state legislature and political campaigns at every level, including the Republican and Democratic national conventions. I interviewed politicians of every stripe, including many gubernatorial and presidential candidates.

One has to be quick. The thrill, and the dread, of the job is writing on deadline. You never get used to it. No matter how advanced in the field you are, deadlines are extremely stressful. When is enough enough? What can you get in a set amount of time? The deadline defines your day. You live by it. Every minute is dictated.

At the end of the day, you go with the best of what you have. Afterwards, it takes a while to calm down. You can't just go from making a deadline at 10 P.M. or midnight to go home and go to sleep. You are too stimulated. It's been too exciting—like after an athletic performance. And you have that same sense of accomplishment. Only once, in my entire career, did I not make deadline. I felt terrible. Yet I finished the story the next day and it turned out to be one of my better stories.

During my years in journalism, I alternated between reporting and editing. As an editor, you respond to but also help fashion the coverage for the day.

A lot goes into this, and having a deep background in reporting helps. You must 5 have quick judgment to assign people stories and be able to respond to things as they come up. You have to know many ways of finding out what's happening. Decisions need to be made about what stories are worth our resources and, once that's decided, how far to go with it: "What do we need to do here?" "Are there enough people covering the story?" "Do we need to send someone to wherever?" The editor makes these decisions.

In addition to being a reporter, I have also been the editor of key sections of the paper: The Book Review and the Op-Ed, or commentary, page. For the Book Review, I assigned all book reviews and oversaw production. For the Op-Ed page, I oversaw a staff that solicited and edited pieces from outside sources—to allow different voices in the paper.

Most recently, I was the deputy of the News Obituary department, which involved a combination of editing and reporting on the major figures of our time. I assigned and oversaw other reporters but often wrote under deadline myself. It was a fun kind of writing—biography, really—and often I had the freedom to choose who to write about. In other roles, I have been an editor in the entertainment and arts section and for a time I was a "special projects editor" in the features part of the newspaper, where I helped plan a major book festival.

I have always liked having choice and flexibility. Some journalists prefer to stay in one special area. They gain expertise—become known for their field. This can be deeply satisfying. Other journalists, like myself, prefer to move around. It's nice when the organization is big—one can move between various jobs yet still build seniority.

I knew what the profession would be like from the time I was in college because I majored in journalism and also I wrote for my college newspaper. I had a basic skill level in writing, which put me in this direction. Comments from teachers such as "well written" tell you something, help you focus on what you're good at. But I also found that I stayed in this field because of the friends I met there. The people you hang out with become as important as the work you do, and I like journalists. They are a smart and funny and skeptical group. They are bright and entertaining. Journalism seemed a good match with my intrinsic abilities and my desire to be with a certain kind of people. And then I became very good at what I did. My annual job reviews are covered with the kind of comments journalists want to hear—"a pro and a self-starter," "a stickler for accuracy," "copy is clear and well organized," "quick to assess the newsworthiness."

Not every day is a thrill and/or a terror. Some days are just boring. There's no 10 story. Everyone is complaining, moping around, depressed. Then the next day, there's a story, and the complaints dry up. Everyone is rushed. When the story is a big one, there is a lot of activity. One thinks, of course, of major disasters or events. But even something like an education bill in the state legislature can be frantic. Lots is happening: a hearing, meetings in the hallways, calls made to check out information, a stop at the teachers' lobby. Journalists need to piece together the story as best they can, try to understand the whole picture. Who is the stronger player? Who will prevail? Is there corruption involved? Whose arms are being twisted? As journalists, we try to talk to people, dig for information. A tape recorder slows us down, so we need to be good at taking notes. We are looking at the clock the whole time. On this kind of a story, by the time I get back to the office, I should have some idea of how to construct the story. Or perhaps I will call in notes to someone on the desk who is keeping track of the bigger picture. I don't work alone, my editors sometimes say when it's time to pull the plug and come back to write. But then sometimes I say to the editor, "I'm finished here, it's time to get it down." Always we are thinking of the clock.

There is a lot of excitement in this job. Things develop. What you think is a story at the beginning of the day may crash, or it may get better and better. Then there's the thrill of finding the right person to talk to, or finding the little lie someone told. Suddenly the picture changes. There's a saying among journalists: "Things don't turn up unless somebody turns them up." It takes grit and smarts to make things turn up, but it's the biggest thrill of all for journalists. Every good reporter and editor gets a rush from turning up something no one wanted us to know.

The best part of the job, though, is the sense of purpose, of "doing good." Journalists are on the side of the people, helping them to know as much as possible to make decisions about how we are governed. It's a shame the media has had a bad reputation in some quarters. Imagine our society without the media, without "news." It's this shared sense of purpose that gives journalists their sense of worth. The goal is to fully cover the important events and decisions of our time. And what could be better than that?

CONNECTING PERSONALLY TO THE READINGS

1. Which kind of work attracted you the most? What was the nature of that attraction? Do you think you have a calling for a certain kind of work? Explain.

2. What kind of person is the journalist? Do you think that you need to be that kind of person to find value in this work? Explain.

3. Looking at this spectrum of jobs, what personal qualities do you think are most important in deriving meaning from each specific kind of work? Explain.

FOCUSING ON THE ARGUMENT

1. The voices here are personalized, reflecting the individuals as much as the jobs. It is this personal tone that gives the interview its credibility. What kind of a person is each individual? How is that person's character reflected in how he or she approaches and describes the work?

2. What details are most telling and why? What qualities of the work does the interviewee highlight to make the work appealing or not?

SYNTHESIZING IDEAS FROM MULTIPLE READINGS

1. How do you think Daniel Levine ("Take This Job and Love It," p. 292) would describe the job skills of the journalist, especially her ability to make deadlines and write clear copy?

2. As a mural painter, Harvey seems to have found a way to express his own ideas and creativity within the strictures of a job he doesn't like. What spirit or view of work does Harvey think is necessary for human dignity on the job? How is this view supported by Gary Soto's

("Black Hair," p. 296) analysis of his summer work and by David Sedaris's ("SantaLand Diaries," p. 303) description of his short stint as a Santa's elf?

3. According to John Berger ("Ways of Seeing," Chapter 8, p. 530), "The meaning of an image is changed according to what one sees immediately beside it or what comes immediately after it." What changes in meaning do you think the muralist created by painting the Nazi storm trooper into the background balcony of the hotel scene in which rich people are seated at tables below? What further changes in meaning did the mural undergo when it became "installed in a hotel"?

4. For the psychiatrist, what makes work meaningful? Do you think that she illustrates the "right livelihood" (self-expression, commitment, mindfulness, and conscious choice) that bell hooks describes in "Work Makes Life Sweet" (p. 285)? Explain.

WRITING TO ACT

1. Write a letter to a former employer about what you learned on the job. What made the experience valuable to you? What aspects of the job could have been changed to help you derive more meaning?

2. Talk with a friend who is doing some soul-searching about work or the work he or she is planning on some day doing. Tell the friend what qualities you think most affect her or his satisfaction. What advice would you give this friend? Write a job description that best combines this person's attributes and the work requirements.

Connecting the Readings to the Artworks

The Trial

1. In "The Physical Genius" (p. 268), Malcolm Gladwell emphasizes that neurosurgeons need visualization, anticipation, and imagination to do their work. Are the same qualities needed for trial work, as depicted here? Explain.

2. Images of power, hierarchy, tradition, and expertise abound in the painting (e.g., the American eagle, the scales, the books and papers). How do specific details suggest the painter's attitude toward these values? Do you think that bell hooks ("Work Makes Life Sweet," p. 285) and David Sedaris ("SantaLand Diaries," p. 303) hold the same view of power? Explain.

3. What view of power, responsibility, and the professions is implied in Daniel Levine's "Take This Job and Love It" (p. 292)? Is it similar to Jack Levine's? Explain.

4. In "The Working Life of a Waitress" (p. 278), Mike Rose discusses the extensive cognitive and social skills (memory, attention, visualization) that a waitress needs in order to be successful. What cognitive skills do the lawyers and judge appear to need? Explain.

New York Office

1. In "Work Makes Life Sweet" (p. 285), bell hooks advises us to love our work, consciously choose what we do, and act with full awareness and care. Does the woman reading the correspondence seem to embody hooks's suggestion? What in her gaze, gestures, posture, and dress make you think so?

2. David Sedaris ("SantaLand Diaries," p. 303) and the muralist both talk about sabotaging their work, mocking the purported objectives of their jobs. What opportunities might this woman have for such sabotage? What might be the motive for doing so?

Dorothy Hodgkin

1. Malcolm Gladwell's "The Physical Genius" (p. 268) describes mental and physical abilities that account for the extraordinary physical genius of a neurosurgeon or a concert cellist, including imagination, anticipation, and preparation. What connection between physical movement and mental acuity does this painting suggest, even though the subject is not a performer? Explain, pointing to specific details.

2. In "Work Makes Life Sweet" (p. 285), bell hooks admonishes us to love our work with a Buddha-like acceptance, finding joy in deliberate actions. Do you think that Dorothy Hodgkin relates to her work the way bell hooks advocates? Explain why or why not. Then explain how both writer and artist help you to define the meaning of work.

Spring Sale at Bendel's

1. In "Nickel and Dimed" (p. 322), Barbara Ehrenreich's experience working at Wal-Mart taught her that women often see shopping as an opportunity to behave as irresponsibly as their children, leaving clothes for others to pick up, trying things on just for fun. In what way does Ehrenreich's wry comment—"The place hasn't been shopped it's been looted"—apply to Stettheimer's depiction?

2. In "SantaLand Diaries" (p. 303), David Sedaris's seasonal job as an elf at Macy's reveals some of the same sardonic views of shoppers that Stettheimer projects. What specific actions in the painting support Sedaris's attitudes? How does the artist make these actions come across as funny, sardonic, or foolish?

Sun and Wind on the Roof

1. Do you think that the woman in Sloan's painting is in harmony with her surroundings? Examine key elements—the subject's face, body, and movement; the clothes on the line, the colors; the dark and light contrasts; and the background. What might Mike Rose ("The Working Life of a Waitress," p. 278) suggest are the sources of this harmony or disharmony?

2. Barbara Ehrenreich ("Nickel and Dimed," p. 322) and bell hooks ("Work Makes Life Sweet," p. 285) might each interpret this painting differently. Why might this be true or not true? Do you think that Ehrenreich's profession as a social critic would affect her interpretations? Explain.

Jersey Homesteads Mural, *Albert Einstein among Other Immigrants*

1. Jersey Homesteads, New Jersey, was a planned community created for Jewish garment workers, sponsored by the Resettlement Administration during Franklin Delano Roosevelt's presidency. Do you think bell hooks ("Work Makes Life Sweet," p. 285) would empathize with the need for a planned community? Explain, drawing attention to images from the mural.

2. How would Soto ("Black Hair," p. 296) and Ehrenreich ("Nickel and Dimed," p. 322) describe the work conditions depicted in this mural? What actions would they likely advocate?

Mural, Great Hall, Detroit Institute of the Arts

1. Historians have long noted that the Industrial Revolution, with its focus on mass production, changed the nature of work. Workers became more machinelike. Do you think that Rivera's mural portrays this idea that workers have become more machinelike? What in the mural and in the readings supports your view?

2. In "Take this Job and Love It" (p. 292), Daniel Levine attacks the supposed myths that low-paying jobs are dead-end, destroying self-confidence. Do you think that Rivera's mural supports or refutes Levine's views? Point to specific elements in the painting to explain your views.

3. In "The Working Life of a Waitress" (p. 278), Mike Rose describes the cognitive and social skills necessary for work as a waitress. Do you think that such skills are in evidence in the painting? Explain why or why not.

El Campesino

1. In "Work Makes Life Sweet" (p. 285), bell hooks describes how low-paying work can be "sweet," depending on one's attitude and consciousness. Do you think that the worker in this picture is oppressed by his work or that he does it with deliberateness? What in the colors, figure, and background supports your view?

2. In "Take This Job and Love It" (p. 292), Daniel Levine thinks that low-paying jobs teach valuable lessons, such as punctuality and responsibility. Do you think that those are the lessons being learned by the field-worker? If so, explain why. If not, explain what other lessons are being learned.

FINDING COMMON CAUSE IN CONTROVERSY
Should the Family Time Flexibility Act Be Supported?

While this chapter asks you to reflect on work from numerous points of view, avoiding simplistic right-wrong thinking, sometimes issues arise that suggest a pro-con debate. Debates are important when one has to choose between supporting or not supporting legislation. Legislation such as the Family Time Flexibility Act (which addresses the treatment of overtime) has created controversy and may affect the daily lives of millions of workers. For this reason, it is important to analyze the arguments for each side, as well as the grounds for these arguments. What follows is an opportunity to sharpen your critical thinking skills by determining which view you think represents our deepest values and concerns. While your ultimate task is to convince readers of your view, persuasion comes after extensive analysis and reflection. Once again the goal is not to dismiss the opposition and win the argument, but to consider, analyze, think through, and determine which side represents our deepest (although not necessarily all of) our values.

The Family Time Flexibility Act specifies that employers can offer workers a choice of overtime compensation in the form of either time-and-a-half vacation hours/days or time-and-a-half pay. If the employee chooses time-and-a-half compensation days, he or she can take the comp days "within a reasonable period," but not at a time when they would "unduly disrupt the operations of the employer." If the employee chooses time-and-a-half overtime pay, employers must pay for that time within thirty days from the end of the calendar year. Supporters claim that the bill offers hourly wage earners the ability to take time off for family care or vacations—a flexibility that government workers have had but workers in the private sector have not. Detractors claim that the bill does not offer real choice because employers can push workers to work more hours, refuse requested compensation days because they "disrupt" operations, and withhold overtime pay until thirty days after the end of the year, which constitutes a free loan. These opposing positions are reflected in the two articles below from different organizations, the Independent Women's Forum and the National Organization for Women. Because the legislation particularly targets women, it is significant that these women's groups hold strongly opposing views.

The two organizations target different facets of the bill to support or condemn. Before you debate the issue, identify all their arguments for and against. Also, look for other perspectives that don't just focus on the employee. For instance, employers also have to benefit. Businesses can easily fold if the flexibility offered workers doesn't also benefit employers. Look for common ground among employers and employees, as well as between the two positions on the bill. Then decide which arguments are strongest and why you think so. In your response, give credence to the opposing side.

DEBORAH PERRY PISCIONE is the president of the Choose to Lead Women's Foundation, an organization that coaches women, through mentoring and advocacy, "to carve their own pathways in work and life." She is also the coauthor (with Democrat Julianne Malveaux) of *Unfinished Business: A Democrat and a Republican Take on the 10 Most Important Issues Women Face.* She appears regularly as a commentator on radio and television shows, and she is also a popular public speaker and lecturer.

The National Organization for Women, founded in 1966, is the largest feminist organization in the United States, with over 500,000 contributing members. Through intensive lobbying, petitions, rallies, and marches, the organization presses for a constitutional amendment that will "protect the rights and choices of women in all sectors of society"; its top priorities include economic equality among all races and genders and the defense of abortion rights.

Motherhood and Comp Time (2003)

BY DEBORAH PERRY PISCIONE

M y kids come first," Le'Shawnda Riley, a 26-year-old, single mother of four told me. "You can always get another job, but if something happens to your kids, nothing's going to bring them back," she lamented.

As a nine-to-five receptionist at a non-profit organization in downtown D.C., Ms. Riley is in an untenable position. She relies on her paycheck to support her family, yet she has to endure the gut-wrenching dilemma of what to do when a child gets sick, needs to go to the dentist, or is performing in a school play she'd like to attend. She is in a bind: her job does not afford her the flexibility to take 'compensatory time' in lieu of payment for overtime hours worked, and it is difficult, time-consuming and costly to secure quality child care in Washington. What's a working mother to do?

The story of Ms. Riley, who has not received a dime of child support since having her children, is appalling yet typical. Many women are not offered workplace flexibility options that could better facilitate balance between work and family. It's not the employers' fault; it's against the law to provide comp time for hourly workers in the private sector. This problem is magnified in one-parent households, where the wage earner literally needs to choose between keeping food on the table and tending to the needs of their children. What kind of choice is that?

There is a glimpse of relief in the Family Time Flexibility Act, recently introduced by Rep. Judy Biggert (R-IL). This bill would allow private sector workers the option of negotiating with their employer to choose comp time or overtime pay, a benefit that has been enjoyed by federal, state, and local public sector workers for years. Since 1977, federal workers have been able to take advantage of this benefit, and state and local public workers since 1985. The bill would match public sector workers' comp time provision of time-and-a-half, meaning for every hour of overtime, the employee is entitled to an hour-and-a-half of either pay or comp time. Choosing comp time in lieu of overtime pay can't be forced on employees.

Representative Biggert's bill amends the 1938, (yes, 1938), Fair Labor Standards Act. The Fair Labor Standards Act needs to be brought into this century. It was written to reflect the workforce during an era when most women did not work outside the home. Needless to say, the composition of the labor force has changed and the world has changed. Today's families face grave challenges, such as dealing with violence in schools, drug addiction, and a justified apprehension about the safety of their neighborhoods. If there were ever a time when children need parents, it is now. Women embrace this belief: 81 percent of women favor compensatory time as an option for greater workforce flexibility, according to the Employment Policy Foundation. However, this is merely a pipedream for some. People are working more and spending less time with their families: according to the International Labor Organization, Americans are working 1,978 hours per year compared to 1,779 hours in 1973.

Private sector hourly wage earners cannot take comp time to attend to the needs of their families until the Fair Labor Standards Act is amended. So, why isn't the Family Time Flexibility Act being rubber-stamped through Congress?

Picture this: an arm wrestling contest between the labor unions and working mothers—and guess who's on the side of labor unions? Feminist groups such as N.O.W who purport to be pro-woman. The unions and feminist groups are using scare tactics to imply that the Family Time Flexibility Act would force employees to work longer hours for less pay and will lose even more control over time spent at work. It's not about control. It's about choices.

Not all labor unions are anti-mother. In testimony before the House Committee on Education and the Workforce, Dennis Slocomb, the Executive Vice President and Legislative Director of the International Union of Police Associations (IUPA) stated "our members want, need, and appreciate the Congressional comp time provision. It allows them to work for compensatory time in lieu of cash overtime which then allows them some control over their schedule: time for family, relief of stress, a day of fishing, a PTA meeting or a ball game comp time is important to the survival of a street level cop."

What is it going to take to provide working single mothers, like Le'Shawnda Riley, the flexibility she deserves? She's not asking for anything more than to be there for her children. Congress should give her a break.

Background: "The Family Time Flexibility Act" (2003)
The National Organization for Women

Winding its way through Congress is regressive Republican legislation that would take away already limited flexibility over hours and wages from workers and hand it to their employers. The House bill, deceptively entitled "The Family Time Flexibility Act" (H.R. 1119), was introduced by Rep. Judy Biggert (R-Ill.) in March. On April 9, it was voted out of the House Education and the Workforce Committee by a vote of 27-22. The similarly titled Senate bill, "The Family Time and Workplace Flexibility Act" (S. 317) was introduced in February by Sen. Judd Gregg (R-N.H.) and has been referred to committee. House Republican leaders have expressed their intentions to bring this corporate-friendly bill to the House floor for a vote in May.

H.R. 1119 and S. 317 constitute an frontal attack on the Fair Labor Standards Act (FLSA), which requires employers to pay overtime to certain employees when they are required to work beyond the normal 40 hour workweek. "The Family Time Flexibility Act" and "The Family Time and Workplace Flexibility Act" are not family-friendly in any way. In fact, they aim to dismantle the most basic family-friendly provision on the books—the 40 hour workweek—giving carte blanche permission to employers to work their employees almost unlimited hours. It is important to note that already the average employee in the U.S. now works 350 hours more per year than does the typical European worker. NOW believes that this legislation is indeed a return to the bad old days when workers were exploited to the maximum. This bill must be stopped in its tracks!

The Bush administration is pushing this bill and related changes to long-standing rules in the Department of Labor that affect workers' rights. Some of these proposals would have profound impacts on millions of workers and would be especially harmful for working women by:

- Excluding previously protected workers who were entitled to overtime by reclassifying them as managers, thereby making them ineligible for overtime pay;
- Eliminating certain moderate-income workers from overtime protections by drastically lowering the maximum salary level at which workers are guaranteed overtime pay for work beyond 40 hours;

- Removing overtime protection from large numbers of workers in aerospace, defense, health care, high tech and other industries; and
- Allowing employers to give even protected workers "comp time" in lieu of overtime pay.

Currently, employers are faced with a substantial disincentive to requiring more than 40 hours of work per week from their employees—time-and-a-half pay. This legislation, however, would remove this disincentive, thereby providing a strong financial incentive for employers to lengthen the workweek. Under these bills, employees working overtime would forfeit their overtime pay for a promise of time off sometime within the next 13 months at their employer's discretion. This takes away employee flexibility both in terms of pay and time off. Those workers using overtime pay to help meet their families' needs are likely to find that opportunities for overtime pay have dried up as employers prefer to give overtime assignments to those who are willing to do it in return for a time-off IOU rather than extra cash in their paycheck.

For businesses doing poorly in this weak economy, this bill is a windfall. In a recent report, the Economic Policy Institute (EPI) explains how, under this bill, employers would essentially take out an interest-free loan from their employees by not paying the[m] for overtime hours worked now in exchange for time off over up to a year from now. According to EPI, "A company with 200,000 FLSA-covered employees might get 160 free hours at $7 an hour from each of them (160 hours is the maximum allowed under the bills). That's the equivalent of $224 million that the company wouldn't have to pay its workers for up to a year after the worker has earned it. Considering that, under normal circumstances, the employer might have to pay six percent interest for a commercial loan of this magnitude, it could save $13 million by relying on comp time to 'borrow' from its employees instead." 5

And if, during that 13 month waiting period, your company happens to be one of the hundreds of thousands of companies that close their doors each year (200,000 in 2000) then you forfeit both the overtime pay and the time off—up to 160 hours. For employees making $10/hour, losing 160 hours of overtime pay is a loss of $2400.

H.R. 1119 and S. 317 pose a serious threat—not only do they seek to undermine workers' most basic rights, they also have friends in high places. The Associated Press reports that "business groups, emboldened by the complete Republican control of Congress and the federal executive branch" are pressing the Bush administration to rewrite labor law—in a way that benefits business and disadvantages workers, we might add. The National Organization for Women opposes this legislation as a serious step backwards in protecting worker rights and harming women and their families. *Please take action now.*

EMPATHIZING WITH DIFFERENT POINTS OF VIEW

Arguments from the Independent Women's Forum, Which Favors the Legislation

1. Working women, who constitute a significant portion of the workforce, are particularly in need of flexible time. Working mothers can benefit by being able to choose to work overtime

hours when it is convenient for them, with the benefit of earning compensatory time-and-a-half hours off when they need them.

2. Federal, state, and local workers have long had the advantage of this benefit. The Family Time Flexibility Act amends the 1938 Fair Labor Standards Act, which is out-of-date legislation, written when the workforce was predominantly male.

3. Scare tactics that assume employers are unfriendly to working mothers hurt men as well as women. Men too need flexible time to be with their families and take a vacation.

4. According to the Employment Policy Foundation, 81 percent of women favor compensatory time as an option for overtime pay.

Arguments from the National Organization for Women, Which Opposes the Legislation

1. Overtime laws currently protect workers against the pressures to receive less or different compensation than time-and-a-half pay. This bill would erode such protections because employees who opted for pay may be passed over for those who would accept time off.

2. Both options for compensation favor the employer. Employers do not have to pay monetary compensation until one month after the end of the calendar year, which constitutes an interest-free loan on the part of employees to employers. And employers do not have to pay compensatory time if it in any way disrupts business.

3. Employees risk losing both monetary and time-off compensation because if the business goes under, employees forfeit both their overtime pay and their time off, up to 160 hours.

4. The 40-hour workweek is itself a protection for families. Overtime bills that encourage businesses to use overtime will further erode that protection.

ADDING MORE INFORMATION (ADDITIONAL ARGUMENTS)

From the Employers' Point of View

1. Sometimes employers need to have employees work overtime. This saves them the cost of hiring and training new workers, whom they may not need for an extended length of time.

2. Overtime provides businesses with increased flexibility. They can immediately increase or decrease the work on a project, allowing them to compete against other companies or businesses.

3. Offering the option of time-and-a-half vacation time in payment for overtime may actually increase the amount of vacation time workers take, as workers can increase their wages with fewer hours. This will make workers more productive on the job.

4. The marketplace determines whether or not salaried employees are being overworked. When the job demands exceed the benefit of the salary, employees can seek other jobs.

From the Employees' Point of View

1. Hourly workers have little power to refuse requests for overtime, and this bill may encourage employers to demand overtime. Although workers are compensated, the loss of family time during high production times has a long-term impact on the psychological health of employees.

2. Employers can deprive workers of compensation for as much as thirteen months for wages and indefinitely for time off. The vague caveat that the employees' comp time not "unduly disrupt" the business could easily be misused.

3. Salaried employees risk never being compensated for their overtime, as businesses that fold cannot be held responsible for this debt to their employees.

SEEKING COMMON CAUSE

1. Both employers and employees benefit when employees like their jobs, feel loyalty to the company, and are productive. It is in the interest of employers to treat employees fairly and compensate them fairly.

2. Both employers and employees benefit when there is minimal turnover of employees.

3. Both employers and employees benefit when the relationship is founded on mutual respect and trust, and trade-offs can be made to benefit both groups.

4. Overtime costs employers as well as employees. Employers typically pay one-and-a-half times the hourly wage. Employees lose recreational and family time. However, both could gain if the overtime is compensated for in appropriate ways.

5. Studies show that workers who put in extensive overtime hours do not work efficiently. It is in the interest of businesses and employees to see that work is done efficiently and that employees have sufficient rest and family and recreation time.

6. As with daycare, employers are trying to make the workplace more attractive to women in order to increase their workforce. Being able to "bank" comp time may be more important to most women than extra money, so it is in the interest of employers to offer such a plan.

7. Both employers and employees have an interest in creating more flexible work plans. There is little incentive for employers to deny employees their requested compensation days. They would face not only class action lawsuits but also the ill will of their employees.

DEBATE ESSAY

Using Web sources in addition to the readings and arguments above, track the arguments for and against this legislation (search "Family Time Flexibility Act"). Note what organizations sponsor particular positions, and identify what their interests might be. Imagine some scenarios in which the Family Time Flexibility Act would help an employee and scenarios in which it would hurt an employee. Write an essay incorporating these scenarios that argues for or against the legislation. Be sure to include opposing points of view.

ADDITIONAL DEBATE QUESTION

The Horatio Alger story—that hard work, in whatever lowly job, eventually leads to success—has been a dominant theme in American life. Gary Soto in "Black Hair" (p. 296) and Daniel Levine in "Take This Job and Love It" (p. 292) hold opposite views on the validity of this theme. They disagree on the value of low-paying, low-skill work. They oppose each other over whether such work increases life skills and self-respect and whether such jobs lead up the employment ladder.

In groups of three or four on each side, debate this issue. Anticipate what the other side might argue. Then offer counterarguments. You may use personal experience, examples from the readings, and critical analyses of opposing views. You might also ask yourself what views the other side assumes, and call these views into question.

Writing a Short Essay

The following short writing projects can prepare you for writing the long essay in the Writing an Extended Argument section or can be done independently.

Writing a Description of an Experience

Describe in detail a job you have held that required imagination or anticipation. What did you need to imagine or visualize in order to perform the work well?

- Describe the job so that a layperson will understand what one does and why one does it.
- Then sum up the role of imagination or visualization in doing the job well. Perhaps form a list of three or four main ideas, in order of importance.
- Then detail these ideas following the order of the list. What might happen if you did not visualize or anticipate? What happened because you did? Describe the whole process. Be sure to use concrete examples and details (use the senses—what you hear, see, feel, smell, and taste).
- Sum up how visualization enabled you to perform the job better.

Imagining an Occupation

- Imagine, and describe in detail, the kind of work you think you would do well. What particular skills or talents do you have that fit you for this work?
- Detail several incidents that reveal the nature of this work.
- Explain what skills, knowledge, or talents fit you for this work. Offer examples that demonstrate this ability.

Contrasting Two Concepts Using Support from the Readings

How might one distinguish between a job and work? Do you think it is possible to transform a low-paying job into work? Explain, referring to the readings.

- First, define "job" and "work" using ideas and examples from the readings. Decide what your position is on this question.
- Give reasons why a job can or cannot be transformed into work, using ideas or examples from the readings.
- Use detailed, concrete examples to illustrate your points. Anticipate what countering views or qualifications to your views writers from this chapter might put forth. Include these anticipated countering views, sum them up in a way the authors would agree represents them fairly, and respond to them.

Seeking Common Ground between Two Opposing Views

In "Work Makes Life Sweet" (p. 285), bell hooks emphasizes the importance of loving what one does, no matter how menial the work. Gary Soto suggests in "Black Hair" (p. 296) that menial work degrades the individual. What common ground can you find between these two views? Explain what assumptions they both might hold about work.

- Summarize the views of both bell hooks and Gary Soto.
- What assumptions do they share, despite their differences?
- What is the significance of this common ground?

Writing an Editorial on the Need to Prepare Students for Changes in the Work World

How do you think computers and the Internet are changing the way work is done? What cognitive skills, such as the ones Mike Rose discusses in "The Working Life of a Waitress" (p. 278), do you think that technology involves? Write an editorial on the importance of these skills, and how schools should prepare students for this kind of work.

- Explain how you think that technology has changed the way work is done.

- Do you think that attitude and imagination are as important to technological jobs as they are to physical genius? Explain.

- Explain what changes (if any) should be made in schooling to better prepare students for the work world of the twenty-first century.

Writing an Extended Argument

The following assignment asks you to incorporate numerous sources and references, as well as the visuals of people working, into a complex argument—that is, to use the readings and visuals to support a view you have arrived at after careful thought and consideration.

The writers and visual artists in this chapter offer various views on the nature of work. One theme seems to be how difficult it is to do work well. From the skillful sewing of bell hooks's aunt in "Work Makes Life Sweet" to the precise knowledge of tire widths that Gary Soto describes in "Black Hair" to the visualization skills of a neurosurgeon to the precision of the scientist portrayed in *Dorothy Hodgkin,* work done well demands attention and effort. Many Americans think that as a worker increases skill, he or she can begin to relax at work. However, many of the jobs described and pictured here often suggest the opposite. Certainly the complex work of a waitress, described so intimately by Mike Rose in "The Working Life of a Waitress," is never relaxed. Consider the journalist who must always write on deadline. Being tense and vigilant is part of the job. Think also of the workers depicted in Diego Rivera's famous mural in Detroit of workers in a factory.

Yet when workers acquire skill, they often seem to achieve a kind of gracefulness and fluidity. Think of the neurosurgeon, the woman hanging clothes (painting by Sloan), the tire thrower, and the muralist. Supporting your views with readings and visuals about various kinds of work, describe the qualities needed for a particular kind of work. How are these qualities alike and different from those needed for other kinds of work? What is the kind of training and attention required for this chosen work?

Your thesis might be an answer to one of these questions:

- What special personal qualities are needed to do domestic work well?

- In what ways does a trial lawyer need to use visualization and anticipation as much as a neurosurgeon?

- What role does playfulness have in being able to perform work well?

- What kind of training or preparation is necessary for good teaching?

Designing the Extended Writing Project

As with other chapters, we add here a reminder about the key elements of a paper. These include your thesis, a structure based on the thesis, detailed descriptions (including quotes and comments on quotes), and discussions of the significance of the thesis. The structure may take many forms and may evolve only after you have written a draft. What follows are reminders about what these elements are and how they might look in schematic form.

A Thesis

A thesis is the point of your essay. It may be a claim, a specific perspective, or a position in a debate.

We offer an example using teaching as our focus. As a student, you have observed various elements of this kind of work and can imagine many others. What thesis or claim could you invent that might explain the qualities and training that are needed to make a good teacher?

EXAMPLES | To teach well, middle and high school teachers require special insight into the motivation of adolescents. More so than subject matter knowledge, these teachers need a keen intuition about individuals and training in adolescent psychology.

Teachers need flexibility and imagination more than they need management skills or subject matter knowledge.

A Structure Based on the Thesis

As we have said elsewhere, an effective way to organize an essay is to follow the order of ideas set forth in your thesis. Sometimes, however, the thesis implies but does not state an idea or ideas that also need to be part of the structure. You might first need to list for yourself the important ideas stated or implied in the thesis and then identify a logical connection among them. You can then use this list as a structure for the paper.

EXAMPLE | What follows is a structure that makes explicit five logically related ideas derived from the first sample thesis above.

- Adolescents are especially concerned with personal identity, with finding their place in a group.
- Teachers need to respond with empathy to individual students who may feel left out of the group.
- Teachers who are successful use a variety of motivations—such as group work, topics that suggest resistance to authority, and common values among different groups of people—to help students feel comfortable in a group and engaged in the lessons.
- Students who feel safe with both the teacher and the students in the class will learn the subject better than students who are uneasy, afraid, or left out.
- Subject matter training is important but not enough for teachers to learn how to reach middle school and high school students.

When you make explicit this logical structure before you write your essay, you will find that the writing goes very easily. The transitions will come naturally, and you will be less tempted to lose focus. As you address the support—including details, examples, and quotations—you should come back to each of these main points, connecting the examples to the main ideas.

Detailed Descriptions

Personal example and details might heighten the impact of such a paper. Especially helpful are quotations from personal experience. What follows is a possible way to provide detail for such a paper.

EXAMPLE | Mr. Wright was the most natural teacher I have known. He had great reverence for his subject, the careful logic of geometry. He explained step-by-step how to do each proof. But his success came less from his detailed knowledge of the steps than through his connections to the students. "Why was this theorem and not another one the appropriate choice?" he would ask. "Tell me more about why you chose to use this theorem . . . ?" he intoned, never looking at his watch. "What other approach could we have used?" Mr. Wright anticipated and voiced all our own thinking and made even our wildest missteps seem logical and normal. He wanted to hear what everyone thought and found reason in each answer. He could then guide us toward approaches that simplified our processes. We never felt "wrong." We never felt patronized. We never felt muddled. We felt like mathematicians.

Conclusion or Significance of the Thesis

The conclusion is a good place to discuss significance. In addition to answering the nagging "So what?" question, a good final paragraph on significance can also involve speculation. What thoughts, questions, or speculations do you want to leave the reader with? Where are you going with your thoughts? For the example here, you could speculate about various actions or implications. Consider these possibilities:

- Teacher training should emphasize interpersonal skills and involve hands-on practice with orchestrating group dynamics.
- Teachers need to learn from each other, visit each other's classes, discuss students more openly, and come together to form a family of help for individuals.
- A teacher who connects with an individual student in a single class can transform that student's life.

Using WEB Resources

To identify recent events that may affect the workplace, check out the following Web sites.

www.dol.gov/

This is the Web site for the U.S. Department of Labor, which is charged with preparing the American workforce for new and better jobs and for administrating and enforcing over 180 statutes. What recent activity or legislation does the Web site identify? What work issue is involved and how do the readings throw light on the issue?

www.aflcio.org

The American Federation of Labor–Congress of Industrial Organizations is America's largest labor union. Its goals are to protect workers, addressing issues such as health care, immigrant worker abuses, job loss, overtime, and workplace rights. What recent issue has surfaced on this Web site? How is it like or different from the issue of compensation for overtime hours that surfaces in the debate?

www.mhhe.com/durkinl

Using the Web for resources on the work world. Go to Web Resources > Chapter 5

GUTZON BORGLUM   Mount Rushmore National Monument, South Dakota (photograph) [1927–1941]

KORCZAK ZIOLKOWSKI   Model for Crazy Horse Memorial humanitarian monument [1948 to present, ongoing]

Over a period of fourteen years, Borglum and his assistants sculpted the monumental faces of four U.S. presidents into the American landscape, carving art out of nature. Do the carvings make you feel that humans' ingenuity rightfully conquers nature or that it wrongfully desecrates it? Explain.

Carved into the Black Hills of South Dakota, the Crazy Horse Memorial is a counterpoint to the U.S. presidents' faces carved on Mount Rushmore. The monument is 600 feet high, with the horse's head 22 stories high and Crazy Horse's head 9 stories high. Why do you think that it is important that this monument was built?

1   Simon Schama states that "to make over a mountain, into the form of a human head is, perhaps, the ultimate colonization of nature by culture" (*Landscape and Memory,* 1995). Do you agree? Explain.

2   It has been suggested that Borglum desired a permanent canvas on which to glorify a new nation. Could the carvings suggest the union of nature and human beings, not necessarily humanity's supremacy over nature? Explain.

3   What do the faces and gaze tell you about each famous president? Why do you think the artist chose to portray the different gazes the way he did?

4   What do the specific details of Crazy Horse's face convey about this man? What Native American values might be implied? Explain.

5   Looking at this model sculpture for the monument, with Crazy Horse's arm outstretched above the horse's mane, what relationship to animals, nature, and other Indians is conveyed? Explain.

6   Compare the model for the carving with the depictions of the U.S. presidents on Mount Rushmore. How do the images of leadership differ? What details emphasize this difference?

DOROTHEA LANGE Tractored Out, Childress County, Texas, June 1938 (photograph)

ALEXANDER HOGUE Crucified Land [1939]

The photograph of furrows and farmhouse against a blank sky conveys Lange's impression of a drought's aftermath. Lange is noted for her photographs of Depression-era men and women trying to live off Dust Bowl lands. What is your first impression of this landscape?

Hogue is known for painting eco-logical themes, especially of dis-asters that follow land misman-agement—drought and floods—with the earth taking the form of living flesh that is dying. His images are stark and abstract, often only indirectly referencing humans, as with his half-covered, tilting houses. What in his use and placement of forms seems particularly significant?

1 Describe the foreground and background and their relative sizes. What objects/images stand out in the foreground? What details in the furrows do you see clearly? What impressions do these sizes and shapes convey?

2 Why do you think that the house is placed in the picture where it is? What relationship does it have to the horizon? To the land in front of it and behind it?

3 How do you know that the house has been abandoned? What does the image of the land tell you about the lives of the people who have left?

4 Unlike Hogue, a painter, Lange, a photographer, framed existing images of nature's devasta-tion, while Hogue created them. How are their tools as artists different yet similar?

5 Describe the objects in the painting (there are no people), especially the scarecrow, plow, and house. Why do you think that they are placed where they are? What might these objects suggest about what has happened to the land?

6 Describe the furrows and ravines surrounding these objects. Why do you think that this image takes up so much of the painting, from foreground to background?

7 The land seems to tilt to the left as does the scarecrow/crucifix. What does this tilting suggest about man's relationship to nature? How does the image of the crucifix heighten this idea?

JASPER FRANCIS CROPSEY Bareford Mountains, West Milford, New Jersey [1850]

Cropsey has created an isolated rural scene, and it conveys a powerful image of tranquility and vulnerability. The golden wheat fields, tiny farmworkers, and sunlit red farmhouse focus attention on the nature of human efforts to cultivate wild land. The darkened mountains and rugged foreground contrast with this manicured, sun-bathed scene.

Brooklyn Museum

1 What does the contrast between the sunlit middle ground and the dark background and foreground suggest about the relationship between humans and nature? Do the shapes of fore-, middle-, and background reinforce or blur this contrast? Explain.

2 The human figures and objects (houses, barns, haystacks, fences, and so forth) in the painting are small. What does their size, color, and placement suggest about the nature and meaning of human endeavor?

3 How does the season (autumn) and time of day (sunset) enhance the sense of human vulnerability? How is the sky portrayed to further that sense of vulnerability?

VIRGINIA A. STROUD   Doesn't Fall Off His Horse [1994]

In illustrating a Native American story about members of one tribe stealing horses from another and a young man gaining his name from the incident, Virginia Stroud creates images of unity among humans, animals, and nature. Color, pattern, shape, size, and the actions of humans and animals reinforce that harmony.

1 The horses dominate the middle ground of the illustration. What characteristics of the horses, in addition to their size and placement, give them prominence?

2 How do the colors, patterns, and placement of the people and the animals connect them to nature?

3 The two figures are secretly unhobbling the horses and putting blankets over their heads to quiet them, before covertly leading them away. Do you think that the horses appear to conspire in the stealth of the two figures? Explain.

ASHER B. DURAND   Kindred Spirits [1849]

A painter of the Hudson River School, Durand depicts a harmonious relationship between a well-known painter and poet in a natural setting. The painting offers a portrait of communion—between artists, who are in conversation, and between men and the natural scene that frames and illuminates them. What else in the painting suggests communion?

1   Describe the interaction between the two men. What do you think they might be discussing? What details convey that they are "kindred spirits"?

2   What effect does the arching tree, framing the vista that the viewer sees, have on the scene? If the painter had removed it, what effect would this have had on the scene?

3   Describe the placement, as well as lighting, of the natural objects or elements in the scene— including the river, waterfall, cliffs, mountains, sky, and rock on which the men stand. What is the effect of this placement and lighting? What does light and placement suggest about the relationship between the men and nature?

FREDERIC EDWIN CHURCH   The Icebergs [1861]

Church, another member of the Hudson River School of painters, was inspired by his trip on a chartered schooner near Newfoundland, as well as by the doomed Franklin expedition in search of the Northwest Passage. Large icebergs fill up the composition, with a prominent, eerily lit form in the center. What is the dominant feeling about nature?

Dallas Museum of Art.

1   The mast and light move the viewer's eye diagonally toward the ice wall on the right, then to the huge iceberg in the center. What is the effect of this movement on how we feel about nature?

2   There are not many signs of human life in the painting. What relationship between humans and nature is depicted here? What details suggest that relationship?

3   Much of the painting is dark, with partial forms of the icebergs lit up in sharp contrast. What feelings about the landscape do such contrasts evoke?

viewer in brilliant color and expansive, idealized forms. Why do you think an artist might want to tackle the challenges of painting (or photographing) the Grand Canyon?

1 The reds and oranges of the painting are deeper and more brilliant than the actual colors of the landscape. How do these colors help viewers to "see" the canyon differently than they would see it on their own? Why do you think Hockney wants the viewer to be aware of this difference?

2 The shapes of the canyon, as well as the trees and sky, are not realistic but idealized. What has been left out? What do you think the painter is suggesting about the relationship between observer and nature by his transformations of the actual shapes?

3 The lines of the sixty separate canvases that form this painting create a grid. What does this grid suggest about the artist's and viewer's role in this landscape? Why do you think Hockney may have wanted to draw attention to this role? Explain.

N A S A   The Blue Marble Earth, Western Hemisphere, digitalized photograph [One of Series, 1970s]

This photograph of Earth depicts the living beauty of the planet. As Lewis Thomas suggests, it looks like a living cell, the white cloud cover part of a membrane that both deflects and absorbs light. Floating alone in space, its aliveness contrasts with the void around it. What other comparisons come to mind when you look at Earth from space?

1 What is surprising about the color of Earth from this perspective? What impression does the "marbling" give?

2 What new perspective does this image provide on our relationship to our environment? Why?

Connecting to Nature

The natural environment affects us all, whether we live in New York City or the open spaces of Montana. How do we experience the natural world? How do we value it, construct it in our minds, give it meaning, and interact with it? In this chapter, a number of issues surface regarding the value of nature. The overarching issue concerns how we connect. Historically, Americans have explored, conquered, plundered, and domesticated nature—bending it to their own purposes. With a vast continent to penetrate, they exploited without much thought to loss—to what generations of deforestation, poor planting techniques, and strip mining would leave in their wake. In the twentieth and twenty-first centuries, Americans are increasingly conscious of the value of open spaces and wilderness areas, especially as such places dwindle. In the tradition of Thoreau, more people find meaning living in and observing nature, and they seek to protect what is fast disappearing. However, such values can conflict with entrenched beliefs in development, civilization, and extraction of resources. Ownership of land, and doing with land as one chooses, has always been part of the European American dream. That dream has often conflicted with Native American views of land, specific places that are not possessions but rather embodiments of the history, beliefs, and everyday survival of the people.

Both the works of art and the essays included here make vivid statements about our relationship to nature. The works of art range from the faces of U.S. presidents carved out of mountains at Mount Rushmore to a pastoral scene on the Hudson River to a stark scene in Texas with minimal human presence to a NASA photo of Earth in space. Nature is different in each image. It is restful and tranquil in some works. It is the source of challenge and self-discovery in other works. And in still others, nature is the empty canvas on which humans paint or carve their visions. The essays have similar scope. They range from rational theories on land use to archaeological views on the environment's role in the demise of civilizations to rhapsodic delight in a wren's song. The essays also include scientists' observations and explorations of life on this planet, providing knowledge that can change our perspective on the natural world.

THE NATURAL WORLD IN THE ARTWORKS

The artworks included here represent several kinds of media, including sculpture carved into a mountain face, paintings, a book illustration, and photography. Implicitly or explicitly, the works embody a vision of the relation between humans and nature. Some depict a harmonious, contemplative relationship. Others depict humankind's desecration of nature, an egocentric destruction for a narrow purpose. Still other works portray nature's space and dimensions, depicting human beings as tiny shapes or present only by implication.

The first work of art is Mount Rushmore Monument, consisting of several granite mountains in South Dakota that have been carved by Gutzon Borglum and his assistants, into faces of four great U.S. presidents. Here, famous men, their ideas, and the artist clearly dominate nature. Scale has been reversed, with humans, who are small and short in comparison with a mountain, depicted triumphantly large and elevated as they emerge from the top of the mountain. The Crazy Horse Memorial, carved almost single-handedly by Korczak Ziolkowski into the Black Hills of South Dakota, is an ongoing humanitarian project that offers a story in counterpoint to Mount Rushmore. Unfinished and dependent on contributions, the memorial reminds us of the exploitation and colonization of Indian lands and culture by Europeans. It celebrates this Native American leader of all-Indian tribes and his valiant leadership at Little Big Horn.

Like the Mount Rushmore Memorial, the painting *Crucified Land* suggests an ego-centric human relationship with nature, but without optimism. Here the artist, Alexander Hogue, comments on humans' degradation of the land and implies that this destruction reenacts the crucifixion of the innocent Christ. A parallel work, the Dorothea Lange photograph *Childress County, Texas, June 1938,* reveals the devastating effects of the Dust Bowl and Depression on the land. The photograph of furrows and farmhouse against a blank sky conveys Lange's impression of what drought has done to the landscape and the people who once lived off this land.

Another work of art reveals nature as a large expanse of rolling mountains and partly tilled lowlands. Jasper Francis Cropsey's *Bareford Mountains, West Milford, New Jersey,* depicts the tiny shapes of humans harmoniously harvesting wheat from a swath of sunlit land. The dark, uncultivated land in the foreground and vast background of dark mountains and illuminated sky suggest humanity's small place in nature.

Nature consistently in harmony and balance with humans and animals is seen in two additional works of art. Virginia A. Stroud, in her illustration from her Native American children's story *Doesn't Fall Off His Horse,* reveals a connectedness among humans, animals, and nature. Image, pattern, and color show the harmony among all three. Asher Durand's painting *Kindred Spirits* suggests a tranquil, meditative scene in which two men, themselves "kindred spirits," share a special connection to nature. The subjects, poet and painter, clearly appreciate the natural environment framed by trees, a rocky crag, and luminous mountains in the background.

In contrast, Frederic E. Church's painting *The Icebergs* depicts a stark and threatening nature, oblivious to humans, portrayed through light and space. The icebergs appear as powerful, mysterious forces moving without reference to people: only by implication— a broken mast—are humans in the picture. David Hockney's *A Bigger Grand Canyon,* a painting also devoid of humans or their actions, offers an enraptured vista of the Grand Canyon, in brilliant colors, emphasizing forms of mountains carved by nature, not humans, over millions of years. In contrast to the human-carved mountains of Mount Rushmore or The Black Hills, these mountains radiate the artist's awe, in terms of color and idealized forms.

Finally, humans are too small to be pictured in NASA's photograph of *Blue Marble Earth, Western Hemisphere,* which captures Earth from space—white clouds swirling above landmasses. The digitalized photograph of Earth depicts the living beauty of the planet, a cell-like image that floats alone in space.

Analyzing the Artwork

The works of art selected here use various elements to communicate humans' relationship to nature: the subjects, the subjects' actions, the background of the painting, objects, color, and light. Because these works emphasize nature, the background or landscape itself is often the dominant "character." Human forms may not even be in the picture. In more abstract works, the shapes and colors also delineate the artist's view of nature. Are the colors vibrant and alive or dark and foreboding? Are the shapes balanced and harmonious or unbalanced and discordant? When you have identified the individual elements of each work, you can then ask what significance each might have.

To identify significance, ask what each element suggests about the relationship of humans to nature. Here are some steps to help you analyze a painting, photograph, illustration, or sculpture that depicts nature:

1. Identify the visual elements that indicate relationships.

   - **The human perspective**   Begin by asking where the human perspective lies in the work. Does the artist depict a person or people looking at the landscape? If there are people in the artwork who are not looking at the landscape, where are they looking? What does the direction of their gaze tell you about their relationship to their surroundings? What are they doing? Where are they positioned in the landscape, and how big are they with respect to the nature around them?

     If the painter has not explicitly depicted any human beings in the landscape, do any objects suggest people's implicit presence? If so, what do the objects imply about the nature of the people, what they are doing or have done, and how they have affected or been affected by the natural scene depicted? If no human-made objects exist, what do the forms and colors tell you about the artist's feelings about the landscape?

   - **The natural perspective**   Look carefully at the portrait of nature. Is it lush and green or starkly colored and dying? Is it tranquil and harmonious or tumultuous and foreboding? Does the artist create signs of the elements, such as wind, rain, heat, or cold? If so, do these signs suggest that the elements are disturbing the setting or complementing it? What are the shapes depicting nature like? Are they rounded and balanced or jagged and off-kilter? Are any of the shapes, colors, or lines in the natural environment reflections of human beings' presence in nature?

   - **Objects, buildings, or animals**   What else has the artist chosen to depict in the scene? Where does the artist place any human-made objects or buildings and how are they depicted? What does each suggest about the actions humans take in the natural world as it is portrayed? Are there any animals or signs of animals in the work of art? If so, describe them. What do their features suggest about human beings' treatment of animals and of nature? Do the animals relate to nature differently than humans do?

2. After you have identified these elements and the relationships between humans and nature that they imply, consider what these relationships suggest about American values.

   - What American values are suggested by the dominant relationship depicted between humans and nature?

- Does the artwork suggest an emergent, possibly different, relationship? If so, what American values does this connection represent?
- If a tension exists, does the artwork indicate any possible common ground between opposing values?

Analysis of a Painting

In the essay "Ice and Light" in this chapter, Barry Lopez analyzes Frederic Edward Church's painting *The Icebergs* (insert 6-6) to help explain his feelings about the Arctic. Lopez begins with the *natural perspective* by describing the ice formations that fill the various areas of the painting—foreground, middle ground, and background. As he describes these areas, Lopez takes the role of the viewer, suggesting how the viewer's eye moves from the large iceberg and grotto in the foreground to the "becalmed embayment" in the middle ground to the "stormy horizon" and "distant icebergs" in the background; he concurrently describes the painting's stark light and dark contrasts, muted colors, and accurate shadings and forms. These descriptions imply a cold, inhuman, supernatural world, inhospitable to human beings.

Lopez then turns to the *human perspective*, recounting how Church believed he had made a mistake not to include humans in the painting; Church later added debris from a shipwreck to the foreground, including a broken mast. These objects, while not human, imply a human perspective. Lopez thinks that the addition of these objects, particularly the mast as symbol for human suffering (the mast as crucifix), shapes our feelings about the landscape. The broken remains of an expedition help us feel how nature, stretching cold and dark into infinity, repels humans' attempts at mastery and mirrors a bleak destiny. While there may seem no common ground between humans and nature, the scene signals an appropriate attitude: humility and awe in the face of forces much greater than ourselves. Such feelings suggest an emergent relationship—of spiritual self-recognition in nature.

THE NATURAL WORLD IN ESSAYS

The essays in this chapter provide multiple perspectives on relating to nature. These perspectives include broad theories of the value of natural landscapes and the threat to our well-being that results from their disappearance. The essays also present personal experiences of living in remote environments and describe heightened observations and a renewed sense of identity. Furthermore, they suggest how different cultures view nature and the diverse roles natural settings play in defining and perpetuating culture.

The first two essays caution against the unbridled use of land for short-term utilitarian purposes. In "Wilderness as a Form of Land Use," Aldo Leopold, from a policy point of view, argues that to preserve the last few wilderness areas, we need a rational land use policy. His seminal work led to the 1964 Wilderness Act that permitted the federal government to protect the "primeval character" of parts of the U.S. landscape. In "The Last Americans," Jared Diamond, a biogeographer, writes about powerful civilizations other than our own that misused land and other resources and then collapsed only decades after reaching their peaks in power and wealth. Figuring prominently in this collapse is environmental degradation.

The next four essays use personal experience to demonstrate the cultural and aesthetic value of nature. Wendell Berry ("An Entrance to the Woods") tells a story of a short trip into nature and his gradual transformation from hurried city life into the slow time and heightened observations of life in nature. In "Heaven and Earth in Jest," Annie Dillard, while living in a small cabin beside Tinker Creek, explores the meaning of the animals and plants, mountains and creeks, around her, using simile and metaphor to communicate her impressions. Leslie Marmon Silko explains in "The Migration Story: An Interior Journey," the cultural value of each rock and bush—the role of each in the stories of the Laguna Pueblo Indians, stories that retell the essential myths and events of the people. Thus, rocks and trees and specific locations *are* the culture, not objects to be used *by* the culture. Barry Lopez ("Ice and Light") describes paintings and cathedrals to communicate his feelings about the icebergs he watches pass in the Canadian Arctic.

The last three essays offer a look at nature through the eyes of natural scientists. These readings teach us how scientists connect to nature, offering perspectives that help us better understand as well as observe and visualize our world. In a selection from her book *In the Shadow of Man*, primatologist Jane Goodall details her work in the forests of Gombe—her work collecting the plants that chimpanzees eat, observing these animals' behavior in their natural habitat, interacting with them as individuals, and discovering tool-using behavior never before observed. In "The World's Biggest Membrane," biologist Lewis Thomas depicts the world from the perspective of the moon, imagining the earth's atmosphere as a membrane—living and breathing, storing and releasing energy, and protecting Earth from deadly ultraviolet light. In "Terminal Ice," Ian Frazier, working with glaciologists, details the scientific features of icebergs and explains the breaking up of vast areas of Antarctica into icebergs the size of Delaware or Connecticut. As a journalist, he records not only scientific facts about ice and the effects of global warming, but also information on how the images of our planet melting enter our consciousness through various media.

Analyzing the Essays

To help you analyze these essays, here are some questions you might ask yourself:

- In the essay, how do nature and the animals in it differ from the human beings?
- What human qualities or values do nature and the animals embody? What qualities of nature do the humans embody? What common qualities do they illustrate?
- In the essay, what relationship is depicted between humans and the natural world?
- What changes in human actions does the essay imply would improve our relationship with the natural world?

Analysis of an Essay

Jane Goodall's piece from *In the Shadow of Man* (p. 402) portrays an increasing closeness between humans and the natural world. Goodall describes her delight in being alone in nature, experiencing the "almost mystical awareness of beauty and eternity" of the African forest. But her focus is on her increasing interactions with and detailed observations of a group of chimpanzees. Goodall describes her relationship with the chimps in terms of human feelings: the chimps increasingly "tolerate" her presence as they become less and less "afraid." And as she comes into closer contact, Goodall depicts individual chimps in terms of human qualities. She gives them individual names and identifies their particular personalities, roles, friendships, mannerisms, and looks, often mentioning a person they remind her of. This experience of similarities between chimp and human culminates in several observations that surprise and delight Goodall. She observes the chimps David Graybeard and Goliath collecting, modifying, and using grass stems as tools to "fish" for underground termites. For scientists, this observation indicates that man is not the sole "tool-using animal." Goodall's detailed scientific observations of primate behavior have helped change our views of these animals, encouraging us to protect not only these families but also their environments.

READING

ALDO LEOPOLD, a pioneer in developing land use policies, argues for the cultural value—in particular, the American cultural value—of wilderness areas. Leopold goes beyond personal experience to theory and argument. He examines the false assumptions that have worked to justify the continual elimination of the wilderness. Among these is the idea that because the development of civilization has depended on conquering wilderness, when we conquer *all* the wilderness we will produce the "ultimate" development (complete annihilation of wilderness). He thus distinguishes between tendencies and ultimates. In making such distinctions, Leopold helps us to identify our unconscious assumptions, to think about what a wilderness area is, and to reflect on the values we don't wish to see lost by poor land use policy. What are your own views about the value of wilderness areas, other than as an economic resource to be developed?

LEOPOLD (1887–1948), often called "the father of wildlife ecology," worked for the United States Forest Service and Forest Product Laboratories before becoming a professor at the University of Wisconsin; at Wisconsin, he helped create the Department of Game Management and was appointed its chair. His books, *A Sand County Almanac* and *Game Management,* earned the philosopher/scientist/teacher an international readership. In 1982, Leopold's children created the Aldo Leopold Foundation, which is committed to the ethical use of land and natural resources.

READING

Wilderness as a Form of Land Use (1925) | BY ALDO LEOPOLD

From the earliest times one of the principal criteria of civilization has been the ability to conquer the wilderness and convert it to economic use. To deny the validity of this criterion would be to deny history. But because the conquest of wilderness has produced beneficial reactions on social, political, and economic development, we have set up, more or less unconsciously, the converse assumption that the ultimate social, political, and economic development will be produced by conquering the wilderness entirely—that is, by eliminating it from our environment.

My purpose is to challenge the validity of such an assumption and to show how it is inconsistent with certain cultural ideas which we regard as most distinctly American.

Our system of land use is full of phenomena which are sound as tendencies but become unsound as ultimates. It is sound for a city to grow but unsound for it to cover its entire site with buildings. It was sound to cut down our forests but unsound to run out of wood. It was sound to expand our agriculture, but unsound to allow the momentum of that expansion to result in the present overproduction. To multiply examples of an obvious truth would be tedious. The question, in brief, is whether the benefits of wilderness-conquest will extend to ultimate wilderness-elimination.

The question is new because in America the point of elimination has only recently appeared upon the horizon of foreseeable events. During our four centuries of wilderness-conquest the possibility of disappearance has been too remote to register in the national consciousness. Hence we have no mental language in which to discuss the matter. We must first set up some ideas and definitions.

WHAT IS A WILDERNESS AREA?

The term wilderness, as here used, means a wild, roadless area where those who are so inclined may enjoy primitive modes of travel and subsistence, such as exploration trips by pack-train or canoe.

The first idea is that wilderness is a resource, not only in the physical sense of the raw materials it contains, but also in the sense of a distinctive environment which may, if rightly used, yield certain social values. Such a conception ought not to be difficult, because we have lately learned to think of other forms of land use in the same way. We no longer think of a municipal golf links, for instance, as merely soil and grass.

The second idea is that the value of wilderness varies enormously with location. As with other resources, it is impossible to dissociate value from location. There are wilderness areas in Siberia which are probably very similar in character to parts of our Lake states, but their value to us is negligible, compared with what the value of a similar area in the Lake states would be, just as the value of a golf links would be negligible if located so as to be out of reach of golfers.

The third idea is that wilderness, in the sense of an environment as distinguished from a quantity of physical materials, lies somewhere between the class of non-reproducible resources like minerals, and the reproducible resources like forests. It does not disappear proportionately to use, as minerals do, because we can conceive of a wild area which, if properly administered, could be traveled indefinitely and still be as good as ever. On the other hand, wilderness certainly cannot be built at will, like a city park or a tennis court. If we should tear down improvements already made in order to build a wilderness, not only would the cost be prohibitive, but the result would probably be highly dissatisfying. Neither can a wilderness be grown like timber, because it is something more than trees. The practical point is that if we want wilderness, we must foresee our want and preserve the proper areas against the encroachment of inimical uses.

Fourth, wilderness exists in all degrees, from the little accidental wild spot at the head of a ravine in a Corn Belt woodlot to vast expanses of virgin country—

Where nameless men by nameless rivers wander
And in strange valleys die strange deaths alone.

What degree of wilderness, then, are we discussing? The answer is, *all degrees.* Wilderness is a relative condition. As a form of land use it cannot be a rigid entity of unchanging content, exclusive of all other forms. On the contrary, it must be a flexible thing, accommodating itself to other forms and blending with them in that highly localized give-and-take scheme of land-planning which employs the criterion of "highest use." By skilfully adjusting one use to another, the land planner builds a balanced whole without undue sacrifice of any function, and thus attains a maximum net utility of land.

Just as the application of the park idea in civic planning varies in degree from the provision of a public bench on a street corner to the establishment of a municipal forest playground as large as the city itself, so should the application of the wilderness idea vary in degree from the wild, roadless spot of a few acres left in the rougher parts of public forest devoted to timber-growing, to wild, roadless regions approaching in size a whole national forest or a whole national park. For it is not to be supposed that a public wilderness area is a new kind of public land reservation, distinct from public forests and public parks. It is rather a new kind of land-dedication within our system of public forests and parks, to be duly correlated with dedications to the other uses which that system is already obligated to accommodate.

Lastly, to round out our definitions, let us exclude from practical consideration any degree of wilderness so absolute as to forbid reasonable protection. It would be idle to discuss wilderness areas if they are to be left subject to destruction by forest fires, or wide open to abuse. Experience has demonstrated, however, that a very modest and unobtrusive framework of trails, telephone line and lookout stations will suffice for protective purposes. Such improvements do not destroy the wild flavor of the area, and are necessary if it is to be kept in usable condition.

WILDERNESS AREAS IN A BALANCED LAND SYSTEM

What kind of case, then, can be made for wilderness as a form of land use?

To preserve any land in a wild condition is, of course, a reversal of economic tendency, but that fact alone should not condemn the proposal. A study of the history of land utilization shows that good use is largely a matter of good balance—of wise adjustment between opposing tendencies. The modern movements toward diversified crops and live stock on the farm, conservation of eroding soils, forestry, range management, game management, public parks—all these are attempts to balance opposing tendencies that have swung out of counterpoise.

One noteworthy thing about good balance is the nature of the opposing tendencies. 15
In its more utilitarian aspect, as seen in modern agriculture, the needed adjustment is between economic uses. But in the public park movement the adjustment is between an economic use, on the one hand, and a purely social use on the other. Yet, after a century of actual experience, even the most rigid economic determinists have ceased to challenge the wisdom of a reasonable reversal of economic tendency in favor of public parks.

I submit that the wilderness is a parallel case. The parallelism is not yet generally recognized because we do not yet conceive of the wilderness environment as a resource. The accessible supply has heretofore been unlimited, like the supply of air-power, or tide-power, or sunsets, and we do not recognize anything as a resource until the demand becomes commensurable with the supply.

Now after three centuries of overabundance, and before we have even realized that we are dealing with a non-reproducible resource, we have come to the end of our pioneer environment and are about to push its remnants into the Pacific. For three centuries that environment has determined the character of our development; it may, in fact, be said that, coupled with the character of our racial stocks, it is the very stuff America is made of. Shall we now exterminate this thing that made us American?

Ouspensky says that, biologically speaking, the determining characteristic of rational beings is that their evolution is self-directed. John Burroughs cites the opposite example of the potato bug, which, blindly obedient to the law of increase, extermi-nates the potato and thereby exterminates itself. Which are we?

WHAT THE WILDERNESS HAS CONTRIBUTED TO AMERICAN CULTURE

Our wilderness environment cannot, of course, be preserved on any considerable scale as an economic fact. But, like many other receding economic facts, it can be preserved for the ends of sport. But what is the justification of sport, as the word is here used?

Physical combat between men, for instance, for unnumbered centuries was an eco- 20
nomic fact. When it disappeared as such, a sound instinct led us to preserve it in the form of athletic sports and games. Physical combat between men and beasts since first the flight of years began was an economic fact, but when it disappeared as such, the in-stinct of the race led us to hunt and fish for sport. The transition of these tests of skill from an economic to a social basis has in no way destroyed their efficacy as human ex-periences—in fact, the change may be regarded in some respects as an improvement.

Football requires the same kind of back-bone as battle but avoids its moral and physical retrogressions. Hunting for sport in its highest form is an improvement on hunting for food in that there has been added, to the test of skill, an ethical code which the hunter formulates for himself and must often execute without the moral support of bystanders.

In these cases the surviving sport is actually an improvement on the receding eco-nomic fact. Public wilderness areas are essentially a means for allowing the more virile and primitive forms of outdoor recreation to survive the receding economic fact of pioneering. These forms should survive because they likewise are an improvement on pioneering itself.

There is little question that many of the attributes most distinctive of America and Americans are the impress of the wilderness and the life that accompanied it. If we have any such thing as an American culture (and I think we have), its distinguishing marks are a certain vigorous individualism combined with ability to organize, a certain intel-lectual curiosity bent to practical ends, a lack of subservience to stiff social forms, and an intolerance of drones, all of which are the distinctive characteristics of successful pi-oneers. These, if anything, are the indigenous part of our Americanism, the qualities that set it apart as a new rather than an imitative contribution to civilization. Many ob-servers see these qualities not only bred into our people, but built into our institutions. Is it not a bit beside the point for us to be so solicitous about preserving those institu-tions without giving so much as a thought to preserving the environment which pro-duced them and which may now be one of our effective means of keeping them alive?

WILDERNESS LOCATIONS

But the proposal to establish wilderness areas is idle unless acted on before the wilder-ness has disappeared. Just what is the present status of wilderness remnants in the United States?

Large areas of half a million acres and upward are disappearing very rapidly, not so 25
much by reason of economic need, as by extension of motor roads. Smaller areas are still relatively abundant in the mountainous parts of the country, and will so continue for a long time.

The disappearance of large areas is illustrated by the following instance: In 1910 there were six roadless regions in Arizona and New Mexico, ranging in size from half a million to a million acres, where the finest type of mountain wilderness pack trips could be enjoyed. Today roads have eliminated all but one area of about half a million acres.

In California there were seven large areas ten years ago, but today there are only two left unmotorized.

In the Lake states no large unmotorized playgrounds remain. The motor launch, as well as the motor road, is rapidly wiping out the remnants of canoe country.

In the Northwest large roadless areas are still relatively numerous. The land plans of the Forest Service call for exclusion of roads from several areas of moderate size.

Unless the present attempts to preserve such areas are greatly strengthened and extended, however, it may be predicted with certainty that, except in the Northwest, all of the large areas already in public ownership will be invaded by motors in another decade.

30

In selecting areas for retention as wilderness, the vital factor of location must be more decisively recognized. A few areas in the national forests of Idaho or Montana are better than none, but, after all, they will be of limited usefulness to the citizen of Chicago or New Orleans who has a great desire but a small purse and a short vacation. Wild areas in the poor lands of the Ozarks and the Lake states would be within his reach. For the great urban populations concentrated on the Atlantic seaboards, wild areas in both ends of the Appalachians would be especially valuable.

Are the remaining large wilderness areas disappearing so rapidly because they contain agricultural lands suitable for settlement? No; most of them are entirely devoid of either existing or potential agriculture. Is it because they contain timber which should be cut? It is true that some of them do contain valuable timber, and in a few cases this fact is leading to a legitimate extension of logging operations; but in most of the remaining wilderness the timber is either too thin and scattered for exploitation, or else the topography is too difficult for the timber alone to carry the cost of roads or railroads. In view of the general belief that lumber is being overproduced in relation to the growing scarcity of stumpage, and will probably so continue for several decades, the sacrifice of wilderness for timber can hardly be justified on grounds of necessity.

Generally speaking, it is not timber, and certainly not agriculture, which is causing the decimation of wilderness areas, but rather the desire to attract tourists. The accumulated momentum of the good-roads movement constitutes a mighty force, which, skilfully manipulated by every little mountain village possessed of a chamber of commerce and a desire to become a metropolis, is bringing about the extension of motor roads into every remaining bit of wild country, whether or not there is economic justification for the extension.

Our remaining wild lands are wild because they are poor. But this poverty does not deter the booster from building expensive roads through them as bait for motor tourists.

I am not without admiration for this spirit of enterprise in backwoods villages, nor am I attempting a censorious pose toward the subsidization of their ambitions from the public treasuries; nor yet am I asserting that the resulting roads are devoid of any economic utility. I do maintain, (1) that such extensions of our road systems into the wilderness are seldom yielding a return sufficient to amortize the public investment; (2) that even where they do yield such a return, their construction is not necessarily in the public interest, any more than obtaining an economic return from the last vacant lot in a parkless city would be in the public interest. On the contrary, the public interest demands the careful planning of a system of wilderness areas and the permanent reversal of the ordinary economic process within their borders.

35

To be sure, to the extent that the motor-tourist business is the cause of invasion of these wilderness playgrounds, one kind of recreational use is merely substituted for another. But this substitution is a vitally serious matter from the point of view of good balance. It is just as unwise to devote 100% of the recreational resources of our public parks and forests to motorists as it would be to devote 100% of our city parks to merry-go-rounds. It would be just as unreasonable to ask the aged to indorse a park with only swings and trapezes, or the children a park with only benches, or the motorists a park with only bridlepaths, as to ask the wilderness recreationist to indorse a universal priority for motor roads. Yet that is what our land plans—or rather lack of them—are now doing; and so sacred is our dogma of "development" that there is no effective protest. The inexorable molding of the individual American to a standardized pattern in his economic activities makes all the more undesirable this unnecessary standardization of his recreational tastes.

PRACTICAL ASPECTS OF ESTABLISHING WILDERNESS AREAS

Public wilderness playgrounds differ from all other public areas in that both their establishment and maintenance would entail very low costs. The wilderness is the one kind of public land that requires no improvements. To be sure, a simple system of fire protection and administrative patrol would be required, but the cost would not exceed two or three cents per acre per year. Even that would not usually be a new cost, since the greater part of the needed areas are already under administration in the rougher parts of the national forests and parks. The action needed is the permanent differentiation of a suitable system of wild areas within our national park and forest system.

In regions such as the Lake states, where the public domain has largely disappeared, lands would have to be purchased; but that will have to be done, in any event, to round out our park and forest system. In such cases a lesser degree of wilderness may have to suffice, the only ordinary utilities practicable to exclude being cottages, hotels, roads, and motor boats.

The retention of certain wild areas in both national forests and national parks will introduce a healthy variety into the wilderness idea itself, the forest areas serving as public hunting grounds, the park areas as public wild-life sanctuaries, and both kinds as public playgrounds in which the wilderness environments and modes of travel may be preserved and enjoyed.

THE CULTURAL VALUE OF WILDERNESS

Are these things worth preserving? This is the vital question. I cannot give an unbiased answer. I can only picture the day that is almost upon us when canoe travel will consist in paddling in the noisy wake of a motor launch and portaging through the back yard of a summer cottage. When that day comes, canoe travel will be dead, and dead, too, will be a part of our Americanism. Joliet and LaSalle will be words in a book, Champlain will be a blue spot on a map, and canoes will be merely things of wood and canvas, with a connotation of white duck pants and bathing "beauties." 40

The day is almost upon us when a pack-train must wind its way up a graveled highway and turn out its bell-mare in the pasture of a summer hotel. When that day comes the pack-train will be dead, the diamond hitch will be merely rope, and Kit Carson and Jim Bridger will be names in a history lesson. Rendezvous will be French for "date," and Forty-Nine will be the number preceding fifty. And thenceforth the march of empire will be a matter of gasoline and four-wheel brakes.

European outdoor recreation is largely devoid of the thing that wilderness areas would be the means of preserving in this country. Europeans do not camp, cook, or pack in the woods for pleasure. They hunt and fish when they can afford it, but their hunting and fishing is merely hunting and fishing, staged in a setting of ready-made hunting lodges, elaborate fare, and hired beaters. The whole thing carries the atmosphere of a picnic rather than that of a pack trip. The test of skill is confined almost entirely to the act of killing, itself. Its value as a human experience is reduced accordingly.

There is a strong movement in this country to preserve the distinctive democracy of our field sports by preserving free hunting and fishing, as distinguished from the European condition of commercialized hunting and fishing privileges. Public shooting grounds and organized cooperative relations between sportsmen and landowners are the means proposed for keeping these sports within reach of the American of moderate means. Free hunting and fishing is a most worthy objective, but it deals with only one of the two distinctive characteristics of American sport. The other characteristic is that our test of skill is primarily the act of living in the open, and only secondarily the act of killing game. It is to preserve this primary characteristic that public wilderness playgrounds are necessary.

Herbert Hoover aptly says that there is no point in increasing the average American's leisure by perfecting the organization of industry, if the expansion of industry is allowed to destroy the recreational resources on which leisure may be beneficially employed. Surely the wilderness is one of the most valuable of these resources, and surely the building of unproductive roads in the wrong places at public expense is one of the least valuable of industries. If we are unable to steer the Juggernaut of our own prosperity, then surely there is an impotence in our vaunted Americanism that augurs ill for our future. The self-directed evolution of rational beings does not apply to us until we become collectively, as well as individually, rational and self-directing.

Wilderness as a form of land-use is, of course, premised on a qualitative conception of progress. It is premised on the assumption that enlarging the range of individual experience is as important as enlarging the number of individuals; that the expansion of commerce is a means, not an end; that the environment of the American pioneers had values of its own, and was not merely a punishment which they endured in order that we might ride in motors. It is premised on the assumption that the rocks and rills and templed hills of this America are something more than economic materials, and should not be dedicated exclusively to economic use.

The vanguard of American thought on the use of land has already recognized all this, in theory. Are we too poor in spirit, in pocket, or in idle acres to recognize it likewise in fact?

45

CONNECTING PERSONALLY TO THE READING

1. Many of Leopold's predictions in 1925 have come to pass. What cultural values do you think have been lost? In the years since Leopold and others set Americans thinking about losing a nonrenewable resource, how has our consciousness of these values changed? (Do you and your parents or friends discuss this loss? Have you felt any loss in your personal life?)

2. Do you think that the U.S. government and U.S. citizens are trying to "balance tendencies" rather than let our last remaining wilderness lands be used for resource extraction and development by commercial interests? Explain.

3. Leopold appeals to our belief in self-direction, reasoned policy, and land use theory. Do you think we can be reasonable and detached about rethinking our views of progress? Explain.

FOCUSING ON THE ARGUMENT

1. Leopold uses definition to get his readers to see the wilderness as more than just an economic resource (lumber, minerals, space for houses, etc.). There are several parts to his definition. Which did you find most convincing? Why?

2. As part of his definition, Leopold uses classification to help readers see wilderness as somewhere between a renewable resource (trees that can be replanted) and a nonrenewable resource (minerals that once extracted are gone). It is renewable in that with maintenance, a wilderness can be used by hikers and naturalists forever. How does this classification further Leopold's argument?

3. Leopold views the value of the remaining wilderness areas as similar to the value of sports: in the wilderness, people can release aggressive tendencies, enjoy themselves, test their own abilities, and so on. Do you find this analogy effective? Why or why not?

SYNTHESIZING IDEAS FROM MULTIPLE READINGS

1. In what ways does Wendell Berry's ("An Entrance to the Woods," p. 372) experience in a small wilderness area support Leopold's argument? What insights does it add to Leopold's views?

2. What values and insights does Leslie Marmon Silko, a Native American, add in "The Migration Story: An Interior Journey" (p. 389) to Leopold's argument that "the rocks and rills and templed hills of this America are something more than economic materials"? How, for the Pueblo Indians, are the hills truly "templed"?

3. Leslie Marmon Silko ("The Migration Story: An Interior Journey"), Wendell Berry ("An Entrance to the Woods"), and Leopold all discuss what is particularly "American" in valuing the land. How do these writers define American valuing of land in similar and different ways?

4. In "The Last American" (p. 362), Jared Diamond shows what can be lost when a resource base is gone. How are Leopold and Diamond alike and different in what they see as a potential loss?

5. How might John Dewey's desire in "The School and the Life of the Child" (Chapter 4, p. 211) to develop children's instincts and activities be applied in classrooms to change young people's concept of "wilderness"?

WRITING TO ACT

1. Think about what criteria a land conservancy should use in selecting lands to protect. Write a letter to a land conservancy, arguing that the agency should use your criteria in selecting which pieces of land to acquire. You might use, as one criterion, Leopold's view of relative value.

2. Develop a land use policy for some land that you know is in dispute. Considering Leopold's view of a "balanced" use of the land, and a rational approach to multiple interests, how would you divide up the use? Write up your plan and submit it to the op-ed section of a local newspaper interested in the dispute.

JARED DIAMOND, like Aldo Leopold in "Wilderness as a Form of Land Use," makes us rethink our assumptions about the environment. For Diamond, we are destroying not just our wilderness areas, and thus our recreational areas, but also our entire ecosystem. We are losing not just opportunities for healthy sport, contemplation, self-knowledge, and aesthetic appreciation, but also the very air we breathe, water we drink, and earth we plant. We are foolishly ignoring the resource base on which any civilization depends. As a geographer and environmental health expert who has researched the archaeology of dead civilizations, Diamond sees our own actions paralleling those of past civilizations that outgrew or destroyed their resource base. Furthermore, he questions our blind assumptions that technology will get us out of this mess. What are your own assumptions about how much faith we can place in technology?

DIAMOND is professor of geography and physiology at the David Geffen School of Medicine at the University of California, Los Angeles. He is particularly interested in integrative and evolutionary physiology, and he has conducted extensive field research in New Guinea for over thirty years. In 1998, he received the Pulitzer Prize for General Nonfiction for the bestselling *Guns, Germs, and Steel: The Fates of Human Societies;* his most recent book is *Collapse: How Societies Choose to Fail or Succeed.*

The Last Americans (2003) | BY JARED DIAMOND

I met a traveler from an antique land
Who said: Two vast and trunkless legs of stone
Stand in the desert . . . Near them, on the sand,
Half sunk, a shattered visage lies, whose frown,
And wrinkled lip, and sneer of cold command,
Tell that its sculptor well those passions read
Which yet survive, stamped on these lifeless things,
The hand that mocked them, and the heart that fed:
And on the pedestal these words appear:
"My name is Ozymandias, king of kings:
Look on my works, ye Mighty, and despair!"
Nothing beside remains. Round the decay
Of that colossal wreck, boundless and bare
The lone and level sands stretch far away.

— "OZYMANDIAS," PERCY BYSSHE SHELLEY

One of the disturbing facts of history is that so many civilizations collapse. Few people, however, least of all our politicians, realize that a primary cause of the collapse of those societies has been the destruction of the environmental resources on which they depended. Fewer still appreciate that many of those civilizations share a sharp curve of decline. Indeed, a society's demise may begin only a decade or two after it reaches its peak population, wealth, and power.

Recent archaeological discoveries have revealed similar courses of collapse in such otherwise dissimilar ancient societies as the Maya in the Yucatán, the Anasazi in the American Southwest, the Cahokia mound builders outside St. Louis, the Greenland

Norse, the statue builders of Easter Island, ancient Mesopotamia in the Fertile Crescent, Great Zimbabwe in Africa, and Angkor Wat in Cambodia. These civilizations, and many others, succumbed to various combinations of environmental degradation and climate change, aggression from enemies taking advantage of their resulting weakness, and declining trade with neighbors who faced their own environmental problems. Because peak population, wealth, resource consumption, and waste production are accompanied by peak environmental impact—approaching the limit at which impact outstrips resources—we can now understand why declines of societies tend to follow swiftly on their peaks.

These combinations of undermining factors were compounded by cultural attitudes preventing those in power from perceiving or resolving the crisis. That's a familiar problem today. Some of us are inclined to dismiss the importance of a healthy environment, or at least to suggest that it's just one of many problems facing us—an "issue." That dismissal is based on three dangerous misconceptions.

Foremost among these misconceptions is that we must balance the environment against human needs. That reasoning is exactly upside-down. Human needs and a healthy environment are not opposing claims that must be balanced; instead, they are inexorably linked by chains of cause and effect. We need a healthy environment because we need clean water, clean air, wood, and food from the ocean, plus soil and sunlight to grow crops. We need functioning natural ecosystems, with their native species of earthworms, bees, plants, and microbes, to generate and aerate our soils, pollinate our crops, decompose our wastes, and produce our oxygen. We need to prevent toxic substances from accumulating in our water and air and soil. We need to prevent weeds, germs, and other pest species from becoming established in places where they aren't native and where they cause economic damage. Our strongest arguments for a healthy environment are selfish: we want it for ourselves, not for threatened species like snail darters, spotted owls, and Furbish louseworts.

Another popular misconception is that we can trust in technology to solve our problems. Whatever environmental problem you name, you can also name some hoped-for technological solution under discussion. Some of us have faith that we shall solve our dependence on fossil fuels by developing new technologies for hydrogen engines, wind energy, or solar energy. Some of us have faith that we shall solve our food problems with new or soon-to-be-developed genetically modified crops. Some of us have faith that new technologies will succeed in cleaning up the toxic materials in our air, water, soil, and foods without the horrendous cleanup expenses that we now incur.

Those with such faith assume that the new technologies will ultimately succeed, but in fact some of them may succeed and others may not. . . . In fact, technology merely constitutes increased power, which produces changes that can be either for the better or for the worse. All of our current environmental problems are unanticipated harmful consequences of our existing technology. There is no basis for believing that technology will miraculously stop causing new and unanticipated problems while it is solving the problems that it previously produced.

The final misconception holds that environmentalists are fear-mongering, overreacting extremists whose predictions of impending disaster have been proved wrong before and will be proved wrong again. Behold, say the optimists: water still flows from our faucets, the grass is still green, and the supermarkets are full of food. We are more prosperous than ever before, and that's the final proof that our system works.

Well, for a few billion of the world's people who are causing us increasing trouble, there isn't any clean water, there is less and less green grass, and there are no supermarkets full of food. To appreciate what the environmental problems of those billions of people mean for us Americans, compare the following two lists of countries. First ask some ivory-tower academic ecologist who knows a lot about the environment but never reads a newspaper and has no interest in politics to list the overseas countries facing some of the worst problems of environmental stress, overpopulation, or both. The ecologist would answer, "That's a no-brainer, it's obvious. Your list of environmentally stressed or overpopulated countries should surely include Afghanistan, Bangladesh, Burundi, Haiti, Indonesia, Iraq, Nepal, Pakistan, the Philippines, Rwanda, the Solomon Islands, and Somalia, plus others." Then ask a First World politician who knows nothing, and cares less, about the environment and population problems to list the world's worst trouble spots: countries where state government has already been overwhelmed and has collapsed, or is now at risk of collapsing, or has been wracked by recent civil wars; and countries that, as a result of their problems, are also creating problems for us rich First World countries, which may be deluged by illegal immigrants, or have to provide foreign aid to those countries, or may decide to provide them with military assistance to deal with rebellions and terrorists, or may even (God forbid) have to send in our own troops. The politician would answer, "That's a no-brainer, it's obvious. Your list of political trouble spots should surely include Afghanistan, Bangladesh, Burundi, Haiti, Indonesia, Iraq, Nepal, Pakistan, the Philippines, Rwanda, the Solomon Islands, and Somalia, plus others."

The connection between the two lists is transparent. Today, just as in the past, countries that are environmentally stressed, overpopulated, or both are at risk of becoming politically stressed, and of seeing their governments collapse. When people are desperate and undernourished, they blame their government, which they see as responsible for failing to solve their problems. They try to emigrate at any cost. They start civil wars. They kill one another. They figure that they have nothing to lose, so they become terrorists, or they support or tolerate terrorism. The results are genocides such as the ones that already have exploded in Burundi, Indonesia, and Rwanda; civil wars, as in Afghanistan, Indonesia, Nepal, the Philippines, and the Solomon Islands; calls for the dispatch of First World troops, as to Afghanistan, Indonesia, Iraq, the Philippines, Rwanda, the Solomon Islands, and Somalia; the collapse of central government, as has already happened in Somalia; and overwhelming poverty, as in all of the countries on these lists.

But what about the United States? Some might argue that the environmental collapse of ancient societies is relevant to the modern decline of weak, far-off, overpopulated Rwanda and environmentally devastated Somalia, but isn't it ridiculous to suggest any possible relevance to the fate of our own society? After all, we might reason, those ancients didn't enjoy the wonders of modern environment-friendly technologies. Those ancients had the misfortune to suffer from the effects of climate change. They behaved stupidly and ruined their own environment by doing obviously dumb things, like cutting down their forests, watching their topsoil erode, and building cities in dry areas likely to run short of water. They had foolish leaders who didn't have books and so couldn't learn from history, and who embroiled them in destabilizing wars and didn't pay attention to problems at home. They were overwhelmed by desperate immigrants, as one society after another collapsed, sending floods of eco- 10 nomic refugees to tax the resources of the societies that weren't collapsing. In all those respects, we modern Americans are fundamentally different from those primitive ancients, and there is nothing that we could learn from them.

Or so the argument goes. It's an argument so ingrained both in our subconscious and in public discourse that it has assumed the status of objective reality. We think we are different. In fact, of course, all of those powerful societies of the past thought that they too were unique, right up to the moment of their collapse. It's sobering to consider the swift decline of the ancient Maya, who 1,200 years ago were themselves the most advanced society in the Western Hemisphere, and who, like us now, were then at the apex of their own power and numbers. . . .

By now, millions of modern Americans have visited Maya ruins. . . .

One of the reasons few people live there now is that the Maya homeland poses serious environmental challenges to would-be farmers. Although it has a somewhat unpredictable rainy season from May to October, it also has a dry season from January through April. Indeed, if one focuses on the dry months, one could describe the Yucatán as a "seasonal desert."

Complicating things, from a farmer's perspective, is that the part of the Yucatán with the most rain, the south, is also the part at the highest elevation above the water table. Most of the Yucatán consists of karst—a porous, spongelike, limestone terrain—and so rain runs straight into the ground, leaving little or no surface water. The Maya in the lower-elevation regions of the north were able to reach the water table by way of deep sinkholes called cenotes, and the Maya in low coastal areas without sinkholes could reach it by digging wells up to 75 feet deep. Most Maya, however, lived in the south. How did they deal with their resulting water problem?

Technology provided an answer. The Maya plugged up leaks on karst promontories by plastering the bottoms of depressions to create reservoirs, which collected rain and stored it for use in the dry season. The reservoirs at the Maya city of Tikal, for example, held enough water to meet the needs of about 10,000 people for eighteen months. If a drought lasted longer than that, though, the inhabitants of Tikal were in deep trouble.

Maya farmers grew mostly corn, which constituted the astonishingly high propor- 15 tion of about 70 percent of their diet, as deduced from isotope analyses of ancient Maya skeletons. They grew corn by means of a modified version of swidden slash-and-burn agriculture, in which forest is cleared, crops are grown in the resulting clearing for a few years until the soil is exhausted, and then the field is abandoned for fifteen to twenty years until regrowth of wild vegetation restores the soil's fertility. . . . The Maya probably achieved . . . high populations by such means as shortening the fallow period and tilling the soil to restore soil fertility, or omitting the fallow period entirely and growing crops every year, or, in especially moist areas, growing two crops per year.

Socially stratified societies, ours included, consist of farmers who produce food, plus nonfarmers such as bureaucrats and soldiers who do not produce food and are in effect parasites on farmers. The farmers must grow enough food to meet not only their own needs but also those of everybody else. The number of nonproducing consumers who can be supported depends on the society's agricultural productivity. In the United States today, with its highly efficient agriculture, farmers make up only 2 percent of our population, and each farmer can feed, on the average, 129 other people.

Ancient Egyptian agriculture was efficient enough for an Egyptian peasant to produce five times the food required for himself and his family. But a Maya peasant could produce only twice the needs of himself and his family.

...And unlike Old World peoples with their horses, oxen, donkeys, and camels, the Maya had no animal-powered transport. Indeed, the Maya lacked not only pack animals and animal-drawn plows but also metal tools, wheels, and boats with sails. All of those great Maya temples were built by stone and wooden tools and human muscle power alone, and all overland transport went on the backs of human porters.

Those limitations on food supply and food transport may in part explain why Maya society remained politically organized in small kingdoms that were perpetually at war with one another and that never became unified into large empires like the Aztec empire of the Valley of Mexico (fed by highly productive agriculture) or the Inca empire of the Andes (fed by diverse crops carried on llamas). Maya armies were small and unable to mount lengthy campaigns over long distances. The typical Maya kingdom held a population of only up to 50,000 people, within a radius of two or three days' walk from the king's palace. From the top of the temple of some Maya kingdoms, one could see the tops of the temples of other kingdoms....

Those are the basic outlines of Classic Maya society, which for all its limitations lasted more than 500 years.... The first physical evidence of civilization within the Maya area, in the form of villagers and pottery, appeared around 1400 B.C., substantial buildings around 500 B.C., and writing around 400 B.C. The so-called Classic period of Maya history arose around A.D. 250, when evidence for the first kings and dynasties emerged. From then, the Maya population increased almost exponentially, to reach peak numbers in the eighth century A.D. The largest monuments were erected toward the end of that century. All the indicators of a complex society declined throughout the ninth century, until the last date on any monument was A.D. 909. This decline of Maya population and architecture constitutes what is known as the Classic Maya collapse.

What happened? Let's consider in more detail a city whose ruins now lie in western   20
Honduras at the world-famous site of Copán. The most fertile ground in the Copán area consists of five pockets of flat land along a river valley with a total area of only one square mile; the largest of those five pockets, known as the Copán pocket, has an area of half a square mile. Much of the land around Copán consists of steep hills with poor soil. Today, corn yields from valley-bottom fields are two or three times those of fields on hill slopes, which suffer rapid erosion and lose most of their productivity within a decade of farming.

To judge by the number of house sites, population growth in the Copán valley rose steeply from the fifth century up to a peak estimated at around 27,000 people between A.D. 750 and 900. Construction of royal monuments glorifying kings became especially massive from A.D. 650 onward. After A.D. 700, nobles other than kings got into the act and began erecting their own palaces, increasing the burden that the king and his own court already imposed on the peasants. The last big buildings at Copán were put up around A.D. 800; the last date on an incomplete altar possibly bearing a king's name is A.D. 822.

Archaeological surveys of different types of habitats in the Copán valley show that they were occupied in a regular sequence. The first area farmed was the large Copán pocket of bottomland, followed by occupation of the other four bottomland pockets.

During that time the human population was growing, but the hills remained uninhabited. Hence that increased population must have been accommodated by intensifying production in the bottomland pockets: probably some combination of shorter fallow periods and double-cropping. By A.D. 500, people had started to settle the hill slopes, but those sites were occupied only briefly. The percentage of Copán's total population that was in the hills, rather than in the valleys, peaked in the year 575 and then declined, as the population again became concentrated in the pockets.

What caused that pullback of population from the hills? From excavation of building foundations on the valley floor we know that they became covered with sediment during the eighth century, meaning that the hill slopes were becoming eroded and probably also leached of nutrients. The acidic hill soils being carried down into the valley would have reduced agricultural yields. The reason for that erosion of the hillsides is clear: the forests that formerly covered them and protected their soil were being cut down. Dated pollen samples show that the pine forests originally covering the hilltops were eventually all cleared, to be burned for fuel. Besides causing sediment accumulation in the valleys and depriving valley inhabitants of wood supplies, that deforestation may have begun to cause a "man-made drought" in the valley bottom, because forests play a major role in water cycling, such that massive deforestation tends to result in lowered rainfall. . . .

Recall that Copán's population was growing rapidly while the hills were being occupied. The subsequent abandonment of all of those hill fields meant that the burden of feeding the extra population formerly dependent on the hills now fell increasingly on the valley floor, and that more and more people were competing for the food grown on that one square mile of bottomland. That would have led to fighting among the farmers themselves for the best land, or for any land, just as in modern Rwanda. Because the king was failing to deliver on his promises of rain and prosperity, he would have been the scapegoat for this agricultural failure, which explains why the last that we hear of any king is A.D. 822, and why the royal palace was burned around A.D. 850. . . .

The Maya history that I have just related, and Copán's history in particular, illustrate 25 why we talk about "the Maya collapse". . . . the disappearance of between 90 and 99 percent of the Maya population after A.D. 800, and of the institution of the kingship, Long Count calendars, and other complex political and cultural institutions. Before we can understand those disappearances, however, we need first to understand the roles of warfare and of drought.

Archaeologists for a long time believed the ancient Maya to be gentle and peaceful people. We now know that Maya warfare was intense, chronic, and unresolvable, because limitations of food supply and transportation made it impossible for any Maya principality to unite the whole region in an empire. . . .

Maya warfare involved well-documented types of violence: wars among separate kingdoms; attempts of cities within a kingdom to secede by revolting against the capital; and civil wars resulting from frequent violent attempts by would-be kings to usurp the throne. All of these events were described or depicted on monuments, because they involved kings and nobles. Not considered worthy of description, but probably even more frequent, were fights between commoners over land, as overpopulation became excessive and land became scarce.

The other phenomenon important to understanding all of these collapses is the repeated occurrence of droughts, as inferred by climatologists from evidence of lake evaporation preserved in lake sediments, and as summarized by Gill in *The Great Maya Droughts*. The rise of Maya civilization may have been facilitated by a rainy period beginning around 250 B.C., until a temporary drought after A.D. 125 was associated with a pre-Classic collapse at some sites. That collapse was followed by the resumption of rainy conditions and the buildup of Classic Maya cities, briefly interrupted by another drought around 600 corresponding to a decline at Tikal and some other sites. Finally, around A.D. 750 there began the worst drought in the past 7,000 years, peaking around the year A.D. 800, and suspiciously associated with the Classic collapse. . . . The southern highlands [above the water table] lost more than 99 percent of its population in the course of the Classic collapse. . . .

. . . Maya warfare, already endemic, peaked just before the collapse. That is not surprising when one reflects that at least 5 million people, most of them farmers, were crammed into an area smaller than the state of Colorado. That's a high population by the standards of ancient farming societies, even if it wouldn't strike modern Manhattan-dwellers as crowded.

Bringing matters to a head was a drought that, although not the first one the Maya had been through, was the most severe. At the time of previous droughts, there were still uninhabited parts of the Maya landscape, and people in a drought area or dust bowl could save themselves by moving to another site. By the time of the Classic collapse, however, there was no useful unoccupied land in the vicinity on which to begin anew, and the whole population could not be accommodated in the few areas that continued to have reliable water supplies.

The final strand is political. Why did the kings and nobles not recognize and solve these problems? A major reason was that their attention was evidently focused on the short-term concerns of enriching themselves, waging wars, erecting monuments, competing with one another, and extracting enough food from the peasants to support all those activities. Like most leaders throughout human history, the Maya kings and nobles did not have the leisure to focus on long-term problems, insofar as they perceived them.

What about those same strands today? The United States is also at the peak of its power, and it is also suffering from many environmental problems. Most of us have become aware of more crowding and stress. Most of us living in large American cities are encountering increased commuting delays, because the number of people and hence of cars is increasing faster than the number of freeway lanes. I know plenty of people who in the abstract doubt that the world has a population problem, but almost all of those same people complain to me about crowding, space issues, and traffic experienced in their personal lives.

Many parts of the United States face locally severe problems of water restriction (especially southern California, Arizona, the Everglades, and, increasingly, the Northeast); forest fires resulting from logging and forest-management practices throughout the intermontane West; and losses of farmlands to salinization, drought, and climate change in the northern Great Plains. Many of us frequently experience problems of air quality, and some of us also experience problems of water quality and taste. We are losing economically valuable natural resources. We have already lost American chestnut trees, the Grand

Banks cod fishery, and the Monterey sardine fishery; we are in the process of losing swordfish and tuna and Chesapeake Bay oysters and elm trees; and we are losing topsoil.

The list goes on: All of us are experiencing personal consequences of our national dependence on imported energy, which affects us not only through higher gas prices but also through the current contraction of the national economy, itself the partial result of political problems associated with our oil dependence. We are saddled with expensive toxic cleanups at many locations, most notoriously near Montana mines, on the Hudson River, and in the Chesapeake Bay. We also face expensive eradication problems resulting from hundreds of introduced pest species—including zebra mussels, Mediterranean fruit flies, Asian longhorn beetles, water hyacinth, and spotted knapweed—that now affect our agriculture, forests, waterways, and pastures. . . .

The cost of our homegrown environmental problems adds up to a large fraction of our gross national product, even without mentioning the costs that we incur from environmental problems overseas, such as the military operations that they inspire. Even the mildest of bad scenarios for our future include a gradual economic decline, as happened to the Roman and British empires. Actually, in case you didn't notice it, our economic decline is already well under way. Just check the numbers for our national debt, yearly government budget deficit, unemployment statistics, and the value of your investment and pension funds. 35

The environmental problems of the United States are still modest compared with those of the rest of the world. But the problems of environmentally devastated, over-populated, distant countries are now our problems as well. We are accustomed to thinking of globalization in terms of us rich, advanced First Worlders sending our good things, such as the Internet and Coca-Cola, to those poor backward Third Worlders. Globalization, however, means nothing more than improved worldwide communication and transportation, which can convey many things in either direction; it is not restricted to good things carried only from the First to the Third World. They in the Third World can now, intentionally or unintentionally, send us their bad things: terrorists; diseases such as AIDS, SARS, cholera, and West Nile fever, carried inadvertently by passengers on transcontinental airplanes; unstoppable numbers of immigrants, both legal and illegal, arriving by boat, truck, train, plane, and on foot; and other consequences of their Third World problems. We in the United States are no longer the isolated Fortress America to which some of us aspired in the 1930s; instead, we are tightly and irreversibly connected to overseas countries. The United States is the world's leading importer, and it is also the world's leading exporter. Our own society opted long ago to become interlocked with the rest of the world. . . .

If all of this reasoning seems straightforward when expressed so bluntly, one has to wonder: Why don't those in power today get the message? Why didn't the leaders of the Maya, Anasazi, and those other societies also recognize and solve their problems? What were the Maya thinking while they watched loggers clearing the last pine forests on the hills above Copán? Here, the past really is a useful guide to the present. It turns out that there are at least a dozen reasons why past societies failed to *anticipate* some problems before they developed, or failed to *perceive* problems that had already developed, or failed even to try to solve problems that they did perceive. All of those dozen reasons still can be seen operating today. Let me mention just three of them.

First, it's difficult to recognize a slow trend in some quantity that fluctuates widely up and down anyway, such as seasonal temperature, annual rainfall, or economic indicators. That's surely why the Maya didn't recognize the oncoming drought until it was too late, given that rainfall in the Yucatán varies several-fold from year to year. Natural fluctuations also explain why it's only within the last few years that all climatologists have become convinced of the reality of climate change, and why our president still isn't convinced but thinks that we need more research to test for it.

Second, when a problem *is* recognized, those in power may not attempt to solve it because of a clash between their short-term interests and the interests of the rest of us. Pumping that oil, cutting down those trees, and catching those fish may benefit the elite by bringing them money or prestige and yet be bad for society as a whole (including the children of the elite) in the long run. . . .

Finally, it's difficult for us to acknowledge the wisdom of policies that clash with strongly held values. For example, a belief in individual freedom and a distrust of big government are deeply ingrained in Americans, and they make sense under some circumstances and up to a certain point. But they also make it hard for us to accept big government's legitimate role in ensuring that each individual's freedom to maximize the value of his or her land holdings doesn't decrease the value of the collective land of all Americans.

Not all societies make fatal mistakes. There are parts of the world where societies have unfolded for thousands of years without any collapse, such as Java, Tonga, and (until 1945) Japan. Today, Germany and Japan are successfully managing their forests, which are even expanding in area rather than shrinking. The Alaskan salmon fishery and the Australian lobster fishery are being managed sustainably. The Dominican Republic, hardly a rich country, nevertheless has set aside a comprehensive system of protected areas encompassing most of the country's natural habitats. . . .

Throughout human history, all peoples have been connected to some other peoples, living together in virtual polders [below-sea-level, reclaimed land in the Netherlands]. For the ancient Maya, their polder consisted of most of the Yucatán and neighboring areas. When the Classic Maya cities collapsed in the southern Yucatán, refugees may have reached the northern Yucatán, but probably not the Valley of Mexico, and certainly not Florida. Today, our whole world has become one polder, such that events in even Afghanistan and Somalia affect Americans. We do indeed differ from the Maya, but not in ways we might like: we have a much larger population, we have more potent destructive technology, and we face the risk of a worldwide rather than a local decline. Fortunately, we also differ from the Maya in that we know their fate, and they did not. Perhaps we can learn.

CONNECTING PERSONALLY TO THE READING

1. Do you agree with Diamond that "our strongest arguments for a healthy environment are selfish"? Explain.

2. Diamond claims that technology may not be able to solve our environmental problems. Do you agree? On what successes and failures do you base your views? Explain.

3. Have you experienced the effects of overpopulation, crowding, or misuse of natural resources in your personal life? Do you have knowledge or experience of political choices with environmental impact that reflect short-term interests? Explain.

FOCUSING ON THE ARGUMENT

1. Diamond uses an exasperated, sometimes sarcastic tone to jar his reader—for instance, "Well, for a few billion of the world's people who are causing us increasing trouble . . ." How does this tone affect the reader? What difference would it make if Diamond had used a matter-of-fact tone?

2. Diamond questions assumptions readers may hold that keep them complacent. These include assumptions that technology will save us and that those distant societies that are collapsing are "weak, far-off, overpopulated" and just "unlucky." Why is it important to address such assumptions? How effective is Diamond in doing this?

3. Diamond makes us look at our civilization through an extended analogy—showing the parallel between our and Classic Maya civilization. He details Maya topography, farming methods, diet, water supplies, transport, population, and political structure—and the collapse of them all. Do you think the parallels are credible? Explain why or why not.

4. Diamond concludes with a comparison of "our whole world" to a polder—reclaimed land in the Netherlands, a country where one-fifth of the farmland is below sea level, requiring extensive environmental efforts. How does this single word sum up Diamond's idea for "good environmental sense"?

SYNTHESIZING IDEAS FROM MULTIPLE READINGS

1. Both Aldo Leopold ("Wilderness as a Form of Land Use," p. 354) and Diamond warn against the destruction of environmental resources. Both look broadly at civilization and history, including American resistance to constraints on individual freedom. Leopold, however, wrote in 1925, Diamond in 2003. What difference in urgency and foreboding do you find in the essays? Explain.

2. In his land use plan, Aldo Leopold ("Wilderness as a Form of Land Use") looks to a rational valuing of land, a policy of "balancing" production needs against recreational needs and deciding which lands need to be reserved for special uses. Why would "balancing" not be enough for Diamond? On what basic premises do they differ and why?

3. Diamond focuses on economic resources in his support of environmental awareness and action. Barry Lopez ("Ice and Light," p. 397), Annie Dillard ("Heaven and Earth in Jest," p. 381) and Wendell Berry ("An Entrance to the Woods," p. 372) value the environment for its beauty, variety, and self-revelation. Do these various reasons reinforce or conflict with one another? Explain.

4. In "The World's Largest Membrane" (p. 416), Lewis Thomas describes the delicate balance needed for Earth's atmosphere to function as a "membrane." How might the misuse of land resources also affect the atmospheric balance?

WRITING TO ACT

1. Write a letter to your local state representative voicing your views on your state's environmental policy or on a recent local decision on the environment that you have researched. Your local newspaper should be a good research tool.

2. The lack of leadership seems a major concern to Diamond. Write an op-ed piece for your local newspaper, detailing the qualities of leadership you think are necessary to forestall the potential destruction of natural resources.

3. The newspapers are full of stories of environmental degradation—such as the increased destruction of sequoias that are hundreds of years old and the high level of pollution in the Arctic. Research any environmental groups that are concerned with an issue you care about. Write to them about your own concerns and how you think you could contribute to their organization.

Transitions from one place to another and from one state of awareness to another are often difficult. They can be jarring or they can be gradual. Would you appreciate a sudden contrast or a gradual introduction to a new environment, especially one in the woods? **WENDELL BERRY** describes an everyday trip into the woods, along the foot trails of the Red River Gorge, Kentucky. He describes a gradual transition, the rambling movements and thoughts of someone increasingly at home in this spot of wilderness. What gradual differences in our selves do we notice when we move from the city into the country? Try to remember some of the feelings you have had on a camping trip or in the woods. Was it difficult to feel at home in this environment? How was your watchfulness increased? Berry thinks we live our civilized lives in the midst of wilderness like a "mollusk lives in his shell in the sea." What do we lose when we ignore the very elements we live in and curl up like mollusks?

BERRY, born in 1934, remains one of the most ardent defenders of rural life and small-scale farming. A poet, essayist, novelist, and English professor at Kentucky State University, Berry also maintains a small farm at Port Kentucky. He is the author of many poetry collections, such as *November Twenty-Six, Nineteen Hundred Sixty-Three* (1964), and the recent *Given: Poems* (2005), and a number of nonfiction titles, including *What Are People For?* (1990) and *The Unsettling of America: Culture and Agriculture* (1996).

An Entrance to the Woods | BY WENDELL BERRY

AN ENTRANCE TO THE WOODS

On a fine sunny afternoon at the end of September I leave my work in Lexington and drive east on I-64 and the Mountain Parkway. When I leave the Parkway at the little town of Pine Ridge I am in the watershed of the Red River in the Daniel Boone National Forest. From Pine Ridge I take Highway 715 out along the narrow ridgetops, a winding tunnel through the trees. And then I turn off on a Forest Service Road and follow it to the head of a foot trail that goes down the steep valley wall of one of the tributary creeks. I pull my car off the road and lock it, and lift on my pack.

It is nearly five o'clock when I start walking. The afternoon is brilliant and warm, absolutely still, not enough air stirring to move a leaf. There is only the steady somnolent trilling of insects, and now and again in the woods below me the cry of a pileated woodpecker. Those, and my footsteps on the path, are the only sounds.

From the dry oak woods of the ridge I pass down into the rock. The foot trails of the Red River Gorge all seek these stony notches that little streams have cut back through the cliffs. I pass a ledge overhanging a sheer drop of the rock, where in a wetter time there would be a waterfall. The ledge is dry and mute now, but on the face of the rock below are the characteristic mosses, ferns, liverwort, meadow rue. And here where the ravine suddenly steepens and narrows, where the shadows are long-lived and the dampness stays, the trees are different. Here are beech and hemlock and poplar, straight and tall, reaching way up into the light. Under them are evergreen thickets of rhododendron. And wherever the dampness is there are mosses and ferns. The faces of the rock are intricately scalloped with veins of ironstone, scooped and carved by the wind.

Finally from the crease of the ravine I am following there begins to come the trickling and splashing of water. There is a great restfulness in the sounds these small streams make; they are going down as fast as they can, but their sounds seem leisurely and idle, as if produced like gemstones with the greatest patience and care.

A little later, stopping, I hear not far away the more voluble flowing of the creek.   5
I go on down to where the trail crosses and begin to look for a camping place. The little bottoms along the creek here are thickety and weedy, probably having been kept clear and cropped or pastured not so long ago. In the more open places are little lavender asters, and the even smaller-flowered white ones that some people call beeweed or farewell-summer. And in low wet places are the richly flowered spikes of great lobelia, the blooms an intense startling blue, exquisitely shaped. I choose a place in an open thicket near the stream, and make camp.

It is a simple matter to make camp. I string up a shelter and put my air mattress and sleeping bag in it, and I am ready for the night. And supper is even simpler, for I have brought sandwiches for this first meal. In less than an hour all my chores are done. It will still be light for a good while, and I go over and sit down on a rock at the edge of the stream.

And then a heavy feeling of melancholy and lonesomeness comes over me. This does not surprise me, for I have felt it before when I have been alone at evening in wilderness places that I am not familiar with. But here it has a quality that I recognize as peculiar to the narrow hollows of the Red River Gorge. These are deeply shaded by the trees and by the valley walls, the sun rising on them late and setting early; they are more dark than light. And there will often be little rapids in the stream that will sound, at a certain distance, exactly like people talking. As I sit on my rock by the stream now, I could swear that there is a party of campers coming up the trail toward me, and for several minutes I stay alert, listening for them, their voices seeming to rise and fall, fade out and lift again, in happy conversation. When I finally realize that it is only a sound the creek is making, though I have not come here for company and do not want any, I am inexplicably sad.

These are haunted places, or at least it is easy to feel haunted in them, alone at nightfall. As the air darkens and the cool of the night rises, one feels the immanence of the wraiths of the ancient tribesmen who used to inhabit the rock houses of the cliffs; of the white hunters from east of the mountains; of the farmers who accepted the isolation of these nearly inaccessible valleys to crop the narrow bottoms and ridges and pasture their cattle and hogs in the woods; of the seekers of quick wealth in timber and ore. For though this is a wilderness place, it bears its part of the burden of human history. If one spends much time here and feels much liking for the place, it is hard to escape the sense of one's predecessors. If one has read of the prehistoric Indians whose flint arrowpoints and pottery and hominy holes and petroglyphs have been found here, then every rock shelter and clifty spring will suggest the presence of those dim people who have disappeared into the earth. Walking along the ridges and the stream bottoms, one will come upon the heaped stones of a chimney, or the slowly filling depression of an old cellar, or will find in the spring a japonica bush or periwinkles or a few jonquils blooming in a thicket that used to be a dooryard. Wherever the land is level enough there are abandoned fields and pastures. And nearly always there is the evidence that one follows in the steps of the loggers.

That sense of the past is probably one reason for the melancholy that I feel. But I know that there are other reasons.

One is that, though I am here in body, my mind and my nerves too are not yet al-   10
together here. We seem to grant to our high-speed roads and our airlines the rather thoughtless assumption that people can change places as rapidly as their bodies can be transported. That, as my own experience keeps proving to me, is not true. In the middle of the afternoon I left off being busy at work, and drove through traffic to the freeway, and then for a solid hour or more I drove sixty or seventy miles an hour, hardly aware of the country I was passing through, because on the freeway one does not have to be. The landscape has been subdued so that one may drive over it at seventy miles per hour without any concession whatsoever to one's whereabouts. One might as well be flying. Though one is in Kentucky one is not experiencing Kentucky; one is experiencing the highway, which might be in nearly any hill country east of the Mississippi.

Once off the freeway, my pace gradually slowed, as the roads became progressively more primitive, from seventy miles an hour to a walk. And now, here at my camping place, I have stopped altogether. But my mind is still keyed to seventy miles an hour. And having come here so fast, it is still busy with the work I am usually doing. Having come here by the freeway, my mind is not so fully here as it would have been if I had come by the crookeder, slower state roads; it is incalculably farther away than it would have been if I had come all the way on foot, as my earliest predecessors came. When the Indians and the first white hunters entered this country they were altogether here as soon as they arrived, for they had seen and experienced fully everything between here and their starting place, and so the transition was gradual and articulate in their consciousness. Our senses, after all, were developed to function at foot speeds; and the transition from foot travel to motor travel, in terms of evolutionary time, has been abrupt. The faster one goes, the more strain there is on the senses, the more they fail to take in, the more confusion they must tolerate or gloss over—and the longer it takes to bring the mind to a stop in the presence of anything. Though the freeway passes through the very heart of this forest, the motorist remains several hours' journey by foot from what is living at the edge of the right-of-way.

But I have not only come to this strangely haunted place in a short time and too fast. I have in that move made an enormous change: I have departed from my life as I am used to living it, and have come into the wilderness. It is not fear that I feel; I have learned to fear the everyday events of human history much more than I fear the everyday occurrences of the woods; in general, I would rather trust myself to the woods than to any government that I know of. I feel, instead, an uneasy awareness of severed connections, of being cut off from all familiar places and of being a stranger where I am. What is happening at home? I wonder, and I know I can't find out very easily or very soon.

Even more discomforting is a pervasive sense of unfamiliarity. In the places I am most familiar with—my house, or my garden, or even the woods near home that I have walked in for years—I am surrounded by associations; everywhere I look I am reminded of my history and my hopes; even unconsciously I am comforted by any number of proofs that my life on the earth is an established and a going thing. But I am in this hollow for the first time in my life. I see nothing that I recognize. Everything looks as it did before I came, as it will when I am gone. When I look over at my little camp I see how tentative and insignificant it is. Lying there in my bed in the dark tonight, I will be absorbed in the being of this place, invisible as a squirrel in his nest.

Uneasy as this feeling is, I know it will pass. Its passing will produce a deep pleasure in being there. And I have felt it often enough before that I have begun to understand something of what it means:

Nobody knows where I am. I don't know what is happening to anybody else in the world. While I am here I will not speak, and will have no reason or need for speech. It is only beyond this lonesomeness for the places I have come from that I can reach the vital reality of a place such as this. Turning toward this place, I confront a presence that none of my schooling and none of my usual assumptions have prepared me for: the wilderness, mostly unknowable and mostly alien, that is the universe. Perhaps the most difficult labor for my species is to accept its limits, its weakness and ignorance. But here I am. This wild place where I have camped lies within an enormous cone widening from the center of the earth out across the universe, nearly all of it a mysterious wilderness in which the power and the knowledge of men count for nothing. As long as its instruments are correct and its engines run, the airplane now flying through this great cone is safely within the human freehold; its behavior is as familiar and predictable to those concerned as the inside of a man's living room. But let its instruments or its engines fail, and at once it enters the wilderness where nothing is foreseeable. And these steep narrow hollows, these cliffs and forested ridges that lie below, are the antithesis of flight.

15

Wilderness is the element in which we live encased in civilization, as a mollusk lives in his shell in the sea. It is a wilderness that is beautiful, dangerous, abundant, oblivious of us, mysterious, never to be conquered or controlled or second-guessed, or known more than a little. It is a wilderness that for most of us most of the time is kept out of sight, camouflaged, by the edifices and the busyness and the bothers of human society.

And so, coming here, what I have done is strip away the human facade that usually stands between me and the universe, and I see more clearly where I am. What I am able to ignore much of the time, but find undeniable here, is that all wildernesses are one: there is a profound joining between this wild stream deep in one of the folds of my native country and the tropical jungles, the tundras of the north, the oceans and the deserts. Alone here, among the rocks and the trees, I see that I am alone also among the stars. A stranger here, unfamiliar with my surroundings, I am aware also that I know only in the most relative terms my whereabouts within the black reaches of the universe. And because the natural processes are here so little qualified by anything human, this fragment of the wilderness is also joined to other times: there flows over it a nonhuman time to be told by the growth and death of the forest and the wearing of the stream. I feel drawing out beyond my comprehension perspectives from which the growth and the death of a large poplar would seem as continuous and sudden as the raising and the lowering of a man's hand, from which men's history in the world, their brief clearing of the ground, will seem no more than the opening and shutting of an eye.

And so I have come here to enact—not because I want to but because, once here, I cannot help it—the loneliness and the humbleness of my kind. I must see in my flimsy shelter, pitched here for two nights, the transience of capitols and cathedrals. In growing used to being in this place, I will have to accept a humbler and a truer view of myself than I usually have.

A man enters and leaves the world naked. And it is only naked—or nearly so—that he can enter and leave the wilderness. If he walks, that is; and if he doesn't walk it can hardly be said that he has entered. He can bring only what he can carry—the little that it takes to replace for a few hours or a few days an animal's fur and teeth and claws and functioning instincts. In comparison to the usual traveler with his dependence on machines and highways and restaurants and motels—on the economy and the government, in short—the man who walks into the wilderness is naked indeed. He leaves behind his work, his household, his duties, his comforts—even, if he comes alone, his words. He immerses himself in what he is not. It is a kind of death.

The dawn comes slow and cold. Only occasionally, somewhere along the creek or on   20
the slopes above, a bird sings. I have not slept well, and I waken without much interest in the day. I set the camp to rights, and fix breakfast, and eat. The day is clear, and high up on the points and ridges to the west of my camp I can see the sun shining on the woods. And suddenly I am full of an ambition: I want to get up where the sun is; I want to sit still in the sun up there among the high rocks until I can feel its warmth in my bones.

I put some lunch into a little canvas bag, and start out, leaving my jacket so as not to have to carry it after the day gets warm. Without my jacket, even climbing, it is cold in the shadow of the hollow, and I have a long way to go to get to the sun. I climb the steep path up the valley wall, walking rapidly, thinking only of the sunlight above me. It is as though I have entered into a deep sympathy with those tulip poplars that grow so straight and tall out of the shady ravines, not growing a branch worth the name until their heads are in the sun. I am so concentrated on the sun that when some grouse flush from the undergrowth ahead of me, I am thunderstruck; they are already planing down into the underbrush again before I can get my wits together and realize what they are.

The path zigzags up the last steepness of the bluff and then slowly levels out. For some distance it follows the backbone of a ridge, and then where the ridge is narrowest there is a great slab of bare rock lying full in the sun. This is what I have been looking for. I walk out into the center of the rock and sit, the clear warm light falling unobstructed all around. As the sun warms me I begin to grow comfortable not only in my clothes, but in the place and the day. And like those light-seeking poplars of the ravines, my mind begins to branch out.

Southward, I can hear the traffic on the Mountain Parkway, a steady continuous roar—the corporate voice of twentieth-century humanity, sustained above the transient voices of its members. Last night, except for an occasional airplane passing over, I camped out of reach of the sounds of engines. For long stretches of time I heard no sounds but the sounds of the woods.

Near where I am sitting there is an inscription cut into the rock:

A • J • SARGENT
fEB • 24 • 1903

Those letters were carved there more than sixty-six years ago. As I look around me I 25 realize that I can see no evidence of the lapse of so much time. In every direction I can see only narrow ridges and narrow deep hollows, all covered with trees. For all that can be told from this height by looking, it might still be 1903—or, for that matter, 1803 or 1703, or 1003. Indians no doubt sat here and looked over the country as I am doing now; the visual impression is so pure and strong that I can almost imagine myself one of them. But the insistent, the overwhelming, evidence of the time of my own arrival is in what I can hear—that roar of the highway off there in the distance. In 1903 the continent was still covered by a great ocean of silence, in which the sounds of machinery were scattered at wide intervals of time and space. Here, in 1903, there were only the natural sounds of the place. On a day like this, at the end of September, there would have been only the sounds of a few faint crickets, a woodpecker now and then, now and then the wind. But today, two-thirds of a century later, the continent is covered by an ocean of engine noise, in which silences occur only sporadically and at wide intervals.

From where I am sitting in the midst of this island of wilderness, it is as though I am listening to the machine of human history—a huge flywheel building speed until finally the force of its whirling will break it in pieces, and the world with it. That is not an attractive thought, and yet I find it impossible to escape, for it has seemed to me for years now that the doings of men no longer occur within nature, but that the natural places which the human economy has so far spared now survive almost accidentally within the doings of men. This wilderness of the Red River now carries on its ancient processes *within* the human climate of war and waste and confusion. And I know that the distant roar of engines, though it may *seem* only to be passing through this wilderness, is really bearing down upon it. The machine is running now with a speed that produces blindness—as to the driver of a speeding automobile the only thing stable, the only thing not a mere blur on the edge of the retina, is the automobile itself—and the blindness of a thing with power promises the destruction of what cannot be seen. That roar of the highway is the voice of the American economy; it is sounding also wherever strip mines are being cut in the steep slopes of Appalachia, and wherever cropland is being destroyed to make roads and suburbs, and wherever rivers and marshes and bays and forests are being destroyed for the sake of industry or commerce.

No. Even here where the economy of life is really an economy—where the creation is yet fully alive and continuous and self-enriching, where whatever dies enters directly into the life of the living—even here one cannot fully escape the sense of an impending human catastrophe. One cannot come here without the awareness that this is an island surrounded by the machinery and the workings of an insane greed, hungering for the world's end—that ours is a "civilization" of which the work of no builder or artist is symbol, nor the life of any good man, but rather the bulldozer, the poison spray, the hugging fire of napalm, the cloud of Hiroshima.

Though from the high vantage point of this stony ridge I see little hope that I will ever live a day as an optimist, still I am not desperate. In fact, with the sun warming me now, and with the whole day before me to wander in this beautiful country, I am happy. A man cannot despair if he can imagine a better life, and if he can enact something of its possibility. It is only when I am ensnarled in the meaningless ordeals and the ordeals of meaninglessness, of which our public and political life is now so productive, that I lose the awareness of something better, and feel the despair of having come to the dead end of possibility.

Today, as always when I am afoot in the woods, I feel the possibility, the reasonableness, the practicability of living in the world in a way that would enlarge rather than diminish the hope of life. I feel the possibility of a frugal and protective love for the creation that would be unimaginably more meaningful and joyful than our present destructive and wasteful economy. The absence of human society, that made me so uneasy last night, now begins to be a comfort to me. I am afoot in the woods. I am alive in the world, this moment, without the help or the interference of any machine. I can move without reference to anything except the lay of the land and the capabilities of my own body. The necessities of foot travel in this steep country have stripped away all superfluities. I simply could not enter into this place and assume its quiet with all the belongings of a family man, property holder, etc. For the time, I am reduced to my irreducible self. I feel the lightness of body that a man must feel who has just lost fifty pounds of fat. As I leave the bare expanse of the rock and go in under the trees again, I am aware that I move in the landscape as one of its details.

Walking through the woods, you can never see far, either ahead or behind, so you move without much of a sense of getting anywhere or of moving at any certain speed. You burrow through the foliage in the air much as a mole burrows through the roots in the ground. The views that open out occasionally from the ridges afford a relief, a recovery of orientation, that they could never give as mere "scenery," looked at from a turnout at the edge of a highway. 30

The trail leaves the ridge and goes down a ravine into the valley of a creek where the night chill has stayed. I pause only long enough to drink the cold clean water. The trail climbs up onto the next ridge.

It is the ebb of the year. Though the slopes have not yet taken on the bright colors of the autumn maples and oaks, some of the duller trees are already shedding. The foliage has begun to flow down the cliff faces and the slopes like a tide pulling back. The woods is mostly quiet, subdued, as if the pressure of survival has grown heavy upon it, as if above the growing warmth of the day the cold of winter can be felt waiting to descend.

At my approach a big hawk flies off the low branch of an oak and out over the tree-tops. Now and again a nuthatch hoots, off somewhere in the woods. Twice I stop and watch an ovenbird. A few feet ahead of me there is a sudden movement in the leaves, and then quiet. When I slip up and examine the spot there is nothing to be found. Whatever passed there has disappeared, quicker than the hand that is quicker than the eye, a shadow fallen into a shadow.

In the afternoon I leave the trail. My walk so far has come perhaps three-quarters of the way around a long zig-zagging loop that will eventually bring me back to my starting place. I turn down a small unnamed branch of the creek where I am camped, and I begin the loveliest part of the day. There is nothing here resembling a trail. The best way is nearly always to follow the edge of the stream, stepping from one stone to another. Crossing back and forth over the water, stepping on or over rocks and logs, the way ahead is never clear for more than a few feet. The stream accompanies me down, threading its way under boulders and logs and over little falls and rapids. The rhododendron overhangs it so closely in places that I can go only by stopping. Over the rhododendron are the great dark heads of the hemlocks. The streambanks are ferny and mossy. And through this green tunnel the voice of the stream changes from rock to rock; subdued like all the other autumn voices of the woods, it seems sunk in a deep contented meditation on the sounds of *l*.

The water in the pools is absolutely clear. If it weren't for the shadows and ripples   35
you would hardly notice that it is water; the fish would seem to swim in the air. As it is, where there is no leaf floating, it is impossible to tell exactly where the plane of the surface lies. As I walk up on a pool the little fish dart every which way out of sight. And then after I sit still a while, watching, they come out again. Their shadows flow over the rocks and leaves on the bottom. Now I have come into the heart of the woods. I am far from the highway and can hear no sound of it. All around there is a grand deep autumn quiet, in which a few insects dream their summer songs. Suddenly a wren sings way off in the underbrush. A red-breasted nuthatch walks, hooting, headfirst down the trunk of a walnut. An ovenbird walks out along the limb of a hemlock and looks at me, curious. The little fish soar in the pool, turning their clean quick angles, their shadows seeming barely to keep up. As I lean and dip my cup in the water, they scatter. I drink, and go on.

When I get back to camp it is only the middle of the afternoon or a little after. Since I left in the morning I have walked something like eight miles. I haven't hurried—have mostly poked along, stopping often and looking around. But I am tired, and coming down the creek I have got both feet wet. I find a sunny place, and take off my shoes and socks and set them to dry. For a long time then, lying propped against the trunk of a tree, I read and rest and watch the evening come.

All day I have moved through the woods, making as little noise as possible. Slowly my mind and my nerves have slowed to a walk. The quiet of the woods has ceased to be something that I observe; now it is something that I am a part of. I have joined it with my own quiet. As the twilight draws on I no longer feel the strangeness and uneasiness of the evening before. The sounds of the creek move through my mind as they move through the valley, unimpeded and clear.

When the time comes I prepare supper and eat, and then wash kettle and cup and spoon and put them away. As far as possible I get things ready for an early start in the morning. Soon after dark I go to bed, and I sleep well.

I wake long before dawn. The air is warm and I feel rested and wide awake. By the light of a small candle lantern I break camp and pack. And then I begin the steep climb back to the car.

The moon is bright and high. The woods stands in deep shadow, the light falling   40
soft through the openings of the foliage. The trees appear immensely tall, and black, gravely looming over the path. It is windless and still; the moonlight pouring over the country seems more potent than the air. All around me there is still that constant low singing of the insects. For days now it has continued without letup or inflection, like

ripples on water under a steady breeze. While I slept it went on through the night, a shimmer on my mind. My shoulder brushes a low tree overhanging the path and a bird that was asleep on one of the branches startles awake and flies off into the shadows, and I go on with the sense that I am passing near to the sleep of things.

In a way this is the best part of the trip. Stopping now and again to rest, I linger over it, sorry to be going. It seems to me that if I were to stay on, today would be better than yesterday, and I realize it was to renew the life of that possibility that I came here. What I am leaving is something to look forward to.

CONNECTING PERSONALLY TO THE READING

1. Berry comments on the current speed of travel: "The faster one goes, the more strain there is on the senses." How do you think that the speed of travel impedes the watchfulness Berry wants us to have?

2. Berry describes a number of feelings of discomfort—severed connections, a sense of unfamiliarity, a sense of the unknowable. What in your own experience is the benefit of such feelings?

3. In stating his purpose for the trip, Berry says that he has "come here to enact . . . the loneliness and the humbleness of [his] kind." Do you think that such a goal has a moral element? Explain.

FOCUSING ON THE ARGUMENT

1. Berry tells the story of a seemingly everyday experience of leaving work and driving to the Red River Gorge foot trails, where he begins an overnight excursion. How does his story draw the reader in?

2. In the story, what kind of persona does Berry project? (watchful? calm? excitable?) What is the appeal of this persona? What kind of relationship do you think he establishes with the reader?

3. Berry observes and describes nature, using telling details. How do these descriptions support his purpose of awakening watchfulness in others?

SYNTHESIZING IDEAS FROM MULTIPLE READINGS

1. According to Leslie Marmon Silko ("The Migration Story," p. 389) and Berry, what moral values arise from experiences in nature?

2. Berry mentions that he cannot help thinking about the distant Indian residents of the Red River Gorge. Leslie Marmon Silko ("The Migration Story," p. 389) connects to previous generations. How are the writers similar and different in the importance they attach to these connections?

3. For Berry, as for Annie Dillard ("Heaven and Earth in Jest," p. 381), one needs to remove oneself physically from the city to experience a different consciousness of nature. Why is this removal so important to each? Explain.

4. The experience in nature Berry describes is one of educating the mind. How might an outdoor education program help the students in Jonathan Kozol's "Savage Inequalities" (Chapter 4), who are locked in decrepit buildings? What might such a curriculum look like?

WRITING TO ACT

1. Identify a public agency in your area focused on conservation or ecology. Find out what local piece of land they are trying to acquire or protect. Visit one you know and care about in your area. Then write a letter supporting the agency's efforts, using Berry's arguments and your own.

2. Research the human and natural history of a protected locale—the people who lived there, what their lives were like, how long ago they lived there, and what changes the landscape has undergone. Write up a short brochure on the local area helping visitors better appreciate what they see.

READING

How do animals and nature make one conscious of the "mystery of continuous creation"? **ANNIE DILLARD** describes simple startling things—her old tomcat's bloody paw prints on her skin, the quiet passivity of the nearby mountains, a frog being sucked alive by a giant water bug. These sensations stimulate her sense of wonder. They help her awaken to what is new, and they provoke her to reflect on the sacred, the beautiful, and the uncertain. Dillard lived near Tinker Creek and wrote about her immediate surroundings. The creeks and mountains have specific local names; and their shapes and qualities have specific meanings. In what ways does this grounding in a specific natural setting help us become more human? How does it help us awaken to intense human feelings not experienced in most of everyday life?

DILLARD is a professor of English and writer-in-residence at Wesleyan University in Connecticut. Her book *Pilgrim at Tinker Creek,* which explores issues of theology and nature, was awarded the Pulitzer Prize in 1975. Dillard has also published a book of poetry, *Ticket for a Prayer Wheel,* and the memoir *An American Childhood,* among other books, essays, and poems.

Heaven and Earth in Jest (1974) | BY ANNIE DILLARD

I used to have a cat, an old fighting tom, who would jump through the open window by my bed in the middle of the night and land on my chest. I'd half-awaken. He'd stick his skull under my nose and purr, stinking of urine and blood. Some nights he kneaded my bare chest with his front paws, powerfully, arching his back, as if sharpening his claws, or pummeling a mother for milk. And some mornings I'd wake in daylight to find my body covered with paw prints in blood; I looked as though I'd been painted with roses.

It was hot, so hot the mirror felt warm. I washed before the mirror in a daze, my twisted summer sleep still hung about me like sea kelp. What blood was this, and what roses? It could have been the rose of union, the blood of murder, or the rose of beauty bare and the blood of some unspeakable sacrifice or birth. The sign on my body could have been an emblem or a stain, the keys to the kingdom or the mark of Cain. I never knew. I never knew as I washed, and the blood streaked, faded, and finally disappeared, whether I'd purified myself or ruined the blood sign of the passover. We wake, if we ever wake at all, to mystery, rumors of death, beauty, violence. . . . "Seem like we're just set down here," a woman said to me recently, "and don't nobody know why."

These are morning matters, pictures you dream as the final wave heaves you up on the sand to the bright light and drying air. You remember pressure, and a curved sleep you rested against, soft, like a scallop in its shell. But the air hardens your skin; you stand; you leave the lighted shore to explore some dim headland, and soon you're lost in the leafy interior, intent, remembering nothing.

I still think of that old tomcat, mornings, when I wake. Things are tamer now; I sleep with the window shut. The cat and our rites are gone and my life is changed, but the memory remains of something powerful playing over me. I wake expectant, hoping to see a new thing. If I'm lucky I might be jogged awake by a strange birdcall. I dress in a hurry, imagining the yard flapping with auks, or flamingos. This morning it was a wood duck, down at the creek. It flew away.

I live by a creek, Tinker Creek, in a valley in Virginia's Blue Ridge. An anchorite's 5
hermitage is called an anchor-hold; some anchor-holds were simple sheds clamped to the side of a church like a barnacle to a rock. I think of this house clamped to the side of Tinker Creek as an anchor-hold. It holds me at anchor to the rock bottom of the creek itself and it keeps me steadied in the current, as a sea anchor does, facing the stream of light pouring down. It's a good place to live; there's a lot to think about. The creeks—Tinker and Carvin's—are an active mystery, fresh every minute. Theirs is the mystery of the continuous creation and all that providence implies: the uncertainty of vision, the horror of the fixed, the dissolution of the present, the intricacy of beauty, the pressure of fecundity, the elusiveness of the free, and the flawed nature of perfection. The mountains—Tinker and Brushy, McAfee's Knob and Dead Man—are a passive mystery, the oldest of all. Theirs is the one simple mystery of creation from nothing, of matter itself, anything at all, the given. Mountains are giant, restful, absorbent. You can heave your spirit into a mountain and the mountain will keep it, folded, and not throw it back as some creeks will. The creeks are the world with all its stimulus and beauty; I live there. But the mountains are home.

The wood duck flew away, I caught only a glimpse of something like a bright torpedo that blasted the leaves where it flew. Back at the house I ate a bowl of oatmeal; much later in the day came the long slant of light that means good walking.

If the day is fine, any walk will do; it all looks good. Water in particular looks its best, reflecting blue sky in the flat, and chopping it into graveled shallows and white chute and foam in the riffles. On a dark day, or a hazy one, everything's washed-out and lackluster but the water. It carries its own lights. I set out for the railroad tracks, for the hill the flocks fly over, for the woods where the white mare lives. But I go to the water.

Today is one of those excellent January partly cloudies in which light chooses an unexpected part of the landscape to trick out in gilt, and then shadow sweeps it away.

You know you're alive. You take huge steps, trying to feel the planet's roundness arc between your feet. Kazantzakis says that when he was young he had a canary and a globe. When he freed the canary, it would perch on the globe and sing. All his life, wandering the earth, he felt as though he had a canary on top of his mind, singing.

West of the house, Tinker Creek makes a sharp loop, so that the creek is both in back of the house, south of me, and also on the other side of the road, north of me. I like to go north. There the afternoon sun hits the creek just right, deepening the reflected blue and lighting the sides of trees on the banks. Steers from the pasture across the creek come down to drink; I always flush a rabbit or two there; I sit on a fallen trunk in the shade and watch the squirrels in the sun. There are two separated wooden fences suspended from cables that cross the creek just upstream from my tree-trunk bench. They keep the steers from escaping up or down the creek when they come to drink. Squirrels, the neighborhood children, and I use the downstream fence as a swaying bridge across the creek. But the steers are there today.

I sit on the downed tree and watch the black steers slip on the creek bottom. They   10
are all bred beef: beef heart, beef hide, beef hocks. They're a human product like rayon. They're like a field of shoes. They have cast-iron shanks and tongues like foam insoles. You can't see through to their brains as you can with other animals; they have beef fat behind their eyes, beef stew.

I cross the fence six feet above the water, walking my hands down the rusty cable and tightroping my feet along the narrow edge of the planks. When I hit the other bank and terra firma, some steers are bunched in a knot between me and the barbed-wire fence I want to cross. So I suddenly rush at them in an enthusiastic sprint, flailing my arms and hollering, "Lightning! Copperhead! Swedish meatballs!" They flee, still in a knot, stumbling across the flat pasture. I stand with the wind on my face.

When I slide under a barbed-wire fence, cross a field, and run over a sycamore trunk felled across the water, I'm on a little island shaped like a tear in the middle of Tinker Creek. On one side of the creek is a steep forested bank; the water is swift and deep on that side of the island. On the other side is the level field I walked through next to the steers' pasture; the water between the field and the island is shallow and sluggish. In summer's low water, flags and bulrushes grow along a series of shallow pools cooled by the lazy current. Water striders patrol the surface film, crayfish hump along the silt bottom eating filth, frogs shout and glare, and shiners and small bream hide among roots from the sulky green heron's eye. I come to this island every month of the year. I walk around it, stopping and staring, or I straddle the sycamore log over the creek, curling my legs out of the water in winter, trying to read. Today I sit on dry grass at the end of the island by the slower side of the creek. I'm drawn to this spot. I come to it as to an oracle; I return to it as a man years later will seek out the battlefield where he lost a leg or an arm.

A couple of summers ago I was walking along the edge of the island to see what I could see in the water, and mainly to scare frogs. Frogs have an inelegant way of taking off from invisible positions on the bank just ahead of your feet, in dire panic, emitting a froggy "Yike!" and splashing into the water. Incredibly, this amused me, and, incredibly, it amuses me still. As I walked along the grassy edge of the island, I got better and better at seeing frogs both in and out of the water. I learned to recognize, slowing down, the difference in texture of the light reflected from mud-bank, water, grass, or frog. Frogs were flying all around me. At the end of the island I noticed a small green frog. He was exactly half in and half out of the water, looking like a schematic diagram of an amphibian, and he didn't jump.

He didn't jump; I crept closer. At last I knelt on the island's winter-killed grass, lost, dumbstruck, staring at the frog in the creek just four feet away. He was a very small frog with wide, dull eyes. And just as I looked at him, he slowly crumpled and began to sag. The spirit vanished from his eyes as if snuffed. His skin emptied and drooped; his very skull seemed to collapse and settle like a kicked tent. He was shrinking before my eyes like a deflating football. I watched the taut, glistening skin on his shoulders ruck, and rumple, and fall. Soon, part of his skin, formless as a pricked balloon, lay in floating folds like bright scum on top of the water: it was a monstrous and terrifying thing. I gaped bewildered, appalled. An oval shadow hung in the water behind the drained frog; then the shadow glided away. The frog skin bag started to sink.

I had read about the giant water bug, but never seen one. "Giant water bug" is re- 15
ally the name of the creature, which is an enormous, heavy-bodied brown beetle. It eats insects, tadpoles, fish, and frogs. Its grasping forelegs are mighty and hooked inward. It seizes a victim with these legs, hugs it tight, and paralyzes it with enzymes injected during a vicious bite. That one bite is the only bite it ever takes. Through the puncture shoots the poisons that dissolve the victim's muscles and bones and organs—all but the skin—and through it the giant water bug sucks out the victim's body, reduced to a juice. This event is quite common in warm fresh water. The frog I saw was being sucked by a giant water bug. I had been kneeling on the island grass; when the unrecognizable flap of frog skin settled on the creek bottom, swaying, I stood up and brushed the knees of my pants. I couldn't catch my breath.

Of course, many carnivorous animals devour their prey alive. The usual method seems to be to subdue the victim by downing or grasping it so it can't flee, then eating it whole or in a series of bloody bites. Frogs eat everything whole, stuffing prey into their mouths with their thumbs. People have seen frogs with their wide jaws so full of live dragonflies they couldn't close them. Ants don't even have to catch their prey: in the spring they swarm over newly hatched, featherless birds in the nest and eat them tiny bite by bite.

That it's rough out there and chancy is no surprise. Every live thing is a survivor on a kind of extended emergency bivouac. But at the same time we are also created. In the Koran, Allah asks, "The heaven and the earth and all in between, thinkest thou I made them *in jest?*" It's a good question. What do we think of the created universe, spanning an unthinkable void with an unthinkable profusion of forms? Or what do we think of nothingness, those sickening reaches of time in either direction? If the giant water bug was not made in jest, was it then made in earnest? Pascal uses a nice term to describe the notion of the creator's, once having called forth the universe, turning his back to it: *Deus Absconditus.* Is this what we think happened? Was the sense of it there, and God absconded with it, ate it, like a wolf who disappears round the edge of the house with the Thanksgiving turkey? "God is subtle," Einstein said, "but not malicious." Again, Einstein said that "nature conceals her mystery by means of her essential grandeur, not by her cunning." It could be that God has not absconded but spread, as our vision and understanding of the universe have spread, to a fabric of spirit and sense so grand and subtle, so powerful in a new way, that we can only feel blindly of its hem. In making the thick darkness a swaddling band for the sea, God "set bars and doors" and said, "Hitherto shalt thou come, but no further." But have we come even that far? Have we rowed out to the thick darkness, or are we all playing pinochle in the bottom of the boat?

Cruelty is a mystery, and the waste of pain. But if we describe a world to compass these things, a world that is a long, brute game, then we bump against another mystery: the inrush of power and light, the canary that sings on the skull. Unless all ages and races of men have been deluded by the same mass hypnotist (who?), there seems to be such a thing as beauty, a grace wholly gratuitous. About five years ago I saw a mockingbird make a straight vertical descent from the roof gutter of a four-story building. It was an act as careless and spontaneous as the curl of a stem or the kindling of a star.

The mockingbird took a single step into the air and dropped. His wings were still folded against his sides as though he were swinging from a limb and not falling, accelerating thirty-two feet per second per second, through empty air. Just a breath before he would have been dashed to the ground, he unfurled his wings with exact, deliberate care, revealing the broad bars of white, spread his elegant, white-banded tail, and so floated onto the grass. I had just rounded a corner when his insouciant step caught my eye; there was no one else in sight. The fact of his free fall was like the old philosophical conundrum about the tree that falls in the forest. The answer must be, I think, that beauty and grace are performed whether or not we will or sense them. The least we can do is try to be there.

Another time I saw another wonder: sharks off the Atlantic coast of Florida. There 20 is a way a wave rises above the ocean horizon, a triangular wedge against the sky. If you stand where the ocean breaks on a shallow beach, you see the raised water in a wave is translucent, shot with lights. One late afternoon at low tide a hundred big sharks passed the beach near the mouth of a tidal river in a feeding frenzy. As each green wave rose from the churning water, it illuminated within itself the six- or eight-foot-long bodies of twisting sharks. The sharks disappeared as each wave rolled toward me; then a new wave would swell above the horizon, containing in it, like scorpions in amber, sharks that roiled and heaved. The sight held awesome wonders: power and beauty, grace tangled in a rapture with violence.

We don't know what's going on here. If these tremendous events are random combinations of matter run amok, the yield of millions of monkeys at millions of typewriters, then what is it in us, hammered out of those same typewriters, that they ignite? We don't know. Our life is a faint tracing on the surface of mystery, like the idle, curved tunnels of leaf miners on the face of a leaf. We must somehow take a wider view, look at the whole landscape, really see it, and describe what's going on here. Then we can at least wail the right question into the swaddling band of darkness, or, if it comes to that, choir the proper praise.

At the time of Lewis and Clark, setting the prairies on fire was a well-known signal that meant, "Come down to the water." It was an extravagant gesture, but we can't do less. If the landscape reveals one certainty, it is that the extravagant gesture is the very stuff of creation. After the one extravagant gesture of creation in the first place, the universe has continued to deal exclusively in extravagances, flinging intricacies and colossi down aeons of emptiness, heaping profusions on profligacies with ever-fresh vigor. The whole show has been on fire from the word go. I come down to the water to cool my eyes. But everywhere I look I see fire; that which isn't flint is tinder, and the whole world sparks and flames.

I have come to the grassy island late in the day. The creek is up; icy water sweeps under the sycamore log bridge. The frog skin, of course, is utterly gone. I have stared at that one spot on the creek bottom for so long, focusing past the rush of water, that when I stand, the opposite bank seems to stretch before my eyes and flow grassily upstream. When the bank settles down I cross the sycamore log and enter again the big plowed field next to the steers' pasture.

The wind is terrific out of the west; the sun comes and goes. I can see the shadow on the field before me deepen uniformly and spread like a plague. Everything seems so dull I am amazed I can even distinguish objects. And suddenly the light runs across the land like a comber, and up the trees, and goes again in a wink: I think I've gone blind or died. When it comes again, the light, you hold your breath, and if it stays you forget about it until it goes again.

It's the most beautiful day of the year. At four o'clock the eastern sky is a dead stratus black flecked with low white clouds. The sun in the west illuminates the ground, the mountains, and especially the bare branches of trees, so that everywhere silver trees cut into the black sky like a photographer's negative of a landscape. The air and the ground are dry; the mountains are going on and off like neon signs. Clouds slide east as if pulled from the horizon, like a tablecloth whipped off a table. The hemlocks by the barbed-wire fence are flinging themselves east as though their backs would break. Purple shadows are racing east; the wind makes me face east, and again I feel the dizzying, drawn sensation I felt when the creek bank reeled. ⟦25⟧

At four-thirty the sky in the east is clear; how could that big blackness be blown? Fifteen minutes later another darkness is coming overhead from the northwest; and it's here. Everything is drained of its light as if sucked. Only at the horizon do inky black mountains give way to distant, lighted mountains—lighted not by direct illumination but rather paled by glowing sheets of mist hung before them. Now the blackness is in the east; everything is half in shadow, half in sun, every clod, tree, mountain, and hedge. I can't see Tinker Mountain through the line of hemlock, till it comes on like a streetlight, ping, *ex nihilo*. Its sandstone cliffs pink and swell. Suddenly the light goes; the cliffs recede as if pushed. The sun hits a clump of sycamores between me and the mountains; the sycamore arms light up, and *I can't see the cliffs*. They're gone. The pale network of sycamore arms, which a second ago was transparent as a screen, is suddenly opaque, glowing with light. Now the sycamore arms snuff out, the mountains come on, and there are the cliffs again.

I walk home. By five-thirty the show has pulled out. Nothing is left but an unreal blue and a few banked clouds low in the north. Some sort of carnival magician has been here, some fast-talking worker of wonders who has the act backwards. "Something in this hand," he says, "something in this hand, something up my sleeve, something behind my back . . ." and abracadabra, he snaps his fingers, and it's all gone. Only the bland, blank-faced magician remains, in his unruffled coat, bare-handed, acknowledging a smattering of baffled applause. When you look again the whole show has pulled up stakes and moved on down the road. It never stops. New shows roll in from over the mountains and the magician reappears unannounced from a fold in the curtain you never dreamed was an opening. Scarves of clouds, rabbits in plain view, disappear into the black hat forever. Presto chango. The audience, if there is an audience at all, is dizzy from head-turning, dazed.

Like the bear who went over the mountain, I went out to see what I could see. And, I might as well warn you, like the bear, all that I could see was the other side of the mountain: more of same. On a good day I might catch a glimpse of another wooded ridge rolling under the sun like water, another bivouac. I propose to keep here what Thoreau called "a meteorological journal of the mind," telling some tales and describing some of the sights of this rather tamed valley, and exploring, in fear and trembling, some of the unmapped dim reaches and unholy fastnesses to which those tales and sights so dizzyingly lead.

I am no scientist. I explore the neighborhood. An infant who has just learned to hold his head up has a frank and forthright way of gazing about him in bewilderment. He hasn't the faintest clue where he is, and he aims to learn. In a couple of years, what he will have learned instead is how to fake it: he'll have the cocksure air of a squatter who has come to feel he owns the place. Some unwonted, taught pride diverts us from our original intent, which is to explore the neighborhood, view the landscape, to discover at least *where* it is that we have been so startlingly set down, if we can't learn why.

So I think about the valley. It is my leisure as well as my work, a game. It is a fierce 30 game I have joined because it is being played anyway, a game of both skill and chance, played against an unseen adversary—the conditions of time—in which the payoffs, which may suddenly arrive in a blast of light at any moment, might as well come to me as anyone else. I stake the time I'm grateful to have, the energies I'm glad to direct. I risk getting stuck on the board, so to speak, unable to move in any direction, which happens enough, God knows; and I risk the searing, exhausting nightmares that plunder rest and force me face down all night long in some muddy ditch seething with hatching insects and crustaceans.

But if I can bear the nights, the days are a pleasure. I walk out; I see something, some event that would otherwise have been utterly missed and lost; or something sees me, some enormous power brushes me with its clean wing, and I resound like a beaten bell.

I am an explorer, then, and I am also a stalker, or the instrument of the hunt itself. Certain Indians used to carve long grooves along the wooden shafts of their arrows. They called the grooves "lightning marks," because they resembled the curved fissure lightning slices down the trunks of trees. The function of lightning marks is this: if the arrow fails to kill the game, blood from a deep wound will channel along the lightning mark, streak down the arrow shaft, and spatter to the ground, laying a trail dripped on broad-leaves, on stones, that the barefoot and trembling archer can follow into whatever deep or rare wilderness it leads. I am the arrow shaft, carved along my length by unexpected lights and gashes from the very sky, and this book is the straying trail of blood.

Something pummels us, something barely sheathed. Power broods and lights. We're played on like a pipe; our breath is not our own. James Houston describes two young Eskimo girls sitting cross-legged on the ground, mouth on mouth, blowing by turns each other's throat cords, making a low, unearthly music. When I cross again the bridge that is really the steers' fence, the wind has thinned to the delicate air of twilight; it crumples the water's skin. I watch the running sheets of light raised on the creek's surface. The sight has the appeal of the purely passive, like the racing of light under clouds on a field, the beautiful dream at the moment of being dreamed. The breeze is the merest puff, but you yourself sail headlong and breathless under the gale force of the spirit.

1. Describe an experience in which you were stunned by a natural event. What was unexpected and why? What thoughts went through your head? What did you wonder about?

2. Dillard compares nature to human sensations—"The creeks are the world with all its stimulus and beauty; I live there. But the mountains are home"—as well as to homely products—"[the steers are] a human product like rayon." Describe a natural scene using similes and metaphors of human feelings and possessions.

3. Describe the slow appearance or disappearance of a natural phenomenon, such as a cliff or tree disappearing into darkness. What series of images did you see? What new sights and thoughts did this slow change provoke?

1. Dillard uses unlikely metaphors to heighten our consciousness of natural events. For instance, she likens a tomcat's bloody paw prints on her skin to painted roses. She then extracts the idea of union (rose) and sacrifice (blood). How do these metaphors draw us into new awareness?

2. Dillard jolts us with unexpected, jarring descriptions—for instance, the inward collapse of a frog being sucked alive by a water bug. What is unexpected in this description? Why do you think Dillard wants to jolt us?

1. Wendell Berry ("An Entrance to the Woods," p. 372) and Dillard both see in nature key principles of life. What differences in their views of the meaning of nature do you see in their different descriptions?

2. Dillard clearly feels at home in nature, but in a different way from how Leslie Marmon Silko ("The Migration Story," p. 389) feels at home in nature. How would you describe that difference?

3. Jane Goodall (*In the Shadow of Man*, p. 402), Leslie Marmon Silko ("The Migration Story," p. 389) and Dillard all write about women who make their homes in nature, not just visit it. Berry ("An Entrance to the Woods," p. 372), Leopold ("Wilderness as a Form of Land Use," p. 354) and Lopez ("Ice and Light," p. 397) describe or defend excursions into nature. What differences in relationships to nature do these women and men project?

4. Dillard plays with metaphors as much as Rosanne Cash in "The Ties That Bind" says musicians play with sounds (Chapter 8, p. 586). Do you think that a writer creating fresh metaphors is like a musician creating a new song? Explain.

1. During a one-week period, write three or four entries in a journal reminding yourself about what your immediate environment teaches you each day. Keep the journal detailed.

2. Write a letter to a friend describing a place so special to you that you learned much about yourself exploring and observing it. Try to convince that friend to spend time in a similarly special place. Ask him or her to share observations and feelings with you.

3. William James said that we perceive what is probable and definite, by which he meant that we typically see what we expect to see. We turn unfamiliar sights into familiar sights, and

blurred or vague images into clear ones. Describe a scene in which what you saw actually surprised or stunned you. Send your description to a nature journal such as *Outside, Nature,* or *National Geographic.*

Our dominant culture once saw humans in opposition to the rugged landscapes and animals of America. When European Americans expanded westward, they viewed the landscape as an impediment to be overcome and the animals as a resource to be exploited. In contrast, American Indians have a long history of interdependence with landscapes and animals. What is the basis of that interdependence? What cultural values arise from it? **LESLIE MARMON SILKO** describes the Emergence and Migration Stories that Laguna Pueblo Indians tell one another. The stories connect the Emergence Place and the Migration Story with an actual landscape, demonstrating how, for the Laguna, specific places are infused with cultural meaning. What have we lost by creating a culture that opposes us to the land?

SILKO is a novelist, short story writer, poet, and screenplay writer. Raised on the Laguna Pueblo Reservation, she often explores her tribal ancestry and mixed ancestry (she is also Pueblo, Mexican, and white) in her writing. Silko is best known for her novel *Ceremony;* she is also the author of *Almanac for the Dead, Storyteller,* and *Gardens in the Dunes,* among other books. This selection is from the longer essay "Landscape, History, and the Pueblo Imagination."

The Migration Story: An Interior Journey (1986)

BY LESLIE MARMON SILKO

THROUGH THE STORIES WE HEAR WHO WE ARE

All summer the people watch the west horizon, scanning the sky from south to north for rain clouds. Corn must have moisture at the time the tassels form. Otherwise pollination will be incomplete, and the ears will be stunted and shriveled. An inadequate harvest may bring disaster. Stories told at Hopi, Zuni, and at Acoma and Laguna describe drought and starvation as recently as 1900. Precipitation in west-central New Mexico averages fourteen inches annually. The western pueblos are located at altitudes over 5,600 feet above sea level, where winter temperatures at night fall below freezing. Yet evidence of their presence in the high desert plateau country goes back ten thousand years. The ancient Pueblo people not only survived in this environment, but many years they thrived. In A.D. 1100 the people at Chaco Canyon had built cities with apartment buildings of stone five stories high. Their sophistication as sky-watchers was surpassed only by Mayan and Inca astronomers. Yet this vast complex of knowledge and belief, amassed for thousands of years, was never recorded in writing.

Instead, the ancient Pueblo people depended upon collective memory through successive generations to maintain and transmit an entire culture, a world view complete with proven strategies for survival. The oral narrative, or "story," became the medium in which the complex of Pueblo knowledge and belief was maintained.

Whatever the event or the subject, the ancient people perceived the world and themselves within that world as part of an ancient continuous story composed of innumerable bundles of other stories.

The ancient Pueblo vision of the world was inclusive. The impulse was to leave nothing out. Pueblo oral tradition necessarily embraced all levels of human experience. Otherwise, the collective knowledge and beliefs comprising ancient Pueblo culture would have been incomplete. Thus stories about the Creation and Emergence of human beings and animals into this World continue to be retold each year for four days and four nights during the winter solstice. The "humma-hah" stories related events from the time long ago when human beings were still able to communicate with animals and other living things. But, beyond these two preceding categories, the Pueblo oral tradition knew no boundaries. Accounts of the appearance of the first Europeans in Pueblo country or of the tragic encounters between Pueblo people and Apache raiders were no more and no less important than stories about the biggest mule deer ever taken or adulterous couples surprised in cornfields and chicken coops. Whatever happened, the ancient people instinctively sorted events and details into a loose narrative structure. Everything became a story.

Traditionally everyone, from the youngest child to the oldest person, was expected to listen and to be able to recall or tell a portion, if only a small detail, from a narrative account or story. Thus the remembering and retelling were a communal process. Even if a key figure, an elder who knew much more than others, were to die unexpectedly, the system would remain intact. Through the efforts of a great many people, the community was able to piece together valuable accounts and crucial information that might otherwise have died with an individual.

Communal storytelling was a self-correcting process in which listeners were encouraged to speak up if they noted an important fact or detail omitted. The people were happy to listen to two or three different versions of the same event or the same humma-hah story. Even conflicting versions of an incident were welcomed for the entertainment they provided. Defenders of each version might joke and tease one another, but seldom were there any direct confrontations. Implicit in the Pueblo oral tradition was the awareness that loyalties, grudges, and kinship must always influence the narrator's choices as she emphasizes to listeners this is the way *she* has always heard the story told. The ancient Pueblo people sought a communal truth, not an absolute. For them this truth lived somewhere within the web of differing versions, disputes over minor points, outright contradictions tangling with old feuds and village rivalries.

A dinner-table conversation, recalling a deer hunt forty years ago when the largest mule deer ever was taken, inevitably stimulates similar memories in listeners. But hunting stories were not merely after-dinner entertainment. These accounts contained information of critical importance about behavior and migration patterns of mule deer. Hunting stories carefully described key landmarks and locations of fresh water. Thus a deer-hunt story might also serve as a "map." Lost travelers, and lost piñon-nut gatherers, have been saved by sighting a rock formation they recognize only because they once heard a hunting story describing this rock formation.

The importance of cliff formations and water holes does not end with hunting stories. As offspring of the Mother Earth, the ancient Pueblo people could not conceive of themselves within a specific landscape. Location, or "place," nearly always plays a central role in the Pueblo oral narratives. Indeed, stories are most frequently recalled as people are passing by a specific geographical feature or the exact place where a story takes place. The precise date of the incident often is less important than the place or location of the happening. "Long, long ago," "a long time ago," "not too long ago," and "recently" are usually how stories are classified in terms of time. But the places where the stories occur are precisely located, and prominent geographical details recalled, even if the landscape is well-known to listeners. Often because the turning point in the narrative involved a peculiarity or special quality of a rock or tree or plant found only at that place. Thus, in the case of many of the Pueblo narratives, it is impossible to determine which came first: the incident or the geographical feature which begs to be brought alive in a story that features some unusual aspect of this location.

There is a giant sandstone boulder about a mile north of Old Laguna, on the road to Paguate. It is ten feet tall and twenty feet in circumference. When I was a child, and we would pass this boulder driving to Paguate village, someone usually made reference to the story about Kochininako, Yellow Woman, and the Estrucuyo, a monstrous giant who nearly ate her. The Twin Hero Brothers saved Kochininako, who had been out hunting rabbits to take home to feed her mother and sisters. The Hero Brothers had heard her cries just in time. The Estrucuyo had cornered her in a cave too small to fit its monstrous head. Kochininako had already thrown to the Estrucuyo all her rabbits, as well as her moccasins and most of her clothing. Still the creature had not been satisfied. After killing the Estrucuyo with their bows and arrows, the Twin Hero Brothers slit open the Estrucuyo and cut out its heart. They threw the heart as far as they could. The monster's heart landed there, beside the old trail to Paguate village, where the sandstone boulder rests now.

It may be argued that the existence of the boulder precipitated the creation of a story to explain it. But sandstone boulders and sandstone formations of strange shapes abound in the Laguna Pueblo area. Yet most of them do not have stories. Often the crucial element in a narrative is the terrain—some specific detail of the setting.

A high dark mesa rises dramatically from a grassy plain fifteen miles southeast of Laguna, in an area known as Swanee. On the grassy plain one hundred and forty years ago, my great-grandmother's uncle and his brother-in-law were grazing their herd of sheep. Because visibility on the plain extends for over twenty miles, it wasn't until the two sheepherders came near the high dark mesa that the Apaches were able to stalk them. Using the mesa to obscure their approach, the raiders swept around from both ends of the mesa. My great-grandmother's relatives were killed, and the herd lost. The high dark mesa played a critical role: the mesa had compromised the safety which the openness of the plains had seemed to assure. Pueblo and Apache alike relied upon the terrain, the very earth herself, to give them protection and aid. Human activities or needs were maneuvered to fit the existing surroundings and conditions. I imagine the last afternoon of my distant ancestors as warm and sunny for late September. They might have been traveling slowly, bringing the sheep closer to Laguna in preparation for the approach of colder weather. The grass was tall and only beginning to change from green to a yellow which matched the late-afternoon sun shining off it. There might have been comfort in the warmth and the sight of the sheep fattening on good pasture which lulled my ancestors into their fatal inattention. They might have had a rifle whereas the

10

Apaches had only bows and arrows. But there would have been four or five Apache raiders, and the surprise attack would have canceled any advantage the rifles gave them.

Survival in any landscape comes down to making the best use of all available resources. On that particular September afternoon, the raiders made better use of the Swanee terrain than my poor ancestors did. Thus the high dark mesa and the story of the two lost Laguna herders became inextricably linked. The memory of them and their story resides in part with the high black mesa. For as long as the mesa stands, people within the family and clan will be reminded of the story of that afternoon long ago. Thus the continuity and accuracy of the oral narratives are reinforced by the landscape—and the Pueblo interpretation of that landscape is *maintained*.

THE MIGRATION STORY: AN INTERIOR JOURNEY

The Laguna Pueblo migration stories refer to specific places—mesas, springs, or cottonwood trees—not only locations which can be visited still, but also locations which lie directly on the state highway route linking Paguate village with Laguna village. In traveling this road as a child with older Laguna people I first heard a few of the stories from that much larger body of stories linked with the Emergence and Migration.[1] It may be coincidental that Laguna people continue to follow the same route which, according to the Migration story, the ancestors followed south from the Emergence Place. It may be that the route is merely the shortest and best route for car, horse, or foot traffic between Laguna and Paguate villages. But if the stories about boulders, springs, and hills are actually remnants from a ritual that retraces the creation and emergence of the Laguna Pueblo people as a culture, as the people they became, then continued use of that route creates a unique relationship between the ritual-mythic world and the actual, everyday world. A journey from Paguate to Laguna down the long incline of Paguate Hill retraces the original journey from the Emergence Place, which is located slightly north of the Paguate village. Thus the landscape between Paguate and Laguna takes on a deeper significance: the landscape resonates the spiritual or mythic dimension of the Pueblo world even today.

Although each Pueblo culture designates a specific Emergence Place—usually a small natural spring edged with mossy sandstone and full of cattails and wild watercress—it is clear that they do not agree on any single location or natural spring as the one and only true Emergence Place. Each Pueblo group recounts its own stories about Creation, Emergence, and Migration, although they all believe that all human beings, with all the animals and plants, emerged at the same place and at the same time.[2]

Natural springs are crucial sources of water for all life in the high desert plateau country. So the small spring near Paguate village is literally the source and continuance of life for the people in the area. The spring also functions on a spiritual level, recalling the original Emergence Place and linking the people and the spring water to all other people and to that moment when the Pueblo people became aware of themselves as they are even now. The Emergence was an emergence into a precise cultural identity. Thus the Pueblo stories about the Emergence and Migration are not to be taken as literally as the anthropologists might wish. Prominent geographical features and landmarks which are mentioned in the narratives exist for ritual purposes, not because the Laguna people actually journeyed south for hundreds of years from Chaco Canyon or Mesa Verde, as the archaeologists say, or eight miles from the site of the natural springs at Paguate to the sandstone hilltop at Laguna.

The eight miles, marked with boulders, mesas, springs, and river crossings, are actu- 15
ally a ritual circuit or path which marks the interior journey the Laguna people made:
a journey of awareness and imagination in which they emerged from being within the
earth and from everything included in earth to the culture and people they became,
differentiating themselves for the first time from all that had surrounded them, always
aware that interior distances cannot be reckoned in physical miles or in calendar years.

The narratives linked with prominent features of the landscape between Paguate
and Laguna delineate the complexities of the relationship which human beings must
maintain with the surrounding natural world if they hope to survive in this place.
Thus the journey was an interior process of the imagination, a growing awareness that
being human is somehow different from all other life—animal, plant, and inanimate.
Yet we are all from the same source: the awareness never deteriorated into Cartesian
duality, cutting off the human from the natural world.

The people found the opening into the Fifth World too small to allow them or any
of the animals to escape. They had sent a fly out through the small hole to tell them if
it was the world which the Mother Creator had promised. It was, but there was the
problem of getting out. The antelope tried to butt the opening to enlarge it, but the
antelope enlarged it only a little. It was necessary for the badger with her long claws to
assist the antelope, and at last the opening was enlarged enough so that all the people
and animals were able to emerge up into the Fifth World. The human beings could not
have emerged without the aid of antelope and badger. The human beings depended
upon the aid and charity of the animals. Only through interdependence could the
human beings survive. Families belonged to clans, and it was by clan that the human
being joined with the animal and plant world. Life on the high arid plateau became viable when the human beings were able to imagine themselves as sisters and brothers to
the badger, antelope, clay, yucca, and sun. Not until they could find a viable relationship to the terrain, the landscape they found themselves in, could they *emerge*. Only at
the moment the requisite balance between human and *other* was realized could the
Pueblo people become a culture, a distinct group whose population and survival remained stable despite the vicissitudes of climate and terrain.

Landscape thus has similarities with dreams. Both have the power to seize terrifying feelings and deep instincts and translate them into images—visual, aural, tactile—
into the concrete where human beings may more readily confront and channel the
terrifying instincts or powerful emotions into rituals and narratives which reassure
the individual while reaffirming cherished values of the group. The identity of the individual as a part of the group and the greater Whole is strengthened, and the terror of
facing the world alone is extinguished.

Even now, the people at Laguna Pueblo spend the greater portion of social occasions recounting recent incidents or events which have occurred in the Laguna area.
Nearly always, the discussion will precipitate the retelling of older stories about similar
incidents or other stories connected with a specific place. The stories often contain disturbing or provocative material, but are nonetheless told in the presence of children
and women. The effect of these inter-family or inter-clan exchanges is the reassurance
for each person that she or he will never be separated or apart from the clan, no matter
what might happen. Neither the worst blunders or disasters nor the greatest financial
prosperity and joy will ever be permitted to isolate anyone from the rest of the group.

In the ancient times, cohesiveness was all that stood between extinction and survival, and, while the individual certainly was recognized, it was always as an individual simultaneously bonded to family and clan by a complex bundle of custom and ritual. You are never the first to suffer a grave loss or profound humiliation. You are never the first, and you understand that you will probably not be the last to commit or be victimized by a repugnant act. Your family and clan are able to go on at length about others now passed on, others older or more experienced than you who suffered similar losses.

The wide deep arroyo near the Kings Bar (located across the reservation border-line) has over the years claimed many vehicles. A few years ago, when a Viet Nam veteran's new red Volkswagen rolled backwards into the arroyo while he was inside buying a six-pack of beer, the story of his loss joined the lively and large collection of stories already connected with that big arroyo. I do not know whether the Viet Nam veteran was consoled when he was told the stories about the other cars claimed by the ravenous arroyo. All his savings of combat pay had gone for the red Volkswagen. But this man could not have felt any worse than the man who, some years before, had left his children and mother-in-law in his station wagon with the engine running. When he came out of the liquor store his station wagon was gone. He found it and its passengers upside down in the big arroyo. Broken bones, cuts and bruises, and a total wreck of the car. The big arroyo has a wide mouth. Its existence needs no explanation. People in the area regard the arroyo much as they might regard a living being, which has a certain character and personality. I seldom drive past that wide deep arroyo without feeling a familiarity with and even a strange affection for this arroyo. Because as treacherous as it may be, the arroyo maintains a strong connection between human beings and the earth. The arroyo demands from us the caution and attention that constitute respect. It is this sort of respect the old believers have in mind when they tell us we must respect and love the earth.

Hopi Pueblo elders have said that the austere and, to some eyes, barren plains and hills surrounding their mesa-top villages actually help to nurture the spirituality of the Hopi *way*. The Hopi elders say the Hopi people might have settled in locations far more lush where daily life would not have been so grueling. But there on the high silent sandstone mesas that overlook the sandy arid expanses stretching to all horizons, the Hopi elders say the Hopi people must "live by their prayers" if they are to survive. The Hopi way cherishes the intangible: the riches realized from interaction and interrelationships with all beings above all else. Great abundances of material things, even food, the Hopi elders believe, tend to lure human attention away from what is most valuable and important. The views of the Hopi elders are not much different from those elders in all the Pueblos.

The bare vastness of the Hopi landscape emphasizes the visual impact of every plant, every rock, every arroyo. Nothing is overlooked or taken for granted. Each ant, each lizard, each lark is imbued with great value simply because the creature is there, simply because the creature is alive in a place where any life at all is precious. Stand on the mesa edge at Walpai and look west over the bare distances toward the pale blue outlines of the San Francisco peaks where the ka'tsina spirits reside. So little lies between you and the sky. So little lies between you and the earth. One look and you know that simply to survive is a great triumph, that every possible resource is needed, every possible ally—even the most humble insect or reptile. You realize you will be

20

speaking with all of them if you intend to last out the year. Thus it is that the Hopi elders are grateful to the landscape for aiding them in their quest as spiritual people.

Notes

1. The Emergence—All the human beings, animals, and life which had been created emerged from the four worlds below when the earth became habitable.
The Migration—The Pueblo people emerged into the Fifth World, but they had already been warned they would have to travel and search before they found the place they were meant to live.
2. Creation—Tse'itsi'nako, Thought Woman, the Spider, thought about it, and everything she thought came into being. First she thought of three sisters for herself, and they helped her think of the rest of the Universe, including the Fifth World and the four worlds below. The Fifth World is the world we are living in today. There are four previous worlds below this world.

CONNECTING PERSONALLY TO THE READING

1. What stories do you recall that seem to define your cultural heritage? Do any of these stories depict the landscape? If so, in what way?

2. Do you have any special places in your experience about which you have developed certain myths or beliefs? Describe them and explain those myths or beliefs.

3. How has the landscape helped to define the beliefs and/or behavior of a special group you belong to? What features of the landscape were most important? Why?

FOCUSING ON THE ARGUMENT

1. Silko describes specific places—mesas, roads, springs—that have cultural significance for the Laguna Pueblo people. What is the effect on the reader of these specific details about boulders, mesas, springs, and river crossings?

2. Silko relies on extensive personal experience and testimony. As a young girl, she heard the stories, and their additions and corrections, about the landscape around her. How do these personal testimonials affect the reader's response?

3. To establish a tone of authority as a cultural anthropologist, what language and conventions of cultural anthropology does Silko use? How do they create the tone?

SYNTHESIZING IDEAS FROM MULTIPLE READINGS

1. According to Silko, the Emergence Story emphasizes the need for a balance between humans and plants and animals—in order for all to survive. How does this view of landscape as communal survival suggest similar themes to those Jared Diamond emphasizes in his warnings about the demise of civilizations in "The Last Americans" (p. 362)?

2. For the Laguna Pueblo people, telling old stories about places, even disturbing stories, helped reassure each person of his or her place in the clan. If for Silko nature bonds a culture together, how does it serve individuals like Wendell Berry ("An Entrance to the

Woods," p. 372) and those individuals Aldo Leopold describes ("Wilderness as a Form of Land Use," p. 354)? Explain.

3. Silko views landscape as a cultural anthropologist. She is trained to look at the myths, stories, and values that surround particular environments for a particular people. In contrast, what background and training does Barry Lopez ("Ice and Light," p. 397) bring to his experiences of a landscape? How do you think this training affects his perceptions?

4. In "Heaven and Earth in Jest" (p. 381), Annie Dillard writes that she thinks of her house "clamped to the side of Tinker Creek as an anchor-hold." (An "anchor-hold" is the home of hermits who seek religious seclusion.) Silko, like Dillard, seems tied to place. What differences do you notice in what place means to them?

5. Stories, like names, tell us who we are. In what ways is Silko's return to her people to record their stories like Itabari Njeri's return to Africa ("What's in a Name?" Chapter 2, p. 71) to find out about herself?

WRITING TO ACT

1. In groups of three to four students, identify a landscape that has cultural meaning to a group of people. You may need to research the history of the land. Write a letter to the owners explaining the meaning of that landscape and why you would like to see it preserved.

2. Write an article for a school newspaper on the need for the kind of balance and interdependence Silko suggests between human life and the life of animals and plants. Use specific examples that relate to places near the school.

3. Choose a scene from a Western movie with which you are familiar (a John Ford movie, for example). What is the cultural meaning of the landscape portrayed?

4. Write a personal essay for possible publication in a journal or magazine such as *Outside*.

READING

BARRY LOPEZ describes a voyage through the Canadian Arctic, especially his encounter with icebergs. To convey his feelings, he uses analogies to nineteenth-century American painting, especially by the Luminists, and Gothic cathedrals. The Luminists' portrayal of vast space and emptiness helps Lopez define his own feelings of loss of ego and silence. These artists depict nature, in particular the Arctic, as light and space, often with few signs of human life. Lopez's discussion of Gothic cathedrals then helps him convey the feeling of spiritual awareness aroused by his solitary encounter with icebergs. Both analogies illustrate Lopez's point about making sense of nature: "we bring our own worlds to bear in foreign landscapes in order to clarify them for ourselves." In what ways has visual art, including old Westerns, influenced your own views of landscapes?

LOPEZ, a former landscape photographer, is an essayist, fiction writer, and avid traveler who writes from a variety of angles about the relationship between humans and nature and how the latter has influenced the former's culture. He has received numerous awards for his work, among them Pushcart Prizes for fiction and nonfiction, a Guggenheim, and an award from the National Science Foundation. He contributes to a wide range of publications, from *The Onion* to the *Paris Review*. This excerpt is taken from his book *Arctic Dreams*.

Ice and Light (1986) | BY BARRY LOPEZ

. . . During the sea-lift passage of the *Soodoc* north through Davis Strait, en route to Little Cornwallis Island, I got in the habit of spending afternoons in the cab of a large front-loader that was chained down on the deck alongside other pieces of heavy machinery. I could sit there out of the wind and occasional rain, looking out through its spacious windows at the sea and ice. Sometimes I would read in the *Pilot of Arctic Canada.* Or I would read arctic history with a map spread out in my lap.

The days among the icebergs passed slowly. I sat in my makeshift catbird seat on the deck, or stood watching in the bows, or up on the bridge with my binoculars and sketchbook.

The icebergs were like pieces of Montana floating past. A different geography, I thought, from the one I grew up knowing.

Icebergs create an unfamiliar sense of space because the horizon retreats from them and the sky rises without any lines of compression behind them. It is this perspective that frightened pioneer families on the treeless North American prairies. Too much space, anchored only now and then by a stretch of bur oak savanna. Landscape painting of the T'ang and Sung dynasties (seventh to twelfth centuries) used this arrangement of space to create the sense of a large presence beyond. Indeed, the subject of such paintings was often their apparent emptiness.

American landscape painting in the nineteenth century, to return to an earlier   5 thought, reveals a struggle with light and space that eventually set it apart from a contemporary European tradition of pastoral landscapes framed by trees, the world viewed from a carriage window. American painters meant to locate an actual spiritual presence in the North American landscape. Their paintings, according to art historians of the period, were the inspirations of men and women who "saw the face of God" in the prairies and mountains and along the river bottoms. One of the clearest expressions of this recasting of an understanding of what a landscape is were the almost austere compositions of the luminists. The atmosphere of these paintings is silent and contemplative. They suggest a private rather than a public encounter with the land. Several critics, among them Barbara Novak in her study of this period in American art, *Nature and Culture,* have described as well a peculiar "loss of ego" in the paintings. The artist disappears. The authority of the work lies, instead, with the land. And the light in them is like a creature, a living, integral part of the scene. The landscape is numinous, imposing, real. It ceases to be, as it was in Europe, merely symbolic.

At the height of his critical and popular acclaim in 1859, Frederic Edwin Church, one of the most prominent of the luminists, set sail for waters off the Newfoundland coast. He wanted to sketch the icebergs there. They seemed to him the very embodiment of light in nature. Following a three-week cruise, he returned to his studio in New York to execute a large painting.

The small field sketches he made—some are no larger than the palm of your hand— have a wonderful, working intimacy about them. He captures both the monolithic inscrutability of icebergs and the weathered, beaten look they have by the time they arrive that far south in the Labrador Sea. Looking closely at one drawing, made on July 1, I noticed that Church had penciled underneath it the words "strange supernatural."

The oil painting he produced from these sketches came to be called *The Icebergs*. It is so imposing—6 feet by 10 feet wide—a viewer feels he can almost step into it, which was Church's intent. In the foreground is a shelf of ice, part of an iceberg that fills most of the painting and which rises abruptly in the left foreground. On the right, the flooded ice shelf becomes part of a wave-carved grotto. In the central middle ground is a becalmed embayment, opening onto darker ocean waters to the left, which continue to a stormy horizon and other, distant icebergs. Dominating the background on the far side of the embayment is a high wall of ice and snow that carries all the way to the right of the painting. In the ocean air above is a rolling mist. The shading and forms of the icebergs are expertly limned—Church was an avid naturalist, and conscientious about such accuracy—and the colors, though slightly embellished, are true.

There are two oddities about this now very famous American landscape painting. When it was undraped at Gaupil's Gallery in New York on April 24, 1861, the reaction was more reserved than the lionized Church had anticipated. But *The Icebergs* differed from the rest of Church's work in one, crucial aspect: there was no trace of man in it. Convinced that he had perhaps made a mistake, Church took the work back to his studio and inserted in the foreground a bit of flotsam from a shipwreck, a portion of the main-topmast with the crow's nest. The painting was then exhibited in Boston, where it was no better received than it had been in New York. Only when it arrived in London did critics and audiences marvel. "A most weird and beautiful picture," wrote a reviewer in the *Manchester Guardian*. England, with its longer history of arctic exploration and whaling and but a few years removed from the tragedy of Sir John Franklin, was certainly more appreciative, at least, of its subject matter.

The second oddity is that Church's painting "disappeared" for 116 years. It was 10 purchased in 1863 by a Sir Edward Watkin, after the London showing, to hang at his estate outside Manchester, called Rose Hill. It then passed by inheritance through Watkins' son to a purchaser of the estate; and then, by donation, to Saint Wilfred's Church nearby (which returned it to Rose Hill with regrets about its size). By 1979 Rose Hill had become the Rose Hill Remand Home for Boys, and *The Icebergs,* hanging without a frame in a stairwell, had been signed by one of the boys. Unaware of its value and seeking funds for the reform school's operation, the owners offered it for sale. The painting was brought back to New York and sold at auction on October 25, 1979, for $2.5 million, the highest price paid to that time for a painting in America. It now hangs in the Dallas Museum of Fine Arts, in Texas.

Church's decision to add the broken mast to *The Icebergs* speaks, certainly, to his commercial instincts, but the addition, I think, is more complex than this; and such a judgment is both too cynical and too simple.

Try as we might, we ultimately can make very little sense at all of nature without resorting to such devices. Whether they are such bald assertions of human presence as Church's cruciform mast or the intangible, metaphorical tools of the mind—contrast, remembrance, analogy—we bring our own worlds to bear in foreign landscapes in order to clarify them for ourselves. It is hard to imagine that we could do otherwise. The risk we take is of finding our final authority in the metaphors rather than in the land. To inquire into the intricacies of a distant landscape, then, is to provoke thoughts about one's own interior landscape, and the familiar landscapes of memory. The land urges us to come around to an understanding of ourselves.

A comparison with cathedrals has come to many Western minds in searching for a metaphor for icebergs, and I think the reasons for it are deeper than the obvious appropriateness of line and scale. It has to do with our passion for light.

Cathedral architecture signaled a quantum leap forward in European civilization. The gothic cathedral churches, with their broad bays of sunshine, flying buttresses that let windows rise where once there had been stone in the walls, and harmonious interiors—this "architecture of light" was a monument to a newly created theology. "God is light," writes a French cultural historian of the era, Georges Duby, and "every creature stems from that initial, uncreated, creative light." Robert Grosseteste, the twelfth-century founder of Oxford University, wrote that "physical light is the best, the most delectable, the most beautiful of all the bodies that exist."

Intellectually, the eleventh and twelfth centuries were an age of careful dialectics, a working out of relationships that eventually became so refined they could be expressed in the mathematics of cathedrals. Not only was God light but the *relationship* between God and man was light. The cathedrals, by the very way they snared the sun's energy, were an expression of God and of the human connection with God as well. The aesthetics of this age, writes Duby, was "based on light, logic, lucidity, and yearning for a God in a human form." Both the scholastic monks in their exegetical disquisitions and the illiterate people who built these churches, who sent these structures soaring into the sky—157 feet at Beauvais before it fell over on them—both, writes Duby, were "people trying to rise above their poverty through dreams of light." 15

It was an age of mystics. When Heinrich Suso, a Dominican monk, prayed at night in church, "it often seemed as if he were floating on air or sailing between time and eternity, on the deep tide of the unsoundable marvels of God." And it was an age of visionaries who spoke of the New Jerusalem of the Apocalypse, where there would be no darkness.

The erection of these monuments to spiritual awareness signaled a revival of cities, without which these edifices could not have survived. (The money to build them came largely from an emerging class of merchants and tradesmen, not royalty.) In time, however, the cathedrals became more and more esoteric, so heavily intellectualized an enterprise that, today, the raw, spiritual desire that was their original impetus seems lost. To the modern visitor, familiar with an architecture more facile and clever with light, the cathedrals now seem dark. Their stone has been eaten away by the acids and corrosives of industrial air. The age of mystics that bore them gave way rather too quickly to an age of rational intellects, of vast, baroque theological abstraction.

A final, ironic point: the mathematics that made the building of the cathedrals possible was carefully preserved by Arabs and Moors, by so-called infidels.

By the thirteenth century, Europe was starting to feel the vastness of Asia, the authority of other cultures. "The dissemination of knowledge," writes Duby, "and the strides made in the cultural sphere had opened [European] eyes and forced them to face facts: the world was infinitely larger, more various, and less docile than it had seemed to their forefathers; it was full of men who had not received the word of God, who refused to hear it, and who would not be easily conquered by arms. In Europe the days of holy war were over. The days of the explorers, traders, and missionaries had begun. After all, why persist in struggling against all those infidels, those expert warriors, when it was more advantageous to negotiate and attempt to insinuate oneself in those invincible kingdoms by business transactions and peaceful preaching?"

This was the philosophy that carried the Portuguese to India, the Spaniards to Peru, and the French and British into the hinterlands of northern North America. Hundreds of years later, a refinement on this philosophy of acquisition propelled Americans, Canadians, and Russians into the Arctic. 20

The conventional wisdom of our time is that European man has advanced by enormous strides since the age of cathedrals. He has landed on the moon. He has cured smallpox. He has harnessed the power in the atom. Another argument, however, might be made in the opposite direction, that all European man has accomplished in 900 years is a more complicated manipulation of materials, a more astounding display of his grasp of the physical principles of matter. That we are dazzled by mere styles of expression. That ours is not an age of mystics but of singular adepts, of performers. That the erection of the cathedrals was the last wild stride European man made before falling back into the confines of his intellect.

Of the sciences today, quantum physics alone seems to have found its way back to an equitable relationship with metaphors, those fundamental tools of the imagination. The other sciences are occasionally so bound by rational analysis, or so wary of metaphor, that they recognize and denounce anthropomorphism as a kind of intellectual cancer, instead of employing it as a tool of comparative inquiry, which is perhaps the only way the mind works, that parallelism we finally call narrative.

There is a word from the time of the cathedrals: agape, an expression of intense spiritual affinity with the mystery that is "to be sharing life with other life." Agape is love, and it can mean "the love of another for the sake of God." More broadly and essentially it is a humble, impassioned embrace of something outside the self, in the name of that which we refer to as *God,* but which also includes the self and *is* God. We are clearly indebted as a species to the play of our intelligence; we trust our future to it; but we do not know whether intelligence is reason or whether intelligence is this desire to embrace and be embraced in the pattern that both theologians and physicists call God. Whether intelligence, in other words, is love.

One day, sitting in my accustomed spot on the cargo deck of the *Soodoc,* I turned to see the second engineer, who had brought two cups of coffee. He was from Guyana. We talked about Guyana, and about the icebergs, some forty or fifty of which were then around us. He raised his chin to indicate and said, "How would you like to live up there? A fellow could camp up there, sail all the way to Newfoundland. Get off at Saint John's. How about it?" He laughed.

We laughed together. We searched the horizon for mirages with the binoculars, but 25 we were not successful. When his break was over, the engineer went back below decks. I hung over the bow, staring into the bow wave at the extraordinary fluidity of that geometry on the calm waters of Melville Bay. I looked up at the icebergs. They so embodied the land. Austere. Implacable. Harsh but not antagonistic. Creatures of pale light. Once, camped in the Anaktiktoak Valley of the central Brooks Range in Alaska, a friend had said, gazing off across that broad glacial valley of soft greens and straw browns, with sunlight lambent on Tulugak Lake and the Anaktuvuk River in the distance, that it was so beautiful it made you cry.

I looked out at the icebergs. They were so beautiful they also made you afraid.

1. When you have been alone in a vast landscape—for instance, at night under a sky lit up by stars—what have been your feelings? How have you described them to yourself?

2. What analogies have helped you to understand your relationship to the vast spaces around you? What in Lopez's comparisons or analogies did you find most helpful?

1. Lopez describes a change that Church made to his painting *The Icebergs*—the addition of a broken mast. How is the mast an example of Lopez's point that as humans we need to "bring our own worlds to bear in foreign landscapes"?

2. Lopez discusses cathedrals as an analogy for humans' "passion for light." How does this analogy convey the need for a "humble, impassioned embrace of something outside the self"? Explain.

3. Even though he uses metaphors himself, Lopez cautions that we risk "finding our final authority in the metaphors rather than in the land." Do you think he makes us feel the authority of the land? If so, how?

4. Near the end of the essay, Lopez returns to his immediate surroundings—the boat in the Canadian Arctic and the forty or fifty icebergs passing by. He ends with his solitary impressions, of beauty and light. Was personal testimony the best way to end this essay on insights and experience beyond the self? Explain.

1. Like Jared Diamond in "The Last Americans" (p. 362), Lopez questions whether or not our civilization has "advanced." These authors, however, use very different arguments to convince the reader. Explain how their reasons differ.

2. In "Wilderness as a Form of Land Use" (p. 354), Aldo Leopold wants a land-use policy that would protect wilderness areas. How might Lopez's description of his experiences, thoughts, and self-assessments in the Canadian Arctic lend weight to Leopold's argument?

3. Both Annie Dillard ("Heaven and Earth in Jest," p. 381) and Lopez use metaphor and simile to communicate the meaning they find in nature. How would you characterize the kinds of comparisons each writer makes? Which do you find more effective? Why?

4. Ian Frazier ("Terminal Ice," p. 408) seems similarly impassioned about icebergs. How does his passion differ from that of Lopez?

5. In "Ways of Seeing," John Berger (Chapter 8, p. 519) claims that when we "see" a landscape, we situate ourselves in it; and when we "see" a work of art from the past, "we situate ourselves in history." Do you think that Lopez has helped us situate ourselves in the Arctic landscape, on his boat? How has he helped us to see in the way Berger means?

1. Using Aldo Leopold ("Wilderness as a Form of Land Use," p. 354) and Lopez as support, as well as information from the Internet, write a letter to a member of Congress voicing concerns you have about the unbridled use of Alaska and other vast spaces for oil drilling and the extraction of other resources.

2. Identify a local place in nature where light and space have had special meaning to you. Describe this place and what it has meant. Using this description as a source of ideas and examples, write an essay for a school paper on the significance of this place as space and light.

3. Diamond ("The Last Americans"), writing about the Maya collapse, seems to exemplify Lopez's idea that we need to "bring our own worlds to bear in foreign landscapes." Using this approach, and perhaps Diamond's ironic style, write about the imminent collapse of a specific environment. Send your piece to a periodical such as *Scientific American, Outside,* or *Nature Conservancy.*

JANE GOODALL, in this selection from *In the Shadow of Man,* recounts an early visit to Africa in which she attempts to gain the trust of a group of chimpanzees. She individualizes the chimps, observing their physical characteristics and personality traits and giving them names. She describes how they act individually but also toward one another and toward her: how they share food, protect one another, dominate one another, and accept one another—and her. These descriptions, while objective and detailed, include expressions of Goodall's own excitement and sense of discovery. Perhaps when we observe animals closely, any animals, we are really trying to find out more about ourselves. What might Goodall be trying to find out about human beings?

GOODALL is an award-winning ethologist and is considered the foremost authority on chimpanzees in the world. Naming instead of numbering the animals she studied, Goodall revolutionized the field of primatology for over twenty-five years. In 1977 she founded the Jane Goodall Institute for Wildlife Research, which attempts to protect chimpanzees and preserve the environment they live in. In addition to *In the Shadow of Men,* Goodall's numerous publications include *Through a Window, The Chimpanzees of Gombe, Reason for Hope,* and a children's series.

Selection from *In the Shadow of Man* (1971)

BY JANE GOODALL

During that month I really came to know the country well, for I often went on expeditions from the Peak, sometimes to examine nests, more frequently to collect specimens of the chimpanzees' food plants, which Bernard Verdcourt had kindly offered to identify for me. Soon I could find my way around the sheer ravines and up and down the steep slopes of three valleys—the home valley, the Pocket, and Mlinda Valley—as well as a taxi driver finds his way about in the main streets and byways of London. It is a period I remember vividly, not only because I was beginning to accomplish something at last, but also because of the delight I felt in being completely by myself. For those who love to be alone with nature I need add nothing further; for those who do not, no words of mine could ever convey, even in part, the almost mystical awareness of beauty and eternity that accompanies certain treasured moments. And, though the beauty was always there, those moments came upon me unaware: when I was watching the pale flush preceding dawn; or looking up through the rustling leaves of some giant forest tree into the greens and browns and black shadows that occasionally ensnared a bright fleck of the blue sky; or when I stood, as darkness fell, with one hand on the still-warm trunk of a tree and looked at the sparkling of an early moon on the never still, sighing water of the lake.

One day, when I was sitting by the trickle of water in Buffalo Wood, pausing for a moment in the coolness before returning from a scramble in Mlinda Valley, I saw a female bushbuck moving slowly along the nearly dry streambed. Occasionally she paused to pick off some plant and crunch it. I kept absolutely still, and she was not aware of my presence until she was little more than ten yards away. Suddenly she tensed and stood staring at me, one small forefoot raised. Because I did not move, she did not know what I was—only that my outline was somehow strange. I saw her velvet nostrils dilate as she sniffed the air, but I was downwind and her nose gave her no answer. Slowly she came closer, and closer—one step at a time, her neck craned forward—always poised for instant flight. I can still scarcely believe that her nose actually touched my knee; yet if I close my eyes I can feel again, in imagination, the warmth of her breath and the silken impact of her skin. Unexpectedly I blinked and she was gone in a flash, bounding away with loud barks of alarm until the vegetation hid her completely from my view.

It was rather different when, as I was sitting on the Peak, I saw a leopard coming toward me, his tail held up straight. He was at a slightly lower level than I, and obviously had no idea I was there. Ever since arrival in Africa I had had an ingrained, illogical fear of leopards. Already, while working at the Gombe, I had several times nearly turned back when, crawling through some thick undergrowth, I had suddenly smelled the rank smell of cat. I had forced myself on, telling myself that my fear was foolish, that only wounded leopards charged humans with savage ferocity.

On this occasion, though, the leopard went out of sight as it started to climb up the hill—the hill on the peak of which I sat. I quickly hastened to climb a tree, but halfway there I realized that leopards can climb trees. So I uttered a sort of halfhearted squawk. The leopard, my logical mind told me, would be just as frightened of me if he knew I was there. Sure enough, there was a thudding of startled feet and then silence. I returned to the Peak, but the feeling of unseen eyes watching me was too much. I decided to watch for the chimps in Mlinda Valley. And, when I returned to the Peak several hours later, there, on the very rock which had been my seat, was a neat pile of leopard dung. He must have watched me go and then, very carefully, examined the place where such a frightening creature had been and tried to exterminate my alien scent with his own.

As the weeks went by the chimpanzees became less and less afraid. Quite often when I was on one of my food-collecting expeditions I came across chimpanzees unexpectedly, and after a time I found that some of them would tolerate my presence provided they were in fairly thick forest and I sat still and did not try to move closer than sixty to eighty yards. And so, during my second month of watching from the Peak, when I saw a group settle down to feed I sometimes moved closer and was thus able to make more detailed observations.

It was at this time that I began to recognize a number of different individuals. As soon as I was sure of knowing a chimpanzee if I saw it again, I named it. Some scientists feel that animals should be labeled by numbers—that to name them is anthropomorphic—but I have always been interested in the *differences* between individuals, and a name is not only more individual than a number but also far easier to remember. Most names were simply those which, for some reason or other, seemed to suit the individuals to whom I attached them. A few chimps were named because some facial expression or mannerism reminded me of human acquaintances.

The easiest individual to recognize was old Mr. McGregor. The crown of his head, his neck, and his shoulders were almost entirely devoid of hair, but a slight frill remained around his head rather like a monk's tonsure. He was an old male—perhaps between thirty and forty years of age (chimpanzees in captivity can live more than fifty years). During the early months of my acquaintance with him, Mr. McGregor was somewhat belligerent. If I accidentally came across him at close quarters he would threaten me with an upward and backward jerk of his head and a shaking of branches before climbing down and vanishing from my sight. He reminded me, for some reason, of Beatrix Potter's old gardener in *The Tale of Peter Rabbit.*

Ancient Flo with her deformed, bulbous nose and ragged ears was equally easy to recognize. Her youngest offspring at that time were two-year-old Fifi, who still rode everywhere on her mother's back, and her juvenile son, Figan, who was always to be seen wandering around with his mother and little sister. He was then about seven years old; it was approximately a year before he would attain puberty. Flo often traveled with another old mother, Olly. Olly's long face was also distinctive; the fluff of hair on the back of her head—though no other feature—reminded me of my aunt, Olwen. Olly, like Flo, was accompanied by two children, a daughter younger than Fifi, and an adolescent son about a year older than Figan.

Then there was William, who, I am certain, must have been Olly's blood brother. I never saw any special signs of friendship between them, but their faces were amazingly alike. They both had long upper lips that wobbled when they suddenly turned their heads. William had the added distinction of several thin, deeply etched scar marks running down his upper lip from his nose.

Two of the other chimpanzees I knew well by sight at that time were David Graybeard and Goliath. Like David and Goliath in the Bible, these two individuals were closely associated in my mind because they were very often together. Goliath, even in those days of his prime, was not a giant, but he had a splendid physique and the springy movements of an athlete. He probably weighed about one hundred pounds. David Graybeard was less afraid of me from the start than were any of the other chimps I was always pleased when I picked out his handsome face and well-marked silvery beard in a chimpanzee group, for with David to calm the others, I had a better chance of approaching to observe them more closely.

Before the end of my trial period in the field I made two really exciting discoveries—discoveries that made the previous months of frustration well worth while. And for both of them I had David Graybeard to thank.

One day I arrived on the Peak and found a small group of chimps just below me in the upper branches of a thick tree. As I watched I saw that one of them was holding a pink-looking object from which he was from time to time pulling pieces with his teeth. There was a female and a youngster and they were both reaching out toward the male, their hands actually touching his mouth. Presently the female picked up a piece of the pink thing and put it to her mouth: it was at this moment that I realized the chimps were eating meat.

10

After each bite of meat the male picked off some leaves with his lips and chewed them with the flesh. Often, when he had chewed for several minutes on this leafy wad, he spat out the remains into the waiting hands of the female. Suddenly he dropped a small piece of meat, and like a flash the youngster swung after it to the ground. Even as he reached to pick it up the undergrowth exploded and an adult bushpig charged toward him. Screaming, the juvenile leaped back into the tree. The pig remained in the open, snorting and moving backward and forward. Soon I made out the shapes of three small striped piglets. Obviously the chimps were eating a baby pig. The size was right and later, when I realized that the male was David Graybeard, I moved closer and saw that he was indeed eating a piglet.

For three hours I watched the chimps feeding. David occasionally let the female bite pieces from the carcass and once he actually detached a small piece of flesh and placed it in her outstretched hand. When he finally climbed down there was still meat left on the carcass; he carried it away in one hand, followed by the others.

Of course I was not sure, then, that David Graybeard had caught the pig for himself, but even so, it was tremendously exciting to know that these chimpanzees actually ate meat. Previously scientists had believed that although these apes might occasionally supplement their diet with a few insects or small rodents and the like they were primarily vegetarians and fruit eaters. No one had suspected that they might hunt larger mammals.

15

It was within two weeks of this observation that I saw something that excited me even more. By then it was October and the short rains had begun. The blackened slopes were softened by feathery new grass shoots and in some places the ground was carpeted by a variety of flowers. The Chimpanzees' Spring, I called it. I had had a frustrating morning, tramping up and down three valleys with never a sign or sound of a chimpanzee. Hauling myself up the steep slope of Mlinda Valley I headed for the Peak, not only weary but soaking wet from crawling through dense undergrowth. Suddenly I stopped, for I saw a slight movement in the long grass about sixty yards away. Quickly focusing my binoculars I saw that it was a single chimpanzee, and just then he turned in my direction. I recognized David Graybeard.

Cautiously I moved around so that I could see what he was doing. He was squatting beside the red earth mound of a termite nest, and as I watched I saw him carefully push a long grass stem down into a hole in the mound. After a moment he withdrew it and picked something from the end with his mouth. I was too far away to make out what he was eating, but it was obvious that he was actually using a grass stem as a tool.

I knew that on two occasions casual observers in West Africa had seen chimpanzees using objects as tools: one had broken open palm-nut kernels by using a rock as a hammer, and a group of chimps had been observed pushing sticks into an underground bee's nest and licking off the honey. Somehow I had never dreamed of seeing anything so exciting myself.

For an hour David feasted at the termite mound and then he wandered slowly away. When I was sure he had gone I went over to examine the mound. I found a few crushed insects strewn about, and a swarm of worker termites sealing the entrances of the nest passages into which David had obviously been poking his stems. I picked up one of his discarded tools and carefully pushed it into a hole myself. Immediately I felt the pull of several termites as they seized the grass, and when I pulled it out there were a number of worker termites and a few soldiers, with big red heads, clinging on with their mandibles. There they remained, sticking out at right angles to the stem with their legs waving in the air.

Before I left I trampled down some of the tall dry grass and constructed a rough hide—just a few palm fronds leaned up against the low branch of a tree and tied together at the top. I planned to wait there the next day. But it was another week before I was able to watch a chimpanzee "fishing" for termites again. Twice chimps arrived, but each time they saw me and moved off immediately. Once a swarm of fertile winged termites—the princes and princesses, as they are called—flew off on their nuptial flight, their huge white wings fluttering frantically as they carried the insects higher and higher. Later I realized that it is at this time of year, during the short rains, when the worker termites extend the passages of the nest to the surface, preparing for these emigrations. Several such swarms emerge between October and January. It is primarily during these months that the chimpanzees feed on termites.

On the eighth day of my watch David Graybeard arrived again, together with Goliath, and the pair worked there for two hours. I could see much better: I observed how they scratched open the sealed-over passage entrances with a thumb or forefinger. I watched how they bit the ends off their tools when they became bent, or used the other end, or discarded them in favor of new ones. Goliath once moved at least fifteen yards from the heap to select a firm-looking piece of vine, and both males often picked three or four stems while they were collecting tools, and put the spares beside them on the ground until they wanted them.

Most exciting of all, on several occasions they picked small leafy twigs and prepared them for use by stripping off the leaves. This was the first recorded example of a wild animal not merely *using* an object as a tool, but actually modifying an object and thus showing the crude beginnings of tool*making*.

Previously man had been regarded as the only tool-making animal. Indeed, one of the clauses commonly accepted in the definition of man was that he was a creature who "made tools to a regular and set pattern." The chimpanzees, obviously, had not made tools to any set pattern. Nevertheless, my early observations of their primitive toolmaking abilities convinced a number of scientists that it was necessary to redefine man in a more complex manner than before. Or else, as Louis Leakey put it, we should by definition have to accept the chimpanzee as Man.

I sent telegrams to Louis about both of my new observations—the meat-eating and the toolmaking—and he was of course wildly enthusiastic. In fact, I believe that the news was helpful to him in his efforts to find further financial support for my work. It was not long afterward when he wrote to tell me that the National Geographic Society in the United States had agreed to grant funds for another year's research.

CONNECTING PERSONALLY TO THE READING

1. What have your own experiences with and observations of animals been like? What thoughts have run through your mind about their relationship to humans?

2. Did you empathize with Jane Goodall? Did you find her work courageous? Dull? Personally challenging? Explain.

3. Can you imagine yourself living alone in the jungle the way she did? What fears do most of us bring to such a setting? Explain.

FOCUSING ON THE ARGUMENT

1. Goodall is a primatologist, yet she describes her emotions and feelings. Do you think that this distracts from the objectivity of her observations? Explain.

2. Goodall describes not "the chimps" but each animal by name. Why is this analogy to humans important to her study of chimpanzee behavior?

3. At the end of this selection, Goodall describes, with telling details, individual chimps using tools. She concludes that humans are not the only tool-making animal. How important are these details in making her conclusions credible? Explain.

4. Goodall's tone reveals elements of awe, humor, surprise, and delight. Why would such variations in tone be appropriate to descriptions of a scientist's increasingly close relationship with a group of chimpanzees?

SYNTHESIZING IDEAS FROM MULTIPLE READINGS

1. The chimps seem in close harmony with their natural environment. How is that harmony similar to and different from the harmony the Laguna Indians achieve with nature, as described by Leslie Marmon Silko in "The Migration Story" (p. 389)?

2. Jane Goodall, like Annie Dillard ("Heaven and Earth in Jest," p. 381) and Ian Frazier ("Terminal Ice," p. 408), observes nature. What details do these writers typically notice? How do the purposes of their observations differ?

3. In places, Goodall describes nature purely in terms of its beauty and vividness, expressing her own delight and gratification. How are her views of nature, the mountains and trees, similar to those of Wendell Berry ("An Entrance to the Woods," p. 372)? What passages most show this?

4. Much of the work Goodall does consists of watching and waiting. The work seems to involve few frills—little and very basic food and shelter, nothing to do but continue her work. How might bell hooks ("Work Makes Life Sweet," Chapter 5, p. 285) view this work? Explain.

5. A single scientist, alone in an African jungle, quietly observing and taking notes, helps change the world's view of humankind's distinctiveness and kinship with other primates. What kind of intelligence do you think Howard Gardner ("Human Intelligence Isn't What We Think It Is," Chapter 4, p. 232) would say that Goodall illustrates? Explain.

WRITING TO ACT

1. Write a job description in which you seek someone with Goodall's qualifications—to continue her work observing chimps in the wild. Explain the benefits of the work.

2. Write a description of a scientist's work as a primatologist, detailing the daily life, using as models the "Voices from the Workplace," Chapter 5, p. 328.

3. Identify agencies or organizations that protect chimpanzees. Write a letter to one such organization, requesting information on its activities. Devise a group project to advance or promote that organization's work.

Merging biology and journalism, **IAN FRAZIER** brings before us images of a melting Antarctica. Careful not to make unsupported attributions, Frazier uses scientific descriptions, images, analogies, history, personal observations, and even fairy tales and movies to help readers visualize what might be happening on our planet. A journalist, he draws attention to the media's role in the problem and its role in environmental politics generally. How might a media expert be helpful in writing about a melting Antarctica?

FRAZIER is a humorist, essayist, and a staff writer for the *New Yorker,* where he contributes feature articles as well as pieces for the "Talk of the Town" and "Shouts and Murmurs" sections; he also writes for other magazines, among them the *Atlantic Monthly.* Frazier's books include *On the Rez, Great Plains, Family, Coyote v. Acme,* and *Dating Your Mom.*

Terminal Ice (2002) | BY IAN FRAZIER

We are melting, like the Wicked Witch of the West. Soon there will be nothing left of us but our hat. From Chile to Alaska to Norway to Tibet, glaciers are going in reverse. Artifacts buried since the Stone Age emerge intact from the ice; in British Columbia, sheep hunters passing a glacier find protruding from it a prehistoric man, preserved even to his skin, his leather food-pouch, and his fur cloak. All across the north, permafrost stops being perma-. In the Antarctic, some penguin populations decline. In Hudson Bay, ice appears later in the year and leaves earlier, giving polar bears less time to go out on it and hunt seals, causing them to be 10 percent thinner than they were twenty years ago, causing them to get into more trouble in the Hudson Bay town of Churchill, where (as it happens) summers are now twice as long. One day in August of 2000 an icebreaker goes to the North Pole and finds, not ice, but open ocean. The news is no surprise to scientists, who knew that the remote Arctic in summer has lots of ice-free areas. For the rest of us, a disorienting adjustment of the geography of Christmas is required.

Globally, there's a persistent trickling as enormities of ice unfreeze. The Greenland ice sheet loses 13 trillion gallons of fresh water a year, contributing a measurable percentage to the world's annual sea-level rise. Every year, the level of the sea goes up about the thickness of a dime. Other meltwater, and the warming of the planet, which causes water to expand, contribute too. A dime's thickness a year doesn't worry most people, so long as it doesn't get worse, which most scientists don't think it necessarily will anytime soon, though who can say for sure? The first nation to ratify the Kyoto Protocol on Climate Change is the island of Fiji, one eye on the Pacific lapping at its toes.

And every year, first attracting notice in the seventies, picking up speed in the steamy eighties and steamier nineties, giant icebergs begin splashing into the news. Usually they arrive in single-column stories on an inside page: "An iceberg twice as big as Rhode Island has broken away from Antarctica and is drifting in the Ross Sea. . . . It is about 25 miles wide and 98 miles long." "The largest iceberg in a decade has broken off an ice shelf in Antarctica . . . as if Delaware suddenly weighed anchor and put out to sea."

Over the years, a number of Rhode Islands and Delawares of ice, and even a Connecticut, drift into type and out again. The more notable ones are sometimes called "celebrity icebergs," and in the cold Southern Ocean (all the biggest icebergs are from Antarctica) an occasional berg has a longevity in the spotlight that a human celebrity could envy. Iceberg C-2—as scientists labeled it—drifts for twelve years and 5,700 miles, nearly circumnavigating Antarctica, before breaking into pieces of non-newsworthy size.

Glaciologists say there's probably no connection between global climate change and the increase in the numbers of big Antarctic icebergs. They say the ice shelves at the edge of the continent, from which these icebergs come, have grown out and shrunk back countless times in the past. Our awareness of the icebergs has mainly to do with satellite technology that allows us to see them as we never could before. Still, when you've recently been through the hottest year of the past six centuries and suddenly there's a 2,700-square-mile iceberg on the loose—well, people talk.

5

. . . Ice plus the *Titanic* spawned nightmares of disaster that never seem to fade. There was a song people used to sing about the *Titanic,* part of which went:

It was on her maiden trip
When an iceberg hit the ship . . .

Of course, the iceberg didn't hit the ship, but the other way around. So forcefully did the iceberg enter our consciousness, however, we assume it must have meant to. Looming unannounced from the North Atlantic on April 14, 1912, it crashed the swells' high-society ball, discomfiting Mrs. Astor, leaving its calling card in the form of a cascade of ice on the starboard well deck, slitting the hull fatally 20 feet below the waterline, and then disappearing into the night. . . .

Northern Hemisphere icebergs like The Iceberg melt quickly once they drift down into the Atlantic, with its warming Gulf Stream. Almost certainly, within a few weeks of shaking up the world, The Iceberg had disappeared. Its ephemerality has only increased its fame; solid matter for just a few historic moments, it continues indefinitely in imaginary realms—for example, as a spooky cameo in the top-grossing movie of all time. The message of The Iceberg, common wisdom has it, concerns the inscrutability of our fate and the vanity of human pride. But when I meditate on ice and icebergs, I wonder if The Iceberg's message might have been simpler than that. Maybe the news The Iceberg bore was more ancient, powerful, planetary, and climatic. Maybe The Iceberg's real message wasn't about us, but about ice.

Icebergs are pieces of freshwater ice of a certain size floating in the ocean or (rarely) a lake. They come from glaciers and other ice masses. Because of the physics of ice when it piles up on land, it spreads and flows, and as it does its advancing edge often meets a body of water. When the ice continues to flow out over the water, chunks of it break off in a process called calving. Some of the faster-moving glaciers in Greenland calve an average of two or three times a day during the warmer months. Icebergs are not the same as sea ice. Sea ice is frozen saltwater, and when natural forces break it into pieces, the larger ones are called not icebergs but ice floes. Icebergs are denser and harder than sea ice. When icebergs are driven by wind or current, sea ice parts before them like turkey before an electric carving knife. In former times, sailing ships that got stuck in sea ice sometimes used to tie themselves to an iceberg and let it pull them through.

A piece of floating freshwater ice must be at least 50 feet long to qualify as an ice- 10
berg, according to authorities on the subject. If it's smaller—say, about the size of a grand piano—it's called a growler. If it's about the size of a cottage, it's a bergy bit. Crushed-up pieces of ice that result when parts of melting icebergs disintegrate and come falling down are called "slob ice" by mariners. Students of icebergs have divided them by shape into six categories: blocky, wedge, tabular, dome, pinnacle, and dry-dock. The last of these refers to icebergs with columnar sections flanking a water-level area in the middle, like high-rise apartment buildings around a swimming pool.

At the edges of Antarctica, where plains of ice spread across the ocean and float on it before breaking off, most of the icebergs are tabular—flat on top, horizontal in con-figuration. In the Northern Hemisphere, because of the thickness of glacial ice and the way it calves, most icebergs are of the more dramatically shaped kinds. Tabular ice-bergs tend to be stable in the water and scientists sometimes land in helicopters on the bigger ones to study them. Northern Hemisphere icebergs, with their smaller size and gothic, irregular shapes, often grow frozen seawater on the bottom, lose above-water ice structure to melting, and suddenly capsize and roll. Venturing onto such icebergs is a terrible idea.

Antarctica has about 90 percent of all the ice in the world; most of the rest of it is in Greenland. Those two places produce most of the world's icebergs—about 100,000 a year from the first, about 10,000 to 15,000 from the other. Glaciers in Norway, Rus-sia, and Alaska produce icebergs, too. The *Exxon Valdez* went aground in Alaska's Prince William Sound partly because it had changed course to avoid icebergs. Scien-tists have not been observing icebergs long enough to say if there are substantially more of them today. They know that the total mass of ice in Greenland has decreased at an accelerated rate in recent years. In Antarctica, because of its size and other fac-tors, scientists still don't know whether the continent as a whole is losing ice or not.

Some people have jobs that involve thinking about ice and icebergs all day long. A while ago I went to the National Ice Center in Suitland, Maryland, and met a few of them. The Ice Center is affiliated with the National Oceanic and Atmospheric Admin-istration, the Coast Guard, and the Navy. The offices of the Ice Center are in one of the many long, three-story government buildings with extra-large satellite dishes on their roofs in a fenced-in, campuslike setting just across the Potomac from Washington. An-tennae poking up from behind clumps of trees add to the spy-thriller atmosphere. The Ice Center's supervisor, a lieutenant commander in the Navy—many of the people who work at the center are military personnel—introduced me to Judy Shaffier, an ice analyst. She is a slim woman in her mid-thirties with a shaped haircut and avid dark eyes accustomed to spotting almost invisible details. An ice analyst looks at satellite images of ocean ice on a computer screen, compares the images to other weather in-formation, and figures out what they mean. "It's a great job, really neat to tell people about at a party or something," Shaffier said. "But it takes explaining. When I say I an-alyze ice, sometimes people don't get that I mean *ice*. They think it must be one of those government-agency acronyms."

Much of the Ice Center is closed to visitors. That's the part where it pursues its main purpose, which is to provide classified information on ice conditions to the military. For example, a nuclear submarine can break through ice 3 feet thick or less; the Center can tell a submarine how close to surfaceable ice it is. Many countries—Japan, Denmark, Great Britain, Russia, France, Sweden—have ice-watching agencies similar to the Ice Center. Any country involved in global ocean shipping needs ice information sometimes. Providing it to merchant ships, scientific expeditions, and the general public is the nonclassified part of the Center's job. . . .

"For us to track an iceberg it must be at least ten nautical miles long," she continued. "We label each one according to the quadrant of Antarctica where it broke off. The quadrants are A through D, and after the letter we add a number that's based on how many other bergs from that quadrant we've tracked since we started doing this back in 1976. The A quadrant, between 90 west longitude and zero, has shelves that calve big icebergs all the time, and we've tracked a lot of bergs from there. A-38 was a recent one. And if a berg breaks up into pieces, any piece that's bigger than ten nautical miles gets its own label, like A-38A, A-38B, and so on."

The subject turned to giant "celebrity" icebergs, and whether she had a favorite.

"In March of 2000 I was sitting at this computer," she said. "Another analyst, Mary Keller, was sitting at the next one, and suddenly she said, 'My God! It's a huge iceberg!' A huge piece had broken off a shelf in the B quadrant since we'd last checked a day or so before. There had been no stress fractures visible in the ice sheet; the calving was completely unexpected. This iceberg was the 15th in B, so we labeled it B-15. I had never seen a berg that size. It was awesome—158 by 20 nautical miles. After it broke off it kind of ratcheted itself along the coast, sliding on each low tide, slowly moving from where it began, and in the process it eventually split into two pieces, one of about 100 miles long and another of about 80. B-15 was the most exciting iceberg I've watched since I've been here."

Shaffier and I spent hours looking at computer images that hopscotched the icy places of the globe. Some of the pictures were visible-light photographs; some were made by infrared imagery that indicated different ice temperatures by color. Iceberg ice is 20 or 30 Celsius degrees colder than sea ice, old sea ice is a few degrees colder than new sea ice; in general, the colder the ice, the more difficult it is to navigate through. In passing, we checked up on B-15A—the giant was partly blocking the entry to West Antarctica's McMurdo Sound, apparently stuck on underwater rocks.

"Let's look at the Larsen Ice Shelf, or what's left of it," Shaffier said. "Did you hear what just happened to Larsen B? The Larsen Shelf is in a part of West Antarctica where local temperatures have gone up 4 or 5 degrees over the past decades, and a few years ago a big part of the shelf, Larsen A, disintegrated almost completely. People said that the rest of the shelf, Larsen B, would probably go in the next two years. Well, a few weeks ago, it went. Over a thousand square miles of ice—*poof.* One day the shelf was there, the next day it started to break up, and 35 days later the satellite images showed nothing but dark water and white fragments where solid white ice used to be. In about a month this major geographic feature of Antarctica ceased to exist." . . .

According to scientists, probably no one has ever heard that sound or been present when a giant Antarctic iceberg calved. Whether that event is even accompanied by sound audible to humans, no one can yet say. Instruments that listen for underwater oceanic sounds sometimes pick up vibrations like a cello bow across strings—only much lower, below human hearing—which are believed to come from the friction of giant icebergs, though none of the vibrations have yet been matched to a specific calving. When giant icebergs run into something, however—when they collide with the ocean bottom or the land—they cause seismic tremors that register at listening stations halfway around the world.

Icebergs are really white. Usually you don't see this kind of white unless you've just been born or are about to die. It's a hazmat-suit, medical-lab, hospital white. There are some antiseptic-blue overtones to it, too, and a whole spectrum of greens where the berg descends into the depths out of sight. In these latitudes, sea and land and sky wear the colors of hand-knit Scottish sweaters: the taupes, the teals, the tans, the oyster grays. Surrounded by these muted shades, icebergs stand out like sore thumbs, if a sore thumb could gleam white and rise five stories above the ocean and float.

I drove hundreds of miles up and down the Newfoundland coast looking for icebergs. When I spotted an iceberg in close, run aground on a point or in a cove, I went toward it in the car as far as I could and then hiked the rest of the way. One such hike led through meadows, down forest trails, and across slippery shoreline rocks all inclined in the same direction. Finally I got to the iceberg, which looked somewhat like a jawbone. It even had tooth-shaped serrations in the right place as it seesawed chewingly in the waves. Gulls on fixed wings shot past the headland entanglements of weather-killed trees, clouds turned in huge pinwheels above, waves crashed, the iceberg chewed. I had forgotten to bring water and my mouth was dry.

Among the small channels and troughs in the rocks, iceberg fragments were washing back and forth. I leaned down and scooped out a flat, oval piece about ten inches long. The sea had rounded and smoothed the hard, clear ice like a sea-smoothed stone. In it were tiny bubbles of air that had been trapped among fallen snowflakes millennia ago; the air had eventually become bubbles as later snowfalls compressed the snow to ice. Bubbles in icebergs are what cause them to reflect white light. Almost certainly, this piece of ice originally was part of the Greenland ice cap. A glacier like the Jakobshavn Glacier on Greenland's western coast probably calved this ice into Baffin Bay, where it may have remained for a year or more until currents took it north and then south into the Labrador Current, which brought it here.

I licked the ice, bit off a piece. It broke sharply and satisfyingly, like good peanut brittle. At places the Greenland ice cap is two miles thick. Climatologists have taken core samples clear through it. Chemical analysis of the ice and the air bubbles in these cores provide a picture of climate and atmosphere during the past 110,000 years. For a period covering all of recorded human history, the Greenland ice timeline is so exact that scientists can identify specific events with strata in the core sample—the year Vesuvius buried Pompeii, say, marked by chemical remnants of the Vesuvian eruption. In ice core samples dating from the Golden Age of Greece, they've found trace amounts of lead, dispersed into the atmosphere by early smelting processes and carried to Greenland on the winds. Lead traces in the ice increase slowly from Greek and Roman times, stay at about the same level during the Middle Ages, go up a lot after the beginning of the Industrial Revolution, crest during the twentieth century, with its leaded automobile fuels, and drop way off after the introduction of unleaded gasoline. Chemicals and other residues in the Greenland ice cores told scientists about temperatures, droughts, the coming and going of ice ages—more about paleoclimates than they had ever known. In particular, they showed how unstable global climate has been, how abruptly it sometimes changed, and how oddly mild and temperate were the recent few thousand years in which people developed civilization. . . .

. . . My own mild fanaticism for icebergs can sometimes be hard to explain to unconvinced acquaintances. I notice the bewilderment in their eyes, and it infects me: Why, exactly, should anyone get so worked up about a piece of ice? Like the Newfoundland faithful of a hundred years ago, each of us sees in an iceberg what we are disposed to see. And yet . . . if icebergs have no significance other than the fanciful notions we project, why do they look as they do? A white iceberg lit by the sun in a field of blue ocean simply *looks* annunciatory. It might as well have those little lines radiating from it—the ones cartoonists draw to show something shining with meaning. In its barefaced obviousness, an iceberg seems the broadest hint imaginable; but what is it a hint of?

25

When I went to the Ice Center, Judy Shaffier gave me a list of ice-watch Web sites run by government agencies in a dozen countries. All across the United States and Canada are institutes and university departments that devote some or all of their resources to studying the world's ice. From the earth and the sky, ever more sophisticated instruments constantly record tiny changes in the ice. A satellite that measures global sea levels, a key part of ice studies, takes 500,000 sea-level readings a day. Laser altimeters deployed on satellites can detect the minutest shifts of ice position with essentially no error. And yet with all this information flooding in, broad conclusions are hard to come by. Science is specialization, and almost no expert in a particular area wants to step out into summary or generalizing. The experts tend to approach big ideas like global warming with the greatest hesitancy. Apparently, nobody wants to be the one to tell us (for example) that our SUVs have got to go.

What science will hazard instead of conclusions is a series of ifs. Ten thousand or 20,000 square miles of ice broken off Antarctica hardly diminishes that continent's total ice area of 5 million square miles, but *if* the shedding of ice continues at an increasing rate, and *if* the ice loss causes the glaciers inland to move faster toward the sea, and *if* seawater flows in where glacial ice used to be and reaches certain sub-sea-level parts of the continent and melts the ice there, and *if* as a consequence the entire West Antarctic Ice Sheet goes—well, then we would have the schnitzel, to speak plainly. That much ice added to the ocean might raise world sea levels anywhere from 13 to 20 feet. Such a rise would submerge parts of the island of Manhattan and of the Florida peninsula, not to mention many other coastal areas worldwide where about half the planet's population lives.

News stories in the months following the *Titanic* disaster examined the preceding few years' weather conditions in the Arctic and North Atlantic and concluded that a number of meteorological features had been "unusual." The winter of 1910–11 had been "unusually" snowy and severe, the summer of '11 and the spring of '12 had been "unusually" warm, the icebergs had drifted "unusually" far south. Such descriptions bring to mind the TV weather forecasters who still speak of temperatures as being "unseasonably" warm; most of the years in the last two decades have been warmer than any recorded in decades previous, so what does "unseasonable" mean nowadays? In fact, from an expanded perspective of time, there is nothing unusual about so many icebergs being as far south as the place where the *Titanic* went down. Over the past millennia, as climatic events came and went, icebergs invaded the Atlantic in armadas. Stones dropped from melting Canadian icebergs have been found in sea sediments off the coast of Portugal. The North Atlantic climate over the last tens of thousands and hundreds of thousands of years has been characterized by periods of continent-wide glaciation, massive melting, and the intermittent huge discharge of icebergs.

As easily as The Iceberg fits a morality tale about human pride, it fits a climatologist's possible scenario of global warming ifs. If increased moisture held in the warmer atmosphere results in more precipitation in the North Atlantic region, and if that precipitation leads to more runoff into the ocean, and if warmer summers result in a greater melting of glacial ice in Greenland, and if lots more icebergs set sail, and if all that leads to a greatly increased amount of fresh water poured every year into the North Atlantic—then, possibly, the complicated process of tropical warm water rising, flowing north, giving off its heat, and cooling and sinking (the process that creates the great ocean currents) will be disrupted. And if those currents stop, and the heat they bring to Northern Europe and parts of the United States and Canada no longer arrives, those regions will very likely become colder, like other places at similar latitudes that ocean currents don't warm.

Of course no one imagined any such scenarios back in 1912. Most people knew little or nothing about climatology. Yet it might turn out that a foreshadowing of major climate change in that part of the world was the real message The Iceberg carried for us out of the North Atlantic night. 30

And then again, maybe not. Discussions of global warming always deal in elaborate, scary possibilities, while always including enough disclaimers and unknowns to blunt the fear. Considering all that's at stake, I want to tell us what we should do immediately to change our lives and avert environmental catastrophe. But I can't bring myself to, somehow. All I can do is put in a good word for the sweeping conclusion and broad generalization. There aren't enough of them around—enough high-quality ones, I mean. I think we have yielded the sweeping-conclusion field to the wackier minds among us. Scenarios based on the Mothman Prophecies are colorful, but not a lot of help in the long run. Sensibly, most of us fort up behind our ever-growing heaps of information. But eventually, and maybe soon, we should draw a conclusion or two about where the globe is heading; and after that, maybe even act.

A lot of what is exciting about being alive can't be felt, because it's beyond the power of the senses. Just being on the planet, we are moving around the sun at 67,000 miles an hour; it would be great if somehow we could climb up to an impossible vantage point and just for a moment actually *feel* that speed. All this data we've got piling up is interesting, but short on thrills. Time, which we have only so much of, runs out on us, and as we get older we learn that anything and everything will go by. And since it will all go by anyway, why doesn't it all go right now, in a flash, and get it over with? For mysterious reasons, it doesn't, and the pace at which it proceeds instead reveals itself in icebergs. In the passing of the seconds, in the one-thing-after-another, I take comfort in icebergs. They are time solidified and time erased again. They pass by and vanish, quickly or slowly, regular inhabitants of a world we just happened to end up on. The glow that comes from them is the glow of more truth than we can stand.

1. To what extent have the media affected your own views about climate change, rising ocean water, and other global changes? Does the media's influence enhance your concern? Explain.

2. Have you seen images or read stories about the Antarctic or Greenland or Alaska? What troubles you the most about potential changes to these remote areas?

1. Frazier uses knowledge from archaeology (once-buried artifacts are uncovered), glaciology, and biology to convey his sense of impending disaster. Yet he combines scientific knowledge with a humorous, almost lighthearted tone ("We are melting"; "people will talk"). What is the effect of this combination on the reader?

2. Frazier looks at melting ice through the eyes of journalists. Some icebergs make the "single-column stories on an inside page," others become "celebrity icebergs." What effect does this analogy of iceberg to media event have on his argument?

3. Frazier combines his media savvy with visual metaphors to heighten our image of ice break-age ("Rhode Islands and Delawares of ice, and even a Connecticut, drift into type and out again"). What metaphors in the essay affect you the most? Explain.

1. Barry Lopez ("Ice and Light," p. 397) and Frazier have different perspectives on icebergs. How do their descriptions differ? What different effects on their readers do they want to achieve?

2. Both Lewis Thomas ("The World's Largest Membrane," p. 416) and Frazier use explicit scientific language and analysis within a frame of metaphor and analogy. Both try to help nonspecialists understand the planet's essential elements—water and oxygen. How are these writers alike in making us feel the fragility of our planet's elements?

3. What fascinates Frazier about icebergs? Does Annie Dillard ("Heaven and Earth in Jest," p. 381) show a similar fascination with elements in nature? Explain.

4. Both Frazier and Diamond ("The Last Americans," p. 362) envision forms of environmental collapse. How are they alike and different in how they depict the collapse and in the causes they identify?

5. Frazier provides a description of what the job of an ice analyst is like. Using bell hooks's ideas about what makes one love the work one does ("Work Makes Life Sweet," Chapter 5, p. 285), explain why ice analysts are likely to love the work they do.

1. Imitating Frazier's tone and integrating your scientific knowledge of ice, write a magazine article on the potential effects of Antarctica breaking into thousands of giant icebergs and heading north. Try to make the article appealing to a large audience, including students your own age.

2. Write a letter to your local state representative encouraging a more active role in reducing emissions that affect the ozone layer.

Using biology and metaphor, **LEWIS THOMAS** helps us see the living, breathing qualities of our Earth, from the perspective of the moon. He compares Earth to a cell and focuses on the cell's membrane to help explain Earth's fragile atmosphere, which is both contained and permeable. Seen as a membrane, something small and everyday, the atmosphere seems to reflect a balance we see everywhere in nature. But our atmosphere also appears threatened. What if the delicate balance between incoming light from the sun and the ozone layer that filters out ultraviolet radiation were thrown off? What if the membrane didn't function anymore? In having us look at tiny blue Earth from the distant, desolate moon, Thomas reminds us that our atmosphere is our life and that it has a fragile container. Why do you think we need such reminders?

THOMAS (1913–1993) sought to combine literary and scientific pursuits throughout his career. He served as dean of both Yale's and New York University's medical schools and as chief executive of the Sloan-Kettering Cancer Institute, while maintaining a private medical practice. Thomas also wrote poetry and lyrical essays on scientific and medical themes. The following excerpt is from a collection of essays written for the *New England Journal of Medicine* and compiled in *The Lives of a Cell: Notes of a Biology Watcher,* which won the National Book Award in 1974.

The World's Biggest Membrane (1973) | BY LEWIS THOMAS

Viewed from the distance of the moon, the astonishing thing about the earth, catching the breath, is that it is alive. The photographs show the dry, pounded surface of the moon in the foreground, dead as an old bone. Aloft, floating free beneath the moist, gleaming membrane of bright blue sky, is the rising earth, the only exuberant thing in this part of the cosmos. If you could look long enough, you would see the swirling of the great drifts of white cloud, covering and uncovering the half-hidden masses of land. If you had been looking for a very long, geologic time, you could have seen the continents themselves in motion, drifting apart on their crustal plates, held afloat by the fire beneath. It has the organized, self-contained look of a live creature, full of information, marvelously skilled in handling the sun.

It takes a membrane to make sense out of disorder in biology. You have to be able to catch energy and hold it, storing precisely the needed amount and releasing it in measured shares. A cell does this, and so do the organelles inside. Each assemblage is poised in the flow of solar energy, tapping off energy from metabolic surrogates of the sun. To stay alive, you have to be able to hold out against equilibrium, maintain imbalance, bank against entropy, and you can only transact this business with membranes in our kind of world.

When the earth came alive it began constructing its own membrane, for the general purpose of editing the sun. Originally, in the time of prebiotic elaboration of peptides and nucleotides from inorganic ingredients in the water on the earth, there was nothing to shield out ultraviolet radiation except the water itself. The first thin atmosphere came entirely from the degassing of the earth as it cooled, and there was only a vanishingly small trace of oxygen in it. Theoretically, there could have been some production of oxygen by photo-dissociation of water vapor in ultraviolet light, but not much. This process would have been self-limiting, as Urey showed, since the wave lengths needed for photolysis are the very ones screened out selectively by oxygen; the production of oxygen would have been cut off almost as soon as it occurred.

The formation of oxygen had to await the emergence of photosynthetic cells, and these were required to live in an environment with sufficient visible light for photosynthesis but shielded at the same time against lethal ultraviolet. Berkner and Marshall calculate that the green cells must therefore have been about ten meters below the surface of water, probably in pools and ponds shallow enough to lack strong convection currents (the ocean could not have been the starting place).

You could say that the breathing of oxygen into the atmosphere was the result of evolution, or you could turn it around and say that evolution was the result of oxygen. You can have it either way. Once the photosynthetic cells had appeared, very probably counterparts of today's blue-green algae, the future respiratory mechanism of the earth was set in place. Early on, when the level of oxygen had built up to around 1 per cent of today's atmospheric concentration, the anaerobic life of the earth was placed in jeopardy, and the inevitable next stage was the emergence of mutants with oxidative systems and ATP. With this, we were off to an explosive developmental stage in which great varieties of respiring life, including the multicellular forms, became feasible.

Berkner has suggested that there were two such explosions of new life, like vast embryological transformations, both dependent on the threshold levels of oxygen. The first, at 1 per cent of the present level, shielded out enough ultraviolet radiation to permit cells to move into the surface layers of lakes, rivers, and oceans. This happened around 600 million years ago, at the beginning of the Paleozoic era, and accounts for the sudden abundance of marine fossils of all kinds in the record of this period. The second burst occurred when oxygen rose to 10 per cent of the present level. At this time, around 400 million years ago, there was a sufficient canopy to allow life out of the water and onto the land. From here on it was clear going, with nothing to restrain the variety of life except the limits of biologic inventiveness.

It is another illustration of our fantastic luck that oxygen filters out the very bands of ultraviolet light that are most devastating for nucleic acids and proteins, while allowing full penetration of the visible light needed for photosynthesis. If it had not been for this semipermeability, we could never have come along.

The earth breathes, in a certain sense. Berkner suggests that there may have been cycles of oxygen production and carbon dioxide consumption, depending on relative abundances of plant and animal life, with the ice ages representing periods of apnea. An overwhelming richness of vegetation may have caused the level of oxygen to rise above today's concentration, with a corresponding depletion of carbon dioxide. Such a drop in carbon dioxide may have impaired the "greenhouse" property of the atmosphere, which holds in the solar heat otherwise lost by radiation from the earth's surface. The fall in temperature would in turn have shut off much of living, and, in a long sigh, the level of oxygen may have dropped by 90 per cent. Berkner speculates that this is what happened to the great reptiles; their size may have been all right for a richly oxygenated atmosphere, but they had the bad luck to run out of air.

Now we are protected against lethal ultraviolet rays by a narrow rim of ozone, thirty miles out. We are safe, well ventilated, and incubated, provided we can avoid technologies that might fiddle with that ozone, or shift the levels of carbon dioxide.

Oxygen is not a major worry for us, unless we let fly with enough nuclear explosives to kill off the green cells in the sea; if we do that, of course, we are in for strangling.

It is hard to feel affection for something as totally impersonal as the atmosphere, and yet there it is, as much a part and product of life as wine or bread. Taken all in all, the sky is a miraculous achievement. It works, and for what it is designed to accomplish it is as infallible as anything in nature. I doubt whether any of us could think of a way to improve on it, beyond maybe shifting a local cloud from here to there on occasion. The word "chance" does not serve to account well for structures of such magnificence. There may have been elements of luck in the emergence of chloroplasts, but once these things were on the scene, the evolution of the sky became absolutely ordained. Chance suggests alternatives, other possibilities, different solutions. This may be true for gills and swim-bladders and forebrains, matters of detail, but not for the sky. There was simply no other way to go.

We should credit it for what it is: for sheer size and perfection of function, it is far and away the grandest product of collaboration in all of nature.

It breathes for us, and it does another thing for our pleasure. Each day, millions of meteorites fall against the outer limits of the membrane and are burned to nothing by the friction. Without this shelter, our surface would long since have become the pounded powder of the moon. Even though our receptors are not sensitive enough to hear it, there is comfort in knowing that the sound is there overhead, like the random noise of rain on the roof at night.

CONNECTING PERSONALLY TO THE READING

1. Have you ever seen photographs of Earth from space? If so, what was your reaction?

2. How does understanding the biology of Earth's atmosphere make you feel about our planet's likelihood of survival? Explain.

FOCUSING ON THE ARGUMENT

1. Thomas is adept at drawing readers in, imagining us observing the way he observes: "If you had been looking for a very long, geologic time. . . ." What is the effect of putting the reader into the picture from the beginning?

2. Thomas uses a single extended analogy to explain the origin and fragility of life on this planet. "It takes a membrane to make sense out of disorder in biology. You have to be able to catch energy and hold it, storing precisely the needed amount and releasing it in measured shares." What is the effect on the reader of this extended comparison of Earth's atmosphere to a membrane?

3. Thomas includes metaphors of everyday utility, management, and finance to make his explanations seem commonsensical, as in "To stay alive, you have to be able to hold out against equilibrium, maintain imbalance, bank against entropy, and you can only transact this business with membranes in our kind of world." What do Thomas's metaphors suggest

about the nature of our atmosphere? Why is an appeal to common sense important to Thomas's argument?

4. Using personification, Thomas tells a story about Earth constructing its own membrane, with oxygen awaiting the emergence of photosynthesis. What is appealing about a story, replete with human motivations, concerning the origin of our atmosphere?

SYNTHESIZING IDEAS FROM MULTIPLE READINGS

1. Both Jane Goodall (selection from *In the Shadow of Man*, p. 402) and Thomas are enthusiastic about their science, using such phrases as "the astonishing thing," "miraculous achievement," "treasured moments," and "exciting discoveries." Do you think the emotion expressed here undermines or enhances your sense of these writers as scientists? Explain.

2. Four writers in this chapter address essential elements of our environment: Barry Lopez ("Ice and Light," p. 397) and Ian Frazier ("Terminal Ice," p. 408) address water (as ice), Aldo Leopold ("Wilderness as a Form of Land Use," p. 354) addresses land, and Thomas addresses air. All four emphasize the pleasure they take in their knowledge or observations. How is that pleasure alike and different among the four writers?

3. Thomas's biology is accessible, reasoned, and significant. How might a course in biology be created, using John Dewey's principles of active learning ("The School and the Life of the Child," Chapter 4, p. 211)?

WRITING TO ACT

1. Using Thomas's metaphors of efficiency and banking, write an essay in his style for your school newspaper that summarizes his ideas and suggests the importance of protecting Earth's "membrane."

2. Write a humorous article for a science journal or for a science section of your local or school newspaper, imagining what would happen if Earth's "membrane" were to break.

Connecting the Readings to the Works of Art

Gutzon Borglum, Mount Rushmore

1. In "Wilderness as a Form of Land Use" (p. 354), Aldo Leopold's discussion of land use may suggest two possible ways of looking at this sculpture: (1) the land has been used by humans to create a park, which now protects it from development, or (2) the land has been decimated by humans to extract resources in the form of tourists. Which do you think most holds true? Explain.

2. According to Leslie Marmon Silko in "The Migration Story" (p. 389), the Laguna Pueblo Indians, like Mount Rushmore's sculptors, also changed the landscape they lived in. Do these changes suggest a different attitude toward nature than the one implied by the creation of Mount Rushmore? Explain.

3. In "Ice and Light" (p. 397) Barry Lopez describes how Frederic Edwin Church first painted *The Icebergs* without any indication of human presence, then later added a broken mast to the foreground to indicate a human presence in the work. How do you think Lopez would view the relationship between humans and nature in Mount Rushmore? Explain.

Korczak Ziolkowski, Crazy Horse Monument

1. In "The Migration Story" (p. 389), Leslie Marmon Silko stresses the importance that Laguna Indians attribute to specific rocks and hills. Do you think Silko would decry the imposition of a monument to Crazy Horse on the sacred Black Hills of South Dakota? Explain.

2. Korczak Ziolkowski was careful to ensure the humanitarian and educational use of the monument. Dedicating his entire life to the project from age thirty-eight, and accepting no salary or federal funding, Ziolkowski almost single-handedly carved or supervised the carving of this enormous project. Yet he developed it with visitor viewing sites in mind, and it attracts thousands of visitors each year. What perspective on this use of the land do you think Aldo Leopold ("Wilderness as a Form of Land Use," p. 354) would hold? Explain.

Alexander Hogue, *Crucified Land*

1. In "Wilderness as a Form of Land Use" (p. 354), Aldo Leopold writes about the need for balancing development with preserving the integrity of the land. He comments that land is a nonrenewable resource. How does Hogue's portrayal suggest that the land has been destroyed beyond renewal? What objects seem to symbolize what is to blame for the devastation? Explain.

2. In "The Last Americans" (p. 362), Jared Diamond sees in the mismanagement of land the seeds of a civilization's demise. How do the objects in the painting, especially the crucifix, the placement of the objects, and the lack of balance in the painting, suggest that Hogue thinks a fundamental balance between humanity and nature has been destroyed? How would Diamond connect such mismanagement with a civilization's demise? Explain.

3. Hogue is noted for his paintings of disasters that follow land misuse: drought and floods. What symbols does the artist use to convey human beings' stubborn beliefs and poor farming practices? What human capacities, identified in Jane Goodall (selection from *In the Shadow of Man*, p. 402), Wendell Berry ("An Entrance to the Woods," p. 372), and Leslie Marmon Silko ("The Migration Story," p. 389) are missing in this portrait of human action?

Dorothea, Lange, *Childress County, Texas, June 1938*

1. In "The Last Americans" (p. 362), Jared Diamond warns us that farming practices that ignore the land and potential weather conditions can contribute to a civilization's collapse. What choices may the farmers have made that could have contributed to this desolation? What in the photograph suggests this view?

2. Most of the writers in this chapter have no experience making a living off the land they describe. How might the people who lived in this house feel about the lives of the writers who extol the beauties of nature? Explain.

Jasper Francis Cropsey, *Bareford Mountains, West Milford, New Jersey*

1. In this painting, a golden strip of light-bathed land reveals human beings' partial cultivation of nature. Do you think that the painting inspires the kind of humility

and awe in the face of nature that Barry Lopez ("Ice and Light," p. 397) experiences looking at icebergs? Explain.

2. In "The Migration Story" (p. 389), Leslie Marmon Silko describes how the landscape reinforces the "continuity and accuracy of the oral narratives" for Laguna Pueblo Indians. Do the people in Cropsey's painting seem tied to natural objects and places in the same way? Explain.

Virginia A. Stroud, Doesn't Fall Off His Horse

1. Jane Goodall (selection from *In The Shadow of Man,* p. 402) shows her understanding and respect for, as well as her ability to interact with, the chimps she studies. Do you think that the relationship between humans and animals that Stroud depicts is similar to the relationship that Goodall describes? Explain.

2. Leslie Marmom Silko, in "The Migration Story" (p. 389), describes the importance of communal narratives in maintaining continuity of cultural values. What cultural values seem embedded in Stroud's story of how a Native American received his name?

Asher B. Durand, *Kindred Spirits*

1. What would Wendell Berry ("An Entrance to the Woods," p. 372) think that the men in the painting were discussing? Explain.

2. The two male artists depicted in the painting do not appear to be living in nature, but rather to be out on a walk. Do they seem to relate to nature differently than do the narrators in Jane Goodall (selection from *In the Shadow of Man,* p. 402) and Annie Dillard ("Heaven and Earth in Jest," p. 381), who live in nature? Explain.

Frederic Edwin Church, *The Icebergs*

1. In "Ice and Light" (p. 397), Barry Lopez notes that in cathedral architecture the relationship between God and humans was depicted in terms of light. Do you think that Church creates a feeling of the supernatural with his use of light? Do any other images in the painting suggest a religious feeling? Explain.

2. In "Heaven and Earth in Jest" (p. 381), Annie Dillard asks, "What do we think of the created universe, spanning an unthinkable void with an unthinkable profusion of forms? Or what do we think of nothingness, those sickening reaches of time in either direction?" Does this painting also inspire you to ask such questions? Explain.

3. Ian Frazier ("Terminal Ice," p. 408) describes icebergs from the point of view of ice analysts as well as naturalists. How does learning about how icebergs are created, their size, and movements affect how you see this painting?

David Hockney, *A Bigger Grand Canyon*

1. Wendell Berry ("An Entrance to the Woods," p. 372) comes to see nature differently while he is living in it and observing it closely. Hockney's vision does not seem to depend on living close to nature and scrutinizing natural events. Do both approaches seem to produce awe and respect? Explain.

2. How might Ian Frazier ("Terminal Ice," p. 408), a scientist and journalist, describe the Grand Canyon? Do you think the knowledge Frazier might provide would change Hockney's vision of the Grand Canyon? Explain.

3. Hockney's painting may well inspire thoughts about the created universe and large expanses of time. Does the painting make you aware of Annie Dillard's "sickening reaches of time in either direction" in "Heaven and Earth in Jest" (p. 381)? Explain why or why not.

NASA, *The Blue Marble Earth, Western Hemisphere*

1. In "The World's Largest Membrane" (p. 416), Lewis Thomas states that "Viewed from the distance of the moon, the astonishing thing about the earth, catching the breath, is that it is alive." Does this photograph make you feel the same way? Explain.

2. Jane Goodall (selection from *In the Shadow of Man,* p. 402) describes the harmony she feels not only with the chimpanzees she studies but also with the physical environment of Africa. Do you think that it is only when we travel very far from our immediate environment that we sense this harmony? Explain.

3. Physical distance evokes new perspectives on nature. Do you think that the "aesthetic distance" of paintings and photographs similarly provoke new perspectives on nature? Explain how these two kinds of "distance" might be similar and different, referring to any of the artwork, and to Jane Goodall (selection from *In the Shadow of Man,* p. 402) and Lewis Thomas ("The World's Largest Membrane," p. 416).

FINDING COMMON CAUSE IN CONTROVERSY: Does the federal government have the right to prevent states from developing land while Congress decides whether to preserve this land as "wilderness"?

Issues of using, restoring, and protecting the natural environment have become the focus of national debate. While the global issues of pollution, diminishing forests and other natural resources, and sustaining the planet seem beyond the scope of a short debate, smaller issues that mirror the larger ones can be debated. As we have noted elsewhere, at times, we need to debate pros and cons to decide on one side over another, especially with legislation. Seeking common ground helps to narrow the focus to core values. Then we can decide which values we most support.

It may seem to you that the value of preserving nature is self-evident. However, a number of readings in this chapter suggest that Americans have fundamental beliefs that lead them to resist the idea that the government should protect land. Among these beliefs are the right to private property, the benefits of progress, the ability of technology to solve problems, the right to improve one's economic well-being, the resistance to government intervention, and trust in the capitalistic enterprise. These beliefs need to be addressed in any federal government policy restricting land use. States, because they represent the interests of local people, may feel that they should have more right to make such decisions than does the federal government. Under what circumstances do you think that the federal government should have jurisdiction over state government? What would be your criteria?

ELIZABETH SHOGREN is a reporter for National Public Radio; she specializes in coverage of environmental issues. For fourteen years, she was a reporter for the *Los Angeles Times,* and during her tenure at the newspaper, she traveled frequently to report on foreign affairs, including the Kosovo crisis in 1999 and the rise of democracy in Russia.

ALDO LEOPOLD ("Wilderness as a Form of Land Use," p. 354) was a pioneer in the environmental movement on land use. He argued that the few remaining wilderness areas in the United States need protection. Leopold's careful definitions, his appeal to reason, and his ability to address potential objections laid the grounds for discussion. The Utah land struggle described in the news article that follows is a modern reincarnation of the concerns Leopold addressed in 1925. The debate over Utah land seems one of state versus federal control, but embodies the same conflict Leopold delineated between extracting resources and preserving a wilderness area. In 1999 the federal Department of the Interior barred vehicle traffic and oil drilling in this area while Congress debated whether it would designate parts of the 2.6 million acres in Utah as a protected wilderness area. Congress has not been able to pass the bill because the Utah delegation opposes it. A suit by the state of Utah led the Department of the Interior to reverse the decision and remove this barrier. The debate seems to mirror Leopold's view of competing "tendencies" (the desire to extract resources versus the desire to maintain cultural values such as beauty and recreation).

How do you imagine that competing "tendencies" or interests could be resolved? Do you think that Leopold's land use theories could help?

The Nation: Tussle over a Western Jewel (1982)

BY ELIZABETH SHOGREN

MOAB, Utah—Monumental red rock walls rise from a canyon rich with ancient juniper trees, tiny pinyon pines and blooming prickly pear cactuses.

Craggy and sometimes whimsical formations—including one in the distinct shape of a Jeep—emerge from the sandstone. In the vast space, only the song of a canyon wren breaks the silence.

The rugged landscape of Goldbar has not been designated wilderness by Congress. But it is among the parcels totaling 2.6 million acres in southern Utah identified in 1999 as candidates for the designation, which protects land from development. Until Congress could consider the matter, the Bureau of Land Management barred vehicle traffic and blocked oil drilling.

Then, in April, Interior Secretary Gale A. Norton put an end to that. To settle a lawsuit brought by the state of Utah, she ordered no more special treatment for those 2.6 million acres. And she directed land managers in all Western states to stop protecting additional parcels of BLM land unless Congress formally declared them wilderness. Goldbar is included in a pending wilderness bill supported by about 150 Republicans and Democrats in the House. But the bill has been blocked because it does not have the support of the Utah delegation, which opposes designating large areas of the state as wilderness.

Battles over such federal lands have raged in the West for decades, but now the parties arguing for less restrictive use have been getting a more sympathetic hearing from the administration.

The Interior Department's about-face was a major victory for rural politicians, oil company executives and others in Utah and elsewhere who want these areas open to resource development and all-terrain vehicles. The decision parallels other administration actions that would remove obstacles to extracting resources—from Alaska oil to West Virginia coal—from federal and private land.

Goldbar's unspoiled beauty and its potential for pro-ducing oil help explain the passions fueling the dispute. Oil companies want to tap into its reserves. Local governments want the money that would bring.

Although Goldbar lies between two popular national parks—Arches and Canyonlands—and is just a couple of miles west of the recreation hub of Moab, hikers can go hours without seeing another person. Through long stretches of slick rock, desert shrubs and huge sandstone boulders, the only signs of previous visitors are cairns (piles of rocks to guide hikers) and occasional tracks from mountain bikes or bighorn sheep.

In a book describing lands with wilderness qualities, the BLM extolled Goldbar's "outstanding opportunities for solitude," one of Congress's main requirements for wilderness. It also found that much of the area remained "natural," with the imprint of humans largely unnoticeable, another main qualification.

Goldbar's sandstone arches, rock-art panels left by aboriginal inhabitants, maze of twisting canyons and spectacular views of the snow-capped La Sal mountains and Arches National Park all support the case for preserving it, environmentalists say.

Even before April's change in policy, however, hikers were not the only ones with access. A dirt road cutting into the heart of Goldbar leads to one of southern Utah's longest-producing oil wells, Long Canyon No. 1.

Liz Thomas, a local environmentalist, said she wished it could remain the only oil well in Goldbar. "There are plenty of places outside of [proposed] wilderness to drill," said Thomas, a lawyer who represents the Southern Utah Wilderness Alliance in Moab. When the BLM permits companies to develop, she said, it forfeits the land's intrinsic value as wilderness without any guarantee of a return. "The oil companies may or may not hit something. But the damage they do will live on and on."

Oil firms said southern Utah's oil fields play only a minor role in overall domestic production. But for Grand County, it's money in the bank. Long Canyon No. 1 has produced millions of dollars in county tax revenue over the last three decades.

Jerry McNeely, a member of the Grand County Council, envisioned more wells pumping to fill the county's treasury. Goldbar overlaps an area known to contain several million barrels of oil.

Modern techniques, McNeely said, enable oil companies to explore for oil and produce it without significantly hurting the scenery. Small oil wells are painted

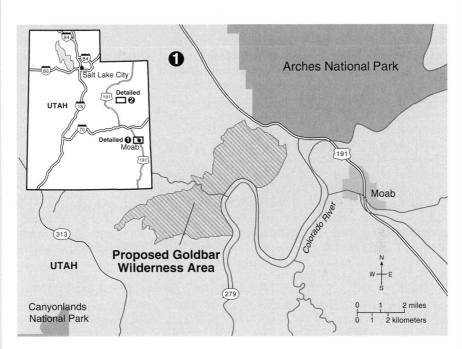

❶

Arches National Park

Salt Lake City

Detailed ❷

UTAH

Detailed ❶
Moab

191

Colorado River

Moab

313

UTAH

Proposed Goldbar
Wilderness Area

N
W ─┼─ E
S

0   1   2 miles
0   1   2 kilometers

279

Canyonlands
National Park

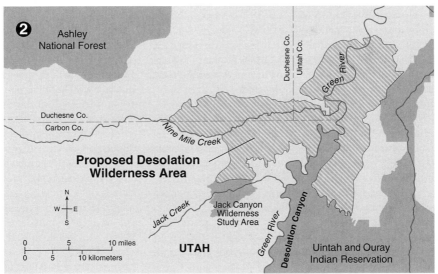

❷ Ashley
National Forest

Duchesne Co.
Uintah Co.

Green River

Duchesne Co.
Carbon Co.

Nine Mile Creek

Proposed Desolation
Wilderness Area

N
W ─┼─ E
S

Jack Creek

Jack Canyon
Wilderness
Study Area

Green River

Desolation Canyon

0   5   10 miles
0   5   10 kilometers

UTAH

Uintah and Ouray
Indian Reservation

to blend with the scenery; horizontal drilling allows drill pads to be established away from the most scenic spots. "I would prefer not to have any wilderness areas," he said. Preserving them, he added, "just stops progress." Stopping development was Congress' intent in passing the 1964 Wilderness Act. Concerned that expanding populations would rob the country of its natural heritage, Congress sought to protect the "primeval" character of wild federal lands for future generations. The law defined wilderness as areas of at least 5,000 acres "where the Earth and its community of life are untrammeled by man, where man himself is a visitor who does not remain."

At first, BLM lands were not included, but in 1976, Congress directed the Interior Department to catalog the "wilderness characteristics" of its lands within 15 years. Since then, 6.5 million acres of BLM land across the West have been designated by Congress as wilderness. Only 30,000 of those acres are in Utah. But the BLM designated an additional 3.2 million acres in Utah for temporary protection as wilderness study areas.

Naturalists argued that many more acres of the state's extraordinary red rock country deserved to be included. . . .

"We're talking about setting aside some of the most scenic jewels in the country," said Heidi McIntosh, the alliance's conservation director. Her group wants 9 million acres—more than one-sixth of the entire state— to be declared wilderness.

Local and state politicians and many others in Utah have said that is too much.

Her group and its supporters in Congress persuaded Bruce Babbitt, President Clinton's Interior secretary, to take a second look at Utah's BLM lands. That effort resulted in the 1999 listing of 2.6 million acres with wilderness characteristics. Babbitt and environmentalists hoped that those acres would be protected until Congress could get around to designating them as wilderness.

The BLM started delaying requests for oil leasing and other development on these lands. The state of Utah sued, contesting the BLM's right to treat those lands as de facto wilderness. Norton settled the suit by agreeing to consider multiple uses for the 2.6 million acres and taking the BLM out of the business of selecting new areas for wilderness protection.

Logan MacMillan, an independent petroleum geologist whose vision for developing oil in a remote area of Utah was thwarted by the dispute over wilderness, welcomed the news.

MacMillan had hoped to produce oil on the northern edge of one of the largest swaths of roadless wild lands in the continental U.S. The aptly named Desolation Canyon is so remote that tourists float down the Green River for four or five days without seeing any sign of civilization. As at

Goldbar, the new policy means oil exploration applications in Desolation Canyon will be considered.

MacMillan agreed that the land affords spectacular vistas. "But I don't believe that should preclude resource development from those lands," he said. "I think oil and gas activity can occur in lands all of us would enjoy being out on."

Marc Smith, executive director of the Independent Petroleum Assn. of Mountain States, said he hoped Norton's new wilderness policy would "signal that the confusion and uncertainty that have surrounded development on federal lands in the West may be improving."

That is also the hope of Utah's rural counties, whose economies have long relied on extracting resources from federal land. The wilderness dispute deterred oil development, leaving local governments such as San Juan County "poorer and poorer," said Ed Scherick, the county's director of personnel and planning. County taxes generated from oil and gas slid from $4.5 million in 1989 to $2.8 million in 2002, officials said.

Tourists have brought in some money, but not enough to fill the hole left by oil production. "Some of this land has to be left for multiple use, or this area cannot sustain itself," Scherick said.

Environmentalists responded that the counties' economic concerns do not justify resource development. "These lands belong to all Americans from coast to coast," McIntosh said. "They're as important to all Americans as the Statue of Liberty is to people in Utah."

EMPATHIZING WITH DIFFERENT POINTS OF VIEW

Try to see the question from both points of view. Take each side in turn, looking at the possible arguments.

Take the side that the Department of the Interior should declare this land protected until Congress votes on a wilderness designation.

- The Goldbar land is nonrenewable. Once destroyed, it cannot be re-created. The area is unique, with red rock formations and deep canyons that lie between two popular national parks. It is so isolated, however, that one can go for miles without meeting another human being.
- Progress and development, although key American values, need limits, in that we may be destroying the very environment that makes living worthwhile.
- A wilderness area can be preserved for countless future generations.
- Oil in Utah plays only a minor role in U.S. oil production.
- Our U.S. natural heritage has already been reduced to a small number of true wilderness areas.
- The 1964 Wilderness Act demonstrates the commitment of Congress to protecting the "primeval character" of such lands. This Wilderness Act represents decades of work by environmentalists and the approval of U.S. citizens and representatives.
- Utah has only a small percentage of Bureau of Land Management (BLM) land that is already designated as wilderness. Only 30,000 of the 6.5 million designated acres lie in Utah. Utah representatives do not face an unfair burden if the tax revenues from a particular county go down.
- The wilderness bill pending in Congress includes sites that have special significance to naturalists. An oil company has already targeted one of the sites.

Take the position that the Department of the Interior should allow development:

- Utah will be particularly hurt economically if all 2.6 million acres are blocked until Congress can consider its wilderness bill.
- It may take years for Congress to make a determination. The land has been under consideration since 1999, and the impending bill has been blocked because of objections from the Utah delegates.
- The counties in which the lands are located need the tax money that has flowed for thirty years. The land overlaps other areas containing several million barrels of oil.
- Utah council representatives claim that oil can be extracted without significantly affecting the environment.

- Setting aside the 2.6 million acres for an unknown number of years is unjust. Such vast amounts of land constitute almost half of the potential new wilderness areas in the United States.
- The Bureau of Land Management has no right to declare the land *de facto* wilderness.
- The Department of the Interior has reversed its decision on the interim use of the 2.6 million acres.

ADDING MORE INFORMATION

- To better understand this debate, search the Internet using keywords such as Goldbar, wilderness protection in Utah, Department of the Interior, land management, and the like. Look for recent editorials and information that support both sides.
- Look at comparable debates. The Mojave National Preserve is composed of mining claims that may soon permit claimholders to purchase the land outright (*Los Angeles Times,* December 4, 2005).

SEEKING COMMON CAUSE

Before taking a final position, look for possible common ground.

- Wilderness areas protect the rights of all Americans to enjoy open space. A balanced federal policy needs to ensure that no one state pays more for such wilderness through loss of potential income or growth than any other state.
- A rational policy of land designation needs to be established so that Congress can pass wilderness bills that no one state can block.
- Long-term interests need to count more than short-term interests.

DEBATE ESSAY

Write an essay for or against the barrier to developing this Utah land. In preparation, first lay out the grounds of the debate, and then decide which side you support and why. Be sure to establish where you think both sides have common interests (using suggestions above or other ideas). Then delineate your arguments, in the order of importance. When you present each argument, be sure to include potential objections and your response to those objections. Explain your position through specific references to facts presented in the article.

WRITING PROJECTS

Writing a Short Essay

The following writing projects can help you prepare for the extended writing project or serve as independent writing projects themselves.

Writing to Understand a Reading

Write a summary of and personal response to any one of the readings in this chapter.

The summary should occupy at least one-third of the paper and should indicate the main point and subordinate points of the article and how they relate. The response should occupy at least one-third of the paper and go beyond opinion to discuss assumptions, concrete evidence, and logical connections.

Writing an Observation

For a period of one week, keep a nature journal. Each day, take about half an hour to observe in a natural setting. Concentrate on your senses. What forms of life do you see? Describe them in detail. What sounds do you hear? Try to compare the sounds to other sounds more familiar. What smells do you notice? Try to eliminate all judgments ("it smelled good") or interpretations ("the bee was angry"). Reread the journal after it is complete, and write about what you think your experiences mean.

Writing a Description

Describe a place in nature that meant a lot to you when you were very young. Detail all of the images that you remember. Make the description as concrete as possible. Then describe how you interacted with the natural setting and what it meant to you. Why do you still remember it? Do the memories play a role in feelings you have today?

Writing to Synthesize

Recall a beautiful natural setting that has been lost over the past five or ten years, because it was either developed, not maintained, or ignored. What accounted for the loss? Do you think that the values or interests that led to the change justified the loss? Referencing readings from this chapter, especially Leopold, Lopez, and Dillard, as well as the artworks, write an essay that communicates both what you think was lost and whether or not you feel the interests justified the loss.

Writing to Compare and Contrast

Compare and contrast the view of human beings' relationship to nature in the carvings on Mount Rushmore and in *Bareford Mountains, West Milford, New Jersey.* Look for themes on which to build your comparison. These might include each artist's view of nature; the depiction of the balance of power between humans and nature; the relationship each artist implies people have to nature (fear, dominance, cohabitation, mutual dependence, and so on); and how each work depicts the benefits of nature.

Writing an Extended Argument

The following assignment asks you to incorporate numerous sources into an interpretation of a landscape painting. You may use any of the readings or other works of art to help you interpret the work. *Topic: What is the relationship between humans and nature depicted in a nineteenth- or early-twentieth-century American landscape painting of your choice?*

Your thesis might emphasize the ideas of one reading over the others, as a way of focusing your essay. The thesis might also be an answer to some of the questions raised in the readings, such as What does nature teach us? How does our sense of time and identity change in nature? How does nature relate to culture?

Your evidence should include detailed discussions of the painting's elements, such as human figures, objects, foreground and background, shapes and colors.

You can also narrow the topic to one of the following questions or one you design:

- What potential conflict or tension does the painting identify in the relationship between the people portrayed and the natural scene?

- What events or narratives does the painting depict or imply? In those narratives, what are people doing? How are they affecting or being affected by the natural setting?

- What do the objects in the painting indirectly tell you about the relationship between humans and nature as the artist envisions it?

Designing the Extended Writing Project

As we suggest with each extended writing project, you should design your project to include key elements of a paper. These include your thesis, a structure based on the thesis, detailed descriptions (including quotes and comments on quotes), and discussions of the significance of the thesis. A working thesis and tentative structure give you a good beginning point before you draft. They may change, however, in the writing process.

A Thesis

Remember that a thesis is the point of your essay. It is a claim or position.

EXAMPLE OF A THESIS | Mount Rushmore represents humanity's need to conquer nature and impose its will upon it.

A Structure Based on the Thesis

You might structure an essay based on this thesis in the following way:

- Many landscapes portray humans as small figures in a posture of contemplation.

- In contrast, Mount Rushmore erases nature to feature the faces of four men.

- The carved faces suggest power, dominance, and superiority.

- The gazes on the carved faces do not connect with one another but look out over the American landscape as individual forces of mind.

- The relationship between human beings and nature is therefore one of individual notions of conquest.

Detailed Description (essays and artwork)

Each of the main points above needs to be supported with details, quotes, and explanations. If you choose to quote or paraphrase ideas from a reading, be sure to cite them. Also, use your own words to introduce quotations. After you have noted a concrete detail from a painting or used a quotation from an essay, comment on how each supports your point.

EXAMPLE | *In contrast, Mount Rushmore erases nature to feature the faces of four men.* The natural shape of the mountain had to be chipped away in order to impose the shape of human heads. These tall mountains, made of granite, no longer look like mountains, with vegetation and soft lines worn down by centuries of natural erosion. Instead, they reveal the sharp lines and cuts from carving implements, which have scraped the stone to smoothness but left scars in the rock. The mountains here are not respected for their evocation of mystery and contemplation, as are the mountains Annie Dillard describes ("Heaven and Earth in Jest," p. 381). Dillard sees in mountains "a passive mystery, the oldest of all" in that they suggest "the simple mystery of creation from nothing"; for her, mountains are "giant, restful, absorbent." In contrast, the artist of Mount Rushmore carved away the mystery and the restfulness of the mountains and gave us instead the furrowed brows and troubled eyes of famous American presidents.

Conclusion or Significance of the Thesis

Writing about significance may be difficult because writers think that significance is self-evident. However, writers do not always make explicit their case for significance. It can help to ask, So what? Who cares? What are the consequences? Who is most affected?

EXAMPLE | How important is humankind's respect for the natural environment? Jared Diamond says that an abuse of natural resources led to the decline of once-flourishing civilizations. Aldo Leopold sees disrespect destroying the last of our wilderness areas. Perhaps Mount Rushmore symbolizes the pride and vanity that may go before the fall. Indeed, the values that Mount

Rushmore projects are not mutuality, mystery, and respect for nature, but rather dominance, superiority, and obliviousness to other life-forms. Such egoism in the face of far stronger forces may well cost us our civilization.

Using WEB Resources

www.offroad.com

This site identifies current attempts to bar vehicles from parkland and off-road sites and seeks to fight this legislation. Read some of the current articles and identify the public use and access arguments expressed. What rights do you think that recreational vehicle enthusiasts have to this land? Do you agree with the arguments presented?

www.blm.gov/nhp/index.htm

This site identifies the various concerns of the Bureau of Land Management, which exists within the Department of the Interior. Some of the programs include the wild horse and burro program and the healthy forests initiative. How might some of these programs come into conflict with supporters of off-road vehicle use? Are there any ideas or values that are common to both parties?

www.mhhe.com/durkin1

Using the Web for resources on Connecting to Nature. Go to Web Resources

The Farnsworth Art Museum Web Site (http://farnsworthmuseum.org)

The Farnsworth Art Museum, located in Rockland, Maine, houses a collection of American fine art, including works by celebrated artists Winslow Homer, Maurice Prendergast, and Andrew Wyeth. It is also devoted to collecting American art related to Maine. While some art museums are resources for quirky artifacts (e.g., the American Visionary Art Museum, http://www.avam.org), others, like the Farnsworth, focus on preserving an artistic heritage. If you have access to the Internet, explore the rest of this site. How do the content, visual images, and writing style reinforce this purpose?

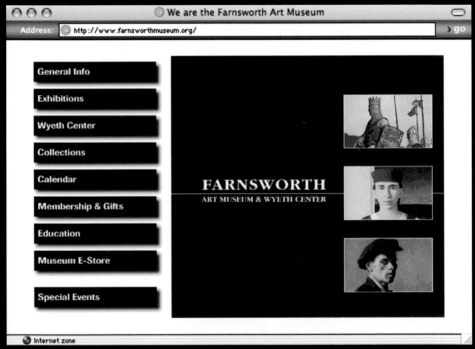

1 How do the colors of Farnsworth's Web pages reinforce your impression of the museum?

2 Both the images and text on these Web pages appear in boxes, like pictures framed on a wall. What are the dominant shapes on these pages? Do they create an impression of serenity, whimsy, wildness, or something else?

3 Compare the presentation of the artwork on these pages with the way Jacob Lawrence's paintings are presented on the Jacob Lawrence: Exploring Stories pages. How are the paintings framed? What text and colors accompany them? How does the presentation of artwork reflect the different personalities of the two sites?

The Guerrilla Girls are an art collective whose goal is to expose racism and sexism in the art world and elsewhere. When making public appearances they wear gorilla masks, hence the pun on "guerrilla" ("warrior"). How do the content, visual appearance, and writing style of this site work together to express political activism?

Jean-Auguste-Dominique Ingres, *The Great Odalisque*. Louvre, Paris.

1   What is the pun on "maximum exposure"? What practice does it allude to?

2   "How women get maximum exposure in art museums" parodies an 1814 French painting by Jean-Auguste-Dominique Ingres, called *Odalisque* ("odalisque" comes from the Turkish word for a female slave in a harem). What makes the Guerrilla Girls' version of this painting a parody? What is their objection to the original painting?

3   Unlike farnsworthmuseum.org, guerrillagirls.com intends not to conserve tradition but to uproot it. How does the site suggest resistance, or even subversion?

4   Compare the fonts used in farnsworthmuseum.org, guerrillagirls.com, and mowa.org. What does this visual cue reveal about the personality of each site?

The Web Site for the Museum of Web Art (MOWA)
(http://www.mowa.org)

MOWA is an online museum of art that is created and experienced on a computer. Un-like most art museums, it is not organized by period, country, or artist, but by "things that move," "things that work," "things that are constant," and "things that change." Visit MOWA online. How is your experience there like and unlike that in a traditional art museum? Which work of arts do you enjoy most and least, and why?

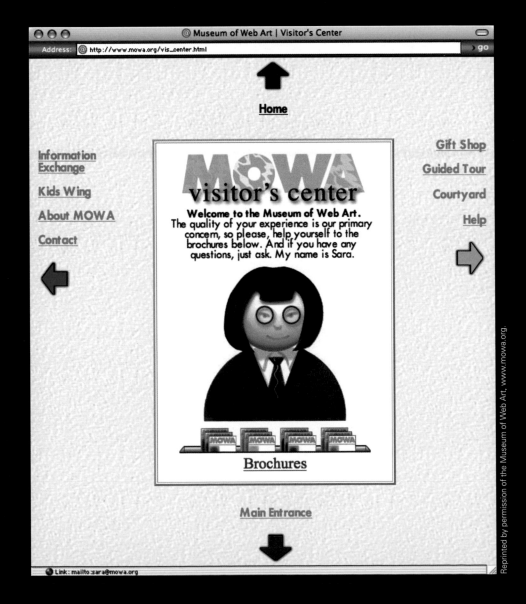

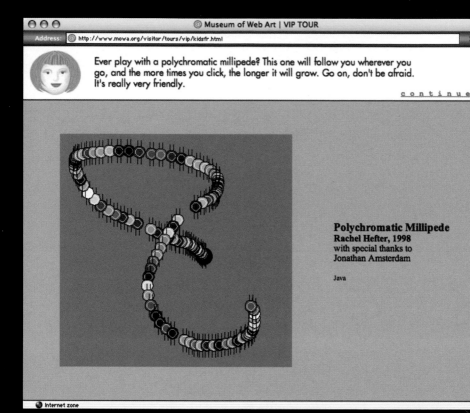

1 What is the effect of including the cartoon images of people—Lillian, who volunteers at the Visitors Center, and Kendra, a tour guide? What would the museum be like if it offered only artwork, without the "people"?

2 How do such elements as mouse rollovers, animation, choice of color, and font style and size help fulfill the purpose of this site?

3 In what ways does MOWA celebrate the new tools and techniques the computer has made available to artists?

4 While the Farnsworth and Jacob Lawrence Web sites are complements to real museums, the Museum of Web Art exists only in cyberspace. How do the three sites reflect this difference?

5 In what ways do the Jacob Lawrence and MOWA sites appeal to young people?

The Jacob Lawrence: Exploring Stories Web Pages
(http://www.whitney.org/jacoblawrence/index.html)

These Web pages were created in conjunction with an exhibit of Jacob Lawrence's work at the Whitney Museum of American Art, New York City. They focus on Lawrence's narrative art, sequences of paintings that tell stories from African American history, and individual works depicting the social life of Harlem, New York (see also *The Library,* insert 2-2). These pages are designed primarily for students and teachers. How do the visual elements (e.g., colors, font, background, composition) suggest that this is the audience?

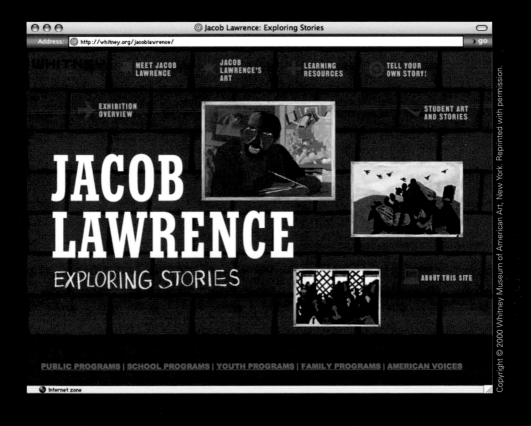

1 What is the effect of using a brick wall as the background for Lawrence's paintings on the home page? How does this image suit the subject of his art?

2 The Learning Resources page is designed much like a Lawrence painting: each section of the page, like each section of the painting, is shaped in an asymmetrical block. How else do this page and the home page repeat elements from Lawrence's painting style?

3 Both this site and guerrillagirls.com are meant to educate the visitor, and issues of social justice are a prominent theme in both. Explore both sites online and compare their treatment of this theme. What is the tone of the text in each site?

Exploring Cyberculture

A new technology often has far-reaching effects: it can influence the way we perceive the world around us, create communities of people who would never have met before, bring places closer together, change our concepts of time and space, give us opportunities to try on new identities, and offer us new ways to act politically. The readings in this chapter analyze how the cultures and practices of the electronic world, especially those that have developed on the Internet and World Wide Web, have enacted a social revolution that is still taking place.

EXPLORING CYBERCULTURE IN THE WEB SITES

This chapter reproduces two pages from each of four Web sites concerned with art: www.farnsworthmuseum.org, site for the Farnsworth Art Museum (whose real-life location is in Rockland, Maine); www.guerrillagirls.com, the site for the activist group Guerrilla Girls (in real life, a group of professionals in the art world, originally based in New York City); www.mowa.org, the Museum of Web Art, an online museum of computer-based art; and the Jacob Lawrence: Exploring Stories site, sponsored by the Whitney Museum of American Art in New York (www.whitney.org/jacoblawrence). Each of these sites represents the power of the World Wide Web in a different way. The Farnsworth site provides access to images from its collection of American art for people who live far from Maine; www.guerrillagirls.com encourages viewers to fight racism and sexism, especially in the art world; www.mowa.org teaches the viewer to appreciate and interact with art that has been created with software; and the Jacob Lawrence: Exploring Stories site helps visitors understand the narrative paintings of African American artist Jacob Lawrence. Each site has a distinct identity, created through deliberate choices of content, images, color, text, and links.

Analyzing the Web Sites

To analyze these Web sites, try to determine the purpose of the site and what kind of audience the site is trying to reach: what can you infer about the age, educational background, social background, or personal interests of the audience? Then look at both the visual elements of the site and the verbal ones. Finally consider how they interact: do language and images reinforce one another, contrast with one another, or seem independent of one another? Because a Web site almost always consists of words and visual elements, you need to look at the language and images both separately and in relation to each other.

Here is a list of other elements to look at as you analyze the Web sites (see also the section on reading Web sites in Chapter 1 of this book):

- **Tone**

  What adjectives would you use to describe the Web page? To describe the prose style(s) of the text? The voice of the speaker? What is your initial reaction to the page?

- **Visual appearance**

  What is the effect of the choice (or lack) of colors? Font style and size? Background image?

  How are text and images laid out on the page?

  What is the effect of the graphic images or lack of them?

  What is the relationship between text and image? Do the images comment on the text, contrast with it, replicate the content, compete with it for attention?

- **Content**

  What kind of information are we given? What information is emphasized? What is downplayed? What is omitted? What is the speaker's attitude toward the content?

- **Links**

  How much does the content rely on links to other Web sites? What kinds of sites are linked to this page? Are the links meant to provide information, give the visitor opportunities to communicate, or sell products?

- **Interactivity**

  Are you an outside observer, or do you interact with these pages? What is the extent and nature of your participation with the content, author, or other users of the pages?

- **Audience**

  Who is the intended visitor, and how can you tell? What is the site's attitude toward the user?

- **Author**

  What, if anything, do you know about the owners of the page? What is their attitude toward the subject of the site?

- **Purpose**

  What are the goals of the pages?

Analysis of a Web Site: The guerrillagirls.com Home Page

Knowing something about the organization Guerrilla Girls—the authors of guerrillagirls .com — helps the viewer understand the Web site. The Guerrilla Girls formed in 1985 as a collective of artists and other art professionals whose mission was to draw attention to discrimination against women artists and artists of color in the art world. Over the years, they expanded their goals to expose racism and sexism in the film world and the culture at large. To protect their personal careers, when making public appearances they wear large gorilla masks, hence the pun on "guerrilla" ("warrior").

Guerrillagirls.com uses language and visual images that express both the Guerrilla Girls' activist goals and their medium of persuasion: humor. The site's purpose is to fight injustice "with facts, humor, and fake fur." The tone, then, is simultaneously serious and funny.

All the images on the site support these purposes: the gorilla mask makes a political statement; it is huge, hairy, snarling, and powerful, with fangs exposed, suggesting that this group is not to be trifled with. At the same time, the mask is funny: it looks incongruous next to the woman's pale, hairless, bejeweled, and therefore most ungorilla-like arm. Likewise, the colors convey both power and humor: they are bright, evoking strength, and garish, suggesting a playful spirit—fire-engine red, hot pink, lime green, screaming purple. Surrounding the clenched fist—and thus drawing attention to this image of political assertiveness—is the name of the site, in letters that seem to move, rather than line up in an orderly row, another image of energy and power. The title points to the site's motto: "re-inventing the 'f' word—'feminism,'" a play on "f word," as well as an announcement of the site's political stance. The images of the posters, books, and Guerrilla Girls in action fill up the page, summarizing the work of this group and presenting a few of the "facts" and instances of the "humor" that make up the site's other pages. Every element here reflects the Guerrilla Girls' hostility to discrimination combined with their strong sense of play, especially through parody.

EXPLORING CYBERCULTURE IN THE ESSAYS

The essays in this chapter address some of the workings of cyberspace and show how computer technology is changing our lives. In "Pyramids and Pancakes," Michael Lewis describes how a fifteen-year-old high school student with no formal legal training functions as a legal expert online, dispensing legal advice to adults who take his help seriously. In this case and others like it, the public trusts knowledge offered by nonexperts, who are strangers, even teenagers. Lewis concludes that on the Internet, professional expertise is no longer the exclusive property of those with specialized training: anyone can be an expert. The Internet is democratizing our culture.

David Weinberger's experience on eBay, which he describes in a selection from *Small Pieces Loosely Joined*, leads him to a similar conclusion; he learns about quilts from the sellers' descriptions of their products and concludes that "the lively plurality of voices sometimes can and should outweigh the stentorian voice of experts." But in addition to promoting an egalitarian view of expertise, the Web, Weinberger believes, changes our notions of space, time, and personal identity. One can access the Web from anywhere in the world, so our traditional concepts of "near" and "far" are irrelevant; we are not held to the same time constraints online as we are in real life (when stores close at certain hours, for example), and since we are usually invisible on the Web, we can craft whatever online identity we want for ourselves.

In "You've Got Blog: How to Put Your Business, Your Boyfriend, and Your Life Online," Rebecca Mead describes an online community and the relationships that develop there, especially a romantic relationship that moves from virtual reality to real life. Her essay illustrates how the line between virtual and real lives is often blurred and how each can spill into the other. Like Mead, Howard Rheingold is intrigued by the computer's ability to elicit rapid and profound social change. Rheingold's article, "How to Recognize the Future When It Lands on You," illustrates a merging of the real and virtual in the way cell phone messaging brings people together. Rheingold argues that cell phones and other mobile computer technologies are a powerful means of collective action, both for good (to overthrow oppressive governments) or ill (mob violence, corporate surveillance of individuals). Like Rheingold, Peter Drucker ("Beyond the Information Revolution") is convinced that computer technology is revolutionizing our social structure, politics, and economy. After illustrating how other technologies, such as the railroad and cotton gin, have transformed our basic social and political structure, he argues that computers are changing the way we buy and sell products, the kind of work we do and value, and the industries we develop.

Nicholas Negroponte also writes about innovative thinking in "Creating a Culture of Ideas," but rather than discuss how computer technologies propagate ideas, he is concerned that our education system foster originality. He argues that creative thinking is essential to the development of new technologies and that schools should encourage students to see from multiple viewpoints, to take risks and even encourage failure as a way of learning, and to share ideas with others. Also concerned about education is Andy Carvin ("Mind the Gap: The Digital Divide as the Civil Rights Issue of the New Millennium"), who argues that the digital revolution is in the hands of those who can financially afford a computer and that those who cannot afford one are being disenfranchised. By positing this gap between those who have computer access and those who don't as a civil rights issue, Carvin emphasizes our legal and ethical responsibility to address this problem, which he ties to education. Adult illiteracy and the lack of technological instruction in schools are two of the problems that must be resolved in order to close the "digital divide."

Students who do have access to computers are the subject of Jennifer Lee's "Nu Shortcuts in School R 2 Much 4 Teachers." Lee's article suggests that instant messaging is changing the way students write, influencing them to use smiley faces and abbreviations like "ppl" for "people" instead of Standard English. Teachers are divided over whether this practice fosters sloppy writing or creativity. Our final selection, Dave Barry's "Selected Web Sites—At Last: Proof that Civilization is Doomed" takes a bemused look at the computer revolution: describing several of the many absurd and apparently pointless Web sites he has visited, he suggests that not all of the computer's contributions to our lives have been profound or even useful. His article reminds us not to take ourselves and our world—virtual or real—too seriously. Like many things in life, cyberspace has the potential to be world changing or utterly ridiculous.

Analyzing the Essays

As you think about the readings, consider these questions:

1. What is the writer's attitude toward the technology he or she is discussing? How can you tell?

2. What problems does the technology create? What advantages does it offer?

3. What kinds of social change does the writer approve and disapprove of?

4. What social conditions best promote constructive change?

5. What social change(s) has the technology brought about?

6. Who benefits from the technology? Who is harmed by it?

7. Does the writer suggest a common ground between technology consumers with opposing interests? If not, can you suggest one?

Analysis of an Essay

As an example of how you might analyze a reading, look at Michael Lewis's "Pyramids and Pancakes." Lewis's point is to show how computer technology can lead to profound social change, in this case, to a shift in our notions of expertise. Marcus Arnold is a fifteen-year-old boy who gives legal advice over the Internet. Though the adults who take his advice know that his legal training consists of hours watching Court TV, they find him so down-to-earth and helpful that they respect him as an authority. Lewis takes pains to show us that Marcus is a fairly typical teenager who lumbers, speaks tersely to his parents, gobbles doughnuts, and provides answers on Askme.com largely as a game—the more accurate his legal information, the higher his score. In giving Marcus a new identity—legal expert—the Internet dispels "the old professional mystique" of lawyering: no longer is legal information accessible only to an educated elite. The Internet thus promotes an egalitarian notion that anyone can do anything and invites us to question the very notion of "expertise." Given that our culture has long relegated professional knowledge—such as journalism, medicine, and law—to those with specific credentials—this shift in thinking is revolutionary. And it illustrates Lewis's contention that the Internet is hosting "a lot of little social experiments."

READING

MICHAEL LEWIS describes an important social change brought about by the Internet: knowledge typically seen as the exclusive domain of professionals can be acquired and delivered by anyone, regardless of credentials. In explaining fifteen-year-old Marcus Arnold's extraordinary success giving legal advice to adults—adults who know Marcus has no legal training—Lewis argues that "at the bottom . . . was a corrosively democratic attitude toward legal knowledge." Why do you think the public is so willing to accept advice from Marcus, in spite of his youth and lack of legal education? If you have given advice to or received advice from strangers on the Internet, what prompted you to do so? How reliable was the information?

LEWIS is a columnist for Bloomberg, a visiting fellow at the University of California, Berkeley, a frequent contributor to the *New York Times Magazine,* and a freelance writer whose work appears in the *New Yorker* and *Slate.* He is the author of the best seller *Liar's Poker* (1989) and *Coach: Lessons on the Game of Life* (2005), among other books.

Pyramids and Pancakes (2001) | BY MICHAEL LEWIS

The strange story of Jonathan Lebed suggested that you couldn't really understand what was happening on the Internet unless you understood the conditions in the real world that led to what was happening on the Internet, and you couldn't understand those unless you went there in person and had a look around.[1] And so it wasn't long after I left Jonathan that I found myself back on the road, heading south from Los Angeles into the desert, to investigate another unintentional insult delivered to the social order by a teenage boy with an AOL account. This one had occurred on a web site maintained by the AskMe Corporation.

The AskMe Corporation had been created in 1999 by former Microsoft employees. The software it sold enabled the big companies that had bought it—3M, Procter & Gamble—to create a private web for their workers. This private web was known as a "knowledge exchange." The knowledge exchange was a screen on a computer where employees could put questions to the entire company. The appeal of this was obvious. Once an AskMe-style knowledge exchange was up and running, it didn't matter where inside the company any particular expertise resided. So long as expertise didn't leave the company, it was always on tap for whoever needed it.

AskMe Corp. soon found that it was able to tell a lot about a company from its approach to the new software. In pyramid-shaped, hierarchical organizations, the bosses tended to appoint themselves or a few select subordinates as the "experts." Questions rose up from the bottom of the organization, the answers flowed down from the top, and the original hierarchy was preserved, even reinforced. In less hierarchical, pancake-shaped companies, the bosses used the software to create a network of all the company's employees and to tap intelligence wherever in that network it happened to be. That way anyone in the company could answer anyone else's questions. Anyone could be the expert. Of course, it didn't exactly inspire awe in the ranks to see the intern answering a question posed by the vice president of strategic planning. But many companies decided that a bit of flattening was a small price to pay to tap into the collective knowledge bank.

The people who created the AskMe.com software believed that it gave companies whose bosses were willing to risk their own prestige and authority an advantage over the hierarchical companies whose bosses were not. They didn't say this publicly, because they wanted to sell their software to the pyramid-shaped organizations, too. But they knew that once the software was deployed, companies that flattened their organization charts to encourage knowledge to flow freely in every direction would beat companies that didn't. Knowledge came from the strangest places; employees knew a lot more than they thought they did; and the gains in the collective wisdom outweighed any losses to the boss's authority.

In short, the software subtly changed the economic environment. It bestowed new rewards on the egalitarian spirit. It made life harder for pyramids and easier for pancakes. 5

Out in the field AskMe Corp.'s salespeople, like salespeople everywhere, found themselves running into the same five or six objections from potential buyers—even when the buyers were pancake-shaped. One was "How do you know that your software won't break down when all of our two hundred thousand employees are using it heavily?" To prove that it wouldn't, AskMe Corp. created a web site and offered a version of its software to the wider public. The site, called AskMe.com, went up on the Web in February 2000, and quickly became the most heavily used of a dozen or so knowledge exchanges on the Internet. In its first year the site had more than ten million visitors, which was striking in view of how peripheral it was to the ambitions of the AskMe Corporation. The company made no money from the site and did not bother to monitor what went on there, or even to advertise its existence. The ten million people who had used the site in its first year were drawn by word of mouth. The advice on the site was freely offered. The experts were self-appointed and ranked by the people who sought the advice. Experts with high rankings received small cash prizes from AskMe.com. The prizes—and the free publicity—attracted a lot of people who don't normally work for free. Accountants, lawyers, and financial consultants mingled their licensed knowledge with experts in sports trivia, fortune telling, and body piercing.

AskMe Corp. didn't think of it this way, but its public web site suggested a question: What is the wider society's instinctive attitude toward knowledge? Are we willing to look for it wherever it might be found, or only from the people who are supposed to possess it? Does the world want to be a pyramid or a pancake?

In the summer of 2000, in a desert town called Perris, halfway between L.A. and Palm Springs, a fifteen-year-old boy had offered his reply to that question, and a thousand or so more besides. His name was Marcus Arnold. His parents had immigrated to Perris from Belize, by way of South-Central Los Angeles. Why anyone would move to Perris from anywhere was not immediately clear: Perris was one of those non-places that America specializes in creating. One day it was a flat hazy stretch of sand and white rock beneath an endless blue sky; the next some developer had laid out a tract of twenty-five thousand identical homes; and the day after that it was teeming with people who were there, mainly, because it was not someplace else. The decision of human beings to make a home of it had little effect on the identity of Perris. Even after the tract houses had been deposited on the desert, Perris was known chiefly as a place to leap onto from an airplane.

Marcus lived with his parents and his twin brother in a small brick house a mile or so from the big drop zone. Over the family's one-car garage, from morning until night, people stepped out of planes and plummeted to earth, and the blue sky above Marcus was permanently scarred by parachutes. Marcus himself was firmly earthbound, a great big bear of a boy. He was six feet tall and weighed maybe two hundred pounds. He did not walk but lumbered from the computer to the front door, then back again. The computer squatted on a faux antique desk in the alcove between the dining room and the living room, which were as immaculately kept as showrooms in a model home. It was the only computer in the house, he said. In theory, the family shared it; in practice, it belonged to him. He now needed as much time on it as he could get, as he was a leading expert on AskMe.com. His field was the law.

The blue screen displayed the beginning of an answer to a question on 10
AskMe.com Marcus had bashed out before I arrived:

> Your son should not be in jail or on trial. According to *Miranda versus Arizona*
> the person to be arrested must be read his rights before he was asked any
> questions. If your son was asked any questions before the reading of his rights

he should not be in prison. If you want me to help you further write me back on this board privately.

The keyboard vanished beneath Marcus's jumbo hands and another page on AskMe.com popped up on the screen. Marcus wanted to show me the appallingly weak answer to a question that had been offered by one of the real lawyers on the site. "I can always spot a crummy attorney," he said. "There are people on the web site who have no clue what they're talking about, they are just there to get rankings and to sell their services and to get paid." Down went his paws, out of sight went the keyboard, and up popped one of Marcus's favorite web sites. This one listed the menus on death row in Texas. Photographs of men put to death by the state appeared next to hideous lists of the junk food they'd ordered for their last meals. Marcus browsed these for a minute or two, searching for news, then moved on, without comment. One of the privileges of adolescence is that you can treat everything around you as normal, because you have nothing to compare it to, and Marcus appeared to be taking full advantage of it. To Marcus it was normal that you could punch a few buttons into a machine and read what a man who was executed by the state this morning had eaten last night. It was normal that the only sign of life outside his house were the people floating down from the sky and into the field out back. It was normal that his parents had named his identical twin brother Marc. Marc and Marcus. And it was normal that he now spent most of the time he was not in school on the Internet, giving legal advice to grown-ups.

Marcus had stumbled upon Askme.com late in the spring of 2000. He was studying for his biology exam and looking for an answer to a question. He noticed that someone had asked a question about the law to which he knew the answer. Then another. A thought occurred: why not answer them himself? To become an official expert he only needed to fill in a form, which asked him, among other things, his age. He did this on June 5—a day already enshrined in Marcus's mind. "I always wanted to be an attorney since I was, like, twelve," he said, "but I couldn't do it because everyone is going to be, 'like, what? Some twelve-year-old kid is going to give me legal advice?'"

"They'd feel happier with a fifteen-year-old?"

He drew a deep breath and made a face that indicated that he took this to be a complicated question. "So when I first went on AskMe," he said, "I told everybody I was twenty, roughly about twenty, and everyone believed me." Actually, he claimed to be twenty-five, which to a boy of fifteen is, I suppose, roughly twenty. To further that impression he adopted the handle "LawGuy1975." People who clicked onto his page found him described as "LawGuy1975 aka Billy Sheridan." "Billy Sheridan" was Marcus's handle on America OnLine.

A few days after he appointed himself a legal expert Marcus was logging onto the Internet solely to go to AskMe.com and deal with grown-ups' legal problems. What sort of legal problems? I asked him. "Simple ones," he said. "Some of them are like, 'My husband is in jail for murder and he didn't do it and I need to file a motion for dismissal, how do I do it?' I have received questions from people who are just, like, you know, 'I am going to be put in jail all of a sudden, can somebody help me plead before they come cart me off,' and it's just, like, well, come on, that's a cry for help. You're not just going to sit there. . . . But most of them are simple questions. 'What's a felony?' Or 'How many years will I get if I commit this crime?' Or 'What happens if I get sued?' 15

Or 'What's the process to file papers?' Simple questions." He said all this in the self-conscious rapid-fire patter of a television lawyer.

Once he became an expert, Marcus's career took on a life of its own. The AskMe rankings were driven by the number of questions the expert answered, the speed of his replies, and the quality of those replies, as judged by the recipients, who bestowed on them a rating of between one and five stars. By July I Marcus was ranked number 10 out of one hundred and fifty or so experts in AskMe.com's criminal law division, many of whom were actual lawyers. As he tells it, that's when he decided to go for the gold. "When I hit the top ten I got some people who were like, 'Congratulations, blah blah blah.' So my adrenaline was pumping to answer more questions. I was just, like, 'You know what, let me show these people I know what I'm doing.'" He needed to inspire even more people to ask him questions, and to reply to them quickly, and in a way that prompted them to reward him with lots of stars. To that end he updated the page that advertised his services. When he was done it said:

> I am a law expert with two years of formal training in the law. I will help anyone I can! I have been involved in trials, legal studies and certain forms of jurisprudence. I am not accredited by the state bar association yet to practice law.. . . Sincerely, Justin Anthony Wyrick, Jr.

"Justin was the name I always wanted—besides mine," Marcus said. Justin Anthony Wyrick Jr.—a pseudonym on top of a pseudonym on top of a pseudonym. Justin Anthony Wyrick Jr. had a more authoritative ring to it, in Marcus's opinion, and in a lot of other people's, too. On one day Marcus received and answered 110 questions. Maybe a third of them came from the idly curious, a third from people who were already in some kind of legal trouble, and the final third from people who appeared to be engaged in some sort of odd cost-benefit analysis.

> **Q:** What amount of money must a person steal or gain through fraud before it is considered a felony in Illinois?
> **A:** In Illinois you must have gained $5001+ in an illegal fashion in order to constitute fraud. If you need anything else please write back! Sincerely, Justin Anthony Wyrick Jr.
> **Q:** Can a parole officer prevent a parolee from marrying?
> **A:** Hey! Unless the parolee has "No Marriage" under the special conditions in which he is released, he can marry. If you have any questions, please write back. Sincerely, Justin Anthony Wyrick Jr.

The more questions Marcus answered, the more people who logged onto the boards looking for legal advice wanted to speak only to him. In one two-week stretch he received 943 legal questions and answered 939. When I asked him why he hadn't answered the other four, a look of profound exasperation crossed his broad face. "Traffic law," he said. "I'm sorry, I don't know traffic law." By the end of July he was the number 3 rated expert in criminal law on AskMe.com. Beneath him in the rankings were one hundred and twenty-five licensed attorneys and a wild assortment of ex-cops and ex-cons. The next youngest person on the board was thirty-one.

In a few weeks Marcus had created a new identity for himself: legal wizard. School he now viewed not so much as preparation for a future legal career as material for an active one. He investigated a boondoggle taken by the local school board and discovered it had passed off on the taxpayer what to him appeared to be the expenses for a private party. He brought that, and a lot more, up at a public hearing. Why grown-up people with grown-up legal problems took him seriously was the great mystery Marcus didn't much dwell on—except to admit that it had nothing to do with his legal training. He'd had no legal training, formal or informal. On the top of the Arnold family desk was a thin dictionary, plus stacks and stacks of court cases people from AskMe who had come to rely on Marcus's advice had mimeographed and sent to him, for his review. (The clients sent him the paperwork and he wrote motions, which the clients then passed on to licensed attorneys for submission to a court.) But there was nothing on the desk, or in the house, even faintly resembling a book about the law. The only potential sources of legal information were the family computer and the big-screen TV.

"Where do you find books about the law?" I asked. 20

"I don't," he said, tap-tap-tapping away on his keyboard. "Books are boring. I don't like reading."

"So you go on legal web sites?"

"No."

"Well, when you got one of these questions did you research your answer?"

"No, never. I just know it." 25

"You just know it."

"Exactly."

The distinct whiff of an alternate reality lingered in the air. It was just then that Marcus's mother, Priscilla, came through the front door. She was a big lady, teetering and grunting beneath jumbo-sized sacks of groceries. A long box of donuts jutted out of the top of one.

"Hi, Marcus, what you doing?" she said, gasping for breath.

"Just answering some questions," he said. 30

"What were you answering?" she asked, with real pleasure. She radiated pride.

"I got one about an appellate bond—how to get one," he said. "Another one about the Supreme Court. A petition to dismiss something."

"We got some chili cheese dogs here."

"That's cool."

Priscilla nipped into the kitchen, where she heaped the donuts onto a plate and 35 tossed the dogs into boiling water. Foodstuffs absolved of the obligation to provide vitamins and minerals cavorted with reckless abandon. Strange new smells wafted out over the computer.

"Where did you acquire your expertise?" I asked.

"Marcus was born with it!" shouted Priscilla. Having no idea how to respond, I ignored her.

"What do you mean?" Marcus asked me. He was genuinely puzzled by my question.

"Where does your information come from?"

"I don't know," he said. "Like, I really just don't know." 40

"How can you not know where knowledge comes from?" I asked.

"After, like, watching so many TV shows about the law," he said, "it's just like you know everything you need to know." He gave a little mock shiver. "It's scary. I just know these things."

Again Priscilla shouted from the kitchen. "Marcus has got a gift!"

Marcus leaned back in his chair—every inch the young prodigy—pleased that his mother was saving him the trouble of explaining the obvious to a fool. It was possible to discern certain lines in Marcus's character, but the general picture was still out of focus. He had various personas: legal genius, humble Internet helpmate, honest broker, ordinary kid who liked the Web. Now he cut a figure familiar to anyone who has sat near a front row in school—the fidgety, sweet-natured know-it-all. What he knew, exactly, was unclear. On the Web he had come across to many as a font of legal expertise. In the flesh he gave a more eclectic performance—which was no doubt one reason he found the Internet as appealing as he did. Like Jonathan Lebed, he was the kind of person high school is designed to suppress; and like Jonathan Lebed, he had refused to accept his assigned status. When the real world failed to diagnose his talents, he went looking for a second opinion. The Internet offered him as many opinions as he needed to find one that he liked. It created the opportunity for new sorts of self-perceptions, which then took on a reality all their own.

There was something else familiar about the game Marcus was playing, but it   45
took me a while to put my finger on it. He was using the Internet the way adults often use their pasts. The passage of time allows older people to remember who they were as they would like to have been. Young people do not enjoy access to that particular escape route from their selves—their pasts are still unpleasantly present—and so they tend to turn the other way and imagine themselves into some future adult world. The sentiment that powers their fantasies goes by different names—hope, ambition, idealism—but at bottom it is nostalgia. Nostalgia for the future. These days nostalgia for the future is a lot more fashionable than the traditional kind. And the Internet has made it possible to act on the fantasy in whole new ways.

Priscilla shouted from the kitchen: "Marcus had his gift *in the womb. I could feel it.*"

Now Marcus had his big grin on. "Welcome to my brain," he said.

"What?"

"Welcome to my brain."

He'd said it so much like a genial host offering his guest the comfortable chair   50
that I had to stop myself from saying "Thanks." Behind him was a long picture window overlooking the California desert—the view was the reason Priscilla loved her house. Beyond that, brown mountains. In the middle distance between white desert and brown mountain, a parachute ripped open and a body jerked skyward.

"Let's try this again," I said.

"Okay," he said, cheerfully.

"Basically, you picked up what you know from watching Court TV shows," I said.

"Basically," he said.

"And from these web sites that you browse."   55

"Basically."

Priscilla shouted out from the kitchen, "How many dogs you want, Marcus?"

"Two and some donuts," hollered Marcus.

"What do you think these people would have done if you weren't there to answer their questions?" I asked.

"They would have paid an attorney," he said. But as he said it his big grin vanished   60
and a cloud shadowed his broad, open face. All of a sudden he was the soul of prudence.

It may well have been that he was recalling the public relations fiasco that followed the discovery by a hundred or so licensed attorneys on AskMe.com the true identity of the new expert moving up their ranks. In any case, he lifted his giant palms toward me in the manner of the Virgin Mary resisting the entreaties of the Holy Spirit, and said, "Look, I'm not out there to take business away from other people. That's not my job."

"But you think that legal expertise is overrated?"

"*Completely.*"

Once Marcus attained his high rankings on AskMe.com, a lot of people he didn't really know began to ask for his phone number and his fee structure. For the first time, for some reason he was unable to explain fully, his conscience began to trouble him. He decided it was time to come clean with his age. To do this he changed his expert profile. Where it had read "legal expert," it now read "15 year old intern attorney expert." A few hours after he posted his confession, hostile messages came hurtling toward him. A few of them came from his "clients," but most came from the lawyers and others who competed with him for rankings and prizes and publicity. A small war broke out on the message boards, with Marcus accusing the lawyers of ganging up on him to undermine his number 3 ranking and the lawyers accusing Marcus of not knowing what he was talking about. The lawyers began to pull up Marcus's old answers and bestow on them lowly one-star ratings—thus dragging down his average. (At the time, third parties could score expert answers; after the incident AskMe.com changed its policy.) Then they did something even worse: asked him detailed questions about the finer points of the law. When he couldn't supply similarly detailed answers, they laid into him. Marcus's replies to the e-mail lashings read less like the work of a defense attorney than of a man trying to talk his torturers into untying him:

"I am reporting your abusive response, for it hurts my reputation and my dignity as an expert on this board."

"Please don't e-mail me threats." 65

"You really are picking on me."

"Leave me alone! I am not even a practicing attorney!"

"Please, I beg of you, stop sending me letters saying that you'll be watching me, because you are scaring my parents."

"I really just want to be friends."

"Can't we just be friends?" 70

To which Marcus's wittiest assailant replied, "In your last two posts you've ended by asking that I be your friend. That's like the mortally wounded gladiator asking to be friends with the lion."

On the one hand, the whole episode was absurd—Marcus Arnold was a threat to no one but himself and, perhaps, the people who sought his advice. To practice law you still needed a license, and no fifteen-year-old boy was going to be granted one. At the same time, Marcus had wandered into an arena alive with combustible particles. The Internet had arrived at an embarrassing moment for the law. The knowledge gap between lawyers and non-lawyers had been shrinking for some time, and the Internet was closing it further. Legal advice was being supplied over the Internet, often for free—and it wasn't just lawyers doing the supplying. Students, cops, dicks, even ex-cons went onto message boards to help people with their questions and cases. At the bottom of this phenomenon was a corrosively democratic attitude toward legal knowledge, which the legal profession now simply took for granted. "If you think about the law," the past chairman of the American Bar Association, Richard S. Granat, told the *New York Times,* in an attempt to explain the boom in do-it-yourself Internet legal services, "a large component is just information: Information itself can go a long way to help solve legal problems."

In that simple sentence you could hear whatever was left of the old professional mystique evaporating. The status of lawyering was in flux, had been for some time. An anthology that will cause elitists to weep will one day be culled from the long shelf of diatribes about the descent into mass culture of the American lawyer at the end of the twentieth century. Separate chapters will detail the advent of the billable hour, the 1977 Supreme Court decision permitting lawyers to advertise their services, and a magazine called the *American Lawyer,* which, in the early 1980s, began to publish estimates of lawyers' incomes. Once the law became a business it was on its way to becoming a commodity. Reduce the law to the sum of its information and, by implication, anyone can supply it. That idea had already traveled a long way, and the Internet was helping it to travel faster. After all, what did it say about the law that even a fifteen-year-old boy who had never read a law book could pass to a huge audience as an expert in it? It said that a lot of people felt that legal knowledge was accessible to the amateur. Who knows: maybe they were right. Perhaps legal expertise was overrated. *Completely.*

By its nature the Internet undermined anyone whose status depended on a privileged access to information. But you couldn't fairly blame the Internet for Marcus Arnold, any more than you could blame the Internet for Jonathan Lebed. The Internet was merely using Marcus to tell us something about ourselves: we doubted the value of formal training. A little knowledge has always been a dangerous thing. Now it was becoming a respectable thing. A general collapse in the importance of formal training was a symptom of post-Internet life; knowledge, like the clothing that went with it, was being informalized. Casual thought went well with casual dress.

Technology had put afterburners on the egalitarian notion that anyone-can-do-anything, by enabling pretty much anyone to try anything—especially in fields in which "expertise" had always been a dubious proposition. Amateur book critics published their reviews on Amazon; amateur filmmakers posted their works directly onto the Internet; amateur journalists scooped the world's most powerful newspapers. There was no reason licensed professionals shouldn't be similarly exposed—after all, they were in it for the money just like everyone else. In late 1999 an outfit in Boston called Forrester Research got the novel idea of going out in the field and talking to doctors about the Internet. The subsequent report was called "Why Doctors Hate the Net." There were many reasons. Patients were pestering doctors to offer advice by e-mail so they didn't have to spend hours hanging around waiting rooms. The doctors hadn't figured out how to get paid to answer e-mails. But if they failed to answer e-mail the patients turned elsewhere for their answers. That was another reason doctors hated the Net: the patients were getting uppity. The Net encouraged patients to believe they knew more than they did. They'd walk into the doctor's office in a state of high indignation armed with some printout from an Internet health care site that utterly disproved that the pain in their gut was, as the doctor had claimed, gallstones. The doctors took their mystique even more seriously than the lawyers—in part because that mystique actually helped them to cure people—and they were displeased to be challenged. But at least their business was not directly threatened. No one was going to put his life in the hands of some web site. Not yet.

And so the situation in which Marcus Arnold found himself in the late summer of 2000, while bizarre, was revealing. Marcus had been publicly humiliated by the real lawyers, but it didn't stop him from offering more advice. He clung by his big mitts to a lower ranking. Then the clients began to speak. With pretty much one voice they said: Leave the kid alone! A lot of people seemed to believe that any fifteen-year-old who had risen so high in the ranks of AskMe.com legal experts must be some kind of wizard. They began to seek him out more than ever before; they wanted his, and only his, advice. Marcus wiped himself off and gave it to them. In days his confidence was fully restored. "You always have your critics," he said. "I mean, with the real lawyers, it's a pride issue. They can't let someone who could be their son beat them. Plus they have a lot more time than I do. I'm always stretched for time. Six hours a day of school, four hours of homework, sometimes I can't get on line to answer the questions until after dinner."

In spite of this and other handicaps, Marcus's ranking rebounded. Two weeks after he disclosed his age, he was on the rise; two weeks later he hit number 1. The legal advice he gave to a thousand or so people along the way might not have withstood the scrutiny of the finest legal minds. Some of it was the sort of stuff you could glean directly from Judge Judy; more of it was a simple restating of the obvious in a friendly tone. Marcus didn't have much truck with the details; he didn't handle complexity terribly well. But that was the whole the point of him—he didn't need to. A lot of what a real lawyer did was hand out simple information in a way that made the client feel served, and this Marcus did well. He may have had only the vaguest idea of what he was talking about and a bizarre way of putting what he did know. But out there in the void, they loved him.

Marcus's father, Melvin, worked at a furniture retail outlet two hours' drive from home, and so wasn't usually around when his son was handing out advice on the Internet. Not that it mattered; he wouldn't have known what Marcus was up to in any case. "I'm not the sort of person who gets on the computer," Melvin said when he arrived home and saw Marcus bashing away for my benefit. "I *never* get on the computer, as a matter of fact." And he said this matter-of-factly, in a spirit in no way defiant or angry, just gently resigned to the Way Things Are. "When I need something from the computer," he also said, "I ask Marcus."

"It just gives me more computer time," said Marcus, and resumed his furious typing.

What with the computer smack in the center of the place, the Arnolds' house didn't allow me to talk to Melvin without disrupting Marcus. When Marcus realized that he was about to be forced to listen to whatever his father might have to say about his Internet self, he lost interest. He called for Marc, and the twin bear-boys lumbered out the front door. On the way out he turned and asked me if I knew anyone in Hollywood he might talk to. "I think what I really want to do," he said, "is be an actor." With that final non sequitur, he left me to cross-examine his parents. 80

The first thing that was instantly clear was that, unlike their son, they were aware that their lives were no longer what anyone would call normal. The Lebeds had proved that if your adolescent child was on line, you didn't need to leave your house to feel uprooted. The Arnolds were already uprooted, so they didn't prove anything. They'd moved from Belize to South-Central Los Angeles. They'd moved from there to Perris for a reason, which Melvin now calmly explained to me. At the family's Los Angeles home Marcus's older brother had been murdered. He'd been shot dead in cold blood by an acquaintance in the middle of a family barbecue. The man who shot him had avoided the death penalty. He was up for parole in 2013. "Marcus didn't tell you about that, did he?" asked Melvin, rhetorically. "In my opinion that's how Marcus got interested in the law. He saw that it wasn't fair."

The Arnolds had moved to Perris shortly after their son's murder. Not long after they'd arrived, Marcus asked for a computer. He'd waited until he crashed the top ten on AskMe.com before he let his parents know why, suddenly, he was up all hours bashing away on the family keyboard. His parents had had radically different reactions to the news. His mother nearly burst with pride—she always knew that Marcus was special and the Internet was giving him a chance to prove it. His father was mildly skeptical. He couldn't understand how a fifteen-year-old boy could be functioning as a lawyer. The truth is, Melvin hadn't taken Marcus all that seriously, at least not at first. He assumed he was reacting to the grief of the murder of his older brother. Then the phone started to ring . . . and ring. "These were grown-up people," said Melvin, still incredulous at the events taking place under his roof. "They call this house and ask for Marcus. These people are like forty, forty-five years old and they're talking to Marcus about their legal problems, but they're not including the parents. That's where I get scared, because it's not supposed to work like that."

"Well . . ." says Priscilla. She scrunched up her big friendly face in what was clearly intended to be disapproval. "They're not acknowledging the fact that he's fifteen. They're acknowledging the fact that he can give them some legal advice."

"But the phone," Melvin said, "it is always ringing. These people want Marcus to give them legal advice. I mean, really, it's like what he does, people do as a *job*. And he's doing it right here. I get so frustrated. I always say, 'Marcus, you're talking too much, you're talking too much.'"

"But that's what attorneys do," said Priscilla, "they talk a lot." 85

Melvin gave up on his wife and turned to me to explain. "I tell him to stay off the phone, stay off the computer. This is the thing I keep on saying to him. Nobody else in this house can ever use the phone. There's no way I can stop him, but still . . ."

"But attorneys talk—that's what they do," said Priscilla.

"I don't use the phone anyway, really," said Melvin. "The calls come, they're never mine, you know. It's always Marcus, Marcus, Marcus—people calling him from everywhere."

They were off and running on what was clearly a familiar conversational steeplechase. "I don't understand," I said. "How do all these people have your phone number?" But neither of them was listening. Priscilla, having seized on her main point, was now intent on spearing Melvin on the end of it. "But that's what he's got to do," she said. "That's what attorneys do! Talk!"

"Yeah, but he's *not* an attorney," said Melvin. He turned to me again in a bid for 90 arbitration. "He drives you nuts with his talk. Nuts!"

"How do they get your phone number?" I asked again.

"But he will be one day," said Priscilla. "He has that gift."

"He's a kid," said Melvin.

"How did they get your phone number?" I asked, for the third time.

Priscilla looked up. "Marcus puts it on the Internet," she said. To her it was the 95 most normal of things.

Melvin took a different view. Maybe it was the distinct feeling he had that a lot of Marcus's "clients" had had to stand in line at a pay phone to make their calls. Or that they always seemed to prefer to wait on hold rather than call back later. Or their frantic tones of voice. Whatever the reason, he didn't like it. "I told Marcus," he said, wearily, "that we don't even know who these people are, they might be criminals out there, that you're not supposed to give them our phone number, our address."

Priscilla furrowed her brow and attempted to conjure concern. "What really scared me one time," she said, less with fear than in the spirit of cooperation, "was this lady that he was assisting with her criminal case. The lady sent him the whole book of her court case. I said, 'Marcus, why would you want to take this upon yourself, you've got to tell this lady you're just fifteen years old.' But he didn't listen to me. The point came that the lady actually wanted him to go to court with her, and I said, 'No, we've got to stop it here, because you don't have a license for that, you don't study law.' He said, 'Mom, you've got to drive me to the court. I know what I'm doing.' I said, 'No way, you don't have a license to dictate the law.'"

I could see that her heart wasn't in this soliloquy. She stopped and brightened, as if to say she'd done her best to meet her husband halfway, then said, "But I think all of this Internet is good for Marcus."

"Do you think Marcus knows what he's doing?" I asked.

"Oh yes, very much," she said. "Because there's a lot of times that we would watch 100 these court shows and he would come up with the same suggestions and the same answers like the attorneys would do."

That appeared to settle the matter; even Melvin could not disagree. Marcus knew his Court TV.

"Can you see him charging for this advice?" I asked.

"At what age?" Melvin said. A new alarm entered his voice.

"Thirty."

"I hope," said Melvin, with extreme caution. "I hope he will do well." 105

"He's supposed to have his own law firm by then," said Priscilla.

Note

1. Jonathan Lebed was a fifteen-year-old charged by the Securities and Exchange Commission with fraud after he used the Internet to manipulate stock prices by recommending (on financial message boards) stocks he had purchased. He made more than $800,000 and had to give back only a portion of it. (Editors' note)

CONNECTING PERSONALLY TO THE READING

1. Many teenagers focus obsessively on a single interest and become expert in it, whether the interest is collecting comic books, following the career of a music group, playing video games, or something else. Do you think Marcus is a typical teenager, do you think he is extraordinary, or is he a combination of the two? Explain your answer.

2. Lewis tells us that Marcus has received some of his legal knowledge from Web sites and most of it from watching Court TV and that he speaks "in the self-conscious rapid-fire patter

of a television lawyer." Do you think Marcus is trying on a role or playing a game, or does he take himself seriously as an amateur lawyer? Or is he doing all three?

3. Considering the pleasure Marcus gets in competing for a high ranking on AskMe.com, his boredom with reading and school, his father's comment that Marcus got interested in the law when "he saw that it wasn't fair," and other details you cull from the reading, what do you think motivates Marcus to act as a legal expert?

FOCUSING ON THE ARGUMENT

1. Lewis uses several metaphors to extend the meaning of his descriptions. How do the following metaphors characterize the companies or people being described: a corporate culture as a pancake; a corporate culture as a pyramid; Marcus Arnold as a lumbering bear with huge paws? What ideas, feelings, or opinions—beyond those that Lewis directly states—do these metaphors give us?

2. Lewis's tone changes throughout the article; he alternately sounds amused, ironic, amazed, and contemplative. Find a section of the article that illustrates one of these tones—or a different one—and explain how the tone reinforces the point of that section.

3. Lewis often quotes Marcus, letting him represent himself in his own words. How do Marcus's style of speaking and word choices characterize him? How do the quotations affect your opinion of Marcus and the knowledge he distributes?

4. The main idea of the article is to show the public's faith in legal advice delivered by someone with no legal credentials, yet Lewis often adds details to his narration that seem unrelated to this point—such as the parachuters who jump in Marcus's neighborhood or Marcus's lunch of chili cheese dogs and doughnuts. Why do you think Lewis includes these details? What do they contribute to the article?

SYNTHESIZING IDEAS FROM MULTIPLE READINGS

1. Both Lewis and David Weinberger (selection from *Small Pieces Loosely Joined*, p. 450) see the Internet as a place where people interact in an egalitarian rather than hierarchical way, where people treat each other as peers rather than according to a system of rank. Do you agree that AskMe.com and eBay.com promote nonhierarchical exchanges of knowledge? Explain why or why not.

2. In arguing that much "expert" information is accessible to amateurs, Lewis calls into question the whole notion of "expertise": " Technology had [. . . enabled] pretty much anyone to try anything—especially in fields in which 'expertise' had always been a dubious proposition." Do you think bloggers like Meg Hourihan (Rebecca Mead, "You've Got Blog: How to Put Your Business, Your Boyfriend, and Your Life Online," p. 456) could be called journalists, even though they lack specific training in journalism? Why or why not?

WRITING TO ACT

1. Join an online discussion group on a topic that interests you; one place to find such a group is groups.yahoo.com. Spend at least two weeks reading the conversation of that group (and posting messages, if you like). Then write a short essay on how knowledge is shared in this group. Whose messages seem most respected, most informative, or most reliable? How is authority conveyed? Do you have any way of determining the credentials of those who give advice or post information?

2. With a small group of other students, create an online discussion group in which you dispense advice on a subject you know well, possibly information on how to find housing on your campus or which are the best restaurants in your area. Then write a few paragraphs explaining what qualifies your group to offer information on this subject—what qualifies you as experts?

DAVID WEINBERGER argues that the Internet and the World Wide Web are a new world in which our familiar expectations of space, time, personal identity, and ways of acquiring knowledge are disrupted. To him, the online world is a strange place: "Even the typical, everyday world of the Web is more alien than it at first seems." How strange do you find the Web and the Internet? In what ways do you behave differently there than you do in the rest of your life? Do you agree with Weinberger that common sense "doesn't hold" on the Internet?

WEINBERGER is a former philosophy professor, vice president of marketing, dot-com founder, and one-man strategic marketing company. During the 2004 presidential campaign, he was Howard Dean's Senior Internet Advisor. Today he is a research fellow at the Berkman Center for Internet and Society at Harvard Law School, and he writes prolifically for *Wired, Salon, USA Today,* the *Guardian,* and other periodicals. His books include the critically acclaimed *Small Pieces Loosely Joined,* which this selection is from, and the bestseller *The Cluetrain Manifesto,* which he wrote with Chris Locke. He also maintains a number of blogs.

Selection from *Small Pieces Loosely Joined* (2002)

BY DAVID WEINBERGER

When Michael Ian Campbell used an online alias, no one was suspicious. After all, choosing a name by which you'll be known on the Web is a requirement for using America Online. Known as "Soup81" to his AOL buddies, the eighteen-year-old Campbell was considered a polite, even kind young man in the Florida town where he lived with his mother. At the end of 1999, he had finished his first semester at a community college and was working in a retail store during the day; at night, he pursued his dream by acting in plays at the Cape Coral Cultural Theater. On December 15, he and millions of others were using America Online's "instant messaging" facility to type messages back and forth to their friends old and new. Instant messaging opens a window on your computer screen in which the letters being typed by your conversant show up as they're being typed. It's like watching over the shoulder of someone typing—even the effect of the Delete key is eerily evident—although that person can be thousands of miles away. Indeed, Soup81 was chatting with sixteen-year-old Erin Walton in Colorado, someone he had never met before. He did know something about her though: eight months earlier, a pair of teenagers had killed thirteen people at Walton's high school, Columbine, in Littleton, Colorado.

After some initial chitchat, Campbell typed a warning onto Walton's screen. Don't go to school the next day, his message said, because "I need to finish what begun [sic] and if you do [go to school] I don't want your blood on my hands."

When Walton, understandably shaken, alerted Columbine's school officials, they closed the school for two days and postponed exams. Three days later, the FBI got a court order in Denver forcing AOL to name the person behind the screen name "Soup81." The agents moved in quickly, questioning Campbell for ninety minutes and taking custody of his computer. A judge ordered Campbell to remain in the county jail without bail until his hearing a few days later.[1]

Campbell's mother blamed this aberrant behavior on the death of her son's father a month earlier. Campbell's lawyer, Ellis Rubin, made up a type of insanity—"Internet intoxication"—to excuse it. But Michael Campbell gave a different explanation. On *The Today Show* a few days later, seemingly trying to puzzle out his own behavior, he said that, as a dedicated actor, he was trying on a role. He was seeing what it would be like to be his favorite actor, John Malkovich.

"Internet intoxication" makes about as much sense as the "Twinkie defense"[2]— Dan White's supposed claim that junk food threw off his moral judgment—but at least it acknowledges that something about the Internet contributed to this event. At the very least, had Campbell met Walton in person, his "channeling" of Malkovich would probably have come off as nothing more than a celebrity impression. The Internet allowed Soup81 to assume a persona and become someone that Michael Ian Campbell wasn't. In fact, Soup81 didn't usually go around threatening people online; this seems to have been an isolated incident. Although Soup81's actions on December 15, 1999, were atypical of the tens of millions of chats that take place every day, it is not at all unusual on the Web for someone to "try on" a personality and to switch personalities from chat room to chat room: behavior that would cause your family to plot an intervention off the Web is the norm on the Web. The very basics of what it means to have a self-identity through time—an "inner" consistency, a core character from which all else springs—are in question on the Web.[3]

Michael Campbell is, of course, an exception, which is why he got onto *The Today Show* and the other 300–400 million users of the Web did not. And that's why he served four months in a Florida jail as part of a plea bargain that also forbade him from using the Internet for three years. Fortunately, Campbell's story is not typical. But even the typical, everyday world of the Web is more alien than it at first seems. Take something as ordinary as visiting eBay. For example, I recently visited eBay after deciding that a quilt would make a perfect—or at least safe—housewarming present for a friend moving into his first house . . .

I type "quilt" into the page's search field. In about one second (I have a cable modem), eBay shows me a page listing the first 50 of 8,179 items for sale that include the word "quilt" in their titles, including books about quilts, fabric for making quilts, quilt designs, and quilt stencils. Daunted by the 164 pages of listings, I search again, this time for "homemade quilt" and narrow the list to 16. That seems so few that I reconsider my search query and realize that I should probably search for "handmade" quilts, not "homemade" ones. Sure enough, I now find 248 items, listed according to which auctions are going to be over first. "Stunning Handmade Quilt w/Brilliant Colors" is closing in two hours and twenty-five minutes; its opening bid of $159 has attracted no takers. Too expensive for me, and apparently also for people who know more than I do about quilts. "NEW HANDMADE SMALL COLORFUL QUILT" closes three hours after that; four bidders have pushed the price to $26.09. The picture is small but the explanatory text has a homey touch:

This quilt measures 56x72 and is very colorful. This quilt is new and will last a lifetime. This would be a perfect fathers day gift, or perfect on back of couch. Please e-mail me with any questions. Shipping will be 5.00. Thank you for looking.

Although the eBay page is formulaic, there's enough context for me to make some tentative judgments. The amateurish prose and layout of the page leads me to assume that the seller isn't full-time in the quilt business. But she seems not to have made the quilt herself because there's no mention of how long it took her and no story about why she made it and why she's now giving it up. Maybe this was a housewarming gift she doesn't like and wants to pass on. Could I be wrong about her? Definitely. But in this case it doesn't matter because the price is too far under the $75 I want to pay for this gift. I may be passing up the bargain of the century, but, as a naïve quilt buyer I have to trust the pricing judgments of the other bidders. I go back to the listing of auctions.

Before I can investigate more offerings, my ten-year-old son slams the door and yells up a cheery "Hey-lo!" and I am distracted for the next couple of hours. It's shortly before dinner when I go back to eBay. On page three there's an auction for a red-and-white quilt currently listed at $66. The picture shows a pattern that I think my friend may like; the design can even be construed as a series of Jewish stars if you catch it at the right angle, which my friend will get a kick out of. The text says:

This is a beautiful quilt made by my Great Aunt. It is in excellent condition. The colors are beautiful. It measures 89 × 72. Buyer pays $10 shipping and insurance.

The page tells me that the starting price for the piece was $40 and four people 10 have bid on it so far. This is getting interesting. So, I click on the rating next to the seller's name and eBay takes me to a page of comments from people who have done business with her. Four people have rated her, all have rated her excellent, and each has written a one-line comment praising her to the skies. But I've bought from eBay before and I know how this works: after the sale, the seller and buyer each get to write a brief evaluation. Anything less than lavish praise is taken as a veiled criticism. Grade inflation has hit eBay.

I didn't win that auction. And although my interactions with eBay were simple, they were based on assumptions that are quite different from my real-world assumptions. I assumed no locality for the seller and bidders beyond an expectation that they were probably all on the North American continent; it's possible that some were in other countries, although the complications of the real-world postal system discourage that. But the distancelessness of the Web is just the most obvious of the disconnects between it and the real world. You could even classify them by using some big concepts from the real world, such as space, time, self, and knowledge:

SPACE

eBay is a Web space that occupies no space. Its "near" and "far" are determined by what's linked to what, and the links are based not on contiguity but on human interest. The geography of the Web is as ephemeral as human interest: eBay pulled together a listings page for me based on my interest in handmade quilts while simultaneously building pages for thousands of others who had other, unpredictable interests. Each of us looked across the space that is eBay and saw a vastly different landscape: mine of quilts, yours of Star Wars memorabilia, someone else's of battery chargers.

TIME

Earlier that morning, while waiting for my wife in our town center, I ducked into a store called Ten Thousand Villages that sells world crafts at prices fair to the artisans.[4] For ten minutes I enjoyed being a Yuppie among the Chilean rainsticks and the Djembe drums from Burkina Faso. Then I saw my wife through the window, left the store, and closed the door behind me. Real-world time is a series of ticks to which schedules are tied. My time with eBay was different. As I investigated different auctions, placed a bid, and checked back every few hours to see if I'd been outbid, I felt as if I were returning to a story in progress, waiting for me whenever I wanted. I could break off in the middle when, for example, my son came home, and go back when I had the time. The Web is woven of hundreds of millions of threads like this one. And, in every case, we determine when and how long we will participate, based solely on what suits us. Time like that can spoil you for the real world.

SELF

Buyers and sellers on eBay adopt a name by which they will be known. The eBay name of the woman selling the quilt I was interested in was "firewife30." Firewife30 is an identity, a self, that lives only within eBay. If she's a selfish bastard elsewhere but always acts with honor in her eBay transactions, the "elsewhere" is not a part of firewife30 that I can know about or should particularly care about. The real-world person behind firewife30 may even have other eBay identities. Perhaps she's also SexyUndies who had 132 "sexy items" for sale at eBay while firewife30 was auctioning her quilt. Unlike real-world selves, these selves are intermittent and, most important, they are written. For all we know, firewife30 started out as firewife1 and it's taken her this many drafts to create a self that feels right to her.

KNOWLEDGE

I began my eBay search ignorant about quilts. By browsing among the 248 quilts for sale, I inadvertently received an education. Yes, I could easily use the Web as a research tool, and at times during my quest I ran down some information—"sashing" is a border around each quilt block,[5] and a good quilter gets 10–12 stiches per inch[6]—but I learned more and learned faster by listening to the voices of the quilters on eBay. I got trained in the features to look for, what quilters consider to be boast-worthy, and what the other bidders thought was worth plunking their money down for. This was unsystematic and uncertified knowledge, but because it came wrapped in a human voice, it was richer and, in some ways, more reliable: the lively plurality of voices sometimes can and should outweigh the stentorian voice of experts.

If a simple auction at eBay is based on new assumptions about space, time, self, and knowledge, the Web is more than a place for disturbed teenagers to try out roles and more than a good place to buy cheap quilts.

The Web[7] has sent a jolt through our culture, zapping our economy, our ideas about sharing creative works, and possibly even institutions such as religion and government. Why? How do we explain the lightning charge of the Web? If it has fallen short of our initial hopes and fears about its transformational powers, why did it excite those hopes and fears in the first place? Why did this technology hit our culture like a bolt from Zeus?

Suppose—just suppose—that the Web is a new world that we're just beginning to inhabit. We're like the early European settlers in the United States, living on the edge of the forest. We don't know what's there and we don't know exactly what we need to do to find out: Do we pack mountain climbing gear, desert wear, canoes, or all three? Of course, while the settlers may not have known what the geography of the New World was going to be, they at least knew that there was a geography. The Web, on the other hand, has no geography, no landscape. It has no distance. It has nothing natural in it. It has few rules of behavior and fewer lines of authority. Common sense doesn't hold there, and uncommon sense hasn't yet emerged. No wonder we're having trouble figuring out how to build businesses in this new land. We don't yet even know how to talk about a place that has no soil, no boundaries, no near, no far.

New worlds create new people. This has always been the case because how we live in our world is the same thing as who we are. Are we charitable? Self-centered? Cheerful? Ambitious? Pessimistic? Gregarious? Stoic? Forgiving? Each of these describes how we are engaged with our world but each can also be expressed as the way our world appears to us. If we're egotistical, the world appears to revolve around us. If we're gregarious, the world appears to be an invitation to be with others. If we're ambitious, the world appears to await our conquest. We can't characterize ourselves without simultaneously drawing a picture of how the world seems to us, and we can't describe our world without simultaneously describing the type of people we are. If we are entering a new world, then we are also becoming new people.

Obviously, we're not being recreated from the ground up. We don't talk in an affect-less voice, express curiosity about the ways of earthlings, and get an irresistible urge to mate once every seven years. But we are rewriting ourselves on the Web, hearing voices we're surprised to find coming from us, saying things we might not have expected. We're meeting people we would never have dreamed of encountering. More important, we're meeting new aspects of ourselves. We're finding out that we can be sappier, more caustic, less patient, more forgiving, angrier, funnier, more driven, less demanding, sexier, and more prudish—sometimes within a single ten-minute stretch online. We're falling into email relationships that, stretching themselves over years, imperceptibly deepen, like furrows worn into a stone hallway by the traffic of slippers. We're falling into groups that feel sometimes like parties and sometimes like battles. We're getting to know many more people in many more associations than the physics of the real world permits, and these molecules, no longer bound to the solid earth, have gained both the randomness and the freedom of the airborne. Even our notion of self as a continuous body moving through a continuous map of space and time is beginning to seem wrong on the Web.

If this is true, then for all of the overheated, exaggerated, manic-depressive coverage of the Web, we'd have to conclude that the Web has not yet been hyped enough.

Notes

1. Dave Bryan, "Parent: Teen Accused of Threatening Columbine Student Was 'Bored,'" AP, December 18, 1999; http://www.newstimes.com/archive99/dec1899/naf.htm.

2. In 1978, former San Francisco supervisor Dan White murdered Mayor George Moscone and supervisor Harvey Milk. White was found guilty of involuntary manslaughter rather than first-degree murder because the

20

jury accepted that he was operating under "diminished capacities." According to the Urban Legends Reference Page, the Twinkie defense was never actually offered. Instead, an expert witness testified that White's abandoning of his usual health-food regime was evidence of his deep depression. The witness did not claim that eating junk food *caused* the depression. Barbara and David Mikkelson, 1999, http://www.snopes2.com/spoons/fracture/twinkie.htm.

3. Sherry Turkle has written two excellent and prescient books on the nature of the self online: *The Second Self: Computers and the Human Spirit* (New York: Simon & Schuster, 1984) and *Life on the Screen: Identity in the Age of the Internet* (New York: Simon & Schuster, 1995).

4. Ten Thousand Villages has a Web presence too, of course, at http://www.tenthousandvillages.com/.

5. http://www.i5ive.com/article.cfm/quilts_and_quilting/37365

6. http://charlotte.med.nyu.edu/jamesdj/photos/crafts.html

7. I purposely conflate the Internet and the Web throughout this book. The distinction is very real from the technical and historical perspectives, but it isn't being observed in the public consciousness: email and home pages seem to be part of the same phenomenon even though the former is the Internet and the latter is the Web.

CONNECTING PERSONALLY TO THE READING

1. Weinberger discusses how the Web provides opportunities for people to try on new identities, even to "switch personalities from chat room to chat room," and argues that such identity switching is "the norm on the web." Describe your own experiences—or those of people you know—with identity switching online.

2. Why does Weinberger believe he uses time differently online than he does in real life? Do you agree that people use time differently online?

3. What does Weinberger mean when he claims that "how we live in our world is the same thing as who we are"? In what ways does your personality define the way you behave in the world or how the world appears to you?

4. Weinberger argues that the Web and the Internet have fallen short of people's initial expectations—it has realized neither their greatest fears nor their greatest hopes. Think of an online experience you had for the first time—for example, your first use of e-mail, chat, an online purchase. What did you imagine the experience would be like before you had it, and in what ways did the experience match or contradict your expectations?

FOCUSING ON THE ARGUMENT

1. Weinberger uses personal experience to illustrate larger issues about how the Web and the Internet are changing people's lives. Pick one of the experiences he recounts and explain the idea about the Internet it illustrates. How engaging do you find this strategy?

2. How useful do you find the analogy between users of the Web and the Internet and the European settlers of the United States? What does the analogy reveal about the experience of using the Web/Internet?

3. Weinberger begins his article by telling a story—of how Michael Ian Campbell issued a threat in an online chat and ended up in jail. How appealing do you find this strategy for opening an essay? In what ways does the story help you anticipate issues that Weinberger raises later?

1. Like Michael Lewis in "Pyramids and Pancakes" (p. 438), Weinberger points out that people readily offer information online, but the individual user must decide how reliable this information is. Why is Weinberger inclined to trust his fellow bidders' knowledge of quilts? Why do you think Marcus's readers trust his legal advice?

2. In what ways does Weinberger rely on the online "reputation systems" that Howard Rheingold talks about in "How to Recognize the Future When It Lands on You" (p. 463)? How do these systems work, and why are they important?

WRITING TO ACT

1. Spend some time on eBay or another online auction site, researching a product that interests you. What did you learn about this product that you didn't know before? If you already knew something about the product, how accurate/reliable did you find the information on eBay? Then write a Web page or pamphlet explaining how to get the most reliable information when making purchases online. Upload your Web page to your class Web site or distribute the pamphlet to your classmates.

2. Write a code of behavior for buyers at online auctions, participants in chat rooms, or people interacting in any other online venue. Post your writing on your class or personal Web site, if you have one, or turn it into a poster and get permission to post it in your campus's computer lab.

READING

REBECCA MEAD's article illustrates one online community, a specific blogging community, and shows how important a place it occupies in the life of one of its best-known participants, Meg Hourihan. In some ways, this group is like many real-life ones: people gossip about each other, develop crushes, play tricks on each other, determine who is popular and who "uncool," and even become celebrities. What impression do you get of this community? How appealing does it seem to belong to a group you know primarily through the Internet?

MEAD is a staff writer at the *New Yorker,* where she has worked since 1997. Her previous jobs include contributing editor at *New York* magazine and writer for London's *Sunday Times.* She continues to write freelance articles, including book reviews, for other publications.

READING

You've Got Blog: How to Put Your Business, Your Boyfriend, and Your Life Online (2000)

BY REBECCA MEAD

1

Meg Hourihan was in a bad mood. She had nothing major to worry about, but she was afflicted by the triple malaise of a woman in her late twenties: (a) the weather was lousy; (b) she was working too hard; and (c) she didn't have a boyfriend. Nothing, not even eating, seemed very interesting to her. The only thing that did sound appealing was moving to France and finding a hot new French boyfriend, but even when she talked about that idea she struck a sardonic, yeah-right-like-I'm-really-going-to-do-that kind of tone.

I know this about Meg because I read it a few months ago on her personal website, which is called megnut.com. I've been reading Megnut for a while now, and so I know all kinds of things about its author, like how much she loved Hilary Swank in "Boys Don't Cry," how she wishes there were good fish tacos to be had in San Francisco, and where she lives. I know she's a feminist, and that she writes short stories, and that she's close to her mom. I know that she's a little dreamy and idealistic; that she fervently believes there is a distinction between "dot-com people," who are involved in the Internet for its I.P.O. opportunities, and "Web people," who are in love with the imaginative possibilities presented by the medium, and that she counts herself among the latter.

Meg is one of the founders of a company called Pyra, which produces an Internet application known as Blogger. Blogger, which can be used free on the Internet, is a tool for creating a new kind of website that is known as a "weblog," or "blog," of which Megnut is an example. A blog consists primarily of links to other websites and commentary about those links. Having a blog is rather like publishing your own, online version of *Reader's Digest,* with daily updates: you troll the Internet, and, when you find an article or a website that grabs you, you link to it—or, in weblog parlance, you "blog" it. Then other people who have blogs—they are known as bloggers—read your blog, and if they like it they blog your blog on their own blog.

Blogs often consist of links to articles that readers might otherwise have missed, and thus make for informative reading: it was via an excellent blog called Rebecca's Pocket that I learned, for instance, that the Bangkok transit authority had introduced a ladies-only bus to protect female passengers from strap-hanging molestation. It also led me to a site devoted to burritos, where I underwent an online burrito analysis, in which my personality type was diagnosed according to my favorite burrito elements: "Your pairing of a meat-free burrito and all those fatty toppings indicates a dangerous ability to live with illusions." Blogs often include links to sites that illuminate the matter at hand. For example, when Meg wrote about planting a plumeria cutting, she linked to a site called the Plumeria Place, which included a picture and a description of the plant.

Many bloggers have Internet-related jobs, and so they use their sites to keep other 5 bloggers informed of the latest news in the world of Web design or copyright law. Jason Kottke, a Web designer from Minneapolis who maintains a site called kottke.org, is widely admired among bloggers as a thoughtful critic of Web culture. (On the strength of the picture transmitted by his Webcam, he is also widely perceived as very cute. If you read around among blogs, you find that Kottke is virtually beset by blogging groupies.) Getting blogged by Kottke, or by Meg Hourihan or one of her colleagues at Pyra, is the blog equivalent of having your book featured on "Oprah": it generally means a substantial boost in traffic, enough, perhaps, to earn the blog a mention on beebo.org, which has functioned as a blog best-seller list. (An example from a blog called fairvue.com: "Jason K. linked to Fairvue. My life is now complete.")

The weblog format of links and commentary has been around for some years, but in the early days of weblogging the sites had to be built by hand, one block of code at a time, which meant that they were produced only by a handful of technology mavens. There were a few weblogs that earned a following among nontech civilians— Jim Romenesko's Medianews, a weblog of stories about the media business, is one;

Arts & Letters Daily, a digest of intellectual affairs, is another—but most remained more specialized. A year and a half ago, there were only fifty or so weblogs; now the number has increased to thousands, with blogs like Megnut getting around a thousand visits a day. This growth is due in large part to Blogger, and a couple of other webloging tools such as Pitas and Editthispage, which have made launching a personal website far simpler.

Most of the new blogs are, like Megnut, intimate narratives rather than digests of links and commentary; to read them is to enter a world in which the personal lives of participants have become part of the public domain. Because the main audience for blogs is other bloggers, blogging etiquette requires that, if someone blogs your blog, you blog his blog back. Reading blogs can feel a lot like listening in on a conversation among a group of friends who all know each other really well. Blogging, it turns out, is the CB radio of the Dave Eggers generation. And that is how, when Meg Hourihan followed up her French-boyfriend-depression posting with a stream-of-consciousness blog entry a few weeks later saying that she had developed a crush on someone but was afraid to act on it—"Maybe I've become very good at eluding love, but that's not a complaint, I just want to get it all out of my head and put it somewhere else," she wrote— her love life became not just her business but the business of bloggers everywhere.

2

Pyra, the company that produces Blogger, has its offices on the ground floor of a warehouse building on Townsend Street in SoMa, the former industrial district that is now home to many of San Francisco's Internet businesses. The company, which was founded last year by Evan Williams (who has his own blog, evhead.com) in collaboration with Meg Hourihan, occupies two computer-filled rooms that face each other across an atrium littered with random pieces of office furniture discarded by Internet startups whose fortunes took a dive when the Nasdaq did, last April. Pyra survived the dive, with some help from venture capitalists, and from Mr. and Mrs. Hourihan, Meg's parents. (More recently, Advance Publications, which publishes the *New Yorker,* invested in Pyra.) Still, Ev and Meg ruefully talk about how they managed to get through the summer of 1999, the season of implausible I.P.O.s, without becoming rich.

"We first met at a party," Meg explained, as she and I sat on a battered couch. Ev rolled his desk chair over to join us. Meg, who grew up in Boston and graduated from Tufts with a degree in English, is voluble and given to gesticulation. She is tall and athletic-looking, and has cropped spiky hair that last spring she bleached white-blond after polling the readers of her blog about her hairstyling options. Meg and Ev dated for a while before deciding that their shared passion for the Internet did not translate into a shared passion for each other; but then Ev drafted Meg to help him start Pyra, the goal of which was to develop a Web-based tool that would help project managers share information with co-workers. (They have since been joined by four other friends.)

"I knew she was very good at helping me think about ideas," Ev said. Ev comes 10 from Nebraska. He once blogged an aerial photograph of the family farm and is taciturn and ironic; he has a beetling brow and a Tintin coif. In 1991, he dropped out of the University of Nebraska–Lincoln after a year and launched his first Internet company, for which he still owes his parents money.

Blogger wasn't part of Pyra's original plan; Ev and a colleague, Paul Bausch, built it for fun, and then launched it on the Web one week in the summer of 1999, when

Meg was on vacation. That fall, Blogger found plenty of users among geeks who were glad to have a tool that made weblogging easier; only recently, though, did Ev and Meg set aside their other Pyra plans. "It took us a long time to realize what we had with Blogger," Meg said.

That afternoon, Meg sat down with me at her computer—I tried to stay out of the range of the Webcam that is trained on her whenever she sits at her desk—and showed me how Blogger works. To use Blogger, it helps to know a little of the computer language html, but, once you've set up your site, adding new chunks of text is as easy as sending an email. Meg clicked open the Blogger inputting box, typed a few words, and showed me how she could hit one button and send the text to her site. The creators of Blogger think it may make posting items on the Web a little too easy; a new term, "blogorrhea," has been coined to describe the kind of entries—"I'm tired" or "This sucks"—that are the work of the unimaginative blogger.

While I was sitting at Meg's desk, I noticed the bookmarks that she had on her Web browser. Among them were evhead.com and kottke.org. She had also marked Jason Kottke's Webcam. Jason Kottke was the object of the crush that Meg had described in her blog a few months earlier. They met last March, at South by Southwest, an alternative-culture conference that takes place in Austin every spring.

"I recognized him immediately," Meg wrote in an email to me. "He was taller than I thought he'd be, but I knew it was him." She had been reading his blog, kottke.org, for ages. "I always thought he seemed cool and intelligent . . . but I thought he was a bit conceited. He was so well-known, and he wrote once about taking some online I.Q. tests and he actually posted his results, which I thought was showoffish."

After meeting Jason, Meg changed her mind: "He seemed not at all conceited like I thought, and actually pretty funny and nice, and cute, much cuter than he ever appeared on his Webcam."   15

Meg made sure she had an excuse to stay in touch. She offered to send Jason a customized version of Blogger code for him to try on kottke.org. Once she got back to San Francisco, she said, "I wrote on Megnut that I had a crush, and he emailed me and said, 'Who's the crush on? Spill it, sister.' So I emailed him back and said it was him. He was really surprised." Meg took further electronic action to advance her aims, and altered her website so that it included her ICQ number—the number someone would need to send her an instant message, even though the last thing she wanted was to be inundated with instant messages from strangers. A couple of days later, Jason ICQ'd her for the first time. ("He fell for my trick," she said.) That night, they instant-messaged for three hours. A week later, she shifted technologies again, and called him on the telephone. Then she invited him to San Francisco, and that was that.

Meg and Jason had been dating for two months when I visited San Francisco, and he was due to arrive from Minneapolis for the weekend. Meg told me about a Web device she uses called Flight Tracker: you type in a flight number, and a map is displayed, with an icon representing the location of the airplane. "I always look at it, and think, Oh, he's over Nebraska now," she said.

I already knew that Meg and Jason were involved, because I'd been reading their websites; although neither of them had written anything about the relationship, there were hints throughout their recent entries. Those hints had also been under discussion on a website called MetaFilter. MetaFilter is a "community weblog," which means that anyone who is a member can post a link to it. Most of the posts to MetaFilter are links to news stories or weird websites, but in early June someone named Monkeyboy had linked to a photograph of Meg and Jason looking into Jason's bathroom mirror. The picture was posted on a website belonging to a friend of Meg's who collects photographs of the mirrors of Web celebrities. Monkeyboy also linked to Megnut's "crush" entry, and to an entry that Jason had written on kottke.org about Meg's site design, and he posted them all on MetaFilter with the words "So what's up with this? I think there's something going on here." This generated a lively discussion, with some bloggers furthering the gossip by linking to other blogs whose authors had confessed to having crushes on Jason, while others wrote in suggesting it was none of anyone's business.

When I looked back at Jason's blog for the period just after he met Meg, I found no references to a romance. Jason's style is a little more sober. But there was one entry in which he seemed to be examining the boundary between his Web life and his non-Web life. He'd written that there were things going on in his life that were more personal than the stuff he usually wrote about in his weblog. "Why don't I just write it down somewhere private . . . a Word doc on my computer or in a paper diary?" he asked himself, and his readers. "Somehow, that seems strange to me though. . . . The Web is the place for you to express your thoughts and feelings and such. To put those things elsewhere seems absurd."

One day, I met Meg and Jason for breakfast. Jason, who is twenty-seven, tall, with 20 short hair and sideburns, was wearing jeans and a "Princess Mononoke" T-shirt. She ordered a tofu scramble and soy latte, he had real eggs. I asked what it was like to have their private lives discussed among the members of their virtual community, and they said they thought it was funny. I asked whether they ever included hidden messages to each other in their blogs, an idea that seemed to surprise them. "Well, I did once use that word 'tingly,'" Meg said. Jason blushed.

A few days later, they stoked the gossip further by posting identical entries on their websites: word-for-word accounts of seeing a young girl on a bicycle in the street, and descriptions of the childhood memories that it triggered. Then a strange thing happened. One by one, several bloggers copied the little-girl entry into their blogs, as if they had seen the child on the bicycle, too. Other bloggers started to write parodies of the little-girl entry. Still other bloggers started to post messages to MetaFilter, asking what the hell was going on with all these sightings of little girls. When I sent Meg an email about this outbreak, she wrote back, "I was especially struck by the number of people who thought it was a big prank pulled by the 'popular' kids to make fun of the uncool kids."

3

There have been some ostentatious retreats from the blogging frenzy: last June, one well-known blogger named Derek Powazek announced in his blog that he wanted no part of it anymore, and that instead of addressing himself to the blogger community at large he would henceforth be writing with only a few friends and family members in mind. This announcement provoked a flurry of postings from neophyte bloggers, who feared they were facing the Twilight of Blogging before they had really had a chance to enjoy the Dawn of Blogging.

The people at Pyra, having generated a blog explosion with their Blogger software, aren't entirely happy about the way blogs have developed. "It's like being frustrated with your kid, when you know he could be doing so much more," Ev told me. He and Meg have been developing different uses for Blogger, including ones from which they might actually make some money. One idea is to install Blogger on the intranets of companies, so that it can be used as a means of letting large groups share information. (Cisco is currently experimenting with using Blogger in-house to keep minutes of project meetings up to date.)

Meanwhile, Meg and Ev have developed a whole new level of celebrity status. Not long ago, a group of bloggers created a community blog called The Pyra Shrine. There are posts about how hot Meg is ("Megnut is da bomb. She's one kewl lady") and whether Ev needs a personal assistant ("You know, to make him coffee and get him stuff. I'd do it. For free, even!"). The whole thing is very silly, and completely irresistible if you're a reader of Megnut or Evhead, or, indeed, if you are the creator of Megnut or Evhead. Meg linked to it on her site recently, and wrote, "O.K., I have to admit, this The Pyra Shrine cracks me up."

It was through The Pyra Shrine that I learned, one day last month, that Jason was   25
moving to San Francisco. ("That's a big sacrifice. He must really love her," one of the Shrine contributors had posted.) I emailed Meg, who told me that Jason had taken a new Web design job and was driving across the country; he was probably in Wyoming at that very moment. I remarked that since he was in a car she couldn't use Flight Tracker to see where he was.

"Oh yeah, it's so bad," she wrote back. "I'm so used to being able to communicate with him, or at least check in in some way all the time (Webcam, Flight Tracker, ICQ, email, etc.) and now there's nothing. Well, except for phone at night, but still, seems like nothing compared with what I've gotten used to."

Later that night, I called Meg, and she sounded excited. "He should be here in three or four days," she said. Having mastered the techniques for having a digital relationship, she was finally ready for an analog one; and she hadn't even had to move to France to get it.

Editor's Note: In 2006, Mead wrote an update on Meg and Jason's relationship ("Meg and Jason," New Yorker, June 5, 2006) in which she reported their move together to New York in 2002, their breakup in 2004, their reconnection in 2005, and on May 28, 2006, their marriage. Thousands of people have viewed photographs of their wedding, which Meg posted on her Flickr page.

CONNECTING PERSONALLY TO THE READING

1. Mead points out that through blogs, one's personal business becomes public. Where else in real life or on the Internet do people share their personal lives with relative strangers?

2. Before Meg and Jason became a couple, they had met both virtually and, a few times, in real life. What impressions of Jason did Meg have from his online persona? How was he like or different in person? Consider your impressions of someone you initially encountered either virtually or through some other medium (e.g., by reading his or her writing or by

listening to a friend talk about him or her) and later met face-to-face. What accounted for any differences in your perception of this person? Do you think that the medium through which we perceive people affects our impression of them?

FOCUSING ON THE ARGUMENT

1. To reach readers who may never have seen a blog, Mead often uses analogies—for instance, she compares the celebrity of getting blogged by Jason Kottke or Meg Hourihan with "having your book featured on 'Oprah.'" Find two other analogies in this article, and show how they clarify Mead's point. What do the analogies tell us about the objects being compared?

2. The article is full of telling details, such as what Meg and Jason ate for breakfast when Mead met with them in San Francisco; the online burrito analysis that Mead tried out; the fact that both Jason and Meg borrowed money from their parents for their Internet business. Pick two or three details from the article, and explain why you think Mead mentions them. Given these details, what do you think Mead thinks of the blogging world she describes? Of Jason and Meg?

SYNTHESIZING IDEAS FROM MULTIPLE READINGS

1. Mead distinguishes between people who are interested in the Internet as a stock investment ("dot-com people") and those, like Meg Hourihan, "who are in love with the imaginative possibilities presented by the medium." Into which category would you put Peter Drucker ("Beyond the Information Revolution," p. 472) and Howard Rheingold ("How to Recognize the Future When It Lands on You," p. 463)? Explain your choice.

2. In "Pyramids and Pancakes" (p. 438), Michael Lewis describes how a teenager is accepted online as an expert on the law. In Meg Hourihan's blogging community, which bloggers have authority, and why? What does it take to be respected as an expert in an online group?

WRITING TO ACT

1. Every day for at least a week visit one of the blogs Mead mentions in her article. Develop an opinion on how this blog functions as a community. Some of the questions you might ask yourself are, How receptive are the contributors to newcomers? What kind of relationships have been developed within the community? What seems to be the purpose of this Web log? Then write an article for your campus newspaper describing your findings.

2. Write a code of behavior for an online community you belong to—a chat room, blog, MOO, e-mail conversation—or if you prefer, for use of any electronic medium in public (e.g., watching TV, talking on a cell phone, using a laptop computer). Then get permission to post your rules of etiquette in the appropriate public space.

3. Create a Web log for your class, where your classmates can post their ideas and respond to one another's postings. Start the conversation by writing a comment about a topic discussed in the course or an event happening in the news or on campus. Add at least one link to your post.

4. On the Web, go to Blogdex and find a Web log on a topic that interests you. Follow the blog for at least a week, and write a response to one of its posts.

HOWARD RHEINGOLD defines "smart mobs" as large groups of people who work cooperatively by communicating electronically. Often these people do not know each other, yet Rheingold believes that they have already produced significant social action; he cites, for example, the Filipino group "People Power II," that in 2001 was able to oust President Estrada through demonstrations organized via cell phone messages. If you or your friends use mobile electronic devices, such as personal digital assistants or cell phones, what effects do these devices have on your (or your friends') life?

RHEINGOLD both worked on and wrote about the earliest personal computers, and he was investigating the influence of online communities in the 1980s, long before most people had heard of the Internet. The former editor of the *Whole Earth Review,* Rheingold also helped found *Hotwired* (of *Wired* magazine) and *Electric Minds.* His books include *The Virtual Community* and *Smart Mobs.* In his spare time, he enjoys painting his shoes.

How to Recognize the Future
When It Lands on You (2002) | BY HOWARD RHEINGOLD

The first signs of the next shift began to reveal themselves to me on a spring afternoon in the year 2000. That was when I began to notice people on the streets of Tokyo staring at their mobile phones instead of talking to them. The sight of this behavior, now commonplace in much of the world, triggered a sensation I had experienced a few times before—the instant recognition that a technology is going to change my life in ways I can scarcely imagine. Since then the practice of exchanging short text messages via mobile telephones has led to the eruption of subcultures in Europe and Asia. At least one government has fallen, in part because of the way people used text messaging. Adolescent mating rituals, political activism, and corporate management styles have mutated in unexpected ways.

I've learned that "texting," as it has come to be called, is only a small harbinger of more profound changes to come over the next ten years. My media moment at Shibuya Crossing was only my first encounter with a phenomenon I've come to call "smart mobs." When I learned to recognize the signs, I began to see them everywhere—from barcodes to electronic bridge tolls.

The other pieces of the puzzle are all around us now but haven't joined together yet. The radio chips designed to replace barcodes on manufactured objects are part of it. Wireless Internet nodes in cafes, hotels, and neighborhoods are part of it. Millions of people who lend their computers to the search for extraterrestrial intelligence are part of it. The way buyers and sellers rate each other on the Internet auction site eBay is part of it. At least one key global business question is part of it: Why is the Japanese company DoCoMo profiting from enhanced wireless Internet services while U.S. and European mobile telephony operators struggle to avoid failure?

When you piece together these different technological, economic, and social components, the result is an infrastructure that makes certain kinds of human actions possible that were never possible before. The "killer apps" of tomorrow's mobile infocom industry won't be hardware devices or software programs but social practices.

The most far-reaching changes will come, as they often do, from the kinds of relationships, enterprises, communities, and markets that the infrastructure makes possible.

Smart mobs consist of people who are able to act in concert even if they don't know each other. The people who make up smart mobs cooperate in ways never before possible because they carry devices that possess both communication and computing capabilities. Their mobile devices connect them with other information devices in the environment as well as with other people's telephones. Dirt-cheap microprocessors are beginning to permeate furniture, buildings, and neighborhoods; products, including everything from box tops to shoes, are embedded with invisible intercommunicating smartifacts. When they connect the tangible objects and places of our daily lives with the Internet, handheld communication media mutate into wearable remote-control devices for the physical world.

Within a decade, the major population centers of the planet will be saturated with trillions of microchips, some of them tiny computers, many of them capable of communicating with each other. Some of these devices will be telephones, and they will also be supercomputers with the processing power that only the Department of Defense could muster a couple of decades ago. Some devices will read barcodes and send and receive messages to radio-frequency identity tags. Some will furnish wireless, always-on Internet connections and will contain global positioning devices. As a result, large numbers of people in industrial nations will have a device with them most of the time that will enable them to link objects, places, and people to online content and processes. Point your device at a street sign, announce where you want to go, and follow the animated map beamed to the box in your palm, or point at a book in a store and see what the *Times* and your neighborhood reading group have to say about it. Click on a restaurant and warn your friends that the service has deteriorated.

These devices will help people coordinate actions with others around the world—and, perhaps more importantly, with people nearby. Groups of people using these tools will gain new forms of social power, new ways to organize their interactions and exchanges just in time and just in place. Tomorrow's fortunes will be made by the businesses that find a way to profit from these changes, and yesterday's fortunes are already being lost by businesses that don't understand them. As with the personal computer and the Internet, key breakthroughs won't come from established industry leaders but from the fringes, from skunkworks and startups and even associations of amateurs. *Especially* associations of amateurs.

Although it will take a decade to ramp up, mobile communications and pervasive computing technologies, together with social contracts that were never possible before, are already beginning to change the way people meet, mate, work, fight, buy, sell, govern, and create. Some of these changes are beneficial and empowering, and some amplify the capabilities of people whose intentions are malignant. Large numbers of small groups, using the new media to their individual benefit, will create emergent effects that will nourish some existing institutions and ways of life and dissolve others. Contradictory and simultaneous effects are likely: People might gain new powers at the same time we lose old freedoms. New public goods could become possible, and older public goods might disappear.

When I started looking into mobile telephone use in Tokyo, I discovered that Shibuya Crossing was the most mobile-phone-dense neighborhood in the world:

80 percent of the 1,500 people who traverse that madcap plaza at each light change carry a mobile phone.[1] I took that coincidence as evidence that I was on the right track, although I had only an inkling of how to define what I was tracking. It had not yet become clear to me that I was no longer looking for intriguing evidence about changing techno-social practices, but galloping off on a worldwide hunt for the shape of the future.

I learned that those teenagers and others in Japan who were staring at their mobile phones and twiddling the keyboards with their thumbs were sending words and simple graphics to each other—messages like short emails that were delivered instantly but could be read at any time. When I looked into the technical underpinnings of telephone texting, I found that those early texters were walking around with an always-on connection to the Internet in their hands. The tingling in my forebrain turned into a buzz. When you have a persistent connection to the Internet, you have access to a great deal more than a communication channel.

A puzzling problem troubles those who understand the possibilities inherent in a mobile Internet: The potential power of connecting mobile devices to the Internet has been foreseen and hyped recently, but with the exception of DoCoMo, no company has yet created significant profits from wireless Internet services. The dotcom market collapse of 2001, accompanied by the even larger decline in value of global telecommunication companies, raised the question of whether any existing enterprises will have both the capital and the savvy to plug the Internet world into mobile telephony and make a successful business out of it.

Forecasting the technical potential of wireless Internet is the easy part. I knew that I should expect the unexpected when previously separate technologies meet. In the 1980s, television-like display screens plus miniaturized computers added up to a new technology with properties of its own: personal computers. PCs evolved dramatically over twenty years; today's handheld computer is thousands of times more powerful than the first Apple PC. Then PCs mated with telecommunications networks and multiplied in the 1990s to create the Internet, again spawning possibilities that neither of the parent technologies exhibited in isolation. Again, the new hybrid medium started evolving rapidly; my Internet connection today is thousands of times faster than my modem of the early 1980s. Then the Web in the late 1990s put a visual control panel on the Net and opened it to hundreds of millions of mainstream users. What's next in this self-accelerating spiral of technological, economic, and social change?

Next comes the mobile Net. Between 2000 and 2010, the social networking of mobile communications will join with the information-processing power of networked PCs. Critical mass will emerge some time after 2003, when more mobile devices than PCs will be connected to the Internet.[2] If the transition period we are entering in the first decade of the twenty-first century resembles the advent of PCs and the Internet, the new technology regime will turn out to be an entirely new medium, not simply a means of receiving stock quotes or email on the train or surfing the Web while walking down the street. Mobile Internet, when it really arrives, will not be just a way to do old things while moving. It will be a way to do things that couldn't be done before.

Anybody who remembers what mobile telephones looked like five years ago has a sense of the pace at which handheld technology is evolving. Today's mobile devices are not only smaller and lighter than the earliest cell phones, they have become tiny multimedia Internet terminals. I returned to Tokyo a year and a half after I first noticed people using telephones to send text between tiny black and white screens. On my most recent visit in the fall of 2001, I conducted my own color videoconference conversations via the current version of high-speed, multimedia, "third-generation" mobile phones. Perhaps even more important than the evolution of color and video screens in telephone displays is the presence of "location awareness" in mobile telephones. Increasingly, handheld devices can detect, within a few yards, where they are located on a continent, within a neighborhood, or inside a room.

These separate upgrades in capabilities don't just add to each other; mobile, multimedia, location-sensitive characteristics multiply each other's usefulness. At the same time, their costs drop dramatically. As we will see . . . , the driving factors of the mobile, context-sensitive, Internet-connected devices are Moore's Law (computer chips get cheaper as they grow more powerful), Metcalfe's Law (the useful power of a network multiplies rapidly as the number of nodes in the network increases), and Reed's Law (the power of a network, especially one that enhances social networks, multiplies even more rapidly as the number of different human groups that can use the network increases). Moore's Law drove the PC industry and the cultural changes that resulted, Metcalfe's Law drove the deployment of the Internet, and Reed's Law will drive the growth of the mobile and pervasive Net.

The personal handheld device market is poised to take the kind of jump that the desktop PC made between 1980 and 1990, from a useful toy adopted by a subculture to a disruptive technology that changes every aspect of society. The hardware upgrades that make such a jump possible are already in the product pipeline. The underlying connective infrastructure is moving toward completion.

After a pause to recover from the collapse of the telecommunications economic bubble of the 1990s, the infrastructure for global, wireless, Internet-based communication is entering the final stages of development. The pocket videophone I borrowed in Tokyo was proof that a high-speed wireless network could link wireless devices and deliver multimedia to the palm of my hand. The most important next step for the companies that would deploy this technology and profit from it has nothing to do with chips or network protocols but everything to do with business models, early adopters, communities of developers, and value chains. It's not just about building the tools anymore. Now it's about what people use the tools to do.

How will human behavior shift when the appliances we hold in our hands, carry in our pockets, or wear in our clothing become supercomputers that talk to each other through a wireless mega-Internet? What can we reasonably expect people to do when they get their hands on the new gadgets? Can anyone foresee which companies will drive change and detect which businesses will be transformed or rendered obsolete by it? These questions first occurred to me on that spring day in Tokyo, but I didn't think about it again until another sight on a street halfway around the world from Shibuya Crossing caught my attention.

Sitting at an outdoor café in Helsinki a few months after I noticed the ways that people were using Japanese "i-mode" telephones, I watched five Finns meet and talk on the sidewalk. Three were in their early twenties. Two were old enough to be the younger people's parents. One of the younger persons looked down at his mobile phone while he was talking to one of the older people. The young man smiled and then showed the screen of his telephone to his peers, who looked at each other and

15

smiled. However, the young man holding the device didn't show his mobile phone's screen to the older two. The sidewalk conversation among the five people flowed smoothly, apparently unperturbed by the activities I witnessed. Whatever the younger three were doing, it was clearly part of an accepted social code I knew nothing about. A new mode of social communication, enabled by a new technology, had already diffused into the norms of Finnish society.

At that moment I recalled the odd epiphany I had experienced at Shibuya Crossing the previous spring. Faint lines began to connect the dots. My internal future-detectors switched from a mild tingle to a persistent buzz.

20

Twice before in the past twenty years I've encountered something that convinced me in an instant that my life and the lives of millions of other people would change dramatically in coming years. On both occasions, I was drawn into a personal and intellectual quest to understand these possible changes. The first experience that propelled me on one of these intellectual expeditions was the sensation of using the graphical user interface that enabled non-programmers to operate computers by pointing and clicking. My 1985 book *Tools for Thought: The History and Future of Mind-Expanding Technology* presented my arguments that the PC could make possible an intellectual and creative expansion as influential as the changes triggered by the printing press.[3]

Within a few years of writing about them, the mind-amplifying gizmos I had futurized about had become part of my own life. My personal computer was a magic typewriter. Then I plugged my PC into my telephone, and I entered into social cyberspace. I spent more and more time online, reading and writing messages to computer bulletin boards, in chat rooms and electronic mailing lists. My 1993 book, *The Virtual Community,* examined the social phenomena I saw emerging from the early days of the Internet era.[4] Because of these previous experiences, I was prepared to pay attention that day in March 2000, when I first watched people in Tokyo thumbing text messages on their mobile phone keypads.

We're only seeing the first-order ripple effects of mobile-phone behavior now—the legions of the oblivious, blabbing into their hands or the air as they walk, drive, or sit in a concert and the electronic tethers that turn everywhere into the workplace and all the time into working time. What if these are just foreshocks of a future upheaval? I've learned enough from past technology shifts to expect the second-order effects of mobile telecommunications to bring a social tsunami. Consider a few of the early warning signs:

- The "People Power II" smart mobs in Manila who overthrew the presidency of President Estrada in 2001 organized demonstrations by forwarding text messages via cell phones.[5]
- A Web site, http://www.upoc.com, enables fans to stalk their favorite celebrities in real time through Internet-organized mobile networks and provides similar channels for journalists to organize citizen-reporters on the fly. The site makes it easy for roving phone tribes to organize communities of interest.
- In Helsinki and Tokyo you can operate vending machines with your telephone and receive directions on your wireless organizer that show you how to get from where you are standing to where you want to go.[6]

- "Lovegety" users in Japan find potential dates when their devices recognize another Lovegety in the vicinity broadcasting the appropriate pattern of attributes. Location-based matchmaking is now available on some mobile phone services.[7]
- When I'm not using my computer, its processor searches for extraterrestrial intelligence. I'm one of millions of people around the world who lend their computers to a cooperative effort—distributing parts of problems through the Internet, running the programs on our PCs while the machines are idle, and assembling the results via the Net. These computation collectives produce enough supercomputing power to crack codes, design medicines, or render digital films.[8]

Location-sensing wireless organizers, wireless networks, and community supercomputing collectives all have one thing in common: *They enable people to act together in new ways and in situations where collective action was not possible before.* An unanticipated convergence of technologies is suggesting new responses to civilization's founding question, How can competing individuals learn to work cooperatively?

As indicated by their name, smart mobs are not always beneficial. Lynch mobs and   25
mobocracies continue to engender atrocities. The same convergence of technologies that opens new vistas of cooperation also makes possible a universal surveillance economy and empowers the bloodthirsty as well as the altruistic. Like every previous leap in technological power, the new convergence of wireless computation and social communication will enable people to improve life and liberty in some ways and to degrade it in others. The same technology has the potential to be used as both a weapon of social control and a means of resistance. Even the beneficial effects will have side effects.

We are moving rapidly into a world in which the spying machinery is built into every object we encounter. Although we leave digital traces of our personal lives with our credit cards and Web browsers today, tomorrow's mobile devices will broadcast clouds of personal data to invisible monitors all around us as we move from place to place. We are living through the last years of the long era before sensors are built into the furniture. The scientific and economic underpinnings of pervasive computing have been building for decades, and the social side-effects are only beginning to erupt. The virtual, social, and physical worlds are colliding, merging, and coordinating.

Don't mistake my estimates of the power of the coming technology with unalloyed enthusiasm for its effects. I am not calling for an uncritical embrace of the new regime, but for an informed consideration of what we're getting ourselves into. We have an opportunity now to consider the social implications of this new technological regime as it first emerges, before every aspect of life is reordered.

Online social networks are human activities that ride on technical communications infrastructures of wires and chips. When social communication via the Internet became widespread, people formed support groups and political coalitions online. The new social forms of the last decade of the twentieth century grew from the Internet's capability for many-to-many social communication. The new social forms of the early twenty-first century will greatly enhance the power of social networks.

Since my visits to Tokyo and Helsinki, I've investigated the convergence of portable, pervasive, location-sensitive, intercommunicating devices with social practices that make the technologies useful to groups as well as individuals. Foremost among these social practices are the "reputation systems" that are beginning to spring up online—computer-mediated trust brokers. The power of smart mobs comes in part from the way age-old social practices surrounding trust and cooperation are being mediated by new communication and computation technologies.

In this coming world, the acts of association and assembly, core rights of free so- 30 cieties, might change radically when each of us will be able to know who in our vicinity is likely to buy what we have to sell, sell what we want to buy, know what we need to know, want the kind of sexual or political encounter we also want. As online events are woven into the fabric of our physical world, governments and corporations will gain even more power over our behavior and beliefs than large institutions wield today. At the same time, citizens will discover new ways to band together to resist powerful institutions. A new kind of digital divide ten years from now will separate those who know how to use new media to band together from those who don't.

Knowing who to trust is going to become even more important. Banding together, from lynch mobs to democracies, taps the power of collective action. At the core of collective action is reputation—the histories each of us pull behind us that others routinely inspect to decide our value for everything from conversation partners to mortgage risks. Reputation systems have been fundamental to social life for a long time. In intimate societies, everyone knows everyone, and everyone's biography is an open, if not undisputed, book. Gossip keeps us up to date on who to trust, who other people trust, who is important, and who decides who is important.

Today's online reputation systems are computer-based technologies that make it possible to manipulate in new and powerful ways an old and essential human trait. Note the rise of Web sites like eBay (auctions), Epinions (consumer advice), Amazon (books, CDs, electronics), Slashdot (publishing and conversation) built around the contributions of millions of customers, enhanced by reputation systems that police the quality of the content and transactions exchanged through the sites.[9] In each of these businesses, the consumers are also the producers of what they consume, the value of the market increases as more people use it, and the aggregate opinions of the users provide the measure of trust necessary for transactions and markets to flourish in cyberspace.

Reputation reports on eBay give prospective auction bidders a sense of the track record of the otherwise anonymous people to whom they may trustingly mail a check. Ratings of experts on Epinions make visible the experience of others in trusting each expert's advice. Moderators on Slashdot award "karma points" that make highly knowledgeable, amusing, or useful posts in an online conversation more visible than those considered less insightful.

Wireless devices will take reputation systems into every cranny of the social world, far from the desktops to which these systems are currently anchored. As the costs of communication, coordination, and social accounting services drop, these devices make possible new ways for people to self-organize mutual aid. It is now technologically possible, for example, to create a service that would enable you to say to your handheld device: "I'm on my way to the office. Who is on my route and is looking for a ride in my direction right now—and who among them is recommended by my most trusted friends?"

Wireless communication technologies and the political regimes that regulate 35 their use are a key component of smart mob infrastructure. One can sit in a restaurant in Stockholm or in the atrium of a business building in San Francisco and connect to unprotected or publicly available wireless networks with a laptop computer. Will ad hoc coalitions of wireless Internet enthusiasts create a grassroots network that can challenge the power of established infrastructure providers? . . .

Loss of privacy is perhaps the most obvious shadow side of technological cooperation systems. In order to cooperate with more people, I need to know more about them, and that means that they will know more about me. The tools that enable cooperation also transmit to a large number of others a constellation of intimate data about each of us. In the recent past, it was said that digital information technology, such as the magnetic strips on credit cards, leaves a "trail of electronic breadcrumbs" that can be used to track individuals. In the future, the trail will become a moving cloud as individuals broadcast information about themselves to devices within ten yards, a city block, or the entire world. Although there is room for speculation about how quickly the new tools will be adopted, certainly over the next several decades inexpensive wireless devices will penetrate into every part of the social world, bringing efficiencies to the production of snooping power. The surveillance state that Orwell feared was puny in its power in comparison to the panoptic web we have woven around us. Detailed information about the minute-by-minute behaviors of entire populations will become cost-effective and increasingly accurate. Both powerfully beneficial and powerfully dangerous potentials of this new tracking capability will be literally embedded in the environment.

Cooperative effort sounds nice, and at its best, it is the foundation of the finest creations of human civilizations, but it can also be nasty if the people who cooperate share pernicious goals. Terrorists and organized criminals have been malevolently successful in their use of smart mob tactics. A technological infrastructure that increases surveillance on citizens and empowers terrorists is hardly utopian. Intrusions on individual privacy and liberty by the state and its political enemies are not the only possible negative effects of enhanced technology-assisted cooperation. In addition, profound questions about the quality and meaning of life are raised by the prospect of millions of people possessing communication devices that are "always on" at home and work. How will mobile communications affect family and societal life? . . .

Before people who hold stakes in tomorrow's technological civilization can hope to address the social challenges posed by smart mob technologies, we have to know what the issues are, what they imply, and useful ways to think about them. . . . I believe that our destiny is not (yet) determined by technology, that our freedom and quality of life do not (yet) have to be sacrificed to make us into more efficient components of a global wealth-generating machine.

I also know that beneficial uses of technologies will not automatically emerge just because people hope they will. Those who wish to have some influence on the outcome must first know what the dangers and opportunities are and how to act on them. Such knowledge does not guarantee that the new tools will be used to create a humane, sustainable world. Without such knowledge, however, we will be ill equipped to influence the world our grandchildren will inhabit.

Notes

1. The Shibuya Crossing in Tokyo, Japan, has the highest mobile phone density in the world. On weekdays an average of 190,000 people and on weekends an average of 250,000 people pass this crossing per day (Source: CCC, Tsutaya), around 1,500 people traverse at each light change, and 80 percent of them carry a mobile phone. <http://nooper.co.jp/showcase/gallery.php?s=4&l=en> (24 January 2002).

2. Karlin Lillington, "Mobile but Without Direction," *Wired News,* 21 September 2000, <http://www.wired.com/news/business/0,1367,38921,00.html> (28 January 2002).

3. Howard Rheingold, *Tools for Thought: The History and Future of Mind-Expanding Technology* (New York: Simon & Schuster, 1985).

4. Howard Rheingold, *The Virtual Community: Homesteading on the Electronic Frontier* (Reading, Mass.: Addison-Wesley, 1993).

5. Arturo Bariuad, "Text Messaging Becomes a Menace in the Philippines," *Straits Times,* 3 March 2001.

6. Lisa Takeuchi Cullen, "Dialing for Dollars," *Time Magazine* 157 (22), 4 June 2001, <http://www.timeinc.net/time/interactive/business/money_np.html> (4 February 2002). See also: Kevin Werbach, "Location-Based Computing: Wherever You Go, There You Are," *Release 1.0* 18 (6), June 2000, <http://release1.ed-venture.com/abstracts.cfm?Counter=8096700> (4 February 2002).

7. "Japan's Lonely Hearts Find Each Other with 'Lovegety,'" *CNN.com,* 7 June 1998, <http://www.cnn.com/WORLD/asiapcf/9806/07/fringe/japan.lovegety/> (26 January 2002).

8. Howard Rheingold, "You Got the Power," *Wired* 8.08, August 2000, <http://www.wired.com/wired/archive/8.08/comcomp.html> (29 March 2002).

9. See: eBay, <http://www.ebay.com>; Epinions, <http://www.epinions.com>; Slashdot, <http://www.slashdot.org>; and Plastic, <http://www.plastic.com>.

CONNECTING PERSONALLY TO THE READING

1. Rheingold believes that computers "are already beginning to change the way people meet, mate, work, fight, buy, sell, govern, and create." Which of these changes have you personally experienced or observed? What is different about the computer-based method of meeting, mating, working, and so on?

2. Rheingold argues that smart mobs can be beneficial or dangerous. What dangers does he see? Have you or has anyone you know suffered as the result of surveillance technology or other "digital traces of our personal lives"?

FOCUSING ON THE ARGUMENT

1. Rheingold uses two concrete personal experiences to anchor more abstract ideas—his speculations about the future. What did he witness in Tokyo and Helsinki, and what ideas about the future did these experiences evoke in him?

2. Rheingold expresses both concern for potential abuse of mobile technologies and enthusiasm for their potential benefits. How would you characterize the tone of this article? What language does Rheingold use to create this tone?

SYNTHESIZING IDEAS FROM MULTIPLE READINGS

1. Rheingold argues that the most influential innovations in computer technology will not be "hardware devices or software programs but social practices." Do you think Peter Drucker ("Beyond the Information Revolution," p. 472) would agree with this assessment? Why, or why not?

2. Rheingold believes that the "key breakthroughs" in computer technology will come, not from known leaders in the computer industry, but from "the fringes," including amateurs. What form of education does Nicholas Negroponte ("Creating a Culture of Ideas," p. 479)

propose that would nurture students' imaginations and thus make this kind of pioneering development possible?

1. Spend a few hours on a Web site in which users publish book reviews or otherwise evaluate other users' work: for example, book reviews on Amazon.com, assessments of buyers and sellers on eBay.com, or reputation of writers on Slashdot.com. Analyze the reviews; then send an e-mail to the owners of the Web site, explaining why you do or do not find the assessments credible.

2. In his description of an interaction he observed among people in a café in Helsinki, Rheingold notes that one person showed an image on his mobile phone to the young members of his group, but did not share it with the older people standing next to them. Rheingold seems puzzled by an act that might seem rude in the United States, but concludes that the behavior was "clearly part of an accepted social code I knew nothing about." Write a social code for the use of mobile phones on your campus. Indicate which actions are acceptable and which are not. Then get permission to post your code in several visible public places.

READING

PETER DRUCKER, in his discussion of the Industrial Revolution, shows how a new technology can quickly create a chain of events that lead to profound social changes: the steam engine, for example, made it easy for textile manufacturers to produce large quantities of cotton fabric. This increased production created a need for more cotton and thus more agricultural workers to grow the cotton plant: the result was the expansion of slavery. Consider two other technologies that Drucker mentions. What was their social and psychological impact, and how did this impact come about?

DRUCKER (1909–2005) was born in Australia and moved to the United States in 1937. He was a professor of social science and management at the Claremont Graduate University in California for more than thirty years. In addition to publishing thirty-five books—most on society and economics—he also wrote a column for the *Wall Street Journal* for twenty years and contributed essays to a wide range of publications, both scholarly and popular. In 2002, he was awarded the Presidential Medal of Freedom.

Beyond the Information Revolution (1999)

BY PETER DRUCKER

The truly revolutionary impact of the Information Revolution is just beginning to be felt. But it is not "information" that fuels this impact. It is not "artificial intelligence." It is not the effect of computers and data processing on decision making, policymaking, or strategy. It is something that practically no one foresaw or, indeed, even talked about ten or fifteen years ago: *e-commerce*—that is, the explosive emergence of the Internet as a major, perhaps eventually *the* major, worldwide distribution channel for goods, for services, and, surprisingly, for managerial and professional jobs. This is profoundly changing economies, markets, and industry structures; products and services and their flow; consumer segmentation, consumer values, and consumer behavior; jobs and labor markets. But the impact may be even greater on societies and politics and, above all, on the way we see the world and ourselves in it.

At the same time, new and unexpected industries will no doubt emerge, and fast. One is already here: biotechnology. And another: fish farming. Within the next fifty years fish farming may change us from hunters and gatherers on the seas into "marine pastoralists"—just as a similar innovation some 10,000 years ago changed our ancestors from hunters and gatherers on the land into agriculturists and pastoralists.

It is likely that other new technologies will appear suddenly, leading to major new industries. What they may be is impossible even to guess at. But it is highly probable—indeed, nearly certain—that they will emerge, and fairly soon. And it is nearly certain that few of them—and few industries based on them—will come out of computer and information technology. Like biotechnology and fish farming, each will emerge from its own unique and unexpected technology.

Of course, these are only predictions. But they are made on the assumption that the Information Revolution will evolve as several earlier technology-based "revolutions" have evolved over the past 500 years, since Gutenberg's printing revolution, around 1455. In particular the assumption is that the Information Revolution will be like the Industrial Revolution of the late eighteenth and early nineteenth centuries. And that is indeed exactly how the Information Revolution has been during its first fifty years.

THE RAILROAD

The Information Revolution is now at the point at which the Industrial Revolution   5
was in the early 1820s, about forty years after James Watt's improved steam engine (first installed in 1776) was first applied, in 1785, to an industrial operation—the spinning of cotton. And the steam engine was to the first Industrial Revolution what the computer has been to the Information Revolution—its trigger, but above all its symbol. Almost everybody today believes that nothing in economic history has ever moved as fast as, or had a greater impact than, the Information Revolution. But the Industrial Revolution moved at least as fast in the same time span, and had probably an equal impact if not a greater one. In short order it mechanized the great majority of manufacturing processes, beginning with the production of the most important industrial commodity of the eighteenth and early nineteenth centuries: textiles. Moore's Law asserts that the price of the Information Revolution's basic element, the microchip, drops by 50 percent every eighteen months. The same was true of the products whose manufacture was mechanized by the first Industrial Revolution. The price of cotton textiles fell by 90 percent in the fifty years spanning the start of the eighteenth century. The production of cotton textiles increased at least 150-fold in Britain alone in the same period. And although textiles were the most visible product of its early years, the Industrial Revolution mechanized the production of practically all other major goods, such as paper, glass, leather, and bricks. Its impact was by no means confined to consumer goods. The production of iron and ironware—for example, wire—became mechanized and steam-driven as fast as did that of textiles, with the same effects on cost, price, and output. By the end of the Napoleonic Wars the making of guns was steam-driven throughout Europe; cannons were made ten to

twenty times as fast as before, and their cost dropped by more than two-thirds. By that time Eli Whitney had similarly mechanized the manufacture of muskets in America and had created the first mass-production industry.

These forty or fifty years gave rise to the factory and the "working class." Both were still so few in number in the mid-1820s, even in England, as to be statistically insignificant. But psychologically they had come to dominate (and soon would politically also). Before there were factories in America, Alexander Hamilton foresaw an industrialized country in his 1791 *Report on Manufactures.* A decade later, in 1803, a French economist, Jean-Baptiste Say, saw that the Industrial Revolution had changed economics by creating the "entrepreneur."

The social consequences went far beyond factory and working class. As the historian Paul Johnson has pointed out, in *A History of the American People* (1997), it was the explosive growth of the steam-engine-based textile industry that revived slavery. Considered to be practically dead by the Founders of the American Republic, slavery roared back to life as the cotton gin—soon steam-driven—created a huge demand for low-cost labor and made breeding slaves America's most profitable industry for some decades.

The Industrial Revolution also had a great impact on the family. The nuclear family had long been the unit of production. On the farm and in the artisan's workshop husband, wife, and children worked together. The factory, almost for the first time in history, took worker and work out of the home and moved them into the workplace, leaving family members behind—whether spouses of adult factory workers or, especially in the early stages, parents of child factory workers.

Indeed, the "crisis of the family" did not begin after the Second World War. It began with the Industrial Revolution—and was in fact a stock concern of those who opposed the Industrial Revolution and the factory system. (The best description of the divorce of work and family, and of its effect on both, is probably Charles Dickens's 1854 novel *Hard Times.*)

But despite all these effects, the Industrial Revolution in its first half century only mechanized the production of goods that had been in existence all along. It tremendously increased output and tremendously decreased cost. It created both consumers and consumer products. But the products themselves had been around all along. And products made in the new factories differed from traditional products only in that they were uniform, with fewer defects than existed in products made by any but the top craftsmen of earlier periods.

There was only one important exception, one new product, in those first fifty years: the steamboat, first made practical by Robert Fulton in 1807. It had little impact until thirty or forty years later. In fact, until almost the end of the nineteenth century more freight was carried on the world's oceans by sailing vessels than by steamships.

Then, in 1829, came the railroad, a product truly without precedent, and it forever changed economy, society, and politics.

In retrospect it is difficult to imagine why the invention of the railroad took so long. Rails to move carts had been around in coal mines for a very long time. What could be more obvious than to put a steam engine on a cart to drive it, rather than have it pushed by people or pulled by horses? But the railroad did not emerge from the cart in the mines. It was developed quite independently. And it was not intended to carry freight. On the contrary, for a long time it was seen only as a way to carry people.

Railroads became freight carriers thirty years later, in America. (In fact, as late as the 1870s and 1880s the British engineers who were hired to build the railroads of newly Westernized Japan designed them to carry passengers—and to this day Japanese railroads are not equipped to carry freight.) But until the first railroad actually began to operate, it was virtually unanticipated.

Within five years, however, the Western world was engulfed by the biggest boom history had ever seen—the railroad boom. Punctuated by the most spectacular busts in economic history, the boom continued in Europe for thirty years, until the late 1850s, by which time most of today's major railroads had been built. In the United States it continued for another thirty years, and in outlying areas—Argentina, Brazil, Asian Russia, China—until the First World War.

The railroad was the truly revolutionary element of the Industrial Revolution, for   15
not only did it create a new economic dimension but also it rapidly changed what I would call the *mental geography*. For the first time in history human beings had true mobility. For the first time the horizons of ordinary people expanded. Contemporaries immediately realized that a fundamental change in mentality had occurred. (A good account of this can be found in what is surely the best portrayal of the Industrial Revolution's society in transition, George Eliot's 1871 novel *Middlemarch*.) As the great French historian Fernand Braudel pointed out in his last major work, *The Identity of France* (1986), it was the railroad that made France into one nation and one culture. It had previously been a congeries of self-contained regions, held together only politically. And the role of the railroad in creating the American West is, of course, a commonplace in U.S. history.

ROUTINIZATION

Like the Industrial Revolution two centuries ago, the Information Revolution so far—that is, since the first computers, in the mid-1940s—has only transformed processes that were here all along. In fact, the real impact of the Information Revolution has not been in the form of "information" at all. Almost none of the effects of information envisaged forty years ago have actually happened. For instance, there has been practically no change in the way major decisions are made in business or government. But the Information Revolution has routinized traditional processes in an untold number of areas.

The software for tuning a piano converts a process that traditionally took three hours into one that takes twenty minutes. There is software for payrolls, for inventory control, for delivery schedules, and for all the other routine processes of a business. Drawing the inside arrangements of a major building (heating, water supply, sewerage, and so on) such as a prison or a hospital formerly took, say, twenty-five highly skilled draftsmen up to fifty days; now there is a program that enables one draftsman to do the job in a couple of days, at a tiny fraction of the cost. There is software to help people do their tax returns and software that teaches hospital residents how to take out a gall bladder. The people who now speculate in the stock market online do exactly what their predecessors in the 1920s did while spending hours each day in a brokerage office. The processes have not been changed at all. They have been routinized, step by step, with a tremendous saving in time and, often, in cost.

The psychological impact of the Information Revolution, like that of the Industrial Revolution, has been enormous. It has perhaps been greatest on the way in which young children learn. Beginning at age four (and often earlier), children now rapidly develop computer skills, soon surpassing their elders; computers are their toys and their learning tools. Fifty years hence we may well conclude that there was no "crisis of American education" in the closing years of the twentieth century—there was only a growing incongruence between the way twentieth century schools taught and the way late twentieth century children learned. Something similar happened in the sixteenth century university, a hundred years after the invention of the printing press and movable type. . . .

THE MEANING OF E-COMMERCE

E-commerce is to the Information Revolution what the railroad was to the Industrial Revolution—a totally new, totally unprecedented, totally unexpected development. And like the railroad 170 years ago e-commerce is creating a new and distinct boom, rapidly changing the economy, society, and politics.

One example: A mid-sized company in America's industrial Midwest, founded in the 1920s and now run by the grandchildren of the founder, used to have some 60 percent of the market in inexpensive dinnerware for fast-food eateries, school and office cafeterias, and hospitals within a hundred-mile radius of its factory. China is heavy and breaks easily, so cheap china is traditionally sold within a small area. Almost overnight this company lost more than half of its market. One of its customers, a hospital cafeteria where someone went "surfing" on the Internet, discovered a European manufacturer that offered china of apparently better quality at a lower price and shipped cheaply by air. Within a few months the main customers in the area shifted to the European supplier. Few of them, it seems, realize—let alone care—that the stuff comes from Europe.

In the new mental geography created by the railroad, humanity mastered distance. In the mental geography of e-commerce, distance has been eliminated. There is only one economy and only one market. . . .

LUTHER, MACHIAVELLI, AND THE SALMON

The railroad made the Industrial Revolution accomplished fact. What had been revolution became establishment. And the boom it triggered lasted almost a hundred years. The technology of the steam engine did not end with the railroad. It led in the 1880s and 1890s to the steam turbine, and in the 1920s and 1930s to the last magnificent American steam locomotives, so beloved by railroad buffs. But the technology centered on the steam engine and in manufacturing operations ceased to be central. Instead the dynamics of the technology shifted to totally new industries that emerged almost immediately after the railroad was invented, not one of which had anything to do with steam or steam engines. The electric telegraph and photography were first, in the 1830s, followed soon thereafter by optics and farm equipment. The new and different fertilizer industry, which began in the late 1830s, in short order transformed agriculture. Public health became a major and central growth industry, with quarantine, vaccination, the supply of pure water, and sewers, which for the first time in history made the city a more healthful habitat than the countryside. At the same time came the first anesthetics.

With these major new technologies came major new social institutions: the modern postal service, the daily paper, investment banking, and commercial banking, to name just a few. Not one of them had much to do with the steam engine or with the technology of the Industrial Revolution in general. It was these new industries and institutions that by 1850 had come to dominate the industrial and economic landscape of the developed countries.

This is very similar to what happened in the printing revolution—the first of the technological revolutions that created the modern world. In the fifty years after 1455, when Gutenberg had perfected the printing press and movable type he had been working on for years, the printing revolution swept Europe and completely changed its economy and its psychology. But the books printed during the first fifty years, the ones called incunabula, contained largely the same texts that monks, in their scriptoria, had for centuries laboriously copied by hand: religious tracts and whatever remained of the writings of antiquity. Some 7,000 titles were published in those first fifty years, in 35,000 editions. At least 6,700 of these were traditional titles. In other words, in its first fifty years printing made available—and increasingly cheap—traditional information and communication products. But then, some sixty years after Gutenberg, came Luther's German Bible—thousands and thousands of copies sold almost immediately at an unbelievably low price. With Luther's Bible the new printing technology ushered in a new society. It ushered in Protestantism, which conquered half of Europe and, within another twenty years, forced the Catholic Church to reform itself in the other half. Luther used the new medium of print deliberately to restore religion to the center of individual life and of society. And this unleashed a century and a half of religious reform, religious revolt, religious wars.

At the very same time, however, that Luther used print with the avowed intention of restoring Christianity, Machiavelli wrote and published *The Prince* (1513), the first Western book in more than a thousand years that contained not one biblical quotation and no reference to the writers of antiquity. In no time at all *The Prince* became the "other best seller" of the sixteenth century, and its most notorious but also most influential book. In short order there was a wealth of purely secular works, what we today call literature: novels and books in science, history, politics, and, soon, economics. It was not long before the first purely secular art form arose, in England—the modern theater. Brand-new social institutions also arose: the Jesuit order, the Spanish infantry, the first modern navy, and, finally, the sovereign national state. In other words, the printing revolution followed the same trajectory as did the Industrial Revolution, which began 300 years later, and as does the Information Revolution today. 25

What the new industries and institutions will be, no one can say yet. No one in the 1520s anticipated secular literature, let alone the secular theater. No one in the 1820s anticipated the electric telegraph, or public health, or photography.

CONNECTING PERSONALLY TO THE READING

1. In describing the sweeping social changes created by the railroad, Drucker indicates that the railroad changed the way people thought: it changed their "mental geography." What specific change is he referring to? How did it come about? Do you think it is possible for a technological innovation to so change people's habits that they perceive the world differently? Why or why not?

2. Consider how you have gone about shopping for clothes, books, music, or other items over the past ten years. Have the places or methods by which you do your shopping changed over time? Why or why not?

FOCUSING ON THE ARGUMENT

1. Drucker uses an extended analogy—comparing the nineteenth-century Industrial Revolution with the modern computer age—to support his argument that we are in the midst of a revolution. Analogies typically serve to make an abstract idea comprehensible; that is, the author compares something the reader is familiar with (e.g., the development of the railroad) with something the reader cannot know (how computers will change the way we think). How useful is the Industrial Revolution/computer age analogy to your understanding of Drucker's assertions about the computer age? What parts of it are most or least helpful?

2. Drucker's essay assumes that the reader is familiar with many of the cultural events he mentions, such as Machiavelli's book *The Prince* or the Protestant Reformation in Europe. Which events were most familiar to you? What information did you have before reading the article that enriched your understanding of the article's references? Which references to historical events were unfamiliar to you?

SYNTHESIZING IDEAS FROM MULTIPLE READINGS

1. Drucker believes that today's educational practices, developed largely in the pre-computer era, are incongruent with the way today's children learn. Do you think Nicholas Negroponte ("Creating a Culture of Ideas," p. 479) would agree with this assessment? Why or why not?

2. John Berger ("Ways of Seeing," Chapter 8, p. 519) discusses how a new technology—the camera—changed the public's relationship to works of art. What changes is Berger referring to, and how do they illustrate Drucker's ideas about the power of technology?

WRITING TO ACT

1. With a group of classmates, write a survey, asking at least twenty people how a particular technology (e.g., online shopping or cell phones) has changed their lives. You might consider limiting your subjects to a specific demographic group, such as college students or people who work in a particular industry. Create five to ten questions to ask this group. Then see if you notice a pattern. Write a brief article describing your findings.

2. Interview your parents, asking them if their shopping habits have changed over the past twenty-five years. For example, have they switched from small grocery stores to large chains, do they browse in bookstores or do most of their book shopping online, do they frequent discount malls or online auctions? Discuss with them the reasons for the change or lack of change. Then write an article explaining your conclusions.

READING

NICHOLAS NEGROPONTE argues that many of the values that the United States holds dear as a culture—a willingness to take young people's ideas seriously, tolerance for differences of all kinds, respect for those who try and fail—nurture in individuals the spirit of innovation. At the same time, however, he argues that our education system and much of the workplace discourages creativity, and he suggests ways of reorganizing these systems so that they cultivate new ideas. Do you agree with Negroponte that homogeneous cultures, with strict norms and shared beliefs, discourage people from thinking creatively, whereas diverse cultures are more hospitable to innovation? Think of a culture that you know, perhaps a student residence or a special interest group you belong to. How diverse is this group? How tolerant is it of those who don't conform to its central beliefs or forms of expected behavior?

NEGROPONTE, computer scientist, founder and chairman of the Massachusetts Institute of Technology's Media Lab, together with the Media Lab faculty, started the One Laptop Per Child project to extend Internet access to students of developing countries. Negroponte designed a $140 laptop for this program. He is also the author of *Being Digital*, a *New York Times* best seller, and *The Architecture Machine*.

Creating a Culture of Ideas (2003)

BY NICHOLAS NEGROPONTE

Innovation is inefficient. More often than not, it is undisciplined, contrarian, and iconoclastic; and it nourishes itself with confusion and contradiction. In short, being innovative flies in the face of what almost all parents want for their children, most CEOs want for their companies, and heads of states want for their countries. And innovative people are a pain in the ass.

Yet without innovation we are doomed—by boredom and monotony—to decline. So what makes innovation happen, and just where do new ideas come from? The basic answers—providing a good educational system, encouraging different viewpoints, and fostering collaboration—may not be surprising. Moreover, the ability to fulfill these criteria has served the United States well. But some things—the nature of higher education among them—will have to change in order to ensure a perpetual source of new ideas.

One of the basics of a good system of innovation is diversity. In some ways, the stronger the culture (national, institutional, generational, or other), the less likely it is to harbor innovative thinking. Common and deep-seated beliefs, widespread norms, and behavior and performance standards are enemies of new ideas. Any society that prides itself on being harmonious and homogeneous is very unlikely to catalyze idiosyncratic thinking. Suppression of innovation need not be overt. It can be simply a matter of people's walking around in tacit agreement and full comfort with the status quo.

A very heterogeneous culture, by contrast, breeds innovation by virtue of its people, who look at everything from different viewpoints. America, the so-called melting pot, is seen by many as having no culture (with either a capital *C* or a lowercase *c*). In rankings of students in industrial countries, U.S. high school students come across as average, at best, in reading, mathematics, and science. And unfortunately, the nation is unrivaled in gun-related crimes among young people. Yet, looking back over the past century, the United States has accounted for about a third of all Nobel prizes and has produced an unrivaled outpouring of innovations—from factory automation to the integrated circuit and gene splicing—that are the backbone of worldwide economic growth.

I see two reasons for this. One is that 5 we do not stigmatize those who have tried and been unsuccessful. In fact, many venture capitalists are more, not less, likely to invest in somebody who has failed with an earlier startup than in someone who is launching his or her first company. The real disappointment is when people do not learn from their mistakes.

The other reason is that we are uniquely willing to listen to our young. In many cultures, age carries too much weight. Experience is rewarded over imagination, and respect can be too deferential. In some cultures, people are given jobs on the basis of age, creating a sedentary environment stifling to the young. Remember the saying "Children are to be seen and not heard"? Well, look at the economic growth created by such "children" as Bill Gates and Michael Dell, to name just two.

That's the good news. But when it comes to nurturing our youth, we have to do better. I am especially concerned about early education, which can (and usually does) have a profoundly negative effect on creativity. In the race to understand what children learn, we are far too enthusiastic about celebrating their successes. What is more fascinating is what children do wrong. Even the concept of "wrong" should get some attention. Though the wind is not made by leaves flapping, as some children guess, the theory is sufficiently profound that it should not be dismissed out of hand. In fact, disassembling erroneous concepts is one of the best ways to find new ideas. The process is akin to debugging a computer program and has almost nothing to do with drill and practice (which is once again becoming a cornerstone of schooling).

Our biggest challenge in stimulating a creative culture is finding ways to encourage multiple points of views. Many

engineering deadlocks have been broken by people who are not engineers at all. This is simply because perspective is more important than IQ. The irony is that perspective will not get kids into college, nor does it help them thrive there. Academia rewards depth. Expertise is bred by experts who work with their own kind. Departments and labs focus on fields and subfields, now and then adding or subtracting a domain. Graduate degrees, not to mention tenure, depend upon tunneling into truths and illuminating ideas in narrow areas.

The antidote to such canalization and compartmentalization is being interdisciplinary, a term that is at once utterly banal and, in advanced studies, describes an almost impossible goal. Interdisciplinary labs and projects emerged in the 1960s to address big problems spanning the frontiers of the physical and social sciences, engineering, and the arts. The idea was to unite complementary bodies of knowledge to address issues that transcended any one skill set. Fine. Only recently, however, have people realized that interdisciplinary approaches can bring enormous value to some very small problems and that interdisciplinary environments also stimulate creativity. In maximizing the differences in backgrounds, cultures, ages, and the like, we increase the likelihood that the results will not be what we had imagined.

Two additional ingredients are needed 10 to cultivate new ideas. Both have to do with maximizing serendipity. First, we need to encourage risk. This is particularly hard in midcareer and often flies in the face of peer review and the mechanisms for corporate advancement. This is simply because risk, on its own, can look pretty stupid. People who look around corners are exposed to failure and ridicule, and thus they must find buoyancy, or support, within their own environment. If they don't, counterintuitive ideas will remain so.

The second ingredient is encouragement for openness and idea sharing—another banality nearly impossible to achieve. At the digital bubble's peak, being open about ideas was particularly hard for computer scientists because people saw riches coming from *not* sharing their ideas. Students would withhold ideas until after graduation. As one person held his or her cards close, another followed, and as a result, many research labs declined in value and effectiveness. In this regard, thank God the bubble has burst.

Not so many years ago, Bell Labs conducted so much research it could easily house some very high-risk programs, including the so-called blue-sky thinking that led to information theory and the discovery of the cosmic microwave background radiation. But the world benefited, and sometimes AT&T did too.

Now, Bell Labs is a shadow of its former self, subdivided several times through AT&T's 1984 divestiture and subsequent split into Lucent, NCR, and the parent firm. Moreover, it is not alone. As the economy sags and companies trim their expenses, some of the first cuts are in high-risk or open-ended research programs. Even if the research budget does not drop, the nature of projects is prone to be more developmental than really innovative. If the trend continues, eventually we will suffer a deficit of new ideas. Already, fewer and fewer big corporations are focusing on new ideas. And the formation of startups has come almost to a standstill.

More than ever before, in the new "new economy," research and innovation will need to be housed in those places where there are parallel agendas

and multiple means of support. Universities, suitably reinvented to be interdisciplinary, can fit this profile because their other "product line," besides research, is people. When research and learning are combined, far greater risks can be taken and the generation of ideas can be less efficient. Right now, only a handful of U.S. universities constitute such "research universities." More will have to become so. Universities worldwide will have to follow.

Industry can outsource basic research, just as it does many other operations. That means innovation has to become a precompetitive phenomenon—something Japan understood in the early 1980s, when its Ministry of International Trade and Industry (now the Ministry of Economy, Trade, and Industry) funded Japanese companies' collaboration on robotics, artificial intelligence, and semiconductor manufacturing. While this approach does not always work, it can be far more effective than most companies assume. Costs are shared, different viewpoints are nourished, and innovation stands a chance for survival in even the worst economic times.

The ability to make big leaps of 15 thought is a common denominator among the originators of breakthrough ideas. Usually this ability resides in people with very wide backgrounds, multidisciplinary minds, and a broad spectrum of experiences. Family influences, role models, travel, and living in diverse settings are obvious contributors, as are educational systems and the way cultures value youth and perspective. As a society, we can shape some of these. Some we can't. A key to ensuring a stream of big ideas is accepting these messy truths about the origin of ideas and continuing to reward innovation and celebrate emerging technologies.

1. Consider the characteristics that Negroponte considers to be essential for innovative think-ing. How has your education helped (or not helped) you to develop these characteristics?

2. Do you agree with Negroponte that, as a culture, the United States does not stigmatize people who fail? Give examples to illustrate your answer.

1. Negroponte begins his article by seeming to argue against the innovativeness he wants to foster: that is, the characteristics he ascribes to innovative people are often "the opposite of what most parents want for their children." How effective is this strategy as an opening? How does it prepare you for the argument that follows, in which he outlines the necessary conditions for fostering innovative thinking?

2. One of Negroponte's rhetorical strategies is a style that is professorial, yet not stuffy, com-bining highly literate word choices and sentence structures with relaxed conversational ones. Find examples of both of these styles in his article and explain what makes them effective or ineffective.

1. Both Howard Rheingold ("How to Recognize the Future When It Lands on You," p. 463) and Negroponte believe that cooperation among people can produce powerful results. What specific kinds of cooperation do they refer to, and what benefits have accrued when people worked together?

2. Like Peter Drucker in "Beyond the Information Revolution" (p. 472), Negroponte draws on experiences from history to illustrate the potential of technological development. Compare one of Drucker's historical references with one of Negroponte's, and explain the point each reference illustrates.

1. Research an important invention, tracing how it developed and who was responsible. Then write a short article showing how the evolution of this invention reflects (or fails to reflect) the conditions Negroponte considers essential to innovation.

2. Think of a course you have taken at any point in your education that has fostered the kind of creativity that Negroponte praises. Write a letter to the teacher or administrator (or both) responsible for the course, explaining why you value what you learned.

ANDY CARVIN believes that the ability to use online media is a basic civil right, one that is cur-rently unavailable to many people in the United States. To correct this problem, the Internet needs to be accessible to all people, not just those who can afford computers; it must also offer information and hospitable online communities that have value to all potential users. In addition, Carvin argues that the Digital Divide is also an education issue: illiteracy must be overcome, and classroom lessons will need to include online interaction. Do you agree that online access is so important that it is a basic civil right? Why or why not?

CARVIN is the program director of the EDC Center for Media and Community, and he coordinates the Digital Divide Network, an online community seeking ways to confront the digital divide; its membership of over 7,000 is composed of activists and business executives, as well as policymakers and academic researchers. In addition to authoring *EdWeb: Exploring Technology and Social Reform,* an online education resource, he also maintains the popular Web log, *Andy Carvin's Waste of Bandwidth.*

Mind the Gap: The Digital Divide as the Civil Rights Issue of the New Millennium (2000)   BY ANDY CARVIN

The Digital Divide is one of the most important civil rights issues facing our modern information economy.

In the years since the start of the Internet Revolution, the American public has been exposed to more than its fair share of overused catchphrases. Way back in the early 1990s, then-Senator Al Gore spoke of an Information Superhighway that would connect the country's citizens to an overwhelming variety of telecommunications opportunities. We read about the near-Messianic coming of a 500-channel universe in which we'll be able to relish a mind-numbing array of programming options, from The Jack Russell Terrier Channel to Ex!, The Ex-Convicts Network. Countless Web sites and multimedia products boast about their "interactivity" when in truth the only interactivity they offer is in choosing which hyperlink to press next. And consider the phrase "click here"—before the advent of the Internet it would have been seen as a completely baffling command. Now it's the Cyber Age equivalent of a welcome mat: Click here and enter the Web site of your dreams.

But despite the media's penchant for beating to death anything to do with the Internet, a new phrase has recently entered the public's online lexicon, one that actually carries significant societal ramifications: the "Digital Divide." In the most basic sense, the Digital Divide is the ever-growing gap between those people and communities who have access to information technology and those who do not (in other words, the haves and have-nots.) The Digital Divide has been on the radar screens of those of us in the policy world for a while now, but over the course of 1999 its profile was raised as more political leaders took an interest in the subject.

The Digital Divide may seem like an intangible concept to some, but studies have begun to articulate it in no uncertain terms. Consider these statistics from the U.S. Department of Commerce:

- Households earning incomes over $75,000 are over twenty times more likely to have home Internet access than those at the lowest income levels.
- Only 6.6 percent of people with an elementary school education or less use the Internet.
- In rural areas, those with college degrees are eleven times more likely to have a home computer and twenty-six times more likely to have home Internet access than those with an elementary school education.
- People with college degrees or higher are ten times more likely to have Internet access at work [than] persons with only some high school education.

Such statistics should not be taken lightly. The Digital Divide is one of the most   5
important civil rights issues facing our modern information economy. As telecommunications increasingly entwines itself with educational, social, financial, and employment opportunities, those communities lacking access will find themselves falling
further behind the rest of society. The Internet has the potential to empower its users
with new skills, new perspectives, new freedoms, even new voices; those groups who
remain sequestered from the technology will be further segregated into the periphery
of public life.

In schools, we've seen the Digital Divide tackled head-on with the implementa-
tion of the E-Rate program. Each year tens of thousands of schools receive over $2 bil-
lion in federal telecommunications subsidies to help support classroom Internet
access. Though some schools still haven't felt the benefits of the E-Rate, many others
have: Over 50 percent of classrooms nationwide now have Internet access. Real
progress is being made.

Whether the issue is in schools or in communities, the Digital Divide is finally
beginning to receive the attention it deserves. But as we try to develop a long-term
strategy for combating the divide, it begs an important question: *Is the Digital Divide
essentially an access issue?* In one sense, of course, the question is a no-brainer. There is
a widening gap between those who have access to information technology and those
who don't; therefore, when dealing with the Digital Divide we need to concentrate on
giving more people Internet access.

But giving people access doesn't instantly solve the manifold woes of our communities and schools. If it did, every kid with Internet access would be getting straight
A's and every adult with access would be gainfully employed and prosperous. It's just
not that simple. Technology access is only one small piece of a much larger puzzle, a
puzzle that if solved might help raise the quality of life for millions of people. None of
us can rightfully say we've found all the individual pieces yet, but some of the pieces
are obvious enough that we can begin to put the Digital Divide puzzle together:

The Digital Divide is about content. The value of the Internet can be directly correlated to the value of its content. If all you can find online is shopping, Pokémon trading
clubs, and porn, you could make a pretty good argument that it's not very important to
give people access to the Internet. As anyone who has used it knows, the Internet can
offer a wealth of opportunities for learning and personal enhancement, but we've only
scratched the surface in terms of its potential. As more underprivileged and disenfranchised communities gain access, the Internet itself must provide the right tools so people are able to take advantage of and use the online medium for more varied purposes,
more learning styles, more languages and cultures. The Internet may feel like a diverse
place, but when compared with the wealth of diversity and knowledge reflected by humanity in the real world, it's still pretty weak. Until the Net contains content that has
true value to all of its potential users it will remain a place for the elite.   10

The Digital Divide is about literacy. As much as we hate to admit it, functional illiteracy amongst adults is one of America's dirty little secrets. Millions of adults struggle
to fill out forms, follow written instructions, or even read a newspaper. A National
Adult Literacy Survey conducted in the early 1990s suggested that as many as 44 million American adults—almost one out of every four—were functionally illiterate, while
another 50 million adults were plagued by limited literacy. We often talk about the

importance of information literacy when it comes to using the Internet. Information literacy is an obviously vital part of the equation, but how can we expect to address and conquer the Digital Divide when nearly half of all American adults can't even process written information competently? Literacy must be tackled at the most basic level in order to afford more people the opportunity to use technology effectively.

The Digital Divide is about pedagogy. Internet access in schools isn't worth a hill of beans if teachers aren't prepared to take full advantage of technology. Research has shown that educators who are resistant to constructivist, or participatory, teaching practices are less likely to utilize the Internet in their lessons, while educators who are more comfortable with constructivist practices are more likely to do so. Teachers who employ more real-world interaction are thus more inclined to employ online interaction. How can professional development be reformed to take these differences into account?

The Digital Divide is about community. One of the greatest strengths of the Internet is in its facility for fostering community. Communities often appear in the most low-tech of places: You can surf the Web until your knuckles implode and yet not feel like you've actually bonded with anyone, but you can subscribe to a simple e-mail listserv and join a gathering of people who have been enjoying each others' wisdom for years. It's paramount for people coming to the Internet for the first time to have opportunities to join existing communities and forge new communities of their own. Public spaces must be preserved online so that people can gather without feeling like direct marketing or more popular and powerful voices are crowding them out. If people can't build meaningful relationships online, how can they be expected to gravitate to it?

These five puzzle pieces—access, content, literacy, pedagogy, and community—may not be enough to complete the entire Digital Divide puzzle, but they go a long way in providing a picture of what's at stake. Giving people access to technology is important, but it's just one of many issues that need to be considered. Schools, libraries, and community centers are taking that first step in getting wired, but they must also consider the needs of the learners, the teachers, and the communities that support them.

We must continue fighting the scourge of illiteracy—among students, their parents, and among the community—by expanding formal and informal opportunities that improve reading and critical-thinking skills. We must demand engaging content from online producers and refuse to buy into mediocre content when it doesn't suit our teaching needs. We must encourage all learners to be creators as well, sharing their wise voices both online and offline. And we must open our schools and libraries to more connections with our communities—no computer lab or training room should sit idle during evening and weekend hours. These are but a few examples of what the education community can do.

The Digital Divide is real, and it will only get worse if we ignore it. Click here to change the world.   15

CONNECTING PERSONALLY TO THE READING

1. Do you know anyone who does not have access to the Internet? Do you agree that that person's life would be improved with such access? Why or why not?

2. Carvin believes one of the most important strengths of the Internet is access to online communities. How important is such access in your life? Explain your answer.

1. Carvin's article can be seen as an extended definition of the expression "Digital Divide." What are some of the different techniques he uses to define this term?

2. Carvin uses several visual devices that are easy to take for granted: division of his article into paragraphs, italics, and a bulleted list. How does each of these devices help the reader follow Carvin's argument? How do they draw attention to parts of the text that Carvin wants to emphasize?

3. How would you characterize Carvin's tone when he talks about each of the following: the media, politicians, and teachers? Does he have a different attitude toward each of these entities? How can you tell?

SYNTHESIZING IDEAS FROM MULTIPLE READINGS

1. Carvin believes that teachers should use "constructivist" practices, in which students work on projects they find meaningful rather than primarily listen to lectures—that is, they learn by doing. Do you think Carvin would approve of the ideas about education that Nicholas Negroponte ("Creating a Culture of Ideas," p. 479) advances? Why or why not?

2. Carvin argues that the Internet offers its users "new skills, new perspectives, new freedoms, even new voices," opportunities he considers empowering. Which specific skills, perspectives, freedoms, or voices do Michael Lewis ("Pyramids and Pancakes," p. 438) and Howard Rheingold ("How to Recognize the Future When It Lands on You," p. 463) discuss? In what ways are these changes empowering?

WRITING TO ACT

1. Research the Digital Divide on the Web, looking for recent statistics on who has and who does not have access to the Internet. Compare your findings with Carvin's. Does the gap between the haves and have nots seem to have widened since 2000, when Carvin published his article? Or has it narrowed or stayed the same? Write an editorial for your local newspaper, describing the Digital Divide as you understand it.

2. Find an organization in your community, possibly a public library, that provides public Internet access. Write a proposal to the organization, suggesting ways to improve or expand this access. For example, you might suggest ways to advertise the availability of computers more widely in your community—targeting a population that doesn't use them. Or you might offer to organize a group of volunteers from your campus who would train people to use the computers or give literacy training to those in the community who have difficulty reading.

READING

JENNIFER 8 LEE, in this article from the *New York Times,* reports on the spread of instant messaging language from online conversation to school papers. For many students, IM-speak is so comfortable that they use it unconsciously. While most teachers regard this abbreviated writing style as inappropriate and even rude in an academic setting, others use it to spark discussion of writing styles. When, if ever, do you write in IM style? What do you like or dislike about this form of writing?

Nu Shortcuts in School R 2 Much 4 Teachers (2002)

BY JENNIFER 8 LEE

Each September Jacqueline Harding prepares a classroom presentation on the common writing mistakes she sees in her students' work.

Ms. Harding, an eighth-grade English teacher at Viking Middle School in Gurnee, Ill., scribbles the words that have plagued generations of schoolchildren across her whiteboard:

There. Their. They're.

Your. You're.

To. Too. Two.

Its. It's.

This September, she has added a new list: u, r, ur, b4, wuz, cuz, 2.

When she asked her students how many of them used shortcuts like these in their writing, Ms. Harding said, she was not surprised when most of them raised their hands. This, after all, is their online lingua franca: English adapted for the spitfire conversational style of Internet instant messaging. Ms. Harding, who has seen such shortcuts creep into student papers over the last two years, said she gave her students a warning: "If I see this in your assignments, I will take points off."

"Kids should know the difference," said Ms. Harding, who decided to address this issue head-on this year. "They should know where to draw the line between formal writing and conversational writing."

As more and more teenagers socialize online, middle school and high school teachers like Ms. Harding are increasingly seeing a breezy form of Internet English jump from e-mail into schoolwork. To their dismay, teachers say that papers are being written with shortened words, improper capitalization and punctuation, and characters like &, $ and @.

Teachers have deducted points, drawn red circles and tsk-tsked at their classes. Yet the errant forms continue. "It stops being funny after you repeat yourself a couple of times," Ms. Harding said.

But teenagers, whose social life can rely as much these days on text communication as the spoken word, say that they use instant-messaging shorthand without thinking about it. They write to one another as much as they write in school, or more.

"You are so used to abbreviating things, you just start doing it unconsciously on schoolwork and reports and other things," said Eve Brecker, 15, a student at Montclair High School in New Jersey.

Ms. Brecker once handed in a midterm exam riddled with instant-messaging shorthand. "I had an hour to write an essay on Romeo and Juliet," she said. "I just wanted to finish before my time was up. I was writing fast and carelessly. I spelled 'you' 'u.'" She got a C.

Even terms that cannot be expressed verbally are making their way into papers. Melanie Weaver was stunned by some of the term papers she received from a 10th-grade class she recently taught as part of an internship. "They would be trying to make a point in a paper, they would put a smiley face in the end," said Ms. Weaver, who teaches at Alvernia College in Reading, Pa. "If they were presenting an argument and they needed to present an opposite view, they would put a frown."

As Trisha Fogarty, a sixth-grade teacher at Houlton Southside School in Houlton, Maine, puts it, today's students are "Generation Text."

Almost 60 percent of the online population under age 17 uses instant messaging, according to Nielsen/NetRatings. In addition to cellphone text messaging, Weblogs and e-mail, it has become a popular means of flirting, setting up dates, asking for help with homework and keeping in contact with distant friends. The abbreviations are a natural outgrowth of this rapid-fire style of communication.

"They have a social life that centers around typed communication," said Judith S. Donath, a professor at the Massachusetts Institute of Technology's Media Lab who has studied electronic communication. "They have a writing style that has been nurtured in a teenage social milieu."

Some teachers see the creeping abbreviations as part of a continuing assault of technology on formal written English. Others take it more lightly, saying that it is just part of the larger arc of language evolution.

"To them it's not wrong," said Ms. Harding, who is 28. "It's acceptable because it's in their culture. It's hard enough to teach them the art of formal writing. Now we've got to overcome this new instant-messaging language."

Ms. Harding noted that in some cases the shorthand isn't even shorter. "I understand 'cuz,' but what's with the 'wuz'? It's the same [number] of letters as 'was,' so what's the point?" she said.

Deborah Bova, who teaches eighth-grade English at Raymond Park Middle School in Indianapolis, thought her eyesight was failing several years ago when she saw the sentence "B4 we perform, ppl have 2 practice" on a student assignment.

"I thought, 'My God, what is this?'" Ms. Bova said. "Have they lost their minds?"

The student was summoned to the board to translate the sentence into standard English: "Before we perform, people have to practice." She realized that the students thought she was out of touch. "It was like 'Get with it, Bova,'" she said.

Ms. Bova had a student type up a reference list of translations for common instant-messaging expressions. She posted a copy on the bulletin board by her desk and took another one home to use while grading.

Students are sometimes unrepentant.

"They were astonished when I began to point these things out to them," said Henry Assetto, a social studies teacher at Twin Valley High School in Elverson, Pa. "Because I am a history teacher, they did not think a history teacher would be checking up on their grammar or their spelling," said Mr. Assetto, who has been teaching for 34 years.

But Montana Hodgen, 16, another Montclair student, said she was so accustomed to instant-messaging abbreviations that she often read right past them. She proofread a paper last year only to get it returned with the messaging abbreviations circled in red.

"I was so used to reading what my friends wrote to me on Instant Messenger that I didn't even realize that there was something wrong," she said. She said her ability to separate formal and informal English declined the more she used instant messages. "Three years ago, if I had seen that, I would have been 'What is that?'"

The spelling checker doesn't always help either, students say. For one, Microsoft Word's squiggly red spell-check lines don't appear beneath single letters and numbers such as u, r, c, 2 and 4. Nor do they catch words which have numbers in them such as "l8r" and "b4" by default.

Teenagers have essentially developed an unconscious "accent" in their typing, Professor Donath said. "They have gotten facile at typing and they are not paying attention."

Teenagers have long pushed the boundaries of spoken language, introducing words that then become passé with adult adoption. Now teenagers are taking charge and pushing the boundaries of written language. For them, expressions like "oic" (oh I see), "nm" (not much), "jk" (just kidding) and "lol" (laughing out loud), "brb" (be right back), "ttyl" (talk to you later) are as standard as conventional English.

"There is no official English language," said Jesse Sheidlower, the North American editor of the *Oxford English Dictionary.* "Lan-guage is spread not because anyone dictates any one thing to happen. The decisions are made by the language and the people who use the language."

Some teachers find the new writing style alarming. "First of all, it's very rude, and it's very careless," said Lois Moran, a middle school English teacher at St. Nicholas School in Jersey City.

"They should be careful to write properly and not to put these little codes in that they are in such a habit of writing to each other," said Ms. Moran, who has lectured her eighth-grade class on such mistakes.

Others say that the instant-messaging style might simply be a fad, something that students will grow out of. Or they see it as an opportunity to teach students about the evolution of language.

"I turn it into a very positive teachable moment for kids in the class," said Erika V. Karres, an assistant professor at the University of North Carolina at Chapel Hill who trains student teachers. She shows students how English has evolved since Shakespeare's time. "Imagine Langston Hughes's writing in quick texting instead of 'Langston writing,'" she said. "It makes teaching and learning so exciting."

Other teachers encourage students to use messaging shorthand to spark their thinking processes. "When my children are writing first drafts, I don't care how they spell anything, as long as they are writing," said Ms. Fogarty, the sixth-grade teacher from Houlton, Maine. "If this lingo gets their thoughts and ideas onto paper [more quickly], the more power to them." But during editing and revising, she expects her students to switch to standard English.

Ms. Bova shares the view that instant-messaging language can help free up their creativity. With the help of students, she does not even need the cheat sheet to read the shorthand anymore.

"I think it's a plus," she said. "And I would say that with a + sign."

CONNECTING PERSONALLY TO THE READING

1. Do you agree with sixth-grade teacher Trisha Fogarty that writing in IM style frees you to think about what—rather than how—you are communicating? Does it foster your creativity?

2. Have you ever received a message in IM form that you had trouble deciphering or sent one that your readers didn't understand? To what extent do you think your social status online depends on your ability to communicate in this way?

1. As a newspaper reporter, Lee relies heavily on interviews for her information and thus quotes her sources liberally. Choose two of the quotations and indicate what values they reveal about their speakers.

2. The article begins with a brief narrative full of concrete details. What are some of those details and how effective is this opening?

3. Can you tell where Lee stands on this issue? Why or why not?

SYNTHESIZING IDEAS FROM MULTIPLE READINGS

1. Choose two of the teachers quoted in this article and discuss whether they subscribe to Nicholas Negroponte's ("Creating a Culture of Ideas," p. 479) ideas about teaching.

2. Lee's article includes a defense of IM by Jesse Sheidower, North American editor of the *Oxford English Dictionary,* which is generally considered the final authority on English. In arguing that IM language is part of a natural evolution of English, Sheidower points to another way computers are rapidly changing our culture. Who is affected by this language? Do you think this language change is as significant as the change in shopping habits that David Weinberger recounts in the selection from *Small Pieces Loosely Joined* (p. 450) or the invention of the camera that John Berger analyzes in "Ways of Seeing" (Chapter 8, p. 519)?

WRITING TO ACT

1. Translate a page of a paper you have written into IM speak. For inspiration, go online to "The English-to-12-Year-Old-AOLer Translator" Web site (http://ssshotaru.homestead.com/files/aolertranslator.html) and see how it translates one of your sentences. Then write an article in which you discuss how the translation affected your paper. Did your ideas become more or less convincing? How did your voice and persona change with the translation? Submit your article about this process for your campus newspaper.

2. With a small group of other students, create a set of guidelines in which you indicate the occasions in which IM language is appropriate and when (if ever) it isn't. Include examples of writing for each guideline. Then create a pamphlet and distribute it on campus or over the Web.

READING

DAVE BARRY's satirical take on the World Wide Web highlights the most absurd uses of this powerful medium. What Web sites have you seen that strike you as simply silly? To what extent do you and people you know use the Web simply to have fun? To what extent do you visit the Web for serious purposes?

BARRY is a popular humor writer whose books include *Babies and Other Hazards of Sex, Dave Barry is from Mars and Venus,* and *Dave Barry in Cyberspace.*

Selected Web Sites
At Last: Proof That Civilization Is Doomed[1] (1996)

BY DAVE BARRY

A common criticism of the Internet is that it is dominated by the crude, the uninformed, the immature, the smug, the untalented, the repetitious, the pathetic, the hostile, the deluded, the self-righteous, and the shrill. This criticism overlooks the fact that the Internet also offers—for the savvy individual who knows where to look—the tasteless and the borderline insane.

I am thinking here mainly of the World Wide Web. Whereas much of the Internet relies strictly on text, the Web is multimedia; this means that if, for example, you're setting up a Web site devoted to exploring the near-universal human fear that a *Star Wars* character wants to consume your gonads, you can present this issue in both words *and* pictures (I'll have more on this issue later in this chapter[2]). You can also greatly advance the frontiers of scientific knowledge regarding Spam.

In researching this chapter, I spent many, many hours exploring the World Wide Web. My time was divided as follows:

ACTIVITY	TIME SPENT
Typing insanely complex Web addresses	2%
Waiting for what seemed like at least two academic semesters per Web page while the computer appeared to do absolutely nothing	93%
Reading snippy messages stating that there is no such Web address	2%
Retyping insanely complex Web addresses	2%
Actually looking at Web pages	1%

As you can see, it can take quite a while for a Web page to appear on your screen. The reason for the delay is that, when you type in a Web address, your computer passes it along to another computer, which in turn passes it along to another computer, and so on through as many as five computers before it finally reaches the workstation of a disgruntled U.S. Postal Service employee, who throws it in the trash. So when browsing the Web, you will almost certainly encounter lengthy delays, which means that it's a good idea to have something else to do while you're waiting, such as reroofing your house.

Anyway, by virtue of being diligent and not having a real job, I was eventually able to get through to quite a few Web pages, and in this chapter I'm going to describe some of the more memorable ones. But before I do, I want to stress three points: 5

- All the pages described here are real; I did not make any of them up, not even the virtual toilet.

---

1. I want to thank the good (weird, but good) people on the *alt.fan* group who suggested many of these sites.
2. This is a good reason to stop reading this chapter right now.

- What you see here represents just a teensy-tiny fraction of the thousands upon thousands of Web pages, with new ones being created constantly. Do not assume, from what you see in this chapter, that *all* Web pages are a total waste of time; the actual figure is only about 99.999997 percent.

- By the time you read this, you may not be able to visit all of these pages. I visited most of them in mid-1996; some of them may have since gone out of existence for various reasons, such as that their creators were recalled to their home planets.

But this chapter is not intended as an exhaustive list: I just want to give you an idea of some of the stuff that's out there. So fasten your seat belt, and let's visit some of the fascinating rest stops on the Information Superhighway. We'll start, appropriately enough, with:

THE TOILETS OF MELBOURNE, AUSTRALIA
http://minyos.xx.rmit.edu.au/~s9507658/toilet/

If you're thinking about taking a trip to Melbourne, Australia, the first question you ask yourself is: "What will the toilets be like?"

The answer can be found at this Web site, which offers *detailed* reviews of selected Melbourne-area toilets. Here are some actual excerpts:

- "What a great day for a drive! Mild weather. A nice lunch. A scenic walk. First-rate toilets."

- "The other notable thing about the toilets was the toilet paper holders. They were Bowscott continuous toilet paper holders that were actually positioned up high enough."

- "On the way we stopped at Eastland shopping centre—home of the best public toilets I have seen so far. They were clean, open, and the toilet roll holders were free moving. As with the Lysterfield Lake toilets, one of the basin-style urinals was positioned lower for kids. The hand dryer was fantastic too. It was a compact, automatic Mirage dryer. Even though it was much smaller than other hand dryers, it blew out plenty of hot air."

And that is not all: From this Web site, you can jump to some of the many, *many* other toilet-related Web sites, including a Virtual Public Restroom ("The Toilet of the Web"[3]), where you can write a virtual message and leave a virtual "poopie."[4]

GIANT COLLECTION OF VIOLA JOKES
http://www.mit.edu/people/jcb/viola-jokes.html

If you're like most people, you frequently remark to yourself: "Darn it! I have an important business presentation to make today, and I would love to 'break the ice' by opening with a viola joke, but I don't know any fresh ones!"   10

Well, you will never have to make that statement again, not after you visit this Web page. This is a *huge* collection of viola jokes. I suppose it's possible that somebody, somewhere, has compiled an even *bigger* collection of viola jokes, but I seriously doubt that this could be done without the aid of powerful illegal stimulants.

Much of the viola-joke humor appears to be based on the premise that viola players are not the brightest or most talented members of the orchestra:

3. http://www.auburn.edu/~carltjm/restroom.html
4. Don't ask.

Q. How can you tell when a violist is playing out of tune?
A. The bow is moving.

Q. What do you call a violist with two brain cells?
A. Pregnant.

Some of the jokes are probably a lot more hilarious if you know something about classical music. I'm sure, for example, that many orchestra professionals slap their thighs when they hear this one:

Q. How do you get a violist to play a passage *pianissimo tremolando?*
A. Mark it "solo."

Ha ha! "Mark it 'solo'!" Whew!

Anyway, I was genuinely surprised by this Web page. I always thought of classical   15
orchestras as somber operations where most of the musicians are very serious and hunched over to the point of bowel disorder. I had no idea that there was this level of wackiness, especially not in the string section. (The woodwinds, of course, are a different story; those dudes and dudettes are out of *control.*)

GUIDE TO CRACKERS
http://mathlab.sunysb.edu/%7Eelijah/cstuff/index.html

This is one of those ideas that you never in a million years would have had yourself, but as soon as you see it, you smack your forehead and say: "Huh?"

This page features photographs of various types of crackers—Cheez-Its, Ritz Bits, etc.—actual size. When you click on a cracker, you go to a page that gives you packaging and nutritional information. You are also encouraged to donate crackers, especially "rare and unusual crackers."

I am *sure* there is a good reason.

HUMAN TESTICLE CONSUMPTION:

Mr. T Ate My Balls

http://www.cen.uiuc.edu/~nkpatel/mr.t/index.html

Chewbacca Ate My Balls

http://www.cen.uiuc.edu/~nkpatel/chewbacca/index.html

There are some things in life that it is better to just not even think about, and one of those things is the question of what, exactly, led to the creation of these pages.

In summary, these pages present pictures of Mr. T and Chewbacca expressing—   20
by means of comic book-style speech and thought balloons—the dramatic theme that they would like to eat your testicles.

For example, in the opening scene of the "Chewbacca Ate My Balls" page, Chewbacca is thinking, "I wish I had some BALLS to munch on . . ." In the next scene, he is thinking: "Your balls are MINE!!" And then, in a dramatic plot development reminiscent of the work of playwright Arthur Miller, Chewbacca thinks, "What? Mr. T already got yours?"

These sites also feature a Guest Book, where visitors can leave comments. The comments that I read were all very complimentary. People really respond to a universal theme like this. I myself had to lie down for a while.

THE SPAM CAM
http://www.fright.com/cgi-bin/spamcam

If you have the slightest doubt that the Internet is good for science, you should look at this page, and then you will have much more serious doubts.

This page is billed as "The page that seeks to answer the question: IS SPAM OR-GANIC?" It presents close-up photographs of scientific experiments showing what happens when Spam and other types of foods are left sitting out for long periods of time. What happens is—get ready for a major scientific breakthrough—everything gets *really* disgusting.

For a while there was also a very popular Web site[5] set up by college students 25 wishing to determine what happens to Twinkies when they are heated with torches, dropped from tall buildings, etc.,[6] but when I tried to check it out, it had been closed down by lawyers. Perhaps by the time you read this book, it will be back in operation again. Or perhaps the entire Internet will have been closed down by lawyers. Or perhaps college students will have started dropping lawyers from tall buildings. You never know with the future.

PIERCING MILDRED
http://streams.com/pierce/

Who says there is no culture on the Internet? You will, after you visit this site. This is a game where you get to select a character—either Mildred or Maurice—and then you pierce that person's body parts, or decorate her or him with designer scars. Mildred and Maurice also sometimes get infected, so sometimes you have to purchase anti-biotic ointment.

You may think this sounds like a fairly perverted game, but ask yourself: Is it *really* that different from Mr. and Mrs. Potato Head?

BANANA LABELS OF THE WORLD
http://www.staff.or.jp/whoiswho/ilkka/bananadir/bananalabels.html

If you thought that there were basically only a couple of types of banana labels, then a visit to this site will quickly convince you that you are a stupid idiot. This site presents pictures of hundreds of banana labels, including labels commemorating historic events such as the 50th anniversary of Miss Chiquita, not to mention a label from a Big Frieda's Burro Banana. This site will also direct you to *other* banana-label pages.[7] And you are invited to send in banana labels, including "virtual banana labels," which I assume means labels for virtual bananas. (My feeling about this is: fine, but they'd better not come out with virtual beer.)

WAVE TO THE CATS
http://hogwild.hamjudo.com/cgi-bin/wave

This is the perfect Web site[8] to show the skeptic who thinks you can't do anything useful or practical on the Internet. At this site, you can click on a button that activates a motor at a remote location; the motor is attached to a large fiberboard hand, which waves back

---

5. http://www.owlnet.rice.edu/~gouge/twinkies.html
6. It turns out that pretty much nothing happens.
7. Of *course* there are other banana-label pages.
8. This is one of many cool sites I found out about through the highly recommended Center for the Easily Amused, located at http://www.amused.com/

and forth at some cats, if the cats happen to be in the room at the time. You can't actually *see* this; you just get the warm feeling of satisfaction that comes from knowing that you are causing a remote, simulated hand to wave at remote, possibly nonexistent cats. You also get a nice "Thank you for your wave" message from the Web page author, as well as his description of the way the cats usually react to the hand ("Master will stare at it when it moves; the other three cats, Callie, Mutant, and Katrina, just ignore it").

I know what you're thinking, but to my knowledge, there currently is no "Spay the Cats" Web site. 30

TROJAN ROOM COFFEE MACHINE
http://www.cl.cam.ac.uk/coffee/coffee.html

If you go to this page, you can, merely by clicking your mouse, see, from anywhere in the world, an up-to-the-second video image of the coffee machine in the Trojan Room of the University of Cambridge Computer Laboratory in England. It would be virtually impossible to calculate the time that has been saved by disseminating this information via the Web, as opposed to previous methods.

CAPTAIN AND TENNILLE APPEARANCES
http://www.vcnet.com/moonlight/CTAPPEARANCES

This page lists upcoming personal appearances by the Captain and Tennille. Using this information, you can find out exactly where this veteran duo will be making their own special brand of musical magic so that you can arrange to be on the diametrically opposite side of the Earth when they perform "Muskrat Love."

CURSING IN SWEDISH
http://www.bart.nl/~sante/enginvek.html

This is the most thorough on-line course in Swedish cursing that I am aware of. It is scholarly, well-organized, and professional-looking; and if your computer has sound, you can click on individual phrases, and your computer will curse at you in Swedish.

Here are some of the practical Swedish curses you can learn on this Web site (I swear I am not making these up):

Han var en jävel på att fiska.
He was bloody good at fishing.
Satan! Ungen pissade på sig!
Hell! The kid wet his trousers!
Pubkillarna var ena jävlar på att pissa.
The guys at the pub were masterly at pissing.
Jag tappade den jävla tvålen
I dropped the f ** king soap.
Det vore himla roligt om du kom till festen.
It would be heavenly if you could take part in the party.
Kukjävel!
F** king f ** ker!
Festen kommer att gå åt skogen!
The party will be a real flop!

And of course the one curse you *constantly* find yourself needing to express whenever you're in Sweden . . . 35

När jag blir av med gipset skall du få se på sjutton!
Just wait until I have gotten rid of the plaster!

DUTCH TRAFFIC SIGNS[9]

http://www.eeb.ele.tue.nl:80/traffic/warning-e.html

Without this site, I would never have known that the Dutch have a traffic sign that means "squalls."

FEDERAL CORPSE SLICE PHOTOS

http://www.nlm.nih.gov/research/visible/photos.html

On this site you can see images taken from the government's Visible Human Project, in which two actual deceased humans, one male and one female, were frozen in gelatin and sliced into very thin slices for the benefit of science. I know what you're wondering: You're wondering where the government got the corpses. You will be relieved to learn that the answer is: not from the Internal Revenue Service Division of Taxpayer Compliance.

Or so they claim.

PEOPLE WITH TOASTERS

http://www.berksys.com/www/promotions/uNurtoaster.html

This page features photographs of people with their toasters.

FABIO

http://redwood.northcoast.com/~shojo/Fabio/fabio.html

This page features photographs of the romantic superstar mega-hunk Fabio with his toaster. 40

No, seriously, the photographs depict the romantic superstar mega-hunk posing in a manner that reveals his deeply passionate sensitive innermost feelings about what a studmuffin he is. What makes this site great is that you can click on the photographs, and, if your computer has sound, Fabio will say things to you, such as "Your caress is my command." Apparently he doesn't realize that you're caressing him with a mouse pointer.

DEFORMED FROG PICTURES

http://www.mncs.k12.mn.us/frog/picts.html

One summer day in 1995 some students at the Minnesota New Country School were on a Nature Studies hike. They started catching frogs, and after a bit they noticed that many of the frogs did not appear to meet standard frog specifications in terms of total number of legs, eyes, etc. So the students started a Frog Project to study this phenomenon. If you visit this Web page, you can read about their work and see actual photographs of the frogs; this will help you to become more aware of the environment, pollution, and other important topics, unless you're the kind of sicko who just wants to look at deformed frogs.

MUSICAL SAND

http://www.yo.rim.or.jp/~smiwa/index.html

If you are interested in information on musical sand (and who is not?), this is really the only place to go. This Web site offers information in both Japanese and a language that is somewhat reminiscent of English. The introduction states:

9. I found this site, along with many other excellent ones, at a *very* useful site called Useless Pages, http://www.chaco.com/useless/index.html. Check it out.

All information concerning Musical Sand in the world ("singing sand" on beach and "booming sand" in desert) will concentrate in this home pages. Singing properties of the sand is very sensitive to pollution, and that may be play a sensor for it.

To my regret, musical sand is on the brink of a critical position to be exterminated. If cleaning air and sea however, musical sand plays wonderful sound with action of wind and wave for us. I make show you World of Musical Sand that Mother Nature polished by spending eternal time.

Think of it: Endangered sand!

If your computer has sound capability, you can actually listen to some singing sand. It is not easy, on the printed page, to describe the eerie, almost unearthly beauty of the sound that the sand makes; the best words I can come up with are "like a vacuum cleaner trying to suck up a dead cow." I for one would hate to see Earth lose a resource like this, and I hereby urge Sting and Willie Nelson to hold some kind of benefit concert.

EXPLODING WHALE
http://www.xmission.com:80/~grue/whale

On this site you can see pictures of the now-famous incident[10] in which the Oregon State Highway Division, attempting to dispose of a large and aromatic dead whale that had washed up on the beach, decided to—why not?—blow it up with half a ton of dynamite.

The theory was that the whale would be converted from one large unit into many small Whale McNuggets, which would then be eaten by seagulls. Unfortunately, this is not what happened. What happened was, following a massive blast,[11] large chunks of rotting whale blubber, some of them large enough to dent a car roof, rained down upon spectators several hundred yards away, and there was *still* an extremely large chunk of dead whale lying on the beach. This was not Seagull Chow. A seagull capable of eating this chunk would have to be the size of the Lincoln Memorial.

The moral here is, if another dead whale washes up on the beach in Oregon, the authorities should probably not turn the disposal job over to the State Highway Division. But if they do, I hope they sell tickets.

WORLD RECORD BARBECUE IGNITION
http://ghg.ecn.purdue.edu/oldindex.html

If this Web page doesn't make you proud to be an American, then I frankly don't know what will. This site presents the ultimate result of the effort by members of the Purdue University engineering department to see how fast they could get the barbecue charcoal ignited at their annual picnic. They started by blowing the charcoal with a hair dryer; then, in subsequent years, they escalated to using a propane torch, an acetylene torch, and then compressed pure oxygen.

At this point, they were lighting the charcoal very fast, but for these guys, "very fast" was not good enough. These guys had a dream, and that dream was to ignite their

10. About ten years ago, I saw a videotape of this incident, made by a local TV station. I wrote a column about it, and somebody unfamiliar with the copyright laws put that column on the Internet. The result is that for years now, people have been sending me my own column, often with notes saying, "You should write a column about this!"
11. Talk about booming sands.

charcoal faster than anybody had ever done before. And thus they hit upon the idea of using liquid oxygen, the kind used in rocket engines. On this Web page you can see photos and video of an engineer named George Goble using long wooden handles to dump a bucket of liquid oxygen onto a grill containing 60 pounds of charcoal; this is followed by a fireball that, according to Goble, reached 10,000 degrees Fahrenheit. The charcoal was ready for cooking in *three seconds*.

Next time Oregon has a whale problem, maybe it should call *these* guys.

FLAMING POP-TART EXPERIMENT
http://www.personal.umich.edu/~gmbrown/tart/

It is a well-known scientific fact[12] that if you put a Kellogg's brand strawberry Pop-Tart into a toaster and hold the toaster lever down so that it can't pop up, after about five minutes, the Pop-Tart will turn into the Blowtorch Snack Pastry from Hell, shooting dramatic blue flames as much as a foot out of the toaster slots.

If you visit this Web page, you can see actual photos of an experiment demonstrating this spectacular phenomenon. I urge you, however, *not* to attempt to duplicate this experiment unless you are a trained science professional using somebody else's toaster, because we are talking about a powerful force with the potential for great destruction. We can only be grateful that the Nazis never learned how to harness it, although historians strongly suspect that they were working on it near the end.

Let me repeat that the Web sites described in this chapter represent just a tiny fraction of what's out there. What you really need to do is get on the Web[13] and start poking around for yourself. You'll quickly discover that what you've read about here exemplifies some of the *saner* thinking going on. So go ahead! Get on the Web! In my opinion, it's WAY more fun than television, and what harm can it do?

OK, it can kill brain cells by the billions. But you don't *need* brain cells. You have a computer.

55

12. This has been verified on the David Letterman show.
13. Don't ask *me* how. I'm not an expert on computers; I only write books about them.

CONNECTING PERSONALLY TO THE READING

1. Barry suggests that all the sites he discusses are trivial. Do you agree with this assessment?
2. Why do you think Barry focuses on goofy Web sites when the Web offers so much more to its users than photographs of people with their toasters and reviews of Australian toilets?
3. Do you think Barry is suggesting that people who theorize about the Web take it too seriously? Or that they exaggerate the Web's potential to improve our lives? Explain your answers.

FOCUSING ON THE ARGUMENT

1. One of Barry's frequent strategies is to disrupt our expectations rhetorically. For example, until the reader gets to the last word, this sentence, "You can also greatly advance the frontiers of scientific knowledge regarding Spam," is a cliché (the tired metaphor of the

Internet as a frontier is familiar to all of us). The trivial subject, Spam, however, takes us in a new, satirical direction, forcing us to laugh at those who regard the Web as a "frontier" of knowledge. Find two other instances of this strategy, where the sentence ends up in a completely different place from where it started.

2. Barry's style is personal: he refers to himself repeatedly as "I" and directly addresses the reader as "you." How appealing do you find this style? What other word choices contribute to the personal style?

SYNTHESIZING IDEAS FROM MULTIPLE READINGS

1. Both Peter Drucker ("Beyond the Information Revolution," p. 472) and Howard Rheingold ("How to Recognize the Future When It Lands on You," p. 463) believe that computers will bring about a social and economic revolution. Do you think Barry would agree with them? Why, or why not?

2. Michael Lewis ("Pyramids and Pancakes," p. 438) and David Weinberger (selection from *Small Pieces Loosely Joined,* p. 450) are both impressed by the way electronic communication has allowed ordinary people to become experts and to share what they know. In what ways do the owners of the Web sites that Barry describes share knowledge and expertise? Do you think their knowledge has value to others? Why or why not?

WRITING TO ACT

1. With a group of classmates, create a Web page on a subject that interests your group. The information and presentation can be silly, serious, useful, or whimsical. Then write a one-page description of your Web site, explaining why you designed it as you did. Indicate the purpose and audience your group had in mind.

2. Interview at least twenty students on your campus, asking them to name and describe their favorite Web sites. Then write an editorial for your campus newspaper in which you categorize the responses. What kinds of sites did students seem to like best, and why? Were these sites primarily practical, playful, informative, entertaining, or something else?

Connecting the Readings with the Web Pages

farnsworthmuseum.org

1. Considering Andy Carvin's ("Mind the Gap," p. 483) analysis of the "Digital Divide," how are those who don't have Internet access put at a disadvantage by being excluded from the Farnsworth museum site and others like it?

2. Consider the social changes that Peter Drucker ("Beyond the Information Revolution," p. 472) attributes to computers. How does access to sites like this one contribute to social change?

3. How does the Farnsworth Art Museum Web site support, contradict, or complicate Dave Barry's ("Selected Web Sites," p. 491) depiction of the World Wide Web?

guerrillagirls.com

1. In "Creating a Culture of Ideas" (p. 479), Nicholas Negroponte argues that innovation comes about from people who are able to make "big leaps of thought," have "multidisciplinary minds," and feel encouraged to share ideas, take risks, and cultivate

the imagination. Do you think guerrillagirls.com has these characteristics? Why or why not?

2. Michael Lewis ("Pyramids and Pancakes," p. 438) and David Weinberger (selection from *Small Pieces Loosely Joined*, p. 450) both describe how the Internet can allow a single person or small group to have a far-reaching effect on others. What potential effect do you think guerrillagirls.com has? How is this effect like or different from the influences of the Internet that Lewis and Weinberger describe?

mowa.org

1. All of the readings in this chapter suggest that computers have changed human behavior in fundamental ways: for example, Howard Rheingold ("How to Recognize the Future When It Lands on You," p. 463) believes that Instant Messaging has revolutionized political activism, Rebecca Mead ("You've Got Blog," p. 456) notes that blogs make people's lives more public than ever before, and Michael Lewis ("Pyramids and Pancakes," p. 468) argues that the Internet allows anyone to be (or seem to be) an expert. Do you think that the way people produce, display, and experience art on the MOWA site represents a cultural shift as significant as those discussed by these authors? Why or why not?

2. Both eBay and MOWA are virtual places that have analogs in real life: the shopping mall and the art museum. How do David Weinberger's (selection from *Small Pieces Loosely Joined*, p. 450) definitions of online space, time, self, and knowledge apply to MOWA?

whitney.org/jacoblawrence

1. Jennifer Lee's article ("Nu Shortcuts in School R 2 Much 4 Teachers," p. 487) tells us that some teachers find that the Internet interferes with their teaching, specifically the teaching of Standard English. In what ways do the Whitney Museum's pages on Jacob Lawrence support teaching and learning?

2. Both Andy Carvin ("Mind the Gap," p. 483) and Jacob Lawrence are concerned with civil rights issues. What differences and similarities do you see in their ideas?

3. In "Creating a Culture of Ideas" (p. 479), Nicholas Negroponte is concerned that education encourage students to be creative. Consider the ways in which he believes teachers can foster students' creativity. Which of these approaches do you see in the Jacob Lawrence pages? Visit the site online; then indicate other ways in which this Web site fosters innovation.

FINDING COMMON CAUSE IN CONTROVERSY: Should it be legal for individuals to download music from file-sharing Web sites (e.g., Gnutella, Kazaa, Blubster, Grokster)?

The article reproduced below, "Piracy Gets Mixed Reviews in Industry," describes the controversy over efforts of the Recording Industry Association of America (RIAA) to punish people who copy music from Internet file-sharing networks and

---

burn them onto their own CDs. Like many debates, this one arises both from a conflict in ideology (how much to regulate the Internet) and a conflict in material gain (whether music publishers should allow their product to be given away). Although it may be hard to find common ground between a long-standing capitalist tradition that protects copyright ownership and the idea prized by many Internet enthusiasts that online materials should be openly shared, both sides have at least one goal in common: to make music widely available to the public. What other common beliefs or interests can you find in this debate?

In September 2003, the RIAA sued 261 people for copyright infringement, arguing that downloading copyrighted music is theft and setting off a passionate debate over what kind of information can be exchanged ethically and legally over the Internet. The article "Piracy Gets Mixed Reviews in Industry" quotes musicians, music industry executives, lawyers, and computer entrepreneurs, among others, who argue in favor of or against illegal downloading of music.

If you have ever downloaded copyrighted music from the Web or if you know people who have done this, do you believe their actions are equivalent to shoplifting? Why, or why not?

ALEX PHAM joined the *Los Angeles Times* staff in 2000; previously, he covered issues ranging from health care and biotechnology to banking for the *Washington Post,* the *Boston Globe, USA Today,* and other newspapers

P. J. HUFFSTETTER specializes in technology but covers a wide range of topics, from politics to environmental issues, for the *Los Angeles Times.*

Piracy Gets Mixed Reviews in Industry

BY ALEX PHAM AND P. J. HUFFSTUTTER

By going to court, the major record labels are showing a united front against music piracy. But the bootlegging of songs online isn't universally reviled by the thousands of people who make their living in the $14-billion U.S. recording industry.

To the chief executive of a rap music label every pirated song means less money in his pocket. To the bass player in an independent band, however, file-sharing networks provide far more exposure than traditional outlets, such as radio. And to the musician who tours with acts such as Beck and Sheryl Crow, the popularity of Kazaa, Morpheus and other online networks ought to persuade the record labels to embrace the Net to reach customers.

A sampling of what rank and file members of the industry had to say:

THE PLAYERS

The fight over online music includes a range of industries and interests.

Chris Gorog

• Chris Gorog

Title: Chairman and chief executive, Roxio Inc.
Position: Pro-digital music technology
Stake: Runs a legal music service and sells CD-burning software

"Anything that Roxio will do in this space will be respectful of artist rights and will be working toward a commercial solution."

• Fred von Lohmann

Title: Senior intellectual property attorney, Electronic Frontier Foundation
Position: Pro-file-sharing technology
Stake: Advocates civil liberties online

"The American public has really spoken on this, and the idea of suing them all into submission is a dead loser."

• Janis Ian

Title: Singer, songwriter
Position: Pro-file sharing
Stake: Sells songs and collects royalties

Janis Ian

"The Internet, and downloading, are here to stay. . . . Anyone who thinks otherwise should prepare themselves to end up on the slag heap of history."

• David Schlang

Title: Chairman, National Assn. of Recording Merchandisers
Position: Anti-piracy
Stake: Sells CDs

"Without exception, we believe artists have the right to be compensated. For that to happen, their work must be protected."

Jack Valenti

• Jack Valenti

Title: Chief executive, Motion Picture Assn. of America
Position: Anti-piracy
Stake: Sells movies

"It is not sharing. It's stealing."

• Wayne Rosso

Title: President, Grokster
Position: Pro-file sharing
Stake: Runs a file-sharing network

"We're a massive distribution arm. It's very powerful, and we happen to have their customers."

Cary Sherman

• Cary Sherman

Title: President, Recording Industry Assn. of America
Position: Anti-file sharing, anti-piracy
Stake: Sells recorded music

"The seriousness of this problem requires us to act quickly and send a loud and clear message that this kind of activity is illegal and has consequences."

• Sarah Deutsch

Title: Vice president, general counsel, Verizon Communications Inc.
Position: Believes RIAA subpoenas violate privacy rights, endanger anonymous speech and threaten public safety by giving a powerful tool to stalkers and other abusers
Stake: Company sells Internet access

"Anyone can claim to be a copyright holder, and anyone can use this process to obtain your identity, whether you've infringed a copyright or not."

Nobuyuki Idei

• **Nobuyuki Idei**
Title: Chairman, Sony Corp.
Position: Pro-technology and anti-piracy
Stake: Sells computers, CD burners, digital music players, music and movies

"They have to change their mind-set away from selling albums and think about selling singles over the Internet for as cheap as possible—even 20 cents or 10 cents—and encourage file sharing so they can also get micro-payments for these files. The music industry has to reinvent itself; we can no longer control distribution the way we used to."

• **Steve Jobs**
Title: Chief executive, Apple Computer Inc.
Position: Pro-technology
Stake: Sells computers, digital music players and downloadable songs

Steve Jobs

"People keep their music collections on their computers. They want to burn CDs and to put their music on portable players. Why shop at a record store?"

Bill Gates

• **Bill Gates**
Title: Chairman, Microsoft Corp.
Position: Pro-technology, anti-piracy
Stake: Sells software and digital media technology

"It reminds me of the early days of the PC industry. The hobbyist clubs would get together and swap the software, and I wrote an open letter—this was back in 1975—saying, 'Gee, come on, you guys, license some of this stuff. It would sure help in terms of invention and new software coming along.' Well, I didn't write that letter in the most politic form. . . ."

Ariana Murray—*Bass player for Earlimart, an independent band*
Los Angeles

People today have new expectations about being able to browse music before they buy. If people are downloading our music, we look at it as a positive thing. For us, it just seems to be a promotional tool. If anything, it's helping us at this point.

Maybe my opinion will change when our record sales start to have a more direct effect on our personal incomes.

At this point, I like the fact that people can listen before they buy the product. Not everyone has the disposable income to go out and buy everything.

I still believe that if a band is really good—if you're writing great songs and you work real hard and tour like crazy—people will buy your record and that's going to help your income.

We put a lot of art into our work. Our record is an enhanced CD with videos on it. That's not something you can download, at least not yet. So we hope that's an incentive for people to own the record.

My reservation about downloading is really an aesthetic one. Imagine if Pink Floyd's "The Wall" came out now. There's this whole idea of concept records, the idea of a record that has a beginning, a middle and an end. There are some records that should be listened to that way. If people download individual tracks, they miss out on the artistry that goes into making the whole.

Tha Realest—
Songwriter/rapper
Chief Executive of 2 Real
Entertainment, a rap label

I've been writing songs since I was in a talent show in fourth grade. That was back in '84 or '85. It was a way to have a conversation with people in the streets, a way to reach out with words. And it got me paid.

I don't download music at all, but bootlegging's been around forever. I know a lot of the kids don't understand it. They don't understand that whole publishing thing. That's what you eat off of, because you don't make huge money when you sign up with the labels. It's the other things that help you get paid. It's the clothing lines and the producing and the publishing. It's the song-writing and the licensing you get from that.

The kids don't see that. I have college kids come up to me all the time, saying, "Hey! I've got this hot bootleg mix CD with your music on it." What he doesn't figure out is he's taking food off my table. They sell the tapes for $10 a pop.

At first, I got mad. Now, I roll with it and use the tapes as a promotional avenue. I go down to the studio once or twice a month, and knock out three to four songs that will just be for these mix tapes. One of these mix tapes might get the word of mouth going, and that's good for me.

Marc Weinstein—
Co-owner, Amoeba Music
stores, Berkeley, California
. . . People who are into music need a way to discover artists, because the radio isn't a very good way to do that. File sharing can be helpful in educating the public.

I'm 46 years old. People [from] my generation have been alienated from the music world. Nothing is played on the radio for us. We have no way of finding out what's new and cool. NPR maybe breaks about one or two interesting things a year that percolate through my generation. But there are so few examples of that.

Stealing—I'm certainly not a proponent of that. Everyone loses out, especially the artists.

But the music industry long ago should have developed a system to help listeners learn about music so they can look up artists and hear what they sound like. Then they can go out and buy what they're interested in.

As far as Amoeba goes, we're doing OK, because people come here to find the unusual stuff, the broad catalog.

It's the chain stores that are hurt by this. People who listen to pop are more likely to shop at chain stores, and they're more likely to take it off the Internet. No one wants to spend $20 to get one song.

Roger Joseph Manning Jr.—*Band member,*
co-founder of Jellyfish and
TV Eyes
Session and tour musician
for Beck, Blink 182, Sheryl
Crow
Woodland Hills, California

The world of recorded media is changing at lightning speeds, and nobody knows what to do about it.

I am on the fence right now about this whole thing. I see where it can be a powerful tool for promoting small and medium artists. On the other hand, all the artists are being ripped off to a degree.

But it's the medium-sized bands and smaller acts that suffer the most from piracy. That scene relies incredibly on sharing and word of mouth.

It's not the Limp Bizkits and the Metallicas. Sure, they can argue losses on paper. So what does that mean? They can't buy their sixth Mercedes?

I make a lot of my living through session work. Many of the bands that I work with are so big that piracy doesn't affect them. The multi-platinum acts still hire me. I don't see them hurting.

But I'm painfully aware and sad about the current state of the business.

We've all been living with the old design where bands sign up with record labels, and musicians end up losing control. In my opinion, that model has ripped off more from musicians [than piracy].

Why not try something else? What have I got to lose by jumping in and experimenting with doing a selected release on a few Web sites?

There has to be some kind of alternative that omits the recording labels so the artist becomes the salesman for his wares. And the Internet could be the vehicle by which he can do that.

Steve Stoute—*Concert promoter and musician manager*
Co-creator of the "Roc Tha Mic" concert tour with rap artists Jay-Z and 50 Cent

I think this tactic is not going to stand up in court. Someone in Omaha, Neb., is going to get sued and go to jail because they swapped a Linkin Park song? They'll sue, the RIAA will sue, everyone will sue, and it'll all come down to being one big scare tactic. Maybe people will learn something. We can only hope.

Look, there's not a direct tie between the health of

concert promoting and downloading on the Internet. If an act's popular, and a song's popular, people are going to download it.

If there's a connection, it's small. The big thing is making sure an act's not overexposed on TV or anywhere else. For us, in concerts, the big thing we deal with is keeping the mystique of an act going.

As live performances on TV shows, and behind-the-scenes and [MTV's] "Cribs" and stuff go up and up, an act's giving more than their music. They're giving bits of themselves away. They're making themselves a lot more accessible to the public now than they did years ago.

The more access you provide to the public, the less there is of the magic of seeing them live and in front of your face. The whole phenomenon of concerts is that you get to see an act live. But if you see them "live" on TV, what's the draw? What's the point?

DIGITAL: THE MUSICAL

A short history of digital music:

Spring 1983: The compact disc goes on sale in the United States, ushering in the digital music age

April 1993: Specifications for MP3 are published as part of an industry standard

June 1994: Aerosmith song "Head First" becomes the first full-length commercial

NEW MEDIUM: Aerosmith, led by Steven Tyler, was the first band to release a song for downloading in 1994.

entertainment product released for downloading

April 1997: Nullsoft releases Winamp, the first popular MP3 player for Windows computers

October 1998: Digital Millennium Copyright Act becomes law, giving copyright holders new tools to battle online piracy

May 1999: Napster debuts, introducing peer-to-peer file sharing to the masses

December 1999: Recording Industry Assn. of America sues Napster Inc. for copyright infringement

April 2000: Metallica sues Napster, USC and others, alleging copyright infringement

July 2000: U.S. District Judge Marilyn Hall Patel orders Napster to stop unauthorized copying of songs, but appeals court puts the ruling on hold

February 2001: 9th Circuit appeals panel rules against Napster

March 2001: First copy-protected CD is released in the U.S.

July 2001: Napster service shuts down

October 2001: RIAA and the Motion Picture Assn. of America sue Kazaa, Morpheus and Grokster for copyright infringement

December 2001: Listen.com launches the

Rhapsody online music service

June 2002: Napster files for Chapter 11 bankruptcy protection

April 2003: RIAA sues four college students for running Napster-like networks. All four settle in May

April 2003: Federal judge rules that Morpheus and Grokster weren't responsible for piracy committed by their programs' users

April 2003: Apple Computer Inc. launches iTunes Music Store

[September 2003]: Record labels sue 261 file sharers

Source: Times research

NEW OUTLET: Apple's Steve Jobs unveils iTunes

Initially, you may see only adversarial viewpoints in this debate. To broaden your view, try to understand the feelings, assumptions, and interests of each side.

Taking the music publisher's side:

- As a business, you have invested a great deal of time, creativity, and money in recording and marketing music. What do you lose when people download your music for free and share it with their friends?
- Your efforts to discourage downloading—by lowering the price of CDs and by using anti-copying technology—have failed. What options do you have to protect your livelihood?
- In what ways is unauthorized downloading and sharing of music simply theft? How does it undermine the system of buying, selling, and profit making that underlies our economy?
- You believe that copyright law treats creative works as private property and is intended to give control of that property (such as music) to its creators. How does the Internet threaten this view of copyright?

Taking the side of a consumer who downloads music through file-sharing programs:

- Have you stopped buying CDs? Or does downloading give you a chance to sample music (e.g., from a new artist) before buying it? What other products might you buy after discovering a new artist online? How does file sharing help the music industry?
- In what ways might you argue that times have changed and that the record industry needs to change, too—and that file sharing is here to stay? How has the Internet changed the buying and selling of products and the sharing of information? What benefits do you see in these changes?
- Imagine that you object to control of the music industry by corporations—by radio programmers, record stores, or music publishers—that decide which music to make publicly available. How does file sharing promote democracy?
- You believe that copyright law is intended to enhance society by encouraging innovation and that the best way to do so is to make creative work accessible to everyone. How does the Internet promote innovation by making information, music, and other creative materials widely available?

ADDING MORE INFORMATION

In developing your own viewpoint on this issue, collect as many ideas and facts as you can. To get a more complete view of the issue consult the Electronic Frontier Foundation (http://www.eff.org), musician Janis Ian's Web site (http://www.janisian.com), and the Recording Industry Association of America Web site (http://www.riaa.org).

As you think about this issue, consider this information:

- In 2002, the record industry believed it lost potential sales worth $10 billion because of illegal downloads.
- After studying the sales of 680 albums over 17 weeks (in 2002), economists Felix Oberholzer-Gee and Koleman Strumpf argued that downloading increased rather than reduced CD sales of the most popular music. Consumers often bought the CD after sampling it first online.
- According to a 2003 study (Pew Internet & American Life Project) of over 2,500 people who download music from file-sharing sites, 80 percent of college and high school students are not concerned about violating copyright law.
- Twenty-five percent of the 6,403 Internet users polled by the Pew Internet & American Life Project (2005) stated that they downloaded music illegally.

- In June 2005, the U.S. Supreme Court, in its case *Metro-Goldwyn-Mayer vs. Grokster Ltd.,* ruled that file-sharing service Grokster intentionally encouraged users to violate copyright law and could be held liable for piracy committed by its users.
- In July 2006, file-sharing service Kazaa paid the movie and music industries over $115 million to settle lawsuits over copyright filed by the RIAA and movie studios. It also agreed to install filtering technologies to prevent users from sharing copyrighted music or film.
- To locate and prosecute those who download copyrighted music, recording companies have to get online services to release personal information about subscribers. In doing so, they commit a privacy violation and open the door for stalkers and other criminals to get such access.
- The first person to be sued for illegal downloading was twelve-year-old Brianna Lahara, who lives in a housing project in New York with her single mother and nine-year-old brother. The record industry agreed to drop charges against her if she paid $2,000 and issued a public apology, which she did.
- Legal online music services such as iTunes, Rhapsody, and Napster offer users access to a large library of digital songs for purchase or for listening (at a low monthly fee—around $10). The selection is large, but vastly smaller than that offered through file sharing.
- Some of the defendants named in lawsuits filed by the RIAA never used file-sharing networks. Without their knowledge, their Internet addresses had been used by their friends, children, or grandchildren to download music.

SEEKING COMMON CAUSE

Before you take a side, first identify the points on which the two sides agree.

1. The music industry and musicians should be compensated fairly for their work.

2. Music should be made widely available to consumers.

3. Opportunities to download music from the Internet are unlikely to go away.

4. "Peer-to-peer" technology, which allows people to share computer files, has many important (and legal) uses besides downloading music.

DEBATE ESSAY

Write a short essay in which you explain why you do or do not think it should be legal to download music from file-sharing Web sites. Consider the interests of all parties affected by these Web sites, including the musicians, music corporations, and the fans. Consider advancing a solution that would accommodate all these interests. If you have relevant personal experience, be sure to include it as well.

WRITING PROJECTS

Writing a Short Essay

The following short writing projects can prepare you for writing the long essay in the Writing an Extended Argument section or can be done independently.

1. Go to a bookstore and spend half an hour or more browsing. Then do the same at an online bookstore (such as barnesandnoble.com or amazon.com). Write a short paper comparing the experiences you had. What were the advantages and drawbacks of each method of

shopping? In what ways were your experiences like or unlike those of David Weinberger (selection from *Small Pieces Loosely Joined,* p. 450)?

2. Go to www.groups.yahoo.com and join a public discussion group on a topic that interests you. After participating for at least two weeks in this group, write a paper analyzing the expertise of the members on the topic of the discussion. What prompts you to trust or doubt the opinions or expertise of the group's contributors?

3. Research the background of someone you regard as a technology or science innovator: for example, George Washington Carver, Ada Lovelace, Thomas Edison, Marie Curie, or Steve Jobs. Compare what you learn about them with the personal characteristics Nicholas Negroponte ("Creating a Culture of Ideas," p. 479) sees as requirements for innovation.

4. Spend a few days observing people in your community using their cell phones. Take notes about when and where they are talking and, possibly, what kinds of things they discuss on their phones in public. Write a paper in which you respond to Howard Rheingold's ("How to Recognize the Future When It Lands on You," p. 463) argument that cell phones are changing our society.

5. Spend an hour or more surfing the Web and see how many Web sites you find that seem as pointless or goofy as the ones Dave Barry describes in "Selected Web Sites" (p. 491). Then write a response to Barry's article.

6. Write a sequel to Dave Barry's article "Selected Web Sites," in which you identify four or more silly Web sites and describe them satirically, as Barry does.

Writing an Extended Argument

Drawing on the four Web sites and at least three of the readings presented in this chapter, discuss one way you believe computers are changing our lives. Be sure to use concrete details from the Web sites and readings—and, if you like, from your own experience—to illustrate your beliefs.

In defining your thesis, answer one of the following questions or pose and answer a question of your own:

1. How is an individual's online identity like or different from his/her face-to-face self?

2. What kinds of relationships or communities develop online, and in what ways are they like or different from face-to-face ones?

3. What social or political changes does computer technology facilitate?

4. How have digital technologies changed the way we perceive time or space?

Designing the Extended Writing Project

The following writing suggestions for constructing a thesis, organizing, adding details, and integrating the thesis and the readings can be generalized to any other writing project you do.

To make your points clearly, we recommend that you follow this strategy:

Narrow the Topic

When you begin your paper you usually need to narrow the topic to a specific question that you answer. The answer to that question is your thesis.

The essay prompt under "Writing an Extended Argument" includes several subquestions, which are designed to help you think of ideas for the essay. These questions are broad, and you will probably write a more interesting and detailed paper if you narrow them down. One way to do this is to pick one question and focus it on a few specific examples.

For example, you might narrow question 1, on online identity, to this: how do owners of Web sites and participants in online discussion groups establish authority? To answer this question, you might analyze the strategies Marcus Arnold (in "Pyramids and Pancakes," p. 438), the sellers on eBay (from *Small Pieces Loosely Joined*, p. 450), and the Web sites farnsworthmuseum.org, guerrillagirls.com, www.whitney.org/jacoblawrence/index.html, and mowa.org use to make their ideas convincing (or unconvincing, if that's what you find). You could also, as a contrast, draw on Dave Barry's description of absurd (and therefore unconvincing) Web sites in "Selected Web Sites—At Last: Proof that Civilization Is Doomed" (p. 491).

Base the Paper's Structure on the Thesis.

One of the most effective ways to organize an essay is to follow the order of ideas set forth in your thesis. There is almost always more than one way to do this. The sample below shows one possibility; the paper based on this outline will have several paragraphs for each section:

THESIS | The Internet allows ideas to travel so quickly that it can provide a ready education for individuals and even lead to rapid political change for society as a whole.

SECTION ONE | Describe how people learn from one another on the Internet. (David Weinberger gets a quick lesson in evaluating quilts; Marcus Arnold—in Michael Lewis's article—shares his legal knowledge; farnsworthmuseum.org teaches visitors about American art.)

SECTION TWO | Discuss how computer technology can engage the public in political action (guerrillagirls.com invites visitors to fight racism and sexism; Rheingold illustrates how individuals have organized politically via cell phones.)

SECTION THREE | Create an analogy between computer technology and an earlier technology, the printing press: the printing press, by making new ideas widely accessible, led to radical social change (Peter Drucker, "Beyond the Information Revolution," p. 472).

SECTION FOUR | Possibly conclude that those without Internet access are being denied opportunities for education and political control (Andy Carvin, "Mind the Gap," p. 483).

Detailed Descriptions of the Web Sites and Readings

Your description of the relevant portions of the readings and Web sites is your evidence and will make up the bulk of the essay. Concrete examples from these sources draw the reader into your argument and are appealing to read, memorable, and convincing. Be sure to describe the readings and Web sites so specifically that a reader who is not familiar with them can picture the Web pages and understand your conclusions about the readings.

In other words, don't stop with a generalization; add concrete information to illustrate it:

Not

Guerrillagirls.com is feisty.

But

Guerrillagirls.com is feisty. On the home page we see a snarling gorilla mask with fangs and an open mouth; the woman wearing the mask seems to be roaring while flexing her biceps. The language is assertive as well: "Do women have to be naked to get into the Met. Museum?" the Guerrilla Girls ask us, their tone outraged and fearless. The lime-green background assaults the eyes. These gorillas are out to fight injustice; they're fighters, *guerrillas.*

Using WEB Resources

Extend the Scope of Your Essay

To add more information to your essay, you might visit Howard Rheingold's Web site (www.rheingold.com) or the blog of Rebecca Blood (www.rebeccablood.net)—both of whom are experts in cyberspace culture—and incorporate some of the information you find there into your paper.

Analyze Another Web Site

Do a Google search (www.google.com) and find a Web site on a topic that interests you. Then analyze its rhetorical features. How convincing does it seem to you? How appealing? What adjectives might you use to describe the personality of this site?

---

www.mhhe.com/durkinl

Using the Web for resources on Exploring Cyberculture. Go to Web Resources

ANNIE LEIBOVITZ   Darci Kistler and Robert La Fosse,
New York City [1990]

Annie Leibovitz's photograph captures the superb technique and power of two ballet dancers, whose bodies are positioned to create a particular effect. What is this effect? How does the contrast of light and shadow enhance it? What do the different textures shown in the photograph contribute to this effect?

1 What specific body positions contribute to the sense of balance that the photograph captures?
2 What is the relationship between the two dancers? How do the lines of their bodies suggest this relationship?
3 The lines of the dancer's arms and legs draw the viewer's eyes toward Kistler's face. What else in the composition reinforces the eye's movement upward?

BARBARA MORGAN   Martha Graham in "Letter to the World"
[1940]

The photograph of Martha Graham dancing *Letter to the World,* a study of Emily Dickinson and her poetry, illustrates the visual element of dance. While dance is made up of motion, the photograph captures one moment of that movement in a still image. The image captured here illustrates the symmetry, balance, and expressiveness of dance. Graham is expressing Emily Dickinson's renunciation of love to become a poet. How does the dancer's body depict the artist as sacrificial victim?

Norton Simon Museum. © Barbara Morgan.

1   What elements of balance and symmetry are created by Graham's body in this photograph? How do they contribute to the feeling of renunciation she projects?

2   What shapes and movement does Graham create with her costume? Do they enhance the feelings of loss projected in her face, arms, and legs?

3   What elements of the photograph suggest the power of art?

4   How does the photograph convey the idea of the human body as the instrument of composition—as a work of art?

ALVIN LANGDON COBURN   Ezra Pound [1917]

To create this photograph of U.S. poet Ezra Pound, Coburn used three mirrors, fragmenting the image into geometric shapes. As poet and artist, Pound and Coburn were both inspired by the industrial progress of the early 20th century and sought to capture the energy of urban life in their work. Coburn achieves an effect of dynamic movement through sequences of triple images. How does this technique affect your impression of Pound? According to the photograph, what kind of man is Pound?

George Eastman House.

1   A poet's gaze can symbolize his artistic vision. Describe Pound's gaze. Where is he looking? What might he be thinking? What is his relationship to the viewer?

2   Why do you think the photographer has left the background black?

3   The photograph contains several triangular shapes that lead the viewer's eyes toward Pound's eyes and forehead. Why do you think Coburn directs the reader's gaze in this way?

JOHN FORD   Still from Stagecoach [1939]

The movie *Stagecoach* is a Western about a group of people traveling by stagecoach through dangerous Indian country. This still shows the stagecoach crossing the mesa escorted by a detachment of cavalry. What dominates the still, however, is not the characters or action, but the vast desert landscape—a large panorama that serves, as Jon Boorstin points out, not so much to develop the plot or characters, as to evoke emotions that "lie beyond words, closer to the moods of music." What emotions does this still evoke in you? What elements of the image create this experience?

Courtesy Everett Collection.

1   How does the setting—the vast expanse of desert and the stark sandstone monoliths in the background—create a sense of danger?

2   The people in the stagecoach appear exposed and isolated, far from the safety of "civilization," which is represented by what we can't see, the town they left and the town they are trying to reach. What images in this still emphasize raw, wild nature?

3   How do the use of light and shadow, the scale of people relative to the background, and the camera angle contribute to making the characters appear vulnerable?

Chagall has stated that "Everything in art must spring from the movement of our whole life-stream . . . including the unconscious." This mural, which covers a wall at New York's Metropolitan Opera House, weaves together images of New York, composers such as Beethoven and Mozart, mythological and Old Testament figures, and characters from such operas as *Romeo and Juliet*. What, according to the mural, are the sources of music?

The Metropolitan Opera, New York.

1 In the center of the mural, the two heads on one body signify Orpheus (whose music charmed the gods) and King David (whose harp playing soothed King Saul), thus unifying Greek mythology and biblical tradition. What other images of unity do you see?

2 What features of the painting suggest the unconscious?

3 How do the shapes, lines, colors, and other elements of the painting evoke music?

insert

Romare Bearden is an African American artist whose collages often reflect aspects of African American culture, in this case, jazz. What do we learn about jazz from this work of art?

1 What is the tone of this collage? What elements of the collage contribute to this tone?

2 Many of the lines of the collage—formed by the trumpets, the microphone, and the men's arms—point toward the woman. What is the relationship among the three musicians?

3 This collage conveys an experience of music in a visual form. The deep primary colors and the flat shapes suggest that the subjects are at one with the music they make. How else does the collage convey this idea?

PABLO PICASSO   Three Musicians [1921]

This painting uses flat squares and rectangles along with bright patterns of color to suggest the combined rhythms of three musicians. Background and foreground, figures and instruments, objects and space, and clothing and body are equally cut into overlapping geometric shapes, suggesting the patterns of musical design.

The Museum of Modern Art, New York.

1   Which shapes and colors in the background are repeated in the foreground? How are the shapes and colors of the objects similar to those that form the musicians themselves? What do these patterns have in common with music?

2   What elements of this painting suggest a spirit of playfulness?

3   Picasso uses small circles for the musicians' eyes, the holes in their instruments, and the musical notes. What three activities do these small circles connect?

ARCHIBALD MOTLEY Blues [1929]

This painting places music in a social setting, a club in Harlem, where people meet, drink, dance, and listen to music. How does the painting suggest social harmony?

Chicago History Museum.

1 Although the musicians sit on the side of the painting, their instruments extend into its center. How does the music tie all the people in the room together?

2 How does color contribute to the mood of this painting?

3 How do the shapes made by the people's bodies suggest the sensuous sound of the blues?

LOUISE NEZ   Reservation Scene [1992]

Rugs serve both a cultural and economic function among the Navajo: they are a traditional art form, and they are also sold, traded, and used in daily life. This work of art is a rug that depicts, among other things, women creating a traditional Navajo rug. What is the process of creating this rug?

Smithsonian American Art Museum. Gift of Chuck and Jan Rosenak and museum purchase made possible by Ralph Cross Johnson. 1997. 124. 189.

1   The woman in the bottom right corner is weaving a traditional Navajo design. What similarities do you see between the colors and patterns in this design and Nez's artwork?

2   What other objects and activities in the work of art are related to the creation and sale of the rug being woven?

3   How do the size and placement of the plants and animals suggest that the people live in harmony with nature?

FAITH RINGGOLD   Dancing at the Louvre [1991]

Ringgold's quilt depicts her family at the Louvre, the most famous art museum in Paris, romping in front of celebrated Renaissance paintings, including Leonardo da Vinci's *Mona Lisa*. Ringgold and her children face the viewer or each other, ignoring the traditional symbols of European culture. What is the significance of this scene?

1   How do the gestures and attitudes of the figures in the paintings differ from those of Ring-gold's family? Why do you think that Ringgold created this contrast?

2   The three paintings all have elaborate frames. How do the frames contribute to the contrast between the background, where the paintings hang, and the foreground, where the family is dancing?

3   What is the effect of conveying this image in a quilt as opposed to an oil painting? What values is the artist suggesting by choosing this medium?

This painting shows us Knight's image of herself as an artist, as well as her model and her painting of the model. How does *Self-Portrait* characterize Knight as an artist?

1 As viewers, we observe Knight observing the model. What does this painting tell us about the act of seeing?

2 In what ways are the three figures in the painting alike or different? What is the significance of these similarities or differences?

3 Do you think Knight identifies with the model, views her from an objective distance, or both? How do the colors and lines of the painting connect the artist to her subject or distance her from it?

MALCAH ZELDIS   A Peaceable Kingdom with Anna Pavlova
[1990]

This painting, which depicts an ideal world, offers stylized images of real historical figures. On the right, for example, are Louis Armstrong and Mother Teresa, and on the left, holding a palette, the artist herself. What other famous people do you recognize here? Why do you think Zeldis has chosen these specific individuals for this painting?

1   Which of the arts are represented here? Why are there so many artists in the "peaceable kingdom"? How do you think Zeldis imagines the role of the artist in society?

2   The painting works by unifying contrasting images. For example, the urban skyline in the background contrasts with, but also helps to frame, the pastoral setting in the foreground, showing us that city and country both oppose and complement each other. What other potentially conflicting images do you see? How does Zeldis reconcile them?

3   The people and animals are grouped together and look out toward the viewer, as if they were sitting for a family portrait. How else does this painting suggest togetherness, harmony? How do the colors and shapes connect the figures to each other?

Exploring the Arts

Both the readings and the works of art in this chapter explore the role of the arts in our lives: how we view a visual medium such as photography, film, or painting (referred to by several of the authors as a "way of seeing"), the place of art in society, and the relationship between artists and their work.

EXPLORING THE "ART" IN THE WORKS OF ART

Some of the works of art in this chapter are included in readings that analyze specific visual images: John Berger's "Ways of Seeing," Wanda Corn's "Ways of Seeing," Jon Boorstin's "The Hollywood Eye," and William A. Ewing's "Dance and Photography." The works of art we have provided separately from these readings are different from the other art in this book in that the works in this chapter address what it means to create and experience art. Annie Leibovitz's *Darci Kistler and Robert La Fosse, New York City, 1990* is a work of art, a photograph, about another work of art, dance. Although a photograph is by nature still, Leibovitz's composition captures movement, the essence of dance, which takes place not in poses, but in the action between each position. The dancers' backs, arms, legs, heads, and hands create an intertwining spiral that evokes movement. At the same time, the eyes, position of the heads, and the arched back suggest emotion, the impetus behind the movement.

Like Leibovitz's photograph, Barbara Morgan's photograph of Martha Graham is both a work of art in itself and a picture of a moment from another work of art, a piece of choreography. In addition, the dance is about what it means to be an artist, specifically, the poet Emily Dickinson. The title of the dance, *Letter to the World*, is the title of a poem by Emily Dickinson, and the dance, choreographed and performed by Graham, is the physical rendition of Graham's belief that the artist renounces the joys of ordinary life to devote herself to art. Like Leibovitz's and Morgan's photographs, the still image from the motion picture *Stagecoach* captures a moment from a moving art form, in this case, film. As Boorstin notes in his essay, spectacular shots like this one give the film "a sense of undeniable reality beyond the screen." In contrast to these images, Alvin Langdon Coburn's photograph of poet Ezra Pound (*Ezra Pound*) takes a still shot—a portrait of a stationary man—and, through blurring and fracturing the image, strives to create a sense of movement. In doing so, Coburn suggests the intensity and energy of the poet's mind.

Like the photographs and the still from *Stagecoach*, the other visual materials in this chapter are works of art about creating and experiencing art. Marc Chagall's *The Sources of Music*, Romare Bearden's *Showtime*, Pablo Picasso's *Three Musicians*, and Archibald Motley's *Blues* all evoke the inspiration behind the creation of music, the joy of producing it, and the experience of hearing it. Chagall's huge mural, thirty by thirty-six feet, which covers a wall at New York's Metropolitan Opera House, celebrates thousands of years of musical history in the Western world. Bearden's collage of three jazz musicians—made of scraps of colored and painted paper—is suffused with the pleasure of making and hearing jazz, an experience that is both spiritual (the lines of the painting point upward) and earthy (the rich colors and solid shapes anchor the figures to the ground). Picasso's painting, which like Bearden's *Showtime* depicts three musicians making music, suggests playfulness and harmony—both in the musicians' relationship with each other and in the musical form itself. Motley's painting *Blues* also suggests joy, somewhat ironically, considering the origin of the blues in the struggles of African American history. In this painting it is not just the musicians who experience joy, but the listeners as well, as they are moved to smile, dance, and share the experience as a community. Here, music brings not only sensuous joy, but also social togetherness.

Louise Nez's rug *Reservation Scene* also depicts social harmony. Here the act of creating art is shown as fully integrated into Navajo culture, rather than as the personal act of a solitary artist. The weaver is part of a much larger scene, full of activity, plants, animals, people, sky, and land, suggesting that the artist is one with her culture. At the same time, the loom is the largest image in this rug—even larger than the three mountains—a scale that might suggest the importance of weaving in Nez's world. Social harmony is also the subject of Malcah Zeldis's painting *A Peaceable Kingdom with Anna Pavlova*. Here music, dance, and painting are essential to a world in which people of different races and cultures and animals of different species all live peaceably together. In addition, both Nez's rug and Zeldis's painting come from a social tradition of folk art that draws on images from daily life and uses bold colors and flat shapes.

Like Nez and Zeldis, Faith Ringgold draws on folk tradition in her work *Dancing at the Louvre:* combining painted images with quilting techniques, her work is inspired by African American slave quilts. At the same time, she parodies the veneration Americans have for European art. In *Dancing at the Louvre,* the young girls dance happily, if irreverently, in front of some of the most celebrated paintings of Renaissance Europe. Ringgold's art of the people thus counters the elitism often identified with the fine art world.

In contrast to these works, Laura Knight's *Self-Portrait* emphasizes the individual artist rather than the artist in society. Knight's artist is shown working indoors and keeping a distance from the model she is painting; she seems alone. *Self-Portrait* is about seeing, that is, about the artist's vision. The painter contemplates her subject in a composition that consists of three planes: the nude model posing on a platform, the painting of this model set on its easel, and Knight herself in the foreground. What does Knight see when she studies the model, and how does she translate that vision into art?

Analyzing Works of Art

Works of art can be analyzed from many different perspectives. They can be viewed in their social and political context, understood against the time in which they were produced. Some have political messages or are closely tied to the biography of the artist. Some works of art make statements about art itself: its role in society or its expression of the artist's personal vision. And works of art are analyzed as aesthetic artifacts, in which their form and other properties are described. Often an analysis of a work of art combines several of these approaches.

As you look at the works of art in this chapter, pay attention to such elements as light and dark, color (if there is any), foreground and background elements, and scale (large or small images). Ask yourself how these physical features of the work of art affect your response to the image. For the photographs of a moving art form—the cinema and dance—note how the image attempts to capture movement, how its composition suggests kinetic energy. What follows are some of the visual elements you might look for as you explore the art in this chapter:

- **Figures** (dress, posture, face, expression, hair, placement) How are the people positioned? What do they look like? How are they interacting?

- **Background/foreground** (location, detail, relation to figure) What does the background look like? Does it frame the central figures or contrast with them? What is emphasized; what is downplayed?

- **Objects** (what they are; why they are there; what they look like or are made of) What do they add to your interpretation of the image? Are they symbolic? What is the relative size of objects to each other? To any people portrayed in the image?

- **Color** (bright, contrasting, monochromatic; associated with certain objects and not others; black and white images, shades of gray, shadows). What is emphasized by the use of color or black and white? What mood does the color or use of black/white evoke?

- **Shape** (sharp, smooth, large, small, rounded, or edged) What mood do the shapes suggest? What emotions do they evoke in the viewer?

- **Context** Where is the work of art displayed? What is its occasion or purpose? Who is the intended viewer? How does the composition of the work of art reflect the materials used in its construction? How is your response to the work of art affected by what you know about the background of the artist or the period or social circumstances in which she or he works?

Analysis of a Painting

Look at Norman Rockwell's painting *Art Critic* (p. 530), which, like most of Rockwell's work, is a narrative painting in a "realistic" style—that is, it tells a story (narrative) through detailed images that resemble what we see in our daily lives (realism). As its title suggests, this is a painting about looking at art, and, in fact, the central images in the painting are all looking intently at something. The composition of the painting moves our gaze elliptically to emphasize the act of looking—from the young man's magnifying glass, to the eyes of the noblewoman in the painting, to the eyes of the men in the larger painting, down the sword to the image of the woman in the museum catalog, down the easel hanging from the art critic's shoulder, and up his bent arm back to the magnifying glass. That is, the lines of the painting control our gaze, making us focus on the elements of the painting that emphasize looking.

The title, too, is about looking and can be seen as a pun: at first glance, the "art critic" is clearly the young man peering at the portrait of a woman; but the "art critic" could also be the art itself, which is not simply looking at the man, but forming a judgment of him. The woman he inspects is in turn inspecting him, and so are the men in the other painting. The woman doesn't seem to take the art critic seriously; her faint smile and raised eyebrows show that she is amused by his intensity, by how earnestly he is studying her. She seems also to be flirting with the young man, thus inverting the usual relationship between a portrait of a beautiful woman and the viewer; in life, the viewer admires, even ogles, the portrait. Here the painting ogles the viewer. In contrast to the woman, the burghers in the other painting are angry, even scandalized by the art critic as if they find his close inspection intrusive and insulting. Both reactions could be seen as a critique of art critics who pick apart a painting rather than experiencing it as a whole. The young man, with his museum catalog, art books, and magnifying glass is a parody of the overly zealous critic.

There is also another art critic in this painting—us. By setting us up to look at the young man looking at a painting that looks back at him, Rockwell invites us to think about our own practice analyzing paintings. Perhaps he is telling us not to take ourselves too seriously. To look too intently at a painting may keep us from being immersed in the world the painting offers: we may notice tiny details, but miss the total experience. The young man, in fact, seems physically boxed in, as if his vision—his understanding of the works of art—is constrained by his narrow gaze through the tiny magnifying glass. The composition of the painting reinforces this idea of constraint: the lines emphasize that the man is boxed in a corner. The vertical lines of the paintings' frames parallel the vertical line where the two walls meet, and the moldings on the wall and the squares of linoleum the man stands on all point toward this corner. Thus, the man's physical position in the corner could be viewed as a metaphor for his narrow brand of art criticism.

Finally, one might look at this painting biographically. Rockwell was often misprized by art critics as shallow, as a painter of simplistic commercial images used primarily as magazine illustrations. Yet in *Art Critic,* he imitates two traditional types of seventeenth-century painting—the portrait of a noblewoman and the Dutch masterpiece—thus showing his technical versatility. Note the resemblance between the painting on the right to Franz Hals's *Regents of the Old Men's Alms House,* reproduced in Berger's "Ways of Seeing" (p. 520). Rockwell's art critic is also an artist. His palette and easel tell us that he has come to the museum not merely to look, but also to learn, probably to imitate the great masters. The art critic is scrutinizing the painting not to pass judgment on it, but to analyze its brush strokes as part of his own growth as a serious artist. Viewed this way, the painting elicits both mockery of the art critic's earnestness and respect for his effort to learn, thus creating common ground between these two responses.

EXPLORING THE ARTS IN THE ESSAYS

The essays in this chapter address the experience of interacting with art, from the audience's viewpoint or that of the artist. John Berger, Mitchell Stephens ("By Means of the Visible"), and Wanda M. Corn all write about how we see visual images. John Berger, focusing on painting, argues that what we see depends on what we already believe: we choose to notice some things and ignore others, and we interpret what we notice according to ideas about the world that we already have. Mitchell Stephens talks about the power of images to affect us: they render complex ideas more efficiently than words can do. Wanda M. Corn, in discussing Norman Rockwell's painting *The Connoisseur,* shows how different artistic styles require different ways of perceiving: abstract expressionists like Jackson Pollock, for example, require an act of "intense looking," in which the viewer "merge[s] psychologically with the painting" and "lose[s] consciousness of his physical self." In contrast, Rockwell's paintings, which tell a story, invite the reader to look closely at individual details rather than be enveloped by the painting as a whole.

William A. Ewing ("Dance and Photography") discusses photography from the artist's point of view, showing how the dance photographer strives to capture the "inner life" of the dancer. With every picture, the photographer makes dozens of decisions—for example, about how to light and frame the subject, or whether the dancer will be moving or still, posed or apparently unaware, in rehearsal or performance. In a similar way, Jon Boorstin describes how the filmmaker's art—full of complex techniques in the use of camera shots, lighting, and sound—makes us believe illusions.

In addition to discussing how the individual perceives visual art, the authors address some of the social implications of the arts. John Berger discusses the democratization of painting—how fine arts are no longer the exclusive property of the wealthy; instead, the camera has made it possible to reproduce images from famous paintings on T-shirts and posters, not only making them widely available, but also allowing the public to alter these images—adding text to a Van Gogh painting, for example. Robert Santelli ("A Century of the Blues"), in detailing the early history of the blues, shows how this musical form evolved from the music slaves brought with them from West Africa; was influenced by spirituals, work songs, and folk music; and incorporated the daily experiences of African Americans in a racist culture. In "The Ties That Bind," Rosanne Cash, a country music singer, describes country music as a form grounded in family relationships and often performed by families. In "When Chickenheads Come Home to Roost," Joan Morgan explores the complex relationship between the disturbing image of women depicted in many of the lyrics of hip-hop music and the cultural circumstances that give rise to such images—a history of violence and oppression directed against African American men. As an African American woman, she seeks a way to reconcile her dismay at the misogyny of these lyrics with her sympathy for the men who write them.

The relationship between the artist and the work of art is also a theme in these readings. John Berger shows how the social context of a painting by Franz Hals—the artist's impoverishment and humiliating dependence on charity—influenced his depiction of the patrons who supported him. Jon Boorstin shows how filmmaking depends on the artist's technical skill and the ability to use sophisticated equipment as well as a sensitive eye and ear. In the same way, William Ewing shows how the photographer must learn a language of images; instead of words and sentences, the photographer creates his art through tone and contrast, double-exposures, blur, and lighting effects. Wanda Corn describes how Norman Rockwell incorporated his understanding of the history and production of other artistic styles into his own painting. Martha Graham, dancer and choreographer, describes the sources of her inspiration, seeing the artist's gift not just in the development of a powerful body and precise technique—though those are essential—but also in such personal characteristics as wonder and openness to life's experience. Rosanne Cash describes how singing onstage with her father allowed her to reconcile conflicts between them. And Robert Santelli shows how generations of blues musicians transmitted their art to each other and transformed it over time. All the writers in this chapter attempt to translate into words the intangible power of art on the artist and audience.

Analyzing an Essay

Look at Rosanne Cash's "The Ties That Bind," an essay that focuses on the relationship between an artist and her art form, in this case country music. Descended from three generations of musicians, and the daughter of renowned country singer Johnny Cash, Rosanne Cash describes how music creates both conflict and reconciliation between her and her family and how she struggles "to make the transition from the creative realms to daily life and back with grace." As a teenager, she tried to distance herself from her family's music background: she would "be an archeologist and move to a kibbutz." But her father's music keeps pulling her back into the family. Her father takes her on a road trip, during which he teaches her his repertoire of songs; his love for this music develops in her both a "passion for songwriting" and a closeness to and appreciation for her father. Then and since, music is the tie that binds Rosanne Cash to her family.

At the same time, family is the tie that binds Cash to music. This connection is not unique to Cash's family; it is the impetus behind country music. Much country music has been written and performed by members of the same family, and family relationships form the basis for its themes—jealous husbands, wayward daughters, saintly mothers, faithful dogs, dying babies. For Rosanne Cash, the song and the singer, art and life, are inseparable. As you read this essay, notice how Cash describes and then reconciles conflicts. What are the different conflicts she recounts? In what ways does music provide common ground between her and her father? What is Cash's attitude toward other kinds of popular music? How does she resolve her discomfort with this music? How does the tone of Cash's writing reflect her desire to resolve conflict?

JOHN BERGER argues that the act of seeing is complex and variable: we see what we choose to see, and our perceptions change according to the context—that is, according to what we expect to see, what we know about what we are looking at, our assumptions about the world around us, when and where we are as well as the physical location of the object, and so forth. Think of something that looked different to you at two different times—possibly two different periods of your life or two different times of day. What accounted for the difference in what you saw?

Born in London in 1926, BERGER served in World War II; a grant from the army helped pay for his education at the Chelsea School of Art. Berger started out as a painter, but he soon branched out into other art forms—especially literary and journalistic ones—and he was the art critic for the *New Statesmen* for a decade in the 1950s. He published *Ways of Seeing*—the television series and the book—in 1972, along with his best-known novel, *G.*, which won the Booker Prize. Today he lives in a small rural community in the French Alps.

Ways of Seeing (1972) | BY JOHN BERGER

The way we see things is affected by what we know or what we believe. In the Middle Ages when men believed in the physical existence of Hell the sight of fire must have meant something different from what it means today. Nevertheless their idea of Hell owed a lot to the sight of fire consuming and the ashes remaining—as well as to their experience of the pain of burns.

When in love, the sight of the beloved has a completeness which no words and no embrace can match: a completeness which only the act of making love can temporarily accommodate.

Yet this seeing which comes before words, and can never be quite covered by them, is not a question of mechanically reacting to stimuli. (It can only be thought of in this way if one isolates the small part of the process which concerns the eye's retina.) We only see what we look at. To look is an act of choice. As a result of this act, what we see is brought within our reach—though not necessarily within arm's reach. To touch something is to situate oneself in relation to it. (Close your eyes, move round the room and notice how the faculty of touch is like a static, limited form of sight.) We never look at just one thing; we are always looking at the relation between things and ourselves. Our vision is continually active, continually moving, continually holding things in a circle around itself, constituting what is present to us as we are. . . .

An image is a sight which has been recreated or reproduced. It is an appearance, or a set of appearances, which has been detached from the place and time in which it first made its appearance and preserved—for a few moments or a few centuries. Every image embodies a way of seeing. Even a photograph. For photographs are not, as is often assumed, a mechanical record. Every time we look at a photograph, we are aware, however slightly, of the photographer selecting that sight from an infinity of other possible sights. This is true even in the most casual family snapshot. The photographer's way of seeing is reflected in his choice of subject. The painter's way of seeing is reconstituted by the marks he makes on the canvas or paper. Yet, although every image embodies a way of seeing, our perception or appreciation of an image depends also upon our own way of seeing. (It may be, for example, that Sheila is one figure among twenty; but for our own reasons she is the one we have eyes for.) . . .

Yet when an image is presented as a work of art, the way people look at it is affected by a whole series of learnt assumptions about art. Assumptions concerning:

Beauty

Truth

Genius

Civilization

Form

Status

Taste, etc.

Many of these assumptions no longer accord with the world as it is. (The world-as-it-is is more than pure objective fact, it includes consciousness.) Out of true with the present, these assumptions obscure the past. They mystify rather than clarify. The past is never there waiting to be discovered, to be recognized for exactly what it is. History always constitutes the relation between a present and its past. Consequently fear of the present leads to mystification of the past. The past is not for living in; it is a well of conclusions from which we draw in order to act. Cultural mystification of the past entails a double loss. Works of art are made unnecessarily remote. And the past offers us fewer conclusions to complete in action.

When we "see" a landscape, we situate ourselves in it. If we "saw" the art of the past, we would situate ourselves in history. When we are prevented from seeing it, we are being deprived of the history which belongs to us. Who benefits from this deprivation? In the end, the art of the past is being mystified because a privileged minority is striving to invent a history which can retrospectively justify the role of the ruling classes, and such a justification can no longer make sense in modern terms. And so, inevitably, it mystifies.

Let us consider a typical example of such mystification. A two-volume study was recently published on Frans Hals. It is the authoritative work to date on this painter. As a book of specialized art history it is no better and no worse than the average.

Regents of the Old Men's Alms House by Hals 1580–1666. Frans Hals Museum, Haarlem, The Netherlands

Regents of the Old Men's Alms House by Hals 1580–1666

The last two great paintings by Frans Hals portray the Governors and the Governesses of an Alms House for old paupers in the Dutch seventeenth-century city of Haarlem. They were officially commissioned portraits. Hals, an old man of over eighty, was destitute. Most of his life he had been in debt. During the winter of 1664, the year he began painting these pictures, he obtained three loads of peat on public charity, otherwise he would have frozen to death. Those who now sat for him were administrators of such public charity.

Regentesses of the Old Men's Alms House by Hals 1580–1666

The author records these facts and then explicitly says that it would be incorrect 10
to read into the paintings any criticism of the sitters. There is no evidence, he says, that
Hals painted them in a spirit of bitterness. The author considers them, however, remarkable works of art and explains why. Here he writes of the Regentesses:

> Each woman speaks to us of the human condition with equal importance.
> Each woman stands out with equal clarity against the *enormous* dark surface,
> yet they are linked by a firm rhythmical arrangement and the subdued diago-
> nal pattern formed by their heads and hands. Subtle modulations of the *deep,*
> glowing blacks contribute to the *harmonious fusion* of the whole and form an
> *unforgettable contrast* with the *powerful* whites and vivid flesh tones where the
> detached strokes reach *a peak of breadth and strength.* (our italics)

The compositional unity of a painting contributes fundamentally to the power of
its image. It is reasonable to consider a painting's composition. But here the composition is written about as though it were in itself the emotional charge of the painting.
Terms like *harmonious fusion, unforgettable contrast,* reaching *a peak of breadth and
strength* transfer the emotion provoked by the image from the plane of lived experience, to that of disinterested "art appreciation." All conflict disappears. One is left with
the unchanging "human condition," and the painting considered as a marvellously
made object.

Very little is known about Hals or the Regents who commissioned him. It is not
possible to produce circumstantial evidence to establish what their relations were. But
there is the evidence of the paintings themselves: the evidence of a group of men and
a group of women as seen by another man, the painter. Study this evidence and judge
for yourself.

Detail from *Regentesses of the Old Men's Alms House.*

Detail from *Regentesses of the Old Men's Alms House.*

The art historian fears such direct judgement:

> As in so many other pictures by Hals, the penetrating characterizations almost seduce us into believing that we know the personality traits and even the habits of the men and women portrayed.

What is this "seduction" he writes of? It is nothing less than the paintings working upon us. They work upon us because we accept the way Hals saw his sitters. We do not accept this innocently. We accept it in so far as it corresponds to our own observation of people, gestures, faces, institutions. This is possible because we still live in a society of comparable social relations and moral values. And it is precisely this which gives the paintings their psychological and social urgency. It is this—not the painter's skill as a "seducer"—which convinces us that we *can* know the people portrayed.

The author continues: 15

> In the case of some critics the seduction has been a total success. It has, for example, been asserted that the Regent in the tipped slouch hat, which hardly covers any of his long, lank hair, and whose curiously set eyes do not focus, was shown in a drunken state.

This, he suggests, is a libel. He argues that it was a fashion at that time to wear hats on the side of the head. He cites medical opinion to prove that the Regent's expression could well be the result of a facial paralysis. He insists that the painting would have been unacceptable to the Regents if one of them had been portrayed drunk. One might go on discussing each of these points for pages. (Men in seventeenth-century Holland wore their hats on the side of their heads in order to be thought of as adventurous and pleasure-loving. Heavy drinking was an approved practice. Etcetera.) But such a discussion would take us even farther away from the only confrontation which matters and which the author is determined to evade.

Frans Hals Museum, Haarlem

Detail from *Regents of the Old Men's
Alms House.*

In this confrontation the Regents and Regentesses stare at Hals, a destitute old painter who has lost his reputation and lives off public charity; he examines them through the eyes of a pauper who must nevertheless try to be objective, i.e., must try to surmount the way he sees as a pauper. This is the drama of these paintings. A drama of an "unforgettable contrast."

Mystification has little to do with the vocabulary used. Mystification is the process of explaining away what might otherwise be evident. Hals was the first portraitist to paint the new characters and expressions created by capitalism. He did in pictorial terms what Balzac did two centuries later in literature. Yet the author of the authoritative work on these paintings sums up the artist's achievement by referring to

> Hals's unwavering commitment to his personal vision, which enriches our consciousness of our fellow men and heightens our awe for the ever-increasing power of the mighty impulses that enabled him to give us a close view of life's vital forces.

That is mystification. . . .

The invention of the camera . . . changed the way in which men saw paintings 20 painted long before the camera was invented. Originally paintings were an integral part of the building for which they were designed. Sometimes in an early Renaissance church or chapel one has the feeling that the images on the wall are records of the building's interior life, that together they make up the building's memory—so much are they part of the particularity of the building.

The uniqueness of every painting was once part of the uniqueness of the place where it resided. Sometimes the painting was transportable. But it could never be seen in two places at the same time. When the camera reproduces a painting, it destroys the uniqueness of its image. As a result its meaning changes. Or, more exactly, its meaning multiplies and fragments into many meanings.

Massaccio (Maso di San Giovanni) (1401–1428). Interior of the Brancacci Chapel. Brancacci Chapel, S. Maria del Carmine, Florence, Italy.

This is vividly illustrated by what happens when a painting is shown on a television screen. The painting enters each viewer's house. There it is surrounded by his wallpaper, his furniture, his mementoes. It enters the atmosphere of his family. It becomes their talking point. It lends its meaning to their meaning. At the same time it enters a million other houses and, in each of them, is seen in a different

context. Because of the camera, the painting now travels to the spectator rather than the spectator to the painting. In its travels, its meaning is diversified. . . .

In the age of pictorial reproduction the meaning of paintings is no longer attached to them; their meaning becomes transmittable: that is to say it becomes information of a sort, and, like all information, it is either put to use or ignored; information carries no special authority within itself. When a painting is put to use, its meaning is either modified or totally changed. One should be quite clear about what this involves. It is not a question of reproduction failing to reproduce certain aspects of an image faithfully; it is a question of reproduction making it possible, even inevitable, that an image will be used for many different purposes and that the reproduced image, unlike an original work, can lend itself to them all. Let us examine some of the ways in which the reproduced image lends itself to such usage.

National Gallery, London

Venus and Mars by Botticelli

Reproduction isolates a detail of a painting from the whole. The detail is transformed. An allegorical figure becomes a portrait of a girl. . . .

Close-up of *Venus and Mars*

Pieter Breughel, the Elder, Procession to Calvary, 1564. Kunsthistorisches Museum, Vienna

Procession to Calvary by Breughel

Paintings are often reproduced with words around them. 25

This is a landscape of a cornfield with birds flying out of it. Look at it for a moment. Then look at the next page.

Van Gogh Museum, Amsterdam

Van Gogh's *Wheatfield with Crows*

This is the last picture that Van Gogh painted before he killed himself.

It is hard to define exactly how the words have changed the image but undoubtedly they have. The image now illustrates the sentence. . . .

Consequently a reproduction, as well as making its own references to the image of its original, becomes itself the reference point for other images. The meaning of an image is changed according to what one sees immediately beside it or what comes immediately after it. Such authority as it retains, is distributed over the whole context in which it appears. . . .

The visual arts have always existed within a certain preserve; originally this preserve was magical or sacred. But it was also physical: it was the place, the cave, the building, in which, or for which, the work was made. The experience of art, which at first was the experience of ritual, was set apart from the rest of life—precisely in order to be able to exercise power over it. Later the preserve of art became a social one. It entered the culture of the ruling class, whilst physically it was set apart and isolated in their palaces and houses. During all this history the authority of art was inseparable from the particular authority of the preserve.

What the modern means of reproduction have done is to destroy the authority of art and to remove it—or, rather, to remove its images which they reproduce—from any preserve. For the first time ever, images of art have become ephemeral, ubiquitous, insubstantial, available, valueless, free. They surround us in the same way as a language surrounds us. They have entered the mainstream of life over which they no longer, in themselves, have power. 30

CONNECTING PERSONALLY TO THE READING

1. Berger argues that historically, the privileged classes have created a mystique about art, treating it as an elite form of expression. What were your attitudes toward art as you were growing up? Do you think art is still remote from the average person, or is it available to everyone?

2. Berger believes that the camera has destroyed the "authority" of art; that is, because the camera has made it possible to reproduce works of art on T-shirts, mugs, and other everyday objects, a work of art can be placed in any context and can thus lose its power to inspire awe. Do you agree with this assessment?

FOCUSING ON THE ARGUMENT

1. Much of Berger's article can be seen as a definition of what it means to "see." What are two ways he defines "seeing"?

2. Berger spends a fair amount of time analyzing two paintings by Franz Hals, *Regents of the Old Men's Alms House* and *Regentesses of the Old Men's Alms House.* What point does he intend us to draw from this analysis? How does this point support his ideas about "seeing"?

SYNTHESIZING IDEAS FROM MULTIPLE READINGS

1. Berger believes that the circumstances under which a painting is created and displayed influence how it is understood by the viewer. Do you think Mitchell Stephens ("By Means of the Visible," p. 550) would agree with him? Give examples from both readings to support your answer.

2. Berger tells us that "every image embodies a way of seeing." What does he mean by this statement, and how might it apply to the movie images Jon Boorstin discusses in "The Hollywood Eye" (p. 561)?

3. Berger argues that changing the context in which we view a work of art can change the way we interpret it. How does the Guerrilla Girls' Web page "Do women have to be naked to get into the Met. Museum?"(Chapter 7, insert 7-4) illustrate Berger's point? In answering this question, compare the Guerrilla Girls' Web page with the Ingres painting (*Odalisque*, Chapter 7, insert 7-4).

4. In "Ice and Light" (p. 396), Barry Lopez compares the way nineteenth-century artists from Europe and the United States painted pastoral landscapes. What is this difference, and how can each be labeled a "way of seeing"?

WRITING TO ACT

1. Find a reproduction of a work of art or other image (e.g., a building on your campus) on an everyday object—such as a mouse pad, umbrella, sheet of stationery, or coffee mug. Then look at the original image (if you have access to it) or a reproduction of the image in a book. How do the different contexts change what you see? Write an editorial in which you explain the effect of reproducing this image onto a common object. You might consider these questions: Does the reproduction devalue the original? Remove its mystique? Make it available for large numbers of people to enjoy? Commercialize it? Or change its effect in other ways?

2. Take a photograph of a building or of people on your campus. Then take another photograph of the same building or people, but change your point of view as photographer. The difference might be a change of angle, light, surroundings, the addition of text to the finished print, or something else. Publish the two images in your school paper, on your Web site, or on a poster, along with a brief text, explaining what you see as the difference between the two images.

READING

WANDA M. CORN describes Norman Rockwell as much more complex, thoughtful, and skilled than many of his critics allow, capable of painting in many styles, appreciative of the abstract art so different from his own narrative realism, and insightful about the relationship between the viewer and the painting. Rockwell (1894–1978) is best known as an illustrator for the covers of *Saturday Evening Post* magazine and as a prolific painter of life in small-town America. His paintings—with their scenes of heroic boy scouts, wholesome children, and earnest shopkeepers—have been extremely popular with the public, but less so with art critics, who derided them for their sentimentality and for portraying a falsely idyllic view of American culture. In analyzing Rockwell's painting *The Connoisseur,* Corn both describes and models for us some of the many ways one can "see" or interpret a work of art. Think of a painting, sculpture, movie, theatrical production, or other performance that you liked, but that others didn't. What do you think accounted for the different reactions?

CORN is the Robert and Ruth Halpern Professor in Art History at Stanford, where her research interests include the art of the Gilded Age and twentieth-century America. She is the author of *The Great American Thing: Modern Art and National Identity* (1999).

Ways of Seeing (1999) | BY WANDA M. CORN

Norman Rockwell cared about the history of art and often put paintings by old and new masters in his paintings. He particularly enjoyed depicting humorous interactions he imagined transpiring between museum visitors and paintings on the walls. Take *Art Critic* [below], a painting about the intense looking that goes on in museums. A young art student in baggy pants and torn sneakers is absorbed in the act of looking. With the aid of a magnifying glass, he studies a piece of jewelry adorning the chest of a woman in an imaginary Rubens portrait. That he is a copyist soon to begin his work Rockwell tells us through the young man's tools. Off a shoulder strap hangs his paint box, a portable easel, and a palette loaded with juicy globs of color rendered so literally that they invite touching to determine whether they are mere illusions or actual peaks of paint. (In Rockwell's oil painting for the illustration, they are in high relief.) Art magazines are tucked under the young man's left arm. Most importantly, in the hand held behind his back, he has a book illustrating the painting in front of him. Therein begins the joke, for in the reproduction, the woman looks straight out at the viewer as she would in an actual portrait. In the Rubens *á la* Rockwell, the woman gazes down upon the young copyist, conveying considerable interest in her young admirer. The respectable burghers in the seventeenth-century Dutch painting on the other wall also react with their eyes. They look disapprovingly

Art Critic, 1955

upon what is transpiring between painter and painting. As our own eyes flit from detail to detail, joining all the other eyes at work, we quickly grasp that Rockwell's humor is about who is looking at whom. While this is easy humor to grasp, it rests upon a fundamental understanding of the nature of the art museum experience. Rockwell understood that museums are about seeing, about viewers using their eyes exclusively to interrogate the works of art in front of them. The humor comes when the figures in the paintings unexpectedly react to and return the viewer's gaze.

But where is the humor in another "looking-at-art" painting by Rockwell, the one called *The Connoisseur*?[1] One's first impression is that little is going on. Rockwell set his stage with a cast of only two: the Painting and the Beholder. The Painting we see head-on; the Beholder, we see squarely from behind. We watch him beholding but are not privy to his reactions, for we cannot see his face. In addition there is one small but important walk-on role in this drama played by the Floor, whose diamonds direct our eyes into the painting and whose ordered forms create a base for the equally ordered Beholder. Given Rockwell's fondness for detail and for faces, the "defaced" viewer and the minimalist composition are the work's most startling features. Let's look carefully at these components as they appear in the original painting, where there is considerable texture and vivid illusionism, qualities diluted in the mass-produced and smaller printed version on the cover of *The Saturday Evening Post* [p. 535].

When Rockwell rendered old-master paintings such as the Rubens portrait and the Frans Hals–like group in *Art Critic,* he imitated the loose brush-work and impasto on a much-reduced scale. Like those who make exquisite small-scale furniture for dollhouses, Rockwell had the ability to miniaturize the style of other painters. His deftness at imitation is particularly impressive in *The Connoisseur,* where he replicated Jackson Pollock's famous drip painting, a non-representational style completely at odds with Rockwell's own meticulous realism. From photographs and a couple of abstractions that the artist gave to friends, we know that Rockwell practiced his mock-Pollock style well in advance of the final painting.[2] He even had some studio fun, having himself photographed as he performed Pollock's characteristic gestures, imitating the famous and much-circulated photographs that Hans Namuth had made of "Jack the Dripper," as *Time* magazine described him [p. 532][3]. Instead of the cigarette that hung from Pollock's mouth in many of Namuth's photographs, Rockwell clenched his pipe between his teeth.

In the final composition, Rockwell created a drip painting that appears to be approximately six feet square, reduced in the painting to one-third this size. It is just a little taller and wider than the height of the Beholder. Recalling Pollock's classic drip paintings of 1947–50 [p. 533], Rockwell's Painting is a tour-de-force of illusionism. One can only marvel at how well he pulled it off. When Pollock created his large canvases, he laid them flat on the ground and walked around them, using the full swing of his arm to create arcs and drips of paint. The size and character of his forms, in other words, bore a direct relationship to the scale of his own body. To replicate such effects in miniature, Rockwell had to give the *illusion* of full arm swings of paint but in fact work up close with smaller instruments. He had to make the reduction without losing the proper relationship of the skeins of paint to the whole.

Even though the surface is not as airy and lacy as an original Pollock, Rockwell got something of the texture and energy right. His drips are appropriately thin, created by

Norman Rockwell painting *The Connoisseur*, 1961

Jackson Pollock painting, 1949

Hirschhorn Museum, Smithsonian Institute, Washington, DC

Jackson Pollock, *Number 3 1949; Tiger,* 1949

something more like a toothbrush than the trowel, knives, paint cans, and sticks that Pollock used, and the larger constellations of paint are proportionately in scale. Magically, the drips lie upon the surface of the canvas and retain their substance as paint. Some of the heavily painted areas have dried and shriveled, just as in Pollock's paintings.

While the painting easily satisfies viewers who know something of Pollock's style but have not been trained in its intricacies, Pollock connoisseurs who have had intimate encounters with the real thing might blanch. For them, the forms would appear too mechanical and cold, the colors too bright, and the surface too densely worked over with the artist's characteristic forms.[4] Furthermore, Pollock's preferred format was not square, but vertical and tall or horizontal and long. "Apocalyptic wallpaper," Pollock critics might well call Rockwell's imitation, using Harold Rosenberg's pungent description of "decorative" action paintings whose forms and surfaces failed to have any existential urgency. Such works "lack the dialectical tension of a genuine act, associated with risk and will," Rosenberg wrote. The artist's "gesture completes itself without arousing either an opposing movement within itself nor his own desire to make the act more fully his own. . . . The result is an apocalyptic wallpaper."[5]

But if we characterize Rockwell as a mimic rather than as a poor abstract painter or Pollock wannabe, then we cannot help but be impressed by the way he used his realist skills to approximate (or illustrate) Pollock's drip style. He even buried a conceit of his own within the Pollockesque swirls. To the right of the man's head, there is an unmistakable P for Pollock in bright red paint; with a little imagination one can also find a much larger (and bloodier) J to the left of the P. The stem of the J is crossed by a horizontal stroke, making not only a second, smaller J but also the shape of the cross. It was well known that Pollock had died in a car crash in 1956, five years before Rockwell conceived this work. On the wall below the Painting, in the same vertical register as the agitated JP, Rockwell signed his own name in sturdy, clean-cut block letters.

This deliberate juxtaposition of Pollock's non-representational artiness with Rockwell's own down-home illustrative skills happens again in the illusionistic body of the Beholder, which so bullishly interrupts the abstract Painting. In meticulous detail and clean realism, the Beholder is classic Rockwell; his body shape, clothes, and the things held in his hands identify his character type. He is conservatively attired, immaculately outfitted in a gray suit that is so perfectly fitted that nary a wrinkle appears across his broad shoulders. His costume not only speaks of his urbanity but also alludes to the male dandy whose aesthetic dress customarily included elegant gloves, an exquisite hat, and a walking stick, represented here by a surrogate umbrella. The soft gray gloves, in particular, give Rockwell's Beholder an air of preciousness and affectation, especially as one is worn while the other is not, a combination that has a long tradition in visual and literary representations of dandies. That our Beholder is a perfectionist in dress is also exemplified by his highly polished black shoes and his starched white shirt peeping above his suit collar and so tightly fitted that his neck bulges slightly out over it. This bit of fleshiness and the thinning gray hair suggest that the Beholder is in the prime of life. His dress evokes professional success (banking or law, perhaps), expensive tastes, and a touch of the esthete. He holds an Art Gallery Guide in his hands, signaling that he frequents galleries.

Exactly where is the Rockwellian humor in this confrontation between city man and abstract painting? *The Connoisseur,* unlike most *Post* covers by Rockwell, is exceedingly deadpan, giving us few directions as to how to react. Indeed, it is so open-ended that viewers read it from a variety of angles.[6] The three letters to the editor of *The Saturday Evening Post* that appeared in the February 17, 1962, issue are a case in point. M. R. Daugherty of Anaheim, California, wondered indignantly why Rockwell wasted his effort on "such junk! The word 'art' has been discounted as much as Uncle Sam's dollar in applying the word to such stuff." Joe F. Akins of Ruston, Louisiana, made his own joke of the cover by reading the Beholder as bewildered and suggesting that it was easy to understand why: for the painting "is obviously hanging upside down." A third writer, Robert J. Handy of Seattle, Washington, complimented Rock-

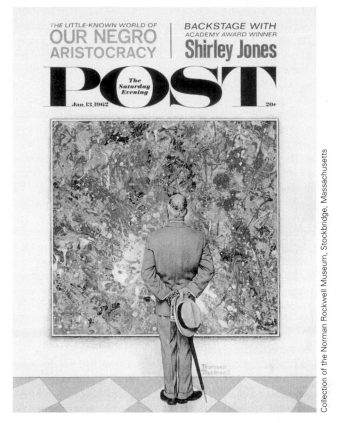

The Connoisseur, 1962

well's modern abstraction—not bad for "just an illustrator"—and praised his sense of humor, a "quality sorely needed in modern art."[7]

The first two of these writers perceived the Painting as the kind of art they did not like or appreciate. The third found it funny, but did not say exactly where he found the humor. All of them implicitly acknowledged the primacy of abstract art in post–World War II American culture. By 1961, when Rockwell created *The Connoisseur,* Abstract Expressionist art had been well covered in the popular press for nearly fifteen years; by the mid-1950s, it had successfully attracted collectors whose passion for this kind of difficult art was itself often newsworthy.[8] All this attention had helped fuel jokes and clichés about abstract paintings: that they could be hung with any side up or be produced by children or monkeys. In such a climate, Rockwell surely intuited that an encounter between a city gentleman and an abstract painting could amuse those for whom modern art was not a regular or necessary part of their universe. But he left the confrontation open to interpretation. *The Saturday Evening Post* readers might easily have found it funny because the world that the contemporary connoisseur occupied

10

was so far removed from the realities of their own lives, or because they believed Rockwell shared their rejection of abstract art. Or they might project onto the male viewer their own bewilderment and anxieties as beholders of paintings whose forms of address they did not understand or find engaging. They might also have found the finely dressed art appreciator a comic figure, he being a type far removed from the middle-brow suburbanites who ordinarily populated the covers of *The Saturday Evening Post*.

There is good slapstick humor, too, in the collision of the chaos and disorderliness of the mock Pollock painting with the tidiness and fastidiousness of the Beholder, whose ordered world extends into the diamond-patterned Floor beneath his feet. The Painting is aggressive and assaulting; the Beholder, rooted to an earthbound tile, is passive and receiving. They are not natural partners but aliens confronting one another. However one wishes to describe it—chaos versus order, color versus line, Baroque versus classical, youth versus age, imagination versus rationality, left brain versus right, female versus male, immateriality versus material—Rockwell vested his illustration of a gentleman's encounter with an abstract painting with some of the grandest and most elementary conflicts in the universe. This is what makes me smile. The Painting is so random and chaotic and the Beholder so balanced and symmetrical. The middle seam in his suit jacket divides his body exactly in half, as does the thin space between his legs. Both arms are pulled behind his back at the same angle and even the folds in his sleeves and pant legs seems to echo one another. Furthermore, his weight is evenly distributed, and his feet are planted like a tree in the middle of the central white diamond on the floor. But then, within all this rigor, there are subtle asymmetries that Rockwell used to animate his stolid composition: the two feet pointing away from the body at slightly different angles and the Beholder's body placed just right of center.

There are also smaller amusements. A little twist of hair that has managed to escape from the Beholder's tidy pate curls into his bald spot like a Pollock swirl of paint; harder to see, there is also a little white tuft at the front center of the Beholder's head that simultaneously belongs both to the hair on the man's head and to the painting's surface. That the Beholder's body remains at attention in the middle of an explosion of white paint is another hilarious passage. How calm and contained he stands in the ejaculatory crossfire of luminous paint!

Given that the miniature Pollock painting is rendered so carefully, even respectfully, what can we deduce, if anything, about Rockwell's personal appreciation of abstract art? If the Beholder is taken as Rockwell's surrogate, then it is all the more significant that the artist did not reveal the one body part we most want to see: the Beholder's face. This is a crucially missing element, since nothing about the Beholder, other than his containment and orderliness, registers any sure reaction to what he is seeing. Because faces are central vehicles for pictorial storytellers—certainly they were for Rockwell—the absence of the man's face warrants further consideration.

To assess the anomaly of Rockwell's faceless Beholder, let us compare him with other representations of connoisseurs looking at works of art. This is an old subject in the history of art, and traditionally the connoisseur's face is vital to the artist's narrative. When the subject first became popular in mid- to late-eighteenth-century England, connoisseurs were often the butt of visual jokes, and their faces carried the comic message. By distending the eyes and noses and exaggerating the wigs of their subjects, satirists such as William Hogarth and James Gillray mocked the pretense and

Unknown Artist, *The Auction,* 1770

greed of English gentlemen and women who formed private collections not because of a passion for art but for status and prestige. In an anonymous print made in London at this time, a group of upper-class connoisseurs, both men and women, stare at a landscape painting being offered for sale, not one of them seeming to notice that the canvas is upside-down [above]. They are grotesquely malformed creatures, analogous to animals who consume everything in sight. They have hooked or pointed noses, barnyard mouths, and intense eyes aimed like arrows at works of art, but seeing nothing. They are acquisitive possessors who do not see.

Alongside this tradition of the connoisseur as blind and foolish, another depicted 15 him as thoughtful and cultured. For artists such as Johann Zoffany in England and,

Honoré Daumier, *Le Connoisseur*, 1860–65

later, Honoré Daumier in France, the act of looking that transpires between a collector and a work of art was a favorite subject. In *Le Connoisseur* [above], Daumier's relaxed collector is seated in the privacy of his home, surrounded by works in his collection. He looks intently upon a small statue of the Venus de Milo standing on a nearby table, his absorption so total that we feel that we are intruding upon his private space.[9] The collector's face, turned to the object under scrutiny, registers appreciation and contentment. The pleasures of beholding, as well as possessing, are visualized further by the beam of light that Daumier uses to bring together the body of the connoisseur with the art he admires as well as the few prints at his side and on the table. Putting everything else in shadow, Daumier literally illuminates the satisfactions that concentrated looking can extract from works of art.

In his connoisseurial portrait of Sidney Janis [p. 539], George Segal renders the same kind of genial looker who expresses his ownership of art—in this case a 1933 Mondrian painting—by gently touching its frame. In the 1950s and 1960s, Janis was a well-known contemporary art dealer in New York; he handled the work of European modernists such as Picasso and Mondrian and also contemporary American artists such as the Abstract Expressionists and Pop artists. By then he had also formed an important collection of modern art that in 1968 went to New York's Museum of Modern

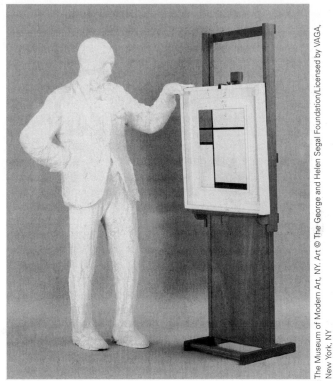

George Segal, *Portrait of Sidney Janis with Mondrian Painting,* 1967

Art.[10] When he sat (or stood, in this case) for his portrait by Segal, he allowed one of the Mondrian paintings in his collection to be worked into the composition. Segal represents him looking kindly and reflectively at the abstract painting on the easel, as if it were a lover. Together the collector and painting form a couple on intimate terms.

In that Rockwell's Beholder is in a public space—most likely a commercial art gallery, given the guide and umbrella in his hand—we must consider yet one more set of representations: cartoons about people in museums and galleries struggling to fathom—and articulate—the meaning of works of modern art. *The New Yorker* magazine specialized in cartoons of this genre and ran them so often that they conditioned audiences to expect humor whenever city viewers were pictured confronting difficult art. These cartoons poked fun both at the befuddled New Yorkers trying to understand abstract art and at the art itself.[11] In one such cartoon, a woman in a gallery of abstract sculpture stands in front of a golf club bent into an abstract shape and calls over to her perplexed husband looking at another work: "Here's one you'll understand." In another cartoon, two well-dressed women sit on a bench in front of a row of abstract paintings, and one says to the other "I wish this bench was in front of something I understood" [p. 540] In these examples, viewers confess their inability to find

"I wish this bench was in front of something I understood."

meaning in abstract works of art, despite their effort. In a Peter Arno example that *The New Yorker* ran in 1961, two city gentlemen of the same type as Rockwell's Beholder study a Pollock painting and render a discriminating if pretentious connoisseurial judgment. One says to the other, "His spatter is masterful, but his dribbles lack conviction" [p. 541].

Cartoons such as these had long been in circulation when Rockwell painted *The Connoisseur.* And his image has all the elements of these cartoons, except that it lacks a punch line. Rockwell does not tell us in words whether his Beholder is bewildered or delighted by what he is seeing; we don't even know if his eyes are open.

So what may we finally conclude about the silent Beholder's encounter with an Abstract Expressionist painting? Did Rockwell's faceless viewer-surrogate express the artist's own indecisiveness about modern art? Was the artist poking fun at connoisseurs of modern art by insinuating that they were dandified and effete? Was Rockwell angered, even threatened, by the popularity of New York School abstraction, expressing it by a joke: a miniature painting executed so well that Rockwell's talents as an illustrator dwarf Pollock's as a fine artist? Or was Rockwell's imitation the sincerest form of flattery, conveying admiration for the abstractionist?[12]

There is some truth, I suspect, to each of these lines of argument, especially if we recall that Rockwell was working in a climate where he and other figurative painters   20

"His spatter is masterful, but his dribbles lack conviction."

such as Andrew Wyeth were roundly criticized for their storytelling. He had cause to defend himself against his detractors and have a little fun with the pieties surrounding abstract art. In the 1950s, the art world feverishly debated the relative merits of abstract art, realist art, and art illustration, and Rockwell, because he was popular, was frequently caught in the crossfire. Clement Greenberg, one of the most vocal critics of the period and a champion of Pollock and other New York School artists, set the terms of the debate. He argued for the aesthetic complexities and challenges of abstract art while protesting the cheapened kitsch culture that he felt dominated America. In Greenberg's lexicon, Rockwell's illustrations were kitsch—that is, popular and commercial artworks that appealed to the masses. His realism was easy, sentimental, and undemanding. When such popular forms become the dominant taste, Greenberg warned, the high arts find it hard to flourish or even survive, and enlightened culture collapses; this was a great danger he felt, in a society as populist and commercial as the United States.[13]

In 1949, Russell Lynes, a writer about contemporary culture, observed how pervasive the debate about the value of modern art, especially abstraction, had become. Even a popular magazine like *Life* was reporting on abstract painters and had sponsored a

Herbert Gehr, *Highbrow, Lowbrow, Middlebrow, Life*, April 11, 1949

serious conference on the nature of modern art.[14] In a long and amusing essay, Lynes suggested that American culture was now divided along lines of taste rather than class. "It isn't wealth or family that makes prestige these days. It's high thinking," he suggested.[15] The country was now broken into three taste groups: highbrow, middlebrow, and lowbrow. Lynes described highbrows as individuals who were challenged by the complexities and intellectuality of modern art, while lowbrows did not care about what was in or out of fashion in art; they just liked what they liked. Middlebrows, on the other hand, took high culture seriously but did not make the fine distinctions of the highbrows. They put reproductions on their walls rather than works of art, and in many respects they had ordinary and eclectic tastes. When it came to modern art, middlebrows could be philistines, lashing out at what they could not easily understand.

The editors of *Life* magazine liked Lynes's *Harper's Weekly* article so much that they digested it for their readers, creating two pictorial charts to categorize the new taste lines.[16] In one of these, they depicted three men standing in front of three pictures [above]. Just as in Rockwell's *The Connoisseur*, we see the men completely from behind and judge their types by their clothes and body postures. To the left, the highbrow man in a suit has his hands drawn comfortably behind his back, his body relaxed as he looks upon a Picasso portrait. In the center, the lowbrow wears a baggy shirt with suspenders; he is short, a bit overweight, and lounges onto one leg. Working class in type, he stares at a pin-up on a calendar. The third man, the middlebrow, stands with tension running throughout his suited body. His hands are drawn in front of him, his shoulders are square, his body type athletic and alert. He looks with assurance at Grant Wood's painting *American Gothic*. He might just as well have been admiring one by Rockwell.

Such postwar arguments set the parameters by which Rockwell was judged by modernist art critics at the time and by art historians today. The latter still are likely to see in the illustrator's work a pandering to philistine audiences, whose antimodern tastes they assume Rockwell shared and nurtured. *The Connoisseur* offers a brilliant corrective to such knee-jerk presumptions. In it, Rockwell makes clear that he knows something about abstract art, and he details for his audience the differences between his very literal style and the abstract one of a modern artist. He found a way to illustrate for a popular audience the different demands that Abstract Expressionist canvases and the covers of *The Saturday Evening Post* made on their viewers. He used *The Connoisseur* to illustrate the theory of looking advocated by the New York School of abstraction and to demonstrate how different it was from the mode of looking embodied within his own illustrations.

A Rockwell painting addresses its viewers directly, relying on many details that are relatively easy to synthesize into a story. The canvases of abstract artists, especially those of the New York School, asked beholders to take time to experience pure form and color. The ideal viewer for Abstract Expressionist work was meditative, someone who slowed down, relinquished external concerns, and put himself into that suspended state Michael Fried has called "absorbed beholding."[17] As Pollock once told an interviewer, he thought viewers should look "passively" at his paintings "and try to receive what the painting has to offer and not bring a subject matter or preconceived idea of what they are looking for."[18] Through such acts of intense looking, the viewer might so psychologically merge with the painting that he would lose consciousness of his physical self (replacing eye-sight with I-site, we might say). Such a theory of transcendence lay behind the New York School's production of very large canvases, so large that they become painted environments, engulfing viewers who engage them from a close vantage point. Customarily, these canvases were hung low and far apart so that viewers would experience each one completely on its own, standing so close that they would have no peripheral vision outside the canvas. They were meant to be completely immersed by large fields of color and painted line.[19]

This, I would submit, is the kind of beholder experience Rockwell illustrated, revealing himself to be far more learned and experienced in abstract art than one might generally suppose. *The Connoisseur* illustrates the relationship between Beholder and Painting that abstract artists imagined and desired. Following this line of argument, let's look one last time at *The Connoisseur*.

Like the Pollock abstractions it imitates, the Painting is very large and was the first thing Rockwell painted. (One can see the vestigial outline of drips under the figure and under the white of the wall at the edges of the canvas.) He then painted the body of the Beholder over the painting so that two thirds of his body was embraced by the abstraction.[20] By tilting the diamond tiles of the Floor upward, Rockwell exaggerated what he had undoubtedly read about painters such as Pollock and Mark Rothko, whose ideal viewers engaged abstract paintings at close hand. He intensified that engagement by adding subtle shadows at all four edges of the canvas, making the Painting appear suspended in front of the gallery wall and pushing into the Beholder's

25

space. Because the Painting is so colorful and dynamic, and so much more aggressive than the Beholder, it threatens to wrap the Beholder in its web. As if a counter force, the modeled body of the Beholder pushes back into the abstract canvas, creating a playful push-pull dynamic that cleverly mimics one of the formalist ideals of the Abstract Expressionist painters.

Locking his two protagonists into an intense pictorial relationship, Rockwell played upon the cliché that opposites attract. In its lock on the Beholder, the abstract Painting also signifies the attacks the New York School made on illustrators like Rockwell, whose gray-suited surrogate—so very realistic in style—stands his ground. But Rockwell's most subtle and sophisticated humor resides in the way he dramatized the nature of looking that Abstract Expressionist canvases invited and depended upon. This was not the kind of looking at details through a magnifying glass that Rockwell depicted in *Art Critic,* an old-master variant of seeing that he practiced as his own. It was rather a contemporary style of absorbed looking that promised transcendence and the experience of bodily loss. Rockwell's down-home emblem of that loss, and of this manner of beholding, is the missing face. The marvel is that Rockwell found a popular and accessible means to illustrate this difficult and innovative style of beholding while remaining true to his own audience's more traditional ways of seeing.[21]

Notes

I thank Tirza Latimer for research assistance; Linda Szekely for helping me in the Rockwell archives; Ken Aptekar, Rolf Diamant, and Nora Mitchell for their clarifying observations; Kris Kelley and Steven Spielberg for making it possible for me to study the painting; and David Cateforis for reading a draft of this essay and suggesting refinements.

1. The painting of *The Connoisseur* was made in 1961 and published on the cover of *The Saturday Evening Post* on January 13, 1962. The fullest discussion of it to date is Karal Ann Marling, *Norman Rockwell* (New York: Harry N. Abrams, Inc., in association with the National Museum of American Art, Smithsonian Institution, 1997), pp. 131–132.

2. None of Rockwell's practice Pollocks appear as polished or as convincing as the one in the final painting. For illustrations of them, see Laurie Norton Moffatt, *Norman Rockwell: A Definitive Catalogue,* 2 vols. (Stockbridge, Mass.: The Norman Rockwell Museum at Stockbridge, 1986), 1:235–236.

3. "The Wild Ones," *Time,* February 20, 1956, pp. 70–75; "Posh Pollock," *Time,* December 15, 1958, p. 58.

4. For example, art historian David Anfam wrote that Rockwell "reduces Pollock's delicate lines to a wall of splashes that leaves the spectator cold." *Abstract Expressionism* (London: Thames and Hudson, 1990), p. 9.

5. Harold Rosenberg, "The American Action Painters," *Art News* 51 (December 1952): 49. My thanks to David Cateforis for reminding me of Rosenberg's coining of this term.

6. I informally polled friends and family as to how they interpreted this image and received a range of answers. Those in my informal group who presumed Rockwell to be an artistically and politically conservative painter consistently felt he had to have been ridiculing modern art. In my final reading of *The Connoisseur,* I think such presumptions stem from a modernist typecasting of Rockwell as a purveyor of middlebrow, kitsch art and not from a close look at his paintings, where he reveals his curiosity about and sympathy for all kinds of art-making, including modern paintings.

7. *The Saturday Evening Post,* February 17, 1962, 5.

8. For an examination of the popular press coverage of Abstract Expressionism, see Bradford R. Collins, "*Life* Magazine and the Abstract Expressionists, 1948–51: A Historiographic Study of a Late Bohemian Enterprise," *Art Bulletin* 73 (June 1991): 283–308.

9. I am indebted here to Michael Fried's descriptions and interpretations in *Absorption and Theatricality: Painting and Beholder in the Age of Diderot* (Chicago: University of Chicago Press, 1988). See especially chapter one, "The Primacy of Absorption."

10. See the catalogue *Three Generations of Twentieth-Century Art: The Sidney and Harriet Janis Collection of The Museum of Modern Art* (New York: The Museum of Modern Art, 1972).

11. See *The New Yorker Album of Art and Artists* (Greenwich, Conn.: New York Graphic Society, 1970) for a large selection of cartoons the magazine has run about modern art. They fall generally into three categories:

those that poke fun at the public's efforts to understand abstract art; those that ridicule the art itself as overblown and egocentric; and those that make the impoverished artist in his garret, slumped in existential angst, the butt of jokes.

12. The editors for *The Saturday Evening Post*, writing of the cover in the table of contents for the January 13, 1962, issue, remarked that it was not clear what the "prosperous-looking art collector" was thinking. "Cover artist Norman Rockwell won't say. 'If I were young now I might paint that way myself,' he explains. 'Recently I attended some classes in modern art techniques. I learned a lot and loved it.'"

13. See Clement Greenberg, "Avant-Garde and Kitsch," *Art and Culture: Critical Essays* (Boston: Beacon Press, 1961), pp. 3–21. On pages 3 and 14, he cites both Norman Rockwell and *Saturday Evening Post* covers as examples of kitsch.

14. "A *Life* Round Table on Modern Art: Fifteen Distinguished Critics and Connoisseurs Undertake to Clarify the Strange Art of Today," *Life*, October 11, 1948, pp. 56.

15. Russell Lynes, "Highbrow, Lowbrow, Middlebrow," *Harper Magazine*, February 1949, pp. 19–28.

16. *Life*, April 11, 1949, pp. 99–102.

17. Fried, *Absorption and Theatricality*, p. 157.

18. "An interview with Jackson Pollock (1950)," in Francis V. O'Connor, *Jackson Pollock* (New York: The Museum of Modern Art, 1967), p. 79.

19. Mark Rothko once recommended that the viewer be as close as eighteen inches to his abstract paintings. John Gage, "Rothko Color as Subject," in Jeffrey Weiss, *Mark Rothko* (Washington D.C.: National Gallery of Art; New Haven, Conn.: Yale University Press, 1998), p. 262.

20. From photographs taken while he was working on *The Connoisseur*, we know that Rockwell carefully thought about how much of the Beholder should be "in" the painting. He used a cutout of the Beholder and moved him up and down against the Painting in order to select the relationship he wanted. See Moffatt, *Norman Rockwell*, p. 236, C505a, for one of his trial runs in which less of the Beholder's legs are in the painting and, as a result, the composition is much less intense. Rockwell at one point also considered putting a second viewer into his painting, a female spectator seen in profile. This idea, too, is less riveting than the final version.

21. It seems appropriate that Steven Spielberg, a filmmaker who is himself a master of special effects and emotional manipulation, owns and treasures this painting as well as others by Rockwell.

CONNECTING PERSONALLY TO THE READING

1. When you first looked at Rockwell's *The Connoisseur* did you find it humorous? Did your reaction to the painting change after you read Corn's analysis? Why or why not?

2. Did reading about the historical context of *The Connoisseur*—the tension between commercial and fine art and between a realist and abstract style in the 1960s art world—change the way you saw the painting? Why or why not?

3. Give an example of "highbrow," "lowbrow," and "middlebrow" art from another art form—such as music, drama, dance, film, or photography. Explain why you categorized each example as you did.

FOCUSING ON THE ARGUMENT

1. Though Corn's purpose is to interpret *The Connoisseur,* she discusses several other paintings and cartoons. How do these discussions help you understand her points about *The Connoisseur*?

2. Corn offers several other critics' interpretations of *The Connoisseur,* some of which seem to conflict with hers. What is her attitude toward these alternative ways of seeing? How does she reconcile them with her own argument?

1. John Berger ("Ways of Seeing," p. 518) believes that what people see in a painting is influenced by assumptions they have about what makes something a work of art—assumptions about "beauty, truth, genius, civilization, form, status, [and] taste." Choose two different critical responses to *The Connoisseur* and show what assumptions about art lie behind them. You might, for example, consider whether a painter whose work appeals to the masses can be considered an artist or whether a viewer's perception of a picture differs if the painter is called an "artist" rather than an "illustrator."

2. Look at Franz Hals's painting, *Regents of the Old Men's Alms House* (reproduced in Berger's "Ways of Seeing"), and Rockwell's version of a Hals painting in *Art Critic.* What differences do you see in the two paintings? How does the fact that Rockwell's version is a painting within a painting affect your response as a viewer? How might John Berger ("Ways of Seeing") or Corn account for the differences you see?

3. In "By Means of the Visible" (p. 550), Mitchell Stephens argues that modern images (such as computer icons and street signs) often take the place of words. How does Corn show us that a narrative painting, such as *The Connoisseur,* can also tell a story without words? Which elements of the painting contribute to the "plot" of the story and "characterization" of the connoisseur?

4. What does it mean to be a "connoisseur" of art? Do you believe that Annie Dillard ("Heaven and Earth in Jest," p. 381) and Wendell Berry ("An Entrance to the Woods," p. 372) are connoisseurs of nature? Why or why not?

WRITING TO ACT

1. Go to a movie or other artistic performance, and write a review of what you've seen. Then read two different reviews of the same event and incorporate them into your argument. Try to find common ground between your viewpoint and those of the other critics.

2. Choose a movie, song, painting, or other work of art that has elicited different reactions on your campus. Write a survey to try to find out what values or assumptions lie beneath people's reactions to this work of art. For example, you might ask people why they were offended, angered, or delighted by the art; or what they would change about it; or what social effects they expect it to have. Poll at least fifteen people. Then write a report, explaining why you think different people saw the work of art differently.

READING

WILLIAM A. EWING's essay describes how dance photographers strive to represent one art form—dance—through another art form—photography. When photographer Barbara Morgan set out to represent Martha Graham's choreography, it was not enough for her to transcribe the dance visually; Morgan sought to capture the personal conflicts and yearnings that motivated Martha Graham's work. For Morgan, photography, like dance, was a form of expression, and her subject, Graham, was more than a dancer, but "a medium through which a greater rhythmic force, that of life itself, pulsed."

Have you ever tried to express an idea or feeling in a photograph you have taken? If so, what effect were you striving for, and what did you do to create it? If not, find a photograph in this book or elsewhere that you find especially moving. What is it about the photograph that appeals to you?

EWING, director of the Musée de l'Elysée in Lausanne, Switzerland, has been curator of many exhibitions in the United States and Europe. He has written several books about photography.

Selection from *Dance and Photography* (1987)

BY WILLIAM A. EWING

Initially Barbara Morgan resisted the blandishments of her husband, Willard, to take up photography. She preferred painting and poetry. She found herself sympathetic to the idea shared by many non-Western peoples that a photograph could steal a person's soul. "I won't be a thief!" she would flatly admonish her husband. But when he brought home a tiny Leica, one of the first in the country, and left it casually lying around, the temptation to give it a try was too much to resist. She soon discovered that the camera was more than a mechanical device; in the hands of an artist it could be used, as could the pen or the brush, in a poetic, expressive way. By the time Morgan met [Martha] Graham in 1935, she had achieved mastery over this new medium, and was looking for new realms to explore.

In an interview in *Dance Life* in 1979 she explained:

> I was moved by her dance (*Primitive Mysteries*) and I wondered if there was a relationship to these Indian rituals. She said "Exactly that. The Indian ritual experiences were one of the most moving experiences of my life." Just like that, bang, I said "Then I'd like to do a photograph book on your dance." She replied, "I'll work with you." Then we began.

It wasn't as a record of the dancer's art that the collaboration excited Morgan, although she could appreciate that it would serve this function; it was the inner life of the dancer which appealed to the poet in Morgan. Graham had learned to use her body to give voice to her innermost conflicts and yearnings.

Morgan evolved an "extinction method" of working, by which she means she would let time pass between seeing the performance and dealing with it. With enough time, "the lesser things would vanish and the intense moment would be right there in my brain. I'd see a pre-vision. Then I'd call Martha up and say I could do it now and we'd set up a time."

In *Deaths and Entrances,* a work inspired by the Brontë sisters, linear time is abandoned as Charlotte (Graham) revisits the past. Morgan created double-images to depict these simultaneous times [photo 1]. In *Letter to the World,* the story of Emily Dickinson's despair and reaffirmation, Morgan located a moment at the juncture of these states of mind [insert 8-2]: the rigidity of the body and the gesture of the arm convey despair; the fluidity of the skirt the hope of spiritual recovery. *War Theme,* on the other hand, held out no such hope [photo 2]. It was not, strictly speaking, a dance. William Carlos Williams had asked Morgan if she could create an image which could accompany one of his poems on the tragedy of the Spanish Civil War. Morgan in turn approached Graham, who agreed to collaborate. After a number of attempts, both were satisfied with one image in particular, in which the body seemed caught in the very instant of its annihilation. In a graphic tonal language of stark black and white (as life fades, light fades, and darkness overwhelms), the life-force yields to destruction.

For Morgan, Martha Graham was a medium through which a greater rhythmic force, that of life itself, pulsed. There were other dancers who had this shamanistic gift, and the photographer worked with them as well—Doris Humphrey, Charles Weidman, Erick Hawkins and Valerie Bettis. Moreover, the essence of dance was not confined to a

Photo 1, Martha Graham in *Deaths and Entrances,* by Barbara Morgan, 1945.

Photo 2, Barbara Morgan's photographs of Martha Graham represent the most celebrated collaboration between photographer and dancer in this century, a collaboration that extended to the creation of the dance *War Theme,* shown in this photograph, designed for the camera alone in 1941.

human vehicle, but could be found in a crowded street, the trunk of a tree, or a corn leaf. But no matter where it was to be found, every image was handled in the bold modernist spirit which the critic Elizabeth McCausland had called for in dance photography only a few years earlier:

> The modern dance is like modern painting and modern sculpture, clean, with crisp edges, of rigid and muscular materials. The photographs of the modern dance must be likewise, with great definition of values, not flowing draperies, with forms solidly modeled in light, but not swept by theatrical or stagey spotlights. . . .

Dance is often described as a language. So too is photography. Dance has movements and gestures; photography has images rendered in tones and contrasts. Dance has positions, *arabesques, jetés;* photography has time exposure, blur, double-exposures, montage. Dance has costumes and decor; photography has texture and grain. One has the stage; the other the frame. Both have lighting effects, illusion and their own chemistry.

In a sense the photographer reinvents his medium whenever he makes a picture. At every stage of the process he must make critical decisions concerning approach, treatment and, ultimately, presentation. Will his subjects be moving or still? Posed, or moving freely? Are they to be caught unawares or asked to participate? Will he work outdoors, on stage, in rehearsal or in the studio? How will he light his subject? How shall he frame it? What camera lens and film format will he use? How long will his exposure last? What might be accomplished with the printing in the darkroom—solarization, for example, or multiple printing? Finally, how shall the work reach the public—in newspapers or specialized magazines, a book or an exhibition? In fact, the options are infinitely more varied than this brief synopsis allows. Although it is seldom perceived as such by the public, photography is a truly plastic art.

CONNECTING PERSONALLY TO THE READING

1. Ewing describes a successful collaboration between dancer Martha Graham and photographer Barbara Morgan. What made this collaboration a success? When you have collaborated with another person on any kind of task, what made the collaboration work well or poorly?

2. What do you think Ewing means when he writes that the public seldom perceives photography as a "plastic art"? Do you agree with this statement? Why or why not?

FOCUSING ON THE ARGUMENT

1. Ewing identifies both dance and photography as languages. What do these art forms have in common with verbal languages? How useful is the analogy to language in helping you understand Ewing's ideas about dance photography?

2. Ewing introduces Morgan to us by telling us a brief story about how she changed her mind about photography. How does this story prepare you for the ideas about photography that come later?

3. Do Ewing's descriptions of Morgan's photographs help you understand the dance pho-tographer's craft? Compare what Ewing says about "Letter to the World," "Deaths and Entrances," and "War Theme" with the photographs of Graham performing these works.

SYNTHESIZING IDEAS FROM MULTIPLE READINGS

1. In "By Means of the Visible" (p. 550), Mitchell Stephens argues that "still images operate under severe handicaps when attempting to embody ideas." What does Stephens mean by this statement? Do you think that Ewing would agree with him? Why or why not?

2. Both Jon Boorstin ("The Hollywood Eye," p. 561) and Ewing discuss the challenges photog-raphers face as they try to create specific effects—for example, manipulating lighting or deciding which camera lens to use. Which challenges do they share? Which challenges are unique to their specific fields, still dance photography (Ewing) and film (Boorstin)?

3. According to Ewing, Morgan believed that the essence of dance existed not just in the human body, but also in other objects—"a crowded street, the trunk of a tree, or a corn leaf." In contrast, Martha Graham ("Blood Memory," p. 591) describes the essence of dance as "the expression of man—the landscape of his soul." What do these two state-ments mean? In what ways do they conflict with, agree with, or complement each other?

4. Nicholas Negroponte ("Creating a Culture of Ideas," p. 478) believes that to be creative, a person must take risks, be open to new ideas, and see things from multiple points of view, including those of other disciplines and cultures. Which of these characteristics do you see in Barbara Morgan, and why?

WRITING TO ACT

1. Barbara Morgan and Martha Graham collaborated on a photograph that illustrated one of William Carlos Williams's poems on the Spanish Civil War. Find a poem or other kind of writing that expresses feelings about a social problem; then take a photograph that repre-sents the feeling this poem evokes in you. Write a brief explanation of what you tried to accomplish in your photograph. Submit the photograph and writing to your campus news-paper or post them on your class Web site.

2. Using a large piece of poster board, create a collage of photographs to express your view of a particular social problem. Get permission to display your poster on campus.

READING

MITCHELL STEPHENS's article discusses the power and limitations of visual images as a form of communication. He argues that while images can efficiently express concrete meanings (e.g., street signs, the icons on a computer desktop), words are more effective for communicating abstractions (e.g., the sentence "I believe"). Think of two images that you encounter often in your life: in which ways are they more or less effective than words?

STEPHENS is professor of journalism and mass communication at New York University. In addition to contributing articles to the *New York Times,* the *Washington Post,* and other newspapers, he has written *A History of the News* (a *New York Times* "Notable Book of the Year"), *The Rise of the Image and the Fall of the World,* and the textbooks *Broadcast News* and *Writing and Reporting the News.* He also writes travel essays for lonelyplanet.com and makes appearances on television and radio, especially NPR.

"By Means of the Visible": A Picture's Worth (1998)

BY MITCHELL STEPHENS

> Painting is much more eloquent than speech,
> and often penetrates more deeply into one's
> heart.
>
> —ERASMUS

Ask the creators of the wilder, more interesting-looking new television commercials, promotional announcements, news videos and even feature films where they found their inspiration, and their answer, more often than not, will contain the same three letters. Director Oliver Stone, when citing the antecedents of the jangled, fast-cut style he used in the movie *Natural Born Killers,* mentioned "commercials and MTV."[1] Don Schneider is senior creative director of the BBDO advertising agency, which has produced some groundbreaking Pepsi commercials, including that attack on the artichoke chef and the old TV. He made a more sweeping confession: "Ninety percent of this has to do with MTV."[2] ABC News took more than ideas from MTV: It hired one of the youth network's talented young producers, David Berrent.

MTV's influence begins, of course, with the music videos themselves—which "might be the only new popular art form in American life," Norman Mailer has suggested.[3] But many of the network's innovations appeared as more substantive supplements to those dizzying collages of guitar strummers and visual metaphors for lust. ABC wooed Berrent after executives saw his documentary *Decade,* a historical look, MTV-style, at the 1980s.

Decade includes a thirty-three-second segment on former President Ronald Reagan's planned "Star Wars" defense system. I make no claims for it journalistically, but in technique and style it is intriguing. An excerpt from a Reagan speech on national security is shown, along with an attack on Star Wars by the late rock musician Frank Zappa. These are sound-bites—the same (except for the use of Zappa as an expert) as might be seen in a traditional news story. But in between, Berrent placed a kind of rock video: While the phrase "guns in the sky" is sung over and over, and Zappa begins to talk, computer simulations of lasers attacking rockets are shown on screen. Those scenes, in turn, are interrupted by flashing, static images: a dollar sign, the symbol warning of possible nuclear contamination, the skull-and-crossbones symbol for danger.

Neither the word *danger* nor its synonyms is vocalized. Berrent clearly is relying on these flashing images not just to illustrate what is being said but to communicate their own meanings. In the introduction to that ABC documentary on churches, Roberta Goldberg, who learned from Berrent, does the same with the shot of three candles being extinguished. These images, the point is, are intended to take the place of words.

Many of the images that decorate our world have similar aspirations. Among the most interesting are the icons that increasingly crowd the edges of computer screens. Small drawings—of a file folder, for instance—first began to replace lines of text on computer displays at a research center run by the Xerox Corporation in the 1970s. The driving force behind this work was Alan Kay, a Ph.D. in computer science, whose dreams for the future of the computer, inspired in part by Marshall McLuhan, included a major role for images. Each icon used on the screen, Kay suspected, was worth not just a word but a whole sentence.[4]

A group of Apple Computer executives and engineers made an expedition to the Xerox center in 1979. They returned with many ideas and then added some of their own. In 1983 Apple released a slow, expensive, unsuccessful, "graphics-oriented" computer named Lisa and then, the next year, a faster, relatively inexpensive, hugely successful computer, using a similar operating system, named Macintosh. The indomitable Microsoft Corporation noticed the idea (Apple suggested, in court, a different verb), and with the success of the Windows operating system in 1990, sets of icons began to appear on most computer screens.[5]

Similar images currently express meanings on traffic signs, rest room doors, Olympic venues and biceps. Armies continue to march under images; the devout of many faiths continue to pray to them. The *Pioneer 10* spacecraft, now embarked on a long journey toward the star Aldebaran, is equipped with a plaque designed to satisfy the curiosity of any aliens encountered along the way—a plaque covered not with words but with images (sketches of a naked man and woman, our solar system, the position of our sun, the hydrogen atom).[6]

Some meanings clearly are better communicated pictorially than verbally, as David Berrent, Alan Kay and most of the world's painters and sculptors have recognized. We live, however, in a culture that, despite the proliferation of images, not only has little faith in their ability but has at times been actively antagonistic toward them.

The Old Testament, characteristically, does not mince words: "Thou shalt not make unto thee any graven image, or any likeness of any thing that is in heaven above, or that is in the earth beneath"—a commandment second only to the demand that no other gods be worshiped before the source of these commandments. An antagonism toward images first appeared here at the beginning of Western culture. It appeared, too, after the development of the alphabet in Greece: Among Plato's targets in the *Republic* is the painter, whom he dismissed as "a magician and imitator." A similar scorn surfaced among Muslims: Muhammed is said to have proclaimed that "the angels will not enter a temple where there are images."[7]

This fury was unleashed, always, by partisans of the word—written or (for Plato)   10
spoken. Behind it was a multifaceted fear: fear, to begin with, *for* the word. Images—easy to understand, fun to look at—inevitably threatened to turn the populace away from the deeper, more cerebral rewards of sacred writings or philosophic discourse.

There was fear too of the magic that seems to lurk in images. They steal likenesses. They do what only gods should be able to do: They recreate the living and preserve the dead. It is hard not to see this as black magic. Images allow us actually to look in on (not just hear about) the familiar from another perspective, an external perspective, often a disorienting perspective—to see ourselves, for example. They are, in this way, inherently unnatural—further evidence of magic.

Then there is the persistent "reality" issue. Images look real but are fake. They pretend to be what they are not. They lie. The portrait is a mute, lifeless substitute for the person; the idol, a primitive and superficial knockoff of the god. But that idol is also attractive and easy to see. It can distract from the more profound but more amorphous glories of the god. A painter, Plato warned, can deceive "children and fools" with mere "imitation of appearance," instead of "truth" or "real things."[8] Images can entrance.

Worse, in imitating "real things," images tend to devalue them. This is what the French theorist Jean Baudrillard called "the murderous capacity of images." Once we begin to lose ourselves in this world of illusions, it can begin to seem as if "truth" and "reality" are just further illusions (deserving of quotation marks). Images, on this level, are, as Baudrillard put it, "murderers of the real, murderers of their own model."[9] The person is now seen as if posing for a portrait. The god is perceived as if just another idol.

"Cursed be the man who makes a graven or molten image," the Old Testament proclaims. We have reconciled ourselves to painting and sculpture by now; nevertheless, echoes of that curse can still be heard in many of the jeremiads launched by television's critics—most of whom retain an almost biblical allegiance to the word. The fear behind that curse undoubtedly was also present in some of the admonitions I heard from my parents: "You've had that thing on all evening!" "You look like you're in some kind of trance!" I'm sure it is present too in some my children have heard from me.

For television also has been judged too easy to watch: not sufficiently challenging, cerebral or deep. It displays a similarly suspect magic: It too captures appearances. Television too is accused of being "unreal," of duping children and fools. And television too has seemed to make the world it portrays—the social and political world—less "real." It has helped fill it with "pseudo-events," to use Daniel Boorstin's often-repeated term. "The shadow has become the substance," Boorstin, with deference to Plato, warned.[10]

Here is a prejudice even Thoth did not face. Video is not only suspiciously new and immature; it is tainted by its reliance upon facile, shallow, unreal, cursed images.*[11]

Oddly, it was a group of thinkers not only steeped in biblical values but influenced by Platonic (or, more precisely, neo-Platonic) values who began to question this fear and scorn.[12] "We do no harm," Pope Gregory I wrote in a letter in 599, "in wishing to show the invisible by means of the visible." In the thirteenth century, Thomas Aquinas outlined an argument in support of "the institution of images in the Church."[13]

The power of the visible has been disparaged and then rediscovered many times since: with the development of painting in the Renaissance (including the use of perspective),[14] with the woodcut and the mechanical reproduction of illustrations, with the arrival of photography.†[15] Over the centuries, those prepared to defend images have produced various calculations of the comparative "worth" of pictures and words. They often seem silly. However, an investigation of the potential of video must begin by confronting the lingering prejudice against images and acknowledging that there *are* some things images do better than words.

Images, to begin with, are marvelously (though never perfectly) accessible. Aquinas explained that the "unlettered" might learn from pictures "as if from books."[16] (Christians were not prepared to ignore the needs of the uneducated, of

15

---

*As James Reston put it, "All cameras tend to corrupt and television cameras corrupt absolutely."
†Wordsworth, one of the disparagers, labeled the use of photographs in newspapers and books "a dumb Art," "a backward movement. . . from manhood,—back to childhood," a "vile abuse!"

children or of fools.) We take advantage of the accessibility of images to aid those who may not understand a particular language—visitors to the Olympics, perhaps, or any space aliens who happen upon *Pioneer 10.*

Another strength of images is their concision—a significant advantage for drivers speeding by or on a crowded computer screen. A native American rock drawing found near a precipitous trail in New Mexico, for example, shows a goat who is climbing but a man on a horse who has fallen.[17] It is difficult to imagine a sign made for the "lettered" that could communicate this warning more efficiently. David Berrent and the others who have begun flashing images on our screens are attempting to exploit this efficiency in their efforts to say a lot in a short time.

Images also can wield great power—religious, tribal, romantic, pedagogic. One of David Berrent's productions for ABC was a public-service announcement on behalf, of all things, of PLUS: Project Literacy U.S. In its thirty seconds, five or six fathers are shown reading to or reading with their children, with scenes from children's books and newspapers gently superimposed on top of them. The fathers explain why this activity is important, but the public-service announcement's power comes not from their words but from the images Berrent has placed before us—images of togetherness, of caring, of warmth.

Aquinas suggested that images can be used to "excite the emotions, which are more effectively aroused by things seen than by things heard."[18] That is why we find images in houses of worship, in military emblems and in tattoos, as well as in public-service announcements. "If the poet can kindle love in man, more so . . . the painter, as he can place the true image of the beloved before the lover," observed Leonardo da Vinci.[19]

There are also understandings, sometimes deep understandings, that can be put into images—accessibly, concisely, powerfully—but are difficult to put into words. The study of botany, zoology, anatomy, geography and astronomy were all advanced during or after the Renaissance by more precise depictions, models, representations and diagrams.[20] "Primates are visual animals," Stephen Jay Gould, the scientist and science writer, has asserted, "and we think best in pictorial or geometric terms. Words are an evolutionary afterthought."[21]

Bill McKibben was appearing on TV. This was an event akin to the Unabomber going on-line or Ralph Nader driving a Porsche. For McKibben, a distinguished environmental writer, had just published an ardent attack on television: a book, *The Age of Missing Information,* based on his experience in watching every program that had appeared on a ninety-three-channel Virginia cable television system during one twenty-four-hour period. McKibben wrote of his concern not only with what TV offers but with what it does not offer: highs, lows, perspective, consciousness of the body, an awareness of death, of the seasons, of nature and of what happens "behind a face." "We use TV as we use tranquilizers," he concluded.[22] But now here McKibben was on the *Charlie Rose Show,* himself part of the dose.

Among those savoring the irony was the *New Republic*'s Robert Wright, who admitted that McKibben looked more "earnest and thoughtful" than he had expected from reading reviews of his book. "TV has won for his cause one small battle that his book alone couldn't have won," Wright observed, "both because I don't have time to read it and because it is missing some kinds of information. (Some very 'natural' kinds of information, like how a person looks when saying what he believes. The written word, we sometimes forget, was invented as a crude if useful substitute for the real thing.)"[23]

That last thought is worth freeing from parentheses. No one, as Wright noted, has been earnest enough to read through, say, all the publications to be found one day on one newsstand (an exercise likely as dispiriting as McKibben's). But we can still come to some conclusions about what the printed word lacks.

Writing's great limitation grows out of its great strength: its abstractness. It is a system of representation, or code, that represents another system of representation, another code: spoken language.[24] The written word *face*—to oversimplify a bit—calls to mind the sound "fās." It is, therefore, two steps removed from that expressive skin sculpture itself.* These steps back needed to be taken and have been hugely productive. Still, it is important to keep in mind the price paid for that abstraction. Printed words may take us, metaphorically at least, "behind a face"; they can help us see what we might not ordinarily see in a face; but they must work hard to tell us what a glance could about the expression on that face. In interpreting the code we make little use of our natural ability to observe: letters don't smile warmly or look intently.

This code, writing, also ignores our ability to find spatial and temporal connections between objects in the world. When we speak with each other, we can point: "That belongs over there." We can demonstrate: "Then she did this with her hair." We can indicate: "You want to give them control over this?" And we can gesture—with a look, a shrug, a grimace. All this information could alternatively be put into words; it could be written down. But in reading it, rather than seeing it, we sacrifice our ability to quickly and intuitively spot relationships—between here and there, this and that, words and gestures, ideas and expressions. We sacrifice our ability to judge earnestness and thoughtfulness, say, by observing people's faces as they speak.

Comparing what he saw on those ninety-three channels to what his senses can pick up in nature or at a circus, McKibben moaned that we are "starved on television's visual Pritikin regimen."[25] This is a point I am anxious to debate. But for the moment it is sufficient to note that, if the measure is *direct* stimulation to our senses, a page of print makes a few moments of television look like a five-course French meal.

Printed prose is "an act of extraordinary stylization, of remarkable, expressive self-denial," stated Richard A. Lanham, who writes on Renaissance rhetoric and contemporary computers.[26] Our eyes were selected over millions of years of primate evolution for their ability to notice, search, compare, connect and evaluate. Increasingly, in the five thousand years since the development of writing, they have been reduced to staring at letters of identical size and color, arranged in lines of identical length, on pages of identical size and color. Readers, in a sense, are no longer asked to *see;* they are simply asked to interpret the code.

Written words, as Aquinas realized but we tend to forget, are hardly a perfect form of communication. No such thing exists. I don't want to overstate the case for images—at least still images—either. Certainly, as the Bible seems to suggest, but for

30

*I am aware of the philosophical critiques that have been launched against such attempts to measure distance from "reality"; however, I don't think they threaten the rather simple point I am making here.

centuries most Europeans tended to forget, nonmoving images have great difficulty conveying certain kinds of meanings. There are limits to what the Dutch humanist Erasmus called their eloquence.[27]

Alan Kay ended up dissatisfied with his experiments in the use of images on computer screens. He had understood, from having read educational theory, that icons were good at helping people "recognize, compare, configure." The success of the Macintosh and Windows operating systems has proven that his understanding was correct. But Kay had a grander ambition: He dreamed of using images to express abstract thought. Kay envisioned a kind of language of images.[28]

That is an old dream. It was long surmised that the mysterious hieroglyphs that could be seen on the Egyptian obelisks that had been dragged to Rome represented such a language of images. "The wise of Egypt . . . left aside . . . words and sentences," wrote Plotinus, the third-century neo-Platonist, "and drew pictures instead."[29] As late as the eighteenth century, the historian Vico assumed that "all the first nations spoke in hieroglyphs."[30]

Behind this notion was the belief, still held by many today, that nature is a "book" with a divine author.[31] If each tree, each ox, has a spiritual message for us, then that message might also be "read" in paintings or even iconic representations of trees or oxen. An image language would be closer to that original divine language. Over the centuries many Europeans attempted to craft such a language.* They produced various occult codes, systems of gestures, systems of concepts, guides to memory and tools for international understanding.[32]

These various image languages all had something in common: To the extent that they tried to communicate meaning effectively without depending on words, they failed. The conviction that the Egyptians had succeeded in this also crumbled. In 1799 one of Napoleon's soldiers in Egypt happened upon an old stone that included an inscription written both in Egyptian hieroglyphic and in Greek. With the "Rosetta stone" Europe finally was able to piece together accurate translations of those mysterious Egyptian writings, and it became clear that not even hieroglyphic had escaped the dominance of language. Instead, like all other successful writing systems, these icons were directly connected to words: For example, they made heavy use, as in King Narmer's name, of phonetic indicators, of homonyms.[33]

Alan Kay's efforts to produce abstract thought from systems of icons on the computer screen failed, too. "All I can say," Kay wrote, "is that we and others came up with many interesting approaches over the years but none have successfully crossed the threshold to the end user." The problem: "In most iconic languages it is much easier to write the patterns than it is to read them," Kay explained.[34]

Here, for example, is the series of hand signals one Renaissance experimenter, the Abbé de l'Epée, used in his language of gestures to indicate the concept "I believe":

> I begin by making the sign of the first person singular, pointing the index finger of my right hand towards my chest. I then put my finger on my forehead, on the concave part in which is supposed to reside my spirit, that is to say, my capacity for thought, and I make the sign for *yes*. I then make the same sign

*The seventeenth-century Jesuit scholar Athanasius Kircher is an example.

on that part of the body which, usually, is considered as the seat of what is called the heart in its spiritual sense. . . . I then make the same sign *yes* on my mouth while moving my lips. . . . Finally, I place my hand on my eyes, and, making the sign for *no,* show that I do not see.

All that is quite clever, even poetic. It must have been great fun to devise but almost impossible for "end users"—those who were watching the abbé's energetic performance—to decipher. That undoubtedly explains why at the conclusion of his elaborate pantomime de l'Epée felt called upon to add one more action: "All I need to do," he stated, "is . . . to write *I believe.*"[35]

If images cannot form languages without a reliance upon words, it is in part because they have a great deal of difficulty escaping the affirmative, the past or present indicative.[36] De l'Epée was able at least to shake his head to put something in the negative; in some traffic signs we use a red diagonal line to say the same thing; but most still pictures must strain to say something as simple as "no" or to ask "why?" or to wonder what might be. They state much more effectively than they negate or interrogate or speculate. Pictures are better, similarly, with the concrete than the abstract, better with the particular than the general. These are significant handicaps.[37]

The other great obstacle to images forming a language of their own stems not from their muteness but from the fact that they tend to say too much. For example, Michelangelo's awe-inspiring depiction at the summit of the Sistine Chapel of God giving life to man through the touch of his finger also can be seen as showing a father-son relationship and perhaps a lover-beloved relationship; it can be seen as showing caring, effort, joy, and undoubtedly numerous other emotions. This richness of meaning is testament to the artist's genius. But if we did not receive some verbal explanation, how could we be expected to "read" this scene as we might read a piece of writing?

Knowing the genre helps. The location of this great fresco tells us that we should search for a religious interpretation in it.[38] But which one? The older man could be saving the younger man; he could be calling him to heaven; he could be giving or taking his soul. To know for sure, we must be directed to a story, to Genesis. Were this scene asked to serve as part of a language without the aid of such a story, how could we pinpoint specific meanings in it?[39] "The image is freedom, words are prison," wrote the film director Jean-Luc Godard, never one to shy from controversy, in 1980. "How are laws decreed today? They are written. When your passport is stamped 'entry to Russia forbidden,' it is not done with an image."*[40] True, but neither the Bill of Rights nor the Declaration of the Rights of Man was composed in images either. The freedom images provide comes at a price.

"The ability of a visual language to express more than one meaning at once," contended Umberto Eco, "is also . . . its limitation." Eco, whose academic speciality is semiotics, the study of systems of signs, called this excess of meaning "the fatal polysemy of . . . images."[41] Aquinas recognized the problem: "One thing may have similitude to many," he wrote. "For instance the lion may mean the Lord because of one similitude and the Devil because of another."[42] How can we develop a lexicon of images if we have no way of determining which of the many possible interpretations of an image is correct? (The perplexing graphics that are supposed to explain to speakers

40

*Oliver Stone has expressed similar sentiments.

of different languages how to operate European appliances provide another example of this problem.)

To use images more precisely without captions, explanations or instructions—without words—it is necessary to rely on the most obvious of images, on clichés: a skull and crossbones, for instance, or a father snuggled up with a book and a child. France's expert on semiotics, Roland Barthes, gave the example of the use of a bookcase in the background of a photograph to show that a person is an intellectual.[43] As a result, as images that try to convey meaning without the use of words become less ambiguous, they also become less interesting, less challenging, and vice versa.

"I don't want there to be three or four thousand possibilities of interpreting my canvas," Pablo Picasso once insisted. "I want there to be only one."[44] However, the artist in his more thoughtful moments undoubtedly realized what anyone who has stood before one of his canvases has likely realized: That is impossible.

Words also can say too much, of course. *Man, woman* or *god,* for example, have no shortage of potential meanings. Dictionaries contain lists of them; occasionally we concoct our own. Writers can never be sure that their words have only one possible interpretation. As our literary theorists have spent a third of a century pointing out, readers bring different experiences and interests to the sentences they read and therefore take different meanings from them.

While working on this book, I reread *Madame Bovary* and, wouldn't you know, [45] began to uncover in Flaubert's novel a series of lessons about images and words. Did he intend for me to read his book this way? Probably not. Nonetheless, Flaubert's problem with me and probably most of his other readers is much less acute than that faced by the authors of potential image languages. With the help (alas) of a translator I was able to get the gist of Flaubert's words. I followed his narrative. I was not so preoccupied with my own concerns that I missed the fact that he had many things to say that are not communications-related.*

Our strategies for reading words are fairly well understood. We can, at least, make use of those dictionaries, with their limited lists of meanings. And the problem of comprehending words is further eased, if never entirely eliminated, by syntax. Using a grammar, the basic structure of which seems built into our genes, we modify the form of our words to signify their relation to their fellows in sentences. And then we narrow their potential meanings further by surrounding them not only with various qualifiers but with prepositions and articles. There are few equivalents for such parts of speech in the realm of the image.

In spoken and written languages, word builds upon word, sentence upon sentence, idea upon idea. The ambiguity of images, on the other hand, is increased by what Alan Kay called their "unsortedness." Painters may have mastered some tricks for guiding our eyes across canvases. But we are not born with, nor have we created, any particularly sophisticated systems for organizing still images to specify or build meanings. "Unlike paragraphs and lists of words, images have no *a priori* order in which they should be understood," Kay noted. "This means that someone coming onto an image from the outside has no strategy for solving it."[45]

---

*Contemporary literary theorists might question in a number of interesting ways my attempt to elude the ambiguities of language here.

This chapter might be helped by a depiction of Thomas Aquinas, Bill McKibben or Alan Kay. It would be useful actually to see how the Abbé de l'Epée looked when he made "the sign of the first person singular." But such concepts as "efficiency," "abstract thought" or "by means of the visible" would be difficult to communicate through still images. And how might an argument composed of such images be organized? Left to right? Up and down? In a kind of circle? Unless, following de l'Epée's lead, such pictures were appended to a written version of the chapter itself, an observer would not know what "strategy" to employ in understanding them.

David Berrent and others of the most interesting workers in video—MTV alumni or MTV watchers—aim a barrage of images at us. Those images can do some things better than words; once we move beyond the scorn and the fears of word lovers, that becomes clear. Certain pictures can put most sentences to shame. But this is as far as I'm willing to go in making the case for still images.

The truth is that I am not one of those folks who spend an inordinate amount of time staring at dew-covered fields, wizened faces, cloud formations, or paintings thereof. It took some decades, and the guidance of a photographer friend, before I learned to notice light, not just the things upon which it shines. I'm good for a few hours in major museums, not a few days. Which is to say that while this is a book that gets rather excited about the potential of image communication, it is not based on a particularly romantic view of images or our visual sense in general.

Some continue to argue that pictures are more honest and profound than words, that they can claim some direct, mystical path to a higher reality. You won't find that argument here. In fact, I've tried to make clear in this chapter that still images operate under severe handicaps when attempting to embody ideas. For certain important purposes, a picture may actually be worth *less* than a single, relatively narrow, well-placed word. I agree with Umberto Eco that some of the most complex uses of images must "still depend (parasitically) on the semantic universe of the verbal language."[46] This, perhaps, is the true "curse" upon those who attempt to communicate through such images, graven or otherwise.

However, Eco did allow for one possible exception to his rule about the limitations of images—an exception even someone who won't pull the car over to gape at a sunset can accept: Eco suggested, with some reservations, that "the images of cinema and television" might escape those limitations.[47]

There is a sense in which David Berrent and his colleagues and successors in video seem better positioned than Michelangelo, Picasso and computer guru Alan Kay might have been to communicate abstract thought unambiguously through images—for motion, sound and computer editing have indeed begun to solve the image's intelligibility problems. And at MTV speeds, in ten or fifteen minutes it is now possible to present *a thousand pictures*.

Notes

1. Cited, John Hartl, "Fractured Reality—Oliver Stone's Latest Manic Movie Mixes Fiction with Today's Headlines," *Seattle Times*, August 21, 1994.
2. Mitchell Stephens, "The New TV," *Washington Post*, April 25, 1993.
3. Norman Mailer, "Like a Lady (Madonna)," *Esquire*, August 1994.
4. Smith and Alexander 231, 235; Kay 193, 201, 202.

5. Levy 69–70, 77–79, 98, 278–79.

6. Arthur Smith 113–14, 121.

7. Book X; Plato, *The Great Dialogues*, 464. Papadopoulo 49.

8. Book X; Plato, *The Great Dialogues*, 463–4. This echoes Plato's attack on orators in the *Gorgias*.

9. Baudrillard 255–56.

10. Boorstin 26–29, 204; see also Mourier 310.

11. Cited, Briggs, *Competition*, 147n.

12. For an investigation of this apparent irony, see Gombrich 154–60.

13. Cited, Freedberg 162–64. For a discussion of the philosophic underpinnings of Aquinas's thoughts on images, see Copleston 47–48, 167–68, 181–83.

14. See Samuel Y. Edgerton Jr. 124–42; Bazin 11; Hogben 186–88; Berger 16.

15. Cited, Crowley and Heyer 195.

16. Cited, Freedberg 162.

17. Gelb 29.

18. Cited, Freedberg 162.

19. Cited, Freedberg 451n.

20. Hogben 188–89.

21. Stephen Jay Gould, "Evolution by Walking," *Natural History*, March 1995.

22. McKibben 147, 189, 190, 197, 198, 211–12.

23. Robert Wright, "Washington Diarist: Channeling," *New Republic*, June 15, 1992.

24. See Aristotle 40 (*De Interpretatione*, 1).

25. McKibben 192.

26. Lanham 9.

27. Cited, Freedberg 50.

28. Kay 196, 202.

29. Plotinus 427.

30. Cited, Eco 166; see also Martin 19.

31. See Gombrich 148–49.

32. Eco 144–76.

33. Eco 144–76.

34. Kay 202.

35. Cited, Eco 173–74.

36. French historian Roger Chartier talked about how images "mirrored" writing; Chartier 19.

37. See Worth.

38. See Gombrich 21 for the importance of genre.

39. William E. Wallace 260–61. For another discussion of possible interpretations of the Sistine ceiling, see Richmond 63–68.

40. Godard 123; translated by Dirk Standen.

41. Eco 174; see also Martin 6.

42. Cited, Gombrich 14.

43. Barthes 201–2.

44. Cited, Alden Whitman, "Picasso: Protean and Prodigious," *New York Times*, April 8, 1973.

45. Kay 202.

46. Eco 174.

47. Eco 175–77.

CONNECTING PERSONALLY TO THE READING

1. Think of a time when you have found writing more efficient than pictures. Then think of a time when you experienced the opposite, when a visual image worked better for you than language did. Explain the effect of the words and images in each case.

2. Stephens cites Thomas Aquinas's belief that images "excite the emotions." Do you find images more emotionally gripping than words or are they equally affecting? Explain your response, giving examples from your personal experience.

FOCUSING ON THE ARGUMENT

1. Stephens includes many examples from a wide range of sources—from the ancient world (e.g., the Bible, the Koran, Plato) to MTV and Pepsi commercials. Indicate which examples you find most convincing and explain what makes them so.

2. Stephens is a journalism professor at New York University, and his essay presents him as a well-read, cultured writer, familiar with works from many different fields, including biology, art, literature, and film. At the same time, he often takes a familiar tone, seeming to draw the reader into a conversation. Which features of the writing style (e.g., his vocabulary, tone, and sentence structure) seem formal and academic to you and which ones familiar and chatty?

SYNTHESIZING IDEAS FROM MULTIPLE READINGS

1. In discussing some of the reasons that different cultures have opposed visual images, Stephens mentions the fear that images "steal likenesses." According to William A. Ewing (in "Dance and Photography," p. 546), Barbara Morgan initially resisted becoming a photographer for the same reason and told her husband, "I won't be a thief!" What beliefs are behind this fear? What prompted Morgan to change her mind?

2. Mitchell Stephens argues that images can often express ideas or experiences that are difficult to put into words. Look over John Berger's article ("Ways of Seeing," p. 518), which is rich in both words and images. Choose an image from the Berger reading and explain what it tells you that Berger's text does not.

3. Quoting Umberto Eco, Mitchell Stephens states, "The ability of a visual language to express more than one meaning at once is also . . . its limitation." Read what Harvey, the mural painter, ("Voices from the Workplace," p. 328) has to say about some of the murals he painted. In what ways do his murals express more than one meaning, and how is this ability both an advantage and a limitation?

WRITING TO ACT

1. Find a television show that defies the criticism that television is not intellectually challenging or, conversely, find one that affirms this criticism. Then write an editorial explaining your findings. Indicate what characteristics make a medium intellectually challenging and which do not.

2. Create a new sign to post on your campus. Your sign should communicate an idea entirely visually, using no language. For example, it might indicate a good place to ride a bicycle, ask people to turn their cell phones off before entering the classroom, or inform students that the computer lab is open for walk-in use. Get permission to post your sign in the appropriate places.

READING

JON BOORSTIN's article shows us how complex a task filmmakers undertake and how much artifice they use to make an image look real. Working with scale, light, background, sound, shots taken close-up or from afar, they juggle hundreds of details to ensure that the viewer enters the world of the film without getting confused or distracted. Think of a scene from a film that you have enjoyed: what made the scene believable to you? How did the scene present the illusion of reality?

BOORSTIN is a writer and producer. He was associate producer on *All the President's Men* and wrote and produced the award-winning thriller *Dream Lover.* His documentary *Exploratorium* was nominated for an Oscar. His latest IMAX film, *Greece: Secrets of the Past,* opened in 2006. He created and produced (with Howard Chesley) the TV series *3 Moons Over Milford,* airing on the Family Channel in the summer of 2006. He is also the author of the novels *Pay or Play* and *The Newsboys' Lodging-House,* winner of the 2003 New York City book award for historical fiction.

The Hollywood Eye (1990) | BY JON BOORSTIN

CREATING A WORLD: LIGHT, SPACE, AND SOUND

The simple pleasure of seeing is so mundane it is easy to underestimate. How much of the enjoyment of even a plot-driven melodrama like *Star Wars* comes from seeing a new world? (The much-touted café scene is a prime example.) John Ford opens *Drums Along the Mohawk* with an eighteenth-century wedding. We don't know the people yet and the words are well worn, but the house has a plain authentic feel and Ford lets the ceremony proceed at a natural pace; we're happy to watch how they tied the knot in the colonies.

On a grander scale, Francis Ford Coppola shows us the Mafia wedding in *The Godfather* and Michael Cimino the wedding in *The Deer Hunter;* David Lean gives us the trooping of the colors in *A Passage to India;* John Ford trails cavalry through the cathedral mesas of Monument Valley in his classic Westerns. Spectacle for its own sake, perhaps, but not empty images. In fact, these are the purest, least literary form of image—the image is the content. The fascination they hold, the feelings they create lie beyond words, closer to the moods of music. And in Hollywood these scenes are almost always heavily scored. This is where movie music comes into its own—where grand, sweeping themes assert themselves and embed in the viewer's consciousness.

Done right, these scenes can sum up the whole emotional experience of a film— and these are moments, don't forget, when character is virtually nonexistent, lost in the magnitude of the epic event. Films work hard to make the audience care about their characters' selfish concerns; these scenes fit the petty creatures into the larger universe, at once revealing their insignificance and making them part of something epic and grand. These moments make movies larger than life.

Eames created his worlds on a tabletop, but creating a world worth watching is usually a big job. Size is crucial. The voyeur in us must feel life encompassing the story, swallowing up the screen. We need spectacle, sweeping panorama, to convince us that the world is out there beyond the edge of the frame. Then when the filmmaker shows us smaller bits we know they aren't just what could be cobbled together, they are all the story needs.

Spectacle is the domain of the long shot, the deep-focus, wide-angle vista with a cast of thousands—impeccably outfitted, for authenticity as well as size grips the imagination. These shots are extemely expensive, often the most expensive in a movie, but the credibility they lend a film is crucial. Producers know them as "money shots"—in the double sense of big payoff and the shots where the cash is right up 5 there on the screen. From a story point of view they are usually insignificant, but to establish a sense of place, a real world for the film, they are indispensable.

The most expensive moment in *Tucker: The Man and His Dream* (Coppola's fable about the little man who battled the moguls of Detroit), in dollars per second of screen time, is the massive gathering outside the Tucker factory the day of the "car of the future's" debut—with scores of period autos and myriad extras in period costume. The shot lasts only a few seconds, and the principals aren't even in it. The most expensive set in *Who Framed Roger Rabbit* is the period street we see for fewer than ten seconds when Benny the Car drives up. (The bulk of the scene plays on a smaller soundstage set built to match.) The most expensive single shot in *All the President's Men* is a shot of Redford changing taxicabs in front of the Kennedy Center. In terms of story, none of these moments comes close to justifying their staggering expense, yet all are money well spent and rarely affordable outside Hollywood. They give the films indispensable substance, a sense of undeniable reality beyond the screen.

And sometimes they do more. If the locale is exotic, epic shots are their own excuse. People love to be taken to a place that's like nothing they've seen before, a real-feeling place with a dense lived-in texture and a sense of evolving vitality, where the most unlikely dress and behavior are taken for granted. The strange truth of the worlds in *The Last Emperor* and *Blade Runner* provides some of the films' principal pleasures. The world itself is reason to see the film.

Here it is less important that something be absolutely real than that it feel authentic. It is the art director's job to determine just how real that is, and because authenticity is the goal the art director draws less on his or her own imagination than on broad research and experience. Art directors, like actors, aren't complimented on their originality but on their "choices."

Even the most outrageous science fiction must ring true; conversely, even the most realistic scene must be subtly altered to give the camera an undiluted sense of reality. In life, we screen out what distracts. Watching film, our eye is less forgiving. The frame implies intention. Flattened out, every part of the image takes on its true visual weight regardless of its significance. The art director must alter reality to make it feel more real on film, whether that means painting a house, planting a tree, or obscuring a sign. If the art director does the job well, his environments are a metaphor for the actions and emotions of the story. Think of the sleek, brooding feel of the Batcave in *Batman* or the jungle-rotten ruins of the Cambodian temple in *Apocalypse Now*.

Light

> "Light can be gentle, dreamlike, bare, living, dead, clear, misty, hot, dark, violent, spring-like, falling, straight, slanting, sensual, subdued, limited, poisonous, calming and pale."
>
> —CAMERAMAN SVEN NYKVIST

The first challenge in creating a credible world, whether it is the entire Forbidden City or Eames' toy trains, is to create a convincing space for that world to inhabit. We mustn't feel we're watching a pageant staged flat for the camera; we are looking through a window onto a three-dimensional universe, an exotic new place with all the depth and solidity of the world we already know. This is as much a problem in the chemistry and mechanics of photography as in the placement of the actors, a cameraman's problem

Still from *Barry Lyndon*

as much as a director's. The director may layer the action in receding planes, or move people up and back, toward the camera and away into the scene rather than in flat tableau; the cameraman's problem is in many ways more subtle and demanding.

To open their screen onto another world cameramen must use all their skill to destroy its flatness. Eames, creating tiny worlds for his spinning tops or his aquarium fish, had a simple rule of thumb: to create a sense of depth, make the background lighter than the foreground. . . . The same rule holds for big films (note that it works for *The French Connection* and *The Wizard of Oz* as well), but for the larger canvas, for Harold Rosson shooting *The Wizard of Oz* or Gregg Toland shooting *Citizen Kane* or Gordon Willis shooting *The Godfather,* creating a sense of space requires a bigger bag of tricks.

Gordon Willis, like other cameramen, haunts art museums. Capturing three-dimensional space on a flat plane, making flat depictions of objects feel round, bathing them in atmosphere—these are problems as old as the Renaissance. There are differences between paint and film—color laws, for example, are additive for paint and subtractive for projected light (a painter mixing all his colors gets black, a cameraman gets white), but in the end, both deal only in light. Both describe how light is reflected or absorbed by objects, and both rely on how light is processed in the brain. Artists light with paint; cameramen paint with light.

A cameraman loves black blacks—they not only impart a rich dense solidity to things, they give the work an anchor, a baseline for the tonal changes the cameraman rings. To reproduce the much broader sensitivity of the eye within the limited palette of film, the cameraman must know exactly how little light must be put on the subject to achieve texture in the shadows and how much can be poured on and still have detail in the highlights. The good cameramen use the full range of their medium, keeping a scene dark save for a single brilliant highlight or juxtaposing a dark scene with a hot, overexposed one.

Still from *The Godfather*

Light defines objects; their relation to each other and the space they occupy is described by the light that etches them. If this light comes from an identifiable source—if it comes from one direction and is explained by a bright window, say, or an overhead lamp—it acts as a unifying force, spreading over its world in a way we recognize, its highlight and shadow telling us where each element resides. Rembrandt and Leonardo are masters of directed light (though we don't see the source); so are Caravaggio and Georges de La Tour. Vermeer adds a layer of subtlety with his fine sense of how light enters a room and infuses the shadows with a reflected glow; Monet's twilight paintings go a step further, imbuing the air itself with the dense luminescence of sunset bouncing in the mist.

Surprisingly, cameramen say that color is easier to shoot than black and white. When the cameraman sets out to create a world, the first problem is to create a sense of depth on a flat plane. This is really a problem in separation: he has to make his subjects stand out from the background and appear to overlap rather than blend into each other. Shooting black and white, the cameraman has only various tones of gray to work with. He or she can put the brightly lit side of an actress' face against a shadowy background, for instance, or can outline her with a specially placed backlight called a liner. Shooting color, however, the cameraman can rely on hue—a pink and a blue that would read as identical grays will stand out clearly from each other, even if they are both lit without highlights or shadows. So the task is simplified. But the good cameraman never forgets the lessons of the painters—that while layering creates

15

depth, layering alone doesn't define space. For that, objects need their own tangible sense of volume, of size and weight, and in color or black and white that means sculpting them with light and shadow. In the words of cameraman Eric Saarinen, "The key to composition is 'light-dark-light.'"

While color separates, it also unifies. Art directors choose the color of every costume and every setting to pull a scene together, to create a dominant mood, to give a sense of completeness to the whole film; cameramen choose a particular color of light for the same reasons. During shooting they carefully control the color temperature of their light to create a yellow-warm or bluish-cold look; then, when the film is all but done, they return for the final step in finishing the film, color-correcting (or "timing") the print. No two scenes in a film will have identical color. Even if the same kind of film stock is used for the whole movie, every production run of that stock is slightly different, every processing bath, each lens has a slightly different color cast; the cameraman has been less than perfect in lighting and exposing every shot. Now, as the lab tries to make its first print of the finished film from the negative, the cameraman has a final chance to adjust the color and brightness of every scene so that all the shots made under all the different conditions feel like a consistent whole. . . .

In the late sixties, as lenses and film stocks became more sensitive and lighting technology evolved powerful new sources, the quartz-halogen lamp and the "nine-light array," cameramen led by Vilmos Zsigmond *(McCabe and Mrs. Miller)*, Haskell Wexler *(The Thomas Crown Affair)*, Vittorio Sterraro *(The Conformist)*, and Gordon Willis (*Klute* and *The Godfather*) could borrow more freely from the painters. Unlike the sky soft light of the early days, when interiors were shot outside under muslin, this

Still from *The Godfather*

Still from *Sunset Boulevard*

light could be manipulated, varied in direction and intensity. What was once an occasional effect became an efficient way of making pictures. Color films took on a new depth and glow, and the cameramen pushed the lower limits of film sensitivity. This new directed soft light allowed lighting to have a natural feel, to wrap around objects and fill in its own shadows; it allowed for rooms to be lit by window light and for light sources to mix and blend the way they do in life.

Even before soft light became practical, the great cameramen honored directed light, and with their mastery they created the same complex texture of reality. But now what only the greats could once achieve we take as commonplace. Even in good television we expect a room will be lit by daylight pouring through the windows and bouncing around as in a painting by Vermeer, creating a rich and vivid space.

Space

To the voyeur's eye, a change of camera angle is a serious event. A cut from one shot to another not only breaks flow, it leaps us from one place to another, forcing us to get our bearings anew within the movie space. Done wrong, this can be a very disorienting experience. It is the editor's job to make these moves invisible; like the cameraman the editor must create a space so solid and convincing that the viewer never feels lost or confused. The editor has to make us feel comfortable that we know, without ever thinking about it, where our actors are and how they face off. Are they looking at each other? If one is speaking, is the other one in earshot? Where are they in the room?

While making cuts, the editor is constantly constrained by the apparent realities 20 of the cameraman's space. The cameraman creates a world, the editor lives within it. If a cameraman gives a scene a strong sense of the source and direction of its light, for example, it is that much easier for the editor to jump around the room—if we leap to a close-up washed in bright highlights, for instance (what a cameraman would call "over key"), we assume the person is near the window; if we then cut to another close-up, lit just as brightly but from the other side, we assume the second person is also close to the window but facing the first.

We rely on these lighting cues more than you might realize. Occasionally, a strong-willed star with a window on her left is convinced her face only looks good lit from the right. The diplomatic or lucky cameraman might be able to have her trade places with her partner, who is lit from the other side by the window; otherwise the cameraman will be forced to "switch keys"—that is, fake it and light her as if the window were on her right anyway. The star will praise the cameraman when she sees the dailies, but the editor will damn him because in spite of all the other clues in the scene, when the editor cuts the scene together the viewer will feel, in some unsettling way, that the two people are facing the same direction instead of facing each other. A brilliant cameraman can light the star just right, maybe bring in some other strong visual clue and get away with it. But it will cause him sleepless nights.

The editor has to uphold not just the integrity of the cameraman's space but the integrity of the actors' behavior. He or she has to make sure they obey the basic laws of time and space. We have to trust that the cigarette an actress lights in one shot is burning when we cut to a different angle ten seconds later (with ten seconds' worth of ash), that her cup of coffee doesn't magically empty, her hair doesn't rearrange itself, her eyeglasses don't pop on and off untouched by human hands. These concerns of "continuity," as they're called, may seem trivial, but they dominate the editor's every decision. The thread of reality must be unbroken or we won't fully give ourselves up to the screen. Our voyeur's eye will set off alarms, and the editor will have committed the gravest of sins: the editor will have pulled us out of the picture.

There is no such thing as perfect continuity, of course. Since every shot is distinct, sometimes filmed out of order, often taken hours or days apart, it is impossible for minute details to match exactly. The expertise of the script supervisor (who is responsible for continuity on the set) as well as the hairdresser, costumer, prop master, and art director is as much to know what won't matter as to catch what will. Must the director retake a shot, perhaps brilliantly acted, because the actor had the cigarette in his right hand instead of his left? Or is the viewer's eye somewhere else, his mind distracted by the emotion, the flaw blurred by the rush of action? Should the editor use the take that matches action or the one with a stronger performance? Is it true, in the refrain of the editing room, "If they're looking at that, we're in trouble"?

Matching is the most obvious continuity problem but not the most disorienting. A sure sign of a neophyte director is a film that is all tight close-ups punctuated by panoramic long shots. Graphically, close-ups and long shots are easier to design and almost always more visually satisfying than the prosaic medium shot. They look better through the viewfinder. Long shots can be composed with a painter's eye for landscape or tableau, while close-ups make for strong compositions—shallow focus at closer distances blurs the background so it doesn't compete with the strong graphics of the face. But while the long shots and close-ups may be handsome, they don't tell a story. Panoramic long shots put us too far away from the actors to read their behavior;

tight close-ups not only overpower all but the most crucial moments, they isolate the character and disorient the viewer. Where is this head, floating among colorful out-of-focus blobs? How far is he from the people he's talking to? Where are they?

In conventional editing, the editor opens with a master shot, the broad angle of spectacle, to ground us and orient the scene, and then jumps into closer angles to tell the story. But not only must the closer angles tell the story, when the editor shifts angles the spatial geometry must hold. Since perception of space changes with distance, with the focal length of the lens and the angle between the camera and the subject (whether the camera is high or low, facing the actor or looking at his profile), much of the cameraman's art is to re-create the apparent reality of the master by altering the relationships in the closer angles. Often what feels like artifice on the set looks more real on film. "Cheat toward the camera" is a common refrain to the actor—look more full into the camera, look away from the actress you are talking to so the audience will believe you are really facing her. . . .

Sound

Close your eyes and your ears will still tell you where you are—indoors or outdoors, in the wilderness or in a backyard or on a street, in an empty church or a busy office, a kitchen or a prison. How much of the frenzy of a trading room comes from the frantic yelling, how much of the calm of a church from its sepulchral silence?

I remember an odd experience, listening to a piano concerto from the cheap seats at the Hollywood Bowl. It was like watching a ball game from the center-field bleachers—I could make out only gross body movements. Luckily, I was watching a flamboyant performer, but the more he flailed away, the more uncomfortable I became, until I realized the problem: I was so far away I was hearing silence when he hit the keys and crescendos when his hands were lifted dramatically in the air.

Usually, we don't even bother to distinguish between the cues that come from our eyes and our ears because, after all, they are a perfect match and perfectly synchronous. But in making a film, capturing sound and image are two entirely different processes. Not only do they not automatically fit, it takes a great deal of effort to bring them together in just the right mix. But our voyeur's ear demands it. When our senses reinforce each other they create a compelling reality; when our senses conflict we tend to trust our eyes (if we don't laugh), but the glories lavished on our eyes are tarnished. If I see a pit bull leaping at me from the screen and hear a kitten's purr, I'll laugh, but how much less terrifying is the pit bull if he is given the barks of a German shepherd or if the barking sounds are muddied and distorted by poor recording or they don't quite match his snarls?

Some student films approach the Hollywood film for visual polish, but I've never seen one that doesn't betray its origins in the sound track. Most other countries don't show our exaggerated respect for sound—in Italy or India, for instance, directors routinely shoot silent and add sound later, crudely but efficiently. They don't need soundproof studios or superquiet cameras, they don't have to shoot more takes because the sound wasn't right. But here in America most scenes are shot and recorded simultaneously, at considerably more trouble and expense, to get that extra correspondence between the visual and aural; here film workers consider a good sound job to be the acid test of a first-rate professional film.

25

Film is edited in two parts, a picture reel and a carefully synchronized matching reel of sprocketed magnetic sound film. Toward the end of the editing process, when the exact sequence and length of shots is accepted as final, the sound editors take over. Their job is to give the sound vivid, consistent, convincing "reality." They pull apart the rough sound track. The different bits of dialogue are separated so they can be rerecorded later to smooth differences in sound perspective, recording levels, and mike timbre. The editors pore over every chance sound, assessing it, replacing it if it doesn't ring true.

Synchronous dialogue almost always sounds more convincing than dialogue added later because subtle differences in performance are reflected in the actor's voice as well as his demeanor. But with other sounds the opposite is usually the case. The laws of sound recording are such that a well-recorded voice usually results in poorly recorded background sounds. The actual background sounds—that is, the sounds as picked up by a microphone and recorded on tape—just don't sound "real." They can be too loud, too harsh, too muddy, or inaudible (I remember doing a film about the making of a lithograph and adding a sound for talc being sprinkled on the stone). Usually, almost every sound effect is replaced—every door slam, car start, key jangle, pouring liquid, paper rustle. Footsteps are added, augmented, or deleted to match the sense of the picture. In fact, one of the hardest decisions is when to use footsteps—sometimes it seems they are indispensable, at other times an annoying distraction.

Whole sound settings are built, layer by layer. When a scene is being shot, the sound recordist makes the crew stand immobile while he records the sound of silence. Editors then build endless loops of this "presence," or "room tone," as an underlying constant for the track, the barely audible background hum which defines a space. On top of that they create whole environments out of ambient sound, turning a silent stage into a noisy tenement, for example, with babies squealing and TVs playing through the thin walls, subways passing underneath, arguments rising from the street. They might add closer sounds on top—the electric hum of a refrigerator, the tick of a clock, the drip of a faucet. A good sound job can require as many as fifteen or twenty reels of "foley effects" (the footsteps, paper rustles, key jingles that match the action we see on the screen) and another forty reels of more generalized background sounds going at once. Editors can compose virtual symphonies of sound effects, more felt than heard by the audience, in support of the image.

Finding just the right sound can be as exacting a task as finding just the right image. *All the President's Men* opens with huge typewriter keys, bigger than the screen, pounding out a date, a visual metaphor for the power of the press. They demanded a special sound, as much larger than life as they were. The sound editor overlaid key hits from a carefully chosen typewriter (he tried half a dozen machines) with the attack sound, the front end, of whip cracks, and the decay sound, the back end, of cannon shots; the mixer took almost four hours to blend them. For *It's a Mad Mad Mad Mad World* Stanley Kramer is said to have sent his effects editor to a gas station halfway to Palm Springs to record a squeaky men's room door because it was the perfect sound for the squeaky wheel on Terry-Thomas' banged-up jeep. Sound editors are connoisseurs of aural tidbits, which they store in large libraries—Chic Ciccolini, for instance, one of the premier sound editors in New York, has a baby cry he's particularly proud of and a deliciously evocative recording of a distant car full of teenagers driving over a manhole cover. They've starred in many sound tracks mixed on the East Coast.

30

As any concertgoer knows, space colors sound. Though sound editors can do wonders, they cannot change the fundamental quality of the sound they are given. Every place has its particular ambience, its blend of absorption and echo which emphasizes certain frequencies, creates certain assumptions of size and mood. If the sound editors are given something recorded in a closet, they can't make it sound as if it were taped in a church, though they might be asked to if forced to replace unacceptable dialogue tracks in the editing, and, indeed, a sophisticated technology exists to help them. They can make a close approximation, but you will hear the difference. Even today, with digital technology and computer-enhanced sound, there is only so much they can fake electronically. In fact, the best way to achieve a larger acoustical effect is still to play the closet track in a large, resonant space and rerecord it from a distance. Sound is too elusive, too complicated to manipulate freely. As the picture editor is at the mercy of the cameraman, the sound editor is at the mercy of the sound recordist.

CONNECTING PERSONALLY TO THE READING

1. Think of a horror movie that you have seen. How did the cinematographer use sound and light or manipulate images to create fear in the viewer?

2. In what ways has this reading changed your impression of filmmaking? If it hasn't, why not?

FOCUSING ON THE ARGUMENT

1. Jon Boorstin's writing is full of contrasts: "the money shots" are expensive and contribute nothing to the story line but "they are indispensable"; "color is easier to shoot than black and white"; "the cameraman creates a world, the editor lives within it." Find another contrast in the reading, and explain how it enriches Boorstin's discussion.

2. Technology is essential to filmmaking, and much of what Boorstin describes is quite technical. Yet he maintains a familiar, accessible tone as if speaking directly to us. Find two elements in his writing style that contribute to this tone and explain how they work.

SYNTHESIZING IDEAS FROM MULTIPLE READINGS

1. Like John Berger ("Ways of Seeing," p. 518), Boorstin is interested in "ways of seeing." What do Boorstin's arguments about how a viewer sees a movie have in common with Berger's comments about viewing paintings?

2. Although Martha Graham (selection from *Blood Memory,* p. 591) developed an exacting modern dance technique, her article emphasizes inspiration and passion as sources for the dancer's art, whereas Boorstin's article focuses on cinematic technique. What is the relationship between technical skill and inspiration in film and dance?

3. Boorstin shows some of the ways filmmakers manipulate scenes to create an effect—for example, to make one image dominate another, establish a mood, or imitate the lighting of a seventeenth-century painting. Advertisers also manipulate the lighting, colors, and composition of their ads to get a certain effect. Look at the Chanel (insert 3-5) and Dior (insert 3-6)

ads. What effects do you think the advertisers were striving for, and what visual techniques did they use? Which of the techniques mentioned in Boorstin's article apply to the ads? In what ways do these techniques create the images that concern Jean Kilbourne ("'The More You Subtract, the More You Add': Cutting Girls Down to Size," p. 149) and Susan Bordo ("The Empire of Images in Our World of Bodies," p. 169)?

WRITING TO ACT

1. View a film and analyze at least three of the elements Boorstin discusses. Then write a film review for your campus newspaper, describing how these technical features influence your perception of the film.

2. Watch a film, possibly a documentary, on a social or political issue. Then create a Web page or write an editorial in which you explain how two or three elements of the filmmaker's craft—the use of light, sound, close-up, and the like—invite the viewer to accept a particular point of view.

READING

JOAN MORGAN is appalled at the hostility toward women expressed in the lyrics of much hip-hop music. But as an African American, she sympathizes with the pain and rage African American men have endured in white culture and sees these lyrics as a necessary expression of these feelings. Do you agree with Morgan that rather than condemn these lyrics, listeners should use them as an opportunity to explore problems caused by racism?

MORGAN was born in Jamaica, moved to New York City as a child, and currently lives in Brooklyn. Her first article for the *Village Voice,* "The Pro-Rape Culture," earned her an award from the New York Association of Black Journalists. She also covered Mike Tyson's rape trial for the *Voice,* and she even appeared in a documentary about Tyson, *The Fallen Champ.* A lifelong hip-hop fan and feminist, Morgan writes about gender and music for a wide variety of magazines and newspapers. Since 2000, she has served as executive editor at *Essence* magazine. *When Chickenheads Come Home to Roost* is her first book.

READING

Selection from *When Chickenheads Come Home to Roost: My Life as a Hip-Hop Feminist* (1999)

BY JOAN MORGAN

L ord Knows our love jones for hip-hop is understandable. Props given to rap music's artistic merits, its irrefutable impact on pop culture, its ability to be alternately beautiful, poignant, powerful, strong, irreverent, visceral, and mesmerizing—homeboy's clearly got it like that. But in between the beats, booty shaking, and hedonistic abandon, I have to wonder if there isn't something inherently unfeminist in supporting a music that repeatedly reduces me to tits and ass and encourages pimping on the regular. While it's human to occasionally fall deep into the love thang with people or situations that simply aren't good for you, feminism alerted me long ago to the dangers of romancing a misogynist (and ridiculously fine, brilliant ones with gangsta leans are no exception). Perhaps the non-believers were right, maybe what I'd been mistaking for love and commitment for the last twenty years was really nothing but a self-destructive obsession that made a mockery of my feminism.

I needed to know, once and for all, if it was in the best interests of me and my sistas to stay in what was—admittedly—a strange and often painful relationship. The time had come for a little heart-to-heart, so I started by writing my homeboy this letter:

You know, Boo,

It's been six years since I've been writing about hip-hop on the womanist tip and I'm still getting asked the same questions. At work, the intelligentsia types want to know if "Given the undeniably high content of sexism and misogyny in rap music, isn't a declared commitment to both, well, incongruous?" And my girls, they just come right out, "You still wit that nigga?"

So I tell them how good you do that thing you do. Laugh and say I'm just a slave to your rhythms. Then I wax poetic about your artistic brilliance and the voice (albeit predominantly male) you give an embattled, pained nation. And then I assure them that I call you out on all of your sexism on the regular. That works until someone, usually a sista-friend, calls me out and says that while all of that was valid, none of it explains why I stayed in an obviously abusive relationship. And I can't lie, Boo, that would stress me. 'Cuz my answers would start sounding like those battered women I write about.

Sure, I'd say (all defensive). It's easy to judge—to wonder what any woman in her right mind would be doing with that wack motherfucka if you're entering now, before the sweet times. But the sweetness was there in the beginning of this on-again, off-again love affair. It started almost twenty years ago, around the time when Tony Boyd all mocked-neck and fine gave me my first tongue kiss in the back of I.S. 148 and the South Bronx gave birth to a culture.

The old-school deejays and M.C.'s performed community service at those schoolyard jams. Intoxicating the crowd with beats and rhymes, they were like shamans sent to provide us with temporary relief from the ghetto's blues. As for sistas, we donned our flare-leg Lees and medallions, became fly-girls, and gave up the love. Nobody even talked about sexism in hip-hop back in the day. All an M.C. wanted then was to be the baddest in battle, have a fly-girl, and take rides in his fresh O.J. If we were being objectified (and I guess we were) nobody cared. At the time, there seemed to be greater sins than being called "ladies" as in "All the ladies in the house, say, Oww!"

Or "fly-girls" as in "what you gonna do?" Perhaps it was because we were being acknowledged as a complementary part of a whole.

But girlfriend's got a point, Boo. We haven't been fly-girls for a very long time. And all the love in the world does not erase the stinging impact of the new invectives and brutal imagery—ugly imprints left on cheeks that have turned the other way too many times. The abuse is undeniable. Dre, Short, Snoop, Scarface, I give them all their due but the mid school's increasing use of violence, straight-up selfish individualism, and woman-hating (half of them act like it wasn't a woman who clothed and fed their black asses—and I don't care if Mama was Crackhead Annie, then there was probably a grandmother who kept them alive) masks the essence of what I fell in love with even from my own eyes.

Things were easier when your only enemies were white racism and middle-class black folk who didn't want all that jungle music reminding them they had kinky roots. Now your anger is turned inward. And I've spent too much time in the crossfire, trying to explain why you find it necessary to hurt even those who look like you. Not to mention a habit called commercialism and multiple performance failures and I got to tell you, at times I've found myself scrounging for reasons to stay. Something more than twenty years being a long-ass time, and not quite knowing how to walk away from a nigga whose growth process has helped define your existence.

So here I am, Boo, lovin' you, myself, my sistas, my brothers with loyalties that are as fierce as they are divided. One thing I know for certain is that if you really are who I believe you to be, the voice of a nation, in pain and insane, then any thinking black woman's relationship with you is going to be as complicated as her love for black men. Whether I like it or not, you play a critical part in defining my feminism. Only you can give me the answer to the question so many of us are afraid to ask, "How did we go from fly-girls to bitches and hos in our brothers' eyes?"

You are my key to the locker room. And while it's true that your music holds some of fifteen- to thirty-year-old black men's ugliest thoughts about me, it is the only place where I can challenge them. You are also the mirror in which we can see ourselves. And there's nothing like spending time in the locker room to bring sistas face-to-face with the ways we straight-up play ourselves. Those are flesh-and-blood women who put their titties on the glass. Real-life ones who make their livings by waiting backstage and slingin' price tags on the punanny. And if our feminism is ever going to mean anything, theirs are the lives you can help us to save. As for the abuse, the process is painful, yes, but wars are not won by soldiers who are afraid to go to the battleground.

So, Boo, I've finally got an answer to everybody that wants to talk about the incongruity of our relationship. Hip-hop and my feminism are not at war but my community is. And you are critical to our survival.

I'm yours, Boo. From cradle to the grave.

I guess it all depends on how you define the f-word. My feminism places the welfare of black women and the black community on its list of priorities. It also maintains that black-on-black love is essential to the survival of both.

We have come to a point in our history, however, when black-on-black love—a love that's survived slavery, lynching, segregation, poverty, and racism—is in serious danger. The stats usher in this reality like taps before the death march: According to the U.S. Census Bureau, the number of black two-parent households has decreased from 74 percent to 48 percent since 1960. The leading cause of death among black men ages fifteen to twenty-four is homicide. The majority of them will die at the hands of other black men.[1]

Women are the unsung victims of black-on-black crime. A while back, a friend of mine, a single mother of a newborn (her "babyfather" —a brother—abdicated responsibility before their child was born) was attacked by a pit bull while walking her dog in the park. The owner (a brother) trained the animal to prey on other dogs and the flesh of his fellow community members.

A few weeks later my moms called, upset, to tell me about the murder of a family friend. She was a troubled young woman with a history of substance abuse, aggravated by her son's murder two years ago. She was found beaten and burned beyond recognition. Her murderers were not "skinheads," "The Man," or "the racist white power structure." More likely than not, they were brown men whose faces resembled her own.

Clearly, we are having a very difficult time loving one another.

Any feminism that fails to acknowledge that black folks in nineties America are living and trying to love in a war zone is useless to our struggle against sexism. Though it's often portrayed as part of the problem, rap music is essential to that struggle because it takes us straight to the battlefield.

My decision to expose myself to the sexism of Dr. Dre, Ice Cube, Snoop Dogg, or the Notorious B.I.G. is really my plea to my brothers to tell me who they are. I need to know why they are so angry at me. Why is disrespecting me one of the few things that make them feel like men? What's the haps, what are you going through on the daily that's got you acting so foul?

As a black woman and a feminist I listen to the music with a willingness to see   10
past the machismo in order to be clear about what I'm *really* dealing with. What I hear frightens me. On booming track after booming track, I hear brothers talking about spending each day high as hell on malt liquor and Chronic. Don't sleep. What passes for "40 and a blunt" good times in most of hip-hop is really alcoholism, substance abuse, and chemical dependency. When brothers can talk so cavalierly about killing each other and then reveal that they have no expectation to see their twenty-first birthday, that is straight-up depression *masquerading* as machismo.

Anyone curious about the processes and pathologies that form the psyche of the young, black, and criminal-minded needs to revisit our dearly departed Notorious B.I.G.'s first album, *Ready to Die.* Chronicling the life and times of the urban "soldier," the album is a blues-laden soul train that took us on a hustler's life journey. We boarded with the story of his birth, strategically stopped to view his dysfunctional, warring family, his first robbery, his first stint in jail, murder, drug-dealing, getting paid, partying, sexin', rappin', mayhem, and death. Biggie's player persona might have momentarily convinced the listener that he was livin' phat without a care in the world but other moments divulged his inner hell. The chorus of "Everyday Struggle": *I don't wanna live no more / Sometimes I see death knockin' at my front door* revealed that "Big Poppa" was also plagued with guilt, regret, and depression. The album ultimately ended with his suicide.

The seemingly impenetrable wall of sexism in rap music is really the complex mask African-Americans often wear both to hide and express the pain. At the close of this millennium, hip-hop is still one of the few forums in which young black men, even surreptitiously, are allowed to express their pain.

When it comes to the struggle against sexism and our intimate relationships with black men, some of the most on-point feminist advice I've received comes from sistas like my mother, who wouldn't dream of using the term. During our battle to resolve our complicated relationships with my equally wonderful and errant father, my mother presented me with the following gems of wisdom, "One of the most important lessons you will ever learn in life and love, is that you've got to love people for what they are—not for who you would like them to be."

This is crystal clear to me when I'm listening to hip-hop. Yeah, sistas are hurt when we hear brothers calling us bitches and hos. But the real crime isn't the name-calling, it's their failure to love us—to be our brothers in the way that we commit ourselves to being their sistas. But recognize: Any man who doesn't truly love himself is incapable of loving us in the healthy way we need to be loved. It's extremely telling that men who can only see us as "bitches" and "hos" refer to themselves only as "niggas."

In the interest of our emotional health and overall sanity, black women have got   15
to learn to love brothers realistically, and that means differentiating between who they are and who we'd like them to be. Black men are engaged in a war where the real enemies—racism and the white power structure—are masters of camouflage. They've conditioned our men to believe the enemy is brown. The effects of this have been as wicked as they've been debilitating. Being in battle with an enemy that looks just like you makes it hard to believe in the basics every human being needs. For too many black men there is no trust, no community, no family. Just self.

Since hip-hop is the mirror in which so many brothers see themselves, it's significant that one of the music's most prevalent mythologies is that black boys rarely grow into men. Instead, they remain perpetually post-adolescent or die. For all the machismo and testosterone in the music, it's frighteningly clear that many brothers see themselves as powerless when it comes to facing the evils of the larger society, accepting responsibility for their lives, or the lives of their children.

So, sista friends, we gotta do what any rational, survivalist-minded person would do after finding herself in a relationship with someone whose pain makes him abusive. We've gotta continue to give up the love but *from a distance that's safe*. Emotional distance is a great enabler of unconditional love and support because it allows us to recognize that the attack, the "bitch, ho" bullshit—isn't personal but part of the illness.

And the focus of black feminists has got to change. We can't afford to keep expending energy on banal discussions of sexism in rap when sexism is only part of a huge set of problems. Continuing on our previous path is akin to demanding that a fiending, broke crackhead not rob you blind because it's *wrong* to do so.

If feminism intends to have any relevance in the lives of the majority of black women, if it intends to move past theory and become functional it has to rescue itself from the ivory towers of academia. Like it or not, hip-hop is not only the dominion of the young, black, and male, it is also the world in which young black women live and survive. A functional game plan for us, one that is going to be as helpful to Shequanna on 142nd as it is to Samantha at Sarah Lawrence, has to recognize hip-hop's ability to articulate the pain our *community* is in and use that knowledge to create a redemptive, healing space.

Notice the emphasis on "community." Hip-hop isn't only instrumental in expos-   20
ing black men's pain, it brings the healing sistas need right to the surface. Sad as it may be, it's time to stop ignoring the fact that rappers meet "bitches" and "hos" daily—women who reaffirm their depiction of us on vinyl. Backstage, the road, and the 'hood are populated with women who would do anything to be with a rapper sexually for an hour if not a night. It's time to stop fronting like we don't know who rapper Jeru the Damaja was talking about when he said:

> Now a queen's a queen but a stunt's a stunt
> You can tell whose who by the things they want

Sex has long been the bartering chip that women use to gain protection, material wealth, and the vicarious benefits of power. In the black community, where women are given less access to all of the above, "trickin'" becomes a means of leveling the playing field. Denying the justifiable anger of rappers—men who couldn't get the time of day from these women before a few dollars and a record deal—isn't empowering or strategic. Turning a blind eye and scampering for moral high ground diverts our attention away from the young women who are being denied access to power and are suffering for it.

It might've been more convenient to direct our sistafied rage attention to "the sexist representation of women" in those now infamous Sir Mix-A-Lot videos, to fuss over *one* sexist rapper, but wouldn't it have been more productive to address the failing self-esteem of the 150 or so half-naked young women who were willing, unpaid participants? And what about how flip we are when it comes to using the b-word to describe each other? At some point we've all been the recipients of competitive, unsisterly, "bitchiness," particularly when vying for male attention.

Since being black and a woman makes me fluent in both isms, I sometimes use racism as an illuminating analogy. Black folks have finally gotten to the point where we recognize that we sometimes engage in oppressive behaviors that white folks have little to do with. Complexion prejudices and classism are illnesses which have their *roots* in white racism but the perpetrators are certainly black.

Similarly, sistas have to confront the ways we're complicit in our own oppression. Sad to say it, but many of the ways in which men exploit our images and sexuality in hip-hop is done with our permission and cooperation. We need to be as accountable to each other as we believe "race traitors" (i.e., 100 or so brothers in blackface cooning in a skinhead's music video) should be to our community. To acknowledge this doesn't deny our victimization but it does raise the critical issue of whose responsibility it is to end our oppression. As a feminist, I believe it is too great a responsibility to leave to men.

A few years ago, on an airplane making its way to Montego Bay, I received another gem of girlfriend wisdom from a sixty-year-old self-declared non-feminist. She was meeting her husband to celebrate her thirty-fifth wedding anniversary. After telling her I was twenty-seven and very much single, she looked at me and shook her head sadly. "I feel sorry for your generation. You don't know how to have relationships, especially the women." Curious, I asked her why she thought this was. "The women of your generation, you want to be right. The women of my generation, we didn't care about being right. We just wanted to win." 25

Too much of the discussion regarding sexism and the music focuses on being right. We feel we're *right* and the rappers are wrong. The rappers feel it's their *right* to describe their "reality" in any way they see fit. The store owners feel it's their *right* to sell whatever the consumer wants to buy. The consumer feels it's his *right* to be able to decide what he wants to listen to. We may be the "rightest" of the bunch but we sure as hell ain't doing the winning.

I believe hip-hop can help us win. Let's start by recognizing that its illuminating, informative narration and its incredible ability to articulate our collective pain is an invaluable tool when examining gender relations. The information we amass can help create a redemptive, healing space for brothers and sistas.

We're all winners when a space exists for brothers to honestly state and explore the roots of their pain and subsequently their misogyny, sans judgment. It is criminal that the only space our society provided for the late Tupac Shakur to examine the pain, confusion, drug addiction, and fear that led to his arrest and his eventual assassination was in a prison cell. How can we win if a prison cell is the only space an immensely talented but troubled young black man could dare utter these words: "Even though I'm not guilty of the charges they gave me, I'm not innocent in terms of the way I was acting. I'm just as guilty for not doing things. Not with this case but with my life. I had a job to do and I never showed up. I was so scared of this responsibility that I was running away from it."[2] We have to do better than this for our men.

And we have to do better for ourselves. We desperately need a space to lovingly address the uncomfortable issues of our failing self-esteem, the ways we sexualize and objectify ourselves, our confusion about sex and love and the unhealthy, unloving, unsisterly ways we treat each other. Commitment to developing these spaces gives our community the potential for remedies based on honest, clear diagnoses.

As I'm a black woman, I am aware that this doubles my workload—that I am definitely going to have to listen to a lot of shit I won't like—but without these candid discussions, there is little to no hope of exorcising the illness that hurts and sometimes kills us.

30

Notes

1. Joan Morgan, "Real Love," *Vibe*, April 1996, p. 38.
2. Kevin Powell, "The Vibe Q: Tupac Shakur, Ready to Live," *Vibe*, April 11, 1995, p. 52.

CONNECTING PERSONALLY TO THE READING

1. Morgan argues that many African American women will not criticize anti-female rap lyrics because they believe such criticism would undermine African American men. Describe another group (of any size) whose members believe that to criticize one another publicly would weaken the group's image in the larger society. How is this attitude enforced?

2. Who or what, according to Morgan, is responsible for the sexism in rap? Who or what do you think is responsible, and why?

FOCUSING ON THE ARGUMENT

1. One of Morgan's strategies is to switch back and forth between two idioms of English, illustrating that she lives in two cultures. How does Morgan's identification with both cultures and their languages help define the conflict she describes in the article?

2. Why do you think Morgan couches some of her ideas in the form of a letter to her "homeboy"? What is the effect of this letter?

1. Mitchell Stephens ("By Means of the Visible," p. 550) and Jon Boorstin ("The Hollywood Eye," p. 561) emphasize that the camera creates illusions that seem like real life: according to Stephens, "Images look real but are fake." The same is often said of other arts. To what extent do you think the violence expressed in many rap lyrics is an artifice, a pose? How can you tell?

2. John Berger ("Ways of Seeing," p. 518) believes that understanding the social context in which a work of art is produced affects our interpretation of the work. How does this observation apply to Morgan's analysis of rap lyrics?

3. Do you think the attitude toward women that Morgan sees in rap lyrics is part of the "laddie" culture that David Brooks ("The Return of the Pig," p. 122) discusses? Why or why not?

1. Analyze the lyrics to a popular song (rap or not), showing how the song illustrates relationships between men and women. Issues you might consider are whether race or racism affect the relationship, whether men are depicted as swaggering or posturing, or whether women are shown using sex as "the bartering chip . . . to gain protection, material wealth, and . . . power."

2. Organize a debate among several members of your class in which you argue whether misogynist rap lyrics should be condemned, understood as reflecting justifiable anger and suffering, accepted as art rather than real-life attitudes, or any other position you find. Help all the sides of the debate craft a position paper reflecting their views.

In this excerpt from his history of the blues, **ROBERT SANTELLI** shows how this musical form is tied to its cultural circumstances. Originating in the South, probably in the late nineteenth century, the blues emerged from the hardships African Americans faced in a slave and, later, Jim Crow society. Its themes and style were influenced by folk music, such as work songs and spirituals, and though rooted in African American life, they are also universal in their personal expressions of love, loss, and struggle. Think of an art form—or a particular work of art (a dance, song, or painting, for example) that is closely connected to historical events or to the experiences of a particular ethnic group. How does knowing this cultural connection affect your experience with this art form?

SANTELLI is the author of nearly a dozen books on American popular music, including *The Big Book of Blues* (1993), *American Roots Music* (2001), and *The Bob Dylan Scrapbook* (2005) and is a frequent contributor to *Rolling Stone* and other pop musical periodicals. Santelli has taught American music history and American Studies at Monmouth and Rutgers Universities in New Jersey and at the University of Washington and was the vice president of education and programming at the Rock and Roll Hall of Fame and Museum before becoming the artistic director at Experience Music Project, the interactive music museum in Seattle.

A Century of the Blues (2003) | BY ROBERT SANTELLI

1903. The place: Tutwiler, a tiny town in the Mississippi Delta, halfway between Greenwood and Clarksdale. It is dusk, and the sky is rich in summer color. The slight breeze, when it visits, is warm and wet with humidity.

William Christopher Handy, better known by his initials, W. C., waits on the wooden platform for a train heading north. Handy, the recently departed bandleader for Mahara's Minstrels, a black orchestra that mostly plays dance music and popular standards of the day, is a learned musician who understands theory and the conventions of good, respectable music. He had joined the Minstrels as a cornet player when he was twenty-two years old and traveled widely with them: the U.S., Canada, Mexico, Cuba. In time, he became their band director. Now, some seven years later, here he is, fresh from agreeing to lead the black Clarksdale band Knights of Pythias.

The train is late, so Handy does the only thing he can do: He waits patiently, trying to stay cool, passing the time with idle thoughts, and scanning the scenery for anything that might prove the least bit interesting. Finally succumbing to boredom, Handy dozes off, only to be awakened by the arrival of another man who sits down nearby and begins to play the guitar. His clothes tattered and his shoes beyond worn, the man is a sad specimen, especially compared to Handy, whose clothes bespeak a black sophistication not often seen in these parts.

The man plays and Handy listens, growing increasingly interested in the informal performance. Handy, of course, has heard many people, black and white, play guitar before, but not the way this man plays it. He doesn't finger the strings normally, instead, he presses a pocketknife against them, sliding it up and down to create a slinky sound, something akin to what Hawaiian guitarists get when they press a steel bar to the strings.

But it isn't just the unusual manner in which the poor black man plays his guitar. What he sings, and how he sings it, is equally compelling. "Goin' where the Southern cross the Dog": Most people around these parts know that "the Southern" is a railroad reference, and that "the Dog" is short for "Yellow Dog," local slang for the Yazoo Delta line. The man is singing about where the Southern line and the Yazoo Delta line intersect, at a place called Moorhead. But something about the way the man practically moans it for added emphasis, repeating it three times, strikes Handy hard; the combination of sliding guitar, wailing voice, repeated lyrics, and the man's emotional honesty is incredibly powerful. Handy doesn't realize it yet, but this moment is an important one in his life, and an important one in the history of American music as well. The description of this incident, written about by Handy thirty-eight years later in his autobiography, is one of the earliest detailed descriptions of the blues ever written by a black man.

Handy called his book *Father of the Blues*. It's a good title for a book—but not, strictly speaking, an accurate one. What Handy did on that railroad platform in Mississippi a century ago was *witness* the blues, not give birth to it. But there's no disputing that he was forever after a changed man. "The effect was unforgettable," he wrote. Even so, he found it hard to bring the blues into his own musical vocabulary. Wrote Handy, "As a director of many respectable, conventional bands, it was not easy for me to concede that a simple slow-drag-and-repeat could be rhythm itself. Neither was I ready to believe that this was just what the public wanted."

But later, during a Cleveland, Mississippi, performance, Handy's band was out-shone—and outpaid—by a local trio playing blues similar to what he heard in Tutwiler. Shortly thereafter, Handy became a believer. "Those country black boys at Cleveland had taught me something. . . . My idea of what constitutes music was changed by the sight of that silver money cascading around the splay feet of a Mississippi string band," wrote Handy.

In 1909 Handy penned a political campaign song, "Mr. Crump," for the Memphis mayor. He later changed the title to "The Memphis Blues" and published it in 1912. The song was a hit. Entrepreneurially savvy, Handy delved deeper into the music, following it with "The St. Louis Blues," "Joe Turner Blues," "The Hesitating Blues," "Yellow Dog Blues," "Beale Street," and other blues and blues-based compositions. Their commercial success made Handy well-off but, more importantly, solidified the idea that the blues could exist in mainstream music settings, beyond black folk culture. The blues had arrived, thanks to W. C. Handy. American music would never be the same.

No one really knows for certain when or where the blues was born. But by the time of Handy's initial success with the music in 1912, it's safe to say it had been a viable black folk-music form in the South for at least two decades. With a couple exceptions, ethnomusicologists didn't become interested in the blues until later, thus missing prime opportunities to document the origins of the music and to record its pioneers. Still, there are enough clues to indicate that the blues most likely came out of the Mississippi Delta in the late nineteenth century.

Like all music forms—folk, pop, or classical—the blues evolved, rather than 10 being born suddenly. So to understand the origins of the blues, you need to take a look at what came before it. You need to go back to the early part of the seventeenth century, when African slaves were first brought to the New World. Europeans involved in the slave trade stripped as much culture from their human cargo as possible before their arrival in the New World. But music was so embedded in the day-to-day existence of the African men and women caught in this horrific business that it was impossible to tear their songs from their souls. In West Africa, where many of the slaves came from, virtually everything was celebrated with singing and dancing: births, marriages, war, famine, religious beliefs, hunts, death. To eliminate music from an enslaved West African was to kill him.

Not that white slave owners in the New World permitted West African music rituals to exist without condition on early plantations along the Eastern Seaboard. Some slave owners forbade any music made by slaves, fearful that rebellious messaging could be encoded in the rhythms and chants. Other slave owners permitted limited music, particularly in the fields. Singing, the owners eventually realized, produced more and better work from the slaves. More liberal slave owners allowed singing and dancing during days of rest and holidays but often under the watchful eye of a work foreman or field master. Then there were those slave owners, a minority to be sure, who actually trained some of their slaves in Western music theory so that they'd be able to entertain guests at white socials and other plantation events. These slaves played stringed, woodwind, and keyboard instruments and created ensembles that played both popular and sacred music.

The earliest indication that slaves other than those specially trained were able to participate in music celebration beyond their own indigenous strains happened in the

"THE ST. LOUIS BLUES"
By W. C. Handy

I hate to see the evening sun go down
I hate to see the evening sun go down
It makes me think I'm on my last go 'round

Feelin' tomorrow like I feel today
Feelin' tomorrow like I feel today
I'll pack my grip and make my getaway

St. Louis woman wears her diamond ring
Pulls a man around by her apron string

Wasn't for powder and this store-bought hair
The man I love wouldn't go nowhere, nowhere

I got them St. Louis blues, just as blue as I can be
He's got a heart like a rock cast in the sea
Or else he would not go so far from me.

church. In the early eighteenth century, during the religious revival period known as the Great Awakening, there existed a desire to make Christians out of the pagan slaves. This missionary zeal swept the American colonies as slaves were taught the teachings of the Bible and spent much of their Sundays in church, albeit a segregated church. While white churchgoers sang hymns with stiff rhythms that required formalized responses from the congregation, Christian slaves sang hymns, too, but were unable to contain their enthusiasm when asked to sing God's praises. Over time, swinging rhythms, hand clapping, foot stomping, and improvised shouts made black Christian music significantly different from the sounds emanating from white churches. The hymns might have been the same, but the singing surely wasn't.

Eventually, black sacred folk songs of redemption and salvation, and of the triumph of hope over despair, created a genre called the Negro spiritual. Songs such as "Go Down, Moses" and "Roll, Jordan, Roll" were sung in the church and in the fields, as slaves seldom regarded the separation of sacred and secular music. The Negro spiritual didn't gain popularity beyond the black community until the 1870s, when Fisk University, a newly appointed black college in Nashville, sought to raise money via a musical tour by its choir. The Fisk Jubilee Singers played not only to white audiences in the United States but also in Europe, prompting attention to the Negro spiritual as a creditable sacred folk-music form.

The blues would borrow from Negro spirituals as well as from field hollers, the most primitive of black music. Field hands didn't exactly holler as much as they whooped, moaned, and sang in sudden and completely improvised ways. A rhythm might come to mind and a melody, too, and then made-up lyrics, perhaps reflecting an approaching storm, a Saturday social, or the resolute stubbornness of a mule. Work songs were more organized musical expressions. Actually, a worker, be it a slave or a post–Civil War sharecropper, could make any song into a work song, if he sang it while working. But many work songs were sung by groups of workers, particularly those picking cotton or laying railroad track or building a levee, who seemed to move in a rhythmic unison. Work songs didn't make the work easier, just a tiny bit more tolerable.

Black folk songs, some of which could be considered work songs, like "John 15 Henry," helped give rise to the blues too. In the song, Henry, a big, strapping black railroad worker, works himself to death trying to outdo a mechanized steel drill. Another song, "Stagolee," (a.k.a. Stagger Lee) tells the tale of a black con man. These musical narratives created characters, outlined plots, and usually contained some kind of lesson for the listener.

Spirituals, work songs, folk songs—these nineteenth-century black music forms were forged with the last of the major blues influences, the minstrel. No other American form is as wrapped in shame as the minstrel, yet there is no doubt of the music's popularity in the nineteenth century, first with white audiences and then with black. Minstrelsy, born in the years before the Civil War, consisted of white singers and actors in corked blackface coarsely ridiculing black southern plantation life for white audiences, many of which were based up North. They lampooned black slang and superstitions, physical features, and virtually everything else connected to the black man's condition in antebellum America. Dancing and singing songs inspired by black folk music, minstrel entertainers portrayed the typical black slave as little more than a clown or ignoramus. After emancipation and the end of the Civil War, whites grew less interested in minstrel shows. Rather than let minstrelsy die (which, admittedly, had created a canon of black-flavored music from the likes of Stephen Foster and other white composers), black singers and dancers eager for the opportunity to scratch out livings as entertainers adopted the form. Using burnt cork on their already dark-skinned faces, which, looking back today, seems to be the ultimate racial insult, black entertainers re-created minstrelsy by presenting the song-and-dance skits to their own people as a form of musical comedy. Black minstrelsy peaked in the late 1870s, and although the traveling minstrel entertainers were black, as were their audiences, the troupes were owned by whites, including Mahara's Minstrels.

> "Music did bring me to the gutter. It brought me to sleep on the levee of the Mississippi River, on the cobblestones, broke and hungry. And if you've ever slept on cobblestones or had nowhere to sleep, you can understand why I began ['The St. Louis Blues'] with 'I hate to see the evening sun go down.'"
> —W. C. HANDY

With so many influences, it is surprising that the blues should be such a "simple" music form—at least on the surface. Lyrically, the blues is about repetition. A first line is sung and then repeated with perhaps a slight variation: "My baby, oh, she left me, and that's no lie/Well, I said my baby, oh, she left me, and no way that's a lie." These two lines are followed by a third line that answers the first two: "Wish my baby'd get back to me, before I lay down and die." Musicologists call this the "A-A-B" pattern. The best blues songwriters pack a whole lot of narrative into such simple lyrical patterns, as the blues has a way of telling its own story. Good love gone bad, evil women and worse men, alcohol, poverty, death, prejudice, despair, hope, the devil, and the search for better days figure into many blues songs. The great bluesman Mississippi Fred McDowell once said, "The blues, it jus' keeps goin' on, goin' on. . . . Know why? 'Cause the blues is the story of life and the spice of life." Mississippi Fred hit it right on the head.

Musically, the blues introduced the "blue" note, one of the most significant contributions to American music made by black culture. These notes are usually made by flattening—lowering by a half step—the third, fifth, or seventh positions of a major scale. Presenting all kinds of emotional possibilities for the musician, blue notes give the blues its special feel, and when they are draped around a blues chord progression, the results can be so rich and *human,* that it satisfies the soul in a way no other music can.

By the late 1890s, it is likely that the blues had taken all its influences and evolved into a form of its own on the plantations that thrived in the Mississippi Delta during this period. Since the blues was born black, the Delta provided the community support necessary for the music to flourish. In the summer, the most tortured of seasons in the Deep South, the large stretch of land known as the Mississippi Delta is as hot as it is flat. During the day, the sun bakes the landscape, much of it below sea level, with nary a rise or hill rump in sight. The seemingly endless fields of cotton, the Delta's principal crop, and the scattered small hamlets, with names like Lula and Bobo, can be paralyzed by the heat and humidity.

The Delta's blues legacy is larger than its physical domain. Only 160 miles long   20
from Memphis to the north, to Vicksburg to the south, and some fifty miles wide, it is not even a true delta, as in the area around the mouth of a river. Rather, it is a remarkably fertile alluvial plain, with soil as dark as the laborers forced to work it. The Delta has its rivers; one of them, the mighty Mississippi, is its western border. One of the more compelling stories of Delta history has to do with man's attempt to keep the Mississippi River out. Long and high levees built by former slaves and sons of slaves in the latter part of the nineteenth and early twentieth centuries kept, more or less, the river from overflowing onto the plantations that grew out of early Delta farms after the land was cleared of its old growth forest.

During the years after the Civil War, known as the period of Reconstruction, the commercial success of cotton made many of the white southern plantation families wealthy. Acres and acres of cotton were planted and picked by black workers and then shipped to Memphis. Having so many fields that needed tending guaranteed work for thousands of black laborers, making the ratio of black to white in the Delta nearly ten to one. Although black workers now had their freedom, in reality they were bound to the plantation, because they worked for a pittance and often owed money to the plantation store for the high-priced goods sold there. Jim Crow laws, the rise of racist organizations such as the Ku Klux Klan, lynchings, and prejudice at every turn made it all but impossible for blacks to enjoy the freedom and dignity that whites did. It was a cruel existence, and the blues documented the black man's woes better than any other form of cultural expression.

The earliest places a person could hear the blues were probably at socials, parties, fish fries, and in juke joints, small shacks on the outskirts of the plantation, where blacks converged on Saturday nights to drink cheap whiskey and dance. The earliest bluesmen were probably local plantation workers who owned a guitar or banjo, had a knack for singing and entertaining, and played for tips. Later, as the blues matured and grew more popular, bluesmen became itinerant entertainers, going from juke to juke, living a life of whiskey, song, women, and wandering.

With its large black population, the Mississippi Delta was the perfect place for the blues to grow, but it wasn't the only place down South where the music thrived. By the turn of the century, the blues had surfaced in west Texas, the Arkansas Delta on the western side of the Mississippi River, Louisiana, and even in Georgia and the Carolinas. The spread of the blues was organic and irregular. The blues pioneers of the late nineteenth and early twentieth centuries had no clue as to the emerging importance of the music they played. There was no way for them to know or even imagine that the blues would have implications far beyond the juke joint, that it would become the foundation for virtually every popular-music form—jazz, rhythm & blues, rock & roll, soul, funk, hip-hop—of the new century. What these blues musicians *did* know was that when they played, people listened, threw some money into their hat, maybe bought them a pint of whiskey. And that was good enough for them.

CONNECTING PERSONALLY TO THE READING

1. Santelli spends some time describing the Mississippi Delta, especially its geography, climate, and people, because he believes that the blues was influenced by the area it came from. What kind of music or other art form is native to the area where you live? How does the region influence the art?

2. Santelli argues that blues is "the foundation for virtually every popular-music form—jazz, rhythm & blues, rock & roll, soul, funk, hip-hop—of the new century." Consider a popular song you like; what elements of the blues do you see in it, if any?

FOCUSING ON THE ARGUMENT

1. Santelli mixes exposition, where he presents facts (e.g., where the blues came from), with description (e.g., the guitar playing at the railroad station), and narration, (e.g., W. C. Handy's first encounter with the blues). What does each of these techniques contribute to the essay?

2. Writers often find it difficult to describe a musical style, yet throughout this essay Santelli defines the blues and attempts to distinguish it from other kinds of music. Find three places that help you understand what the blues is, and explain how each one contributes to the overall definition.

SYNTHESIZING IDEAS FROM MULTIPLE READINGS

1. Like Santelli, John Berger ("Ways of Seeing," p. 518), writing of painting, believes that art is influenced by the context in which it is created—such as historical events of the period or the circumstances of the artist. In what ways do the quotations from musician W. C. Handy in Santelli's article and Berger's analysis of the Franz Hals painting illustrate this belief?

2. In "The Hollywood Eye" (p. 561), Jon Boorstin discusses how the techniques of cinematography—light and sound, for example—create a specific artistic effect. Santelli does the

same for the blues, discussing its rhythm, pattern of rhyme, "blue note," and chord progression. Listen to a blues piece; then show how these technical elements contribute to its emotional impact. How do these elements illustrate Boorstin's point that the technique of a work of art creates an illusion for the audience?

3. Santelli shows how blues evolved throughout African American history, arguing that elements of African and early African American culture are still evident in the blues form. What elements of her ancestors' culture does Louise Erdrich still see today ("The Names of Women," p. 76)? What kept both cultural traditions alive?

WRITING TO ACT

1. Research a musician or other artist from your community, and create a Web site, video, or pamphlet describing this person's art. Consider the personal background of the artist, his/her training or influences, and, if possible, include samples of the work of art. Show the relationship between this artist and the community.

2. Listen to the music of W. C. Handy, Bessie Smith, or any other blues musician. Write an article in which you show how this music does or does not conform to the definition of blues that Santelli gives us.

READING

ROSANNE CASH, a country music artist and daughter of the late country musician Johnny Cash, writes about how making music together creates a bond among musicians. She believes that this bond is especially important to country music, which has a tradition of exploring family ties and which is often passed down from one family member to another. But she also argues that such a bond can be created not just by music, but also by any "shared passion" and that it occurs not just among family members, but also between any people who share this passion. Think of an interest you have that you care deeply about and that you share with someone else. Does this "shared passion" create a special bond between you? Why or why not?

CASH (b. 1955) has had eleven number one hits on the country music charts; her most recent album is *Black Cadillac,* which has had cross-over success. She is also the author of the short story collection *Bodies of Water.*

READING

The Ties That Bind (2000) | BY ROSANNE CASH

From the time I was six until I was 12, my family lived on a barren hilltop in Southern California in the tiny town of Casitas Springs, between Ventura on the ocean and Ojai at the mountains. Although we were isolated, we had a lot of deliveries up there on the mountain: the milkman, the Jewel Tea truck (a traveling store of candy, powdered drinks, snacks and bulk white-trash kinds of food) and the Helm's bakery truck—my favorite. I always ran outside when the Helm's truck bumped across the cattle grate at the top of our drive. One day I bolted out through the garage to greet the driver just as he flung open the back doors like it was a gypsy wagon. I practically swooned before the hundreds of cakes, pies, tarts and breads.

"Do you take the truck home at night?" I asked.

"Yes." He smiled at me.

"How do you keep from eating all this stuff when you get home?"

"Well, if you're around it all day, you want to get away from it when you go home at   5
night. Does your daddy sit around and sing all day when he comes home off the road?"

I pondered for a moment. "Well, no."

It was the answer he expected, and so I gave it, but what I was thinking then, and what I understand more clearly now, is that it's not just the singing you bring home with you. It's the constant measuring of ideas and words, if you are a songwriter, and the daily handling of your instrument, if you are a musician, and the humming and scratching and pushing and testing of the voice, the reveling in the melodies, if you are a singer. More than that, it is the straddling of two worlds, and the struggle to make the transition from the creative realms to daily life and back with grace. My father is, and does, all of that. I do too, although I cannot claim my father's profound originality and influence. (Indeed, I go by the maxim that genius does what it must and talent does what it can.)

I belong to an extended family of musicians whose members sprawl across three generations. Some occupy positions of great acclaim (my father and my stepmother's family, the Carter Family), others of anecdotal obscurity (my maternal uncle, "Wildman" Ray Liberto, a former raucous honky-tonk piano player). At 16, I did not intend to take my place among them. Tradition was anathema to me; I understood that real rebellion would be to take a straight, nonmusical path. My mother had had a strict Italian Catholic upbringing, which pretty much defined her views about a woman's place in the world, and my father was an enormously visible performer. I had a fierce though silent desire to live a different life. I would not be a housewife, nor would I seek fame as a singer. I would be an archeologist and move to a kibbutz (odd choice for a Catholic girl, and so much the better). Change and newness: That defined life as far as I was concerned.

Then, when I was a day out of high school, my father took me on the road. It was something of a graduation gift, and a chance to catch up on some lost time with my dad. And it was a serious education: traveling the world, watching him perform, singing on the bus. He made a list of 100 Essential Country Songs, which he instructed me to learn, a wide-ranging list that ran from the old history lesson songs like "The Battle of New Orleans" through classics like Hank Williams's "I'm So Lonesome I Could Cry." I was ushered into a treasury of song, and it was thrilling to learn more about my father through his great love for this music. I learned to play guitar from my stepmother's sister, Helen, and from Mother Maybelle Carter, and from Carl Perkins, all of whom were on the road with Dad at the time. Each day, I spent many hours in dressing rooms, practicing chords and the old songs they taught me. I discovered a passion for songwriting that remains undiminished to this day and that led me into my life as a writer and singer—into my family's vocation.

I lasted 2½ years on that bus until, too much feeling the constraint a young girl   10
feels in the constant presence of a parent, I moved to London and then came home and went to college. But an important part of my heart and soul was given form and expression on that bus, and I came to realize how a shared passion forges deep bonds between people, defining a family more deeply than blood connection alone can do.

At the heart of real country music lies family, lies a devotion to exploring the bonds of blood ties, both in performance and in songwriting. Of course, there have been families in pop music (the Jacksons, the Beach Boys, Heart, Hanson). Parents and children have sung all manner of music together or in succession—Judy Garland and Liza Minnelli, Nat King Cole and Natalie Cole, Tim Buckley and Jeff Buckley, Loudon Wainwright III and his son, Rufus. But the community of country music emphasizes the family connection, revels in it, and there seems to be less rivalry, less need for the children to break away on their own musical terms (although that was an impulse I struggled with for the first 15 years of my career). Country treats family as a rich and fascinating source of material for its songs.

The Carter Family is the prototypical country music family, both for its artists and in the wide-ranging subjects of its songs, but there have been many, many more examples since the Carters began singing in the 1920s. It seems that members of every possible variation of the extended family have pursued careers separately, together and successively. (This is also true in bluegrass and gospel, close cousins to country.) As a teenager, I saw the Earl Scruggs Revue perform perhaps 20 times and held my breath for those moments when laconic Earl would glance at one of his sons, who had just performed a phenomenal solo, in a fleeting moment of approbation. Doc and Merle Watson also had a special resonance for me as performers. They were so close—in their genetic gifts, in their attitudes and quiet respect for each other—that it was a privilege to be in their audience. I was certain that they treated each other the same offstage as on. When Merle died in 1985, it was painful to imagine the enormity of the loss for Doc. He lost not only his son but his musical soulmate. I was thrilled recently to discover that Doc now plays music with Merle's son.

It was riveting to watch the Judds at the height of their career work out their mother-daughter tensions on stage. Every subtle gesture—mom stroking Wynonna's hair and the almost imperceptible flinch it provoked, or the intense glances from one to the other that were ignored—spoke reams, and every adult daughter in the audience would relate. In my own performing, I've found it impossible to stay mad at someone you love when you are on stage with them. Arguments and grudges melt away under the spotlights and the audience's gaze. I feel that I should somehow be better on stage, more magnanimous, for the sake of the audience, and sometimes I *am* better. One of the sweetest moments of my life occurred several years ago, the last time my dad played Carnegie Hall. I had been a little angry with him the day before the show and had brought up some old grievances, which he listened to gracefully. He invited me to sing "I Still Miss Someone" with him the next night. I demurred. The day of the performance, I had a fierce headache and told him I could not do it. I went to his hotel that evening before the show, and he asked again. I declined, but as I watched him walk out of the room I suddenly realized what it meant to him and agreed to sing the song. That night, as we sang together, all the old pain dissolved. I felt the longing to connect completely satisfied. Under the lights, in the safety of a few thousand people who loved us like crazy just then, I got something from my dad that I'd been trying to get since I was about six years old. It was truly magic, for both of us. I don't think we've ever been so close.

Performed by families and often about family, traditional country music spares nothing and no one in its gaze. In the deeply maudlin early country songs about dead babies, for example, lie the hard truths about mountain life. The best in this tragic bunch—according to my dad, anyway—is an old tune called "The Railroad Engineer." The engineer's baby is sick, but he has to go to work and drive ol' No. 9, or whatever it is, so he bids his wife:

Just hang a light when I pass tonight—
Hang it so it can be seen.
If the baby's dead, then show the red;
If it's better, then show the green.

Happily the engineer sees green, but most babies did not fare so well in the early Appalachian songs, which were a way to count the losses and gather comfort.

Mother is the most revered member of the family in traditional country music, 15 the person whose mention holds the greatest emotional charge. The "country classic of them all" (again, according to Dad) is "Sweeter Than the Flowers," co-written by Ervin Rouse, who also wrote "Orange Blossom Special." It begins:

Yes, as far as I can remember
She'll remain the rose of my heart.
Mam took sick along in December;
February brought us broken hearts.
The reason we've not called a fam'ly reunion,
We knew she wouldn't be there,
But since we've thot it all over, Mama
We know that your spirit is there.

If this is not wrenching enough, the song continues (with a line that boasts one of the all-time great rhymes):

No, no, there's no need to bother;
To speak of you now would only hurt father.

This couplet just kills me, so to speak.

But modern country music is shiny and rich and rather shallow, and naturally it speaks less of desperate loss. The dead have all but disappeared, though they occasionally surface. Back in the '80s, George Jones's "He Stopped Loving Her Today" had everyone swooning with morbid joy. Babies are more likely to be celebrated in birth than in demise (as in Loretta Lynn's "One's on the Way").

Still, the family faded in country as sexual heat began to obsess most singers and songwriters, just as it does in pop music. Anyone who has listened to old honky-tonk knows that this has always been a theme of country, but today it is *the* theme: The airwaves are soggy with songs about romance, desire, longing for love, love that got away, love gone wrong, standing up to or by your man or woman, loneliness, frustration, carnal passion, lovers' quarrels, and on and on. It's all real stuff, certainly, and good fodder for song, but the hormonal flushes of love affairs are not the only thing going on in a life. Lost from view are the other potent relationships, forged of blood and shared history, rich with emotional content, ripe for exploration. As Bruce Springsteen—one of the most family-inspired songwriters of the past two decades—said in "Highway Patrolman," "Nothing feels better than blood on blood." Certainly that has informed my own writing. I've written about my children in "Carrie," "Child of Steel" and "Mid-Air"; about a baby I lost in "Just Don't Talk About It"; and about my dad in "My Old Man."

I owe you, Mom. 20

As I was writing this, I called my dad to ask him about the old songs. I asked him about songs about mothers, babies, brothers and sisters, fathers and grandparents. He gave me titles, years and the names of the recording artists, and then sang them to me over the phone, verse by verse, more excited by each new recollection. Out of time, he told me to call back the next morning so we could talk about the songs "for a long time."

"I know *all* of them!" he said happily. I thought about those old songs all night and called him back first thing the next morning so he could sing the entirety of "Sweeter Than the Flowers" to me. He paused at the end as I scribbled down the lyrics.

"There's a whole other group of songs, if you're interested," he said.

"About who?" I asked.

"Dead dogs," he answered, solemnly, and rattled off a list of titles. I laughed. But   25
what I was thinking about was that bakery truck and how I had lied to the driver. We do take our deliveries home at night, and everything comes inside, and we're not shy about getting our fill.

CONNECTING PERSONALLY TO THE READING

1. Cash's father is eager to pass on to her his knowledge of country songs. Think of a family you know that takes pains to transmit tradition—whether artistic heritage, family customs, ethnic history, language, or another aspect of family culture to its children. Why is it important to the older generation to keep the tradition going? How receptive is the younger generation to this tradition, and why?

2. Cash argues that sex and romance have dominated the lyrics of recent country songs. Think of songs from any musical style that do not take sex and romance as their primary theme. What are these songs about? Do you see a pattern in the topics of these songs?

FOCUSING ON THE ARGUMENT

1. Cash begins and ends her essay with a story about a bakery delivery truck. How does this story illustrate the major idea of the essay?

2. Cash's essay is full of telling details—e.g., Wynonna Judd reacting to having her hair touched. Pick one such detail and show how it enriches this essay—for example, does it make the writer more sympathetic to us, or does it clarify her ideas or feelings or help us understand the people she describes?

SYNTHESIZING IDEAS FROM MULTIPLE READINGS

1. Both Martha Graham (selection from *Blood Memory,* p. 591) and Rosanne Cash write about their personal relationship with their art form. What similarities or differences do you see in the way they value what they do as artists?

2. Joan Morgan (selection from *When Chickenheads Come Home to Roost,* p. 572) and Rosanne Cash both write about popular music forms that emerge from a particular subculture of the United States. What conflicts does each writer see in her relationship to the musicians she describes—Cash's relationship with her father and Joan Morgan's with the

African American rappers she listens to? How does each move from experiencing conflict to finding common cause? What accounts for the change in each case?

3. Much of Cash's article describes how she initially rejected, later accepted, and finally came to appreciate her family. In what ways does her experience resemble and differ from that of Caffilene Allen ("First They Changed My Name," p. 65)? What conclusions did each woman draw in exploring her personal history?

WRITING TO ACT

1. With two or three other people, write and perform a song. If no one in your group plays a musical instrument, rewrite the lyrics to a song. Then write a short essay, describing how the collaboration affected the relationship among the group members. For example, did the experience make you feel closer? Did it create, unveil, or resolve conflicts?

2. Listen to some of the music of Johnny Cash, Rosanne Cash, or the two of them performing together. Then write a review of this music, considering how the songs themselves or the particular performance illustrates any of the assertions Cash makes in her essay.

READING

MARTHA GRAHAM believes dance engages the dancer's self-discipline, intellect, body, and spirit. In this excerpt from her autobiography, she argues that the dancer experiences life intensely and that the qualities that make a great dancer—curiosity, openness to experience, and an appetite for living—are also the qualities that give anyone, dancer or not, a full, rich life. If you are a dancer or other artist, what characteristics do you see as important for your art? If you are not an artist, what qualities in a dancer or other performer do you value, and why?

GRAHAM (1894–1991) was a pioneer of modern dance and one of the foremost dancers/choreographers in the United States. As a female choreographer, she attracted much criticism and acclaim in the 1920s. She founded the Martha Graham School of Dance in 1927. Many of her ballets celebrated great women in history, including Joan of Arc and Emily Dickinson. She danced for the final time at the age of seventy-six, and she continued to choreograph until her death at ninety-six. Graham was the first recipient of the Presidential Medal of Freedom.

| Selection from *Blood Memory* (1992) | BY MARTHA GRAHAM |

I am a dancer.

I believe that we learn by practice. Whether it means to learn to dance by practicing dancing or to learn to live by practicing living, the principles are the same. In each it is the performance of a dedicated precise set of acts, physical or intellectual, from which comes shape of achievement, a sense of one's being, a satisfaction of spirit. One becomes in some area an athlete of God.

To practice means to perform, in the face of all obstacles, some act of vision, of faith, of desire. Practice is a means of inviting the perfection desired.

I think the reason dance has held such an ageless magic for the world is that it has been the symbol of the performance of living. Even as I write, time has begun to make today yesterday—the past. The most brilliant scientific discoveries will in time change and perhaps grow obsolete, as new scientific manifestations emerge. But art is eternal, for it reveals the inner landscape, which is the soul of man. . . .

People have asked me why I chose to be a dancer. I did not choose. I was chosen to be a   5
dancer, and with that, you live all your life. When any young student asks me, "Do you think I should be a dancer?" I always say, "If you have to ask, then the answer is no." Only if there is one way to make life vivid for yourself and for others should you embark upon such a career . . . You will know the wonders of the human body because there is nothing more wonderful. The next time you look into the mirror, just look at the way the ears rest next to the head; look at the way the hairline grows; think of all the little bones in your wrist. It is a miracle. And the dance is a celebration of that miracle.

I feel that the essence of dance is the expression of man—the landscape of his soul. I hope that every dance I do reveals something of myself or some wonderful thing a human being can be. It is the unknown—whether it is the myths or the legends or the rituals that give us our memories. It is the eternal pulse of life, the utter desire. I know that when we have rehearsals, and we have them every day, there are some dancers, particularly men, who cannot be still. One of the men in my company is not built to be still. He has to be moving. I think at times he does not know what he is doing, but that is another matter. He's got the essence of a man's inner life that prods him to dance. He has that desire. Every dance is a kind of fever chart, a graph of the heart. Desire is a lovely thing, and that is where the dance comes from, from desire. . . .

Outside my studio door, in my garden, is a tree that has always been a symbol of facing life, and in many ways it is a dancer. It began as a sapling when I first moved here and although a wire gate was in its way, it persisted and grew to the light, and now thirty years later it is a tree with a very thick trunk, with the wire embedded within. Like a dancer it went to the light and carried the scars of its journey inside. You traverse, you work, you make it right. You embody within yourself that curiosity, use that avidity for life no matter whether it is for good or for evil. The body is a sacred garment. It's your first and your last garment; it is what you enter life in and what you depart life with, and it should be treated with honor, and with joy and with fear as well. But always, though, with blessing.

They say that the two primary arts were dance and architecture. The word "theatre" was a verb before it was a noun—an act, then a place. That means you must make the gesture, the effort, the real effort to communicate with another being. And you also must have a tree to shelter under in case of storm or sun. There is always that tree, that creative force, and there is always a house, a theatre.

Trees can be the most beautiful things in the world, particularly when they are not in leaf. There is one tree where the road cuts through Central Park from the East to the West Side. Each passage I make during the seasons shows it in a different aspect of becoming. When it is out of leaf, it becomes so old and so striking, rather like my favorite No mask, of an old woman who had once been very beautiful. Each time I see that tree I salute it for its power, and its mystery.

The spine is your body's tree of life. And through it a dancer communicates; his   10
body says what words cannot, and if he is pure and open, he can make of his body a tragical instrument.

That tension, that intensification of a body in its stillness and in its movement, I feel reflected in our studio. At one time a creek ran through this property, and I believe the land still holds some of that hidden water. The Greeks felt that where there was a spring, a manifestation of the flow of life, there also was a goddess who could either be placated or offended. It is a strange force that at times seems alive under our building. Even in the studio, we have had a little shoot of plant life come up out of the floor just near the piano. It is another world and we accept it as a gift.

I am absorbed in the magic of movement and light. Movement never lies. It is the magic of what I call the outer space of the imagination. There is a great deal of outer space, distant from our daily lives, where I feel our imagination wanders sometimes. It will find a planet or it will not find a planet, and that is what a dancer does.

And then there is inspiration. Where does it come from? Mostly from the excitement of living. I get it from the diversity of a tree or the ripple of the sea, a bit of poetry, the sighting of a dolphin breaking the still water and moving toward me . . . anything that quickens you to the instant. And whether one would call that inspiration or necessity, I really do not know. At times I receive that inspiration from people; I enjoy people very much and for the most part feel it is returned. I simply happen to love people. I do not love them all individually, but I love the idea of life pulsing through people—blood and movement.

For all of us, but particularly for a dancer with his intensification of life and his body, there is a blood memory that can speak to us. Each of us from our mother and father has received their blood and through their parents and their parents' parents and backward into time. We carry thousands of years of that blood and its memory. How else to explain those instinctive gestures and thoughts that come to us, with little preparation or expectation. They come perhaps from some deep memory of a time when the world was chaotic, when, as the Bible says, the world was nothing. And then, as if some door opened slightly, there was light. It revealed certain wonderful things. It revealed terrifying things. But it was light. . . .

The life of a dancer is by no means simple. It is comparatively short. I am not an   15
example of that, but I could not do certain things beyond a certain point. Old age is a pain in the neck. I didn't want to grow old because I didn't realize that I was growing old. I feel that it is a burden and a fearful thing and one I have to endure. It is not a thing to be treasured or to be loved. It is by any means a difficulty to bear.

When I stopped dancing, it was not a conscious decision. I realized that I did not have the strength or the ability to build into the interior and the soul of the artist. Before I began to dance I trained myself to do four hundred jumps in five minutes by the clock. Today, there are so many things I can't do. I get absolutely furious that I cannot do them. I didn't want to stop dancing and still do not want to. I have always wanted a simple, direct, open, clean, and wonderful life. That has been my time.

There are always ancestral footsteps behind me, pushing me, when I am creating a new dance, and gestures are flowing through me. Whether good or bad, they are ancestral. You get to the point where your body is something else and it takes on a world of cultures from the past, an idea that is very hard to express in words. I never verbalize about the dance as I create it. It is a purely physical risk that you desire to take, and that you have to take. The ballet I am doing now is a risk. That is all I can say because it isn't fulfilled yet. I let no one watch, except for the dancers I am working with. When they leave I am alone with the ancestral footsteps.

Somewhere very long ago I remember hearing that in El Greco's studio, after he died, they found an empty canvas on which he had written only three words: "Nothing pleases me." This I can understand.

At moments I think that it is time for me to stop. I think of Mallarmé's image of the swan, the beautiful swan, who stayed too long in the winter water until the ice closed around his feet, and he was caught. I wonder, sometimes, if I have stayed too long. Perhaps I am just being afraid. . . .

I do not feel myself unique by any means, but I do know that I agree with Edgard   20
Varèse—and I'm going to use a word that I never use regarding myself or anybody else. And that word is genius. Varèse, a wonderful French composer, who wrote some music for me, opened up new areas of musical strength in the way he used percussion that I had never experienced before. He said, "Martha, all of us are born with genius, but most people only keep it for a few seconds."

By genius he meant that curiosity that leads to the search for the secret of life. That is what tires me when I teach and I come away alone. Sometimes you will see a person on the stage who has this oneness with himself—it is so glorious it has the power to stop you. It is a common gift to all of us but most people only keep it a few moments.

I can never forget the evening I was staying late at the school, and the phone rang. I was the only one there and I picked it up to hear a mother ask about classes for her child. "She is a genius. Intuitive. Unique. It must be nurtured now." "Really," I answered. "And how old is she?" Her mother replied, "Two years old." I told her that we only accepted children at nine (today much earlier, thanks to vitamins and computers and home training). "Nine!" she cried. "But by nine she will have lost all of her genius." I said, "Madame, if she must lose it, it is best she lose it young."

I never thought of myself as being what they call a genius. I don't know what genius is. I think a far better expression is a retriever, a lovely strong golden retriever that brings things back from the past, or retrieves things from our common blood memory. I think that by every act you do—whether in religion, politics, or sex—you reveal yourself. This, to me, is one of the wonderful things in life. It is what I've always wanted to do—to show the laughing, the fun, the appetite, all of it through dance.

In order to work, in order to be excited, in order to simply be, you have to be reborn to the instant. You have to permit yourself to feel, you have to permit yourself to be vulnerable. You may not like what you see, that is not important. You don't always have to judge. But you must be attacked by it, excited by it, and your body must be alive. And you must know how to animate that body; for each it is individual. I remember the great Russian ballet teacher Volkova, who had fled during the Russian Revolution and was teaching in Denmark. Interestingly enough, she never learned a word of Danish, only English. A young man did a series of extraordinary leaps across the floor. He looked back at Volkova for the praise he knew was his, and she said, "It was perfect. But too effective."

When a dancer is at the peak of his power he has two lovely, fragile, and perish-   25
able things. One is the spontaneity that is arrived at over years of training. The other is simplicity, but not the usual kind. It is the state of complete simplicity costing no less than absolutely everything, of which T. S. Eliot speaks.

How many leaps did Nijinsky take before he made the one that startled the world? He took thousands and thousands and it is that legend that gives us the courage, the energy, and arrogance to go back into the studio knowing that while there is so little time to be born to the instant, you will work again among the many that you may once more be born as one. That is a dancer's world.

My dancer's world has seen so many theatres, so many instants. But always I have resisted looking backward until now, when I began to sense that there was always for my life a line through it—necessity. The Greek myths speak of the spindle of life resting on the knee of necessity, the principal Fate in the Platonic world. The second Fate weaves, and the third cuts. Necessity to create? No. But in some way to transcend, to conquer fear, to find a way to go on.

How does it all begin? I suppose it never begins. It just continues.

CONNECTING PERSONALLY TO THE READING

1. Think of an activity that you do in which you or someone you know strives toward perfection. What does such an effort require of a person? Do you think perfection is a valuable goal, or do perfectionists simply court frustration? Explain your answer.

2. Graham values simplicity, spontaneity, and the ability to live in the moment. What do you think she means by these characteristics? Do you agree that they are essential for anyone to enjoy life? Why or why not?

FOCUSING ON THE ARGUMENT

1. Graham's opening paragraph is four words long. What is the effect of this opening? How does it illustrate her idea about what it means to be a dancer?

2. Graham often makes unusual connections between things: for example she describes a tree in her garden as "a symbol of facing life, and in many ways . . . a dancer." Find two such connections and explain what you think Graham means by them.

SYNTHESIZING IDEAS FROM MULTIPLE READINGS

1. In "Ways of Seeing" (p. 518), John Berger points out that what we see when we look at an image depends on what we already know about it. The same can be said of reading; what we take away from a reading owes a great deal to what we already know about the subject. What did you know about dance before you read Graham's article? In what ways did this knowledge or lack of knowledge help or hinder your understanding of her ideas?

2. Do you think that Graham would agree with William Ewing's statement (in "Dance and Photography," p. 546) that dance is a "language"? Why or why not?

3. As dance photographer and dancer/choreographer, Barbara Morgan (in William Ewing's "Dance and Photography") and Martha Graham had a very successful collaboration. What ideas about modern dance do they share?

1. Go to a dance performance and notice how technically skilled the dancers are and how emotionally committed they seem to be. Then write a review of the performance for your campus newspaper.

2. Think of an activity you do that takes training, skill, and personal characteristics such as self-discipline, a sense of wonder, or excitement. Write a one-page manifesto in which you explain, as Graham does in the reading, why each of the characteristics you name is important. Share your work with others who engage in the same activity.

Connecting the Readings with the Works of Art

Annie Leibovitz, *Darci Kistler and Robert La Fosse, New York City, 1990*

1. In analyzing Norman Rockwell's painting *The Connoisseur,* Wanda Corn ("Ways of Seeing," p. 529) argues that the painting reveals Rockwell's response to abstract art. Noting the composition, lighting, and mood of Leibovitz's photograph, what ideas about classical ballet do you think Leibovitz holds? About ballet dancers?

2. In "Blood Memory" (p. 591), Martha Graham asserts that "movement never lies." What do you think Graham means by this statement, and how might you apply it to Leibovitz's photograph? What truth does Leibovitz show in capturing a moment from a movement, a dance?

Barbara Morgan, Martha Graham Dancing *Letter to the World*

1. William Ewing ("Dance and Photography," p. 546) quotes critic Elizabeth McCausland's statement that photographs of modern dance should be "solidly modeled in light, but not swept by theatrical or stagey spotlights." Do you think Morgan's photograph would satisfy this requirement? Why or why not?

2. According to Mitchell Stephens in "By Means of the Visible" (p. 550), a major strength of images over words is their concision and immediate emotional value. What conciseness and immediate emotional value is expressed here? Explain.

John Ford, still from the movie *Stagecoach*

1. John Berger ("Ways of Seeing," p. 518) indicates that "seeing . . . comes before words," that it "establishes our place in the surrounding world." How does this still perform such a function for the audience of this movie?

2. Mitchell Stephens ("By Means of the Visible," p. 550), having identified the advantages of images over words, then lists their detractions. He notes that images are problematic in that they are inherently fake—"they lie" and thus devalue reality. Further, they can provoke an unlimited number of interpretations, creating confusion. Looking at the still, do you think that the image devalues reality? Can you identify some of the diverse possible interpretations that might create confusion? Explain.

Alvin Langdon Coburn, *Ezra Pound*

1. William Ewing ("Dance and Photography," p. 546) describes Barbara Morgan's effort to capture Martha Graham's state of mind when she photographed her danc-

ing. What state of mind do you think Coburn reveals in his photograph of poet Ezra Pound? How does his photograph achieve this effect?

2. According to Jon Boorstin in "The Hollywood Eye" (p. 561), an important consideration in shooting a film is to "create a sense of depth on a flat plane," a task which includes making the subject stand out from (rather than blend into) the background. Although Coburn is creating a still photograph, he has a similar challenge. How does he solve this problem?

Marc Chagall, *The Sources of Music*

1. In "By Means of the Visible" (p. 550), Mitchell Stephens points out that some meanings are communicated more effectively through pictures than through words. What ideas about music does Chagall's painting evoke, and how does his medium, painting, convey these ideas? Do you think that the same ideas could have been communicated just as well in words?

2. John Berger ("Ways of Seeing," p. 518) explains how the setting in which a work of art appears (e.g., in a museum or on a T-shirt) affects the viewer's experience with and appreciation of this work of art. How does knowing that Chagall's mural occupies a huge wall at the Metropolitan Opera House in New York City affect your interpretation of this painting?

Romare Bearden, *Showtime*

1. In "Ways of Seeing" (p. 518), John Berger argues that what we see when we look at a work of art is affected by what we know. How is your reaction to Bearden's collage influenced by what you already know or have experienced with jazz? With music in general?

2. Martha Graham (selection from *Blood Memory*, p. 591) believes that dance expresses the human soul and that it is "a symbol for the performance of living." Given how Bearden depicts a musical performance, do you think that she might say the same thing about music? Why or why not?

Pablo Picasso, *Three Musicians*

1. In "The Ties That Bind" (p. 586), Rosanne Cash describes how making music together creates a personal tie among musicians. Describe how Picasso's painting establishes the same idea through shape, line, and color.

2. In "Ways of Seeing" (p. 518), John Berger comments that when an image is presented as a work of art, people view it according to assumptions about art that they already have. What assumptions about art do you have, and how do they affect what you see in Picasso's painting and how you respond to it?

Archibald Motley, *Blues*

1. Robert Santelli writes, in "A Century of the Blues" (p. 579), that blues lyrics are built on repetition: "A first line is sung and then repeated with perhaps a slight variation." How does Motley's painting represent this quality visually?

2. What images of African American community, especially relationships between men and women, does Joan Morgan describe in the selection from *When Chickenheads Come Home to Roost* (p. 572)? How are these images like or different from those depicted in Motley's painting? What, according to Morgan and Motley, is the function of music in this community?

Louise Nez, *Reservation Scene*

1. This weaving is full of images of community. How does the rug connect the people to each other and to the other figures being depicted? How does the rap music Joan Morgan (selection from *When Chickenheads Come Home to Roost*, p. 572) describes connect African Americans to each other and to their shared history?

2. In "By Means of the Visible" (p. 550), Mitchell Stephens argues that visual images are often meant to take the place of words. To what extent does the image woven into Nez's rug take the place of words? What story does the rug tell?

Faith Ringgold, *Dancing at the Louvre*

1. For Martha Graham (selection from *Blood Memory*, p. 591), there is "blood memory that can speak to us," particularly for the dancer who feels an "intensification" of life and body. In what ways does the African American family depicted in the quilt seem to be expressing in dance a kind of "blood memory" in the face of European tradition?

2. In "Ways of Seeing" (p. 518), John Berger discusses the importance of the drama of a work of art, the contrast between the artist and the subject. He discusses how Frans Hals—destitute at eighty, yet commissioned to paint the Regents and Regentesses of a charity house—plays out this drama in his paintings. How is a drama played out in Ringgold's quilt?

Laura Knight, *Self-Portrait*

1. In "By Means of the Visible" (p. 550), Mitchell Stephens points out that Plato distrusted the painter as an imitator and deceiver and depreciated the portrait as "a mute, lifeless substitute for the person." What is the basis for these objections? In what ways does Knight, using color, line, and shape, compensate for the fact that her portrait, unlike a real person, cannot move or speak?

2. Explain how this statement from John Berger's article, "Ways of Seeing" (p. 518), might apply to Knight's painting: "We never look at just one thing; we are always looking at the relation between things and ourselves."

Malcah Zeldis, *A Peaceable Kingdom with Anna Pavlova*

1. John Berger (in "Ways of Seeing," p. 518) observes that when text accompanies a picture it affects our interpretation of the picture. How does knowing the title of Zeldis's painting influence what you see in it? If you did not know the title of Zeldis's painting, how might you interpret it differently?

2. In "Ways of Seeing" (p. 529), Wanda M. Corn points out that Norman Rockwell's work speaks directly to the viewer, "relying on many details that are relatively easy to synthesize into a story." The same could be said of Zeldis's painting. Tell the story you see in this painting. Then compare it to the story told in a work of art with a similar theme, Judy Chicago's "Rainbow Shabbat" (insert 2-8).

FINDING COMMON CAUSE IN CONTROVERSY
How much license should a documentary filmmaker take in editing, juxtaposing, and otherwise reconstructing events?

Michael Moore's film *Bowling for Columbine* has generated sharply opposing reactions: some critics believe it distorts the facts about gun control supporters; others regard it as a legitimate form of documentary, one that combines interpretation with indisputable fact. Despite the controversy evoked by this film, it is possible to examine the reasoning on both sides and identify points of agreement. Whatever position you take on this issue is likely to be most credible when it acknowledges shared beliefs.

READING

In his 2002 Academy-Award winning documentary, *Bowling for Columbine,* writer and filmmaker Michael Moore attacks the gun culture in the United States. He sees this culture as responsible for the thousands of shootings in this country every year, particularly the 1999 shootings at a high school in Littleton, Colorado, where two high school students opened fire on students and teachers, killing fourteen people. Moore created a documentary that includes attacks on the National Rifle Association (NRA) and Charlton Heston, its president.

At question is Moore's use of techniques to persuade an audience, techniques that some claim may not be appropriate to a documentary. These viewers note that a documentary, by standards set by The Academy of Motion Picture Arts and Sciences, is supposed to be a nonfictional movie. Asserting that Moore has deliberately distorted facts, these critics fault Moore for such practices as cutting footage from two different speeches to make it appear as if the footage came from one. Other viewers, in defense of Moore, claim that all television and movies, including documentaries and news stories, are heavily edited, blending fact, interpretation, and entertainment. **David Hardy**, an Arizona lawyer who specializes in gun issues and who has worked for the National Rifle Association, claims that Michael Moore has not created a documentary.

Hardy maintains the Web site www.mooreexposed.com and is the author of *Michael Moore Is a Big Fat Stupid White Man.* He is at work on a documentary of his own about the Bill of Rights.

Bowling for Columbine: Documentary or Fiction?

BY DAVID T. HARDY

Michael Moore's "Bowling for Columbine" won the Oscar for best documentary. Unfortunately, it is not a documentary, by the Academy's own definition.

The injustice here is not so much to the viewer, as to the independent producers of real documentaries. These struggle in a field which receives but a fraction of the recognition and financing of the "entertainment industry." They are protected by Academy rules limiting the documentary competition to nonfiction.

Bowling is *fiction*. It makes its points by deceiving and by misleading the viewer. Statements are made which are false. Moore leads the [viewer] to draw inferences which he must have known were wrong. *Indeed, even speeches shown on screen are heavily edited so that sentences are assembled in the speaker's voice, but which were not sentences he uttered.* Bowling uses deception as its *primary* tool of persuasion and effect.

A film which does this may be a commercial success. It may be entertaining. But it is not a documentary. One need only consult Rule 12 of the rules for the Academy Award: a documentary is a *non-fictional* movie.

The point is *not* that Bowling is biased. 5 No, the point is that Bowling is deliberately, seriously, and consistently *deceptive*.

1. **Willie Horton.** The first edition of the webpage had a section on falsification of the election ad regarding Willie Horton (the convict, not the baseball star). This was one of the earliest criticisms of Bowling—Ben Fritz caught it back in November, 2002.

To illustrate politicians' (and especially Republican politicians') willingness to play the "race card," Bowling shows what purports to be a television ad run by George Bush, Sr., in his race against Governor Dukakis. For those who weren't around back then—Massachusetts had a "prison furlough" program where prisoners could be given short releases from the clink. Unfortunately, some of them never came back. Dukakis vetoed legislation which would have forbidden furlough to persons with "life without parole" sentences for murder, and authorities thereafter furloughed a number of murderers. Horton, in prison for a brutal stabbing murder, got a furlough, never returned, and then attacked a couple, assaulting both and raping the woman. His opponents in the presidential race took advantage of the veto.

The ad as shown by Moore begins with a "revolving door" of justice, progresses to a picture of Willie Horton (who is black), and ends with dramatic subtitle: "Willie Horton released. Then kills again."

Fact: Bowling splices together two different election ads, one run by the Bush campaign (featuring a revolving door, and not even mentioning Horton) and another run by an independent expenditure campaign (naming

Horton, and showing footage from which it can be seen that he is black). At the end, the ad a là Moore has the customary note that it was paid for by the Bush-Quayle campaign. Moore intones "whether you're a psychotic killer or running for president of the United States, the one thing you can always count on is white America's fear of the black man." There is nothing to reveal that most of the ad just seen (and all of it that was relevant to Moore's claim) was not the Bush-Quayle ad, which didn't even name Horton.

Fact: Apparently unsatisfied with splicing the ads, Bowling's editors *added* a subtitle "Willie Horton released. Then kills again."

Fact: Ben Fitz also noted that Bowling's editors didn't bother to research the events before doctoring the ads. Horton's second arrest was not for murder. (The second set of charges were aggravated assault and rape).

I originally deleted this from the main webpage, because in the VHS version of Bowling Moore had the decency to remove the misleading footage. But as Brendan Nyhan recently wrote in Spinsanity, he put it back in in the DVD version! He did make one minor change, switching his edited-in caption to "Willie Horton released. Then rapes a woman." Obviously Moore had been informed of the Spinsanity criticism. He responded by correcting his own typo, not by removing the edited in caption, nor by revealing that the ad being shown was not in fact a Bush-Quayle ad.

2. **NRA and the Reaction to Tragedy.** A major theme in Bowling is that NRA is callous toward slayings. In order to make this theme fit the facts, however, Bowling repeatedly distorts the evidence.

A. **Columbine Shooting/Denver NRA Meeting.** Bowling portrays this with the following sequence:

Weeping children outside Columbine;

Cut to Charlton Heston holding a musket and proclaiming "I have only five words for you: 'from my cold, dead, hands'";

Cut to billboard advertising the meeting, while Moore intones "Just ten days after the Columbine killings, despite the pleas of a community in mourning, Charlton Heston came to Denver and held a large pro-gun rally for the National Rifle Association;"

Cut to Heston (supposedly) continuing speech . . . "I have a message from the Mayor, Mr. Wellington Webb, the Mayor of Denver. He sent me this; it says 'don't come here. We don't want you here.' I say to the Mayor this is our country, as Americans we're free to travel wherever we want in our broad land. Don't come here? We're already here!"

The portrayal is one of an arrogant protest in response to the deaths—or, as one reviewer put it, "it seemed that Charlton Heston and others *rushed to Littleton to hold rallies and demonstrations* directly after the tragedy." The portrayal is in fact false.

Fact: The Denver event was not a demonstration relating to

10

Columbine, but an annual meeting ... whose place and date had been fixed years in advance.

Fact: At Denver, the NRA cancelled all events (normally several days of committee meetings, sporting events, dinners, and rallies) save the annual members' meeting; that could not be cancelled because corporate law *required* that it be held. [No way to change location, since you have to give advance notice of that to the members, and there were upwards of 4,000,000 members.]

Fact: Heston's "cold dead hands" speech, which leads off Moore's depiction of the Denver meeting, was not given at Denver after Columbine. It was given a year later in Charlotte, North Carolina, and was his gesture of gratitude upon his being given a handmade musket, at that annual meeting.

Fact: When Bowling continues on to the speech which Heston *did* give in Denver, it carefully edits it to change its theme.

Moore's fabrication here cannot be described by any polite term. It is a lie, a fraud, and a few other things. Carrying it out required a LOT of editing to mislead the viewer. . . .

Moore has actually taken audio of seven sentences, from five different parts of the speech, and a section given in a different speech entirely, and spliced them together. Each edit is cleverly covered by inserting a still or video footage for a few seconds.

First, right after the weeping victims, Moore puts on Heston's "I have only five words for you . . . cold dead hands" statement, making it seem directed at

them. As noted above, it's actually a thank-you speech given a year later in North Carolina.

Moore then has an interlude—a visual of a billboard and his narration. This is vital. He can't go directly to Heston's real Denver speech. If he did that, you might ask why Heston in mid-speech changed from a purple tie and lavender shirt to a white shirt and red tie, and the background draperies went from maroon to blue. Moore has to separate the two segments.

Moore's second edit (covered by splicing in a pan shot of the crowd) deletes Heston's announcement that NRA has in fact cancelled most of its meeting: 15

> "As you know, we've cancelled the festivities, the fellowship we normally enjoy at our annual gatherings. This decision has perplexed a few and inconvenienced thousands. As your president, I apologize for that."

Moore then cuts to Heston noting that Denver's mayor asked NRA not to come, and shows Heston replying "I said to the Mayor: As Americans, we're free to travel wherever we want in our broad land. Don't come here? We're already here!" as if in defiance.

Actually, Moore put an edit right in the middle of the first sentence, and another at its end! Heston really said (with reference [to] his own WWII vet status) "I said to the mayor, well, my reply to the mayor is, I volunteered for the war they wanted me to attend when I was 18 years old. Since then, I've run small errands for my country, from Nigeria to Vietnam. I know many of you here in this room could say the same thing."

Moore cuts it after "I said to the Mayor" and attaches a sentence from the end of the next paragraph: "As Americans, we're free to travel wherever we want in our broad land." He hides the deletion by cutting to footage of protestors and a photo of the Mayor before going back and showing Heston.

Moore has Heston then triumphantly announce "Don't come here? We're already here!" Actually, that sentence is clipped from a segment five paragraphs farther on in the speech. Again, Moore uses an editing trick to cover the doctoring, switching to a pan shot of the audience as Heston's (edited) voice continues. What Heston said there was:

20

> "NRA members are in city hall, Fort Carson, NORAD, the Air Force Academy and the Olympic Training Center. And yes, NRA members are surely among the police and fire and SWAT team heroes who risked their lives to rescue the students at Columbine.
>
> *Don't come here? We're already here.* This community is our home. Every community in America is our home. We are a 128-year-old fixture of mainstream America. The Second Amendment ethic of lawful, responsible firearm ownership spans the broadest cross section of American life imaginable.
>
> So, we have the same right as all other citizens to be here. To help shoulder the grief and share our sorrow and to offer our respectful, reassured voice to the

national discourse that has erupted around this tragedy."

I recently discovered that Moore has set up a new webpage to respond to a chosen few points of criticism, one of which is his, er, creative editing of Heston's speech. . . . Basically, Moore contends that he didn't mean for the viewer to get the impression that "cold dead hands" was spoken at Denver—that just "appears as Heston is being introduced in narration." As for the rest, well, "Far from deliberately editing the film to make Heston look worse, I chose to leave most of this out and not make Heston look as evil as he actually was." Sure. That's why he left out:

> "As you know, we've cancelled the festivities, the fellowship we normally enjoy at our annual gatherings."
>
> "So, we have the same right as all other citizens to be here. To help shoulder the grief and share our sorrow and to offer our respectful, reassured voice to the national discourse that has erupted around this tragedy."
>
> "NRA members are, above all, Americans. That means that whatever our differences, we are respectful of one another and we stand united, especially in adversity."

EMPATHIZING WITH THE VIEW THAT MOORE'S FILM IS NOT A TRUE DOCUMENTARY

According to David Hardy (www.hardylaw.net/Truth_About_Bowling.html), Moore has done the following:

- spliced images from two different sources to create a single erroneous image.
- made a sequence of cuts to imply false relationships between events.

Bowling for Columbine: Documentary or Fiction?

- deliberately disguised these cuts by panning or narration.
- left out the contexts of speeches so as to distort their meaning.
- gone beyond bias to deception.

EMPATHIZING WITH THE VIEW THAT MOORE HAS PRODUCED A WORTHY DOCUMENTARY

Other critics disagree with Hardy:

- According to Dan Robey, *Bowling for Columbine* should not be read as a traditional documentary: "fusing flashy news reports, bizarre situations, ironic twists, tense interviews, and South Park style animation, [the movie] is a documentary for a new generation." (www.tech.mit.edu/V122/N51/Bowling_for_Col.51a.html)

- Robey argues that Moore wants to force us to think about significant issues. Furthermore, because Moore "doesn't present a final thesis," he doesn't allow viewers to "reject or adopt his views."

- Kevin Mattson, writing in *Dissent Magazine* (Spring 2003), notes that the "complaints about Moore's work often have more to do with politics than a commitment to factual accuracy." Many of the documented errors come from *Forbes* magazine, a conservative publication that has not been interested in recording inaccuracies of Republican Party spokespeople.

- Mattson also observes that Moore's methods derive from his need to make the film entertaining. Moore is quoted as saying, "I always assume that only 10 to 20 percent of people who read my books or see my films will take the facts and hard-core analysis and do something with it. If I can bring the other 80 percent to it through entertainment and comedy, then some of it will trickle through."

- Mattson argues that today it is the norm to blur the line between news and entertainment. Moore's work reflects the irony and cynicism typifying our postmodern culture.

- One also might argue that rather than being deceptive, Moore cuts and splices decontextualized images to make a larger point. For instance, he does not intend for us to connect Bill Clinton's bombing of the Sudan directly to the high school shooting, but rather intends to show that we live in a violent culture where guns and weaponry proliferate—a culture that makes school violence understandable, if not inevitable.

- One Web site indicates that few commentators note what Moore has accurately captured in *Bowling for Columbine.* For instance, Moore has outtakes that show that the scene in which he receives a gun in return for opening up a bank account is accurate. The outtake shows the bank employee telling Moore he "can pick the gun up immediately from their vault." (Critics had argued that the bank scene had been staged, that guns were not given out without background checks, and that clients needed to drive two hours to pick up the gun.) (www.kuro5hin.org/story/2003/9/24/53736/8924)

ADDING MORE INFORMATION

1. The *American Heritage Dictionary of the English Language* defines a documentary as "a work, such as film or television program, presenting political, social, or historical subject matter in a factual and informative manner and often consisting of actual news films or interviews accompanied by narration." (Fourth edition, 2000, Houghton Mifflin Company.)

2. The Academy of Motion Picture Arts and Sciences defines a documentary in this way:

An eligible [for the Oscars] documentary film is defined as a theatrically released nonfiction motion picture dealing creatively with cultural, artistic, historical, social, scientific,

economic or other subjects. It may be photographed in actual occurrence, or may employ partial re-enactment, stock footage, stills, animation, stop-motion or other techniques, as long as the emphasis is on fact and not on fiction.
(http://www.oscars.org/77academyawards/rules/rule12.html)

3. Of the twenty-five awards *Bowling for Columbine* received from U.S. and international film organizations, fifteen were specifically in the "documentary" category:

- Academy Awards, USA, 2003, Oscar, Best Documentary
- American Cinema Editors, USA, 2003, Eddie, Best Edited Documentary Film
- Amsterdam International Documentary Film Festival, 2002, Audience Award
- Broadcast Film Critics Association Awards, 2003, BFCA Award, Best Documentary
- Chicago Film Critics Association Awards, 2003, CFCA Award, Best Documentary
- Dallas/Fort Worth Film Critics Association Awards, 2003, DFWFCA Award, Best Documentary
- Florida Film Critics Circle Awards, 2003, FFCC Award, Best Documentary
- Golden Trailer Awards, 2003, Golden Trailer, Best Documentary
- Independent Spirit Awards, 2003, Independent Spirit Award, Best Documentary
- Kansas City Film Critics Circle Awards, 2003, KCFCC Award, Best Documentary
- Las Vegas Film Critics Society Awards, 2003, Sierra Award, Best Documentary
- National Board of Review, USA, 2002, NBR Award, Best Documentary
- Online Film Critics Society Awards, 2003, OFCS Award, Best Documentary
- São Paulo International Film Festival, 2002, Audience Award, Best Documentary
- Toronto Film Critics Association Awards, 2002, TFCA Award, Best Documentary

The other awards are as follows:

- Atlantic Film Festival, 2002, Audience Award
- Bergen International Film Festival, 2002, Audience Award
- Bodil Awards, 2004, Bodil, Best American Film (*Bedste amerikanske film*)
- Cannes Film Festival, 2002, 55th Anniversary Prize
- César Awards, France, 2003, César, Best Foreign Film (*Meilleur film étranger*)
- Kinema Junpo Awards, 2004, Kinema Junpo Award, Best Foreign Language Film Director
- San Sebastián International Film Festival, 2002, Audience Award
- Sudbury Cinéfest, 2002, Audience Award
- Vancouver International Film Festival, 2002, Most Popular Film
- Writers Guild of America, USA, 2003, WGA Award (Screen), Best Screenplay Written Directly for the Screen

4. Charlton Heston's Speech to the National Rifle Association, May 4, 1999, Denver, Colorado: http://www.freedaily.com/articles/990504n1.html

5. Dziga Vertov, a widely acclaimed documentary filmmaker and theorist, wrote about producing documentaries:

I am the camera's eyes. I am the machine that shows you the world as I alone see it. Starting from today I am forever free of human immobility. I am in perpetual movement. I approach and draw away from things—I crawl under them—I climb on them—I am on the head of a galloping horse—I burst at full speed into a crowd—I run before running soldiers—I throw myself down with the aeroplane—I fall and I fly at one with the bodies falling or rising through the air. (*Kino Eye: The Writings of Dziga Vertov,* ed: Annette Micheleon. University of California Press, Reissue Edition, August 1995)

6. Joris Ivens, in his book *The Camera and I,* writes:

I was surprised to find that many people automatically assumed that any documentary film would inevitably be objective. Perhaps the term is unsatisfactory, but for me the distinction between the words "document" and "documentary" is quite clear. Do we demand objectivity in the evidence presented at a trial? No, the only demand is that each piece of evidence be as full a subjective, truthful, honest presentation of the witness's attitude as an oath on the Bible can produce from him.

SEEKING COMMON CAUSE

Before you decide on your position, consider possible common ground between the opposing views.

- Both sides might agree that we need a definition of *nonfiction* in film, one that would clarify what constitutes stepping over the line. In nature photography, photographers routinely alter nature before photographing it. News programs routinely imply causal relations by juxtaposing images and commentary.

- Film distinctions such as *fiction* and *nonfiction* change with the times, as the style, tone, and methods of film evolve. Both sides might agree that such changes in style affect documentaries. What changes would both sides agree to as not affecting the category of *documentary*?

- Both sides might agree that MTV has changed the technique and style of journalism. Mitchell Stephens ("By Means of the Visible," p. 551) identifies some of these changes when he discusses David Berrant's documentary *Decade,* a historical look at the 1980s. For example, many of the images that appear while a person is speaking in this film don't just "illustrate what is said" but "communicate their own meanings."

DEBATE ESSAY

If possible, view the film *Bowling for Columbine.* Using the evidence from the Web sites mentioned above (and from the movie, if you have seen it), decide whether you think *Bowling for Columbine* is a legitimate documentary. Has it overstepped the boundary between nonfiction and fiction?

WRITING PROJECTS

Writing a Short Essay

The following short writing projects can prepare you for the extended writing project or be written as independent essays.

Summarizing a Reading and Applying It to a Work of Art

Write a summary of one of the readings and apply its ideas to a work of art you have liked (for example, a movie, poem, painting, photograph, or piece of choreography).

The summary of the reading should occupy at least one-third of the paper and indicate the main points and evidence the author uses.

The application should occupy the rest. It should

- explain how the reading's main points apply to the work of art
- use details from the work of art as evidence

Comparing Works of Art with Similar Subjects

Below are pairs of works of art with similar subjects or themes. Choose one pair and compare the way each artist depicts this theme. What impression do you get of the people, objects, or events you see in the works of art? What attitude toward the subject does the artist portray? If there is more than one person shown, what is the relationship between them? What techniques does the artist use to create these impressions? In describing the works, use the guidelines for analyzing art in the introduction to this chapter and in Chapter 1.

- Mary Cassatt, *The Child's Bath* (insert 1-5); Henry Ossawa Tanner, *The Banjo Lesson* (insert 1-6)
- Patricia Rodriguez, Irene Perez, Graciela Carillo, *Fantasy World for Children,* (insert 2-6); Winslow Homer, *Snap the Whip* (insert 4-7)
- Laura Knight, *Self-Portrait* (insert 8-11); Frida Kahlo, *Self-Portrait on the Borderline between Mexico and the U.S.* (insert 2-7)
- David Hockney, *A Bigger Grand Canyon;* (inset 6-7); John Ford, still from *Stagecoach* (insert 8-4)

Viewing Images in Context

Bring to class three prints or photocopies of a photograph of your friends or family. Write a paragraph describing the occasion for the photograph, the relationships among the people in it, and any other information that would create a context for the photo.

Give two of your classmates copies of the photograph without telling them anything about it and without showing them your paragraph. Have each of them write a caption for the picture. Afterwards, share your paragraph with them.

Using this experience as evidence, write a brief essay explaining John Berger's statement that words affect the viewer's interpretation of an image.

Responding to Someone Else's Interpretation

Michael Moore's *Bowling for Columbine* generated numerous Web sites that either defamed the documentary or praised it. Choose a painting, television show, film, or other work of art that has received a lot of publicity, and read what others have had to say about it in newspaper reviews, chat rooms, blogs, or elsewhere. Then write a response to these opinions.

In doing so, follow these steps:

- Summarize other people's views, identifying the main issues they raise.
- Explain your response to these views.
- Discuss the details in the work of art that support each interpretation.

Comparing Art and Lived Experience

Compare the reality portrayed in a particular work of art (for example, an outdoors scene, an object, a person, an emotion, a relationship) with your own life experience of this reality.

- Begin with the reality of the work of art. Describe it, using concrete details—for example, for a play, you might describe costumes; for a movie, lighting; for a poem, rhythm; for a painting, color.
- Next, explain how your life experience of the subject (for example, how it feels to be out in the desert or mountains, or the relationship between a mother and her child) is like or different from what you see in the work of art. How does the mood or overall effect of the work differ from what you're familiar with in your life?
- Show how the similarities and differences you see are related to ideas in any two of the readings. Use the readings to show the significance of your comparison.

Reacting Personally to Art

According to Mitchell Stephens in "By Means of the Visible" (p. 550), some cultures fear the magic in images and suppress them; they fear that images can "steal likenesses" by pretending to be what they're not. Consider a film, song, piece of choreography, photograph, or painting that you have reacted to strongly. How does the work of art make you feel? Does it in any way "steal" from reality as you experience it? Explain.

- Begin by explaining what Stephens means by "stealing likenesses."

- Then describe the work of art and your reaction to it.

- Finally, explain whether you think the images or lyrics "stole" likenesses.

Writing an Extended Argument

The following assignment asks you to support a thesis using several sources from this chapter, choosing among the readings, works of art, debate, and Web sites. Use the sources to explain, support, and provide details for the paper.

Write an essay in which you elaborate on the following quotation:

> Every image embodies a way of seeing. Even a photograph. For photographs are not, as is often assumed, a mechanical record. Every time we look at a photograph, we are aware, however slightly, of the photographer selecting that sight from an infinity of other possible sights. . . . The photographer's way of seeing is reflected in his choice of subject. The painter's way of seeing is reconstituted by the marks he makes on the canvas or paper. (John Berger, "Ways of Seeing," p. 519)

Designing the Extended Writing Project

What follows are suggestions for constructing a thesis, organizing your material, elaborating on your ideas, and providing examples of them.

The Thesis

The thesis is a sentence or two that asserts the main point of your paper. In this case, your thesis will be a sentence that states what the quotation means.

Suppose you are writing about this statement from Jon Boorstin's "The Hollywood Eye":

> [In film] even the most realistic scene must be subtly altered to give the camera an undiluted sense of reality. . . . The art director must alter reality to make it feel more real on film, whether that means painting a house, planting a tree, or obscuring a sign. (p. 563)

Your thesis might be this:

In "The Hollywood Eye," Jon Boorstin discusses a paradox: to make a scene seem real, the film-maker must resort to artifice.

A Structure Based on the Thesis

Here's one possible structure for the essay on Berger's statement:

Section 1. Introduce your thesis.

Section 2. Elaborate on the thesis; you might explain Berger's idea in more detail, using examples from his essay.

Section 3. Briefly discuss other writers from this chapter whose ideas complement Berger's.

Section 4. Describe several of the works of art reproduced in this book to illustrate the idea in the quotation. You might, for example, compare three works with a similar subject to show how three different artists "see" the same thing differently.

Section 5. Briefly indicate the significance of the thesis—for example, you could relate Berger's point about the visual arts to the work of other artists—of dancers, musicians, or poets.

Following this structure, an outline of the essay on the statement from Boorstin's article might look like this (each section would have one or more paragraphs):

EXAMPLE

Section 1: In "The Hollywood Eye," Jon Boorstin discusses a paradox: to make a scene seem real, the filmmaker must resort to artifice (thesis).

Section 2: Boorstin shows how the use of light, color, flat images, and three-dimensional shapes, as well as extensive editing, paradoxically distorts images in order to make them look authentic. (elaboration of your thesis)

Section 3: In discussing still images, Mitchell Stephens and William A. Ewing also argue that the photographer carefully constructs a picture to make it "real" for the viewer. (other writers whose views complement Boorstin's)

Section 4: To give an impression of on-the-spot reality, Michael Moore uses a handheld camera in many scenes of *Bowling for Columbine.* (Here, you would detail the use of the handheld camera in scenes throughout the movie—for example, by moving the camera to follow the people he inter-views, Moore makes the scene look not slick or scripted, but spontaneous and sincere).

Section 5: It is not just painters, photographers, and filmmakers who use artifice to create an im-pression of authenticity—dancers, musicians, and other artists do the same thing. (Here you might briefly mention William A. Ewing's description of the dancer's "positions . . . , costumes . . . , lighting effects . . . , [and] illusion" and Robert Santelli's description of the blues musician's "slid-ing guitar, wailing voice, repeated lyrics"). (significance of your thesis)

Detailed Description

Your evidence consists of one or a combination of these devices: detailed descriptions of the works of art, summary and paraphrase of ideas from the readings, quotation, and information from other sources you may consult. The paragraph below illustrates the thesis "In 'The Hollywood Eye,' Jon Boorstin discusses a paradox: to make a scene seem real, the filmmaker must resort to artifice." Notice the specific details.

EXAMPLE

To give an impression of on-the-spot reality, Michael Moore uses a handheld camera in many scenes of *Bowling for Columbine.* In one scene, Moore follows Charlton Heston into the interior of Heston's house, where the camera then canvasses the gun memorabilia on the walls. The camera jostles as Moore follows Heston. Moore pans to the expansive views the home commands, the floor-to-ceiling glass windows, and the expensive home interiors. The camera continues to bob-ble as it focuses on Heston's face, recording his grimaces and frowns, and then follows him as he walks away. The effect is similar to that of a home movie—the order in which we see these im-ages seems random, unscripted, as if we the viewers are there watching the scene unfold as it happens. Here artifice creates the impression of unedited reality.

Conclusion

What is the significance of your thesis? What does it add up to? In this final section of your paper, you need to connect your thesis to something a little outside the scope of your discussion without introducing an entirely new idea that needs support.

Here are some suggestions for the paper written with the sample thesis ("In 'The Hollywood Eye,' Jon Boorstin discusses a paradox: to make a scene seem real, the filmmaker must resort to artifice").

- Move slightly away from the subject to show how the thesis applies in a different context. In Section 5 of the outline on p. 609, we relate Boorstin's idea to arts other than film: "It is not just painters, photographers, and filmmakers who use artifice to create a impression of authenticity—dancers, musicians, and other artists do the same thing."

- Imagine the social or political consequences of the thesis. For example, the ease with which a filmmaker can manipulate an audience with illusions raises questions about how much we can believe what we see on the news.

- Reflect on the philosophical implications of the thesis. For the Boorstin quotation, you could observe that everyone sees "reality" differently and that few, if any, perceptions are universal.

- Relate the thesis to a historical or cultural fact, such as Mitchell Stephens's observation that some cultures distrust images, believing that they "steal" from reality.

Using WEB Resources

1. Explore the companion Web site to the Public Broadcasting Corporation's production of the television program *Jazz:* http://www.pbs.org/jazz. On the home page, the site identifies jazz as "the purest expression of American democracy." After studying the history of jazz and noting its effect on other arts and other facets of U.S. culture, explain why you think jazz is described this way.

2. Study the information on the Web site http://www.womenfolk.com/historyofquilts/afam .htm. Note the history and varied functions of quilts and quilt making in the United States, especially the background of African American quilts. In what ways is Faith Ringgold's work of art part of a tradition of American quilt making?

www.mhhe.com/durkinl

Using the Web for resources on Exploring the Arts. Go to Web Resources

Text Credits

Chapter 2

Excerpts from *The Language of Discretion* by Amy Tan. Copyright © 1990 by Amy Tan. Reprinted by permission of Amy Tan and the Sandra Dijkstra Literary Agency.

"Public and Private Language" from *Hunger of Memory: The Education of Richard Rodriguez* by Richard Rodriguez. Reprinted by permission of David R. Godine, Publisher, Inc. Copyright © 1982 by Richard Rodriguez.

"From Outside, In" by Barbara Mellix originally appeared in *The Georgia Review*, Volume XLI, No. 2 (Summer 1987). Copyright © 1987 by The University of Georgia, © 1987 by Barbara Mellix. Reprinted by permission of Barbara Mellix and The Georgia Review.

"First They Changed My Name" by Caffilene Allen. Reprinted by permission of Dr. Caffilene Allen.

"What's In A Name?" by Itabari Njeri from *Los Angeles Times Magazine,* January 29, 1989. Reprinted by permission.

"The Names of Women" by Louise Erdrich was first published in *Granta 41,* September 1992. Copyright © 1992 by Louise Erdrich. Reprinted by permission of The Wylie Agency.

"Transformation" from *Talking to High Monks in the Snow* by Lydia Minatoya. Copyright © 1992 by Lydia Minatoya. Reprinted by permission of HarperCollins Publishers.

"From A Native Daughter" by Haunani-Kay Trask from *The American Indian and the Problem of History* edited by Calvin Martin. Oxford University Press, 1987. Reprinted by permission of Haunani-Kay Trask.

Excerpts from "What Global Language?" by Barbara Wallraff. First published in *The Atlantic Monthly,* November 2000. Copyright © Barbara Wallraff. Reprinted by permission of the author.

"The Dilemma of Black English" by Ken Parish Perkins from *Fort Worth Star Telegram,* July 13, 1998. Reprinted by permission.

Chapter 3

"Myth of the Sexual Athlete" by Don Sabo from *Changing Men,* vol. 20. Copyright © 1989. Reprinted by permission of Sage Publications, Inc.

"Just Walk On By" by Brent Staples. Reprinted by permission of the author. Brent Staples writes editorials for *The New York Times* and is author of the memoir, *Parallel Time: Growing Up in Black and White.*

"The Return of the Pig" by David Brooks from *The Atlantic Monthly,* April 2003. Reprinted by permission.

"Beer Commercials: A Manual on Masculinity" by Lance Strate from *Men, Masculinity and the Media,* edited by Steve Craig. Copyright © 1992. Reprinted by permission of Sage Publications, Inc.

"Best of Times, Worst of Times: Cindy Jackson speaking to Danny Danziger" by Danny Danziger. Reprinted by permission of Danny Danziger.

"My Brown Face" by Mira Jacob from *Body Outlaws: Rewriting the Rules of Beauty and Body Image,* edited by Ophira Edut. Copyright © 2003 by Mira Jacob. Reprinted by permission of Seal Press.

"The More You Subtract, the More You Add" is reprinted and edited with the permission of The Free Press, a Division of Simon & Schuster Adult Publishing Group from *Can't Buy My Love: How Advertising Changes the Way We Think and Feel* by Jean Kilbourne. Copyright © 1999 by Jean Kilbourne. All rights reserved.

"The Empire of Images in Our World of Bodies" by Susan Bordo is reprinted with permission from *Unbearable Weight: Feminism, Western Culture and the Body, 10th Anniversary Edition*. Copyright © 2004. Excerpted from the new 10th anniversary preface.

"Dividing the Consumer Pie" by Danae Clark from *Gender, Race and Class in Media: A Text-Reader*. Copyright © 1995. Reprinted by permission of Sage Publications, Inc.

"Why the *M* Word Matters To Me" by Andrew Sullivan from *Time Magazine*, February 10, 2004. Copyright © 2004 TIME Inc. Reprinted by permission.

"Death Blow to Marriage" by Stanley Kurtz in *National Review*, February 5, 2004. Copyright © 2004 by National Review Online, www.nationalreview.com. Reprinted by permission.

Chapter 4

"School: The Story of American Public Education" by David Tyack from *School: The Story of American Public Education* by Sarah Mondale and Sarah Patton. Copyright © 2001 Sarah Mondale and Sarah Patton. Reprinted by permission of Beacon Press, Boston.

"Learning in the Key of Life" by Jon Spayde from *Utne Reader*, May/June 1998. Reprinted with permission from *Utne* magazine.

"Savage Inequalities of Public Education in New York" from *Savage Inequalities* by Jonathan Kozol. Copyright © 1991 by Jonathan Kozol. Used by permission of Crown Publishers, a division of Random House, Inc., and by permission of the author.

"The Merits of Meritocracy" by David Brooks from *The Atlantic Monthly*, May 2002. Reprinted by permission of the author.

"Who Is This Child?" by Robert Barr from *Phi Delta Kappan*, January 1996. Reprinted by permission of the author, Robert Barr, Senior Analyst, Boise State University.

"Human Intelligence Isn't What We Think It Is" by Howard Gardner from *US News & World Report*, March 19, 1984. Copyright © 1984 U.S. News & World Report, L.P. Reprinted with permission; "Human Intelligence Isn't What We Think It Is" by Howard Gardner from *Multiple Intelligences* by Howard Gardner. Copyright © 1993 by Howard Gardner. Reprinted by permission of Basic Books, a member of Perseus Books, L.L.C.

"Epilogue: Lilia" is reprinted with the permission of The Free Press, a Division of Simon & Schuster Adult Publishing Group, from *Lives on the Boundary: The Struggles and Achievements of America's Underprepared* by Mike Rose. Copyright © 1989 by Mike Rose. All rights reserved.

"Forget Classrooms" by Michael J. Lewis from *The Chronicle of Higher Education*, July 11, 2003. Copyright © 2003. Reprinted by permission of the author.

"She's Almost Too Good to Be True, and to Prove It, She's Going to Sue" by Hans Alhoff from *Los Angeles Times*, May 7, 2003. Reprinted by permission of the author.

Chapter 5

"The Physical Genius" by Malcolm Gladwell from *The New Yorker*, August 1999. Reprinted by permission of the author.

"The Working Life of A Waitress" from *The Mind at Work* by Mike Rose. Copyright © 2004 by Mike Rose. Used by permission of Viking Penguin, a division of Penguin Group (USA) Inc.

"Work Makes Life Sweet" from *Sisters of the Yam: Black Women and Self Recovery* by bell hooks. Copyright © 1993 by Gloria Watkins. Reprinted by permission of South End Press and Between the Lines.

"Take This Job and Love It" by Daniel Levine from *Policy Review: Journal of American Citizenship*, May-June 1997, No. 83. Reprinted by permission of The Heritage Foundation.

"Black Hair" by Gary Soto from *Living Up the Street* published by Laurel Leaf Books (New York: Bantam Doubleday Dell), 1992. Copyright © 1985 by Gary Soto. Used by permission of the author.

"SantaLand Diaries" from *Holidays on Ice* by David Sedaris. Copyright © 1997 by David Sedaris. Used by permission of Little, Brown and Co., Inc.

Excerpt from "Selling in Minnesota" from *Nickel and Dimed: On (Not) Getting By in America* by Barbara Ehrenreich. Copyright © 2001 by Barbara Ehrenreich. Reprinted by permission of Henry Holt and Company, LLC.

"Mural Painter" by Harvey from *Sabotage in the American Workplace: Anecdotes of Dissatisfaction, Mischief and Revenge*, edited by Martin Sprouse. Copyright © 1992 Pressure Drop Press. Reprinted by permission of the editor.

Chapter 6

Chapter 7

"Selected Web Sites" from *Dave Barry in Cyberspace* by Dave Barry. Copyright © 1996 by Dave Barry. Used by permission of Crown Publishers, a division of Random House, Inc.

"Piracy Gets Mixed Reviews in Industry" by Alex Pham and P.J. Huffstutter from *Los Angeles Times,* September 9, 2003. Reprinted by permission.

Chapter 8

Chapter 1 from *Ways of Seeing* by John Berger. Copyright © 1972 by John Berger. Used by permission of Viking Penguin, a division of Penguin Group (USA) Inc.

"Ways of Seeing" by Wanda M. Corn originally published in Maureen Hennessey and Anne Knutson, *Norman Rockwell: Pictures for the American People,* New York, NY: H.N. Abrams, 1999. Reprinted by permission of the author. Wanda M. Corn is the Robert and Ruth Halperin Professor in Art History, Stanford University.

Excerpts from *Dance and Photography* by William A. Ewing. Copyright © 1987 Thames & Hudson Ltd., London. Reprinted by kind permission of Thames & Hudson Ltd., London.

"By Means of the Visible" from *The Rise of the Visible, the Fall of the Word* by Mitchell Stephens. Copyright © 1998 by Mitchell Stephens. Used by permission of Oxford University Press, Inc.

Excerpts from *The Hollywood Eye: What Makes Movies Work* by Jon Boorstin. Reprinted by permission of the author.

"From Fly Girls to Bitches and Hos" is reprinted with permission of Simon & Schuster Adult Publishing Group from *When Chickenheads Come Home to Roost: My Life as a Hip Hop Feminist* by Joan Morgan. Copyright © 1999 by Joan Morgan. Originally appeared in *VIBE* Magazine. Epigraph from "When Black Feminism Faces the Music and the Music is Rap" by Michele Wallace from *The New York Times,* July 29, 1990. Copyright © 1990 by The New York Times Co. Reprinted with permission.

Definition of "documentary" is adapted and reproduced by permission from *The American Heritage Dictionary of the English Language,* Fourth Edition. Copyright © 2006 by Houghton Mifflin Company.

"A Century of the Blues" by Robert Santelli from *Martin Scorsese Presents the Blues: A Musical Journey,* forward by Peter Guralnick. Reprinted by permission of the author.

"The Ties That Bind" by Rosanne Cash. Copyright © 2000 by Rosanne Cash. Reprinted by permission of the author.

Excerpt from *Blood Memory* by Martha Graham. Copyright © 1991 by Martha Graham Estate. Used by permission of Doubleday, a division of Random House, Inc.

"Bowling for Columbine: Documentary of Fiction?" by David T. Hardy. Reprinted by permission of the author.

Photo Credits

Page 32: Herscovici/Art Resource, NY. © 2007 C. Herscovici, Brussels/Artists Rights Society (ARS), New York. HMSG 66.3199; **141:** © Dave Benett/Getty Images; **150, 151, 152, 153, 154, 155, 156, 157, 158, 159, 160, 161, 162, 163, 164, 165:** Image courtesy of The Advertising Archives; **247:** Collections of the University of Pennsylvania Archives; **249:** © Jeff Goldberg/Esto. All rights reserved.; **502:** (left) © Vaughn Youtz/ZUMA/Corbis, (top center) © AP Images, (bottom center) © John Hayes/Reuters/Corbis, (right) © AP Images; **503:** (left) © Reuters/Corbis, (top center) © Kim Kulish/Corbis, (center) © Reuters/Corbis; **505:** © John Atashian/Corbis; **506:** (bottom right) © Chris Hardy/San Francisco Chronicle/Corbis; **520, 521, 522, 523:** Foto Marburg/Art Resource, NY; **524:** (top) Scala/Art Resource, NY, (bottom) © The McGraw-Hill Companies, Inc./John Flournoy, photographer; **525:** (both) Art Resource, NY; **526:** (top) Erich Lessing/Art Resource, NY, (bottom) Art Resource, NY; **527:** (top) Art Resource, NY, (bottom) Image courtesy of The Advertising Archives; **530:** Photo courtesy of the Norman Rockwell Museum, Stockbridge, Massachusetts. Permission granted by the Norman Rockwell Family Agency LLC.; **532:** (top) Photo courtesy of the Norman Rockwell Museum, Stockbridge, Massachusetts. Permission granted by the Norman Rockwell Family Agency LLC., (bottom) © Martha Holmes/Time Life Pictures/Getty Images. © 2007 The Pollock-Krasner Foundation/Artist Rights Society (ARS), New York; **533:** Hirshhorn Museum, Smithsonian Institution, Washington, DC. Gift of Joseph H. Hirshhorn, 1972 (72.235). © 2007 The Pollock-Krasner Foundation/Artist Rights Society (ARS), New York; **535:** Photo courtesy of the Norman Rockwell Museum, Stockbridge, Massachusetts. Permission granted by the Norman Rockwell Family Agency LLC. © 1962 SEP: Licensed by Curtis Publishing, Indianapolis, IN. All rights reserved. www.curtispublishing.com; **537:** Reproduced from the Collections of the Library of Congress, Washington, DC; **538:** The Metropolitan Museum of Art, New York, H. O. Havemeyer Collection, Bequest of Mrs. H. O. Havemeyer, 1929 (29.100.200); **539:** The Museum of Modern Art, NY, Sidney and Harriet Janis Collection. Digital Image © The Museum of Modern Art/Licensed by SCALA/Art Resource, NY. Art © The George and Helen Segal Foundation/Licensed by VAGA, New York, NY.; **542:** © Time Life Pictures/Getty Images; **548:** (both) © Barbara Morgan, The Barbara Morgan Archive; **564:** Courtesy Everett Collection; **565, 566, 567:** Paramount/The Kobal Collection

Insert Credits

Insert 1-1: © Museum of Fine Arts, Boston, Massachusetts, USA, Gift of Robert Treat Paine, 2nd. 31.33

Insert 1-2: © Brooklyn Museum/Corbis

Insert 1-3: Smithsonian American Art Museum, Washington, DC. Gift of the Harmon Foundation. 1967.59.669. Smithsonian American Art Museum, Washington, DC/Art Resource, NY

Insert 1-4: Wadsworth Atheneum Museum of Art, Hartford, CT. © 2007 The Georgia O'Keeffe Museum/Artist Rights Society (ARS), New York

Insert 1-5: The Art Institute of Chicago, Robert A. Waller Fund, 1910.2. Reproduction, The Art Institute of Chicago.

Insert 1-6: Hampton University Museum

Insert 1-7: Museum purchase in part through the Smithsonian Institution Collections Acquisition Program. 1995.40. © 1988 Pepon Osorio. Smithsonian American Art Museum, Washington, DC/Art Resource, NY

Insert 1-8: The Montreal Museum of Fine Arts. Purchase, Horsley and Annie Townsend Bequest, 1983.1. Photo The Montreal Museum of Fine Arts, Brian Merrett. SODART (Montreal) 2007. Art © Estate of Leon Golub/VAGA (New York). Courtesy Ronald Feldman Fine Arts.

Insert 2-1: © Stephen Scott Young. Courtesy of Surovek Gallery, Palm Beach, FL.

Insert 2-2: Smithsonian American Art Museum, Gift of S.C. Johnson & Son, Inc. 1969.47.24 © 2007 The Jacob and Gwendolyn Lawrence Foundation, Seattle/Artists Rights Society (ARS), New York

Insert 2-3: Smithsonian American Art Museum. Museum purchase through the Smithsonian Institution Collections Acquisition Program. 1995.94 © Carmen Lomas Garza. Photo: M. Baldwin

Insert 2-4: Japanese American Museum, Los Angeles.

Insert 2-5: Courtesy Tomie Arai. © Tomie Arai

Insert 2-6: © Mujeres Muralistas, courtesy of Patricia Rodriguez

Insert 2-7: © Christie's Images/Corbis. © Banco de México and INBA Mexico, 2007

Insert 2-8: Through the Flower/Judy Chicago. © 2007 Judy Chicago/Artists Rights Society (ARS), New York

Insert 3-1: Image courtesy of The Advertising Archives

Insert 3-2: Photo courtesy of Lowe Worldwide

Insert 3-3, 3-4, 3-5, 3-6, 3-7, 3-8: Image courtesy of The Advertising Archives

Insert 4-1, 4-2: Courtesy of the author

Insert 4-3: Courtesy Utah State University. Photographer Donna Barry

Insert 4-4: © Alain Jaramillo

Insert 4-5: © Doug Snower Photography

Insert 4-6: © Michael T. Sedam/Corbis

Insert 4-7: © Butler Institute of American Art, Youngstown, OH, USA, Museum Purchase 1918/Bridgeman Art Library

Insert 4-8: Photo by Alan Bauer/www.alanbauer.com

Insert 5-1: The Art Institute of Chicago. Gift of Mr. and Mrs. Edwin E. Hokin and Friends of American Art, 1954.438. Reproduction, The Art Institute of Chicago. Art © Jack Levine/Licensed by VAGA, New York, NY

Insert 5-2: Montgomery Museum of Fine Arts, Montgomery, Alabama, The Blount Collection

Insert 5-3: National Portrait Gallery, London

Insert 5-4: Philadelphia Museum of Art, Pennsylvania, PA, USA/Bridgeman Art Library

Insert 5-5: Maier Museum of Art. Fine Arts Fund, 1947.

Insert 5-6: Scala/Art Resource, NY. Art © Estate of Ben Shahn/Licensed by VAGA, New York, NY

Insert 5-7: Detroit Institute of Arts/Bridgeman Art Library © Banco de México and INBA Mexico, 2007

Insert 5-8: © Daniel DeSiga

Insert 6-1: (top) © C. Borland/PhotoLink/Getty Images, (bottom) Mike Wolforth/Getty Images

Insert 6-2: (top) Reproduced from the Collections of the Library of Congress, Washington DC, (bottom) Gilcrease Museum, Tulsa, OK

Insert 6-3: © Brooklyn Museum/Corbis

Insert 6-4: From 'Doesn't Fall Off His Horse' by Virginia Stroud, © 1994 by Virginia A. Stroud. Used by permission of Dial Books for Young Readers, A Division of Penguin Young Readers Group, A Member of Penguin Group (USA) Inc., 345 Hudson Street, New York, NY 10014. All Rights Reserved.

Insert 6-5: © Granger Collection

Insert 6-6: Dallas Museum of Art. Anonymous gift. 1979.28

Insert 6-7: National Gallery of Australia. © David Hockney

Insert 6-8: © Brand X Pictures/PunchStock

Insert 7-4: Réunion des Musées Nationaux/Art Resource, NY

Insert 8-1: © Annie Leibovitz. Courtesy Contact Press.

Insert 8-2: Norton Simon Museum, Gift of the Artist. © Barbara Morgan, The Barbara Morgan Archive.

Insert 8-3: George Eastman House

Insert 8-4: Courtesy Everett Collection

Insert 8-5: The Metropolitan Opera, New York. © 2007 Artists Rights Society (ARS), New York/ADAGP, Paris

Insert 8-6: Courtesy Romare Bearden Foundation. Art © Romare Bearden Foundation/Licensed by VAGA, New York, NY

Insert 8-7: The Museum of Modern Art, New York, Mrs. Simon Guggenheim Fund. (55.1949). Digital Image © The Museum of Modern Art/Licensed by SCALA/Art Resource, NY. © 2007 Estate of Pablo Picasso/Artists Rights Society (ARS), New York

Insert 8-8: Chicago History Museum. The Collection of Valerie Gerrard Browne. © Valerie Gerrard Browne.

Insert 8-9: Smithsonian American Art Museum. Gift of Chuck and Jan Rosenak and museum purchase made possible by Ralph Cross Johnson. 1997.124.189. Smithsonian American Art Museum, Washington, DC/Art Resource, NY

Insert 8-10: © Faith Ringgold. Image courtesy of Faith Ringgold.

Insert 8-11: National Portrait Gallery, London. © 2007 Laura Knight/Artists Rights Society (ARS), New York/DACS, London

Insert 8-12: © Malcah Zeldis/Art Resource, NY